ACLS History E-Book Project

Reprint Series

The ACLS History E-Book Project (www.historyebook.org) collaborates with constituent societies of the American Council of Learned Societies, publishers, librarians and historians to create an electronic collection of works of high quality in the field of history. This volume is produced from digital images created for the Project by the Scholarly Publishing Office and the Digital Library Production Service at the University of Michigan, Ann Arbor. The digital reformatting process results in an electronic version of the text that can be both accessed online and used to create new print copies. This book and hundreds of others are available online in the History E-Book Project through subscription.

Many of the works in the History E-Book Project are available in print and can be ordered either directly from their publishers or as part of this series. For information refer to the online Title Record page for each book. Inquiries regarding this series can be directed to info@hebook.org.

ACLS
HISTORY E-BOOK

http://www.historyebook.org

UITGAVEN VAN HET
NEDERLANDS HISTORISCH-ARCHAEOLOGISCH INSTITUUT TE İSTANBUL

Publications de l'Institut historique-archéologique néerlandais de Stamboul
sous la direction de
E. van DONZEL, Machteld J. MELLINK, C. NIJLAND et
J. J. ROODENBERG

LII

THE 1703 REBELLION AND THE STRUCTURE OF OTTOMAN POLITICS

THE 1703 REBELLION AND THE STRUCTURE OF OTTOMAN POLITICS

by

RIFA'AT ALI ABOU-EL-HAJ

NEDERLANDS HISTORISCH-ARCHAEOLOGISCH INSTITUUT
TE İSTANBUL
1984

Witte Singel 24
P.B. 9515
2300 RA Leiden
NEDERLAND

I.S.B.N. 90 6258052 1
Printed in Belgium

To the memory of my father Ali Mustafa Sultani
and to the memory of Cengiz Orhonlu

ACKNOWLEDGEMENT

Many individuals and institutions facilitated my work on this book. The Başbakanlık Arşivi in Istanbul, the Public Record Office and the British Museum in London, provided space for research and supplied microfilms; the Österreichische Nationalbibliothek and the Berlin Staatsbibliothek supplied microfilms. The Near East Center of the University of California at Los Angeles, through the courtesy of its then Director Speros Vryonis, allowed me full access to the University's research facilities during two quarters of 1975. A Summer Grant and a Creative Leave from California State University at Long Beach, along with permission for extended academic leaves over the last eight years freed me from my teaching responsibilities to do both the research and the writing of this book.

If he is lucky, a scholar's teachers beyond graduate training are his students and professional friends. The former allow him to learn as he teaches, perhaps the most exciting and most gratifying of all learning; the latter by sacrifice of time and effort respond with encouragement and care to his speculations and creative efforts, however tentative. Here I wish to record my gratitude to my students in general and to my colleagues Afaf Lutfi al-Sayyid Marsot, Albert Hourani and Andreas Tietze in particular.

My psychohistorical and psycho-social education has been enriched by the seminars offered by Roger Gould, M.D., at the Neuropsychiatric Institute of the University of California Medical School, Los Angeles, in 1971 and 1972; by the seminars which Peter Loewenberg taught both in the History Department at the University of California at Los Angeles and jointly with the Southern California Psychoanalytic Institute between 1972-76; and by the several informal dialogues held in Los Angeles by a group of social scientists and psychoanalysts in 1972-78.

Richard Stehr edited the manuscript of this book and Joan Mortenson did the typing of the final draft. Dr. van Donzel, Dr. Erdbrink and Mr. Rault were kind and untiring in the time and effort which they put in the final editing of this work.

NOTE ON TRANSLITERATION

For a number of Ottoman historical terms a not completely modernized Turkish spelling has been used. The reader will find *hass* instead of *has*, *tekaüd* instead of *tekaüb*. All forms, however, are to be found in Redhouse, *Turkish-English Dictionary*.

When not functioning as titles or parts of personal names, the terms are printed in italics. Those Ottoman historical terms, however, which have an accepted English form, are printed in Roman characters, e.g. "pasha households".

TABLE OF CONTENTS

PROLOGUE

Most standard interpretations of Ottoman politics and, indeed, of Islamic politics in general emphasize the domination of the individual ruler through his charisma, character and style rather than the structure which supported him and underlay the continuity of governmental processes. The present study was undertaken partly to correct this imbalance without losing sight of the impact of the individual dynast on the historical moment.

The 1703 rebellion was chosen for the light it could shed as much on the structure and processes of Ottoman politics as on the sultan, Mustafa II. Since contemporary sources are woefully inadequate for the reconstruction of normal political life in the second half of the seventeenth century, it becomes necessary to examine it in the "abnormal" instance. Through both a narrative of the rebellion and a close study of the memberships and associations of the component political substructures in each alignment, we are able to observe Ottoman polity as it fragmented into competing sovereignties, each vying for exclusive representation of Ottoman public interests. Here we note that the incidence of large scale violence is associated not with the immediate point of dissolution, but rather with the succeeding period of reconstruction, when there ensues a deadly competition over who qualifies for membership in the new polity.

The following interrelated propositions and theses guided the research for this study:

1. The rebellion does not represent a class or corporate conflict (e.g., *ulema* vs. palace or bureaucracy vs. military). Rather, it consisted of a struggle between coalitions of factions drawn from various groups—a struggle between composites, including those normally considered "disenfranchized" (e.g., the inhabitants of Istanbul and theological students):

2. The vizier and pasha households (*kapı*, pl. *kapılar*) from which, in part, the leadership of the rebellion was drawn are here recognized as having been a growing and dominant, if not actually quite new, substructure in Ottoman political life for at least the preceding half century. Their preeminence was partly evidenced by their increasing control over a large share of key positions in the central and the provincial administrations.

3. The internal and external policies of the Ottoman sultans were as much interrelated as they were bound by the exigencies of the historical moment. The frontier ideology, though now less reflective of political reality, continued to serve as the language through which historically bound decisions are interpreted.

INTRODUCTION

On Tuesday, July 17, 1703, six hundred Istanbul-based armorers (*cebecis*), set out from their barracks in defiance of their superiors' orders, marched unhindered to the military parade grounds of the city and planted their regimental banners—a symbolic act of revolt[1]. This act of defiance was occasioned by directives for their immediate dispatch as part of an expeditionary force to suppress a local revolt in Western Georgia (then composed of tribute paying-vassal states of the dynasty)[2].

The ostensible reason for the armorers' insurrection was their pay, which had fallen several installments in arrears. That this insurrection was for them not a mere financial matter is witnessed by the fact that no sooner had they reached the parade grounds than they called on their comrades to agree on the matter of bringing to justice those who had betrayed the Muslim faith and its chief instrument, the Ottoman Sublime state[3].

The armorer's bid to take justice into their own hands did not go unheeded, for within three days they had succeeded in attracting to their cause the religious, civil, and military orders of the city. From this innocent beginning the insurrection exploded into a full rebellion, which brought about the replacement of the current sultan. Mismanagement of state affairs—all Ottoman sources agree—was the primary cause of the insurrection[4]. Their list of reasons, however, was confined

[1] Silihdar Mehmed Ağa, *Nusretname* (translation by I. Parmaksızoğlu), 2 vols. Istanbul, 1962-69, II, 140 ff., and *Nusretname*; Istanbul: Beyazit Umumi Kütüphanesi ms. 2369, 285a ff. Since Parmaksızoğlu's translation leaves out occasionally some names, and sometimes whole sections of the original, throughout this study, his translation was checked out against the original Ottoman. Hereafter cited as Silihdar, *Nusretname* with volume and page number for the translation/folio number for the manuscript.

[2] A detailed description of the campaign preparations based primarily on Ottoman archival sources is given in appendix II below.

[3] By the second half of the seventeenth century delays in payment by the Ottoman treasury had become the normal practice.

[4] The standard chronicles used for the reconstruction of the rebellion are: Silihdar, *Nusretname*; Defterdar Mehmed Efendi, *Zübdetül-vakayi'* Istanbul, Süleymaniye Kütüphanesi ms., Esad Efendi 2382 (hereafter cited as Defterdar, *Zübdet*); Raşid, *Tarih-i Raşid* 6 vols., Istanbul, 1282 (hereafter cited as Raşid, *Tarih*); these are supplemented by two anonymous histories in Berlin: *Tevarih-i Sultan Süleyman (II)* Berlin, Staatsbibliothek, Diez A quarto 75 (hereafter cited as *Anonymous History* Berlin Diez A quarto 75) and *Kitab-ı Edirne Vak'ası* Berlin, Staatsbibliothek, Diez A quarto 5 (hereafter cited as *Anonymous History*, Berlin Diez A quarto 5). In addition to the accounts of the

to the most immediate precipitants. Human frailties constituted their main focus. The chronicler, Silihdar Mehmed Ağa, our main contemporary witness to these events — with first-hand knowledge of court life owing to his office in the palace — was uniquely qualified to enumerate the current explanations, which his contemporaries accepted, for the confrontation that brought to an end the reign of his sovereign. The first controversy centered on the decision of Mustafa II to recall Feyzullah Efendi, the sultan's former tutor, from his exile in Erzurum[5]. No sooner had the old mentor arrived in the capital than the sultan had him elevated to the office of *şeyhülislâm*. Feyzullah, not content with this office, eventually came to dominate both the religious bureaucracy and the government, allowing no one, high or low, to make decisions without his consent. None of Mustafa II's grand viziers was free from his direct meddling in the daily workings of government. The degradation of the highest executive office is summed up in the designation of the last incumbent as the lackey of the *şeyhülislâm*[6].

The second controversy our chronicler recorded centers on the choice of Edirne as the seat of government. By choosing Edirne, the sultan was shunning the first capital, Istanbul, with all that the court's absence implied economically to the city's life and livelihood. As the official explanation had it, the territorial clauses of the treaties of Karlowitz and Istanbul (1699 and 1700) were still in the stage of implementation and required close scrutiny by the government. Owing to Edirne's proximity to the newly designated borders, the court preferred it over Istanbul as the center for monitoring the final acts of the commissions for border demarcation and border differentiation. Although this contention was true, neither the sultan nor his mentor had much liking for life in Istanbul. Mustafa II preferred Edirne thanks to its easy access to his favorite hunting grounds[7]. The more likely explanation for shunning Istanbul was the presence of a large "army" of demobilized government officials and soldiers[8].

rebellion related by these contemporary sources the following were consulted: Naima, *Tarih-i Naima* 6 vols. Istanbul, 1283 (hereafter cited as Naima, *Tarih*); Şefik Efendi, *Şefikname şerhi* Istanbul, 1290 (hereafter cited as Şefik, *Şefikname*); and in London, Public Record Office, State Papers 97/21 (Sutton Papers) (hereafter cited as P.R.O., S.P., 97/21). For Ottoman archival sources see bibliography below.

[5] The causes are systematically listed in Silihdar, *Nusretname*, II, 140-141/285a. The former mufti had been previously linked to the rebellion of 1687 as a partisan of Mehmed IV (Silihdar, *Tarih*, II, 342 "*Sultan Mahmede canibdarlık*").

[6] "*vezir bizim kendi çırağımız*". *Ibid.*

[7] *Ibid.*

[8] Anonymous History, Berlin A quarto 75, 237b and Istanbul, Başvekalet Arşivi, Mühimme Defteri (Registers of General Public Affairs), 114, 80a and 87a (hereafter this series is cited as Mühimme Defteri).

The most acute controversy centered on the treatment Mustafa II and Feyzullah meted out to the *ulema*[9]. The *şeyhülislâm*, as head of the religious bureaucracy, promoted the interests of his immediate and extended family over more experienced and deserving *ulema*. Posts which required several years of training at the mosque colleges, and a concomitant maturity of judgment, were assigned to men who were barely out of adolescence[10].

The *şeyhülislâm*'s violations of protocol, precedent, and experience in preferring his favorites touched the *ulema*'s pockets as well as their sensibilities and made them amenable to the use of force in ousting the mufti and his sovereign. It seemed that Feyzullah was bent on establishing an *ulema* dynasty which would carry out and perpetuate his work and would influence not only the *ilmiye* but also the court of the Ottoman sultans, the theoretical center of power. This idea was suggested by the way he went about appointing his own men to key positions in both the civil and religious bureaucracies. The key illustration of his ambition can be seen from the almost unprecedented letter of appointment Feyzullah obtained from his master, making his eldest son, Fethullah, *mufti-designate* in the event of the incumbent's demise[11].

All contemporary and near contemporary sources agree that mismanagement of state afairs was the primary cause of the rebellion[12]. They would disagree with Silihdar's assertions only over minor details, such as whether or not Rami Mehmed, the incumbent grand vizier, set off the spark which ignited the fire of rebellion. Some exonerate him outright, while others omit him entirely from their considerations of the rebellion's causes. They all agree that the selfish and personal ambition of Feyzullah was the major factor in the insurrection. Another was fate, part of the ineffable divine plan, though elevated to heights beyond either human control or human comprehension.

At no point do these sources explain the wider and underlying factors that contributed to the rebellion and its timing. Even modern writers do not devote much attention to the phenomenon of either rebellion or revolution in Ottoman history. Basing his treatment on meagre evidence and secondary sources, Şerif Mardin can still dismiss an experience such as the Ottomans had in 1703 as a

[9] Silihdar, *Nusretname*, II, 142-143/285a-b.

[10] Normally it took about thirty years of service in progressively higher posts before one attained high office in the *ilmiye* bureaucracy. For example, Başmakcızade Ali Efendi (1639-1712) attained his first *kadi*ship at the age of fifty, that of *nikabet* (headship of Prophet's descendants) at fifty-three and the office of *şeyhülislâm* at sixty-seven. Detailed biography in Şeyhî, *Vakayi'ül-fuzalâ*, Vienna, Österreichische Nationalbibliothek, ms. H.O. 126 (hereafter cited as Şeyhî, *Vakayı'*).

[11] Purported copy of the *berat* of appointment is in Şefik, *Şefikname*, 11-14.

[12] Defterdar, *Zübdet*, 416a-419b; Silihdar, *Nusretname*, II, 140-144/285a-b; Raşid, *Tarih*, III, 11-17; Naima, *Tarih*, VI Naima's appendix, pp. 2-58.

mere flash "in the pan caused by accumulated grievances and aimed at obtaining concessions, not a real clash of institutionalized privileged groups as in Europe"[13]. L. V. Thomas, in his study of the late seventeenth-century historian, Naima, follows his subject's opinion and attributes the conflict to Feyzullah's nepotism and his attempt "... as mufti to become the chief administrative official of the state"[14]. The rebellion of 1703 is viewed as an encounter between conservatives (especially the "rigidly orthodox ulema") and liberals, represented by Köprülü Amcazade Hüseyin and Rami Mehmed respectively[15]. These two sides are said to have shown their true colours in their respective reactions to the defeat at Zenta. At that point the liberal side favored making peace, if for no other reason than to give the state more time to muster resources for the next battle with the powers of the Holy League.

The majority of the conservatives in Ottoman society, however, could not tolerate the peace treaties which had been arranged by Amcazade and Rami Mehmed. Here, Thomas asserts that the "... opposition was principally interested in furthering its own fortunes at home, and their criticism of Köprülü's handling of foreign affairs was, to that degree, rather a blind for domestic intrigue than bona fide conviction that the Ottomans could at once successfully fight Europe without prior reform at home"[16].

Beyond pointing out that the conflict divided the factions between conservative (clerical) and liberal (i.e., Köprülü), Thomas does not offer any further differentiation between the various factions involved in the political dynamics of this period.

When viewed in terms of underlying factors, the rebellion of 1703 can be partially explained as the failure of "peaceful" resolution of political conflict — the frustration of contending elites and coalitions over who would control the day-to-day activities of government[17]. At stake was not only power but also the vast patronage which devolved to the successful contenders. The problem is further complicated by the contradiction between the Ottoman theory of power — wherein the sultans were absolute rulers — and the reality that evolved in the second half of the seventeenth century.

[13] Şerif Mardin, "Power, Civil Society and Culture in the Ottoman Empire", *Comparative Culture and Society*, IX, (1969), 269.

[14] L. V. Thomas, *A Study of Naima*, New York, 1972, 84 (hereafter cited as Thomas, *Naima*).

[15] *Ibid.*, 67.

[16] *Ibid.*

[17] For a study of the model of political conflict as the normal for political life see, for example, James Rule and Charles Tilly, "1800 and the Unnatural History of Revolution", *Journal of Social Issues*, 28.1 (1972), 49-76 and their bibliography (hereafter cited as Rule and Tilly, "1800 ... Revolution").

The theory and the reality were thought to have coincided in the sixteenth century under Süleyman Kanunî, (the lawgiver, 1520-1566). The institution devised to support this absolutism was the *devşirme* slave system[18]. After training in the palace schools and at other designated locations, the most qualified men were assigned to key positions of power, command and responsibility, according to their merit and ability. Thus, grand viziers and pashas in both the central and the local administration, and the highest commanders of the standing army were normally graduates of this system.

Although mainly devised to create absolutely loyal servants for the dynasty — to counter the growing authority and challenge which the *uç beyleri* (leaders of the march warriors) posed to the dynasty in the 1450s — the slave system, in turn, began to threaten the authority of the sultans. The purported near absolute power that the graduates of this "institution" exercised over both the government and the palace reached its climax in 1622 with the deposition and assassination of Osman II, under whom recruitment for the system had been curtailed and the continued existence of the institution threatened.

Part of the explanation for the decline of the *devşirme* system has to be sought in the changed fortunes of the Ottoman state from 1566 on. By that date the Ottomans had reached the effective limits of their expansion at the expense of Christian Europe. (The exceptions to this generalization are Ottoman conquests in the Ukraine and Podolia under Köprülüzade Fazıl Ahmed.)

With the cessation of expansion there was less need for, and reliance upon, the military arm (the *kapı kulları*) for administration. The foundations for a new alternative to the *gulam* system were already laid in the sixteenth century. The sources for this alternative were the vizier and pasha households (*kapılar*), which were known to have had large staffs of their own, both slave and Muslim born[19, 20].

Late in that century, complaints were already being lodged at the court against the preferential treatment some of the associates of these households were receiving

[18] See Halil İnalcık, "Ghulām", *Encyclopaedia of Islam*, Second Edition, 1954-). See also "Devshirme" in *Ibid.* (hereafter reference to this edition will be cited as *E.I.*²).

[19] H. A. R. Gibb and H. Bowen, *Islamic Society and the West*. I., Parts I and II (London, 1950-57). (Hereafter cited as Gibb and Bowen, *Islamic Society*.)

[20] In a recent article Joel Shinder suggests that the bureaucracy (especially the *defterdarlık*/ Finance Ministry) tended to dominate political life in the period following Süleyman I and right into the first half of the seventeenth century. "Career Line Formation in the Ottoman Bureaucracy, 1648-1750: A New Perspective". *Journal of the Economic and Social History of the Orient*, 1974, XVI, 217-37. (Hereafter cited as Shinder, "Ottoman Bureaucracy 1649-1750".)

in assignments to lucrative governmental positions. At that stage of its development the phenomenon was still rather sporadic[21].

In seeking an explanation for the shift in recruitment from the *devşirme* system to the *kapılar*, we should, in part, be guided by how at least one contemporary observer viewed the changed needs of the Ottoman state late in that century. Mustafa Naima (ca. 1665-1716) avers that with the end of expansion the Ottoman state needed men with the specialized experience provided by administrative assignments[22]. The type of training the vizier and paşa *kapılar* furnished was in the bureaucratic, financial and military fields. Pashas and viziers depended on *timars*, *zeamets* or *hass* assignments for their maintenance. The care and bookkeeping operations for these financial sources were assigned to their personal subordinates. Some of these men were trained in the military arts and were expected to command the household troops which each vizier and pasha contributed in partial fulfillment of his obligation to serve the Ottoman state[23]. In contrast to the *devşirme* system, the "graduates" of the vizier and pasha households (*kapılar*) can be characterized by flexibility and a sense of both initiative and independence.

Ideally, the training of slaves was aimed at the production of men who were absolutely loyal to the Ottoman family and bound to it in their life, person and fortunes. Those reared and educated in that system were either purchased directly in the slave market or came from non-Muslim young sons of Ottoman subjects or taken as prisoners of war and were expected to shed all previous ties with family and culture. They underwent a long period of rigorous training and acculturation before graduation into a career they were most qualified for in terms of natural ability and experience[24].

One wonders about the emotional and psychological make-up of men who had been wrenched in their childhood from their home and life styles to be brought up in a totally different faith, culture, and language. At the very least we should expect men who feared attachments and were emotionally guarded, if not actually highly dependent and rigid. Here we can also note that generally the personality-type which the palace training produced met the goals of the system's founders: viz. the creation of men who were completely dependent on the sultans.

[21] For a preliminary study of the *kapılar* see Rifa'at Ali Abou-El-Haj, "The Ottoman Vezir and Paşa Households", *Journal of the American Oriental Society* (1974), 94.4, 438a-447b (hereafter cited as Abou-El-Haj, "Vezir and Paşa Households"). For examples from the 16th century, see A. Tietze, *Mustafa 'Ali's Description of Cairo of 1599*, Vienna, 1975.

[22] Naima, *Tarih*, I, author's introduction 2-65, especially 49-52.

[23] Gibb and Bowen, *Islamic Society*, I, 151-53.

[24] İnalcık, "Gh̲ulām", *E.I.*[2].

The political and material advantages that devolved to the viziers and pashas directly and indirectly, through the assignment of their household affiliates to government posts, should not be ignored. As the administration of the Ottoman state became more oriented towards *kapılar* and less towards the palace, it became more and more imperative for the prudent vizier or pasha to have his own men assigned to key positions in the administration. At one stroke he would unburden himself of their financial upkeep and have loyalists working for his personal advantage in government[25].

By the end of the seventeenth century nearly half of all the key posts in the central and provincial administration of the Ottoman state were staffed by men who were trained in, raised by or attached to at least one vizier-pasha household[26]. Along with this predominance in service went political power and influence. Mehmed IV was deposed, and later barred from the succession, following a direct confrontation with the vizier and pasha households (*kapılar*). Even his sons, Mustafa, who became sultan in 1695, and Ahmed, who succeeded in 1703, had been denied the throne on at least two prior occasions following their father's ousting in 1687[27].

As sultan, Mustafa II seemed determined either to circumvent or completely neutralize the power structure which had evolved into political predominance during the previous half century. The potentially violent confrontation that ensued between the ruler and the households took eight years to come to a head. No single faction could be credited with carrying out the rebellion, least of all the one drawn from the households. Rather, the rebellion drew on a coalition of factions drawn from the various corporations that constituted Ottoman society (especially the *ulema*, military, and merchants of Istanbul). Each faction had its own immediate and, sometimes, longstanding, grievances against the government. Although invariably the incumbents were able to give *ad hoc* justifications for each move that may have alienated a faction, the latter perceived these moves as constituting a policy to exclude them from power, privilege and the fruits of service.

The very disparate interests of the component parts brought together in 1703 made for an uneasy coalition that was bound to fall apart with Mustafa II's

[25] Naima alludes to these advantages. L. V. Thomas, *Naima*, 105. Sixteenth century English grandees favored, in a similar fashion, the expansion of the bureaucracy to accommodate their personal followers.

[26] For statistics see Abou-El-Haj, "Vezir and Paşa Households", 442a-43a.

[27] For a brief reconstruction of these events see Abou-El-Haj, "Vezir and Paşa Households", 443a-444b which is based mainly on Silihdar Mehmed Ağa, *Silihdar Tarihi*, 2 volumes, Istanbul, 1928, II, 278-333, 483, 569-70 (hereafter cited as Silihdar, *Tarih*) and Defterdar, *Zübdet*, 119a-141b.

deposition[28]. Though the transformation of power was effected with a minimum of bloodshed, the differences between the various elements in the coalition far outstripped the similarities, and violence ensued. Several factions — asserting either their supremacy or the privileges and advantages they had gained through the rebellion — eliminated other factions. The exception to this deadly competition was the *kapılar*. The affiliates of these *kapılar* who entered on the rebel side and those who served Mustafa II's government survived well into the regime of Ahmed III[29].

The complexity of the evolved Ottoman political structure can be discerned in terms of the incrustations of privilege and advantage which accrued to faction and corporation through ad hoc grant or rebellion. Over the years a certain balance had been reached, a balance of forces and accommodations of the various layers of privilege. A "reformer" like Mustafa II had to contend not only with the historically accumulated prerogatives but with the delicate balance of power among the various factions of Ottoman society. Interference in one segment would usually tip the scale in favor of at least one other, and possibly threaten the whole structure of checks and balances. A rebellion, on the other hand, would serve as a wedge, providing the opportunity either to reassert one's threatened position or consolidate newly won but not quite institutionalized positions at the expense of others (including the dynasty).

In a political system where, at least theoretically, all power is vested in the ruler, the personality of the incumbent becomes an important factor in the style if not the conduct of the government. By a stroke of good fortune Prince Mustafa grew up into full adulthood unencumbered by the handicaps that had arrested the growth of his predecessors. It is partly due to this comparatively healthy growth and development that we attribute his taking the initiatives in 1695 to reverse the political trends which had evolved before his reign. His ally and mainstay in the ensuing struggle was his former mentor, Feyzullah Efendi. As the tale of their relationship unfolds, however, it becomes clear that the sultan had not shaken off his childhood dependence on the old mufti. By the end of the reign neither the threat to his throne nor the disruption of public life would persuade Mustafa II to abandon the attachment and trust which he vested in Feyzullah[30].

[28] Discussed in the next two parts of the present study.
[29] For percentages see p. 87 below.
[30] A psychoanalytically informed treatment of Mustafa II's personality and how his personality was fit for the historical moment is attempted in R. A. Abou-El-Haj, "The Narcissism of Mustafa II (1695-1703): A Psychohistorical Study", *Studia Islamica*, XL, (1974) (hereafter cited as Abou-El-Haj, "Mustafa II: A Psychohistorical Study"). Additional suggestions and modifications are added in the present study.

The arena of foreign policy was where the new sultan chose to test the coalition he had forged. All his hopes were pinned on the successful execution of an aggressive military strategy. But Mustafa II was not satisfied with observing and managing the campaigns from a safe and comfortable distance, as his father Mehmed IV had been. Instead — like his sixteenth-century ancestor heroes — he chose to stand personally at the head of the army in the field. The general popularity of his martial stance must have been quite apparent. By focusing on foreign affairs, Mustafa II raised a minimum of legal and constitutional questions, since here the prerogatives of the sultans were beyond doubt.

However, it was on the outcome of his military ventures that the final results of his internal policy hinged. If his military thrusts against the Christian powers succeeded, his bid to ignore the evolved political structure, which he inherited from his immediate predecessors, would have been vindicated. Even with his adventures ending in failure, Mustafa II tried to maintain an active role in the conduct of government affairs.

Amcazade Hüseyin, the nephew of Mehmed, the first Köprülü and founder of the vizier-pasha household (*kapı*) par excellence, was chosen as the chief executive who could minimize the humiliations of the peace treaties that had to be signed following fourteen years of war. Although the choice of this fourth Köprülü was an obvious concession to the *kapılar*, Hüseyin was not left alone to put Ottoman affairs in order; Feyzullah Efendi was placed in a position as another executive in competition with the new grand vizier. It is perhaps in reaction to this diffusion of executive power — and the resultant administrative fragmentation which must have ensued — that we encounter the first covert, though reported, attempt at ousting the mufti.

The failure of that endeavour paved the way for the removal of Mustafa II. Amcazade Hüseyin, however, proved no match for the well-entrenched mentor. Neither did his two successors in office[31]. With no peaceful recourse open to them, a faction of the vizier and pasha households (*kapılar*) (in coalition with several elements from the corporations of Ottoman society with their own grievances to air against the government) opted for an open rebellion. At first it seemed that the rebels would be satisfied with the removal of the mufti, but the sultan's apparent failure to carry this out forced them to depose Mustafa II as well.

The paucity of modern research in the social and economic history of the Ottoman state in general, and of this particular period specifically, precludes a comprehensive explanation for the rebellion of 1703. Here the rebellion is treated

[31] These events are briefly analysed in Abou-El-Haj, "Vezir and Paşa Households", 444a-446a.

mainly for the light it sheds on the structure of Ottoman politics in the second half of the seventeenth century. The model adopted for explaining it is one of political conflict[32].

To date, the standard framework for the explanation and analysis of Ottoman polity has been the charismatic one. The polity's dynamic is tied mainly to the character of the incumbent ruler. His qualities, negative or positive, are indelibly printed on the political history of his reign. What is ignored in this type of treatment is that the substructures that evolved over the years came to supplement the personal rule of the sultans. Thus, whereas the charismatic treatment and model thrive in unstable conditions, the substructures provide continuity of both procedure and service.

Here it is contended that the system of confining to "cages" (sg.: *kafes*) princes who were potential heirs to the Ottoman throne also served to prevent the rise of sultans with charismatic qualities, and that the practice was introduced as much to assure less tumultuous succession as it was to serve the purposes of the evolved political substructures in their bid to control power. One of the chief qualities of a charismatic leader is his insistence on his own procedures and structures to the exclusion of preexisting ones, but to the historically evolved substructures continuity is at the heart of good government. Charismatic leaders, on the other hand, thrive on instability, as they seem to provide their own form of continuity[33].

As a substructure of Ottoman politics, the *kapı* must have developed with at least the tacit, if not active, encouragement of the dynasty. Through a policy of confiscations the sultans in the fifteenth and sixteenth centuries were able to curb the power of viziers and pashas who graduated from the palace service[34]. Since these men where regarded as the personal slaves of the sultans, their effects following dismissal or demise were turned over to the royal treasury (*enderun hazinesi*).

By seizing their wealth through this policy, the dynasty was effective in curtailing the palace graduates' capacity for self-perpetuation. As the palace turned to recruit Muslims in its service, the policy of confiscations was also extended to Muslim-born officials. These men were viewed by the sultans as their household

[32] The theoretical orientation for the study of the rebellion is taken primarily from Rule and Tilly, "1830...Revolution".

[33] On charismatic authority see H. H. Gerth and C. Wright Mills (eds.), *From Max Weber: Essays in Sociology*, New York, 1958, 245-62.

[34] For a general treatment of the sultans' policy of confiscations see "Müsadere", in *İslam Ansiklopedisi*, Istanbul, 1940- (hereafter cited as *İ.A.*). A more specific treatment for the period under discussion in Abou-El-Haj, "Vezir and Paşa Households", 446a-b footnote 36, and below.

slaves (kul, pl. kullar) and therefore subject to the same regulations[35]. If, however, this policy—which was applied at least throughout the second half of the seventeenth century—was meant to curb the *kapılar* from perpetuating themselves, it failed.

Apparently, neither the sultans nor their chief administrators were seriously interested in the rigorous application of the policy of confiscations. Several loopholes were available. One was the conversion of personal property into inalienable family endowments (*evkaf-ı zürriye*), a practice which had its early start in at least the sixteenth century. Revenues from these endownments were turned over to the descendants' heirs[36]. The sultans, in turn, violated the policy by turning over the household of a deceased vizier to his son[37].

Yet the law of confiscation was not abandoned, although in a large number of cases only its letter was followed. The pretense was maintained that every effort was expended in collecting estates and effects for the royal private purse. Once the law had been enforced, and with the pardoning of the officer in question, no further confiscations were allowed. A corollary to the law was a statute of limitations.

From these observations it is obvious that the sultans were not interested in rendering their demoted high officials or their heirs totally destitute. Numerous officials, following dismissal from office, were awarded retirement (*tekaüd*) benefits from the royal domains (*hass*) or direct cash from one of the numerous government monopolies (e.g. *gümrük*, customs). Even officials in between assignments were allowed to draw on their official benefits until their next appointment[38]. As for the children and heirs of deceased high officials, they challenged the legality of the confiscations and almost invariably were allowed to retain some, if not all, of what they claimed[39]. In cases where the viziers or pashas fell prisoner to the enemy, their families kept at least part of their property[40].

The relationship between the sultans and the *kapılar* had become one of mutuality and interdependence by the second half of the seventeenth century, as is especially

[35] Even Köprülüzade Mustafa was not immune from this practice. Details in Silihdar, *Tarih*, II, 598.

[36] Details in Gibb and Bowen, *Islamic Society*, I.I., 168 ff.

[37] Such was the case of Birunsuz Mehmed Bey who following his father's demise was given the rank of Karaman, awarded the *sancak* of Alâiye and authorized to carry over his father's *kapı*. The case of the perpetuation of Ispanakcı Ismail's *kapı* through his son is recorded in Mühimme Defteri 114, 10b and is also reported in Silihdar, *Nusretname*, II, 131/283a.

[38] High *ulema* who were awaiting assignment were also assigned interim livings from the revenues of several *kadılık*s.

[39] E.g. Fındık Mehmed's orphans have a petition in Mühimme Defteri 106, 155 (dated April, 1695).

[40] E.g. Atlubeyzade Mehmed who was taken prisoner while defending fort Kenin. His *çiftlik* money was assigned to his household and family. Mühimme Defteri 106, 237 (dated August, 1695).

evident in the claims for military assistance that rulers made on the households during the campaigns. The children of viziers and pashas were called upon to provide men, material, and sometimes even their own persons for military service[41].

The patchy nature of the available sources on the processes and dynamics of Ottoman politics makes the study of the phenomena in their normal state quite impossible. For the half century under consideration only echoes of challenges and conflicts among the existing structures are registered in the chronicles[42].

[41] For 1107/1696 campaign, each one of the following, according to his or/her means, was expected to provide *piyade* and *süvarı*:

		Men Provided
1	Boşnalık Ibrahim Hanoğlu Ali Bey	500
2.	Cevan Kapıcıbaşıoğlu Ahmed	200
3.	Köprülüzade Numan Bey	150
4.	Mıhalbeyoğlu (Yenişehir ayanından) Ömer	50
5.	Turhanbeyoğlu Hâcc Mustafa	100
6.	Mü'menzade	30
7.	former Büyük tezkereci	50
8.	Widow and son of Mahmudbeyoğlu	150
9.	Çatrazade Mustafa Bey	25
10.	Canarslan Paşazade Hüseyin	25
11.	Şah Gazipaşaoğlu	25

Silihdar, *Nusretname* I, 148-49/232a, supplemented by Mühimme Defteri 108, pp. 188-89, 248; Raşid, *Tarih*, II, 361; Defterdar, *Zübdet*, 313a. For the same campaign, the following officials were expected to provide men:

1.	Istanbul defterdarı	20
2.	Defterdar başı	10
3.	Tersane emini	50
4.	Darbhane emini	20
5.	Istanbul ağası	20
6.	Gümrük emini	40
7.	Tophane nazırı	10
8.	Istanbul bostancı başısı	50
9.	Edirne bostancı başısı	50

Mühimme defteri 108, 189-90.

It is quite obvious that the court expected the group of sons of viziers and pashas to deliver a larger share of the men for the campaign of 1107 than even the second echelon of the Ottoman central and palace administration.

[42] Three examples are cited in illustration of political conflicts in the second half of the seventeenth century. The first two point to challenges to Köprülü growing authority. In 9 Safer, 1074 (12 Sept., 1663), Reisülküttab Şamizade Mehmed tried to undermine Köprülüzade Fazıl Ahmed's position at the court by accusing the grand vezir of incompetence. He even had a replacement at hand in the person of his own *damad* Vali of Nicopolis Nikebolu Kadızade Ibrahim. When a report of the reisülküttab's machinations reached Fazıl Ahmed, he had Şamizade Mehmed and his son-in-law executed. (Details in Silihdar, *Tarih*, I, 276-77.) The second incident relates the growing jealousy, power and wealth of Fazıl Mustafa (Silihdar, *Tarih*, II, 567). Finally, early in the reign of Mustafa II when the sultan himself challenged the monopoly on power which the incumbent grand vezir Sürmeli Ali, an affiliate of the Sokollu Household, had exercised (Silihdar, *Nusretname*, I, 7/214a and 26-28/217a-b).

But the echoes remain as enigmatic traces, mere hints, rarely followed by analysis or explanation. The breakdown and fragmentation of Ottoman polity in the wake of the 1703 rebellion and its reconstitution immediately afterward provide a picture of Ottoman political structure — the various combinations of alignments and alliances that constituted the polity before, during, and after the rebellion. This treatment makes it possible to move from a flat tableau filled with un-dimensional men propelled by wooden motives to one of conflict over real issues, like whether the *nizâm-ı âlem* (world order) was better served by a charismatic leader or an evolved, but oligarchic, structure. One stood for reform aimed at self-aggrandizement, the other for continuing the representation of broader interests than the dynasty's.

The uprising that triggered the rebellion in 1703 was led by the *cebecis*, a contingent of the standing army ordered from Istanbul to quell a rebellion in western Georgia. Trouble had been brewing for some time in this area. A chain of events of both internal and international magnitude had forced the Ottoman court to take drastic actions. The 1703 expedition was one attempt to stem the tide of receding Ottoman power in the Caucasus[43].

Between March and July of that year most of the military preparations for launching the Georgia campaign were readied. In the middle of July the five janissary *odas* assigned to the expeditionary force embarked under the direction of *seğmen başı* Haşımoğlu Murtaza[44]. When the *cebecis*' turn for embarking came, they refused. Murtaza was challenged to produce the armorers' pay which had fallen ten installments in arrears. In April, owing to diversion of payments to other services, this *ocak* could not be paid in time. A month later, despite attempts to make up part of the shortages through contributions from the sultan's private treasury, not enough cash could be found to meet the *cebeci* payroll in full. This time the deficit was attributed to embezzlement by the head of the *ocak*, *cebeçi başı* Hasan, and his two assistants, who were all dismissed[45]. The *cebecis*, though, had resolved by oath not to leave Istanbul until they had received full compensation for past services[46].

Realizing that this act of insubordination could not pass unpunished, they locked the *cebehane* (armory), which was under their supervision, and barricaded them-

[43] For the Georgia campaign see appendix II.

[44] As indicated in footnotes 4 and 8 above, the analysis of the 1703 rebellion is based on Silihdar, Raşid, Naima and the two Berlin anonymous histories, the Sutton papers in the P.R.O., in addition to Mühimme Defteri 114 and the Vienna copy of Rami Mehmed's public letters. Silihdar's narrative in *Nusretname*, II, 140-184/285a ff. served as the main outline for the present study, supplemented by Defterdar and other contemporary and near contemporary sources.

[45] The explanation is in Defterdar, *Zübdet*, 416a. The *kaymakam* of Istanbul communicated this state of affairs to the grand vezir in Edirne. The latter's response was to have Hasan Ağa removed and forced to pay from his own estate to cover the *cebeci* pay. The *sürre emini* Ibrahim Ağa was given the office of *cebeci başı*. Sultanic orders to the *kaymakam* are in Mühimme Defteri 114, 74b (dated Muharrem 1115/May 1703) and the appointment of Ibrahim in *Ibid.*—Sutton reports in P.R.O., S.P. 97/21, 136b that on July 19, Thursday, 30,000 "dollars" (*guruş*) were sent to the *kaymakam*.

[46] *Ibid.* Sutton reports that the *cebecis* rejected the offer to be paid by saying "they could be paid when they pleased".

selves in their quarters near the Aya Sofya Mosque[47]. The evening of Tuesday, July 17, was spent in deliberations. Although no records of what was discussed are extant, the *cebeci*s' aims and plans of action are apparent from the decisions they made during the following days.

In Istanbul the central government was represented by the grand vizier's deputy (*kaymakam*), Abdullah. It was from this quarter that the *cebeci*s expected disciplinary action for their defiance of orders. Since standing alone they would have been doomed to failure and easy suppression, they took measures to assure the generalization of their cause beyond their specific grievance.

Within the military establishment proper the *cebeci*s had two options: to render neutral or recruit the janissaries as allies. Without the latter's alliance, any rebellion would have been doomed to premature failure. Anticipating an attempt at this alliance, the *kaymakam* blocked the *cebeci* access to the janissary *oda*s. Thus, when the armorers marched in full battle gear on Wednesday from their barracks to the Et Meydanı (parade grounds adjacent to the janissary quarters), they found the gates shut. Undeterred in their determination to gain access to the Meydan and establish contact with the janissaries, the *cebeci*s forced open one of the gates, Yeniçeri Meydan Kapısı, and struck their regimental colors in the middle, signaling their readiness to meet force with force.

On the way to the parade grounds the *cebeci*s created a major commotion and panic in the city. Expecting trouble, merchants and shopkeepers closed their establishments. The unemployed and the curious, having nothing better to do, joined the march to the Meydan. There they heard the *cebeci*s justify their insurrection, not in terms of corrupt officials entrusted with handling their back pay, but of punishment to be meted out to those who betrayed the state[48].

At this stage the names of those accused of this serious charge were not revealed. In fact, once they bound some of the city's inhabitants and members of the *ulema* corps to their cause, the *cebeci*s retreated from this serious accusation and confined themselves to championing justice[49]. In effect, the *cebeci*s were uniting their cause with that of certain elements of Istanbul society already harboring grievances against specific officers of the incumbent government. As outlined by contemporary Ottomans, the aggrieved can be broken down into two groups — the *ulema*, *meşayih* and the inhabitants and merchants of the city.

[47] Şefik, *Şefikname*, 26-27.

[48] "*Devlet hayinlerini istemeziz*", Silihdar, *Nusretname*, II, 146/286a.

[49] The first rallying cry was perhaps not without purpose. There are indications that it would not have drawn as quick a response as was desired at that desperate moment in the rebellion. Such a serious charge would have required substantiation for which there was neither the time nor the audience.

Şeyhülislâm Feyzullah, the head of the corporation of *ulema*, was the target of the first group's complaints. Controlling the religious bureaucracy, Feyzullah had the final say in who occupied the highest posts in the system. Normally these offices were reserved for men of learning, experience, and seniority, but—in violating of all known set precedents and accepted "ancient customs"—this *şeyhülislâm* had been able to elevate his sons, relations, and followers to the highest and most lucrative ranks of the *ilmiye* without regard to age, education, or experience[50].

The malcontents could point to Seyyid Fethullah, the eldest of his five sons, as an example. At the age of twenty-five he held the *mevleviyet* of Selânik. Thereafter, in rapid succession, he held the *sadaret* of Anadolu, the rank of Rumeli, the *nikabet* (headship of the Prophet's descendants), and finally the rank of *şeyhülislâm*. Thus, within the span of four years, he managed to attain what, under normal circumstances, would have taken him no less than twenty[51]. In assigning offices to his immediate and extended family and entourage, Feyzullah not only removed deserving, experienced, and learned men but deprived some of them of taking their normal turn at the most rewarding posts in the system. The discontented among the *ulema* saw their cause, then, as one of justice—justice in the fair assignment of posts in accordance with known precedents and justice against the flagrant nepotism practiced by the head of their corporation.

[50] A quotation from a contemporary source could perhaps serve to convey the outrage of the ulema at Feyzullah's nepotism: "He had eight sons. One the *nakib* (Fethullah)... another the Anadolu kazaskeri, another with the rank of Anadolu (served as the) *Şehzade hocası* (preceptor of the heirs-apparent), another with the rank of Anadolu.... Of his relations (*akriba*) at the ages of ten and fifteen, respectively, each having served as *müderris* (teacher) at the Süleymaniye (Mosque schools). Dede Efendi (made it as) Rumeli kazasker, two of his *damads* made it as Istanbul kadis, and of the rest of them (his relations) and entourage (*taallûkat*/hangers on), it is impossible to count who made it as *molla* (religious bureaucracy), and who made it as *müderris*.... While those who (normally) would spend seventy or eighty years of their individual lives in the lower ranks before attaining their high hopes for the *kazaskerlik*, his sons, who were not even twenty or thirty years of age each, had their hands kissed by these elderly ones. (That was apparently not enough) since Ebezade Abdullah, the former *kazasker* of Rumeli, was sent into exile at Cyprus, Yahya Efendi to Aleppo, and Mirza Efendi to Sinop. For three or four years each their families suffered hardships. The *müderris* who was not one of (the mufti's) followers spent four to five or sometimes even seven to eight years in waiting in one or another of the honorific grades before getting to attain the next actual step...". Anonymous History, Berlin Diez A quarto/75, 234b-235a.

[51] Charges against Feyzullah and his family and followers in *Ibid.*, and Silihar, *Nusretname*, II, 142-43/285a-b. The nomination of Fethullah to the office of Şeyhülislâm took place on Ramazan 24, 1113 (February 24, 1702), only one and a half years prior to the outbreak of the rebellion. As an example of Fethullah's meddling in non-*ilmiye* affairs, evidence of one example should suffice. He was instrumental in shifting the assignment of Divriki Ibrahim (formerly bey of Divrik, *Çavuş başı* and a well known *gazi* of provincial military background) from the eyalet of Şehrizor to that of Cyprus, Defterdar, *Zübdet*, 403a and Raşid, *Tarih*, II, 557. For biography of Ibrahim see Mehmed Süreyya, *Sicili-i Osmanî*, 4 volumes, Istanbul, 1308. Volume I, 118 (hereafter cited as Süreyya, *Sicil*) and Silihdar, *Nusretname*, II, 120/281b.

Their grievances were not against violations of principle but against specific, identifiable, and concrete abuses of office.

The inhabitants and, especially, the merchants of Istanbul blamed Feyzullah for the extended absence of the court from the city[52]. On March 21, 1701, Mustafa II had decreed the transfer of the seat of government from the first capital to Edirne. Presumably, two purposes were served by this move.

First, the business of the border commissioners, noted above, would be more easily expedited.

Second, the sultan was still receiving diplomatic representatives from the powers of the Holy League concerning ratifications of the peace treaties. This, too, would be further facilitated by the proximity of Edirne to the international frontier[53].

In the wake of the rebellion Silihdar Mehmed wrote that he was sceptical about the reasons the court offered for its absence from Istanbul. Peace had already been established with the Christian powers, and there was no diplomatic reason for the sultan's absence from the first capital. Mustafa II, however, had been persuaded by the *şeyhülislâm* to leave the city. According to contemporary sources, Feyzullah wished to isolate the sultan from the aggrieved and unemployed *ulema* and others who resided in Istanbul. In fact, Mustafa II showed every sign of permanent settlement in Edirne. The imperial harem was transferred to the second capital, and residencies were prepared for all three newly-betrothed princesses and their spouses to settle in Edirne[54].

To the people of Istanbul this permanent settlement meant economic deprivation, because the merchants who supplied the palace and high government officials were denied their rightful source of livelihood. The location of the court was no idle matter, and when Ahmed III acceded to the throne following the ouster of Mustafa II in 1703, his primary promise was that the court would never reside at Edirne, but would remain in Istanbul[55].

[52] Silihdar, *Nusretname*, II, 142/285a, Anonymous History, Berlin Diez A quarto/75, 236a-b.
[53] For a detailed discussion of the negotiations which led to the peace treaties see R. A. Abou-El-Haj, *The Reisülküttab and Ottoman diplomacy at Karlowitz* (Princeton Ph.D. dissertation, 1963, available through University Microfilms) (hereafter cited as Abou-El-Haj, *Reisülküttab and Karlowitz*) and R. A. Abou-El-Haj, "Ottoman Diplomacy at Karlowitz", *Journal of the American Oriental Society*, 87, 1967. Both international and internal (ideological) repercussions of the peace treaties can be consulted in R. A. Abou-El-Haj, "The formal Closure of the Ottoman Frontier in Europe: 1699-1703", *The Journal of the American Oriental Society*, 89, 1969 and Ottoman indulgence in make-believe both before and at the negotiations is discussed in *idem.*, "Ottoman Methods of Negotiation: The Karlowitz Case", *Der Islam*, 51, 1974 (hereafter cited as Abou-El-Haj, "Ottoman Methods of Negotiations").
[54] As citations in footnote 52 above.
[55] Anonymous History, Berlin Diez A quarto 5, 44a-b.

The grievances of the *ulema* and the capital's residents would not, however, warrant as sweeping and serious an accusation against the incumbent government as the *cebeci*s had leveled early in their insurrection. It was perhaps with this in mind that the rebels had to abandon temporarily the slogan of treason for a demand for justice. Contemporary sources indicate that redress of their grievances against Feyzullah and economic relief remained the rebels' chief rallying points to the very end. These served to bind significant elements of the Istanbul inhabitants and the *ulema*—with *their* concrete grievances—to a common cause with the *cebeci*s, a bid for justice.

To rally the *ulema* it was necessary to have one of their chiefs in the rebel camp. Thus, no sooner had the *cebeci*s' banners been struck at the Et Meydanı than a mission was dispatched to fetch the kadi of Istanbul, who was the highest ranking member of this corporation left behind by the court[56].

That same day, the *kaymakam* Abdullah and the *seğmen başı*, Murtaza, hearing of the *cebeci* outbreak, finally decided to meet force with force. A three-fold course of action was planned: to convene the loyal *ulema* and Istanbul's prominent statesmen at the Top Kapı palace, issue a call for the standing army (mainly janissaries) to assemble at the double, and pick-up the sacred banner of Eyyubu Ansari for rallying forces to suppress the *cebeci*s' sedition[57]. (The flags with religious significance served as a rallying symbol—the prophet's flag had the highest such significance—that of Eyyub was of a secondary order of significance.)

While all those assembled at the *saray* spent the evening there for their own security, the *seğmen başı* went over to the *Ağa Kapısı* (Janissary Ağa's residence) to muster the troops loyal to the sultan. The *bostancı başı*, Edirneli Mehmed, was sent to fetch the sacred banner[58].

Thursday, July 19, proved the most decisive date in this first phase of the insurrection. According to plan, Murtaza assembled and armed the janissaries and the *ocak ağaları* at the break of dawn and marched them to the Top Kapı palace. To his great surprise he found the Bab-ı Humayun (one of the main gates to the *saray*) locked and closely guarded. Probably uninformed of the *kaymakam*'s plan, Arnavut Osman, the *saray ağası*, had given orders to seal the palace gates against everyone. Failing to gain access through the Bab-ı Humayun, the *seğmen başı* tried the Demir Kapı, also in vain. While retracing his steps back to the

[56] Defterdar, *Zübdet*, 421a and Silihdar, *Nusretname*, II, 147/286a. It is perhaps ironical that this Seyyid Mahmud Efendi was a *damad* of Feyzullah Efendi. Silihdar, *Nusretname*, II, 143/285b.
[57] *Ibid.*, and Defterdar, *Zübdet*, 420b.
[58] Silihdar, *Nusretname*, II, 147/186a.

Bab-ı Humayun, Murtaza found himself face to face with contingents of the rebel *cebecis*[59].

The encounter between the military forces of both sides proved crucial, for the *seğmen başı* had with him contingents of the janissaries he had gathered that morning to defend the palace against an expected attack by the *cebecis*. While he was putting these contingents together, the *cebecis* received word of his intentions, though too late to prevent his departure for the palace. Thus, when they marched under their regimental banner to the Ağa Kapısı, they found it closely guarded in the wake of the departed janissaries.

The Janissary Ağa's residence, which also served as a prison, was stormed, and all prisoners were freed to join the *cebecis*. From there they marched against the *kaymakam*'s residence where—again owing to faulty intelligence—they failed to find the *kaymakam*. When the *cebecis* insisted on entering to search for him, the guard fired at them, and several *cebecis* were hit. Incensed at this attack, the *cebecis* stormed the *kaymakam*'s residence, gained access to the ground and building, and eventually pillaged the palace of all its belongings.

From that point, each violent move escalated and brought the *cebecis* closer to the point of no return. From the *kaymakam*'s palace they marched on to the Top Kapı palace for their fateful confrontation with the *seğmen başı* at the Bab-ı Humayun. Subsequent decisions on both sides hinged on the outcome of this encounter. Murtaza had returned to the palace for its defense and the possible suppression of the insurgents. Both sides were fully armed. One false move on the part of the *cebecis* would spell their doom and the end of their insurrection.

Finally, however, the encounter ended peacefully, as men on both sides—out of loyalty to brothers-in-arms—were not ready to take arms against one another. This left Murtaza exposed and without protection. When he tried to escape, he was easily intercepted and dragged to Et Meydanı[60].

From the first outbreak of the insurrection the *seğmen başı* had tried in vain to appease the *cebecis* and prevent the spread of sedition to other sectors of both the military and civilians. When he failed, he had to use force to suppress the insurrection. The *cebecis*, and especially the janissaries—mindful that a show of legality was necessary—would have preferred to have Murtaza on their side. This was a vain gesture.

[59] Defterdar, *Zübdet*, 420b.

[60] Silihdar, *Nusretname*, II, 148/286a; P.R.O., S.P. 97/21, 136b (Sutton reports, "the Janissaries who were held by the (*seğmen başı*) broke out and joined rebels and put down segban basi.") and Anonymous History, Berlin Diez A quarto/75, 238a-39b.

He, in turn, tried to appease them by promising to intercede with the sultan for their pardon should they put down their arms. Since he would not join the rebellion, the janissaries turned their violence against him. Their commitment to the rebellion was made contingent upon the *ağa*'s execution. His death not only rid the rebels of the last remaining major military officer openly loyal to the incumbent government, but seems to have cemented the coalition of the two major military components, without whom the rebellion would have been doomed to an early failure.

Contemporary Ottoman authors do not explain the alacrity with which major elements of the military orders joined the rebellion. Thus, although the specific grievances of the *cebeci*s (namely their back pay) are spelled out quite clearly, no hint is given to account for the defection of the Istanbul-based janissaries, by far the most powerful and prestigious contingents in the Ottoman standing army. It is one of the arguments of this book that the Karlowitz treaty—with their attendant demobilization of the armed forces—and the wide-spread unemployment of the military[61] following a decade and a half of war, were the major underlying causes of the military forces' alignment with the rebel *cebeci*s. Mustafa II, who had opted to test his proposed political reforms in the battlefields of southeastern Europe, had failed in his mission.

The military failure, culminating in the rout of Ottoman forces at Zenta in 1697, was papered over and hidden from the general public for several years until the demarcation agreements were put into effect. The speed with which Mustafa II recognized the major territorial losses (e.g. Hungary), as well as the demarcations of a political linear frontier between the Ottomans and their Christian neighbors, brought home the full impact of the military failure[62]. Mustafa II, then, stood to be blamed for the military failure at Zenta because of his readiness to recognize the laws and precedents of the Christian powers and because of the consequent territorial losses allowed by the peace treaties[63].

[61] The registration of troops and of military claimants on the Ottoman treasury which accompanied the demobilization were carried in the grand vizierate of Amcazade Hüseyin (1697-1702) and through the tenures of his successors Dal Taban Mustafa and Rami Mehmed. Anonymous History, Berlin Diez A quarto/75, 162a-164b; Defterbar, *Zübdet*, 398a-b and Raşid, *Tarih*, II, 553; and Silihdar, *Nusretname*, II, 133/283b (the last for Rami Mehmed dated in A.H., 1114).

[62] There is evidence which suggests that steps were taken to blunt the impact of the territorial concessions. For example, the evacuated garrison of Fort Kamenets-Podolsk was forbidden permission to cross into Ottoman territory proper. Instead it was broken up into smaller units which were assigned to forts and garrisons on the Ottoman border: e.g., Kılburun, Akkerman, Yanık Hisar, Özü/Oczakow, Kili, Bender and Babadağ. In the language of the order: "... bir ferdi ahar mahalla dağılıp gitmemek üzere cema'atleri zabitlerine tenbih ü nizam verip...". For the official register of the evacuation, reassignment and provisioning of the garrison for the interim consult Istanbul: Başvekâlet Arşivi, Maliye Defteri (financial register) 6006, 90-109 (hereafter cited as Maliye Defteri).

[63] Abou-El-Haj, "Ottoman Methods of Negotiation" and *idem.*, "Mustafa II, A Psychohistorical Study".

Since 1683-84 the ranks of the armed forces, both regular (janissaries, *cebeci*s and others) and auxiliary (para-military, such as the *levend*s, *sipahi*s, *arnavut*s) were swollen to meet the military requirements of the Ottoman state, i.e., facing external aggression and *for* internal security. For instance, the number of registered janissaries had doubled by the year 1697. Under each of the grand viziers who served after Zenta there were attempts at a more careful accounting in the registration of troops. These inspections (*yoklamalar*) were aimed at the demobilization of the overgrown military establishment and the lightening of the financial burdens of the overextended Ottoman treasury[64].

When the news of the janissaries' defection and the *seğmen başı*'s subsequent assassination reached *kaymakam* Abdullah, a report was dispatched to Edirne informing the government of the most recent events. The *ulema* and statesmen who were assembled at the Top Kapı palace were released. Abdullah himself went into hiding[65]. His departure signaled the collapse of the government effort to suppress the rebellion from Istanbul. The release of the men of the *ilmiye* tended to strengthen the rebels' hand, coinciding as it did with the dispatches that were sent out under the seal of the captive kadi of Istanbul inviting the *ulema* to join the rebels at the parade grounds. As an incentive for the uncertain and reluctant a provision was added, explaining in no uncertain terms that, besides dragging them by force into the Et Meydanı, their homes would be sacked[66].

On Friday, July 20, four days after the *cebeci* insurrection, the *ulema*, *molla*s and *meşayih* joined the armed force at Orta Cami'i, the janissary regimental mosque. Some apparently arrived quite voluntarily at the parade grounds following their release from the palace[67]. The great majority, however, appeared only after receiving the rebel "invitation". What seems to have concerned them, even at this juncture in the rebellion, was the conduct and aims of the rebels. To the

64 Three months prior to the outbreak of the insurrection we find the incumbent grand vizier Rami Mehmed engaged in the final accounting for the registration and inspection of troops. The number of soldiers and their salaries, excluding North Africa, were put at 292,947 men and their yearly salaries and expenditures at 25,893 *kese*s of *akçe*s. Silihdar, *Nusretname*, II, 113/283b. Demobilization was ordered under Amcazade Hüseyin (1697-1702). Anonymous History, Berlin Diez A quarto/75, 237a is the only source to claim demobilization of troops as one of the causes for the rebellion.

65 Abdullah sent his report to the *rikâb* (court) on Thursday July 19, 1703 and arrived in Edirne on July 22. Defterdar, *Zübdet*, 421b, and Silihdar, *Nusretname*, II, 150/286b. For the correspondence between the court and Abdullah over the matter of *cebeci* salaries and eventual instructions for the suppression of the revolt by force see Vienna: Österreichische Nationalbibliothek, Mss. H.O. 179 (vol. I) and A.F. 159 (vol. II), "Münşeat-i Rami Mehmed" (hereafter cited as Rami Mehmed, "Münşeat") 133a-b and 204a-b.

66 Silihdar, *Nusretname*, II, 150/286b.

67 Defterdar, *Zübdet*, 421b.

mind of the *ulema* it was of paramount importance that the decisions made and the actions carried out conformed to the *şeriat* law[68].

The malcontents assured them at every stage that the sanction of the sacred law would be sought, especially since their own aims were not dissimilar to those of the *ulema*, namely the demand for justice — i.e., the removal of Feyzullah and company and the return of the court to Istanbul. From this point on, two themes dominate the activities of the *ulema*, the military, and the representatives of the merchants and people of Istanbul: the sincerity of the various elements of the coalition to conform with the *şeriat*, and whether the insurrection-turned-rebellion would turn into an outright *hurûc ala s-sultan* (withdrawal of allegiance from the sultan).

The first text of the two themes appeared simultaneously on the first Friday following the outbreak of the insurrection. The day is generally the Muslim occasion for public prayers, in which the *hutbe* is a critical element. The prayers were usually given in the name of the incumbent ruler as a sign of his imamate of the Muslim community and its sovereign — as leader of the faithful in prayer, defender of the faith, upholder of both justice and the *şeriat*[69]. Thus, the Friday prayers served as an occasion for renewal of allegiance and loyalty to the ruler.

But a dilemma arose among those assembled at the Meydan. Some felt that the conduct of the government did not warrant holding public prayers on that day. Others were of the contrary opinion, reasoning that the grievances which united them were all directed against the *şeyhülislâm* and not the sultan. The question was finally posed before the most eminent of the *ulema* present, Başmakcızade Ali, who had served until quite recently as the *kazasker* of Rumeli. This âlim answered in the customary abstract response of the canonical opinion (*fetva*) that one of the necessary principles of the propriety of holding the Friday prayers is the equity of the sultan, viz. his justice. Since the banner of revolt had been unfurled against the incumbent ruler on the assumption he had failed in maintaining the precepts of justice (*namus-ı adalet*), in what ways could the Friday prayers be deemed justified and proper?[70]

The first step in the direction of a *hurûc ala s-sultan* had been taken. The question left unanswered at this early stage was whether this first step should be immediately escalated into an outright declaration of their intention to replace the incumbent sultan, or should the matter be left for later events to occasion it. Armed with a legal sanction against holding public prayers that day, the rebels' case was thus strengthened against the moderates in this dispute.

[68] *Ibid.*
[69] Silihdar, *Nusretname*, II, 150-51/286b
[70] *Ibid.*

An interpretation of the *fetva* needs to be raised at this point. It is not quite clear from contemporary sources whether it was meant to be restrictive or comprehensive. If restrictive, it would have meant a tentative injunction and, therefore, temporary prohibition against holding prayers, with the attendant withholding of the weekly *hutbe* until justice and equity had finally been upheld by the ruler. Following this interpretation Mustafa II would only have to dismiss Feyzullah and return the court to Istanbul. On the other hand, the more comprehensive interpretation of the *fetva* would have meant a permanent injunction against holding public prayers as long as Mustafa II held office. This would have amounted to a *fetva* of deposition, an interpretation the soldiers and rebels were not quite ready to admit at this juncture—at least not openly and publicly.

There is evidence that both these interpretations were understood and used. However, this early in the rebellion the rebels chose not to press the second alternative, consistent with their declared intention of deposing Feyzullah and returning the court to Istanbul. The second alternative interpretation was kept in reserve for future use.

Whatever the intended implications of the *fetva* may have been, the very fact that it was issued at all was of decisive importance for the development of the rebellion. Up to this point the protest appeared merely as a unilateral one against the infractions and corruptions of certain officials of the incumbent government. The legal opinion served two purposes. It gave the rebellion a much needed stamp of legitimacy and sealed the union between the military elements and the *ulema*. Those in rebellion could now appeal to, and eventually command, the allegiance of whatever elements remained uncommitted[71].

One curious but consistent feature of the narrative of the rebellion in contemporary Ottoman sources requires explanation. Up to this point, the rebellion is portrayed by all Ottoman contemporaries as spontaneous, anonymous and leaderless—especially in the search for a legal opinion on the holding of public prayers. However, once the *fetva* was issued, declaring that the dissidents at least had legal grounds for their protest, leaders began to emerge openly. It is quite obvious that by this point the situation in Istanbul had deteriorated to such an extent that disorder and chaos threatened to disrupt life. Thus, ostensibly, responsible leadership would emerge, if only to avert the evils of civil war. In reality an alternate authority was in the making at this stage. It is here that the

[71] The most reluctant of the military elements to join the rebellion were the *bostancıs*, the palace guard. Their presence on the side of the rebels was of paramount importance, for it may be recalled that the *bostancı* commander had earlier been instructed by the *kaymakam* Abdullah to fetch the flag of the Eyup Mosque. Since he had that banner, and given its symbolic value for rallying the troops to the side of the rebellion, it became paramount for the leaders to see the *bostancıs* and their commander on the rebel side. Silihdar, *Nusretname*, II, 153/287a.

actual split in Ottoman polity may have been felt. The obvious threat of its fragmentation would have jeopardized the course of the rebellion and subverted the specific goals and purposes of the various factions in the coalition.

These observations are borne out in part by the men who emerged as leaders, the pattern of their behavior, and the policies they promulgated from this point on. Practically every one of the measures the contenders took with the incumbent government was marked by deliberateness and measured action—i.e., control. Thus, Çalık Ahmed Ağa, a former *kul kâhyası* (elected deputy *ağa* of the janissaries), deliberately refrained from breaking away from the Edirne government[72], despite his wish to get the *ağalık* of the janissaries. Instead, he curbed his ambition for the moment and took the office of *seğmen başı*, mainly as a replacement for the deceased Murtaza. By shunning the office of *yeniçeri ağası* (general of the janissaries), Çalık Ahmed indicated reluctance on the part of the rebel leadership to exercise sovereign power at that juncture. Later on we see the same hesitancy in the selection of Sohrablı Ahmed as the replacement for Abdullah Pasha, the Istanbul *kaymakam*.

Although less restrained in the selection of *ulema* to fill the highest posts of the *ilmiye* corporation, the same leadership, nevertheless, continued to act as though Mustafa II's authority was not in jeopardy. To them it was a foregone conclusion that Mustafa II would accept their demand for the dismissal of Feyzullah and his entourage, the religious bureaucracy, and confirm *their* nominees as replacements.

Başmakcızade Ali Efendi, the *âlim* who had just issued the *fetva* on the propriety of Friday's prayers, was returned as *mufti* to replace Feyzullah[73]. This Ali Efendi had once been the protégé of Ebusaidzade Feyzullah Efendi who, along with several other *ulema*, was instrumental in deposing Mustafa II's father, Mehmed IV, in 1687[74]. His star began to rise in 1690 but came to a quick fall in 1695[75]. He staged a comeback during the latter part of Amcazade Hüseyin's vizierate when he returned to occupy several high positions[76].

All indications point to a lack of sympathy between Ali Efendi and the sultan. It seems that this *âlim* was much more in sympathy with the Köprülü coalition

[72] Silihdar, *Nusretname*, II, 151/286b.

[73] For a short biography see Ms. Vienna H.O. 126, II, 167b-168b.

[74] Silihdar, *Tarih*, II, 295-98, 565-69; and 565-69 which shows him as an ally of Köprülüzade Fazıl Mustafa, warning the latter of the plot to replace ailing sultan Süleyman II without the grand vizier's consultation. Rasid, *Tarih*, II, 283 and Defterdar, *Zübdet*, 276b and Silihdar, *Nusretname*, II, 31.

[75] First as *nakib* (1690), then Rumeli *kazasker* (to 1693). Silihdar, *Tarih*, II, 510 and 735.

[76] 1700-1701. Silihdar, *Nusretname*, II, 43, 92/271b, 278a.

and pattern of government and was, therefore, opposed to the one Mustafa II tried to promulgate upon his accession. There are indications that point to Ali Efendi's implication in Köprülü Amcazade Hüseyin's attempt to depose Mustafa II[77].

The rebel choice for *kazasker* (chief judge) of Rumeli was Tevki'i-zade Mehmed Efendi, who had served as *kadı* of Istanbul in April 1693, and reached the rank of Anadolu five years later, though never holding the office itself[78]. The selection of Mehmed Efendi reflects another pattern in contrast to that of Ali Efendi's nomination for muftiship. Whereas the latter may not have been sympathetic to either Mehmed IV or his son Mustafa II—owing to their antipathy to the Köprülü—Mehmed Efendi championed the deposed Mehmed IV and his sons in their bid to have at least one of them returned to the throne in 1690-91. The *molla*, who once served as Imam to Kara Mustafa[79], was exiled for his advocacy of Mehmed IV's cause[80].

But the accession of Mustafa II was no blessing for him either. The new ruler did not recognize his earlier, though unsuccessful, support for the former sultan, and for the duration of the son's reign, Mehmed Efendi remained at the outer borders of the higher bureaucracy of the *ilmiye*[81]. He must have arrived at the conclusion that under Mustafa II's reign, and especially with Feyzullah at the helm, he had little chance to improve his position and, therefore, finally opted to associate himself with the challenge being posed to Mustafa and his government in July 1703[82].

What emerges from this comparison between the rebels' choices to fill these two high posts in the *ilmiye* is instructive. It shows that, like all other "professional" groups in Ottoman society, the members of the *ilmiye* did not act either consistently or monolithically. In the case of Tevki'i-zade Mehmed Efendi, in fact, we have an *âlim* who changed his "affiliation" when it suited his interest and what he

[77] Başmakcızade Ali was dismissed from the *kazaskerlik* of Rumeli only two weeks following the implication of Kıblelizade Ali Bey, nephew of the grand vizier, in his attempt at contacting Prince Ahmed (subsequently Ahmed III), the incumbent sultan's brother, for the purpose of sounding him out on the anticipated change in government. Silihdar, *Nusretname*, II, 92/278a.

[78] Short biography in Ms. Vienna H.O. 126, II, 153a-b.

[79] Şefik, *Şefikname*, 198.

[80] Silihdar, *Tarih*, II, 565-69.

[81] In 1693, and only for five months, he served as Istanbul Kadi. Silihdar, *Tarih*, II, 697 and Ms. Vienna H.O. 126, II, 153a-b.

[82] Anonymous History, Berlin Diez A quarto 5, 4 a-b reports that as an indication of the high reputation and prestige of this âlim Tevfikzade Mehmed was initially invited by the rebels to mediate with the *seğmen başı* Haşımoğlu Murtaza. His acceptance of rebel nomination to Rumeli Kazaskerlik is detailed in both Silihdar, *Nusretname*, II, 151-52 and Anonymous History, Berlin Diez A quarto 5, 16a-b.

considered to be that of the *ilmiye* and, therefore, of the state. Later on we see even Başmakcızade Ali reverse himself and his affiliations, separate himself from the rebel cause, and opt for a neutral position by resigning the office of mufti, just conferred upon him by the rebels[83].

The rebel nominees for the offices of Anadolu chief judge and *nakib* were Yahya Efendi[84] and Ibrahim Efendi[85], who had been frustrated by Feyzullah Efendi even though they had come up through the ranks expecting appointment to the highest *ilmiye* posts. Ibrahim Efendi had served two terms as kadi, once for Selânik (Salonica) in 1694 (prior to Mustafa II's accession) and once for Şam (Damascus) in 1699-1700, before being nominated for the *nikabet* by the rebels[86]. Yahya Efendi, on the other hand, served as *kadı* of Istanbul in 1697-98[87] and then remained without appointment to office until the rebellion. At ages sixty-six and sixty-four respectively, Ibrahim Efendi and Yahya Efendi, with only occasional appointments to high office under Mustafa II, must have felt slighted. Though not much is known about Ibrahim's background, Yahya came from a prominent, political *ulema* family. Both his grandfather, Abdurrahim Efendi, and his father, Mehmed Efendi, had been involved in the removal of sultans (Ibrahim [in 1648] and Mehmed IV [in 1687])[88, 89].

83 Silihdar, *Nusretname*, II, 157-58/288a. Ali Efendi was obviously not willing to openly associate himself with the covert intentions of the rebels. It is quite probable that he feared the implications of such an association for his future career.

84 A short biography in Ms. Vienna H.O. 126, II, 184a-b.

85 A short biography in Ms. Vienna H.O. 126, II, 161a-b.

86 *Ibid.*, and Silihdar, *Nusretname*, III, 157-58/286a.

87 Silihdar, *Nusretname*, I, 246, 336/247a, 260a.

88 Şefik, *Şefikname*, 115-16.

89 One of the most politically active of the ulema of this period is Hakimbaşızade Yahya Efendi, the son of Halebli Salih Efendi, Mehmed IV's court physician. Silihdar openly associates Yahya Efendi with being instrumental in the removal of grand vizier Ismail in October, 1688. Silihdar, *Tarih*, II, 359. Less than a year later, in September, 1689, he is described as having an active role in the crucial discussions with grand vizier Bekri Mustafa following the fall of Niş. Silihdar, *Tarih*, II, 475. To the Janissary ağa Koca Mahmud's suggestion that the ulema should join the military ranks in order to add their numbers and prestige to the effort to recover lost territory, Yahya Efendi lectured him on the four part "constitutional" division of the Ottoman body-politic (peasants, merchants, soldiers and ulema) and their preordained functions (to the military *taife* he recalled, "your business is to preserve and protect the people who reside within Islamic lands and to repulse the enemy who occupies Islamic lands". To the ulema: "We are bound to our business of applying and facilitating the Prophet's canonical laws [*ahkâm-ı şer'i nebevî*] to forbid and impede the violators of God's people and preserve their rights in conformity with the requirements of the *şeriat* against those who do not uphold God's command!"). Although the grand vizier is reported to have agreed with Yahya Efendi's affirmation of rigid societal stratification and definition of functions of the various corporations, he "remained suspicious of Yahya Efendi, among others, fearing that they may be plotting his removal from office". Defterdar, *Zübdet*, 173b-174a and Raşid, *Tarih*, II, 90-92. Yahya Efendi is reported to have taken part in his removal a short month later (October, 1689). Defterdar, *Zübdet*, 177b. Later that same year, this same Yahya is reported to have sided with Köprülüzade Mustafa in the dispute which the latter had with *Darüssaadet ağası* Mustafa and

Once the rebel nominees for the high *ilmiye* posts had been named, there was one other high post still vacant in the government at Istanbul. It may be recalled that the Kaymakam Abdullah had fled the city as soon as he heard of the assassination of the *seğmen başı* Murtaza. Consistent with their principle of not appropriating the sovereignty of the Edirne government, the rebels, at this stage, only appointed a replacement for Abdullah. Their choice was Sohrablı Ahmed Pasha, also known as Kavanoz (Fatty). He was of Russian origin and a convert to Islam. His career was typical of a great number of Ottoman high officials in the seventeenth century. After seeing service as a slave in the household of Silihdar Hüseyin Pasha (d. 1687)[90], he entered the inner service of the sultan's palace for at least nine years[91].

In December, 1687, he was granted vizieral rank and given the government of Basra province[92]. After holding several more governorates[93], he was removed

succeeded in his plea with the sultan for the ağa's dismissal. Raşid, *Tarih*, II, 116-118. His partnership for the Köprülüs is further illustrated by his divulgence to Fazıl Mustafa of a plot by the latter's opponents to replace the ailing Süleyman II with their own candidate in order to preclude the grand vizier's candidate. Silihdar, *Tarih*, II, 565-69. Following the demise of Fazıl Mustafa at Slankamen, Yahya Efendi is found again giving political advice to the newly appointed grand vizier Kadi Ali. This time, however, the advice was not appreciated and Yahya was removed from office. Defterdar, *Zübdet*, 216a and Raşid, *Tarih*, II, 166-68. His outspoken opinions and daring did not earn him either the admiration or love of high officials. At Mustafa II's accession, Yahya Efendi had been removed from office due to his unparallelled outspokenness of the truth and his daring ("beynel emsal kelam-i hakk tefevvühünde... meşhur ve bu güne cesaretlerinden naşi... ba'is-i tenafür-i tab'-ı hümayun") (Defterdar, *Zübdet*, 277a-b). He was required to confine himself to Aleppo, his native town. Mühimme Defteri 105, 58. Although recalled from exile early in Mustafa II's reign, Yahya did not desist from political "intrigue". In April, 1702, he is accused of having been seen with Amcazade Hüseyin's nephew, Kıblelizade Ali Bey. The latter had just been exiled from the court after being implicated in the heinous crime of having tried to reach crown-prince Ahmed to sound him out on replacing Mustafa II. Yahya was returned to Aleppo again in exile. Anonymous History, Berlin Diez A quarto/75, 294a. One of the first acts of the rebel mufti Imam Mehmed following his confirmation by Ahmed III was to recall Yahya from exile. Anonymous History, Berlin Diez A quarto 75, 276a. L. V. Thomas claims that Yahya, Ramı (Mehmed) and (Amcazade) Hüseyin "were united in opposition against Elmas Mehmed" (Mustafa II's hand-picked grand vizier), but he gives no evidence in support of this alliance. *Naima*, 54, note 47.

90 This Hüseyin, also known as Kız Hüseyin, was born c. 1616 in Istolice or Istoliza (modern Stolac) in Herzegovina of Bosnian origin, i.e. a Christian convert. In his teens he entered the *gılman* corps of the old imperial palace at Edirne. After serving close to forty years in the inner service of the palace he graduated to the governorate of Aleppo that proved to be one of a series of provincial appointments mainly in eastern provinces. He also had a son who also attained the title of pasha. For his various assignments as governor and for notations of his more significant activities consult Silihdar, *Tarih*, I, 391, 556, 559, 561, 622, 636, 760 and II, 5, 114, 217, 241, 248, 265. Short biographies in Silihdar, *Tarih*, II, 293-94 and Süreyya, *Sicil*, II, 197.

91 Süreyya, *Sicil*, I, 235.

92 Silihdar, *Tarih*, II, 308. Defterdar, *Zübdet*, 139b specifies that he paid into the *enderun* treasury the *câ'ize* (present!) of 150 *kese akçes* for the Basra post and for the *tuğ-ı hümayun* (rank of pasha) 45 *kese akçe* to the total of 195 *keses*.

93 Five governorates. Silihdar, *Tarih*, II, 350, 553, 605, 792.

in 1695 from the Diyar Bekir and deprived of the rank of vizier for his incompetence in providing troops for Mustafa II's first military campaign[94]. He was returned to public service under the vizierate of his brother-in-law, Amcazade Hüseyin[95]. Ahmed had apparently managed to get himself berothed to Hüseyin's sister with her father's consent but not her brother's[96].

Though technically unattached to the palace, Ahmed had hitched his star to that of the most powerful household in the land. His fortunes and misfortunes both would be tied to those of the Köprülü's. He would rise to lucrative posts while a Köprülü was the incumbent vizier and lose them with their departure[97]. During the last year of his brother-in-law's vizierate, Ahmed managed to get himself elevated to the prestigious, though by then mainly ceremonial, post of *nişancı*[98], but was removed when Hüseyin resigned in 1702. (Typically, from that point on he was known alternately as Kavanoz and Nişancı Ahmed.)

Although most of the contemporary Ottoman observers agree on the specific details of Ahmed Pasha's career, none of them seem surprised that an in-law of the Köprülüs would accept the rebel nomination to the *kaymakamlık* (rank of *kaymakam*) and thereby associate himself and the Köprülüs with the rebel cause[99]. And though none of these same observers even try to explain why, we shall see later in the narrative that the rise of Nişancı Ahmed was part of a pattern of rebel nominations involving several Köprülü sympathizers and affiliates in various capacities in the alternate government which the rebels were rapidly putting together. Here we will just touch upon some of our observations:

The emergence of this Köprülü client at the head of the rebel government signaled the overt entry into the coalition of a new element, which had been lying dormant. With the further unfolding of the rebellion we find more individuals who had held office under the Köprülüs openly associating themselves with the rebellion. The irony of replacing Abdullah Pasha, himself a Köprülü, with a Köprülü client should not escape our attention. Abdullah was the son-in-law of

94 Silihdar, *Nusretname*, I, 45/219b and Mühimme Defteri 106, 195.

95 Silihdar, *Nusretname*, I, 302/255a.

96 Hüseyin's father died in August, 28, 1687. The grand vizier is reported to have said of his brother-in-law, "peder-i merhum bizim Ayşeyi şu herife vermiş benim rızam yok idi". (My father gave our Ayşe to this "chap," I myself would not have consented to it.) For how contemporaries viewed him, see Anonymous History, Berlin Diez A quarto 75, 282a-284b.

97 Silihdar, *Nusretname*, II, 9, 25, 90-92/ 267a, 269b, 277b-278a.

98 Silihdar, *Nusretname*, II, 119/281b-282a. On the diminished status of the Nişancı see Abou-El-Haj, *Karlowitz and Reisülküttab*, 31-33 and 55-56, notes 39-42.

99 Anonymous History, Berlin Diez A quarto 75, 282a claims that with the outbreak of the revolt and the escape of *kaymakam* Abdullah, no (responsible) vizier was left in the city. Out of necessity he (Ahmed Pasha) was brought from retirement and made *kaymakam*. In the early stages of the rebellion he is reported as being *memnun olmayip* (quite unhappy) and *havfa tabi'* (subject to fear).

Feyzullah and, from all indications, this association seems to have been forced on Abdullah. Suffice it to note that Feyzullah exercised some control over the Köprülü family through his office of guardian over the vast Köprülü endowments[100].

One of the major theses of this study is that the Köprülüs were but one element, a political substructure, which emerged from the middle of the seventeenth century and vied with the Ottoman dynasty over the rulership of the state. We will point out later, however, that Köprülü family members and sympathizers could also be found serving the incumbent government. This tendency illustrates another thesis advanced by this study: that the rebellion was as much an *inter*-elite as it was an *intra*-elite conflict. Its dynamics point to a conflict not between classes rigidly held together, but between contenders drawn from parts of practically all elements of Ottoman society.

As the news of the rebellion spread outside the capital proper, it began to attract the discontented in great numbers. Each of the following men seems to have had a very specific grievance against either a high official or a specific policy of the incumbent government.

Karakaş Mustafa Ağa[101], a *timar sipahi* (received his pay as a *sipahi* by collecting taxes on a *timar*), had been deprived of his livelihood by the *telhisçi* of Feyzullah Efendi, Belinli Mehmed Ağa[102]. When the aggrieved Karakaş arrived in Edirne to protest, he was harassed with such threats that he returned, quite defeated, to settle at Üsküdar. While he was biding his time, the rebellion broke out, and in it he saw his chance to take vengeance on Feyzullah. This same Mustafa was later to be credited with organizing and maintaining order throughout the rebellion[103].

Two other virtual unknowns entered the rebellion at this stage[104]: Mustafa Efendi, also known as Ladikli Deli Emir Mustafa[105], and Ahmed Ağa, known

[100] The *nezaret* of Feyzullah over the Köprülü *evkaf* is mentioned in Mühimme Defteri 106, 243. Feyzullah as muftı had the *nezaret* of over 100 *vakf*s by 1697-98. A list of these is given in Maliye Defteri 6006, 8b-9a.

[101] Silihdar, *Nusretname*, II, 153-54/287a.

[102] *Ibid.* Anonymous History, Berlin Diez A quart 75, 236a-b lists him as one of the causes of the rebellion. He is supposed to have held a *malikane* in Adana which gave him a revenue of 80 *kese*s *akçe*.

[103] Defterdar, *Zübdet*, 422b calls Karakaş Mustafa a daredevil who had talent for organization.

[104] *Ibid.*, is the only source that adds the names of Yekçeşm Yusuf, Musili, Çelebi Mehmed and Selim. Silihdar, *Nusretname*, II, 154/287a.

[105] Mustafa Efendi who subsequently was appointed as *Imam-ı Sultani* for Ahmed III was one of the ulema executed by order of the new monarch. Anonymous History, Berlin Diez A quart 75, 296a-b and Silihdar, *Nusretname*, II, 209-10/296a. He was regarded by our earlier source as the *baş u buğ* of the *seyyid*s and responsible for assembling 2,000 ulema for the rebel cause at *Meydan-ı Lahm*. Anonymous History, Berlin Diez A quart 75, 240a-b.

as Durcan, a janissary who resided at Büyük Çekmece. It is not clear why contemporary sources add the names to the long and impressive list of distinguished men who sided with the rebellion. Perhaps it was to demonstrate the grandiose designs that nonentities could harbor and how these "riff-raff" of Ottoman society could take advantage of troubled times to feed their personal ambitions without regard to public interest[106].

Or was it perhaps to have someone to blame for the crude behavior of the rebels. Perhaps the sources were trying to justify the elite's joining the rebellion by seeing them as the one element that could restrain and guide Ottoman society through a difficult but inevitable transition[107]. Since the chroniclers were subsidized by these same elite of Ottoman society, it is quite understandable why they would try to advance the cause of the higher "classes".

Without either explanation or justification the names of two experienced middle-ranking officers of the regular army are also mentioned on the side of the rebels. They are Yekçeşm Deli Musili Ağa, who had held the *seğmen başı* office several times[108], and Çelebi Mehmed Ağa, who had previously held the offices of *zağarcı başı* (head of one of the janissary companies), *kul kâhyası* and *seğmen başı*[109]. It is quite obvious that at least one chronicler was showing there was further augmentation of responsible rebel leadership with middle and high ranking officers and ex-officers of the regular armed forces, men who would play a crucial and steadying role in the course of the rebellion.

By this juncture the first of a two-stage strategy had been completed. Ostensibly, the rebels posed as reasonable men who had very specific bones of contention with officers of the incumbent government. It would seem then that had the sultan complied with the simple request of the rebels, there would have been no further difficulties.

At the same time, however, a nucleus of an alternate authority was in the making with de facto appointments being made to the *ilmiye* and other branches of

106 Contemporary observers treat these virtual unknowns, especially from the military, with condescension and disdain.

107 Given the fact that the chroniclers were subsidized by the elite of Ottoman society, it is quite understandable why they would try to advance the cause of the higher "classes" of that society. For example, Mustafa Naima Efendi. His first patron was Amcazade Hüseyin to whom he dedicated the first preface of his chronicle. Following the death of the grand vizier he was attached to Moralı Hasan to whom he dedicated the second preface to the very same work. Thomas, *Naima*, 31-34, 42-48.

108 The first time in October, 1693, Silihdar, *Tarih*, II, 735; the second time in May, 1695, Silihdar, *Nusretname*, I, 30/217b and the third time in 1701-02, Silihdar, *Nusretname*, II, 89/272a. Defterdar, *Zübdet*, 422b claims that Musili entered the rebellion quite early. Short biography in Süreyya, *Sicil*, IV, 498.

109 For a short biography see Süreyya, *Sicil*, IV, 209.

government. (We have noted earlier that replacements for the mufti, *kaymakam*, and *seğmen başı* had already been selected.) There seems to have been no question in the minds of those who effected these changes that their actions were legitimate. Although they may have been acting under the guise of jealousy for maintaining public order, they were, in fact, acting in a sovereign manner, thereby narrowing the sultan's alternatives for action.

Once the first stage had been weathered, the question of the legitimacy of the sultan and that of his government would be raised in the rebel councils[110]. Yet there is no public record of it. Only reasonable options seem to have been offered the sultan to save his throne and government.

The next most crucial business for the rebels concerned minimum demands of the government. It is not quite clear from available sources how many meetings were held and who the participants were. It *is* clear, however, that when the petition to the sultan was finally penned it did not reflect all the issues voiced by the deliberators, or all the real motives that impelled them.

Both in its draft and final forms[111] the petition listed two conditions to be met before the rebels would put down their arms, i.e., Feyzullah and his entourage had to be dismissed and the sultan and his court had to return permanently to Istanbul. In the final draft the return of the government to the capital and the delivery of Feyzullah alive became mandatory conditions. While deliberating the final draft, some of the *ulema* tried to revise the order of priority, placing greater weight on the return of the court to Istanbul. They were overruled. Eventually, an ultimatum was appended, requiring both the response and return of the court to Istanbul within five days of the petition's issuance[112]. From all available sources it is fairly clear that most of the eminent *ulema* did not act with complete freedom or without intimidation. In its essentials and tone the final draft of the petition reflected the thinking of the more radical and extreme elements of the rebellion.

The most threatening extant version of the petition reads: "Let the *padişah* know that upon the receipt of our letter, Feyzullah Efendi should be taken and dispatched in chains to Istanbul. And if there is need for a padişah, let him come along and if there is another answer, let him make so known"[113].

110 Silihdar, *Nusretname*, II, 154-56/287a-b.

111 A copy in Silihdar, *Nusretname*, II, 155/287b.

112 *Ibid.*

113 "... Feyzullah Efendi varakamız vusulünde ahz edup kayd u bend ile Istanbula irsal ve padışahlık gerek ise ma'an gelesin ve eğer bir ahar cevabın var ise ona göre bildüresin". Anonymous History, Berlin Diez A quarto 5, fol. 10b. "In this petition they did not altogether lose their respect to the sultan, as it was positively reported upon the grounds, yt. when the said Petition was read to the People and Souldiery, upon their hearing the expression of requesting the Gr. Sigr. to return hither, they cried out, they did not request it, but require it", P.R.O., S.P. 97/21, 136b.

The final draft of the petition was read aloud (Saturday, July 21) to the assembled representatives of the various dissident groups[114]. It was this version that was finally agreed upon, signed and sealed by some three hundred men representing, among others, the *ulema*, *ocak* officers and *esnaf* of the city[115]. The number of signatories and the orders they represented were meant to impress upon Mustafa II not only the depth of rebel unity, but also the breadth of the coalition and the support for their cause. These nuances could be demonstrated by examining the backgrounds of some of the men chosen to deliver the petition.

The most prominent member of the delegation was Türk Hasan Efendi, and a glimpse at his biography might help us discern why he was chosen for the task. He did not enter the *ulema* corps through the usual path of either birth (i.e., family) or the *medrese*, but rather via the palace, where he first served in the *gılman-ı hassa* (previously reserved for slaves)[116]. Having been born at Safranbolu (Zaʿferan Bolu) to a Muslim family, he earned the rank of *kalfa* before enrolling in the *ilmiye*.

In May, 1690, he aligned himself, through his father-in-law, Ibrahim Efendi (the Imam of former sultan Mehmed IV), with the faction that was sympathetic to returning ex-sultan Mehmed IV (or one of his sons) to the vacant throne[117]. But Köprülüzade Mustafa Pasha wanted Ahmed II to be sultan—and Hasan, his father-in-law, Ibrahim, and their allies were exiled to Cyprus.

Türk Hasan was released only after the demise of Ibrahim Efendi[118]. At the outbreak of the rebellion he was between appointments, having served most recently as kadi of Egypt. The selection of an *âlim* who had quite obviously championed Mehmed IV and his immediate family must have been meant as a signal to Mustafa II that the rebellion was not confined to those who may have originally opposed Mustafa II's accession to the Ottoman throne, but included men who were once allies of that branch of the Ottoman dynasty.

One other feature of Türk Hasan's background may suggest further reasons for his choice. Since he was well-known at the court, owing both to his sympathies

[114] It was read by Taşcızade Abdullah to the rebel mufti Ali Efendi, the great *mollas*, *meşayih* and *müderrisler*, commanders of the *ocaks* and the *ayan* and *sadat* of the capital. Defterdar, *Zübdet*, 423a. This Taşçizade Abdullah was a close associate of Imam Mehmed Efendi, the rebel replacement for Başmakcızade Ali Efendi, Anonymous History, Berlin Diez A quarto 75, 296a-b. He was of Bosnian origin. When he entered Istanbul he was already an adult. He is reputed to have chosen the *va'z* (preaching) branch of the *ilmiye*... Şefik, *Şefikname*, 151-52. During one of Mustafa II's campaigns, he and another *âlim*, Himmetzade Abdullah Efendi, were invited to join the sultan. *Ibid.*

[115] The figure is quoted from Anonymous History, Berlin Diez A quarto 75, 241a-b.

[116] Ms. Vienna H.O. 126, II, 162a-b and Şefik, *Şefikname*, 149.

[117] Silihdar, *Tarih*, II, 565-69.

[118] Silihdar, *Tarih*, II, 600.

toward and services in the palace, he would gain access to the sultan more easily than someone barely known at the court or known for his hostility to Mustafa II and his family[119].

Taşçızade Abdullah Efendi was another member of the *ulema* delegation sent with the petition. Having served as *va'iz* during the campaigns of Mustafa II, he, too, was well-known at the court. The rebels, therefore, thought he would not be considered unwelcome by Mustafa II[120].

Of the other *ilmiye* petitioners, Isa Efendi is worthy of note. He was a member of the *derviş* (mystical) order of the Halvetiye[121]. Since Feyzullah Efendi was also a known member of that order, is it possible that inclusion of these two members served as a signal by its representatives of their disassociation from the *mufti* due to their unhappiness with him? At the very least it would indicate that the Halvetiye order sympathized with the protesters against Feyzullah, for once the Istanbul side decided to march against Mustafa II, Himmetzade Abdullah Efendi[122]—one of the most respected members of the Halvetiye, and an open critic of Mehmed IV's passion for the hunt—marched along with them[123].

Of the other "classes" represented in the delegation the military assigned two from each main division of the regular armed forces (janissaries, *sipahi*s, *cebeci*s, *topçu*s, etc.). And the trades and merchants of the city also assigned two men from each of their divisions. When the *harcırah* (travel allowance) was alloted to them, the delegates left for Edirne—their journey beginning in mid-afternoon, Saturday, July 21, 1703[124].

Before following their course and fate, and before analyzing the position of the incumbent government, it is important to evaluate contemporary versions of what transpired at the sessions which were held by the rebels to spell out their demands of Mustafa II. What was left out of the petition, and out of contemporary narratives, is perhaps more important than what was included. Nearly all the sources single out Feyzullah as the main target of personal hostility and antagonism. His royal mentor is portrayed as blameless, except for his extended absence from Istanbul. Consequently, it would seem, his return to the capital

[119] Hasan's choice may indicate the triumph of the moderates in having their own spokesman sent to head the delegation.

[120] Same sources as in n. 114 above.

[121] Ms. Vienna H.O. 126, II, 218b-219a. It should also be noted that a member of the *halvetiye* order, Isazade Ömer Efendi, was also one of the petitioners. Biography in Ms. Vienna H.O. 126, II, 217b. See also Silihdar, *Nusretname*, II, 156/287b.

[122] Ms. Vienna H.O. 126, II, 213b-216a and Anonymous History, Berlin Diez A quarto 75, 253b.

[123] Silihdar, *Tarih*, II, 245-48.

[124] Silihdar, *Nusretname*, II, 156/287a.

would have been sufficient to abate any ill-feeling which may have been harbored against him.

Only one of the Ottoman sources consulted hints at direct criticism of Mustafa II. Here the royal sovereign is blamed for his handling of the most recent war and subsequent peace treaties with the Holy League. The evacuation and abandonment of the Podolian fort of Kamenets-Podolsk by Ottoman forces in implementing the peace treaty with Poland was singled out for the heaviest criticism[125]. From supplementary sources it can be accurately stated that not only were these criticisms voiced but Mustafa II's competence as sultan was openly questioned, especially regarding the amount of territory the Ottomans had to surrender and the "Christian" laws (read European) by which their sovereign was guided. There was no doubt, then, in the minds of those attending the deliberations on the petition that as soon as Mustafa II had complied with their request to return and hold court in Istanbul, he was not expected to continue very long in office.

Why is it, then, that when Mustafa II was being tried for the equivalent of high treason[126], the rebels could not spell out the charge against him quite so openly? One suggestion can be offered in explanation: It is quite obvious that at this stage the rebel coalition was not firmly bound and, therefore, not so secure. (Just as obviously, there were elements that would have opted for an open declaration of the rebellion aimed at the ousting of the sultan.)

But cooler heads prevailed. Mustafa II was invited to return to Istanbul, ostensibly to carry out the normal business of government—with only the slightest hint of what would be in store for him once he returned. In fact, there is evidence that following the session where Mustafa II's competence was questioned, the rebel coalition began to fragment. Feigning illness, Başmakcızade Ali, the rebel nominee for mufti, begged to be relieved—his main motive being one of disassociation from the faction favouring the deposition of Mustafa II.

Emphasizing the extraordinary nature of the events that Istanbul was experiencing, the normal life of the city was drastically curtailed. Shops, closed since the first outbreak against the incumbent government, were ordered to remain shut, with the exception of butchers, bakers, grocers, and public baths. A discriminatory, though limited, curfew was imposed on the movements of minors, women, and members of non-Muslim *millet*s[127].

As rebel intentions became more and more obvious, the unity of their coalition

[125] Anonymous History, Berlin Diez A quarto 5, 7a.

[126] For the circumstances and details see Abou-El-Haj, "Ottoman Methods of Negotiation". These same charges are also discussed below.

[127] Silihdar, *Nusretname*, II, 156/287b.

began to be threatened. In order to ensure the initial unity which had evolved out of the *cebeci* insurrection, steps were taken to protect the interests of the coalition members. Various merchant groups had, quite early in the rebellion, demonstrated their discontent with the government by entering the rebellion with their banners and their *kâhyas* in the vanguard. To safeguard their shops, guards were assigned to police the bazaars of the city. To further cement the coalition, a covenant was made involving the symbolic sharing of salt and bread before the Koran and a sword[128].

All these measures point to an atmosphere which was heavy with the anticipation of drastic change. They indicate fear of relaxation of tension lest there be a loss of momentum and the possibility of counter-movements rising to crush the rebellion. Every possible measure was taken to ensure that a business-as-usual atmosphere would not prevail. Finally, these measures show that the situation was much graver and involved more than just returning the sultan to Istanbul and deposing Feyzullah[129].

We have already noted the resignation of Başmakcızade Ali from the office of *şeyhülislâm*. Ill health and old age were the ostensible reasons for his request to be relieved of the high honour. As recorded by contemporary sources, the purported illness was close to paralysis which had left Ali's capacities for movement and speech quite impaired[130]. Yet, within the same year — but under more auspicous circumstances — this same Ali Efendi would gladly accept the mantle of office from Ahmed III[131]. Only one of our sources admits that Ali wanted to separate himself from the machinations of the rebel leadership, especially in their plan to oust Mustafa II[132].

For Ali's replacement the rebels chose Imam Mehmed Efendi, who had served as *şeyhülislâm* for seventy days[133] — partially coinciding with Mustafa II's reign — only to be dismissed to make way for Feyzullah Efendi[134]. The career of this *âlim* further indicates that the corps of the *ulema* did not act quite as monolithically

[128] Silihdar, *Nusretname*, II, 157/187b-288a. Defterdar, *Zübdet*, 423b specifies that heads of the ulema, *sadat*, *ocak* commanders and leaders of the city were brought for taking an oath and making a covenant (symbolically) over a sword, bread, salt and a copy of the Koran.

[129] The fickleness of the Istanbul crowd and the still precarious nature of the coalition required both symbolic and concrete coercive measures to ensure and guarantee support of all members of the initial coalition.

[130] Anonymous History, Berlin Diez A quarto 75, 247a. "Tamla şeklinde hastalık... harakete ve nutuka macalı kalmayıp... halk kendisinden meyus olmuşlar".

[131] Anonymous History, Berlin Diez A quarto 75, 296a-b and Silihdar, *Nusretname*, II, 209-10, 296a.

[132] Anonymous History, Berlin Diez A quarto 75, 247a.

[133] Silihdar, *Nusretname*, II, 158/288.

[134] Silihdar, *Nusretname*, I, 31/217b.

as once believed[135]. Mehmed Efendi had served in the capacity of second and third *imam* for Mehmed IV, Mustafa II's father. This association, though, did not jeopardize his future career, as he attained the office of judge of Rumeli twice[136], before finally being raised to the highest *ilmiye* post of *şeyhülislâm*[137]. Thus, despite his association with the discredited sultan, Mehmed IV, this *âlim* managed well to adapt himself to the political regimes that followed the ouster of the sultan, without experiencing any recrimination.

Was this flexibility and adaptability the reason for Mustafa II's suspicion of him? Although we do not know the answer, we can perhaps understand Imam Mehmed Efendi's hostility to Feyzullah, who replaced him, and to Mustafa II, who deprived him of his post well short of his full term of service[138].

The defection of Başmakcızade Ali and his replacement by Imam Mehmed signaled a significant change in rebel policy. Up to this point all those appointed to high office by the rebels were considered as replacements for vacant positions (e.g., *seğmen başı* and *kaymakam*) or were named because of the rebel demand for the dismissal of Feyzullah and his family. But now, for the first time, we witness assignments to high offices corresponding to those in Edirne.

On Sunday, July 22, the day following the dispatch of the rebel petition, Çalık Ahmed—who had just been elevated to the *seğmen başılık*—was invited (by whom we are not told) to head the janissary corps on the leadership's own authority[139].

We have seen how the rebel coalition was formed. It was composed of four elements: the military, the *ulema*, the vizier and pasha households, and the inhabitants and merchants of the capital. Each element had its own specific grievances against the incumbent government. Though the rebels had most of the standing army on their side and were obviously quite capable of effecting the deposition of Mustafa II and his government, they took every precaution to minimize confrontation. Yet plans were set for a full-scale military takeover should the necessity arise. While Feyzullah Efendi was the apparent butt of all rebel complaints, there was an attempt at accomplishing a smooth and unchaotic change. Finally, as we noted, all the paraphernalia of an alternate authority must have been set up quite early in the rebellion.

135 His biography in Ms. Vienna H.O. 126, II, 338b-339b.

136 In April, 1688 and in June, 1694. Defterdar, *Zübdet*, 142 and Silihdar, *Tarih*, II, 746.

137 In March, 1695. Silihdar, *Nusretname*, I, 21/216.

138 On May 27, 1695, Imam Mehmed Efendi was expected to settle at his home in Istanbul and was consoled with Konya *Kadılığı* for his livings. Silihdar, *Nusretname*, I, 31/217b.

139 So were Maanoğlu Saleh, who got the office of *sipahiler ağası*, and Gavur Hasan who got the office of *silihdar*. Silihdar, *Nusretname*, II, 158/288a. Saleh was a personal friend of Çalık Ahmed and is reputed to have contributed thirty *kese*s of his own monies quite early to the rebel cause. *Ibid.*

In a subsequent part of our study we will delineate the Edirne government's response to the early manifestations of the rebellion and assess the resources it could muster to face the formidable forces the rebels seemed to have gathered against it. Here we will note the point in time that the government began to suspect that the rebellion was not merely about back pay for the *cebeci*s.

While the rebels claimed that all they wanted was the dismissal and trial of Feyzullah and the return of Mustafa II and his government to Istanbul, no overt action was taken and no statement issued about their actual intentions for the sultan's ouster. The government, meanwhile, maintained a façade of accommodating rebel demands for the mufti's ouster and the return of the court to Istanbul. Mustafa II went as far as having the rebel nominees for high office confirmed by decree, asking only that the *ulema* members appear at the court in the traditional manner for their formal installation before the sultan. But the government also had its own conditions. The sultan would promise to return to Istanbul but only if the Istanbul crowd dispersed and all "classes" and factions returned to their normal habitats and activities.

Though pretending to accommodate them, the sultan was taking no chances. Preparations for a military confrontation were immediately put into effect. Besides sending orders to forces not committed to the rebel cause, a decree was circulated, mainly in Europe, for the blockade of all points of entry leading into Edirne. In taking these precautions, the incumbent government betrayed its own suspicions of the rebels' real intentions.

ENCOUNTER

Initially, the authorities at Edirne seemed to have underestimated the seriousness of the outbreak in Istanbul. In response to the first reports from *kaymakam* Abdullah, the government advised appeasement[140]. Abdullah was instructed to assemble the *ulema* and loyal leaders of the city for deliberations on the most appropriate measures to cope peaceably with the emergency. To facilitate their task, a large sum of money was sent to meet the *cebeci* payroll[141]. However, these last measures were taken on Monday, July 23, two days after the rebel delegation was dispatched for Edirne. Thus, the courier who carried the government's last message to Abdullah never reached his destination[142].

In the meantime, further disturbing news was received in Edirne. *Seğmen başı* Murtaza had been assassinated, and Abdullah, the government's highest ranking representative in Istanbul, was in flight. A meeting was held at the grand vizier's residence with representatives of the highest officers of the *ilmiye*, *seyfiye* and *kalemiye*. Following a short period of deliberation, firmer measures were recommended against the rebels, especially as it was felt that Murtaza's murder should not pass unpunished[143], (as though every violation of the law were taken as such a major threat to law and order that people would be encouraged to take the law into their own hands).

Nevertheless, the escalation of the sedition into an outright rebellion caught the Edirne government quite unprepared. It made its first overt move the following day, Tuesday, July 24, when a sub-delegation—consisting of a deputy of Türk Hasan Efendi and an Istanbul-based *bostancı*—arrived at the grand vizier's headquarters to report the imminent arrival of the Istanbul delegation[144]. Here, Ottoman sources are not in full agreement over what happened. Some claim that Feyzullah recommended that the delegation be halted, the petition taken from it, and all arrested and sent into exile[145]. On the following day, Wednesday, the

140 Silihdar, *Nusretname*, II, 135/283b.

141 Silihdar, *Nusretname*, II, 159/288a, and Defterdar, *Zübdet*, 423b. The *cebeci* problem goes back to May, 1703, when officers of the *cebecis* were dismissed for embezzlement. Rami Mehmed, "Munşeat", II, 133a-b.

142 The *kul kâhyası* Abdullah reached Silivri, but found it inadvisable to proceed when he heard that people in Istanbul had broken out in rebellion and joined the *cebecis*. Defterdar, *Zübdet*, 423b.

143 Silihdar, *Nusretname*, II, 160-61/288a.

144 Silihdar, *Nusretname*, II, 161/288b and Defterdar, *Zübdet*, 424b.

145 Silihdar, *Nusretname*, II, 161-62/288b. Orders in Mühimme Defteri 114, 116, show that the fort

recommendation was apparently translated into a mandate to the Edirne *bostancı başı* to carry out the interception at Hafsa[146].

This was the most consistent version of what happened. The blame is put squarely on the mufti's shoulders. The sultan was reputedly passive throughout, while the grand vizier Rami Mehmed Pasha was a reluctant instrument of Feyzullah's machinations. According to the same version; Mustafa II came alive on Thursday[147] when he took the initiative and called Rami Mehmed to the palace to give an account of the most recent developments in Istanbul and of the rebel delegation's fate. The ruler was reportedly angered by the incarceration of the rebel delegation and demanded an explanation for the unceremonious manner in which they were treated. Rami Mehmed is purported to have said that in this matter, like all those pertaining to public affairs, he was completely guided by the mufti, as ordered by the sultan. Thus, the mufti was blamed for dictating the arrest warrant.

Mustafa II, finally realizing that the mufti had indeed exceeded his legitimate authority, had Feyzullah dismissed. Orders were issued for his exile from Edirne. With Feyzullah's removal the Edirne government was playing along with the rebels' presentations that the mufti was the chief and only target of all the discontented in Istanbul[148]. Accordingly, Mustafa II and Rami Mehmed are portrayed as both conciliatory and genuinely accommodating to the rebels. The grand vizier, obviously aware of the five day limit placed on meeting their demands, could not wait until the actual exile of the mufti to report to Istanbul. Çöbek Ahmed Ağa, one of his trusted *ağa*s, was dispatched on Thursday with an informal message reporting the deposition of Feyzullah and the full compliance of the court with the new nominations for the *ilmiye* posts[149]. The grand vizier's man was followed two days later with an official messenger armed with nomination *berat*s for the rebel replacements, of both the *ilmiye* and other branches of government[150]. Edirne expected the new mufti, the two *kazasker*s, and the *nakib* to proceed to the court for their formal confirmation in the sultan's presence.

commander and its prison commander were informed of the arrest of Şaban and Süleyman (both military officers with the rebel delegation) and all men sent with the delegation from Istanbul. (Order dated July 24 - August 3, 1703).

146 Silihdar, *Nusretname*, II, 161/288b.

147 Silihdar, *Nusretname*, II, 162-63/288b.

148 Silihdar, *Nusretname*, II, 161/288b.

149 Silihdar, *Nusretname*, II, 162/288b. Defterdar, *Zübdet*, 424b claims that the memo was dated July 27 (Friday). This would indicate that the grand vizier was fully aware of the rebel deadline of five days wait for a response from Edirne to the petition.

150 Silihdar, *Nusretname*, II, 163/288b. For an example, the orders to each of the rebel ulema nominees were carried by *Küçük Mirahor* Selim. Copies of these letters can be seen in Rami Mehmed, "Münşeat" II, 211b.

Although the Edirne government was able to maintain a united front in the face of the *cebeci* insurrection and the ensuing first stage of the rebellion, from this point on it began to show signs of fragmentation. This breakdown becomes less surprising when it is studied against the political background of Mustafa II's eight-year reign. It has already been noted that Mustafa II's accession signaled a reversal in Ottoman politics. His ultimate aim was to free himself to exercise the day-by-day control over state affairs[151].

Mustafa ascended the throne on a note of sweeping change in the way the state's domestic and foreign affairs were run. He declared his absolute determination to "... go on the campaign and *cihad* in person"[152]. In justification of this unusual step he declared that "... since my father's sultanate, no ruler had taken to the field of battle in person — thereby the giaurs have attacked the Ottoman state from four directions, capturing Muslim lands and taking Muslim prisoners"[153].

The blame for the failure of Ottoman arms is placed squarely on the shoulders of his father's predecessors, Mustafa's two uncles, Süleyman II and Ahmed II, who had been dragged out of the *kafes* (harem cage) to ascend the throne of the house of Osman. During the short reign of these sickly and deranged princes a powerful coalition led mainly by the Köprülü house, its satellite viziers, and paşas, among other grandee houses, had managed to conduct state affairs on behalf of the dynasty and palace[154]. These grandees and their household staffs bear the highest blame for the failure to withstand the incursions of the powers of the Holy League against Muslim territory in southeast Europe. There is a personal dimension to the antipathy between Mustafa II and the Köprülüs. Mustafa II's father, Mehmed IV, had been removed from office in 1687 by a rebellion led by a Syavuş Pasha[155], the personal slave of Köprülü Mehmed, and the latter's son Fazıl Mustafa. Although Siyavuş was assassinated during the ensuing violence[156], Fazıl Mustafa managed to return to power and block ex-sultan Mehmed IV from staging a comeback[157].

151 These observations are explored in Abou-El-Haj, "Vezir and Paşa Households".

152 Raşıd, *Tarih*, II, 298-99.

153 *Ibid.*

154 Discussed in Abou-El-Haj, "Vezir and Paşa Households"

155 Abaza Siyavuş served both grand viziers Fazıl Ahmed and Kara Mustafa in various capacities. Silihdar, *Tarih*, I, 523, and II, 63, 129 and especially the biography 399-400. A veteran of the Vienna campaign, he is accused by Cantemir of having conspired against grand vizier Sarı Süleyman and having taken part in the conspiracy to depose Mehmed IV. *The history of the growth and decay of the Othman Empire*, London, 1756 (hereafter cited as Cantemir, *The history of the... (Othman Empire)*, 341-42 note 89. Silihdar, though acknowledging his piety, describes him in very unflattering terms: He is devoid of intelligence, political wisdom and sagacity. Silihdar, *Tarih*, II, 400.

156 Silihdar, *Tarih*, II, 333. Although his wife, Ayşe (daughter of Köprülü Mehmed), and his two sons were spared, the rest of his harem were taken as booty by the unruly soldiers. Defterdar, *Zübdet*, 141a-b. Biography in Süreyya, *Sicil*, III, 117.

157 Silihdar, *Tarih*, II, 318-22, 483.

Mustafa II's bid to take the conduct of state affairs into his own hands signified the reversal of a pattern of rule set quite firmly for nearly half a century by Köprülü Mehmed. When the first Köprülü had been invited to the office of grand vizier, internal strife and disaffection was nearly paralyzing the Ottoman state. While an endemic inter-elite conflict had practically debilitated the power of the central administration, a Venetian naval blockade came quite close to denying Istanbul water access to the Mediterranean. Under the circumstances Köprülü Mehmed was able to procure a carte blanche guaranteeing him unencumbered control over the business of government[158].

The most politically pointed of his preconditions for accepting high office relates to public administration appointments. He would countenance no interference in his placement of men in either the lowest or highest rungs of government service. Even the sultan himself was expected to abstain. This renunciation had far-reaching implications, since the prerogative for appointments had always been the ruler's. The Ottoman administration, especially, had been the exclusive preserve of the palace, in the person of the *kullar* and the military, for at least a century.

Mehmed and his successor, Fazıl Ahmed, were to have no apparent problem in staffing the highest posts of the government with men of their own choosing who were both loyal and qualified to perform their duties. Although we cannot say with any great assurance to what extent these appointees were the personal puppets of Mehmed Pasha, an incomplete survey of those holding office under Fazıl Ahmed and Kara Mustafa (his own successors to the office of grand vizier, 1664-1683) indicates that, rather than turning exclusively to the palace or the military, these last two grand viziers resorted just as frequently to the households of the viziers and paşas to staff the highest and most important positions of the central and provincial administration[159].

The half century following the ascendance of Köprülü Mehmed was mainly dominated by grand viziers who were either drawn from his own descendants,

[158] List of conditions in Seyyıd Ibrahım el-Müderris, "Sülale-i Köprülü" 6 (3b-4a).

[159] In this footnote and throughout the remainder of the book the following abbreviations are used to designate the following:

B.Z. : Beyzade. Sons and relatives of founder of the *kapı*.
V.H. : Vizier-Pasha Household. All others attached to the *kapı*.
P. : Palace. Graduates of the Palace.
M. : Military. Those who originated in the military establishment.
C. : Civilian. Those who originated in the bureaucracy.

	1664-1676: Fazıl Ahmed					1676-1683-84: Kara Mustafa				
	B.Z.	V.H.	P.	M.	C.	B.Z.	V.H.	P.	M.	C.
Central	3	1	8	3	2	2	10	8	1	–
Eyalet	1	20	44	13	4	7	13	9	7	–
Sancak	1	2	8	1	1	13	6	3	2	2

For sources see note 182 below.

like his sons Fazıl Ahmed and Fazıl Mustafa, his nephew, Amcazade Hüseyin, his son-in-law Kara Mustafa and members of their various *kapılar* (Kara Ibrahim, Abaza Siyavuş, Arabacı/Kadı Ali, and Namazcı Ali) or men drawn from other vizier and paşa households.

The de facto concession of powers to the elder Köprülü set the standard for all grand viziers in the next fifty years. However, this pattern did not pass unchallenged[160]. The first royal challenge came in 1684. As an accretion to the reforms of the first two Köprülüs, the Ottoman sultanate was finally capable of taking the initiative against the Habsburgs and Europe. The comparatively successful bid to regain the military initiative had been brought to a peaceful halt in 1664 with the treaty of Vasvar.

Hostilities resumed, however, in 1683—through the agency of the Köprülü protégé, Kara Mustafa—with the Ottomans extending the lines of the battle to the very walls of Vienna. Kara Mustafa's defeat and the ensuing disastrous Ottoman retreat challenged the Köprülü formula for rule, and their undisputed quarter-of-a-century power monopoly was discredited.

Kara Mustafa himself was executed—an unfortunate decision since the grand vizier was recognized by his contemporaries as a capable administrator. The next three years saw Mehmed IV try to take matters into his own hands, only to find himself ousted—deprived of power and office[161].

The events leading to the expulsion of Mehmed IV point, through direct and circumstantial evidence, to the Köprülüs' complicity in the incitement of the rebellion. The grand viziers Kara Ibrahim and Bosnevi Süleyman, Kara Mustafa's successors, failed to stem the inexorable tide of Habsburg expansion at the expense of Ottoman territory in Europe[162]. Moreover, the state treasury—almost exhausted from preparations for the 1683 campaign—was nearly empty in 1687. Troops on the front lines of battle were rarely paid, and when they were it was usually several installments short of their full salaries[163].

The rebellion started as an insurrection of the military against the grand vizier Bosnevi Süleyman, who obviously could not deliver on the many, and apparently contradictory, promises he had made regarding their recompense[164]. As he fled

[160] E.g. Fazıl Ahmed was challenged quite unsuccessfully in 1663 by Şamizade Mehmed, the *reisülküttab*, on behalf of his own damad Kadizade Ibrahim. For details, see Silihdar, *Tarih*, I, 276-77.

[161] These observations are based mainly on Silihdar, *Tarih*, I, 757, II, 1-2, 15, 18-39, 42-45, 85-93, 102 and 121.

[162] Silihdar, *Tarih*, II, 201, 225-26, 249, 273.

[163] Defterdar, *Zübdet*, 119a-120b and Raşid, *Tarih*, I, 1514-16.

[164] Silihdar, *Tarih*, II, 278-79.

the insurrection, officers reached his predecessor, Kara Ibrahim, who had been exiled by Mehmed IV in 1685[165]. They hoped to reinstate him as grand vizier. Mehmed IV had him executed — the apparent reason being his alleged readiness to accommodate the insurrectionists once he took office. The terms of the agreement are not given by the sources, but it should be kept in mind that Kara Ibrahim, once the *kâhya* of Kara Mustafa, remained loyal to the Köprülüs after he took high office in 1684.

Following the failure at Vienna and the execution of Kara Mustafa, his *kaymakam* in Edirne, Köprülüzade Mustafa suffered only a temporary setback. He was removed from his post as deputy to the grand vizier only to be returned a few months later as a vizier of the *kubbe*. Mustafa eventually retired as vizier at his own request[166].

Undaunted by the sultan's precipitous reaction to their potential nominee for the grand vizierate, the rebels turned to a commander closer at hand as their grand vizier-elect: Abaza Siyavuş, another Köprülü loyalist, once the slave of Köprülü Mehmed and subsequently his son-in-law. Their second choice revealed their partisanship perhaps even more than their first[167]. However, almost immediately following the rebel announcement of their choice to replace Bosnevi Süleyman, Fazıl Mustafa was recalled to fill the post of deputy to the grand vizier at the court. By this gesture Mehmed IV showed that the rebellion had gone beyond control and that he was harboring the vain hope that this Köprülü heir would shield him from the rebels and save his throne[168].

Why would the Köprülüs at this stage turn against Mehmed IV and cooperate with the rebel demand for his replacement? Although he was the very sultan who had conceded power to the elder Köprülü in 1656, Mehmed must have realized that the family and the *kapılar* had become the dominant factor in both Ottoman politics and government. His one chance to regain power came with the failure of Kara Mustafa at Vienna.

In discussing the decision to lay siege to the Habsburg capital, Ottoman sources accuse Kara Mustafa of misleading the court by marching onto Vienna when in fact he had given the sultan the impression he was headed for the siege of a less important fort nearer by[169]. In other words, Kara Mustafa had not only

[165] Silihdar, *Tarih*, II, 283-84.
[166] Silihdar, *Tarih*, II, 222 and 232. He accepted the minor post of commander of Boğaz Hisarı and the island of Sakız with *hasslar*.
[167] Biography in Süreyya, *Sicil*, II, 399-400.
[168] Silihdar, *Tarih*, II, 284 "Baban ve karındaşın sadaretinde rahat olmuşıdım. Sen dahi şu ʿulunmuş, ateş itfasına çare görmek gereksin duam seninle biledir".
[169] Silihdar, *Tarih*, II, 1-2, 18-19, 28-31, 38-39.

disobeyed imperial orders but had gone beyond his mandate. If this were indeed the case it would show that Kara Mustafa had acted in a manner independent of the court's wishes. It was a clear indication of the level of freedom the Köprülüs had attained in the conduct of Ottoman state affairs.

If, on the other hand, Kara Mustafa had kept the sultan appraised of his true plans—which is more likely—then Mehmed IV must have subsequently changed his own version in order to extricate himself from the inevitable consequences of the defeat. The credulity with which the sultan's accusation was received by those close to the court should indicate the growing opposition to the power monopoly the Köprülü household had attained in the previous quarter of a century.

The jealousy that the court and other elite elements in Ottoman society felt toward the Köprülüs' power can be illustrated by an incident which touched upon the accumulated wealth of that house. One of the innumerable prerogatives of the sultans was the right to confiscate the property of dismissed, deceased or discredited officers. However, when Köprülü Mehmed died the sultan did not exercise the option, nor did he do so fully with the death of Fazıl Ahmed. Thus, the wealth accumulated by the first two Köprülüs remained untouched. But with the treasury in want of cash, the sultan's attention was drawn to the untapped wealth of the Köprülüs then invested in Fazıl Mustafa, the family heir[170]. The informant, *Imam-ı Sultanî* Ibrahim[171], hinted that instead of leaving so much wealth to rot in the Köprülü coffers, the Ottoman state could make better use of it.

Whether the royal hostility was due to the jealousy of the sultan himself or that of his immediate circle is a moot question. Nevertheless, Mehmed IV must have felt compelled to curtail the Köprülü power, and the debacle at Vienna served as the opportune moment for carrying out his design. This was an unfortunate move on Mehmed IV's part, for in 1687 he had to turn to Köprülü Fazıl Mustafa to save himself and his throne from the wrath of the rebels. At their encounter the ruler admonished his subject to do his upmost to dampen the fire of the rebellion, reminding him that his father's and brother's loyal service had pleased the sultan and the dynasty. He told him that if he aspired to the heights and rewards which they had received, he would have to help subdue the rebellion[172].

The chronicler's account of the events following this encounter between Fazıl Mustafa and Mehmed IV are somewhat muddled. It is not quite clear whether

[170] Silihdar, *Tarih*, II, 567.
[171] Also known as Edirnevi Ibrahim, the father-in-law of Türk Hasan Efendi who served as the rebel chief delegate to Mustafa II.
[172] Silihdar, *Tarih*, II, 284. Ottoman text in note 168 above.

Mustafa failed in his mission to dissuade the rebels from removing his royal master or was actually reluctant to pursue the matter with them. There is persuasive evidence to show that Fazıl Mustafa was active not only in the deposition of Mehmed IV but also in denying the throne to either of Mehmed's sons[173]. If the role of Fazıl Mustafa in the events of 1687 is obscured by the complex of rebellion, turmoil, and fluidity which ensued, his role as grand vizier in denying the throne to either of ex-sultan Mehmed's sons in 1691 is quite explicit.

The incumbent sultan, Süleyman II, Mehmed IV's brother, who had succeeded in 1687, suffered from a severe case of dropsy, and his ill health was a constant worry to the grand vizier. In 1691, when it became quite obvious that Süleyman II would die, Fazıl Mustafa was advised by his supporters to make sure that the ailing sultan was not left behind in Istanbul, lest his death bring back to the throne ex-sultan Mehmed IV or one of his eligible sons. To deny the loyalist element the chance to choose its own monarch, the grand vizier was persuaded to take Süleyman II with him to Edirne where final control over the succession would presumably remain in the Köprülü hands.

During deliberations over the succession the possibility of Mehmed IV's (or his sons') return was raised but quickly scotched as a bad risk. Mehmed had reigned for forty-odd years with proven incompetence. His sons, according to Fazıl Mustafa, were much too spoiled during their father's sultanate to be effective rulers. The choice fell to Prince Ahmed, Mehmed IV's brother, who had become, after quite a long confinement in the harem cage, an expert at (politically harmless) "pietistic and ascetic exercises"[174]. Köprülü opted for the passive weakling over the strong-willed and independent candidate. And so, when Süleyman II died, Prince Ahmed — the son of Sultan Ibrahim and the handpicked choice of Fazıl Mustafa — was raised to the throne. The grand vizier now had a malleable monarch who would leave him in complete control over state affairs.

The return to the Köprülü formula of rule lasted into the first few weeks of Mustafa II's reign. Soon after Ahmed II's accession Fazıl Mustafa died at the battle of Islankamen[175], the culmination of the Ottomans' resurgent recovery

[173] Silihdar, *Tarih*, II, 483, 569-70. Cantemir puts it quite bluntly: "The choice of any of these was dangerous to the Vizir. For if Mahomet (IV) was restored, he was apprehensive for his life, since he was thought to be no inconsiderable manager of the sedition which had deposed him; if either of his sons were chosen, he was afraid lest these youths, having been liberally educated in the palace, contrary to the custom of the rest of the shezade, and being instructed in the administration of the government, might divest him of the vizirship and absolute command". *The history of the... Othman Empire*, 377.

[174] Silihdar, *Tarih*, II, 569-70.

[175] Silihdar, *Tarih*, II, 591-93.

from the military retreats of the previous six years (Belgrade was now back in Ottoman hands, as was much of Serbia). His successors to the office of grand vizier—Arabacı Ali and Çalık Ali—were, respectively, members of Fazıl Mustafa's and Kara Mustafa's households. In fact, the four years preceding Mustafa II's accession were dominated mainly by *kapı* graduates, two of whom were of the Köprülü faction[176].

When Mustafa II ascended the throne in February 1695, the incumbent grand vizier was Sürmeli Ali, also a *kapı* graduate, having been raised by a retainer of the famous sixteenth-century grand vizieral family of the Sokollus[177]. Thus, while Mustafa II was determined from the start of his reign to exercise the ancient prerogatives of reigning and ruling, the grand vizier was equally determined to undermine the ruler's hasty bid to take the mantle of the *gazi*[178], in the tradition of the sixteenth-century warrior-sultans. Despite serious shortages in supplies and treasure, Mustafa II would not be swayed from his determination to carry out that same spring a personal campaign into enemy territory[179].

Within the first five months of his sultanate Mustafa II resolved this impasse with his grand vizier by having Sürmeli Ali dismissed and eventually executed[180]. Elmas Mehmed was raised to the office of grand vizier. The contrast between the life histories of these two men is telling. Ali had been a *kapı* graduate and had attained the rank of paşa after serving as *başdefterdar* (finance officer), while Mehmed was brought up at the palace and graduated right into public service[181]. The sultan's encounter with Sürmeli Ali is symbolic of the former's intimidation of those who had helped deny Prince Mustafa the throne in 1687 and 1691 and dominated political life in the sultanates of his two uncles, Süleyman II and Ahmed II.

[176] The exception was Bozoklu Mustafa who was raised in the palace. He was grand vizier from March, 1693 to March, 1694 and died in 1698.

[177] I. H. Uzunçarşılı, *Osmanlı Tarihi* (Ankara, 1954), III, ii, 441.

[178] Cantemir openly states the case of Sürmeli Ali as one who tried to imitate Fazıl Mustafa by depriving prince Mustafa of the throne, and in favor of having Ahmed II's son Ibrahim elevated to the throne. "... his only reason for defrauding Mustafa II of the throne was, that he feared to lose the absolute power he had enjoyed under Ahmed II over the state and army, if a prince of vigor and versed in affairs, as Mustafa was, should obtain the crown". *The history of the ... Othman Empire*, 396.

[179] Silihdar, *Nusretname*, I, 7/214b. Sürmeli Ali's advice to the sultan was to desist from joining the campaign that year. "Bu yıllık asitanede rahat olup ...".

[180] Silihdar, *Nusretname*, I, 28/217b. Silihdar quotes Mustafa's anger at Ali in the following words: "... sağ oldukça ateşim sönmez". (As long as he is safe (alive) my fire (and anger) would not abate.) *Ibid.*, 31/217b. Within three weeks of his dismissal one of the *kapıcıs* was handed the order for the former grand vizier's execution: "... vezir-i âzam sabık Ali paşa dammi mubah olmağla ol zalımın varup bila-aman cezayın verip ser-i maktu'ın der devletmedarim getirmek babında hatt-i hümayun ...". Mühimme Defteri 106, 93.

[181] His father Sadık Reis was a naval officer (*gemi reisi*). His first assignment outside the palace, in May, 1688, was that of the *Nişancı*. Silihdar, *Tarih*, II, 361.

Significantly, no overt challenge to Mustafa II's assertion of power was recorded following the dismissal and execution of Sürmeli Ali. From 1695 to 1697 he tried to mold the various elements of the Ottoman elites, including the vizier and pasha households, into subordinate instruments of the dynasty in its rejuvenated efforts to regain what was lost to the European powers over the previous twelve years. When translated into internal political policy, Mustafa II's measures meant reverting from dependence on the vizier and pasha households to the old policy of drawing on the palace and the military in staffing the highest posts of government.

The clearest evidence of this shift can be illustrated by comparing the backgrounds and affiliations of the men who held high office prior to Mustafa II's reign with those holding office during the first two years of the reign, when the palace and the royal mentor Feyzullah dominated. From at least 1683, we have already noted, the trend of appointments had been one of drawing on men from the vizier and pasha households nearly as much as from the palace and the military to staff the highest posts of the central and provincial administration of the Ottoman state.

In a survey of appointments to fifteen preselected high positions in the twenty-year period, 1683-1703, the central government turned nearly 40 percent of the time to the *kapılar*, 26.3 percent and 21.3 percent, respectively, to the palace and the military, and 12.5 percent to civilians[182].

Upon his accession Mustafa II proceeded not only to remove a grand vizier whose affiliation fit the new pattern noted above, but also to reverse the trend of the previous two decades. For the first two years he drew more heavily and more frequently on the military and the palace to fill the highest posts of the central administration[183].

In a survey of the same fifteen preselected posts Mustafa II's government turned 18.18 percent of the time to the *kapılar*, and 45.45 percent and 9.1 percent, respectively, to the palace and the military. The ultimate success of Mustafa II's policies, as with all sultans bent on personally managing state affairs, rested on *his* performance and that of his key appointees in the conduct of government. Here

182 For the *eyaletler* (34 in number) the percentages are: 41.90; 38.50; 15.70 and 3.70. These observations are based on a biographical survey of all men who held office between 1683-1703. The official biographies were gleaned mainly from contemporary sources: especially Silihdar, *Tarih* and *Nusretname*; Defterdar, *Zübdet*; Mühimme defteri nos. 106-114. These were supplemented by Süreyya, *Sicil*; Raşid, *Tarih*; and M.S. Vienna H.O. 126. The statistical information was first published in 1974 in Abou-El-Haj, "Vezir and Paşa Households", 442a-443b.

183

	V.H.	P.	M.	C.
1683-1703	39.50	26.30	21.30	12.50
1695-97	18.18	45.45	9.10	27.27

Appendix I below provides a list by name, office, year and affiliation of the chief officers of the central & provincial administrations, 1683-1703.

an analysis of Mustafa II's upbringing and personality might shed some light on how and why he differed from his royal predecessors and explain his course of action and decisions[184].

Mustafa II was in his early thirties when he acceded to the throne. Unlike his two predecessors, he had grown into adulthood during the unusually long reign of his own father, Sultan Mehmed IV. Consequently, he and his younger brother, Ahmed, grew up without the encumbrances of the harem cage to which all potential heirs to the Ottoman throne (and hence rivals of the incumbent) were confined.

There the princes' growth and development were almost literally arrested, making them moral and intellectual incompetents. Such was the fate of Prince Süleyman. Born in 1642, he acceded to the throne in 1687, having spent almost forty of his forty-five years removed from contact with the outside world. The effect of this confinement on his personality was most telling. When he was fetched by a palace official for the accession ceremony, he refused to leave the *kafes* for fear that this was part of his brother's plot to lure him out of the harem and destroy him. Despite assurances to the contrary—and viziers, *ulema* and officers of the armed forces waiting to swear allegiance at his inauguration—he said, quite pathetically, "If it has reached the point of my destruction, tell me, so that I can perform my (final) prayers first"[185].

As with all princes, Mustafa, on reaching the age of six, was assigned a tutor who initiated him into the world of learning and of adults. Emir Efendi, his mentor of only eight months, died and was succeeded by Seyyid Feyzullah, an *âlim* the young prince grew up to depend on into adulthood[186]. As a measure of Feyzullah's profound and enduring influence, no sooner had Mustafa become sultan than orders were sent recalling his old mentor from exile. Within only two months of his accession, Mustafa elevated Feyzullah to the highest post of the *ilmiye*. In a short time Feyzullah's control had penetrated so deeply into all government affairs that he was dubbed "*sahibürreaseteyn*" [holder of the two headships] (the *ilmiye* and the central administration).

The sultan's dependence on his old tutor—not only for advice but for actual administrative management and guidance—is best illustrated by a directive Mustafa II issued in 1703 to his new grand vizier, Rami Mehmed, admonishing him to be guided by the mufti in all state affairs[187].

[184] What follows is an outline with revisions of Abou-El-Haj, "Mustafa II: A Psycho-historical Study". Biographical data were drawn from Silihdar, Raşid, Cantemir and Richard Knolles (and P. Rycaut), *The Turkish History*, 3 vols. (London, 1687-1700).

[185] Silihdar, *Tarih*, II, 295-98, 569-70.

[186] Sabra Meservey presents the most elaborate treatment of Feyzullah in English. *Feyzullah Effendi: An Ottoman Şeyhulislam* (Princeton University Ph.D. dissertation, 1966).

[187] Şefik, *Şefikname*, 18.

There seems, however, to be an emotional dimension to this attachment and dependence. Late in his reign, Mustafa turned a deaf ear to the outcries of corruption and nepotism leveled at his old tutor and would not relinquish him until the sultan's own mother made it clear to him that he had to choose between Feyzullah and the throne[188].

This attachment is more surprising as the sultan's childhood points to a free and liberal upbringing. According to one contemporary, the prince was spoiled and unharnessed, he indulged in eating only for the purposes of riding and hunting, and took music lessons to facilitate his revelry[189]. Though this description does not come from an unprejudiced observer[190], it does show the measure of freedom and development this prince was allowed away from the stupefying confines of the *kafes*.

Whatever evidence we have on Prince Mustafa's parents points to a rather weak father and a mother mainly preoccupied with herself and her place in her husband's affections. Mehmed IV was himself a mere child when he ascended the throne. During his minority and early adulthood his mother acted as his regent. It was she who abdicated her son's royal prerogatives in 1656 in favor of Köprülü Mehmed. The young monarch remained a mere figurehead primarily concerned with hunting. In his one attempt at independent action he proved himself such an utter incompetent that power had to be wrested from his hands before the Ottomans were almost physically thrown out of southeastern Europe[191].

Mustafa's mother, on the other hand, was apparently a strong woman who was quite conscious of the transitory and precarious nature of her place in the sultan's affections. Accordingly, she is said to have resorted to every possible female guile to keep herself in Mehmed IV's good graces[192]. In his adult life—in spite of the free and liberal upbringing that should have given him autonomy—Prince Mustafa, like most Ottoman sultans before and after him, showed complete deference to his mother. Thus, the mother, like the grandmother, came to play a significant role in some of the crucial decisions of his reign, including the final dismissal of the old mufti, which her son could not bring himself to carry out[193].

The posture of independence masking an actual dependence, combined with the strong suggestion of indulgence early in childhood, points to a disturbance in

188 Anonymous History, Berlin Diez A quarto 75, 244a.
189 Silihdar, *Tarih*, II, 569-70.
190 This observation was made in 1691 by grand vizier Köprülüzade Mustafa in justification of his nomination of Ahmed II instead of princes Mustafa and Ahmed.
191 Abou-El-Haj, "Mustafa II: A Psychohistorical Study", 127.
192 *Ibid.*, 128.
193 Anonymous History, Berlin Diez A quarto 75, 244a.

early development when adaptive modes are first said to be established[194]. Those displaying this lack of autonomy are quite likely to have failed to internalize normal early frustrations—character forming structures which help the child cope with his inner and outer worlds. The lack of internalization of the parental model at about the sixth year of growth leaves the child, and eventually the adult, in a constant yearning for an alter ego to provide the leadership and approval he needs to function effectively.

The idealization of Feyzullah the mentor by the adult sultan, and the latter's need for external sanction, implies that as a child of five or six Prince Mustafa may have experienced some traumatic disruption in his relationship with his mother. We have already noted that at the age of six it was normal for young princes to be introduced to the world of learning and of men. This marked a stage in their growth and development. It also constituted the beginning of their separation from their mothers and women attendants. Significantly, in the development of his personality, it was at this point that Prince Mustafa was first introduced to Feyzullah Efendi[195]. The old mentor's return in 1695 to a place of influence and prominence at the court of his old pupil can be explained from within the psychology of the ruler. There are, however, historical factors independent of Mustafa's personal needs which also account for and complement the emotional one offered above.

First, it was not the usual practice for a sultan to turn exclusively to the şeyhülislâm for advice on matters outside the realm of the religious bureaucracy. The chiefs of the *ilmiye* were indeed consulted, but only in conjunction with men of affairs (viziers, paşa, commanders, and even civil bureaucrats) in the very highest councils of government. Contemporary sources do not give any direct explanation for Mustafa II's new departure. Some, in fact, show that other sultans in the past had taken the chief of the *ilmiye* into their confidence.

It should be kept in mind that when Mustafa finally acceded to the throne it was almost as a last resort. On two prior occasions when he was eligible to assume the sultanate—and capable of serving in that post—he was blocked. Thus, when his uncle Ahmed II died in 1695, prince Mustafa was the oldest member of the Ottoman dynasty who was sound in body and mind and, therefore, the most eligible to accede. His elevation to the throne, when it did come, was more a matter of established precedent and tradition than of choice.

194 This assessment of Mustafa's personality is informed by the psychoanalytic studies and theories of Heinz Kohut, "Forms and Transformations of Narcissism", *Journal of the American Psychoanalytic Association*, XIV, 1966 and *The Analysis of the Self* (New York, 1971).

195 Silihdar, *Tarih*, I, 556.

It is quite probable that Mustafa turned to Feyzullah partly because he distrusted the loyalty of those in power during the reigns of his two uncles. Furthermore, such a coalition would have tried to dissuade not only Mustafa but any ambitious sultan from embarking upon an expansionist policy. Feyzullah was not only unencumbered by such an association but — by the very nature of his call as a member of the *ilmiye* — would have been more dedicated to the "old" ideals and practices of the Ottoman state.

It is with this background in mind that one has to view Mustafa's early ambition to be not only the figurehead of the state but its leader in battle as a *gazi*, intent upon the resumption of Ottoman initiatives. He also set the style for simple living, foregoing the luxuries usually attending sultans on campaign[196] and sharing the humble soldier's diet[197]. Moreover, he championed justice by personally acting as a judge[198]. If not exactly fanatical, he was, like all potential reformers, puritanical and moralistic, forbidding his soldiers the pleasure provided by camp followers, be they male or female[199].

In short then, Mustafa believed that the Ottoman state needed the right leader who continued to have faith in its ideology and was not unmindful of the precedents and postures of the great sultans of the dynasty. Guided by Providence, that leader would inevitably assure the recovery of the glories of the Ottoman state. He must have been encouraged to believe that *he* was that leader, surely not by the realistic, though ambitious, statesmen of the day, for the state had just sustained some very serious setbacks at the hands of the Christian powers. At best the advice of these statesmen would have been caution, not outright confrontation bordering on suicide. It had to be someone with the orientation and thinking of Feyzullah who would encourage, no matter how unrealistically, the revival of the old Ottoman *gazi* ideals and traditions for guidance of the princes in their conduct of state affairs.

As a student, Mustafa must have been taught what was expected of him as the future ruler of the Ottoman state and given models of former illustrious sultans as historical realizations of the ideal ruler. These lessons were not wasted on him, for upon his accession he fancied himself as the new Süleyman Kanunî[200], the *gazi* saviour of the state who would extricate it from its recent disasters.

The makebelieve of Mustafa early in his reign served him well through two

196 Silihdar, *Nusretname*, I, 7/214a.
197 Silihdar, *Nusretname*, I, 40/219a.
198 Silihdar, *Nusretname*, I, 42/219a.
199 Silihdar, *Nusretname*, I, 146-231b.
200 Raşid, *Tarih*, 299. "In the first eight years of his reign, my great grand father Süleyman Han, did not only send his viziers on campaigns against the enemy, but went on every *gaza* himself...".

campaign years (1695-97)[201]. The audacity of Ottoman military actions, unexpected by the Habsburgs, netted Mustafa some minor victories in the recovery of forts and redoubts along the Tamışvar and Transylvania frontier. These daring exploits, which earned Mustafa the coveted title of *gazi* (infidel-fighter), were brought to a sudden halt by the annihilating defeat of Ottoman forces at Zenta in the third year of campaigning.

Acting contrary to the best available advice, the sultan and his hand-picked grand vizier, Elmas Mehmed, took the most direct route and exposed themselves to a confrontation for which they were ill prepared. Ottoman forces were caught by surprise, pressed into a corner and routed. The sultan, though personally safe, lost his grand vizier and most of his commanders, some of them seasoned veterans of the 1683 campaign. In assessing the defeat of 1697, one contemporary source blames the lack of cooperation between men of state and Elmas Mehmed, Mustafa II's personal choice for grand vizier[202]. The chronicler further ascribes to these elements jealousy and ill will toward the palace favorite, which he feels undermined Mustafa II's military policies.

Were these the same men who were rebuffed at the time of the sultan's accession? The chronicler is not clear. However, to extricate himself from the embarrassment of defeat, he turned, like his father before him, to a Köprülü to serve in this time of trouble.

Amcazade Hüseyin managed in five years of service not only to achieve a fairly equitable peace settlement, but also to give the Ottomans respite from nearly fifteen years of war. No sooner had he taken office than he reversed his predecessor's pattern of recruitment for high office. During his five-year vizierate, Hüseyin's appointees from the vizier and pasha households numbered almost twice those of palace and military origin, i.e., 54 percent were drawn from the *kapılar* as opposed to 29 percent from the palace and military[203].

[201] Mustafa's campaigns and the disaster at Zenta are discussed in Abou-El-Haj, *Reisülküttab and Karlowitz* and "Ottoman Diplomacy". On make-believe following defeat see "Ottoman Methods of Negotiation". (For example, the defeat at Zenta is completely glossed over by contemporary Ottoman sources: "... üç defa bizzat nemçe üzerine azimet buyurulup mansuren avdet olunmuş idi". (Three times he [Mustafa II] campaigned in person against the Austrians and returned victorious.) Mustafa had been victorious only on two campaigns, the third ended up in the disaster at Zenta. Of the peace negotiations, the same source reports: "... cevanib-i arba'adan hücum eden düşmanlar kendileri sulha taleb ibram ve ilhah eylediler". (The enemies came from four sides, insisting on making peace.) Anonymous History, Berlin Diaz A quarto 75, 144a and 148a-b.

[202] Raşid, *Tarih*, II, 407.

[203] What follows were the patterns of appointments during the grand vizierates of Amcazade Hüseyin and Elmas Mehmed.

	V.H.	P.	M.	C.
Amçazade	54.00	16.66	12.50	16.66
Mehmed	18.18	45.45	9.10	27.27

Had Hüseyin hoped to have a free hand in the management of state affairs by reversing the recruitment policy, he was fated to be disappointed. Though willing to turn to a Köprülü for the task of recovery and reconstruction, Mustafa II would not allow him complete freedom of action. Feyzullah remained at the sultan's side and, until his demise in 1703, intruded into state affairs with the open blessings of the palace. Some contemporaries note that Feyzullah's influence began to increase following the defeat at Zenta.

The change is attributed to the sultan's withdrawal from taking an active part in the direction of state business and coincided with the growing ambition of Feyzullah and his family. Mustafa II's character seems to have undergone a radical transformation from one of ambition, arrogance and piety to one of ambivalence, indecisiveness, and narcissism bordering on perversion[204].

Feyzullah Efendi and his entourage acted as a counter-weight to the inevitable growth in power of Amcazade Hüseyin. Contemporaries only hint at the tension between these men. Proof of the conflict has to be called from indirect evidence.

Echoes of discontent and unrest with the government are registered under several disguises and in different forms[205]. Measures were taken to foil the development of a coalition of the kind that managed the deposition of Mehmed IV in 1687.

Since the Köprülüs were the most likely to provide credible leadership against the incumbent sultan, several marriage alliances were arranged between daughters of Mustafa II and Feyzullah and sons of the Köprülüs[206]. Even these gestures

[204] The near disintegration of character here suggested can be attributed partly to Mustafa II's failure to achieve his goals for himself and for the state. [His withdrawal which coincided with the fortieth year of his life suggests a reopening of his identity crisis which hits the hardest those who had failed in the introjection of adaptive structures in early childhood. The above observations are based on Eliott Jaques, "The Mid-Life Crisis", *International Journal of Psychoanalysis*, 46.4, 1965 and a lecture by Roger Gould, M.D. on the mid-life crisis, delivered in 1973 at Beverly Hills, California, U S.A.]

[205] *Cebeci* discontent over their salaries was not something new. Five years earlier, Raşid notes that the *cebecis* were unhappy about the inability of the treasury to meet their pay. *Tarih*, II, 437. See also Defterdar, *Zübdet*, 349a. The sources record instances of *molla*s voicing disguised criticism of the government's handling of state affairs In each case the protestor was sent into exile as a means of silencing him. E.g., Defterdar, *Zübdet*, 411b.

[206] Köprülüzade Fazıl Mustafa's two sons:

a) Abdullah Bey who was married to one of Feyzullah's daughters. Cantemir comments this Abdullah was elevated to high office at age 18. *The history of the ... Othman Empire*, 433 note 44. Ottoman sources state quite clearly that Abdullah was elevated to the deputy's post due to the fact that the mufti did not trust the incumbent, Yusuf. Even then, i.e., a year and a half before 1703, there were rumors of an impending rebellion. Defterdar, *Zübdet*, 389a, 411b; Silihdar, *Nusretname*, II, 88, 119/277b, 281b and Raşid, *Tarih*, II, 524, 878-79.

b) Numan Bey who was engaged to marry Ayşe Sultan. He was made into the 6th vezir of the *kubbe altı* then appointed to the government of Erzurum, and Anadolu. A palace was built for Ayşe of drawing the Ottoman dynasty and that of Feyzullah closer to the Köprülüs failed to silence the discontent of the family and its allies with Feyzullah and his master.

An incident that occurred in 1702 suggests there were efforts being made to effect change in leadership. A few months prior to Amcazade Hüseyin's resignation as grand vizier, two of his men were relieved of duty and orders were issued for their execution. One of them was Hüseyin's nephew, Kıblelizade Ali, who was caught attempting to make contact with Prince Ahmed, Mustafa II's brother. He was immediately removed from the office of *mirahor-ı evvel* (master of the sultan's horses), escorted from Edirne to Istanbul, and executed[207]. His uncle pleaded for his life, but to no avail. In fact, the grand vizier himself was saved only by the entreaties made on his behalf by the *valide sultan* (the queen mother) with the sultan[208].

Two weeks after the removal of Ali, Amcazade Hüseyin's *kâhya*, Şehrizorlu Hasan, was dismissed because—according to contemporary observers—he had incurred the sultan's anger[209]. As a pretext, Hasan was assigned to the government of one of the Asiatic provinces, but orders were issued to a palace executioner to overtake him. The condemned man managed to escape and to hide for more than a year, surfacing at the outbreak of the rebellion as one of its chief lieutenants[210].

Why did Kıblelizade Ali try to contact Prince Ahmed in the harem, at a great risk to his own life? And why would the court insist on removing Hüseyin's *kâhya* and eventually insist on his destruction? It is quite probable that Hüseyin must have finally decided—much like his cousin, Fazıl Mustafa, before him—to get rid of both the sultan and the mufti, having despaired of Feyzullah's

in Edirne that was modelled on the *Saray-ı Atik* in Istanbul. Silihdar, *Nusretname*, II, 37, 46, 119, 142/270b, 271b, 281b-282a, 285a.

Ali Bey (son of Kara Mustafa, besieger of Vienna) was betrothed to Safiye Sultan and was given the governorate of Crete. A palace was built for Safiye, similar to the one built for her sister in Edirne. Silihdar, *Nusretname*, II, 120, 142/282a, 285a.

207 Silihdar, *Nusretname*, II, 90, 116/277b, 281b; Raşid, *Tarih*, II, 531 and Defterdar, *Zübdet*, 393a. Anonymous History, Berlin Diez A quarto 75, 293a-294a gives a slightly different explanation for Ali's execution. Cantemir, *The history... of the Othman Empire*, 429, note 38 calls Ali the son of Amcazade's sister and a "favourite".

208 Silihdar, *Nusretname*, II, 116/281b.

209 Defterdar, *Zübdet*, 391b. Silihdar, *Nusretname*, II, 92/278a, points out that it was the mufti who was instrumental in the dismissal of Hasan and for the eventual orders to have him executed.

210 Silihdar, *Nusretname*, II, 120/281b. Orders for his arrest are in Mühimme Defteri 114, 2a and 12a. The order to the Istanbul Kaymakamı for Hasan's execution is afterwards cancelled. *Ibid.*, 53a. An order to the *vali* of Diyar Bekir requires that Hasan be imprisoned. *Ibid.*, 73a. From the above it would seem that Hasan must have had some very powerful friends at the center of power to intervene on his behalf.

interference in state affairs and Mustafa's inability or refusal to curb his mentor's ambition and greed.

These revelations threatened Hüseyin's position. Two months following the removal of his *kâhya*, the grand vizier—pleading ill health—asked to be relieved of his duties[211]. Amcazade Hüseyin was granted his wish but placed under house arrest at his *yalı* near Silivri[212].

Dal Taban Mustafa and Rami Mehmed, the last two grand viziers, were handpicked by the mufti[213]. With Hüseyin out of the way Feyzullah's dominance reached its zenith. We have already noted that his ambition was not confined to the period of his own life. The mufti wished to perpetuate his family in the family in the headship of the *ilmiye* for at least the lifetime of Mustafa II. Since he was the monarch's senior by more than twenty years, he wanted to assure the continuation of his family influence after his own death. In 1702, only a few months before the execution of Kıblelizade Ali Bey, Feyzullah, as we have noted earlier, obtained the patent for the office of *şeyhülislâm designate* in his first son's name[214]. To further insure his family's influence on Mustafa II's progeny, Feyzullah had another son[215] appointed tutor (*hoca*) to Mahmud, Mustafa's first born and heir-apparent to the sultanate.

In short, Feyzullah indicated—through the betrothals of princesses and his own daughter to the Köprülü sons, his active participation in state affairs, and his attempt to insure that his influence would be perpetuated at the court through his own sons—that he did not see himself in the traditional role of the *âlim*. Instead, he acted for all practical purposes like any vizier or pasha of the previous half century, with the same ambition to perpetuate himself and family in office and assure continued political domination. Feyzullah came close to establishing a *kapı* with the staffs, and paraphernalia that went with such an establishment, without formally crossing corporate lines.

Having perhaps chosen the Köprülü household as his model, it would be expected that Feyzullah received his most vehement and concentrated opposition from that quarter. Indeed, it is quite likely that Feyzullah's ambition to head both the *ilmiye* and *seyfiye* corporations may have finally convinced Amcazade Hüseyin to attempt to rid himself of the mufti. Failing to concince the sultan to restrain

211 Silihdar, *Nusretname*, II, 118-19/281b.
212 Raşid, *Tarih*, II, 542 claims that *çavuş başı* Budur Mustafa, one of Amcazade Hüseyin's men, was also dismissed about the same time as was Kıblelizade Ali, and probably for the same reasons.
213 Silihdar, *Nusretname*, II, 118, 129/281b and 285a.
214 Silihdar, *Nusretname*, II, 89/277b.
215 His name is Hasan Efendi, Silihdar, *Nusretname*, II, 90-92/277b-278a.

Feyzullah made him consider the more drastic measure of replacing Mustafa II with his brother, Prince Ahmed[216].

Feyzullah's ambitions proved too much to bear, even to his hand-picked grand viziers. Dal Taban Mustafa was removed as grand vizier and executed within four months of his appointment for conspiring to depose the mufti, provoking a rebellion in the Crimea and threatening to resume war against Russia[217].

Dal Taban started his career as a messenger (*karakulak*) in the household of Kara Ibrahim Pasha. (Kara İbrahim, at that point, served as the *rikab kaymakam*[218]. He had also been attached to a household — that of Kara Mustafa[219], then third vizier and eventually grand vizier and besieger of Vienna in 1683 — before entering public service.) Dal Taban Mustafa entered the military and eventually reached the highest ranks: *cebeci* and janissary *başılık*s[220]. From there he entered the provincial administration, first as head of several *sancak*s and then of half a dozen *eyalet*s[221].

He served with distinction in at least two of his assignments. In 1697, while governor of Bosnia, he carried out successfully military raids into both Habsburg and Venetian territory right up to the last few weeks before the signing of the peace treaty at Karlowitz. Since he was known to be hostile to the peace treaties, Mustafa was assigned to governorships in Asia, where he managed to suppress several rebellions before being selected by Feyzullah for the grand vizierate[222].

By settling on Dal Taban Mustafa as his nominee to succeed Amcazade Hüseyin, the mufti had picked someone who was a known associate, and perhaps ally, to the Köprülüs. By the time of his nomination, however, Dal Taban Mustafa had been removed from the capital and court for almost ten years. His long absence from the court, and his known hostility to the peace treaties negotiated mainly by Amcazade Hüseyin, may have left him without reliable contacts and

216 Was Kıblelizade Ali sounding him out on his feelings towards Feyzullah? This question is raised in light of the fact that prince Ahmed was in his childhood also tutored by Feyzullah. When the prince became sultan in 1703, he is supposed to have admonished his brother Mustafa on his undue dependence on their mutual mentor. Naima, *Tarih*, VI, Author's appendix, pp. 26-27.

217 For a discussion of Daltaban Mustafa's motives and plans, see Abou-El-Haj, "Closure of Ottoman Frontier", 471a-475b.

218 Whereas Cantemir claims that Mustafa was a janissary who had been brought up at the "court" of (Köprülüzade) Fazıl Ahmed, Süreyya claims that he had grown up in Kara Mustafa's circle, and that he eventually became Kara Mustafa's *telhisçi*. Cantimer, *The history of the... Othman Empire*, 414, note 30; Süreyya, *Sicil*, III, 412. The Anonymous History, Berlin Diez A quarto 75, 204b reports his *intisab* to Kara İbrahim.

219 An. *kâhya*. Silihdar, *Tarih*, I, 563.

220 Silihdar, *Tarih*, II, 196, 237, 238, 423, 510, 615.

221 Silihdar, *Tarih*, II, 645 and *Nusretname*, I, 105/227a; 206/240a; 209-10/240b; 311-15/256b; 317-20/257a-b; II, 9/267a; 31/270a; 116/281b.

222 Silihdar, *Nusretname*, II, 118/281b.

completely dependent on the mufti. Yet, when he arrived as the grand vizier designate, Dal Taban Mustafa was met by two men who had served with him in the *kapı* of Kara Ibrahim and had moved on to find service with Amcazade Hüseyin. When the latter was relieved of his office, Dal Taban Mustafa's cohorts remained[223].

According to contemporary sources, the first two months of his grand vizierate Dal Taban Mustafa devoted to reviving and upholding social rituals. He demonstrated a penchant for tradition by his insistence on applying laws on dress which distinguished *zimmis* from Muslims, women from men, and viziers from non-viziers[224]. Amcazade Hüseyin had apparently ignored these laws that, presumably, could have created social havoc in the highly structured society of the day[225]. Mustafa also showed interest in the conditions of the armed forces, especially the financial status of those who were pensioned off and demobilized following the war[226].

A little more than three months after his nomination to the office of grand vizier, Dal Taban Mustafa was implicated in two plots — the assassination of Feyzullah[227] and the incitement of rebellion and separatist tendencies in the Crimea and the Bucak[228]. Trouble in the Crimea and among the Tatars began brewing just after the peace treaties were signed and ratified in 1699 and 1700.

The bone of contention was the frontier between the Tatars on the one hand and the Poles and Russians on the other. Until the treaties were signed, the Tatars had freedom to raid and move across the open and undifferentiated frontier between the lands of Islam and these two Christian powers. Where possible, the peace agreements stipulated the demarcation of linear boundaries which facilitated the closure of the frontier, except for strictly authorized and legitimate purposes, such as trade and commerce[229].

The economic hardship these restrictions caused the Tatars, and their suspicion that Russia was about to launch another attack on them, encouraged the Crimean

[223] Zülfikarzade Kara Osman, the son of the Ottoman envoy to Vienna (1687-89) and Doyğun Mustafa. Raşid, *Tarih*, II, 540.

[224] Anonymous History, Berlin Diez A quarto 75, 186a; Defterdar, *Zübdet*, 399a, 401a and 404a and Silihdar, *Nusretname*, II, 121/282a.

[225] The grand vizier's penchant for conformity, tradition and social stratification may point to his upstart origins. It is perhaps for this same reason that Ottoman sources also mention his social conservatism.

[226] Defterdar, *Zübdet*, 298a-b.

[227] Silihdar, *Nusretname*, II, 140/285a.

[228] Silihdar, *Nusretname*, II, 122-29/282a-283a. Defterdar, *Zübdet*, 409b-410a attributes his dismissal to his laxity with the Tatar rebellion, whereas Raşıd, *Tarih*, II, 574 states quite bluntly that Dal Taban had collaborated with the Tatar rebels.

[229] Abou-El-Haj, "Closure of the Ottoman Frontier".

and Bucak Tatars to contemplate a preemptive attack, with or without Ottoman blessings. Their several appeals to Mustafa II to heed their warnings of an imminent Russian attack were met with complete skepticism by Feyzullah Efendi. Dal Taban Mustafa seemed to be their last resort. The grand vizier, in turn, took this opportunity to subvert the 1699 and 1700 arrangements. This he did by encouraging the Tatars to plan for war with a promise of full Ottoman support under his own leadership. When his plan was discovered, Dal Taban Mustafa was forced into preparing the suppression of his Tatar allies, thereby dissuading others from joining the insurrection. Immediately thereafter the grand vizier was removed from office and beheaded[230].

Rami Mehmed occupied the office of grand vizier for seven short months[231]. He was a bureaucrat who had returned to government "civil" service after a stint of several years in the *kapı* of Musahib Mustafa, a companion of Mehmed IV and his son-in-law. Since he was not a newcomer to government service[232], the grand vizier demonstrated quite early in his career an understanding of the nuances and delicacies of political power. His main claim to leadership was his service as head of the Ottoman peace delegation, 1697-1700[233]. By the time he was offered the office of grand vizier, the mufti's influence had penetrated so far into the executive branch of service that Rami Mehmed was openly regarded as Feyzullah's lackey and protégé[234].

The drastic measures Mustafa II and his mentor had to resort to following the fall of Amcazade Hüseyin, and the rapid changes that took place in the office of grand vizier, serve to indicate the heightening political tension within the central government and suggest the court's growing struggle to maintain its hold over the day-to-day business of state affairs.

Some Ottoman contemporaries believed that a conspiracy to oust the mufti and sultan was being hatched between sympathetic elements from both sides[235].

230 Silihdar, *Nusretname*, II, 130/283a.

231 His official biography for the years up to 1698 is treated in Abou-El-Haj, *Reisülküttab and Karlowitz*, 25-59 and more recently in *İ.A.*

232 He entered the grand vizier's chancery at twelve years of age. Anonymous History Berlin Diez A quarto 75, 200b-201b.

233 Details in Abou-El-Haj, *Reisülküttab and Karlowitz*, especially 60-132, and "Ottoman Diplomacy", 501a-512b.

234 "Sadr-ı azam çırağımızdır". Şefik, *Şefikname*, 17.

235 Rami Mehmed is singled out as being chief plotter on the sultan's side with Moralı Hasan as the second culprit. Silihdar, *Nusretname*, II, 129, 141-42/285a. Following the rebellion and accession of Ahmed III the same Moralı Hasan, when he became grand vizier, defended Rami Mehmed and indicated to the sultan his usefulness for the state in the following manner: "The state needs someone (of Rami Mehmed's caliber). During the disturbance (*gavga*) he did not leave my side. Throughout he and I were in total agreement about serving your majesty...". Anonymous History, Berlin Diez A quarto 75, 291a-b.

Although it would be futile to try to resolve conclusively the question of premeditation at this point, there is plenty of evidence to suggest that a great deal of sympathy and understanding, if not outright affinity, existed between some of the leaders of the government at Edirne and the provisional one in Istanbul.

The most telling evidence can be culled from an examination of the backgrounds and affiliations of some of these men. Amcazade Hüseyin's successors continued his policy of drawing on the vizier and pasha households (*kapılar*) to man the highest posts in the central administration[236]. Perhaps the most significant fact to emerge from exploring the background of some of the men of the rebellion and those who served the government is that a good number of them belonged to—or had been associated with—the *kapı* of the last Köprülü grand vizier[237].

Since it was quite clear that the sultan could not overnight purge the men who were sympathetic to the vizier and pasha households in general, or the Köprülü one in particular, some measures had to be taken to ensure the royal hold on government.

We have already noted that late in the grand vizierate of Amcazade Hüseyin marriage alliances were arranged between the young Köprülü heirs and the daughters of Mustafa II and Feyzullah. In the last year of Mustafa II's reign we see the same sons-in-law assigned to sensitive posts in the government. Köprülüzadeler Abdullah and Numan were given the *kaymakam*ate of Istanbul and the *vali*ship of Anadolu, respectively, while Kara Mustafa's son, Genç Ali, was appointed *beylerbeyi* of the critical frontier fort at Tamışvar[238]. We also witness at this juncture the assignment of other key government positions of men related by marriage to either the sultan and the mufti but drawn from the palace and the military. The imperial swordbearer, Çorlulu Ali, betrothed to Princess Emine Sultan, was graduated from the palace service with a *paşalık* and the rank of third vizier of the *kubbe*[239]—and Kara Mehmed Ağa, whose son was betrothed to the mufti's daughter, was assigned to the *cebeci başılık*[240].

236

	V.H.	P.	M.	C.
Amcazade Hüseyin	54.00	16.16	12.50	16.16
Dal Taban Mustafa / Rami Mehmed	65.00	7.00	7.00	21.00

237 This includes Sohrablı Ahmed and Şehrizorlu Hasan, the rebel grand vizier and his deputy. Rami Mehmed himself was a highly favored and trusted member of Amcazade Hüseyin's government.

238 Reference in footnote 206 above.

239 Anonymous History, Berlin Diez A quarto 45, 18a-b.

240 Cantemir, *The history of the ... Othman Empire*, 417. Defterdar, *Zübdet*, 340b describes him as having *kemâl-i intisab* (perfect clientship) with the mufti. As *kassab başı*, Kara Mehmed had become a very wealthy man. Immediately following the accession of Ahmed III he was tapped for 150 keses akçe as a contribution for payment of the *cülusiye* (accession) gift to the troops. Anonymous History, Berlin Diez, A quarto 75, 265a.

These appointments bear witness to the obvious anticipation of a continuing challenge to the court's growing authority. As a gauge of its confidence in the adequacy of those measures, the government reacted with what seemed like indifference, when the disaffection against it was first translated into the *cebeci* insurrection and eventual rebellion. It thus focussed mainly on the financial problem of the *cebeci* protest, expecting that all the difficulties it had would end with the dispatch of a few money bags to appease them[241]. However, when the *seğmen başı* was assassinated, firmer measures were taken[242]. Even when the actual news of the rebellion was brought home to Edirne in the form of the petition, the government—still defying political realities—had the delegation arrested and sent into eventual exile[243].

It is perhaps just as obvious that these government measures were not taken without a great amount of tension and anxiety. At some point following the detention of the rebel delegation, Mustafa II is purported to have awakened to the dangerous consequences of the government's reactions.

According to one contemporary Ottoman version, the sultan was angered by the wanton defiance of his subjects in the arrest of their delegation. When he confronted the grand vizier with this accusation, Rami Mehmed placed the full blame on the mufti.

While this illustrates the extent the mufti's political influence had reached by 1703, another contemporary version of the encounter exposes Feyzullah's financial corruption[244]. When the sultan suggested to Rami Mehmed that the court would require money to transfer the government to Istanbul in compliance with rebel demands, the grand vizier revealed the bankruptcy of the treasury.

After the *defterdar* confirmed Rami Mehmed's contention the sultan approached the mufti, who purportedly offered him seventeen thousand *kese*s of *akçe*s to finance the move. Mustafa II is said to have been quite surprised at the mufti's instant wealth, as the latter had always pleaded poverty whenever the sultan

[241] *Kul kâhyası* Abdullah was dispatched to Istanbul with 30 *keses akçe*. Defterdar, *Zübdet*, 423b and Silihdar, *Nusretname*, II, 159/288b.

[242] Defterdar, *Zübdet*, 424a states then and there it was decided to prepare for punishment of the rebels who had assassinated the *seğmen başı*. Some of the retired pashas were recalled and were given new assignments: Ahmed *paşa kâhyası* Hasan was given the command of Bosnia; Esir Ibrahim was given Niğde Sancağı; Kurd Mehmed to Manisa Sancağı. Other orders were dispatched to the eyalets recalling commanders and their troops to assemble for the defense of the Edirne government. Defterdar's contentions are confirmed by the official correspondence in Mühimme Defteri 114, 116-117. Of those recalled were: Hasan of Hodaverdi and Sultan Önü; Hodaverdi of Işkodra, Prizrin and Dukagin; Hasan, formerly of Belgrade; Ali of Belgrade and Ibrahim, the beylerbeyi of Rumeli.

[243] According to a copy of the official correspondence in Mühimme Defteri 114, 116a, dated: 24 July to 3 August, 1703.

[244] Anonymous History, Berlin Diez A quarto 4 5, 18a-b.

brought up financial matters. When Feyżullah was thus confronted with his own pleas of povery, he reportedly became tongue-tied.

The sultan then turned to the *defterdar* for an explanation. It was only at this point that the sources of Feyzullah's wealth were defined in terms of "... *malikâneler*. Each month he gets that many [*kese*s] and each year that much [income]"[245]. Mustafa II is said to have been unable to contain his anger and finally confessed he had been duped by the mufti. Now that his abuse of political power and his financial corruption were finally revealed, Mustafa II had him immediately removed from office and escorted out of the city[246].

These two reports do not explain Mustafa II's motive for taking the reins of power into his own hands. At the most they illustrated to contemporaries in very concrete terms the mufti's supposed political incompetence, financial corruption, and deceptiveness. Instead of complying with the subjects' wishes by handing the mufti over to them, Mustafa II sent his mentor to a secure spot outside Edirne and out of reach of the rebels[247]. At the same time he took measures to secure his own position by preparing for an eventual military confrontation[248]. Thus, the public protestations of the government are contradicted by contemporary official correspondance of both the sultan and his grand vizier. Whereas publicly the mufti was condemned for the high-handed way he acted, the official dispatches saw the rebellion in Istanbul as primarily the result of a misunderstanding between the mufti and Istanbul *ulema* over appointments within the *ilmiye* bureaucracy[249].

His removal from the court and transfer to a secure point was viewed as a way of appeasing the *ulema* and avoiding the further spread of discontent with Mustafa II's regime among the rest of the population[250]. (It was thus described not as *nefiy* [exile] but rather as *nakl* [removal]—while dispelling the discontent was depicted as *def*ʿ*-i fetret* [fending against festering].) It is quite obvious that Mustafa II must have hoped that the rebellion would subside due to Feyzullah's "dismissal" and that he could then feel free to recall his mentor at some appropriate point in the immediate future.

245 *Ibid.*
246 Anonymous History, Berlin Diez A quarto 75, 244b.
247 Ramı Mehmed, "Münşeat", II, 120a-b. In a letter addressed to the vali of Ozü, commanders of Belgrade and Timişvar, dated in July/August, 1703.
248 Starting as early as July 25, 1703, orders were dispatched to no less than twenty commanders. Rami Mehmed, "Münşeat", 207a-211b; 213a-215b; 217a-218a; 219a-220b; 221b.
249 In the dispatches the conflıct between the mufti and the ulema is described as "... şeyhülislam Feyzullah Efendi hazretlerile asitān-ı sa'adetde olan ulema efendiler beyninde menasib-i 'aliyyeye müteallik ahvalından naşi bazı mertebe-i münafi vuku' bulundugundan ...". Rami Mehmed, "Münşeat", II, 210a-b.
250 *Ibid.*

The discrepancy between the sultan's public pretensions and actual motives was not completely lost on the leaders of the rebellion. In all subsequent transactions between the two sides they showed distrust in the government's words and deeds. It was hard for the government to conceal completely its defensive and military precautions. In the next few days the more the Istanbullus insisted on the sultan's immediate compliance with their very specific demands, the more elusive he and the government in Edirne became. Until the actual confrontation of their armed forces, each side tried to act reasonably—showing the other the propriety of its stance.

In the end, attempts at reaching some common ground were not only vain, but became progressively more perfunctory. Ultimate purposes were getting less and less clear, and each side moved farther away from reaching an understanding with the other. This interval was used for consolidation of both position and support, and excuses were found to accuse the other party of ill faith and ill intentions. In the span of a few days, no less than three official delegations were sent from Edirne to Istanbul (e.g., on July 26 and another on July 28), but on Friday no official reports reached Istanbul from Edirne. Since that day had been designated by the rebels as their deadline for receiving the court's response to their petition, public prayers were again blocked as an assertion that justice and equity did not prevail in the land[251].

Towards evening scouts were sent out as far as Çekmece in hope of getting word of the delegation. Finally, a report was received that the mufti had been sent into exile (which was false, as he was not exiled until after July 29) and that the same news would be delivered officially the next day by the government's messengers, the *mirahor-ı sani* Selim Ağa, and the grand vizier's *tezkireci*, Mustafa Efendi[252].

On Saturday, however, only Cöbek Ahmed, one of Rami Mehmed's *ağa*s, arrived at rebel headquarters with the informal but conciliatory report of the mufti's dismissal. While a debate ensued over accepting his credentials—since he had no knowledge of their delegation's existence or whereabouts—suddenly a *bostancı* appeared. He had been sent to Istanbul as part of the delegation's escort[253] and now verified what the rebels had feared. At Silivri, some 12 miles out of Istanbul, the delegation was met by the *kul kâhyası* Abdullah, who had been sent with

251 Silihdar, *Nusretname*, II, 163/289a. July 27, 1703.

252 Silihdar, *Nusretname*, II, 164/289a. Defterdar, *Zübdet*, 425b does not go into detail about this period of fluctuation. Rather, he relates that before any of the Edirne messengers arrived the rebels had apparently received word that their delegation had been placed under arrest and conducted into exile.

253 Reported only by Silihdar, *Nusretname*, II, 164-65/289a.

instructions to the *kaymakam* Abdullah to pay the *cebeci*s with the funds he was carrying with him. When he saw that the *cebeci* protest had grown into a rebellion, he did not dare take another step in the direction of Istanbul.

When they reached Çorlu, a few miles from Edirne, the *efendiler* deemed it wise to send an anticipatory note to the grand vizier and the *reis efendi* informing them of the delegation's imminent arrival with a petition for the sultan. Two men were chosen as a subdelegation, the *bostancı*—who was narrating the progress of the rebel mission's journey to Edirne—and the *çuhadar* of Türk Hasan Efendi (the chief of the mission). These two men entered Edirne on Tuesday, July 24, and immediately delivered their message. While they were awaiting a reply, one of the men of the *reis efendi* advised them to flee, since orders had apparently been prepared for the arrest of the entire delegation and pay and provisions issued to the soldiers for a forceful suppression of the rebellion. To make their escape easier, the *bostancı* and his companion separated—with the former, after some difficulty, arriving at Istanbul[254].

To those assembled at the Meydan it was quite obvious that an outright contradiction existed between the grand vizier's conciliatory instructions and the reported harshness of the government's response to the Istanbul mission. While one pointed to accommodation, the other showed bad faith and ill intentions. The "coincidence" of the grand vizier's *ağa* arriving with his positive report, and the *bostancı* with his negative one, may not have been strictly fortuitous. Here, as in the next episode, we discern an attempt on the Istanbul side to counter every sign of conciliation from Edirne as concrete and direct evidence of the untrustworthiness of the other side.

For a while the *bostancı*'s report prevailed over the *ağa*'s. Some men were inclined to take drastic action—like the execution of the grand vizier's *ağa*—as a sign of their utter contempt for the Edirne government. But cooler heads prevailed, and two other recommandations were accepted: to draw up a new petition and to await the arrival of the *mirahor-ı sani* before taking any further drastic measures.

The petition took most of Saturday and the evening of the 28th to draft. Forty men representing the *ocak*s, *ilmiye*, and other orders of Ottoman society would be assigned to deliver it to the sultan in person. Since the *mirahor-ı sani* was expected on Sunday, it was also decided to await his arrival before sending the new petition. Hopes were quite high that this second government envoy would be able to resolve once and for all the contradictory reports of the previous day.

254 *Ibid.*

True enough, a memo was received early Sunday from the *mirahor* requesting an escort from each *ocak* to meet him at Küçük Çekmece (as was the custom for sultanic envoys)[255]. The rebel leaders obliged, and shortly after breakfast he was escorted into the Et Meydanı. When the sultan's message was delivered to the assembly, they found it did not allay their fears and suspicions. Feyzullah had been removed, but the rebels were not allowed to press charges against him. Furthermore—although the court had indicated readiness to return to Istanbul, as indicated in their first petition—Mustafa II made his return contingent upon the dispersal of the rebel assembly[256].

To the rebels the most serious problem was the lack of information on the whereabouts of their delegation. The *mirahor-ı sani*, who had been dispatched without any knowledge of the mission's arrival or exile, could shed very little light on this matter. All these factors, when added to the *bostanci*'s earlier one, pointed to foul play and led to the suspicion that the sultan had no real intention of accommodating the rebels.

Two subsequent reports further confirmed rebel suspicions and finally crystalized their petition against the government in Edirne. The *bostancı*'s report was confirmed that same day with the arrival of a *sipahi* who had been assigned as escort to the first Istanbul mission[257]. While the *bostancı*'s report may have been based on hearsay, the *sipahi* was an eyewitness to the delegation's fate from its arrival at Hafsa to its arrest a few miles from there (on Tuesday, July 24) by the Edirne *bostancı başı* and his men. He even claimed that the government had intended to have the delegation slaughtered to the last man.

The second piece of intelligence came from Mustafa Efendi, the grand vizier's *tezkereci*, who had been dispatched along with the *mirahor* with official messages from the sultan and the grand vizier. Since the two had separated during their trip, the *tezkereci* arrived late that day following the receipt of the *sipahi*'s report. When Mustafa was brought before the *ulema* at Orta Camii and questioned about the fate of the delegation, he volunteered that the reports of the *bostancı* and *sipahi* were indeed correct, for he himself—as the grand vizier's *tezkereci*—had written the order for the arrest and exile of the delegation[258].

255 Silihdar, *Nusretname*, II, 166/289a-b.

256 According to Defterdar, *Zühdet*, 426a, the rebel interpretation of the imperial rescript did not differ from their interpretation of the grand vizier's memo which was brought by Çöbek Ahmed. The intention of Edırne was under the circumstances to disperse the rebel assembly. Furthermore, the sultan had no intention of returning to Istanbul.

257 Reported in Silihdar, *Nusretname*, II, 166-67/289b.

258 Silihdar, *Nusretname*, II, 166-67/289b. This report, which is found only in Silihdar, points to Rami Mehmed's sympathies with the rebel cause. Otherwise, why would his trusted secretary speak so plainly to the rebels. Or was it in fact that Rami Mehmed intended to convey to the rebel side the actual plan of the sultan for not delivering the mufti and that he had no intention of returning

The *sipahi*'s report further cemented the rather loosely held coalition of the various groups in Istanbul. The abuse of their delegation was taken as an open challenge. The rebels felt especially insulted since the sultan, in contrast, had received—with all due honor and pomp—the "infidel" delegations that came to ratify the recently signed peace treaties[259].

The abuse of the Muslim delegation by a Muslim court served as the necessary ingredient for issuing a *fetva*, binding all those involved in the rebellion to unite in their action—surviving or perishing together. Thus, the oath and covenant that bound the *ulema*, *meşayih*, soldiers, and *halk* were now renewed with a vengeance, for anyone who saw fit to break away from this front was termed a traitor and, therefore, subject to the death sentence[260].

Concrete measures, openly showing the rebels acting in a sovereign manner, were then taken for the first time. Members of the *ilmiye* who were nominated by Istanbul to the three highest posts of the corporation were confirmed as both de facto and de jure holders of their respective assignments. In addition, and again acting on their own authority, the Istanbullus filled significant positions, e.g., the *kadı*ship of Istanbul went to Köprülü partisan Beyler Hocası Ahmed Efendi (who had served as the tutor for Kara Mustafa's sons) and the office of *seğmen başı* to Koca Musili[261].

For grand vizier designate the rebels elevated Sohrablı Ahmed[262], the Istanbul Kaymakam and the brother-in-law of the late grand vizier Amcazade Hüseyin. Until this point in the rebellion the people of Istanbul had apparently counted on Rami Mehmed to act as a moderating influence on the sultan. With the grand vizier's *tezkereci* directed to draw up their delegation's orders of exile they decided to abandon him along with the sultan[263].

At this stage an additional leader appeared in the person of a former vizier. Şehrizorlu Hasan, who had also served in the late Amcazade Hüseyin's government as the grand vizier's *kâhya* and had been hiding since his removal from office, reappeared in Istanbul to be listed as one of the commanders of the rebellion. It may be recalled that this is the same Hasan who had escaped the executioners sent after him at the behest of Feyzullah. Sohrablı Ahmed assigned Hasan as his *kaymakam* in Istanbul[264].

to Istanbul? It is just as likely then that the troops' movements in and by Edirne were conveyed at this time to the rebels.

259 Silihdar, *Nusretname*, II, 167/289b. "kafirden gelen ilçiye ri'ayet ve ikram iderler, ümmet-i Muhammad rusulune bu hakaret ve 'azāb olur mu?".

260 *Ibid.*

261 *Ibid.*

262 Silihdar, *Nusretname*, II, 168/289b.

263 *Ibid.*

264 Defterdar, *Zübdet*, 428a-b tries to point out the importance of this addition to the rebel cause

Earlier it had been established that each party to the dispute had decided (quite early) on its ultimate goal. The provisional government would depose and replace Mustafa II, and the Edirne government would resist that anticipated move. Yet each side, biding for time, acted as though its goals were not so drastic and spent time and effort to establish the genuineness of its declared goals.

These maneuvers obviously indicated that neither side had consolidated sufficient support. Had either side declared its position from the very start (the people of Istanbul had done so on two occasions when certain elements had openly aired their intentions, only to be suppressed almost immediately, especially by Çalık Ahmed) panic would quite likely have struck the majority of the population, and insubordination could have spread throughout the land. With disorder and dislocation it would have been impossible for either side to obtain the necessary support or successfully carry out its operations. (Typical reactions of individuals under these circumstances would be fear and avoidance of being caught in the middle of the inevitable conflict, resulting in the mass departure of families from the urban centers.)

Perhaps just as significant as the above factors is the example of the rebellion of 1687 when, for a few months, chaos and terror reigned supreme, caused much loss of life and property, and almost completely halted government transactions[265]. Order was restored only with the final deposition of Mustafa II's father and elevation of his weak uncle Süleyman II. The vivid memories of the insecurity that prevailed in Istanbul and Edirne sixteen years earlier—when the rebels had openly declared their intention to remove the incumbent sultan—must have played an important role in obscuring the intentions of both parties to the 1703 vonflict.

Since a strictly military solution was sought at the outset in 1687, here it would seem an attempt was made to effect a smooth transition from one reign to the next. In addition we see the *ulema* playing a much more important role at practically each step. Their opinion was sought and solicited before every significant move: on the efficacy of holding Friday prayers, and upon receiving news of the arrest of the rebel delegation by the Edirne government.

The clearest example of the rebel leaders' and the *ulema*'s mutual interests can be seen following the return of Türk Hasan from exile[266]. Despite the former

by stating that Hasan was capable of attracting and binding the *levend* with one word. Silihdar, *Nusretname*, II, 170-71/290a.

265 Silihdar, *Tarih*, II, 278-333 has the best description of this rebellion that spanned several months.

266 Anonymous History, Berlin Diez A quarto 75, 250a-251a. Also Silihdar, *Nusretname*, II, 170/290a. Defterdar, *Zübdet*, 428a-b, maintains that the rebel mission was accused of having been compromised with royal gifts and presents.

head of their delegation returning with what looked like a moderate and conciliatory response from Edirne, the leaders decided to seek the deposition of Mustafa II. Consequently, Hasan was maligned and repudiated as having been compromised by the sultan. Rather than acting as their partisan, Hasan was accused of acting as a mediator. Under threat of death he then was ordered to keep close to his home.

Rumors were spread that the next sultan would be Prince Ibrahim, the son of the late Ahmed II, instead of Ahmed, the brother of Mustafa II[267]. (Both of the latter two were sons of the same mother, and it was thus reasoned that the mutual mother would continue to exert influence under Ahmed III as she had done under Mustafa II.) When the rumors reached the point where people began talking about swearing allegiance to Prince Ibrahim, Çalık Ahmed stepped in and squelched the story. His objections were based on Ibrahim's minority (he was only eleven years old) and on the principle that seems to have guided every responsible leader in the rebellion: no illegal or extra-legal action would be tolerated. Instead, for every action that might have been construed as a sovereign act, legal sanction was nearly always sought[268]

There was a pragmatic corollary to this principle—the feeling that even at this late a point in the rebellion, the change in government could not be carried off. Thus, every precaution and preparation was taken to muster all necessary support from all significant quarters for the drastic actions they were about to take.

With the *ulema* this was done with both intimidation and confrontation on the one hand and cajoling on the other, lest the lack of *ulema* sanction should lead to unnecessary bloodshed and chaos. First, the case against Mustafa II had to be made to appear not only as legal, but also as the logical outcome of his own conduct and behaviour. Questions were raised about his sincerity and truthfulness[269], e.g., "Why hasn't he ridden [to us] as soon as he heard of our request... [for him to depart from Edirne and come to settle in Istanbul]?" Then it was reasoned that while "in two days, the body of one of his deceased sons arrived from Edirne for burial... yet he did not show up [even though we had given him four to five days]. Furthermore, he let the mufti escape free without being

[267] Anonymous History, Berlin Diez A quarto 75, 251b claims that the arguments took place in Istanbul itself and not on the road. Silihdar, *Nusretname*, II, 177/391a-b claims that the same took place as the rebel troops were approaching Edirne.

[268] This tendency demonstrates as much the legalistic bent of the Ottoman mind as it does the fear on the part of the leaders of the rebellion to take actions which might be construed as contrary to the *şeriat*. Underlying both was an obvious hesitancy to take independent actions which could lead to chaos.

[269] Anonymous History, Berlin Diez A quarto 75, 252a.

brought to us for trial". Following these open speculations, they declared their lack of faith in the sultan.

It is at this point, our chronicler reports, that the *ulema* began in earnest to fear a *hurûc ala s-sultan* (withdrawal of allegiance)[270]. While they were ascertaining the meaning of such a state of affairs, rumor had it that some people in Istanbul were intent on raiding the city of Edirne and burning its houses to the ground. (It is reported by our source that the *serdengeçtis*, irregular forces who were regarded as *erazil* [rabble], were intent on acting on this threat.)

At this juncture the *ulema* were made to intervene, while at the same time defining their role in the rebellion[271]: "Comrades, we have corresponded [i.e., written petition and given *fetvas*] on your behalf. ... Then, as now, you claimed that the case [against Mustafa II and the mufti] should be tried in accordance with the *şeriat* [canon law]. Yet now you are saying that you intend to raid and loot Edirne. Our aim is not fighting [to achieve our goal] but rather bringing the whole matter of the conflict with Mustafa II peacefully to a successful end. [*Bizim muradımız kital ile olmayıp sühulet iş başarmakdur.*] Since all Muslims are brothers, and we are all Muslims and of the same persuasion, to allow the sword to decide issues is contrary to the *şeriat* and is not suitable to us. ...".

The *ulema* saw their role primarily as one of mediation in the hope that change could take place fairly peacefully. From the military there came an immediate disclaimer[272]: "*Hâşa sümme hâşa*" [God Forbid!] that such words should be uttered from any of us. Our case is indeed one of canon law. There are fifty to sixty thousand men assembled. If one of these is found acting contrary to the *şeriat* may he be deprived of wife and child [literally: *bir avrada oğlana erişip* (separated from wife and child)]. Has anyone's honour been injured? Has anyone's money or effects been taken? Why do you speak in this manner [when, in fact, nothing of the sort has taken place)?" It was made clear, however, that troops were to march to Edirne. Should they be shot at they would respond in kind.

The *ulema* finally conceded to military pressure and openly espoused the rebel cause, the deposition of Mustafa II—perhaps as much for the justness of the case against him as for the fear that their own opposition could eventually cause even greater harm than the simple matter of removing a sultan. Their unequivocal support came in the form of canonically binding *fetvas*. Four of these will be presented in order to discern some of the specific grievances mustered against Mustafa II and some of the justifications accepted in the *şeriat* for removal of

270 Anonymous History, Berlin Diez A quarto 75, 254a-b.
271 Anonymous History, Berlin, Diez A quarto 75, 254b.
272 Anonymous History, Berlin, Diez A quarto 75, 254b-255a.

a sultan. In the following presentation the flowery language of the *fetvas* is skipped in favor of the succinct summary.

The first question posed to the mufti was:

"The padişah of Islam, may Allah extend his shadow over humanity, while for the greater glory of Allah and in mercy for Allah's creatures he has been entrusted [with their welfare], he leaves what he was entrusted with, and with the excuse of hunting departs from his capital city and roams [without aim] throughout the Muslim lands; if he has burdened his subjects with his injustice and inequity and without *şeriat* justification wasted the [Muslim] treasure, are said measures sanctioned in the *şeriat*?"

"*Yoktur* [It is not]", the rebel mufti Imam Mehmed answered laconically[273].

By this first opinion Mustafa II was accused of leaving his trust of looking after the welfare of Muslims to others, allowing injustice and inequity to reign supreme while roaming the hunting grounds of the realm, and burdening his subjects by wasting the revenues of Islam on his own pleasures (and those of his family in the form of lavish expenditures on his daughters' weddings).

While the first *fetva* tried to pinpoint the sufficient cause for a sultan's removal, the second defined the status of those who resist an unjust ruler.

"If from amongst the Muslims, a group rises in revolt against an unjust *Imam*, in order to end his injustice, is such a group considered a seditious one [*ehl-i bagy*]?"

Once assured of the legality of their stance in bearing arms against an unjust ruler, the rebel leaders took up the status of those who support an unjust ruler:

"If a group of Muslims rise in revolt against the injustice of the *Imam*, is the aid given by the remaining people to the *Imam* against those in revolt considered appropriate?"

This time the response from the mufti was: "*Olmaz* [Not appropriate]!"[274]

While the above three *fetvas* covered the grievances against Mustafa II in the traditional abstract manner of the legal opinion[275], the fourth (which comes to

[273] "Padişah-ı Islam... hazretleri t'azıman lı-'amr allah ve şafakatan 'ala halk-ı allah ıle me'mur bihi terk ve sayd u şikar bahanesile makar-ı saltanatını olan beldeden huruc ve haraket ve bilad-ı muslımin içinde tevaf edüb re'aya ve berayaya tekālif-ı şāka ile zulm u te'addi ve bigayr-ı vech şer'ī beytül-malī izā'et olsa müşār ileyhin bu vech üzere harakatıne musağ-ı şer'i varmıdır", "El-cevab: Yoktur". "Ketabahu Mehmed al Sadik 'ufiya anhü; ketabahu al-fakir Mehmed 'ufiya 'anh". Written by (former mufti) Mehmed Sadek and [*fetva emini* (Galipoli/Semavkalı)] Mehmed. Anonymous History, Berlin, Diez A quarto 75, 255a-b.

[274] Anonymous History, Berlin, Diez a quarto 75, 255b.

[275] *Ibid.*, 255a-b.

us from non-Ottoman sources) spelled out in very specific terms some of the charges leveled against Mustafa II. The question referred not only to the circumstances of the recent peace treaties, but to their subsequent ratifications and implementations[276].

By the summer of 1703 the territorial clauses of these treaties mainly resulted in the loss of Hungary, Transylvania, Morea, Podolia, and parts of the Crimea. Furthermore, the ensuing border demarcations finally spelled the closure of the frontier that in the past had fostered the expansion of Ottoman holdings in Europe. In the light of the disastrous agreements and territorial demarcations Mustafa II was charged with having compromised his mandate by accepting the peace treaties.

The question was then posed whether or not the Muslims were bound by the agreements Mustafa II had signed, especially with regard to handing over so many cities and provinces to the enemy. Here, the legitimacy of continuing in office a ruler who had conceded so much land and had conducted peace negotiations in accordance with European (i.e., Christian) law was being challenged.

With the first *fetva* the rebels managed to have Mustafa II declared an unjust and irresponsible sultan-*imam* whose wastefulness and neglect of duty had lost him the allegiance of his subjects. The second and third were canonical justifications of the actions which the rebels had taken in denying allegiance to him and in undermining the legal position of men and forces on the imperial side. With the fourth Mustafa II was accused of accepting dictation from the Christian powers by acquiescing to the peace treaties of 1699 and 1700 and of betraying Ottoman ideology by implementing the border demarcations that spelled the final closure of the frontier.

The above examples illustrate not only the interdependency of the *ulema* and the military, but also the tempering role the *ulema* tried to play in the rebellion, where the reasonableness and logic—if not the legality—of the rebels' ultimate goal finally received the proper sanction. In Edirne the same qualities of moderation were attached to the grand vizier, Rami Mehmed, though some of them were supposedly exhibited by the sultan as well.

Of all those involved in the events of 1703, the grand vizier perhaps most typified the qualities of reason and moderation. Almost all his contemporaries agree that Rami Mehmed was quite an unambitious man. To illustrate his

[276] Sutton is our source for this report. P.R.O., S.P. 97/21, 133. The English ambassador at the Ottoman court indicates that he obtained it from the secretary of a member of the secret council which was held (prior to the dispatch of the rebel petition to Edirne) in Istanbul. In the author's estimate this council sat in judgment on Mustafa II's reign.

modesty, some of his contemporaries point to the numerous times he declined to accept the honorific though quite prestigious title of vizier — the highest distinction attainable in the nonreligious service of the Ottoman state. (A cynical view of his refusal would attribute it to the high price one had to pay for achieving the patent for this title.)

The offer came sometime after he had successfully conducted the Ottoman's delicate and sensitive negotiations that led to the peace treaties of Karlowitz and Istanbul. His reluctance to accept the high honour can be partly attributed to his interest in retaining the office of *reisülküttab*, a position which — though subordinate to the grand vizier — had attained great importance by the end of the seventeenth century. By the time he had been elevated to that post Rami Mehmed was especially expert at dealing with foreign powers. He served nearly eight continuous years in that capacity before being elevated to the grand vizierate.

Prior to his return to government service in 1686, Rami Mehmed served in various capacities in the household of Musahib Mustafa Paşa (died 1686), a favorite of Mehmed IV and his son-in-law. The chief qualities of the careers he had been committed to until 1703 were those of liaison, mediation, and conciliation. If his personality may be measured by the career he followed, it would probably be accurate to conclude that Rami Mehmed was not a person to welcome situations that required independence and decisiveness.

It is in the light of this observation that his reluctance to accept the rank of vizier, which preceded every appointment to high executive position, can be further understood. Thus, when he accepted the office of grand vizier in 1703, it was less a matter of choice than necessity or coercion. The Ottoman state was about to be thrust into a "civil war" by the machinations of the incumbent grand vizier, Dal Taban Mustafa, in his desperate attempt to rid himself of Feyzullah Efendi[277].

It was in the aftermath of these troubles that Rami Mehmed was catapulted to high office[278]. It is likely that no other Ottoman official was at hand who would accept the curtailed powers the grand vizierate had undergone due to the influence of the sultan's mentor. As long as Feyzullah was in control, Rami Mehmed played a rather insignificant role in the conduct of state affairs. When

[277] Further implications are explored in Abou-El-Haj, "Ottoman Methods of Negotiation" and "Closure of the Ottoman Frontier".

[278] Defterdar, *Zübdet*, 406a-407b, considers this matter of some importance since he devotes considerable space to it in his otherwise laconic chronicle. Immediately thereafter, Defterdar provides an alternate explanation: Rami Mehmed was catapulted to higher office in anticipation of the dismissal of grand vizier Dal Taban Mustafa, and, indeed, shortly thereafter Rami Mehmed was offered the office of grand vizier.

the rebellion broke out he could not even save the Istanbul delegation from the humiliation and degradation to which Feyzullah subjected it. After the mufti's removal, however, the grand vizier took on a more active role, though mainly one of moderating the differences between the two sides. Although he could not openly agree and sympathize with the grievants from Istanbul, he was not considered hostile to them.

His attitudes were best portrayed by a contemporary who was sympathetic to the grand vizier. Here the Edirne government's position is interpreted not only as logical and reasonable but conforming to the sanctions of the *şeriat*. Thus, the sultan requested that Istanbul nominees for high *ilmiye* offices be dispatched to Edirne not only for official installation but for the performance of the *mevlid*, which could not be carried out without their appearance at the court[279] (the counter-argument for Istanbullus not holding public prayers until justice reigned in the land).

To the rumor that "the sultan was intent upon unleashing his armed forces against the Istanbullis"[280], Rami Mehmed is reported as having had the reasonable answer: "God forbid! [iyazen billâh]. It is not for fighting Muslims. The assembling of troops is simply for combating the *eşrar* [brigands] [*haydut*s in Europe and *celali*s in Anatolia who had been around for some time]. I [myself,] do not accept a falling out between Muslims. Their blood is like my own blood, their life is like my own life, and their property is like my own property. [*Anların kanı kanımız gibi, canı canımız gibi, malı malımız gibidir* (I would not tolerate the shedding of their blood, the taking away of their lives or the destruction of their property)] ... all these rumots and all this dissension will sow hatred amongst Muslims which would serve only the benefit of our mutual enemies [the Christians]. May Allah change this dissension into unity, amity and affection".

In thus assessing Rami Mehmed's role in the events leading up to the military confrontation between the Edirne and Istanbul sides, this same source persisted in portraying him as being more concerned with preserving life and avoiding dissension.

The sultan's moderation is illustrated by his willingness to be completely guided by the *şeriat*[281]. He is quoted as stating that "whatever is required by it I am

[279] Anonymous History, Berlin, Diez A quarto 75, 246a.

[280] For this and subsequent quotations see, Anonymous History, Berlin, Diez A quarto 75, 249b-250a.

[281] "Şer'-i şerif inkiyadımız kamāldır. Şar'an ne iktiza ederise razīyım kat'ā mühalafetimiz yoktur. Giflatımıza hasbile kusurumuz olmuş ise fīmā ba'd kullarımızın hilaf-ı marzaları olan ilerde bulunmayıp kendilere yaramayanlar bize dahi yaramaz". Anonymous History, Berlin, Diez A quarto 75, 251a.

willing to accept without wavering. If due to my *gaflet* [heedlessness] and inattention I have failed [in my responsibilities], then in the future I will be guided by them. Whatever they find unsuitable will be unsuitable to us".

Yet, despite all this moderation and reasonableness on the part of both grand vizier and sultan, the mufti was removed from their reach instead of being delivered to the rebels to stand trial. The court remained in Edirne, making the return of the sultan contingent upon the dissipation of the rebellion. The verbal protestation of good will voiced by Rami Mehmed and Mustafa II was in direct contrast to their actions. The military preparations in Edirne purportedly made the Istanbul forces finally determined to march against the sultan and achieve by force what they could not achieve by peaceful means.

The alignment of forces, equipment and resources[281] on both sides should throw

[282] *War Equipment*

Istanbul	*Edirne*
20 *kolunburna topu*	
40 *şahî darbzen*	
2 *havan*	
1 *barut-ı sıyah*	
	Silihdar, *Nusretname*, II, 171-172/290a
20 *top-ı kolunbur*	
10 *top-ı şahî*	
30 *top-ı bayağı*	
4 *havan topu*	
400 *kumbara-yı deste*	
400 *kumbara topu*	
1400 *barut*	
6000 *kazma*	
12000 *kürek*	

Anonymous History, Berlin, Diez A quarto 4 5, 36b. (This is the main source for Joseph von Hammer, *Geschichte des Osmanischen Reiches*, 10 vols., Pest, 1827-1835, vol. II, 82 [hereafter cited as von Hammer, *G.O.R.*].)

Extraordinary Payments-Gifts

Istanbul	*Edirne*
5 dollars to each man	7 dollars to old janissaries
	5 dollars to new janissaries

P.R.O., S.P. 97/21, 137a.

40 *akçe* each to janissaries and *serdengeçti*s	
25 *akçe* each as *teraki* to the *bayrakdar*s	
10 *akçe* each to *sipahlar*	
10 *akçe* each to *silihdarlar*	
10 *akçe* each to *seyyidler*	

Anonymous History, Berlin, Diez A quarto 75, 253a-b.

	7 *guruş* each to the janissaries
	100 *kese akçe* for the *sipahilar* and *silihdarlar*
	1000 *altun*s to *ağa* of the janissaries
	1000 *altun*s to Çakırcı Hasan Paşa, Commander of Edirne forces
	3 *kese akçe* to *kul kâhyası*

some light on the ultimate outcome of the by now inevitable confrontation. While one or two sources exaggerated as 100,000 the number of men each side could muster, most contemporaries agree that the Istanbul side had 60,000 to 70,000 men, including 20,000 to 25,000 members of the regular armed forces, and the Edirne side only 20,000 to 30,000 in all[283]. Although von Hammer quoted a much higher figure for the Edirne side, the sultan's desperation for more men and their continued loyalty could be illustrated by three directives issued by the sultan five days before the actual confrontation. To bolster Edirne's meager forces, a contingent from the palace bodyguards (*baltacıs*, *arz ağaları*, among others) was released by Mustafa II[284].

Perhaps more significant, both constitutionally and psychologically, was the unprecedented order addressed to the holders of *zeamet*s and *timar*s in Rumeli promising to award in perpetuity these benefits to them and their descendants[285].

2 *kese akçe* to *ağırcı baçı*
2 *kese akçe* to *sansuncu başı*

Silihdar, *Nusretname*, II, 170-174/290a-b.

283 (*Men mustered:)

Istanbul	*Edirne*
20,000 accounted for	-
60,000 total stated	—
Silihdar, *Nusretname*, II, 169/290a.	
20,700 soldiers	20,000
900 *sadat*	1,000 others
1,000 others	Raşid, *Tarıh*, III, 50-51
60-70,000 men	30,000
P.R.O., S.P. 97/21, 137a	P.R.O., S.P. 97-21, 137a
21,600 soldiers	80,000 soldiers
1,000 others	
von Hammer, *G.O.R.*, II, 82.	
61,000 soldiers	—
1,000 *sadat*	- -
Anonymous History, Berlin, Diez A quarto 75, 253a-b.	
100,000 men of all kinds	—
50,000 plus soldiers	—
Anonymous History, Berlin, Dıez A quarto 5, 3a-b, 15a.	
25,000 soldiers	—
900 *sadat*	—
1,000 plus *softa* and *esnaf*	—

Defterdar, *Zübdet*, 428b.

284 Silihdar, *Nusretname*, II, 174/291a.

285 In a letter addressed to vizier Hasan Paşa, commander sent agaınst the Istanbul rebels, he is instructed: "... Rumeli eyaleti askeri... hâliyâ me'mur oldukları hususda dahı mezburlardan (askerler) sadakat ve istikamet ve gayret ve hamiyet ile hizmet me'mul-ı hümayun olmağla haklarında avatif-ı seniye-i padişahâne zuhura getirilip ba'del-yevm fevt olanlarının ziamet ve timarı oğulları var ise tamamen oğullarına yoksa oğlu oğullarine ve karındaşlarına onlar dahı yoksa akrabalarına verilip ecnebiyeye verilmemek üzere ferman olunmağla imdi ... emir-ı şerifimi ... kıraat ve mezmun-i münifi i'lan u işa'at edip...". Rami Mehmed, "Münşeat", II, 222a-b, dated August 17, Friday (Ramazan II., 4, 1115).

To ensure their service and retain the loyalty of the few janissaries on his side, the sultan guaranteed them, forever, exemption from demobilization and any "future obligations" (meaning obscure)[286].

Despite these desperate measures the Edirne side could only bring together a maximum of 30,000 men, mainly from the auxiliary forces of Rumeli. There are even hints that in spite of the promises of future rewards and privileges to these armed forces, including actual cash payments, Edirne had a hard time holding on to them[287]. (The sources refer to deserters from Edirne who fled after receiving cash from the sultan, only to be arrested by the Istanbul forces before the actual confrontation took place.)

While contemporary sources list a formidable array of some sixty pieces of field artillery, several thousand hand grenades, six thousand picks and axes, and less than twelve thousand shovels for the Istanbul side, none list Edirne's material. This observation lends further support to the suggestion made earlier that most of the armed forces Edirne could call on consisted mainly of provincial and auxiliary irregular troops and very few from the regular armed forces.

Given the disparity between the military preparedness of the two sides and the unreliability of the Edirne forces, Mustafa II's determination to proceed with the military confrontation could be construed as no more than an out-and-out bluff. Every trick for breaking the Istanbul coalition against him was tried, from the attempt at subverting the Istanbul *ulema* to the projected posture of reasonableness and moderation.

Thus, when only hours separated the two forces, the government in Edirne tried one last tactic to accomodate the rebels. The sultan sent the *serasker* (commander) of the Edirne forces to sound out the Istanbul on their demands[288]. Their reply came in the form of the *fetva*s outlined and discussed earlier which gave them legal sanction for seeking the sultan's removal.

Mustafa II and his advisors failed in their efforts to avert an armed confrontation. Within a little over a month from the outgreak of the rebellion the armed forces of the two sides stood face to face on the plains of Hafsa, outside Edirne. Given

[286] "... bu ta'ıfe-i gabiyenin defi'inda uğur-ı hümayunda hizmetde bulunan kullarımın fima ba'd esamileri çalınmayıp cümle tekâliften muaf olsunlar. Bu hatt-ı hümayunum ocağınızda hıfz olunup mucibince ila maşaallah amel oluna". Şefik, *Şefikname*, 192-94.
[287] Four or five men arrested in Istanbul claimed to have fled Edirne after having been paid by the sultan. At their interrogation they claimed that the government was paying 30 *guruş* each to certain types of soldiers, e.g., *tufeng* and *postal sarıca seğmen*. They further claimed that most of those registered in Edirne were from the Croats, Arnavuts, Çobans and Çıtaks, i.e., mainly auxiliary and irregular troops. Anonymous History, Berlin, Diez A quarto 5, 15a-b.
[288] Silihdar, *Nusretname*, II, 178/291b.

the buildup for it, when the confrontation did take place it was anti-climatic[289]. The suspected unreliability of the Imperialist soldiers was proven, when following their sworn oath of undying loyalty and support for the sultan, they contacted the Istanbul side.

At a prearranged hour a loud explosion was heard (by one account the simultaneous firing of one thousand muskets), signaling both sides to join hands[290]. Abandoned, unprotected and helpless, Mustafa II and his commanders scattered. Most of his top advisors disappeared into hiding and the sultan, himself, returned to the palace at Edirne.

His official chronicler, Silihdar Mehmed, tried to cheer him up by reminding him that his ancestors had weathered worse storms than that, and from more heinous criminals. But Mustafa replied:

"It is not the same. All is lost. Words are of no use now. My viziers along with my soldiers have joined hands with the rebels. May God save me from their evils [evil intentions]. May He have them all burn in hell!"[291]

This bitterness dissipated, however, when he met his weeping mother, the *Valide Sultan*, as he was about to enter the harem. To her he described his predicament in more neutral terms:

"The soldiers have deposed me. In my place as *padişah* they set my brother Sultan Ahmed. *Allah mübarek eyleye* [May God bless him]. I entrust the safety of my children and women to him"[292].

The events culminating in Mustafa II's removal were marked essentially by a minimum of disorder or violence. Ahmed III's accession, however, inaugurated an escalation in both. The comparative order and control that had characterized the rebels' actions in the previous few weeks, gave way to vandalism and near anarchy as various elements tried to take the law into their own hands and made conflicting demands on the very government they helped create.

Each component part expected the government to serve its interests—sometimes to the exclusion of all others. Thus, all elements expected to be not only members

[289] Silihdar, *Nusretname*, II, 182/392, 292a. P.R.O., S.P. 97/21, 130ff. has a slightly different version.

[290] Anonymous History, Berlin, Diez A quarto 75, 261a.

[291] Silihdar Mehmed addressing Sultan Mustafa II: "niçin böyle mey'ūs olursunuz? Fitne olagelmişler eslâfınız erazil ve eşkiya elinden ne zahmetler çekmişdir?". Mustafa II: "Yok, yok, iş bitti. Söz tükendi. Vüzeramla kul ağalarım gelen eşkiya ile yekdil yekcihattir. Şerlerinden cenāb-ı hak bariye sığındım. Cümlesine kahr ü helāk eyleye". Silihdar, *Nusretname*, II, 183-84/292a.

[292] To the Valide sultan, he said: "Kul beni tahtdan indırmişler. Yerıme karındaşım sultan Ahmed Padişah eylemişler. Allah mübarek eyleye. Evladlarım ve hassa cariyelerim kendiye Allah emaneti olsun". Silihdar, *Nusretname*, II, 184/292a.

of the polity, but also of the government. A skeletal narrative and analysis of these events may clarify how and why the coalition, which made the change in government possible, fell apart and indicate the measures the new government took to ensure the reconstruction of a unified Ottoman polity.

The conflict between the government and the element that began to challenge it from within centered on three main general problems: out-and-out vandalism for personal gain and the attendant insecurity upon the fall of legitimate power; the accession gift and the meeting of financial obligations incurred by the previous government; and finally and perhaps most significantly, the question of who would make the final decision on appointments, and from which group or faction these appointments would mainly be drawn.

One of the first acts of the new government was to order the loyalist forces to depart from the city within a prescribed period of time and return to their home bases. Those who did not would be executed[293]. Although this was a wise decision in that it averted a real confrontation between the troops Mustafa II had assembled and those who came from Istanbul, it put Edirne at the mercy of the latter.

Anticipating raids and vengeance on them, important government officials and leaders fled the city. The inhabitants who remained hid their valuables, and members of their households were spirited off to their country residences (*çiftliks*)[294]. Before going into hiding, the grand vizier, Rami Mehmed, manumitted his slaves[295], but did not have time to secure his family from danger and humiliation at the hands of the rebels. In the end his immediate family was removed from the grand vizier's *saray* in Edirne with only the clothes on their backs. They were eventually reduced to living in Rami Mehmed's home in Eyüp, district of Istanbul, since all his property had been confiscated, as was traditional, to the benefit of the public treasure[296].

[293] "ve Edırnede müctemi' olan Rumeli askerine ve Yürük-...ızın verilip nefīr-i 'ām ve sa'ir askerden akşamadek bir ferd bulunur ise katl olunur deyü dellallar nidā olunup ol gün dağılıp İstanbuldan gelenler kaldı". Anonymous History, Berlin, Diez A quarto 75, 262b.

[294] *Ibid.*

[295] To help them avoid the humiliation of capture and violation, those women slaves who had known his bed, he gave away to be married to Muslims.

[296] All his effects, including an invaluable library of one thousand bound volumes, rare and unduplicable, were taken from his homes in Edirne and Istanbul. The total market value of his effects came to 1,000 *keses akçe*, of which only 100 were in cash. As evidence of his honesty, the chronicler points out that Rami Mehmed had refused to accept the *cā'izes* (gifts) to which grand viziers were traditionally entitled from new office holders (amongst others). The dearth of cash was due to the fact that since his elevation to the grand vizierate, he had spent no less than five hundred *keses* on the poor and on his own household. Anonymous History, Berlin, Diez A quarto 75, 261a-b.

However, not all the valuables sequestered from the former grand vizier and other high officials of the late government ended up in the public treasure[297]. The rebels, especially Karakaş Mustafa and Durcan Ahmed, either managed to take valuables outright for themselves—before the registrars of confiscations visited these homes—or got themselves included among the registrars and split the most valuable items between them.

Although contemporary Ottoman sources rarely give total numbers in describing the confiscations and raids, one indicates no less than sixteen hundred homes raided by the troops from Istanbul[298]. Feyzullah Efendi's family and entourage were especially singled out for the most intense destruction.

The mufti's flight from the rebels was intercepted[299]. He and his sons were put through rigorous interrogation, mainly to elicit the whereabouts of their liquid assets. Eventually, the father was subjected to a humiliating execution[300]. Except for Fethullah, the aspirant to the office of mufti who was also executed, the lives of the rest of his family were spared[301]. Their homes, and even the homes of their women relations that under normal circumstances would have been immune from raids, were not spared[302].

To stem these individual acts of vandalism and return a modicum of security to life in the two major Ottoman cities, the new government first had to take steps to remove its own soldiers from the city and the streets by hastening their return

[297] Anonymous History, Berlin, Diez A quarto 75, 263b.

[298] These figures are given on the authority of Muslimzade Efendi, the *kâtib* of the *mahkeme* of Edirne, by the author of Anonymous History, Berlin, Diez A quarto 75, 264a.

[299] Anonymous History, Berlin, Diez A quarto 75, 266a-27b.

[300] When the rebels asked the ulema for a *fetva* for Feyzullah's execution, they were informed quite inaccurately that, to date, no mufti had been executed. The removal and, sometimes banishment of a mufti had always been deemed sufficient. This same source then proceeds to point out that Feyzullah's enemies devised a method by which they could ensure his execution. First they had the *nakibüleşraf* (Seyfizade Ibrahim), in his capacity as the head of the descendants of the Prophet, send an officer on his behalf to deprive the mufti and his sons of their green turbans (which was the accepted and external signal that they were *seyyid*s), and then they prepared orders appointing each one of them to a *sancak* (enrolled as military men, which status removed their immunity from execution). In prison a *ferman* was sent to each, informing him that the sultan had bestowed on him the *beylik* (commander of *sancak*). The next day, Feyzullah himself was brought out and beheaded, even "before the words of the *şehadet* (profession of Islam) were departed from his lips". [Anonymous History, Berlin, Diez A quarto 75, 268b]. In another version, Feyzullah was first paraded before the troops, presumably to assure them that it was indeed the mufti who was about to be beheaded. To make doubly sure, his severed head was paraded to the troops also. [Anonymous History, Berlin, Diez A quarto 5, 42a-b]. The humiliation was carried even further when the mufti's body was dragged before Christian priests who both chanted and burnt incense. (The implication is that he did not die as a Muslim). Anonymous History, Berlin, Diez A quarto 75, 267b and 168a.

[301] Silihdar, *Nusretname*, II, 197/296a and Anonymous History, Berlin, Diez A quarto 75, 270b-271a and 281b.

[302] Anonymous History, Berlin, Diez A quarto 75, 255b-256a and 264a.

to their respective headquarters. Before any of them would budge from his station in Edirne, however, each demanded the accession gift and/or his back pay and promotion[303]. As soon as the accession payments and other financial obligations were met, the soldiers were ready to disperse to their assigned headquarters. The financial obligations of the new government, however, did not end there[304]. By the time all those who could make financial claims on the

[303] The *cülusiye bahşişi* (coronation accession gift) was a customary donation from the new sultan to certain elements of the standing army on the occasion of his accession. At Sultan Ahmed's there arose a problem which apparently was frequently raised on such occasions over whether the lists of those eligible was flexible. One interpretation quoting the *kanun* of Süleyman I stipulated only the *odalı yeniçeri*s (janisseries stationed in the barracks of Istanbul) and those assigned to certain forts on the frontier were so entitled. Since this was the interpretation which was favored by the palace, it was suggested then that the commanders of the *oda*s would, using both the registers and their personal knowledge, proceed to specify the individuals entitled to receive the coronation gift. The *serdengeçti*s (volunteers recruited ad hoc by janissary commanders from outside the *ocak* and hence had the nebulus status of being in the corps but not of it) protested this interpretation, claiming that in accordance with their register, they too were included in this benefit. (Apparently not all protested, some, in fact, complied and tried to disassociate themselves from those who did not.) The helplessness of Ahmed III and his government in the face of these challenges is evidenced by their compliance; in the end both the *odalı*s and *serdengeçti*s were paid a whopping sum of over 1.5 million akçes. (Close to 200,000 sterling pounds, according to Sutton, P.R.O., S.P., 97-21, 141a.) Wright puts it at 1,537,666 piasters. However, Ottoman sources place it at 3,688 purses. Since the Ottoman treasury was practically empty, the *defterdar* had to devise an ingenious method to collect not only enough money for the *cülusiye* but also for payment of arrears for soldiers. In the end he needed to raise over 7,000 keses. For the accession gift, he collected: 2,000 from the *İç Hazinesi* and from monies from Egypt and the sultanic *hasslar*, 500 from the Valide Sultan, 500 from confiscated effects of Rami Mehmed and Feyzullah and others, 100 from Mehmed Efendi, the *kâhya* of the Valide Sultan, 200 from Muhsinzade Mehmed Efendi and *divan hocaları* as a loan, 150 from *Kassab Başı* Mehmed Ağa. Since this total (3,450) fell short of what was needed, the *defterdar* took one of the *kâtib-i şer'* [clerk in Muslim law court] and paid a visit to the Edirne *Bedestan*. The trusts and orphan funds which were deposited there were tapped in order to raise the rest of the money. Our source is careful to point out that nothing illegal or unethical was done here, for to guarantee the payment of this "loan", jewelry and precious items, presumably from the inner treasury, were placed at the Bedestan in the form of *rehin*/pawn. Anonymous History, Berlin, Diez A quarto 75, 265a-b. Defterdar Mehmed Efendi confirms the need for raising not only 3,688 but also one thousand more keses for distribution to the *serhadli* janissaries. Defterdar, *Zübdet*, 437a. When the court finally entered Istanbul it had to raise more money, not only for accession gifts but also for more back pay. Defterdar (*Ibid.*) places the needed amount at 2,600 *keses*. Raşid, *Tarih*, III, 75-76, agrees essentially with the above figures, so does Silihdar, 293b. Wright puzzles over the sources for the 3,600 additional *keses* needed. Defterdar Mehmed does not provide him with an answer. Anonymous History, Berlin, Diez A quarto 75, gives a detailed list of the sources of the revenue.

[304] Soon after the court's arrival in Istanbul two to three thousand *çalık yeniçeri*s (struck off the lists) took advantage of the fluidity of the situation, occupied the janissary *oda*s and demanded to be reenlisted in the books as fullfledged janissaries — thus giving them equal title to the *cülusiye*. Although these latter claimants were finally disbursed without gaining either recognition for the status they demanded or for pay, the government was less successful with the *bostancı*s (palace guard) who felt that it was their turn to demand the full twelve installments due them. (The *bostancı* challenge to the new government nearly cost the corps its existence. Given the sensitivity of their role in defending the sultan and guarding the palace, Ahmed III felt he could not trust them anymore. He ordered the dissolution of the corps of *bostancı*s, its members to be made janissaries.

government were satisfied, more than seven thousand purses had been collected and disbursed[305].

The main problem facing reconstituted authority in Istanbul—and one that occasioned the greatest escalation in violence—was the question of who made decisions on appointments and from whom appointments were drawn. The answer to the second question gives a clue to the first. Sohrablı Ahmed's administration turned more frequently to the military for appointments to high central government offices than to any other single group within the rebel coalition. This constituted a clear overturning of a trend established at least two decades previous.

For the fifteen preselected offices already referred to in earlier observations, the rebel government turned 64.29 percent of the time to the military group as against 28.57 percent and 7.14 percent, respectively, to the households and the palace. For the period of 1683-1703, the military's share stood at 21.3 percent to the palace's 26.3 percent and the households' nearly 40 percent even.

This reversal of the trend was reflected, according to practically all contemporary sources, in the predominance of the military at every turn in the life of Sohrablı Ahmed's government. As proof of the military's preeminence, these sources agree that not only high officers (e.g., Çalık Ahmed, the janissary *ağa*) but also those of lower rank (e.g., Karakaş Mustafa and Durcan Ahmed) managed to allocate themselves the most lucrative benefits, as well as to confirm and appoint people of their own choosing[306].

The breakdown of the rebel coalition is attributed to the unreasonable ambition and perhaps greed of these officers[307]. Çalık Ahmed, the rebel janissary *ağa*, was

A fresh crop of *bostancıs* was to be brought into being through the *devşirme*, and to that effect, Yusuf Ağa, the former *Kul Kâhyası*, was so ordered. At this point the elders of the corps protested that the dissolution of the *bostancıs* would constitute an injustice to themselves since they had served the dynasty quite faithfully for stints of thirty to forty years. They figured that since they had nothing to do with the recent sedition the injustice was further compounded. It is interesting to note that they attributed the ill behavior of members of the corps to the change in the practice of recruitment. In the past, they argued, those who became *bostancıs* were drawn from the *devşirme* of Rumeli only. Then it was possible to train them in the proper ways and manners. Now, they went on to explain, recruitment was made from *ecnebîs* ["foreigners", who presumably were not as amenable to the training and disciplining traditionally associated with the old system]. It is never explained who these foreigners were, but we are to presume that they refer to Muslim-born recruits from both Anatolia and Rumeli. Although the order for dissolution was not rescinded, the elders were allowed to retain their status and, presumably, their benefits and seniority. Anonymous History, Berlin, Diez A quarto 75, 272a-b.

305 Anonymous History, Berlin, Diez A quarto 75, 270a, maintains that already before the *bostancıs*' claim on the government, its daily obligations due to the *cülusiye*, promotions and retirements amounted to three *yük*s each day [or 300,000 *akçe*s].

306 Anonymous History, Berlin, Diez A quarto 75, 263b.

307 Anonymous History, Berlin, Diez A quarto 75, 263a-b; Defterdar, *Zübdet*, 341a; Silihdar, *Nusretname*, II, 202-203/296a-b; Raşid, *Tarih*, III, 95-98; and P.R.O., S.P., 97/21, 160a.

not satisfied with making the most important decisions from behind the scenes. He wanted to do it openly and in no uncertain terms demanded the grand vizierate from the sultan and his entourage[308].

Having come up through the military ranks, he had the commoner's direct touch, which seemed to offend one of Ahmed III's palace retainees who was more used to the deliberate and less direct approach required by Ottoman etiquette[309].

Durcan Ahmed, another janissary, though a *serdengeçti* (irregular), also figured prominently quite early in the rebellion and demanded that he be given the rank of vizier[310]. Although objections were raised to elevating him to such a high and lucrative post without his first serving in any of the intermediary ones[311], he was finally awarded the rank he demanded and the governorate of Sivas with two *tuğ*s (horsetails).

However, Çalık Ahmed, Durcan Ahmed, and no less than nine identifiable military leaders met with a violent end[312]. At one point Çalık Ahmed is supposed to have boasted: *bu devlet bana münhasırdır*,—which amounts to saying: I am the state![313] The issue between the government and these military leaders was

308 *Ibid.*

309 Silihdar, *Nusretname*, II, 202-03/295a. Silihdar points out that Çalık Ahmed approached him several times on account of the grand vizierate. At one point he tells Silihdar, that the padişah had promised it to him. Here the author indicates his impatience with the *yeniçeri ağası*'s persistence. Silihdar is also quite derisive of the military mens' lack of knowledge of Ottoman etiquette. This comes out in his report of the events leading up to the *cebecis*' petition to Ahmed III when they insisted on delivery of the petition to the sultan in person. When they came before Ahmed III, the petition was so poorly written that they had to supplement it with verbal explanations. Silihdar, *Nusretname*, II, 198-200/293b. That Silihdar was not exaggerating in his description of the rebel military's lack of etiquette and crudeness can be illustrated from another contemporary source which claims that Çalık Ahmed, himself, did not treat the Silihdar Ağa (i.e., Silihdar the author) with proper etiquette. Anonymous History, Berlin, Diez A quarto 75, 278a-279a.

310 Anonymous History, Berlin, Diez A quarto 75, 241a-272a.

311 An intermediary rank would have been that of *beylerbeyi*.

312 1. Balıkcıoğlu Ibrahim, member of the *ocak*s, referred to by our sources as *başzorba* (head brigand) was given the *sancak* of Akşehir in Anatolia and executed. Silihdar, *Nusretname*, II, 201.
2. Subaşi Ali was exiled and executed. *Ibid.*
3. Div Ali, rebel *kul kâhyası*, was given the *sancak* of Bursa and disappeared before his arrival at his assignment having received word of his impending doom. *Ibid.*, 204. He was discovered in April, 1707, and executed. *Ibid.*, 235.
4. Süleyman, *muhzır ağası*, was exiled to Belgrade and eventually executed at Bihać. *Ibid.*, 204. Şefik calls him *amid-i eshab-i bagiy* (head of the men of the rebellion/sedition). *Şefikname*, 288-89.
5. Ma'anoğlu Salih, *sipahlar ağası*, executed following the revolt of *serdengeçtis*, among others, in reaction to the dismissal of Çalık Ahmed and the grand vezir Sohrabli Ahmed. Silihdar, *Nusretname*, II, 208.
6. Boşnak Ibrahim, *cebeci başı*, exiled to Bagdat and executed upon arrival there. *Ibid.*, 210.
7. Çilesiz/Küçük Ali, one of the rebel *cebecis*, taken to Kızıl Ada and executed there. *Ibid.*
8. Karakaş Mustafa, exiled to Mecca, found in Egypt and executed there. *Ibid.*
9. Kara Bıçak Mehmed, a *cebeci* friend of Küçük Ali, was executed. Şefik, *Şefikname*, 295.

313 Silihdar, *Nusretname*, II, 202/295a.

one of testing the qualifications of those who are to become members in the polity and, therefore in the government. Of the military group a few seem to have had political ambition. The rest acted as though their most immediate concern was their pay.

Once a substantial number of the standing army received their pay, they ceased to exist as a cohesive group. In fact, the government had taken the precaution of weeding out dissident elements from the standing armed forces through a new registration following the court's arrival in Istanbul[314]. Thus, when the issue was challenged, those officers with political ambition, like Çalık Ahmed, were quickly isolated and eventually eliminated one by one[315].

Only after the annihilation of the rebellion's military leadership, did anyone challenge the conduct of the palace and the new government that succeeded the short-lived one of Sohrablı Ahmed[316]. Elements of the janissary corps, the *serdengeçti*s and the *cebeci*s especially, met with commander of the *sipahlar* Saleh Ağa, a close associate of Çalık Ahmed, to discuss the fate of the fallen leaders of the rebellion[317]. Some bewailed their condition and the betrayal of the covenant they had taken at the beginning of the rebellion. Some reasoned that had they remained united, the janissary *ağa* would still be in his preeminent position along with the grand vizier, Sohrablı Ahmed.

It had become apparent to those assembled that the new government was bent on extirpating the last of those taking part in the rebellion. Some suggested a new confrontation with that government by demanding the reinstatement of Çalık Ahmed and Sohrablı Ahmed. There was, however, a significant disagreement with this suggestion, especially from the janissaries:

"We are pleased with the padişah and with the [new] grand vizier [Moralı Hasan]. The coronation donative and salaries they have paid us, and they have promised

[314] Silihdar, *Nusretname*, II, 197-98/294b-295a.

[315] Çalık Ahmed was removed very early in the reign of Ahmed III. Since there was fear that his removal might precipitate trouble among his followers at a time the government did not feel strong enough to handle it, it took the precaution of isolating him and removing him from the court and capital immediately after his dismissal to the post of governor of Cyprus, away from the potential base of his support in the barracks of Istanbul. Therefore, when he finally accepted his new assignment and requested permission to spend time in the city to settle his personal affairs before embarking to Cyprus, this was refused. From the palace he was taken by prearranged transportation by ship to his destination and eventual execution upon arrival in Cyprus. Silihdar, *Nusretname*, II, 202/295a. Silihdar, with obvious hostility to the men of the rebellion, relishes in his detailed description of the fall of Çalık Ahmed and the other men of the rebellion and describes how they were picked out one by one and eventually put to death. Having been the chronicler for ex-sultan Mustafa II, he did not enjoy Ahmed III's confidence for very long.

[316] Eighty-eight days. Silihdar, *Nusretname*, II, 205/295b.

[317] Silihdar, *Nusretname*, II, 207-08/295b and Anonymous History, Berlin, Diez A quarto 75, 288a-b.

us our full wages as they fell due. ... [You claim not to trust the sultan and the grand vizier, but whenever you needed money, you turn to them and they lived up to their promise. ...]. To whom would you appeal to get posts [*menasıb*]? The *vilâyets* [appointments to the provincial governorates] and the *menasıb* are clearly within the padişah's prerogative. Accordingly, the dismissal from posts and appointments is also. ... We have no bones to pick with either the padişah or the grand vizier. ..."[318].

There was obviously no significant interest among the military in mounting a concerted effort to get appointments to the major government posts or, for that matter, to exercise leadership of the government. In the end this signaled a lack of the need to wield sovereignty, which was immediately reflected in major cutbacks in recruiting the military for high office.

Although less powerful than the military, the rebel-appointed *ulema* proved no less of a political nuisance. Within five months of Ahmed III's accession, and only ten weeks from Çalık Ahmed's fall, three *ulema* holding high office in the rebel government were dismissed—one being executed and the other two sent into exile[319]. Most contemporary Ottoman sources vaguely attribute these changes to these men's close association with the rebellion.

Two, however, specify political motives. One of those exiled and eventually executed, the mufti Imam Mehmed Efendi, reportedly had addressed himself thus to the new grand vizier, Moralı Hasan: "Pasha, my son, your having earned the vizirate has the consensus of the *ümmet* [Muslims]"[320].

This was construed as direct interference with the sultan's prerogative and resulted in the removal of the rebel mufti. The other explanation attributes to all three

[318] Silihdar, *Nusretname*, II, 207/295b. Dated December, 1703.

[319] Imam-ı Sultanî Mehmed Efendi was singled out not only for exile but also for execution. None of our sources gives any kind of explanation for the exceptional treatment given this *âlim*. It is perhaps not insignificant that the otherwise complete and celebrated biographical dictionary of the ulema, Şeyhî, has no entry for him. Raşid is enigmatically silent on this point. Silihdar explains the changes at this point in vague terms. The three ulema are accused of having entered the rebellion voluntarily, presumably as opposed to those who entered due to *maslahat* (the public interest, and perhaps involuntarily, but in order to guide the rebellion into the least destructive path) or *zarurat* (necessity, coercion as in the case of Başmakcızade Ali, the rebel nominee for mufti for a few days). Still this explanation does not illuminate the drastic measures taken in either the case of Mehmed Efendi or that of Ladikli Mustafa who also was executed. This latter was one of the first ulema to join the rebellion and is dubbed by one of the sources as the leader (*baş u bug*) of the *seyyids* who had assembled with some two thousand ulema early in the rebellion. Incidentally, some of the sources call Mustafa "*müteseyyid*" (pretender to title of *seyyid*, a form of denigration). Anonymous History, Berlin, Diez A quarto 75, 240a-b.

[320] "Paşa oğlum, senin vezaretin icma-i ümmetle olmuşdur". Raşid, *Tarih*, III, 120-21. Şefik, *Şefikname*, 293 obviously drew on Raşid and used essentially the same wording except for the substitution of the phrase, "şu me'mûriyet-i celileyeye na'iliyetin ..." for *vezaret*.

dismissed members of the *ulema* undue influence over the military[321]. Both explanations have the common denominator of residual and undue independence and influence acquired mainly through the role these men played in the rebellion. They were, in effect, challenging the sultan's claim to unencumbered sovereignty.

Apparently, Ahmed III was able, quite early in his reign, to appease and eventually weaken the unity of the merchants and inhabitants of the city of Istanbul who were among the mainstays of the rebellion. Since their chief grudge against the former government related to Mustafa II's strong preference for residing in Edirne, to the economic detriment of Istanbul, the new ruler took it upon himself to rectify that problem. He vowed that no sultan thereafter would either settle or live in Edirne[322]. Even during European compaigns the sultan would spend no more than three days and nights in the city of Edirne and then only in the royal tents, avoiding residence in the palace. As proof of Ahmed III's sincerity, no one was appointed to the office of *bostancı başı* (commander of palace guards) for that city's palaces.

Sohrablı Ahmed and Şehrizorlu Hasan, the two pashas of the rebellion, seem to have been encumbered the least by this association. Ahmed was dismissed to serve with full honours the following year, while Hasan was retained in various capacities by succeeding grand viziers[323].

[321] Anonymous History, Berlin, Diez A quarto 75, 296a-b. The sultan's unhappiness with the mufti is first attributed to the fact that he had harbored Taşçızade Abdullah Efendi, a *va'iz* at Sultan Beyazit Mosque, who had uttered words which must have been construed as critical of the policies of the new government of Moralı Hasan. A ferman was issued for his arrest and exile. When the mufti was confronted with the statement that the said *va'iz* was invited to the mufti's house, he confirmed that he had actually invited him, but the man had not arrived. The government agent was able to get confirmation of the fact that the said *va'iz* had indeed arrived at the mufti's house and that the latter had hidden him. Taşçizade Abdullah was captured and exiled. When the news of the said incident reached the janissary *ocak*s, leaders there are supposed to have come to Moralı Hasan with the following plea: It is agreed that if the mufti (Imam Mehmed), the *Imam-ı Sultanî* (Ladikli Mustafa) and the *kadı* of Istanbul (Beyler Hocası Ali) are not exiled, we (the leaders) won't be able to control the *ocak*s (Müftü, hünkâr imami ve Istanbul kadısı ittifak üzeredir nefi olunmadukça ocağı zabt edemeziz).

[322] This order was issued as an imperial ferman and disseminated by town criers to all corners of the city of Edirne: "ba'delyevm padişahın biri ise gelip bu şehirde karar eylemeyip ve sakin olmıya ve bostancı başı vaz olunmıya ve devletden sefer olmadıkça Edirnede kimesne oturmiya... ve kendiler otağ-ı meymenet asarlarında üç gün ve üç gece meks ü aram edip saraylarına girmemişlerdir". Anonymous History, Berlin, Diez A quarto, 5, 44a-b.

[323] Ahmed was spared, according to one source, for the help he extended in the dismissal and eventual execution of Çalık Ahmed, the janissary *ağa*. He was put in prison for three days and then was sent to Sakız Adası with enough *Hass* income for his livings. Silihdar, *Nusretname*, 209/296a, Defterdar, *Zübdet*, 341a, Sutton, P.R.O., S.P. 97/21, 160a. Sutton contends that Ahmed was made to refund 300 purses of money to the treasury. A year later, he was given the command of fort Lepanto, where he served until his death. Silihdar 297b/II, II, 218. Hasan Paşa, on the other hand, served in no less than four posts before his demise. From the post of Istanbul *Kaymakamı* he went on to serve as *Defterdar* with the rank of vizier, then to Rumeli governorate, and finally

Although other pashas may have been suspected by their contemporaries of harbouring sympathy for the rebellion, none came forward until the actual military confrontation between the armed forces of Istanbul and Edirne[324]. The affiliation of Sohrablı Ahmed and Şehrizorlu Hasan with the household of the late grand vizier Köprülü Amcazade Hüseyin was well known. The comparatively mild treatment meted out to them and other paşas suspected of sympathizing with their cause[325], coupled with the central government's reversal of the rebel policy of recruitment for high office, suggests clues to which, in the final analysis, would benefit most from the rebellion of 1703.

It has already been noted that as long as Çalık Ahmed held sway over the government, the military filled the highest positions of the central administration. After his removal and the subsequent departure of Sohrablı Ahmed there was a progressively heavier dependence on the affiliates and staffs of the vizier and pasha households to fill these same positions. By the end of Kalaylıkoz Ahmed's grand vizierate, the third of the reign, the government filled nearly six times as many posts from the households than from the military — 62.5 percent to 12.5 percent. This represents a complete reversal of the rebel government policy when the military was looked to 64.29 percent of the time and the households only 28.57 percent. The palace recruits fared even worse under the rebel government — 7.14 percent as opposed to 25 percent under Kalaylıkoz Ahmed's government.

Following the suppression of the rebellion Ahmed III returned to the recruitment policy which had been instituted for most of the half century prior to the accession of Mustafa II. When Ahmed III returned to the Köprülü policy of recruitment, he also brought back the vizier and pasha households into a position of predominance in Ottoman politics.

to the command of Fort Belgrade. His execution was apparently unrelated to his association with the rebellion. Berlin Anon. 215, 284a, 297a; Silihdar, *Nusretname*, II, 209/210/296a, 297b. This Hasan was apparently a good friend of former grand vizier Rami Mehmed. Upon the reappearance of the latter from hiding, Hasan helped in the return of Rami Mehmed's properties and *malikane*s. Anonymous History, Berlin, Diez A quarto 75, 291b.

324 Mustafa II lamented to Silihdar the fact that his viziers and commanders had abandonned him on the battlefield. Silihdar, *Nusretname*, II, 183-84/290b-291a.

325 The two prime suspects were grand vizier Ramı Mehmed and Moralı Hasan, (the latter the brother-in-law of both Mustafa II and Ahmed III). Rami Mehmed went into hiding only to be pardoned by Ahmed III and, through the intervention of Moralı Hasan, was returned to the rank of pasha and assigned to the government of Cyprus and eventually to that of Egypt before he was retired in 1707. Silihdar, *Nusretname*, II, 208/297a; Anonymous History, Berlin, Diez A quarto 75, 290b-291b; and Maliye Defteri 3159, 122b.

POSTSCRIPT

The study of the 1703 rebellion provides us with a rare view of Ottoman polity at work within a given time dimension. Guided by a conflict model of politics, we can witness the dynamics of this polity at a particular historical moment. Since Ottoman sources do not reveal contemporary power structures it is impossible for historians to reconstruct normal Ottoman political processes. It is only in the case of rebellion—i.e., the disruption of these processes—that we are afforded a partial reconstruction.

The rebellion itself was occasioned by the failure to peacefully resolve the conflict over the question of membership in the government. This failure resulted in a split in Ottoman polity and the rise of two alternate authorities, each claiming exclusive hold over sovereign power. It is contended in this study that the grounds for this impass had been set eight years earlier by the new sultan. Ignoring the political realities of his day, Mustafa II resolved to revive the practice of serving as his own chief minister.

In this book it is argued that the political structure that prevailed during the half century prior to this sultan's accession came to be dominated by the vizier and pasha households. The year 1656 is the critical date in the development of this substructure of Ottoman politics. It is at this point that Mehmed IV renounced his executive prerogatives to Köprülü Mehmed. Although the renunciation was given on an emergency basis (the Venetians were threatening the city of Istanbul, and the military elements had rendered internal political life nearly chaotic by their intransigence), this grand vizier's successors managed to preserve the new power arrangement.

Although the *kapılar*'s potential for competing with the palace and the military as alternate sources for providing trained men for high office can be traced back to the end of the previous century, it was only in the second half of the seventeenth century that the households came to command the lion's share of appointments. Changes in both the international standing and domestic policies of the Ottoman state explain, in part, the predominance of the *kapılar* over the traditional sources of recruitment. Although the ideology of the ever-expanding frontier was kept alive, the sultans had by the early seventeenth century adopted a defensive posture. Except for minor additions in the Ukraine under Fazıl Ahmed no significant territorial acquisitions had been made since Süleyman Kanunî's in the sixteenth entury. The changed status and needs of the Ottoman state required different skills in its administrators.

These changes point to the progressive insufficiency of training in the martial arts — either palace or military — to meet the needs of a government growing in complexity. In the meantime, the *devşirme* system which was created in the fifteenth and sixteenth centuries supposedly to assure the sultans' absolute power had — with the elimination of the balance of power at the center — come to dominate both palace and administration. We have already noted the dynasty's disenchantment with the *devşirme* and janissaries. We also noted that a young sultan in the third decade of the seventeenth century had tried in vain, and fatally, to abolish the *devşirme* system of military recruitment. At the very least this indicates the system's growing obsolescence. This neglect, in turn, may have added to the shortage of properly trained men to staff even the military and central governmental posts, previously the preserve of the palace.

Men from all walks of life were therefore attracted to the entourage of the viziers and pashas. Those who came young were provided with the best training available for government service[326]. Here they would find assembled some of the best minds of the day and have contact with the high and mighty of Ottoman society in the persons of the vizier and pasha household guests. If the head of the *kapı* happened to be an in-law of the sultan's, the household and its staff would, in all probability, have been known to members of the royal house.

The *kapı* provided a slave, a young *şagird* (scribal apprentice) or even a full-grown savant with employment, protection, training, and the right contacts for entry into government service. In return, the head of the *kapı* expected the graduates' continued loyalty to his own person and interests while they were in office[327]. The retainees not only served as skilled administrators of the households, but

[326] Thomas, *Naima*, 148, describes the kind of *meclis* which the viziers and pashas held at this time. At the one which Amcazade Hüseyin held the chronicler, Naima, read his own work. Perhaps the best illustration of the *kapı* as a training "institute" during the second half of the century is that of Musahib Mustafa, the patron of Rami Mehmed. Nabi Efendi, one of the most prominent poets and literary men of this period, was also attached to the same household. Rami Mehmed, who entered the *kapı* later than had Nabi, followed in the latter's footsteps and occupied the administrative positions which were vacated by Nabi as he was getting promoted to the next rung of *kapı*-service. When Musaheb Mustafa died, both Nabi and Rami Mehmed went on the pilgrimage. Rami Mehmed, then, returned to government service in the grand vizier's chancery, while Nabi went into retirement. E. J. W. Gibb, *A History of Ottoman Poetry* (London, 1904), III, 325-26. "Nabi Efendi" and "Rami Mehmed" in *İ.A*. What is perhaps of special significance about Musahib Mustafa is the fact that he was the son-in-law of Mehmed IV. When Mustafa died, his wife was given in marriage to Moralı Hasan, who was both the friend of Rami Mehmed and the grand vizier who succeeded the rebel leader, Sohrablı Ahmed. Silihdar, *Tarih*, II, 498, and *Nusretname*, II, 205/295b. Also see Abou-El-Haj, *Reisülküttab and Karlowitz*.

[327] Thomas, *Naima*, 96-97.

many proved sufficiently qualified even to meet the needs of the provincial and central administrations. By the end of the seventeenth century nearly all internal and foreign policy matters were directed by men of the *kapıs*. The administrations of the sultans who preceded Mustafa II illustrate this point. Mustafa's father, Mehmed IV, was known to have marched with his chief lieutenants as far as the closest hunting grounds and then go off on his own to indulge in his passion for the game, while the grand viziers proceeded to the battlefield[328]. While Mehmed IV was allowed to make only martial gestures — earning him the undeserved though coveted title of *gazi* (infidel-fighter) — his brother, Süleyman II and Ahmed II, left state affairs completely in the hands of their subordinates. The *kapı* phenomenon was not, however, confined to the Köprülü family, as illustrated by at least forty other documented households during the period 1683-1703[329].

[328] This was especially true during the grand vizierates of Fazıl Ahmed and Kara Mustafa

[329] The forty-odd are:

Ahmed (Defterdar)
Ahmed (Melek)
Ahmed (Salt)
Ahmed (Sohrablı)
Ali (Arabacı)
Alı (Çalık)
Ali (Kadı)
Ali (Kılıç)
Alı (Sofu)
Ali (Soyulcu)
Ali (Sürmeli)
Cafer (Büyük)
Kasım
Mehmed (Ahmedpaşaoğlu)
Mehmed (Rami)
Mehmed (Seyyidîzade)
Mustafa (Bozuklu)
Mustafa (Daltaban)
Mustafa (Ferari)
Mustafa (Ferari/Kara)
Mustafa (Kara)
Mustafa (Kıblelizade)
Mustafa (Midillili)
Mustafa (Musaheb)

Fereng
Halil (Koca/Arnavut)

Hüseyin (Gür)
Hüseyin (Ma'anoğlu)
Hüseyin (Silihdar)
Hüseyin (Topal)
Ibrahim (Kara)
Ibrahim (Mısırlızade)
Ibrahım (Han/Sokollu)
Ibrahim (Şeytan/Melek)
Ismaıl (Karayılanoğlu)
Mustafa (Tekfurdağlı)

Ömer (Koca)
Osman (Yeğen)
Salih (Arap)
Sıyavuş (Abaza)
Süleyman (Sarı)

This list is confined to vizıers and paşas whose family members or household members came to hold central and *eyalet* level appointments. The Ottoman state had close to forty *eyalets* at this point, and these were divided into approximately 270 *sancaks*. Gibb and Bowen, *Islamic Society*, I, I, 143, note 1 and Evlıya Çelebi, *Narrative of Travels in Europe, Asia and Africa*, London, 1834, 90ff. From the chronicles available to the author, some thirty-five men of the *kapı halkı* of Kara Mustafa were isolated. Of these no less than six attained the rank of pasha:

Kara Ibrahim
Çerkes Ahmed
Çerkesli/Celeb Hasan
Çalık Ali
Tokatlı Mahmud

Besides allowing us perhaps only a glimpse of Ottoman political life in on-going history, the rebellion of 1703 points to specific changes and continuities. It clearly shows that the palace and the military had taken secondary roles in both the formulation and execution of policy. There are indications that men who began their careers in these two services became more reluctant to take on posts in the public administration, preferring retirement or some other avenues of "public" service[330]. A measure of the military's growing insignificance as a source of authority in the late seventeenth century can be illustrated from the rebellion's aftermath by the reluctance of the officers to defend their men and by these soldiers' indifference to the fate of their leaders. We have noted that once the accession money due to them and their salaries had been met, those of the military front ceased to act as one unit. The developing quarrel between the new sultan and the military officers over the occupation of significant posts was not deemed sufficiently important for a united stand. The military survivors of the rebellion could not provide an alternate method to the one which gave the sultan the sole prerogative for appointment to high office.

The rebellion points to the reduced stature and powers of the sultan. He was no longer the independent agent who sought and kept his own counsel. If the business of government were to be carried out with any kind of efficiency, and if he wished to have a hand in government himself, the ruler had to seek the advice of "interested parties" and heed their counsel. (Ahmed III was especially critical of his brother Mustafa II for the latter's nearly complete reliance on and trust in Feyzullah.)[331]

The erosion of the sultan's powers and standing can be further illustrated from Mustafa II's last desperate actions. In his final bid to keep the throne this ruler was willing to barter his constitutional and executive prerogatives. Loyalist troops were exempt from the *esame* inspections and obligations and spared any kind

Deli Ömer

Kara Ibrahim who succeeded Kara Mustafa to the office of grand vizier and served in that capacity for two years, had a *kapı* of whose *halk* seven men attained the rank of pasha:

Hazinedar Ibrahim	Dal Taban Mustafa
Gürci/Gür Ibrahim	Uzun Ali
Büyük Cafer	Cadı Yusuf
Kürd Şahin.	

[330] Silihdar Mehmed, the author of one of our major sources for this period, was offered a vizierate and a governorate to go with it. He declined for fear of doing injustice to the inhabitants. Instead, he chose retirement. Silihdar, *Nusretname*, II, 211/296a. Our second example is *Oda başı* Mustafa, who was born in Rumeli and migrated to Istanbul. There he entered the 20th *bölük* of *Dergâh-ı âli yeniçerileri* as the *karakulak*. He then became first *vekil-ı aşçı* and then *oda başı*. He retired with a *vazife* and eventually married the daughter of Şeyh Yahya Efendi. He entered the *ilmiye* after having studied under Şeyhülislâm Ali. He died in 1703. Biography from Şeyhî, "Vekayi'", II, 210a.

[331] Naima, *Tarih*, VI, author's appendix 26-27.

of doubt as to their, and their descendents' title to their original *timar*s (usufructs). (Ahmed III, in turn, had to abandon Edirne as an alternate seat of government, on his own behalf and on that of his successors, in response to rebel demands.) Furthermore, nepotism was now institutionalized with set limits to which one could take advantage of his position to advance his family and entourage—even those who were the special favorites of the sultans[332].

If Mustafa II had been bent on centralism (and there is some evidence that he had been [Appendix II]) he failed miserably. The rebellion of 1703, in fact, paved the way for more decentralization. The rebellion further secured the predominance of two substructures of Ottoman polity: the vizier and pasha households, and the *ulema*. We have noted a number of critical political incidents where the *ulema* took an active part. In the second half of the century one such *ulema* family even took a hand in deposing three sultans.

The vizier and pasha households came to dominate the grand vizierates which followed Ahmed III's accession to power. We have given evidence of the chief executives' return to the old policy of recruiting men from the *kapılar* to staff most of the high government posts. It is perhaps significant to note that the systematic elimination of the rebellion's military leaders was viewed by contemporaries as the reasonable result of their "heinous" crime. Their demise was taken as a signal for the end of the rebellion. The peaceful departure of Sohrablı Ahmed from the center of power is barely mentioned in these same sources. His chief lieutenant in the rebel command, Şehrizorlu Hasan, was kept on by the government of Ahmed III and eventually executed in circumstances not related to the rebellion.

The adoption of a structural approach to the delineation of the Ottoman political community of the last two decades of the seventeenth century and a dynamic approach in the analysis of the forces at play in the 1703 rebellion allows for one broad conclusion serving as a final hypothesis. With very few exceptions, the most recent general interpreters of Ottoman political history are still guided by the basic principle of charismatic leadership and, therefore, accept palace administrative dominance as set forth in the previous two centuries by Mehmed the Conqueror and Süleyman Kanunî, respectively. The interpretations are based on the assumption that the sultan through the *devşirme* system had monopolized power. Any historical deviation from this classical norm through the evolution of political substructures responding to historical demands—whether from within or without the palace—is treated as a sign not of vitality, but of decline and disintegration. Here we face a paradox reminiscent of the historically evolved

[332] As, for example, the flagrant abuse of the practice by Feyzullah.

"Marxist dilemma": the triumph of the proletariat signals the end of both history and politics. In the Ottoman case, however, the paradox has to be stood on its head. While the *devşirme* system of administration headed by a charismatic figure is treated as an historically determined phenomenon (hence, the ideal norm), the political substructures which developed in the seventeenth and eighteenth centuries[333] are viewed primarily as aberrations (hence, symptoms of decline and corruption). This line of argument is based on the absurd assumption that in these latter two centuries Ottoman society had reached a state of stagnation[334].

The approach to and the results of this study point to a need for skepticism not only about the ahistorical treatment outlined above but also about the validity of the whole framework of understanding earlier Ottoman political developments. Is it useful to continue to accept the standard generalization which accords the fifteenth and sixteenth century sultans exclusive and unchallenged control over state affairs? Should we not reopen the question and expand the hypothesis in search of other political structures which may have vied with the dynasty and the *devşirme* system? The general feasibility of this proposition has not been the main focus of this study. Only future probes into the eras of the giant *gazi*-sultans will determine its probity.

[333] E.g., Albert Hourani, "The Changing Face of the Fertile Crescent in XVIII Century", *Studia Islamica*, VIII (1957), gives a dynamic treatment of the Arab world in this highly suggestive article.
[334] E.J. Hobsbawm explores this idea of stagnation in his article, "The Social Function of the Past: Some Questions", *Past and Present*, 55, (1972), 3-17.

APPENDIX I
List of Office Holders
1683-1703

Central Administration

İstanbul Kaymakamı	*Year**		*Affiliation, etc.*
Tokatlı Mahmud	inc.**	V.H.	of Kara Mustafa
Kara Hasanağazade Mustafa	1095	M.	
Boşnak Recep (Şatir)	1097	V.H.	Sarı Süleyman
Fazıl Mustafa	1099	B.Z.	Köprülü
Nişancı Ismail	1099	P.	
Kötü Eğri Omer	1099	M.	
Çalık Ali (Namazcı)	1101	V.H.	Kara Mustafa
Amcazade Hüseyin	1102	B.Z.	Köprülü
Çelebi İsmail (Voyvoda)	1103	M.	
Boşnak Hüseyin	1103	C.	
Kandilci Hüseyin	1104	P.	damad of Karayılanoğlu İsmail
Kalaylıkoz Ahmed	1105	P.	
Amcazade Hüseyin	1105	B.Z.	Köprülü
Midillülü Mustafa (Esir)	1105	V.H.	Fazıl Mustafa
Çerkes Osman	1106	P.	Damad. Umatullah Sultan***
Diramalı Çelebî Ibrahim	1108	M.	
Helvacı Yusuf	1109	P.	
Çerkes Osman	1112	P.	same as 1106 above
Helvacı Yusuf	1114	P.	
Abdullah	1114	B.Z.	Köprülü
Rikab Kaymakamı			
Kara Ibrahim	inc.	V.H.	Ferari Mustafa and Kara Mustafa
Musahib Mustafa	1096	P.	Damad. Hatice d. of Mehmed IV.
Divrikli Mehmed	1096	V.H.	Köprülü Mehmed
Bosnevi Süleyman (Sarı)	1096	P.	(Cantemir calls him Köprülü creature; Silihdar favors the Palace.)
Boşnak Recep (Şatir)	1097	V.H.	see 1097 İstanbul Kaymakamı
Fazıl Mustafa	1098	B.Z.	Köprülü

* A.H. year of appointment.
** Incumbent on 25 Zilhice 1094.
*** *Damad* capitalized indicates an in-law of the Dynasty.

Arnavut Hüseyin (Beğli)	1100	P.	
Çelebî Mehmed	1100	V.H.	
Moralı Ali (Türk)	1101	P.	
Beyzade Ali	1103	P.	damad of Fazıl Mustafa
Bozoklu Mustafa	1103	P.	
Osman	1104	V.H.	Fazıl Ahmed
Çerkes Osman	1105	P.	see 1106 Istanbul Kaymakamı
Abdullah	1105	V.H.	Sürmeli Ali
Elmas Mehmed (deputy)	1105	P.	his father Sadik a naval *reis*
Selanikli Ahmed (Rum)	1105	P.	
Elmas Mehmed	1106	P.	see 1105 above
Moralı Hasan	1106	P.	Damad. Married Hatice widow of Musahib Mustafa
Bozoklu Mustafa	1109	P.	
Moralı Hasan	1110	P.	as 1106 above
Ali (Kıbtı)	1115	P.	

Nişancı

Nişancı Ismail	inc.	P.	
Elmas Mehmed	1099	P.	see 1105 Rikab Kaymakam
Karanfilzade Ali (deputy)	1100	C.	
Keresteci Mehmed	1106	V.H.	Sürmeli Ali
Karanfilzade Ali	1106	C.	
Bahrî Mehmed	1109	P.	
Sohrablı Ahmed	1110	V.H.	Silihdar Hüseyin. Entered *enderun* service; damad: Amcazade Hüseyin
Abdullah	1114	B.Z.	Köprülü
Kara Bekir	1114	C.	Belonged to Amcazade Hüseyin's circle
Ali	1115	C.	Brother-in-law of Amcazade Hüseyin

Vezir-i Âzam

Kara İbrahim	1094	V.H.	see rikab kaymakamı 1094
Sarı Süleyman	1097	V.H.	see rikab kaymakamı 1096
Abaza Siyavuş	1098	V.H.	Köprülü Mehmed and his damad
Bozoklu Mustafa (nominated)	1099	P.	
Nişancı Ismail	1099	P.	
Bekrî Mustafa	1099	M.	
Fazıl Mustafa	1101	B.Z.	Köprülü
Arabacı Ali	1102	V.H.	started in *ilmiye*, joined Koca Halil's *kapı* then Fazıl Mustafa's
Bozoklu Mustafa (nominated)	1103	P.	
Çalık Ali	1103	V.H.	Kara Mustafa
Bozoklu Mustafa	1104	P.	
Sürmeli Ali	1105	V.H.	Sokulluzade Ibrahim Han
Elmas Mehmed	1106	P.	his father Sadik a naval *reis*
Amcazade Hüseyin	1109	B.Z.	Köprülü

Daltaban Mustafa	1114	V.H.	(Cantemir identifies him as a janissary who was brought up at Fazıl Ahmed's court) Kara Ibrahim
Rami Mehmed	1114	C.	

Yeniçeri Ağaları

Bekrî Mustafa	inc.	M.	
Arnavut Zülfikar	1095	M.	
Çolak Hasan	1097	M.	
Bekrî Mustafa	1098	M.	
Cadi Yusuf	1098	V.H.	Kara Mustafa
Cerrah Mustafa	1099	P.	
Harputlu Ali	1099	V.H. ?	Fazıl Mustafa
Cerrah Mustafa	1099	P.	
Ali	1099	M.	
Musa (nominated)	1099	P.	
Bosnevî Hasan	1099	P.	
Üsküplü Mahmud	1099	M.	
Malatyalı Bekir	1101	M.	
Kadı Ali	1101	V.H.	Fazıl Mustafa
Çikoğlu Mehmed	1102	V.H.	Fazıl Mustafa
Eğinli Mehmed	1103	P.	
Daltaban Mustafa	1103	V.H.	same as g.v. 1114 above
Celebî Ismail	1103	M.	
Curcu Abdullah	1104	M.	
Koca Murad	1105	M.	
Çerkes Yusuf	1106	P.	
Baltazade Mahmud	1106	M.	
Diramalı Çelebî Ibrahim	1109	M.	
Kürd İbrahim	1109	M.	
Doğramacı Mehmed	1112	M.	
Tellak Ali	1114	V.H.	Amcazade Hüseyin
Trabluslu Osman	1115	M.	
Çalık Ahmed	1115	M.	

Kapudan Paşa

Bozoklu Mustafa	inc.	P.	
Boşnak Ahmed	1095	V.H. ?	
Mısırlızade Ibrahim	1097	M.	
Kalaylıkoz Ahmed	1100	P.	
Mezzomorto Hüseyin	1101	M.	
Mısırlızade Ibrahim	1101	M.	
Helvacı Yusuf	1103	P.	
Amcazade Hüseyin	1106	B.Z.	as g.v. 1109 above
Mezomorto Hüseyin	1106	M.	
Abdülfettah	1113	M.	
Aşçı Mehmed	1114	V.H.	Mısırlızade Ibrahim

Sipahiler Ağaları

Kabakulak Ahmed	inc.	M. ?	
Abaza Siyavuş	1095	V.H.	see g.v. 1098
Siyavuş	1095	V.H.	Defterdar Ahmed
Arnavut Hüseyin	1095	P.	
?			
Deli Piri	1099	M.	
Sarı Ali	1099	M. ?	
Yumak Mehmed	1099	V.H.	Musaheb Mustafa
Sarı Ali	1101	M.	
Kalın Ali	1101	V.H.	Fazıl Mustafa
Ömer	1101	V.H.	Fazıl Mustafa
Gümüş Mehmed	1102	M.	
Kalın Ali	1103	V.H.	as 1101 above
Kurd Ahmed	1104	V.H.	Kadı Ali
?			
Deli Mehmed	1106	P.	
Ahıskalı Abdulbaki	1107	V.H.	Tekfurdağlı Mustafa
Haci Mustafa	1107	V.H.	also damad of Kara Mustafa
Osman (Zülfikaroğlu)	1110	V.H.	Kara İbrahim
Ibrahim Ağa	?	?	
Çorlulu Abdullah	?	?	
Tellak Ali	1114	V.H.	Amcazade Hüseyin
Telhisci Mehmed	1114	V.H.	Amcazade Hüseyin
Kermetcioğlu Mehmed	1114	V.H.	Sofu Ali
Ma'anoğlu Saleh	1115	V.H.	Ma'anoğlu Hüseyin Bey

Cebeci Başı

Koca Fazlı	inc.	M.	
Abaza Siyavuş	inc.	V.H.	as g.v. 1098 above
Koca Fazlı	1095	M.	
Yusuf	1097	M.	
?	?	?	
Koca Murad	1100	M.	
Daltaban Mustafa	1100	V.H.	as g.v. 1114 above
Seyyid Ahmed	1101	V.H.	Fazıl Mustafa
İkinci Hüseyin	1103	V.H.	Sarı Süleyman
Ismail	1103	M.	
Kalın Ali	1104	V.H.	Fazıl Mustafa
Kaftancı Mehmed	1105	V.H.	Çalık Ali
Selanikli Ahmed (Rum)	1105	P.	
Hazinedar İbrahim	1106	V.H.	Kara İbrahim and Sarı Süleyman
Ali	1106	M.	
Abdul-Rahman (Sari)	1107	M.	
Mustafa	1108	M.	
Filibeli Mehmed	1109	M.	
Ahmed	1110	M.	

Divrikli Mustafa	1110	M.	
Kaftancı Mehmed	1111	V.H.	as 1105 above
Kiremetcioğlu Mehmed	1113	V.H.	Sofu Ali
Hasan	1114	M.	
Paşnak İbrahim	1115	V.H.	Rami Mehmed
Kara Mehmed	1115	M. ?	his son married daughter of Feyzullah Efendi

Baş Bakı Kullu

Siyavuş Ağa	inc.	V.H.	Defterdar Ahmed
Doğancı Hüseyin	1095	?	
Matmat Osman	1098	M.	
Hüseyin	1099	V.H.	Musaheb Mustafa
Süleyman	1099	V.H.	Damad of Defterdar Mehmed
Sarı Osman	1099	V.H.	Soyulcu Ali
?	1104	?	
Gümüş Mehmed	1105	M.	
Fazlı	1105	C.	
Yusuf	1106	C.	
Ibrahim (Hazinedar)	1106	V.H.	Kara İbrahim and Sarı Süleyman
Sarı Osman	1108	V.H.	as 1099 above
Şehrizorlu Hasan	1109	V.H.	Kara İbrahim and Amcazade Hüseyin
?	1113		
?	1115		

Büyük Mirahor

Sarı Süleyman	inc.	V.H.	see g.v. 1097 above
Şahin Mustafa	1095	P.	
Boşnak Recep	1095	V.H.	Sarı Süleyman
Voynuk Mehmed	1099	M.	
Küçük Hasan	1099	M.	
Ömer	1099	M.	
Dayazade Omer	1099	P.	
Taslak Ismail	1102	P.	
Baltacı Ibrahim	1104	P.	
Çalık Ahmed	1106	P.	
Çerkes Mehmed	1109	P.	
Kıblelizade Ali	1112	B.Z.	son of Kıbleli Mustafa and nephew of Amcazade Hüseyen
Boşnak Yusuf	1113	P.	
Çalık Ahmed	1114	P.	
Celeb Abaza Ahmed	1115	V.H.	Sohrablı Ahmed
Kalfa Mehmed	1115	P.	

Çavuş Başı

Kadıköylü Mehmed	inc.	P.	?
Boşnak Ahmed	1095	P.	

Çalid Ali	1096	V.H.	as g.v. 1103 above
Haci Ali	1096	V.H. ?	
Hasseki Mustafa	1097	P.	
Yeğen Mehmed	1098	V.H.	Abaza Siyavuş
Fetvacı Hüseyin	1099	M.	
Zülfikar	1099	C.	
Hacioğlu Mehmed	1099	V.H. ?	
Salt Ahmed (Bazirgan)	1099	P.	
Ermeni Mehmed	1099	P. ?	
Şehrî Mehmed	1101	P.	
Şatırlı Ibrahim	1101	V.H.	Fazıl Mustafa
Ali Ağa	1101	?	
Çaturzade Ali	1102	V.H.	Fazıl Mustafa
Şehrî Mehmed	1102	P.	
Mustafa	1102	M. ?	
Eyüp Ağa	1104	V.H.	Fereng Bey
Hacı Mustafa	1105	V.H.	brother of Elmas Mehmed
Arnavut Abdi	1106	P.	
Divrikli Ibrahim	1108	V.H. ?	
Haci Mustafa	1110	V.H.	as 1105 above
Yusuf	1113	V.H.	Amcazade Hüseyin
Telhisçi Mehmed	1113	V.H.	Amcazade Hüseyin
Hazinedar Osman	1114	?	
Çirağı Ali	1115	P.	

Kapıcılar kâhyaları

Gazazzade Ahmed	inc.	P.	
Şatır Boşnak Recep	1095	V.H.	Sarı Süleyman
Hazinedar Osman	1095	V.H.	Kara Ibrahim
Şamlı Abdizade Mehmed	1097	V.H.	Sarı Süleyman
Kaysarıyalı Ibrahim	1099	M.	
Çerkes Mehmed	1099	P.	
Baltacı Hasan	1099	P.	
Çerkes Yusuf	1103	P.	
Arnavut Abdi	1104	P.	
Baltacı Hasan	1105	P.	
Eyüplü Hassan	1106	P.	
Kıblelizade Ali	1109	B.Z.	nephew of Amcazade Hüseyin
Veli	1112	P.	
Karakaşzade Ismail	1115	B.Z.	

Silihdar Ağa

Küçük Hasan	inc.	P.	
Sefer	1095	V.H.	Midillili Mustafa
Kürd Şahin	1097	V.H.	Kara İbrahim
Dursun Mehmed	1097	V.H.	Kasım
Süleyman	1099	?	
Germiyanoğlu Mehmed	1099	M.	

Tekkeli Ahmed	1099	M.	
Kalın Türk Ali	1101	V.H.	Fazıl Mustafa
Deli Ibrahim	1101	M.	
Kürd Ahmed	1103	V.H.	Arabacı Ali
Sarı Osman	1104	V.H.	Soyulcu Ali
Gümüş Mehmed	1104	M.	
Sarı Osman	1105	V.H.	as 1104 above
Kürd Ahmed	1106	V.H.	as 1103 above
Osman Ağa	1107	V.H.	Kara İbrahim and Amcazade Hüseyin; son of Zülfikar
Ali Ağa	1110	V.H.	Amcazade Hüseyin
Kadızade Abdullah	1112	P.	
Süleyman	1114	B.Z.	son of Kara İbrahim
Çatırzade Ahmed	1115	V.H.	Fazıl Mustafa

Defterdar başı

Mağnisalı Mahmud	inc.	C.	
Divrikli Mehmed	1095	V.H.	Köprülü Mehmed
Kıncı Ali	1096	C.	
Seyyid Mustafa	1098	C.	
Doğancı Hüseyin	1098	P. ?	
Ramazan	1099	C. ?	
Fındık Mehmed	1099	P. ?	
Sürmeli Ali	1100	V.H.	as g.v. 1105 above
Kel Yusuf	1101	C.	
Girli Ismail	1101	C.	
Sürmeli Ali	1102	V.H.	as g.v. 1105 above
Canib Ahmed	1103	C.	
Kalın Ali	1104	V.H.	Fazıl Mustafa
Girli Ismail	1104	C.	
Köse Halil	1105	C.	
Canib Ahmed	1106	C.	
Ebübekir	1107	C.	in Amcazade Hüseyin's circle
Köse Halil	1107	C.	
Boşnak Sari Mustafa	1110	P.	
Canib Ahmed	1112	C.	
Muhsinzade Mehmed	1114	C.	
Boşnak Sarı Mustafa	1114	P.	
Sarı Mehmed	1114	C.	in circle of Kılıç Ali

Reisülküttab

Laz Mustafa (Telhisçi)	inc.	V.H.	Kara Mustafa
Fereng Mustafa	1095	P.	eventually served as *kāhya* to Melek Ahmed
Yeğen Mehmed	1097	V.H.	Kara İbrahim
Nazmi	1098	C.	
Fereng Mustafa	1099	P.	
Sami Ahmed	1100	C.	

Kara Bekir Efendi	1101	C.	
Rami Mehmed	1106	C.	in Musahib Mustafa's household
Küçük Mehmed	1108	C.	
Rami Mehmed	1109	C.	
Abdi (Şeyhîzade)	1114	C.	served in households of Kara Mustafa, Amcazade Hüseyin and Daltaban Mustafa
Abdul-Kerim	1114	C.	

GOVERNORS OF *EYALETLER*/PROVINCES

Adana

Divrikli Mehmed	inc.	V.H.	Köprülü Mehmed
Çerkes Ahmed	1095	V.H.	? brother-in-law of Kara Mustafa
Arap Haramuş Mehmed	1101	?	
Gürcü Mehmed	1101	P.	Damad of Murad IV
Büyük Cafer	1103	V.H.	Kara İbrahim
Çerkes Ibrahim	1104	P.	? Damad. Fatmah Sultan sister of Mustafa II
Kalaylıkoz Ahmed	1107	P.	
Amcazade Hüseyin	1107	B.Z.	see g.v. 1109 above
Daltaban Mustafa	1108	V.H.	see g.v. 1114 above
Fazlı	1108	C.	
Gürcü Süleyman	1109	P.	
Divrikli Mustafa	1113	M.	
Seyyid Ahmed	1114	B.Z.	
Boşnak Sarı Mustafa	1115	P.	

Erzurum

Kız Hüseyin	inc.	P.	
Gümrükçü Abdin	1096	?	
Kalaylıkoz Ahmed	1098	P.	
Türk Ali	1099	P.	
Şahin Mustafa	1099	P.	
Dursun Mehmed	1099	V.H.	Kasım
Çalık Ali	1101	V.H.	as g.v. 1103 above
Kötü Eğri Omer	1101	M.	
Binamaz Halil	1102	?	
Beyzade Ali	1103	P.	brother of Ferari Kara Mustafa and married to daughter of Fazıl Mustafa
Gürcü Mehmed	1105	P.	
Midillili Mustafa	1106	V.H.	Fazıl Ahmed
Ahıskalı Abdul-Baki	1107	V.H.	Tekfürdağlı Mustafa
Dursun Mehmed	1110	V.H.	see 1099 above
Dirameli Ibrahim	1110	M.	

Numan	1112	B.Z.	Köprülü
Yeğen Mehmed	1114	V.H.	Kara İbrahim
Köse Halil	1114	C.	

Eğer

Boşnak Osman (Sarhoş)	inc.	V.H.	?
Boşnak Osman	1096	P.	

Anadolu

Hazinedar Hasan	inc.	V.H.	?
Gürcü Mehmed	1098	P.	also known as Mağrulzade
Hazinedar Hasan	1099	V.H.	id.
Erzurumlu Ömer	1099	V.H.	Kara Mustafa
Ahmed	1101	V.H.	Kara Mehmed
Malatyalı Bekir	1101	M.	
Kemankeş Ahmed	1102	?	
Çelebî Ismail	1103	M.	also known as Voyvoda
Hüseyin	1103	P.	?
Mısırlızade Ibrahim	1104	M.	
Daltaban Mustafa	1107	V.H.	as g.v. 1114 above
Mısırlızade Ibrahim	1108	M.	
Kalın Ali (Türk)	1109	V.H.	Fazıl Mustafa
Seyyid Ömer	1109	M.	
Mısırlızade Mehmed	1110	B.Z.	Damad. Fatma Sultan d. of Mehmed IV
Eyüp	1111	?	
Arnavut Abdi	1112	P.	
Daltaban Mustafa	1114	V.H.	as g.v. 1114 above
Numan	1114	B.Z.	Köprülü

Bosnia

Osmanpaşoğlu Ahmed	inc.	B.Z.	
Boşnak Osman	1095	P.	
Fındık Mustafa	1095	V.H.	Hüseyin
Abaza Siyavuş	1096	V.H.	as g.v. 1098 above
Boşnak Ahmed (Serhoş)	1097	V.H.	?
Atlübeyzade Mehmed	1097	B.Z.	
Macı Ali	1099	M.	
Yeğen Osman	1099	M.	
Topal Hüseyin	1099	M.	
Büyük Cafer	1102	V.H.	Kara Ibrahim
Mehmed	1103	V.H.	Topal Hüseyin
Dizdarzade Ahmed	1109	V.H.	Mehmed as 1103 above
Daltaban Mustafa	1109	V.H.	as g.v. 1114 above
Köse Halil	1110	C.	
Sefer	1114	M.	also known as Seyfullah
Doğramacı Mehmed	1115	M.	

Budin

Şeytan İbrahim (Melek)	1095	C.	Damad. Rukiye Sultan, Murad IV's daughter
Arnavut Abdi	1096	M.	relation of Hocazade Hasan
Osmanpaşaoğlu Ahmed	1096	B.Z.	same as 1096 above

Basra

Şair Abdi	inc.	P.	
Gümrükçü Hüseyin	1097	P.	
?	1098	?	
Sohrablı Ahmed	1099	V.H.	Silihdar Hüseyin. Entered Palace service; damad of Amcazade Hüseyin
Şair Abdi	1099	P.	
Doğancı Hüseyin	1099	?	
Eğriçelioğlu Halil	1100	?	also known as Findıklı
Osmanpaşaoğlu Ahmed	1101	B.Z.	
Kâhya Hasan	?	V.H.	?
Salt Ahmed	1103	P.	
Bezirgân Halil	1103	V.H.	brother of Salt Ahmed
Beyzade Ali	1105	P.	brother of Ferari Kara Mustafa, damad of Köprülü/Fazıl Mustafa
Bezirgân Halil	1105	V.H.	as 1103 above
Kâhya Hasan	1107	V.H.	?
?			
Kâhya Hasan	1107	V.H.	?
Beyzade Ali	1112	P.	as 1105 above
Yeğen Ali	?	?	?
Aşcıoğlu Ali	1115	V.H.	Mısırlızade İbrahim

Bağdad

Dirmeli İbrahim	inc.	M.	
Öküz Ömer	1095	P.	
Boşnak Serhoş Ahmed	1098	V.H.	?
Öküz Ömer	1099	P.	
Baltacı Hasan	1101	P.	
Salt Ahmed	1102	P.	
Koca Omer	?	?	
Ahmed	1103	V.H.	Koca Ömer
Ahıskalı Ahmed	1104	V.H.	Öküz Ali
Beyzade Ali	1105	P.	brother of Ferari Kara Mustafa, damad of Fazıl Mustafa
Kalaylıkoz Ahmed	1105	P.	
Beyzade Ali	1106	P.	same as 1105 above
Çelebî Ismail	1109	M.	
Dal Taban Mustafa	1111	V.H.	as g.v. 1114 above
Topal Yusuf	1114	?	Damad. Fatmah Sultan daughter of Mehmed IV

Habeş

Mehmed	?	?	
Abaza Mustafa	1106	M.	
Mısırlı Mehmed	1106	B.Z.	
Gümrükçü Siyavuş	1107	C.	?
Süleyman	?	?	

Halep

Çerkes Ahmed	inc.	V.H.	? brother-in-law of Kara Mustafa
Tekfurdağlı Bekri	1095	M.	
Şeytan Ibrahim	1096	C.	Damad. Rukiye Sultan daughter of Murad IV
Arnavut Abdi	1096	M.	
Boşnak Ahmed	1097	V.H.	? known as *kâhya*
Abaza Siyavuş	1097	V.H.	as g.v. 1098 above
Hazinedar Hasan	1098	V.H.	?
Yeğen Osman	1099	M.	
Hazinedar Hasan	1099	V.H.	?
Yeğen Osman	1099	M.	
Arap Recep	1100	M.	?
Arnavut Halil	1100	M.	?
Topal Hüseyin	1103	M.	
Büyük Cafer	1104	V.H.	Kara İbrahim
Dursun Mehmed	1106	V.H.	Kasım
Büyük Cafer	1107	V.H.	as 1104 above
Çerkes Osman	1108	P.	Damad. Umetullah, daughter of Mehmed IV
Kanicalı Osman	1108	P.	
Moralı Hasan	1109	P.	Damad. Hatice Sultan daughter of Mehmed IV
Eyüplü Hasan	1110	P.	
Beyzade Ali	1111	P.	brother-in-law of Ferari Kara Mustafa
Çerkes Mehmed	1112	P.	
Çetrefiloğlu Yusuf	1114	B.Z.	
Çerkes Mehmed	1115	P.	

Diyarbekir

Şeytan Ibrahim (Melek)	inc.	C.	Damad. Rukye Sultan daughter of Murad IV
Abaza Siyavuş	1095	V.H.	as g.v. 1098 above
Kız Hüseyin	1096	P.	
Büyük Cafer	1097	V.H.	Kara İbrahim
Osmanpaşaoğlu Ahmed	1099	B.Z.	
Öküz Ömer	1099	P.	
Osmanpaşaoğlu Ahmed	1099	B.Z.	
Kemankeş Ahmed	1101	?	
?	1102	?	

Çalık Ali	1102	V.H.	as g.v. 1105 above
Şahin Mehmed	1103	P.	
Kalaylıkoz Ahmed	1105	P.	
Bazirgân Halil	1105	V.H.	brother of Salt Ahmed
Beyzade Ali	1105	P.	brother of Ferari Kara Mustafa. Damad of Fazıl Mustafa
Çerkes Osman	1105	P.	Damad. Umetullah Sultan daughter of Mehmed IV
Divrikli Ismail	1105	V.H.	? brother of Şeytan İbrahim
Şeyhoğlu Ahmed	1106	P.	?
Sohrablı Ahmed	1106	V.H.	Silihdar Hüseyin. Entered Palace service; damad of Amcazade Hüseyin
Şahin Mehmed	1106	P.	
Topal Hüseyin	1107	M.	
Daltaban Mustafa	1108	V.H.	as g.v. 1114 above
Kavukçu Ibrahim	1108	M.	
Dursun Mehmed	1109	V.H.	Kasım
Çetrefiloğlu Yusuf	1110	B.Z.	
Mısırlızade Mehmed	1111	B.Z.	Damad. Fatmah Sultan daughter of Mehmed IV
Çetrefiloğlu Yusuf	1112	B.Z.	
Topal Yusuf	1112	?	Damad. Fatmah Sultan daughter of Mehmed IV
Kürd Ibrahim	1114	M.	
Eyüplü Hasan	1114	P.	

Rakka

Kâhya Ali	inc.	V.H.	?
Boşnak Ahmed	1096	M.	
?	?	?	
Gürcü Süleyman	1099	P.	
Erğentli Süleyman	1099	P.	
Aşçı Mustafa	1105	P.	
?	?	?	
Kadızade Hüseyin	1107	?	
Kürd Ahmed	1107	V.H.	Kadı Ali
Topal Yusuf	1108	?	Damad. Fatmah Sultan daughter of Mehmed IV
Daltaban Mustafa	1110	V.H.	as g.v. 1114 above
Beyzade Ali	1111	P.	brother of Ferari Kara Mustafa; damad of Fazıl Mustafa
Eyüplü Hasan	1111	P.	
Çerkes Osman	1114	P.	

Rumeli

Hocazade Hasan	inc.	M.	
Kadıköylü Mehmed	1095	P.	?
Çelebi Ismail	1095	M.	

Gümrükçü Hüseyin	1096	P.	
Zinel	1097	B.Z.	
Osmanpaşazade Ahmed	1098	B.Z.	
Yeğen Osman	1099	M.	
Öküzöldüren Ahmed	1099	V.H.	Musaheb Mustafa
Kemankeş Ahmed	1099	?	
Deli Veli	1099	V.H.	maternal uncle of Yeğen Osman
Zurnapa Mustafa	1100	M.	
Arnavut Mustafa	1101	M.	
Arnavut Cafer	1102	B.Z.	
Arnavut Mahmud	1103	B.Z.	
Arnavut Süleyman	1107	B.Z.	
Arnavut Cafer	1108	B.Z.	
Arnavut Abdi	1109	P.	
Kandilci Hüseyin	1112	P.	damad of Karayılanoğlu İsmail
Hazinedar Ibrahim	1114	V.H.	Kara İbrahim and Sarı Süleyman

Silistre

Fazıl Mustafa	inc.	B.Z.	Köprülü
Hüseyin	1095	P.	
Arap Recep	1098	M.	
Kara Mustafa	1099	V.H.	Yeğen Osman
Arap Recep	1100	M.	
Boşnak Hüseyin	1100	C.	
Mısırlı Mehmed	1101	B.Z.	
Çerkes Ahmed	1101	V.H.	? brother-in-law of Kara Mustafa
Topal Hüseyin	1102	M.	
?			
?			
Çetrefilzade Yusuf	1107	B.Z.	
Çerkes Ibrahim	1107	P.	Damad. Fatmah Sultan daughter of Mehmed IV
Ibşir Hassan	1108	P.	
Kandılcı Hüseyin	1108	P.	
Hazinedar Ibrahim	1109	V.H.	Kara İbrahim and Sarı Süleyman
?			
?			

Sivas

Kadızade Hüseyin	inc.	B.Z.	
Boşnak Mustafa	1096	P.	
Büyük Cafer	1096	V.H.	Kara İbrahim
Osmanpaşazade Ahmed	1097	B.Z.	
Şair Abdi	1097	P.	
?			
Gedik Mehmed	1099	P.	
Mirzazade Mehmed	1099	?	
Şeyhoğlu Ahmed	1100	P.	
Gürcü Süleyman	1101	P.	

Öküz Ömer	1102	P.	
Erzurumlu Omer	1102	V.H.	Kara Mustafa
Helvacı Yusuf	1103	P.	
Genç Mehmed	1103	P.	
Şeyhoğlu Ahmed	1104	P.	
Kalaylıkoz Ahmed	1104	P.	
Bostancı Mahmud	1104	V.H.	Bozoklu Mustafa
?			
?			
Mehmed	?		
Kandilci Hüseyin	1106	P.	
Dursun Mehmed	1107	V.H.	Kasım
Çetrefilzade Yusuf	1108	B.Z.	
İsmail (Küçük)	1109	B.Z.	
Aşçı Mustafa	1110	P.	
Erğentli Süleyman	1113	P.	
Mehmed	1114	?	

Şam

Boşnak Osman	inc.	P.	
Dirameli Ibrahim	1095	M.	
Şahin Mehmed	1096	P.	
Şahin Mustafa	1096	P.	
Gürcü Ibrahim	1097	V.H.	Kara İbrahim
Arap Saleh	1097	B.Z.	
Hamza	1099	C.	
Salt Ahmed	1099	P.	
Bozoklu Mustafa	1101	P.	
Abaza Murtaza	1102	?	
Bozoklu Mustafa	1102	P.	
Gürcü Mehmed	1103	P.	
Mıdıllılı Mustafa	1104	V.H.	Fazıl Ahmed
Çelebî Ismail	1104	M.	
Şahin Mehmed	1105	P.	
Çelebî Ismail	1105	M.	
Kanicalı Osman	1106	P.	
Bozoklu Mustafa	1108	P.	
Şamlu Ahmed	1109	B.Z.	
Mısırlı Mehmed	1110	B.Z.	Damad. Fatma Sultan d. of Mehmed IV
Çerkes Hasan	1110	P.	
Arslan Mehmed	1113	B.Z.	
Çerkes Osman	1114	P.	
Kürd Mehmed	1114	M.	
Trabluslu Osman	1115	M.	

Şehr-i Zor

?	inc.		

Amcazade Hüseyin	1095	B.Z.	as g.v. 1109 above
?			
Kadioğlu Hüseyin	1097	B.Z.	
Çerkes Ahmed	1098	V.H. ?	brother-in-law of Kara Mustafa
Dülvar	1101	M.	
Arnavut Hüseyin	1102	P.	
Kâhya Hasan	1103	V.H.A.	
Siyavuş	1104	?	
Hayre Ali	1106	M.	
Boşnak Hasan	1108	V.H.	Topal Hüseyin
Erğentli Süleyman	1109	P.	
Topal Yusuf	1110	?	Damad. Fatma Sultan d. of Mehmed IV
Çetrefilzade Yusuf	1112	B.Z.	
Şehrizorlu Hasan	1113	V.H.	Kara İbrahim and Amcazade Hüseyin
Divrikli Ibrahim	1114	V.H.	
Haşim Mehmed	1114	P.	
Erğentli Süleyman	1114	P.	
Eyüplü Hasan	1115	P.	

Trablus Şam

Defterdar Hasan	inc.	C.	relation of Kara Mustafa
Niğdeli Ali	1095	?	
Arnavut Hüseyin	1098	P.	id.
Gümrükçü Abidin	1099	?	also known as Şeyhoğlu
Arnavut Hüseyin	1099	P.	
Hamza	1099	P.	
Kıncı Ali	1101	C.	
Bozoklu Mustafa	1102	P.	
Beyzade Ali	1103	P.	brother of Ferari Kara Mustafa, damad of Köprülü Mustafa
Sürmeli Ali	1103	V.H.	as g.v. above
Arslan Mehmed	1105	B.Z.	also known as Matrakçızade
Boşnak Mustafa	1114	P.	

Trabzon

Kinci Ali	1099	C.	
Sümnücü Mustafa	1099	?	also known as Pehlivan
Kalaylıkoz Ahmed	1102	P.	
Anğurlu Ali	1104	M.	
Hasan	1104	?	
Ömer	1104	M.	
Haşim Mehmed	1105	P.	
Demurli Ali	?	P.	
Ömer	?	P.	
Bağdatlı Mehmed	1107	B.Z.	also known as Kara
Mısırlı Mehmed	1110	B.Z.	Damad. Fatma Sultan d. of Mehmed IV

Ahıskalı Abdul-Baki	1110	V.H.	Tekfurdağlı Mustafa
Seyyid Ömer	1111	M.	

Kars

Boşnak Mustafa	?	?	also known as Celeb
Şehsüvaroğlu Mehmed	1096	B.Z.	

Temeşvar

Çerkesli Hasan	inc.	C.	also known as Celeb, Defterdar
Seyyidi Ahmedpaşaoğlu Mehmed	1095	B.Z.	
Osman Ağa	1095	V.H.	Ahmedpaşaoğlu Mehmed
?			
Gürcü Ibrahim (Gur)	1097	V.H.	Kara İbrahim
Büuük Cafer	1099	V.H.	Kara İbrahim
Kandilci Hüseyin	1102	P.	
Fındık Mustafa	1103	V.H.	Gür Hüseyin
Topal Hüseyin	1104	M.	?
Kandilcı Hüseyin	1104	P.	Damad of Karayılanoğlu İsmail
Deli Ömer	1108	M	
Büyük Cafer	1108	V.H.	Kara İbrahim
Arnavut Süleyman	1109	B.Z.	
Çetrefilzade Yusuf	1109	B.Z.	
Ahmed	1110	?	
Hazinedar Ibrahim	1111	V.H.	Kara İbrahim and Sarı Süleyman
Maktulzade Ali	1114	B.Z.	son of Kara Mustafa. Damad: Safiye Sultan daughter of Mustafa II
Yusuf	1114	?	

Kars

?			
?			
Boşnak Mustafa	?	?	
Şehsüvaroğlu Mehmed	1096	B.Z.	
?			
?			
Ayazmalı Ahmed	1099	P.	
?			
?			
?			
Niğde Ali	1104	?	
Boşnak Hüseyin	1104	C.	
Hasan	1104	?	
Cerrah Mustafa	1105	P.	
Devrikli Ismail	1106	V.H. ?	brother of Şeytan İbrahim
Bağdatlı Mehmed	1107	B.Z.	
Salih	1109	?	
Mustafa	?	?	

Murtaza	1114	?	
Arslan	?	?	

Kıbrıs

?			
?			
Baba Hasan	1097	M.	
Boşnak Ahmed	?	M.	also known as Çıfutoğlu
Çolak Ahmed			
Halebli Ahmed	1101	?	
Kinci Ali	1102	C. ?	
Sürmeli Ali (Dimotkalı)	1103	V.H.	as g.v. 1105 above
Sarıkçı Mustafa	1103	?	
Distarı Mehmed	1104	?	
Kalaylıkoz Ahmed	1104	P.	
Kandilci Hüseyin	1105	P.	damad of Karayılanoğlu İsmail
Boşnak Hüseyin	1106	C.	also known as Ferari
Bahrî Mehmed	1108	P.	
Midillili Mustafa	1109	V.H.	Fazil Ahmed. Also known as Esir
Midillili Ismail	1110	V.H.	Amcazade Hüseyin
Seyyid Ahmed (Emir)	1111	B.Z.	?
Devrikli Ibrahim	1114	V.H.	? Brother of Şeytan İbrahim

Karaman

Abdül-Mümen	inc.	?	
Rüstem	1095	V.H.	Kara Mehmed
?			
?			
Nigdeli Ali	1098	?	
Kara Mustafa	1099	V.H.	Yeğen Osman
Buzoğlan	1099	V.H.	?
Kemankeş Ahmed	1100	?	
Dursun Mehmed	1101	V.H.	Kasım
Çelebî Ismail	1102	M.	
Eğriçeli Halil	1103	?	known as Voyvoda
Şeyhzade Ahmed	1104	P.	?
Gürcü Mehmed	1104	P.	also known as Mağrulzade
Fındık Mustafa	1105	V.H.	Gür Hüseyin
Hısım Mehmed	1106	P.	
Genç Mehmed	1107	P.	
Amcazade Hüseyin	1107	B.Z.	as g.v. 1109 above
Çerkes Ibrahim	1108	P.	Damad. Fatmah Sultan d. of Mehmed IV
Mısırlı Mehmed	1108	B.Z.	
Eyüplü Hasan	1109	P.	
Dirameli Ibrahim	1110	M.	also known as Çelebî
Kanıcalı Osman	1110	P.	
İzmitli Mustafa	1111	V.H.	?

Eyüp	1112	?	
Çavuş Halepli Ali	1113	?	
Kırşehirli Arap Ömer	1114	?	

Kameniçe

Arnavut Abdi	inc.	M.	
Bozoklu Mustafa	1095	P.	
Tokatlı Mahmud	1095	V.H.	Kara Mustafa
Bozoklu Mustafa	1095	P.	
Boşnak Hüseyin	1097	C.	
Yeğen Ahmed	1100	V.H.	?
Kahraman	1100	V.H.	relation of Crimean Han

Kandiye

Soyulcu Ali	inc.	P.	
Burunsuz Ahmed	1095	M.	
Seyyid Mustafa	1096	C.	
Zülfikar	1097	M.	
Fazıl Mustafa	1099	B.Z.	Köprülü
Çalık Ali	1100	V.H.	as q.v. 1103 above
Şeyhoğlu Ahmed	1101	P. ?	
?			
?			
Fındık Mehmed	1103	P. ?	
Şahin Ismail	1105	M.	also known as Ispanakçı/Çelebî
Çalık Ali	1107	V.H.	as 1100 above
Helvacı Yusuf	1112	P.	
Maktulzade Ali	1113	B.Z.	son of Kara Mustafa. Damad Safiye Sultan d. of Mustafa II
Köse Halil	1114	C.	
Maktulzade Ali	1114	B.Z.	as 1113 above
Şahin Ismail	1114	P.	as 1105 above
Kalaylıkoz Ahmed	1114	P.	

Kanica

Konakçı Hasan	inc.	V.H.	Musahib Mustafa
Bekrî Mustafa	1095	M.	
Fındık Mustafa	1098	V.H.	Gür Hüseyin

Keffe

?			
?			
?			
Koca Murad	1100	M.	
Mehmed	1105	?	
Moralı	1106	P.	Damad. Hatice Sultan d. of Mehmed IV

Tatar Murtaza	1106	B.Z.	
Tumanlı İsmail	1111	P.	
Abdürrahman	1114	M.	

Maraş

Ömer (Deli)	inc.	C. ?	
Şeyhoğlu Ahmed	1095	P. ?	
?			
?			
Boşnak Ahmed	1098	M.	also known as Çıfutoğlu
Moralı Ali (Türk)	1099	P.	
Hüseyin	1099	V.H.	Musahib Mustafa
?			
Erğentli Süleyman	1101	P.	
Yumak Mehmed	1102	V.H.	Musahib Mustafa
Arnavut Ali	1103	P.	
Malatyalı Bekir	1103	M.	
?			
Bozoklu Hasan (Tokmak)	1105	B.Z.	? from grand vizier Bozoklu Mustafa's home town
Şamlı Ahmed	1105	B.Z.	Arab Salihpaşaoğlu
Çokalı Ahmed	1107	P.	?
Yünüs	1108	B.Z.	?
Dimur Halil	1109	B.Z.	?
Arapgir Ahmed	1112	M.	
Kanicalı Osman	1114	P.	

Mısır

Hamzeh	inc.	P.	
Baltacı Hasan	1098	P.	
Moralı Hasan	1099	P.	Damad. Hatice Sultan d. of Mehmed IV
Boşnak Ahmed (Serhoş)	1100	V.H.	?
Moralı Ali	1102	P.	
Kalın Ali (Türk)	1105	V.H.	Fazıl Mustafa
Hazinedar Ali	1106	?	
Çelebî Ismail	1106	M.	
Boşnak Hüseyin	1109	C.	known as Ferari
Kara Mehmed	1110	V.H.	Amcazade Hüseyin

Mora

Şahin Mustafa	1095	P.	
Ispanakçı Ismail	1095	P.	also known as Karayılanoğlu
Halil	1096	?	
Şahin Mustafa	1096	P.	
Musahib Mustafa	1096	P.	
Mustafa	1097	M.	also known as Kara Hasanağaoğlu

Ispanakçı Ismail	1097	P.	
Devrikli Mehmed	1098	V.H.	Köprülü Mehmed
Arnavut Halil	1099	M.	
Dirameli Ibrahim	1106	M.	
Arnavut Halil	1107	M.	
Mısırlızade Ibrahim	1107	M.	
Çakırcı Hasan	1108	P.	also known as Çavuşoğlu
Eyüp	1109	V.H.	Koca Halil (Arnavut)

Mosul

Deli			
Deli Emir Mehmed	1094	?	
?			
?			
?			
Sohrablı Ahmed	1099	V.H.	Silihdar Hüseyin. Entered Palace service. Brother-in-law of Amcazade Hüseyin
Ömer	?	?	
Niğdeli Ali	1101	?	
Midillili Mustafa	1102	V.H.	Fazıl Ahmed
Şeyhzade Ahmed	1104	P.	
Erğentli Süleyman	1106	P.	
Kâhya Hasan	1108	V.H.	?
Beyzade Ali	1109	P.	brother of Ferari Kara Mustafa, damad Köprülü Mustafa
Çetrefilzade Yusuf	1111	B.Z.	
Kürd Ibrahim	1112	M.	
Aşçı Mustafa	1114	P.	
Topal Yusuf	1115	P.	Damad. Fatmah Sultan d. of Mehmed IV

Varad

Gürcü Mehmed	inc.	P.	also known as Mağrulzade
Kadıköylü Mehmed	1095	P.	
Hayre Ali	1099	M.	
Çavuşoğlu Mehmed	1099	?	
Şahin Mehmed	1102	?	

Van

Öküz Ömer	1095	P.	
Büyük Cafer	1095	V.H.	Kara İbrahim
Büyük Mustafa	1096	P.	
Moralı Ali	1096	P.	
Kalaylıkoz Ahmed	1098	P.	
Bahrî Mehmed	1099	P.	
Osmanpaşaoğlu Ahmed	1099	B.Z.	

Öküz Ömer	1099	P.	
Bosnevî Hasan	1099	P.	
Erzurumlu Omer	1101	V.H.	Kara Mustafa
Dursun Mehmed	1102	V.H.	Kasım
Öküz Ömer	?	P.	
Divrikli Ismail	1103	V.H. ?	brother of Şeytan Ibrahim
Midillili Mustafa	1104	V.H.	Fazıl Ahmed
Şamlı Mehmed (Abdioğlu)	1105	V.H.	Sarı Süleyman
Beyzade Ali	1105	P.	brother of Ferari Kara Mustafa; damad of Köprülü/Fazıl Mustafa
Gürcü Mehmed	1106	P.	also known as Mağrulzade
Çetrefilzade Yusuf	1107	B.Z.	
Dursun Mehmed	1108	V.H.	as 1102 above
Kanicalı Osman	1109	P.	
Kalın Ali	1109	V.H.	Fazıl Mustafa
Kanicalı Osman	1111	P.	
Çelebî Ismail (Voyvoda)	1112	M.	
Dirameli Ibrahim	1112	M.	
Aşçı Mustafa	1113	P.	
Arnavut Abdi	1114	P.	
Çerkes Osman	1115	P.	Damad. Umetüllah Sultan d. of Ahmed IV

Yanova

Seyyidîzade Mehmed	inc.	B.Z.	
Osman	1095	V.H.	Seyyidîzade Mehmed
Osmanpaşaoğlu Ahmed	1095	B.Z.	
Boşnak Ahmed	1096	V.H.	? also known as Kâhya
Şahin Mehmed	1096	P.	
Boşnak Cafer	?	M.	
Göleli Mehmed	1108	M.	?
?			
?			
?			
Hazinedar Ibrahim	1113	V.H.	Kara İbrahim and Sarı Süleyman
Kandilci Hüseyin	1114	P.	damad. Karayılanoğlu İsmail (also known as Ispanakci)
Ispanakçı' Ismail	1114	P.	
Hazinedar Ibrahim	1114	V.H.	as 1114 above
Helvacı Yusuf	1114	P.	

APPENDIX II

Georgia Campaign

The uprising which triggered the rebellion of 1703 took place four years from the signing of the treaties of Karlowitz and Istanbul and was led by one of the military contingents ordered to suppress a rebellion in Western Georgia[1].

South of the Caucasus, Ottoman suzerainty had been recognized by three principalities: Mingrelia (Dadian for the Ottomans), Guria (Guriel), and Imeretia (Açık Baş). By the early part of the eighteenth century the Ottoman sultans were in the habit of selecting and appointing the princes for these principalities. In return, these rulers were expected to pay an annual tribute[2]. In accordance with Ottoman Imperial practice, the principalities were regarded as tributary states, and therefore enjoyed internal self-rule, exemption from Ottoman-Muslim settlement on their lands and from further taxation. To secure and protect Ottoman interests in Western Georgia, the Muslim Georgian dynastic family of the Jakilis, based in Çıldır (Akhaltsikche), was created with Ottoman blessing in 1625, within striking distance from the capitals of the three principalities[3].

The immediate cause for the Ottoman intrusion in Western Georgia was occasioned by a local power struggle which threatened Ottoman suzerainty[4]. Prince Mamia, of Guria and Mingrelia, had (in an attempt at incorporating Imeretia within his own domain) assassinated in succession two princes of the said principality who had been directly appointed by the sultan (a certain Simon/Svimon and his brother George/Giorgi)[5]. The picture is further

[1] Late in 1702, Raşid reports that problems in Georgia were already brewing. The reader is left with the impression that the envoys of Guriel prince had been sent to prison following receipt of news that Guriel commanders had been engaged in activities which were contrary to the "ahd u peyman" (treaty with the Ottoman state). Raşid, *Tarih*, II, 561.

[2] Defterdar contends that the envoys from Guriel were imprisoned late in 1702. Since payments of the *cizye* (tribute) had not been forthcoming for some time from the prince of that principality, his envoys were incarcerated. Defterdar Mehmed Efendi adds that the same prince was accused of indulging in "untoward" activities. *Zübdet*, 405a.

[3] This *beylerbeyi* family, known alternatively as Atabeg-Jakili House, was established by Sap'ar paşa (Beka III), 1625-35, who was the first of his line to convert to Islam. He was installed as pasha with two horse-tails. A Gugushvili, "Kings of Georgia", *Georgica*, I, 142-44.

[4] M.-F. Brosset, *Histoire de la Georgie*, II, i. & ii., 300-301.

[5] Ottoman official correspondence describes the struggle in Georgia in the following manner: Simon, former prince of Imeretia (Açık Baş), had earlier departed Imeretia. When he tried to return, he was assassinated somewhere between Imeretia and Guriel. His assassination had been perpetrated by Mamia, prince of Guriel and Mingrelia (Dadian/Odiş).

The Ottoman state had appointed Giorgi (a brother of Simon) in his stead as prince. İshak (the beylerbey of Çıldır) was ordered to conduct the newly appointed prince to his principality. When they reached the town-fort of Bağdad (Bagrad/Bağdadcık) in Imeretia, Mamia sent safe-conduct for the said prince and Abaschidze provided the escort. However, Giorgi disappeared and was assassinated in transit. Mühimme Defteri 114, 25b-26a.

complicated by another claimant to the princely throne of Imeretia, a certain Abaschidze. This latter contender was himself a *tavat* (local nobleman) who had cooperated with others of his class in the assassination of the last prince of Imeretia.

Although within the context of Ottoman West Georgian relations of the previous half century these unilateral acts do not seem to have been either unusual or uncommon, the disproportionately massive military response which followed portends a probable change in Ottoman Imperial policy in Georgia. The ostensible aims of the Ottoman court consisted simply of the elimination of these contentious princes and the elevation of a loyal prince to the vacant seat at Mingrelia. An unusually large expeditionary force was mounted between March and July, 1703, requiring the participation of all the provincial troops of eastern and north-eastern Anatolia, along with substantial contingents of the standing armies based in the provinces and at the capital[6]. The commander in chief of this expeditionary force, Halil Pasha, was instructed to enter Georgia from the West, secure Guria, capture Mamia and proceed from there into Imeretia. There, he was expected to drive out Abaschidze and secure the principality for an Ottoman-backed prince. Explicit instructions were given to the commander of Çıldır and other eyalets in the south, to aid Halil by securing the mountain passes before marching north into West Georgia[7].

The most unusual articles in Halil Pasha's instructions are those relating to the Imeretian forts of Kutais and Bağdadcık[8]. Implied in these articles were the termination of self-rule in Guria and the substantial curtailment of autonomy in Imeretia[9]. Halil is ordered to conquer (*tamamile zabt*) Guria, eject Abaschidze from Imeretia, and secure and garrison forts Kutais and Bağdadcık with contingents of the standing army. A replacement for Abaschidze in Imeretia was named by the court, but there was no provision made for the Guria court. According to one contemporary chronicler, Guria had already been disignated a *malikane* for the benefit of the *şeyhülislâm* (Feyzullah)[10]. Imeretia's autonomy would be further compromised by the presence of Ottoman garrisons at its capital Kutais, and one of its major provincial towns Bağdadcık[11]. The creation of a *timar* out of the lands in the vicinity of the latter town even before 1703, suggests rather conclusively that even before the expeditionary force was mounted in 1703, there was a substantial revision in Ottoman policy with reference to Imeretian autonomy[12].

[6] For Çıldır, Mühimme Defteri 114, 27a, 29a, 19b, 30b, 49b and 75a-b. For Erzurum, Mühimme Defteri 114, 26a, 75a-b, 102b-103a. For Kars, Mühimme Defteri 114, 30a, 75a-b and Rami Mehmed, "Münşeat", II, 76a-b. For Trabzon, Mühimme Defteri 114, 26a, 27b, 47b and 75a-b. For Janissary *odas* and other regiments of the standing army, Mühimme Defteri 114, 6b, 31b, 32a, 41b, 42a, 42b, 63b, 47a and 47b Rami Mehmed, "Münşeat", II, 68a-b; 79a.

[7] Mühimme Defteri 114, 27a.

[8] Mühimme Defteri 114, 25b-26a.

[9] *Ibid.*

[10] Silihdar, *Nusretname*, II, 132/283b. "... Gürcistanda Guriel memleketi şeyhulislâm efendi kendiye malikane...".

[11] Mühimme Defteri 114, 25b-26a.

[12] Mühimme Defteri, 114, 30b. Halil, commander of the expeditionary force, was informed of the disposition of this *timar*. Originally the land, located in Imeretia villages near Bağdad, had been owned by a Christian monk who with his brother had resorted to "brigandage". Thenceforth they fled. The land was awarded as a *timar* for life (*mülk-timar*) to a certain Ömer. The latter had apparently donated the income forthcoming to him from the *timar* for the rebuilding of fort Bagrad. Halil was instructed further to examine the lands of the said *timar* in order to determine whether it would be suitable for meeting the needs of the fort and its garrison. (The stated income from the timar was only 15,000 *akçes*.)

The outright conquest of Guria and the growing direct control of Imeretia may have come as a response to Ottoman losses in Europe over the previous fifteen years. It followed a pattern of consolidation of Ottoman control over fluid frontier zones which had the tendency of becoming potential areas of power vacuum[13]. This state of the frontier provided temptations for its neighboring power, Russia, in 1700's[14]. Furthermore, extension of direct Ottoman control in Georgia at the expense of the tribute paying princes opened the region for economic settlement and exploitation and kept restless elements of the military establishment pre-occupied on the frontier.

[13] William McNeill, *Europe's Steppe Frontier*, Chicago (1964).

[14] On the Russian involvement in West Georgia's troubles see especially Silihdar, *Nusretname*, I, 344-47/ 261a-b. Here, it is reported that as early as 1698, a Georgian prince was sent to the Muscovite Czar in the hope of aid in the capture of fort Kutatais.

BIBLIOGRAPHY

Archival Sources

Başbakanlık Arşivi (Istanbul), Maliye Defteri: 3159, 6006.
——, Mühimme Defteri: 105, 106, 108, 114.
Public Record Office (London), State Papers 97/21, The Sutton Papers.

Manuscript Sources

Staatsbibliothek (Berlin), Diez A quarto 75, "Anonymous History". (Kitab-i Tevarih-ı Sultan Suleyman. Bin doksan dokuz senesinin bin yüz on senesinden söyler.)

Staatsbibliothek (Berlin), Diez A quarto 5, "Anonymous History". (Kitab-i Edirne Vakasi. On beş senesi olan eşkiyalin hekayetlerin söyler.)

Köprülü Kütüphanesi (İstanbul), Hafiz Ahmed Kitabi no. 212. (Ibrahim Al-Müdderis; Tarih-ı Sulale-i Köprülü.)

Beyazıt Umumi Kütüphanesi (İstanbul), no. 2369, (Silihdar Mehmed Ağa, Nusretname.)

Österreichische Nationalbibliothek (Vienna), H.O. 126 (Şeyhî, Vakayi'ül-fuzalâ.)

Österreichische Nationalbibliothek (Vienna); H.O. 179, (Rami Mehmed, Münşeat, vol. I.); A.F. 159, (Rami Mehmed, Münşeat, vol. II.).

Süleymaniye Kütüphanesi (İstanbul), Esad Efendi 2382, (Defterdar Mehmed Efendi, Zübdetül-vakayi'.)

Printed Sources

ʿAlī, see Tietze below.

Abou-El-Haj, R. A.: *The Reisülküttab and Ottoman Diplomacy at Karlowitz*. Ph.D. Dissertation, Princeton University, 1963.

——, "Ottoman Diplomacy at Karlowitz", *Journal of the American Oriental Society*, vol. 87.4 (1967).

——, "The Formal Closure of the Ottoman Frontier in Europe: 1699-1703", *JAOS*, vol. 89.3 (1969).

——, "Ottoman Methods of Negotiation: the Karlowitz Case", *Der Islam*, 51.1 (1974).

——, "The Narcissism of Mustafa II (1695-1703): A Psychohistorical Study", *Studia Islamica*, XL (1974).

——, "The Ottoman Vezir and Paşa Households, 1683-1703: A Preliminary Report", *JAOS*, 94.4 (1974).

Alderson, A. A.: *The Structure of the Ottoman Dynasty*. Oxford, 1956.

Allen, W. E. D.: *A History of the Georgian People*. London, 1932.

Brosset, M. F.: *Histoire de la Georgie*. 5 vols. St. Petersburg, 1849-58.

Cantemir, Dimitri: *The history of the growth and decay of the Othman Empire*. London, 1756.

Danişmend, I.: *Izahlı Osmanlı tarihi kronolojisi*. 4 vols. Istanbul, 1947-55.
Encyclopaedia of Islam. New Edition, 1954-.
Evliya Çelebi: *Narrative of Travels in Europe, Asia and Africa*. London, 1834 (reprint, 1968).
Flügel, Gustav: *Die Arabischen, Persischen, und Türkischen Handschriften der Kaiserlich-Königlichen Hofbibliothek*. Wien, 1865.
Gibb, E. J. W.: *A History of Ottoman Poetry*. 6 vols. London, 1900-09.
Gibb, H. A. R. and Harold Bowen: *Islamic Society and the West*. I, i and ii, London, 1950 and 1957.
Gould, Roger: "Mid-life Crisis", lecture delivered at Beverly Hills, California, U.S.A., 1973.
Guyushvili, A.: "The Chronological-Geneological Tablets of the Kings of Georgia", *Georgica*, I, 2 and 3 (1936).
Hammer-Purgstall, Joseph von: *Geschichte des Osmanischen Reiches*. 10 vols. Pest, 1827-35.
Hobsbawm, E. J.: "The Social Function of the Past: Some Questions", *Past and Present*, 55, (1972).
Hourani, A.: "The Changing Face of the Fertile Crescent in the XVIIIth Century", *Studia Islamica*, VIII (1957).
İslâm Ansiklopedisi. Istanbul, 1940-.
Jaques, Elliott: "Death and the Midlife Crisis", *International Journal of Psychoanalysis*, 46.4 (1965).
Kahane, H. and R. and A. Tietze: *The Lingua Franca in the Levant*. Urbana, Ill., 1958.
Knolles, Richard (and P. Rycaut): *The Turkish History*. 3 vols. London, 1687-1700.
Kohut, Heinz: *The Analysis of the Self*. New York, 1971.
Mardin, Şerif: "Power, Civil Society and Culture in the Ottoman Empire", *Comparative Culture and Society*, XI (1969).
Lang, D. M.: *A Modern History of Georgia*. London, 1962.
McNeill, William: *Europe's Steppe Frontier*. Chicago, 1964.
Meservey, Sabra F.: *Feyzullah Efendi · An Ottoman Şeyhülislâm*. Ph.D. Dissertation, Princeton University, 1966.
Naima, *Tarih-i Naima*. 6 vols. Istanbul, 1281-83.
New Cambridge Modern History. Vols. IV (1970), V (1961) and VI (1970), Cambridge, U.K.
Parry, Vernon J.: "Elite Elements in the Ottoman Empire", in Rupert Wilkinson, Ed., *Governing Elites*. New York, 1969.
Pitcher, D. E.: *An Historical Geography of the Ottoman Empire*. Leiden, 1972.
Silihdar Mehmed Ağa: *Nusretname*. (Translation into modern Turkish by İsmet Parmaksızoğlu). 2 vols. Istanbul, 1962-69.
Silihdar Mehmed Ağa: *Silihdar Tarihi*. 2 vols. Istanbul, 1928.
Raşid: *Raşid Tariḫi*. 6 vols. Istanbul, 1282.
Rule, James and Charles Tilly: "1830 and the Unnatural History of Revolution", *The Journal of Social Issues*, 28.1 (1972).
Shinder, Joel: "Careerline Formation in the Ottoman Bureaucracy 1648-1750: A New Perspective", *Journal of the Economic and Social History of the Orient*, XVI (1974).
Sumner, B. H.: *Peter the Great and the Ottoman Empire*. London, 1949.
Şefik Efendi: *Şefikname*. Istanbul, 1290.
Mehmed Süreyya: *Sicil-i Osmanî*. 4 vols. Istanbul, 1308-15.
Tietze, Andreas: *Mustafā ʿAlī's Description of Cairo of 1599*. Vienna, 1975.
Thomas, L. V.: *A Study of Naima*. New York, 1972.
Uzunçarşılı, I. H.: *Merkez ve Bahriye Teşkilâtı*. Ankara, 1948.
——, *Osmanlı Tarihi*. III, i. Ankara, 1951.
Wright, Walter L.: *Ottoman Statecraft*. Princeton, 1948.

INDEX

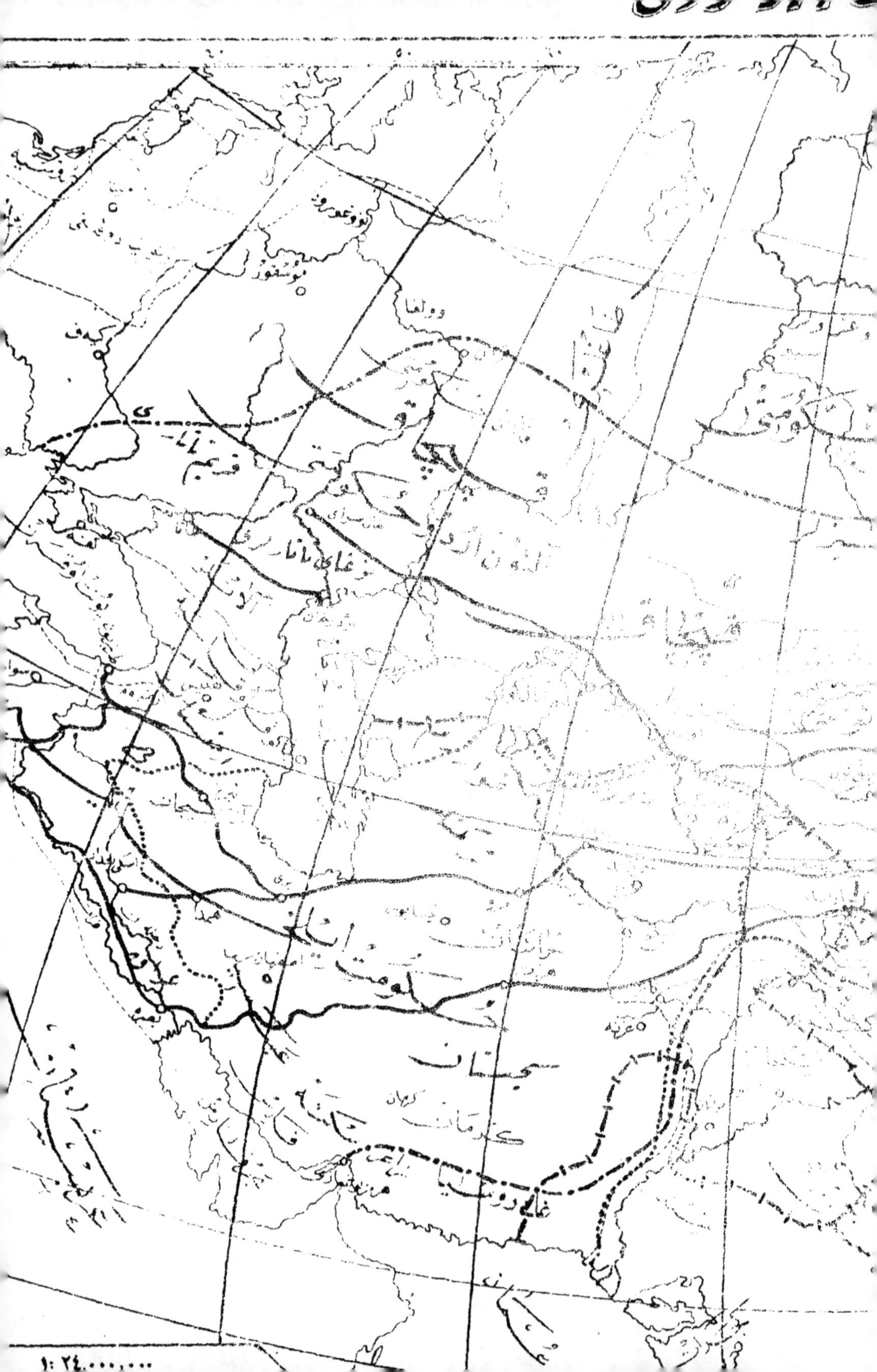
1: ٢٤.٠٠٠,٠٠٠

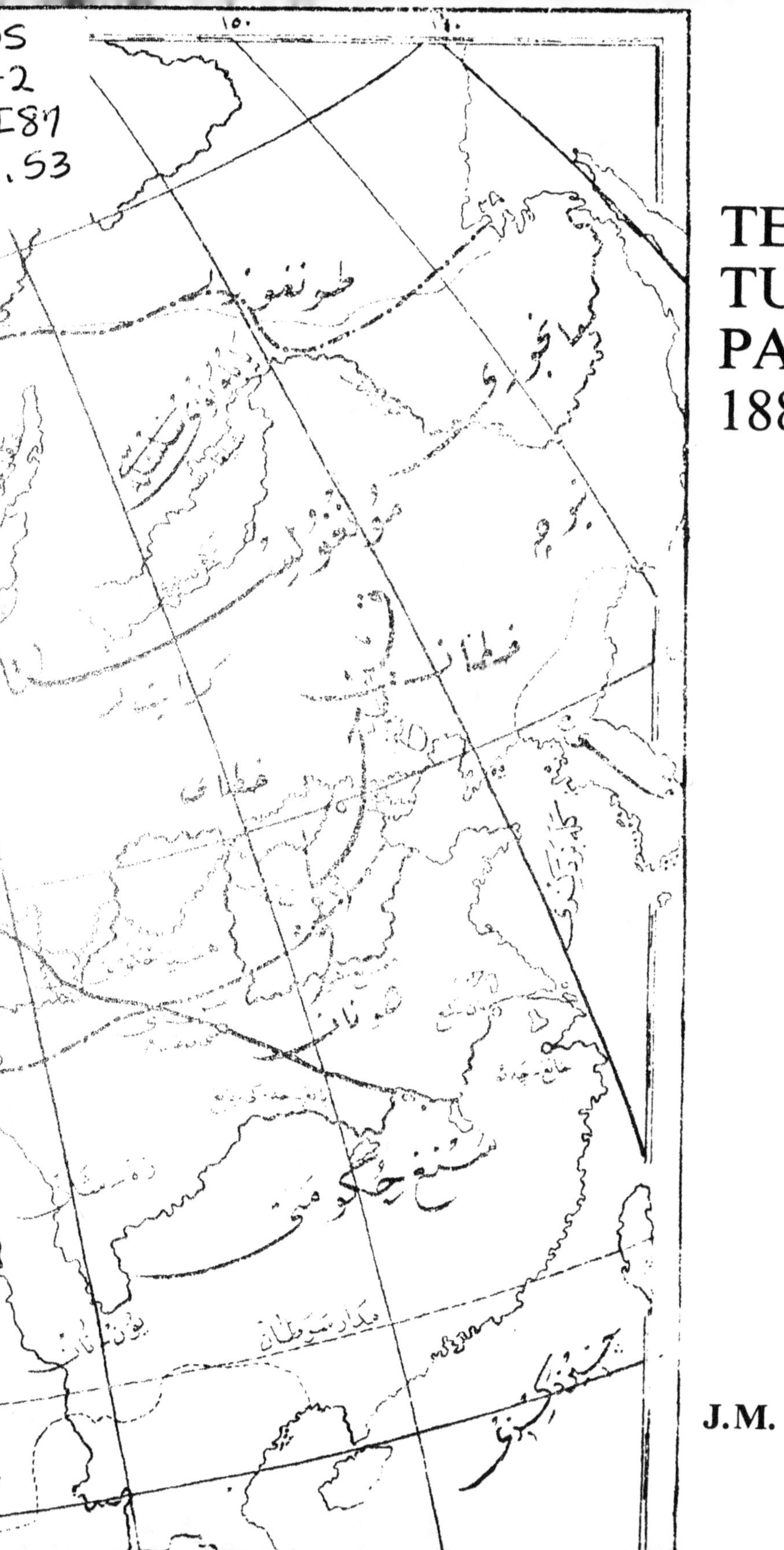

TEKİNA
TURKIS
PATRIOT
1883-1961

J.M. LANDAU

Cover illustration: A map of Turkish groups in the Ottoman Empire and in the Diaspora, published just before the First World War.

UITGAVEN VAN HET
NEDERLANDS HISTORISCH-ARCHAEOLOGISCH INSTITUUT TE İSTANBUL

Publications de l'Institut historique et archéologique néerlandais de Stamboul
sous la direction de
E. van DONZEL, Machteld J. MELLINK, C. NIJLAND et J.J. ROODENBERG

LIII

TEKİNALP, TURKISH PATRIOT
1883-1961

Tekinalp
At the time of the First World War

In the late 1950s

TEKİNALP, TURKISH PATRIOT
1883-1961

by

JACOB M. LANDAU

NEDERLANDS HISTORISCH-ARCHAEOLOGISCH INSTITUUT
TE İSTANBUL
1984

Nederlands Instituut voor het Nabije Oosten
Witte Singel 24
postbus 9515
2300 RA LEIDEN

ISBN 90 6258 053 X
Printed in Belgium

CONTENTS

ACKNOWLEDGEMENTS

This study could not have been written without the help and advice of members of the family of the late M. Cohen-Tekinalp, his friends and acquaintances, scholars and librarians in Turkey and abroad. My assistant, Avner Levy, was particularly helpful. The Harry S Truman Research Institute for the Advancement of Peace, at the Hebrew University of Jerusalem, allocated generous grants which helped finance, in part, the necessary research. Dr. E. van Donzel, Director of the Nederlands Instituut voor het Nabije Oosten, Leiden, and his staff have graciously agreed to publish this book and have done everything within their power to see this task through; of the staff, Dr. C. Nijland has been particularly helpful. Professor Barbara Flemming, of Leiden, has read a large part of the manuscript and commented on it. A fellowship from the Nederlands Institute of Advanced Study, Wassenaar, enabled me to carry out a part of the research required for this volume. I am deeply grateful to them all.

J.M.L.

NOTE ON TRANSLITERATION AND PRONUNCIATION

Turkish materials in Roman script have been rendered as they appeared – even in cases where official orthography has since changed. Ottoman script has been adapted to modern spelling, as used currently in the Republic of Turkey.

Modern Turkish is a phonetically written language, in which *a* is pronounced as *a* in *mama; c* as *j* in *jar; ç* as *ch* in *cherry; g* hard, as in *good; ğ* is a barely audible glottal stop; *i* as *ee* in *beef; ı* (dotless) as *u* in *podium; ö* and *ü* as in German; *ş* as *sh* in *ship.*

ABBREVIATIONS

CZA – Central Zionist Archives, Jerusalem

FO – Foreign Office series in the PRO

İM – *İktisadiyat Mecmuası*, Istanbul

PRO – Public Record Office, London

1. INTRODUCING THE SUBJECT

One of the lesser-known intellectuals who have contributed markedly to the evolution of Ottoman and Turkish nationalism in the twentieth century is Moiz[1] Cohen, *alias* Munis Tekin Alp or Tekinalp. Despite his important role, Tekinalp's career has been mentioned only rarely and briefly[2] – if at all – by Turkish historians of their own national movement. Some, like Professor Niyazi Berkes, have downgraded him to a mere "Istanbul businessman."[3] Perhaps the reason for this attitude lies in the fact that Tekinalp's writings were published over a long stretch of sixty years in several languages, as books and articles in numerous journals, thus compounding difficulties in developing a balanced and comprehensive overview.

Re-examination of most of his published output,[4] interviews with his family and acquaintances,[5] and perusal of his manuscript diaries[6] have enabled me to attempt understanding the career of this remarkable personality and evaluating his role in the nationalist movement of the late Ottoman Empire and the Republic of Turkey. The representative selection of Tekinalp's works which follows this analysis is arranged chronologically and spans most of his life. Insofar as possible, the samples have been rendered in their original languages, to afford a better grasp of Tekinalp's personal view and style; those in Judeo-Spanish and Turkish have, in addition, been translated into English, in an appendix.

TEKİNALP'S LIFE

Born just about a hundred years ago, Tekinalp (1883-1961) lived during one of the most interesting periods of Ottoman and Turkish history; most of his time was spent in such foci of nationalist activity as Salonica and Istanbul, thus rendering his involvement in national affairs easier to understand. Moiz, the son of Ishak Cohen, was born in Serres[1] into an orthodox Jewish family. He was the youngest of nine children, having been preceded by five sisters and three brothers, one of whom became Rabbi of Serres, another a cobbler and the third a grocer; the girls received only a limited education, as was then customary. Theirs was, in many respects, a Sephardic version of the "Fiddler-on-the Roof" family,[2] from which only the young Moiz broke away. He went to Salonica to study at a school run by the *Alliance Israëlite Universelle*, a philantropic association set up by French Jews in 1860 to promote education among Jews in the Orient.

One may only surmise the reactions of this young man from Serres upon first arriving in the capital of Macedonia, which at that time had begun to undergo rapid modernization: new roads and railway lines improved contact with the outside world, modern suburbs were being constructed to offset the ravages of periodic fires, new schools were erected and the water supply, medical facilities and city transportation developed apace, while a number of industries and the new harbour were prospering. Intellectual life, no less than material transformation, posed political challenges as well: Turks and Greeks were maneuvering for positions of power and Jews, who accounted for more than half of Salonica's population, were very much in evidence as well. Furthermore, some Turks were busily preparing for the so-called Young Turk revolution, later to guide its progress. Western European ideas were becoming increasingly popular, offering bewilderingly attractive options to the intellectual.[3] Tekinalp's diaries of his Salonica years well reflect his own infatuation with several of the then prevailing ideological currents.

At the same time, however, he went on to study for the Rabbinate of the Salonica Jewish Teachers' College; he was ordained as a rabbi but never actually officiated in that capacity. He then studied law, first at the modern three-year *École Impériale de Droit*, inaugurated in Salonica in December 1907,[4] and later in Istanbul. Moiz Cohen was studious by nature, but also had to earn a living, as he was assisting his family in Serres. More than once, this situation moved him to record in his diaries such phrases as: "Je me reproche d'avoir négligé l'étude. Je me propose de me rattraper."[5] Furthermore, even at that time, he experienced some doubts regarding his vocation; self-questioning about his own religious sentiments is obvious from his energetic search for a more satisfying ideological commitment. Since 1905, he wrote in the *Asır* (Era), later renamed the *Yeni Asır* (New Era) newspaper, which he served as contributor and co-editor for five years, publishing a number of articles on socio-economic topics in this journal and others. Soon afterwards, he established and presided over the *Tamim-i Lisan-ı Osmani Cemiyeti* (The Society for Universal Adoption of the Ottoman Language).[6]

In 1907, Cohen read a number of works on socialism and prepared to write his own book on the subject[7] – an intention which was never realised. At about the same time, he joined and became active in the freemasons,[8] along with several other Salonica Jews.[9] Two years later, he attended a World Zionist Congress in Hamburg, as a delegate from Salonica, but could not agree with the Zionist aim to establish a Jewish state in Palestine; he would have preferred to see the Jews immigrate to – and thereby strengthen – various parts of the Ottoman Empire.[10] Since the Zionist movement evidently preferred to encourage Jewish immigration to Palestine, rather than to Anatolia, it appears that he quickly dissociated himself from it. Instead, he entered into correspondence with Israel Zangwill, the noted British Jewish writer, who had set up a rival organisation, the Jewish Territorial Organisation, which favourably considered Jewish settlement projects in other parts of the world. His letters to Zangwill and others indicate that he was ready to act as an intermediary between this organisation and the Central Committee of Union and Progress;[11] nothing resulted from this venture, however. As he tells us in his diaries, he gradually drifted away from Jewish activities, with the exception of his continued participation in the *Club des Intimes*, an official body of the Jewish community in Salonica.[12] While its rival, the *Club Nouveau*, focused on Jewish matters, with occasional sympathy for Zionism,[13] the *Club des Intimes* was avowedly non-Zionist and occasionally anti-Zionist,[14] eagerly supporting the Government's policy of Ottomanising the Empire's minorities.[15]

Cohen, who had been active since 1908 within the committee of Union and Progress, hailed the Young Turk revolution of July 1908 with the following comments in his diary: "Une révolution pacifique a éclaté dans le pays qui a abouti à la promulgation de la Constitution. Ce changement aura sans doute une certaine influence sur mon propre avenir."[16] He indeed soon (1910) became a Member of the Provincial General Council (*Meclis-i umumi-yi | vilayet*). Although generally active in politics, he was not primarily involved in decision-making within the Committee of Union and Progress; he never penetrated the inner circle in which another Salonica Jew, Emanuel Carasso, was so active. Cohen was perceptive enough to realise that he was making little political headway within the Committee of Union and Progress.[17] He therefore devoted himself to his own writing and to promoting fraternity among Turks and Jews (his writings will be discussed in subsequent chapters). Insofar as this rapprochement was concerned, Cohen frequently visited the *Club Ottoman Union et Progrès* in Salonica. According to his diaries,[18] in May 1910, he set about – with characteristic vigour – establishing a *Ligue d'Ottomanisation* among local Jews, based upon the above *Club des Intimes.* In September of that year, he even organised a joint excursion of twenty members of the *Club des Intimes* to Cavalla to fraternise with the *Club Ottoman Union et Progrès* there.[19] In the following year, his writings strenuously advocated foundation of a *Ligue Patriotique* of Turks and others to support the Government's policies.[20]

His Salonica period was relatively brief but had a profoundly stimulating effect on Cohen's formative years. His residence there ended with the town's conquest by the Greeks in 1912, whereupon he spent a few months in Vienna, but soon afterwards settled in Istanbul, the Empire's capital. He taught law and political economy at Istanbul University, part-time, during the years 1914 to 1918, but made his living chiefly in the tobacco-exporting business, devoting to it only as much time as necessary to maintain his growing family (his wife and their three children – Isaac, Thérèse and Guillaume – the youngest of whom was born in 1914), a particularly important factor in light of the rapid increase in Turkey's cost-of-living index during the First World War and the War of Independence which followed it (from 100 points in 1914 to 1256 in 1922).[21] Nevertheless, it appears that Cohen remained interested primarily in intellectual activity, of which Istanbul was the undisputed centre for residents and new immigrants alike. His frequent contacts then included such leading writers as Ziya Gökalp and Celal Sahir. He had met and became impressed by the former in Salonica, although he never really became close to him then nor during their subsequent journalistic collaboration in Istanbul.[22] The latter, on the other hand, was a constant companion and associate in literary enterprise. During his Istanbul years, Cohen contributed essays on cultural and political themes to several leading magazines, such as *Türk Yurdu, Türk Derneğı* and *Yeni Mecmua*. During the First World War, he published an economic weekly, *İktısadiyat Mecmuası,* organ of the *İktisat Derneği* (Economics Association) which he had set up in 1916,[23] editing this periodical, which was partly Government-financed, until 1918. In it, he strove to familiarise his readers with the basic ideas of a national economy. He also established another association, *Türk Birliği* (The Union of Turks) and began writing several books (to be discussed below) before and during the war years.

From 1916 to 1922, Cohen had been active in the *Duhan Türk Anonim Şirketi* (The Turkish Tobacco Company Ltd.), gaining experience which proved valuable when he moved over to the large, Geneva-based Hermann Spierer Tobacco Company. He made his mark in this company upon representing it, as legal consultant, in a claim against Lloyd's of London. The company maintained that their loss of that tobacco in the burning of Izmir was the result of accident, whereas the insurance firm argued that it had been an act of war. Soon afterwards, he became the company's director for Turkey, supervising the exports of Turkish tobacco; later, he even served as secretary-general of the Turkish tobacco dealers' society. During part of the 1930s, moreover, he also managed the Turkish affairs of Omnipol, a subsidiary of the Czechoslovak firm, Skoda.

Having become an ardent Kemalist after the end of the First World War, he officially assumed the name of Munis Tekinalp (formerly, Tekin Alp had merely been his penname), wrote on Kemalism and lectured at the People's Homes established by the new regime. Among the Turkish intellectuals in the Republic, he was friendly with dedicated Kemalists like Yunus Nadi, editor of the daily *Cumhurıyet*, but also with others adhering to alternative schools of thought, such as Ahmet Emin Yalman, editor of *Vatan* and Zekeriya and Sabiha Sertel, active socialist thinkers and editors of *Tan.*

Although Tekinalp was hit very hard financially in 1942 by the *Varlık Vergisi,* a special tax imposed on Turkey's minorities, his loyalty to the regime and to the Republican People's Party never wavered. During 1945-1950, he was a Member of the Municipal

Council of Istanbul, serving on a committee for reorganising public services, among others; he reportedly promoted and introduced trolley-bus service in the city. In 1954 and 1957, Tekinalp ran unsuccessfully, as one of the party's parliamentary candidates from Istanbul. During the 1950s, most of his public functions centred in Istanbul's *Tüccar Derneğı* (Merchants's Association), which he served as secretary-general for a time, strenuously attempting to steer it in more liberal directions.[24] In this respect, he participated in the association's monthly, *Türkiye İktisat Mecmuası*, published in Istanbul since 1948, contributing numerous articles of social and economic interest. He also wrote occasionally in various magazines and several dailies, primarily *Cumhuriyet, Vatan, Akşam, Hürriyet, Son Posta* and others.

Throughout his life, Tekinalp attempted to be a model Turk. In 1908, having renounced the temptation of other ideologies, he became a patriotic Turk, remaining committed (with certain variations to be considered below) to this outlook unreservedly. Having little to do with the Jewish community or with Judaism in general (he even sent his children to non-Jewish schools), he was even more insistent upon overall Turkification than he had been in his Salonica days. In 1928, he founded the *Millî Hars Birliği* (National Culture Union) – an organisation for promotion of the Turkish language – in Istanbul, together with two other Jews, Nissim Matsliah and Dr. Samuel Abrevaya, as well as several non-Jews, including the above mentioned Yunus Nadi.[25] In 1934, Tekinalp and two other Jews, Hanri Soriano and Marsel Franko, established the *Türk Kültür Cemiyeti* (Turkish Culture Association) for the same purpose.[26]

The *Ten Commandments* which Tekinalp prepared and distributed among Jews and others in Turkey ('Think Turkish, speak Turkish, pray Turkish,' etc.), although ridiculed by some – who termed them *The Ten Commandments of Moses*, evidently referring to Tekinalp's given name of Moiz – constitute a rather lucid indication of his general outlook, which was emulated by a small number of Armenians and Greeks who, like him, were connected with the Republican People's Party and the People's Homes. In 1935, some of them established an Association of Secular Christian Turks in Istanbul, committed to Turkish language and culture and to the fusion of minorities into the larger Turkish nation.[27] Among Turkey's Jews, however, particularly those of his own generation, Tekinalp was virtually unique in this respect; Abraham Galante, the noted historian of Ottoman Jewry, was the only prominent Jew besides Tekinalp to propagate such views actively.[28] In his *Vatandaş, Türkçe konuş!* (Compatriot, speak Turkish!),[29] Galante also fervently pleaded for everyone in Turkey to speak Turkish, addressing himself primarily to the minorities (Greeks, Armenians, Jews) and calling for a public effort in this respect.

Tekinalp's dedication to Turkism earned him membership in the prestigious *Türk Dil Kurumu* (Academy of the Turkish Language) and other scholarly societies. It therefore appears somewhat difficult to understand why in 1956, upon his retirement from business, Tekinalp left Turkey and spent his last years in Nice, on the French Riviera, at a boarding-house near the home of his nephew (the cobbler's son), a devoutly orthodox clothing manufacturer. Before leaving Istanbul forever, he petitioned the Turkish Ministry for Foreign Affairs for the post of Honorary Consul in Nice,[30] no doubt in order to maintain his contacts with Turkey – but was turned down. Nevertheless, he kept in touch with developments in his homeland by regularly reading the Turkish press, although he himself wrote less than he had before. He continued to contribute to the above *Türkiye İktisat Mecmuası* and some other periodicals, also finding time to correspond regularly with such old friends as J. Nehama, the historian of Salonica's Jews. During his last years, Tekinalp was joined in Nice by his daughter-in-law, Guillaume's wife, and their children. In 1961, Tekinalp died and was buried in the Jewish cemetery of Nice, thus disproving the rumour that he had converted to Islam;[31] while Tekinalp was indifferent to all religions – and even averse to them to some degree – his burial in a Jewish cemetery is conclusive proof that Tekinalp, a patriot Turk, lived and died in the religion of his own ancestors.[32]

3. INTELLECTUAL ACTIVITY AND WRITINGS

Tekinalp's intellectual activity, carried on virtually uninterrupted throughout his entire life, was most unusual – to say the least. He was directly interested in many fields, including politics, public administration, law, economics and business, journalism, Ottoman history and literature, freemasonry, Jewish tradition and Zionism (the last two only early in his life). He was fluent in Turkish, French, German and Judeo-Spanish, and fairly well-versed in Hebrew, modern Greek, English and Italian. Tekinalp lectured occasionally, but was at his best in conversation, rather than public address; he maintained regular contact with some of the most influential Turkish intellectuals of his time. A voracious reader of newspapers, magazines and books, he also seems to have been a compulsive writer.[1] Words he once wrote in his diary during his youth have held true for the rest of his life: "Comme je ne suis pas habitué à être sans occupation, ça me gêne énormement."[2]

Tekinalp's works range over many subjects and were written in both Ottoman and modern Turkish, as well as French, German, English and Judeo-Spanish. In addition to several books, he published numerous articles, at home and abroad, a complete list of which is not easy to compile. The difficulties are enhanced by his having signed them variously as M. Cohen, Moiz Cohen, Tekin, Tekin Alp, Tekinalp or M. Tekinalp. His own *hal tercümesi* mentions his books alone, as does the only summary attempt to list his works, undertaken by Professor Cavit Orhan Tütengil soon after Tekinalp's death.[3] My own 'Preliminary List of Tekinalp's writings,' in an appendix to the present study,[4] is still incomplete. The present chapter will attempt to outline his writings, *grosso modo,* while subsequent ones will aim at more detailed analysis.

Tekinalp's writing career commenced at the young age of fourteen with a contribution in 1897 to a Turkish children's journal, *Çocuklara Rehber*.[5] It is uncertain whether he published anything (and if so, what) in the years which immediately followed; it is reasonable to assume that he devoted most of his time to completing his studies. From 1906 on he began to write occasionally for the Salonica newspaper *Yeni Asır*, concentrating chiefly upon economic and legal issues and later on political ones as well.[6] A research paper he had prepared during his legal studies was published in Salonica (probably in 1909 or subsequently)[7] as a small book entitled *Teşebbüs-ü şahsî ve tevsî-i mezuniyet* (Private initiative and the broadening of authorisation). Tekinalp had established contact with several members of the Committee of Union and Progress in Salonica approximately two years before their revolution. The success of this revolution emboldened him to support their aims in writing in other Ottoman journals, such as the Salonica *Ittihad ve Terakki* (from late 1908) or the Istanbul *Tesvir-i Efkâr* and *Le Jeune Turc* (in 1909). The Ottomanist ideology he had espoused served as the main theme of his discourse at the Ninth World Zionist Congress, which convened in Hamburg in December 1909 – his only real venture into Zionist activities. The lecture was delivered in French, but has survived only in German translation in the proceedings of the Congress.[8] In 1910, Tekinalp explained these visions of Ottomanism to his coreligionists in the Salonica Judeo-Spanish magazine *La Epoca.*[9]

It appears that this was the approximate period during which he decided to write for foreign journals as well, while continuing his journalistic activity in the Ottoman Empire. His first attempt resulted in a lengthy and interesting treatise on the problems of the Ottoman Empire at that time and of intellectual ferment amongst its elites. The article, entitled "Les Turcs à la recherche d'une âme nationale,"[9a] covered thirty-five pages of the August 1912 fascicle of the Paris magazine *Mercure de France* and was considered important enough to be translated for the Istanbul *Türk Yurdu*, an Ottoman political magazine with Pan-Turk leanings. There is some question regarding authorship, however, as the article was signed with a pseudonym, P. Risal. We are not aware that Tekinalp used this pseudonym, which was later employed by J. Nehama,[10] except once, several years earlier, when he authored (in Paris also) an essay about the Turkish press. The *Türk Yurdu*, introducing its Turkish translation,[11] was apparently unaware that Risal was a pseudonym; however, both Tekinalp and Nehama still resided in Salonica at the time and were as yet probably unknown to the editors of *Türk Yurdu*. Withal, the article's French style vastly differs from Nehama's: furthermore, Tekinalp cited it so frequently as his own in his *hal tercümesi* and other works that one tends to take him at his word.[12] It appears highly unlikely that he would have usurped the authorship of an article by his good friend Nehama. As to the origin of this pseudonym, one may surmise that it was an anagram of L'ASIR, the name of Tekinalp's newspaper together with the French definite article.

Soon after settling in Istanbul in early 1913, Tekinalp became involved in local intellectual circles and was driven to fervid writing activity just before and during the First World War. His output during those years was remarkable in quality and quantity alike: it commenced with a lecture in Vienna, in May 1913, on Balkan Jews – actually a memoir on Ottoman Salonica's Jewish community, later published in an Austrian Jewish organ.[13] It is likely, however, that his most important work at the time was *Türkler bu muharebede ne kazanabilirler? Büyük Türklük: en meşhur Türkçülerin mütalaatı* (What can the Turks gain in this war? Pan-Turkism: Opinions of the most famous Pan-Turkists). Published in 1914, probably soon after the Ottoman Empire's entry into the war, the book presented a forceful case for Pan-Turkism, the ideology Tekinalp had meanwhile adopted[14] along with Enver Pasha and several other leaders of the Committee of Union and Progress. One year later, the book was published in a considerably enlarged German edition as *Türkismus und Pantürkismus,*[15] amplified and probably translated by the author and representing another manifestation of his efforts to interpret Turkish nationalism to the world (as he had done three years earlier in French). While the Turkish edition was signed with his own name, M. Cohen, the German one bore the pseudonym Tekin Alp, undoubtedly in order to render it more convincing to readers. The second part of the German edition comprised the translation of the Turkish work, while its first part consisted of new material. One year later, the German version was translated into English[16] anonymously (probably by the known Orientalist E. Denison Ross[17]) for British intelligence, under the title *The Turkish and Pan-Turkish ideal.*[18] It comprised the entire German version, except for the testimonials about Pan-Turkism by Ottoman men of letters which were appended to the Turkish and German editions. Foreign Office officials in London found it "very useful,"[19] as did British war propaganda staff, as expressed in the London monthly *The Round Table*[20] and in its reprint entitled *Turkey: A Past and a Future.*[21]

Turan, also published in Istanbul in 1914, is yet another lengthy exposition – in Turkish – of the ideas of Pan-Turkism, focusing upon the happy lands of Turan, alleged home of all peoples of Turkic origins and considering political implications for the future. Here, however, we must first settle the question of authorship: *Turan* has been attributed to Tekinalp by the catalogues of Turkey's most reputable libraries, including the National Library in Ankara, as well as by bibliographical studies[22] and works by various scholars.[23] Nevertheless, there are two problems to be solved. Firstly, the book is signed Tekin, a pseudonym never used by M. Cohen beforehand or subsequently; secondly, neither his later writings nor his *hal tercümesi* ever refer to this work or list it as his own. Nevertheless, *Turan* may indeed have been written by Tekinalp, as the arguments it advances are known to be his own. Furthermore, we may well understand that during the Kemalist period, when so-called Turanism was anathema to the regime in Turkey, he would hardly have wished to advertise his authorship of such a book. Although this evidence is not fully conclusive, we may accept, with reservation, the claim that Tekinalp is the author of *Turan*.

During the entire First World War period, Tekinalp busily wrote articles, chiefly for periodicals, on a number of selected topics, of which several are prominent. Firstly, he apparently continued to view himself as interpreter of the Ottoman Turks to Europe and vice versa. In 1914, he contributed articles about life in Germany to the scholarly *Bilgi Mecmuası* of Istanbul, while two years later, he translated into German some representative nationalist Turkish writing for the *Oesterreichische Rundschau* of Vienna.[24] Secondly, he commented on political and military developments in *İçtihad*, a prestigious Istanbul fortnightly, during 1914; later on, he wrote optimistically on the same topics for the Istanbul weekly *Yeni Mecmua*, undoubtedly in order to raise his readers' morale. Thirdly, between 1916 and 1918, he set up and edited the Istanbul weekly *İktisadiyat Mecmuası*, for which he wrote regularly on Ottoman economics and finances (and occasional book reviews) in Turkish, with frequent translations into French or German. These he supplemented with contributions on kindred subjects in the Istanbul weekly *Yeni Mecmua*. Some articles were sent for publication in the German *Wirtschaftzeitung der Centralmächte.*[25] Views propounded in those articles, chiefly those published in the *İktisadiyat Mecmuası* and the *Yeni Mecmua*, advocated a 'national economy' to solve many of the Ottoman Empire's troubles.[26]

Tekinalp appears to have concluded his journalistic activity in the Ottoman period in 1919: two articles on "Yeni Osmanlılık" (New Ottomanism), published in the Istanbul weekly *Büyük Mecmua,*[27] appropriately called on the Turks to start a new period in their history. The difficult years for Turkey, which followed during its War of Independence, were perhaps even more traumatic for Tekinalp himself, who had to adapt to a new regime led by people with an ideology different from those he had formerly espoused. He appears however to have adapted quite rapidly, having ultimately become an ultra-Kemalist. Nevertheless, he seems to have written few articles between 1920 and 1944;[28] instead, he prudently devoted himself to authoring three well-written books, published at eight year intervals, all relating to the new Turkey that was in formation.

Tekinalp's efforts at furthering overall Turkification, particularly among Turkish Jews, have already been mentioned. He had written articles in *Yeni Asır* to that end and, as early as 1908, had been commended for it by the Salonica Judeo-Spanish newspaper *La Epoca.*[29] He had founded associations for that purpose and had apparently disseminated the idea there. In 1928, he published an entire book on the subject (partly based on his own articles in the press), *Türkleştirme* (Turkification), which appeared in Arabic script just before the change in the Turkish alphabet. This unfortunate timing may have led to the book's obscurity, despite its considerable merits. The author's plans to bring out a French translation[30] never materialised. Tekinalp's credo that Turkification of all ethnic minorities was a vital task for promoting national identification, although received with mixed feelings by some of the members in those communities, proved his good faith and bolstered his individual standing with the new regime.

Tekinalp's next and much larger book, *Kemalizm,* was published first in Turkish in 1936. It enjoyed a better fate than *Türkleştirme* and was translated into French one year later – as *Le Kemalisme*, with a preface by Edouard Herriot – and subsequently apparently in 1938[31] into Czech as well. A chapter was later translated into English by Professor Elie Kedourie.[32] Tekinalp's discussion of Kemalism was obviously not the first to be published in Turkey or abroad. As early as 1921, Berthe Georges-Gaulis, a well-known French Turcophile, mentioned Kemalism in her *Le nationalisme turc,*[33] although her approach was mainly descriptive. Similarly, Mediha Muzaffer's *İnkılâbın ruhu* (The spirit of the revolution)[34] was published three years before Tekinalp's *Kemalizm*, but provided a rather brief survey only. Tekinalp's *Kemalizm* was more profound and objective than earlier works, as observed by a renowned Turkish historian, Professor Ömer Barkan, in a review at that time.[35] Furthermore, it provided the first detailed analysis of Kemalism ever to appear in Turkish or in French. Although soon followed by other studies,[36] *Kemalizm* was surely a pioneer work in its field – in terms of both scope and depth.

Tekinalp appeared certain not only of Kemalism's past and present but of its future as well. Partially basing himself on Yakub Kadri's novel, *Ankara*, he attempted to predict that the Kemalist state of 1942 (hardly a long-range prediction) would be utopia of continuing progress, as "the past is the mirror of the future."[37] Tekinalp was to have an opportunity to verify his image of Kemalism's future in his next book, *Türk ruhu* (The Spirit of the Turks), published in 1944. He had prepared a French translation of this book as well, but only the Turkish version appeared in print. The greater part of this volume is a study of the past history and literature of the Turks, although the last few chapters do deal with the Kemalist period, repeating and elaborating upon several of the arguments Tekinalp had raised in earlier works.[38]

In the following years, Tekinalp returned to journalism and, during the subsequent dozen-odd years, published numerous articles in various magazines, especially the Istanbul dailies *Tan* and *Vatan*, the *Dünya ve Türkiye*, the Ankara *İller ve Belediyeler Dergisi*, the Jewish community's French organ *L'Etoile du Levant,* and others. Mostly, however, he wrote for the Istanbul monthly which he had founded in 1948 and had edited for some time, the *Türkiye İktisat Mecmuası*, organ of the *Tüccar Derneği*, contributing articles in Turkish which dealt primarily with economic and financial affairs, but expressed an obvious commitment to social issues. It was this attitude that dictated his relatively liberal stand: Tekinalp consistently advocated a limited etatism, recommending private initiative for economic enterprises capable of acting on their own. Some of his articles, however, were about cultural matters, a subject towards which he displayed growing concern in his later years. As many have discovered, *on retourne toujours à son premier amour.* Not coincidentally, the last essay he ever wrote (to our knowledge), from his retirement in Nice, combined his interests in economy and culture. It was published in 1959, two years before his death, in the *Bilgi* monthly of Istanbul (organ of the Teachers' Union of Turkey) and was entitled "Ziya Gökalp'te tesanütçülük" (Solidarity in Ziya Gökalp),[39](a theme he had already entertained quite a few years earlier. Its *Leitmotif* was one which he had frequently advocated: what Turkey really needed was a spirit of solidarity, for the collective good, rather than concentration upon narrow, individual interests.

4. TEKİNALP THE PATRIOT

In most of his deeds and virtually all his writings, Cohen-Tekinalp emerges as first and foremost a Turkish patriot. His belonging to a minority group may well have intensified this patriotic activity, once the commitment was made, a rather commonplace phenomenon in the Middle East. We need mention only the role of another Jew, James Sanua, in Egyptian nationalism, or that of Michel Aflak, a Christian, in Syria. Analysis and propagation of nationalism was undoubtedly the central theme of most of Tekinalp's early works and many of his later ones as well. The British Foreign Office, attempting to use Tekinalp's works on nationalism for its own purposes, characterised them in 1916 as "rather technical; but well-written, with some learning."[1] This description was not far off the mark, although it failed to emphasize his ardent patriotism. One of his earliest essays, "Band-ı-mahsus" (A special article), published in the Salonica *İttihad ve Terakki* in 1908,[2] passionately called for an Ottoman boycott of Austrian goods, to punish Austria-Hungary and aid the Ottomans. His first detailed elaboration of patriotism, in the lengthy article "Les Turcs à la recherche d'une âme nationale," commenced with the following phrase, "Dans l'immense empire des Turcs osmanlis, l'éternel négligé est le prétendu dominateur."[3] His passionate attachment to the Turkish national cause and land underwent a certain evolution; it was generally supportive of the government's ideology at the time, but never flagged in its basic patriotic commitment. Subsequent chapters will devote more space to analysis of the various aspects of this nationalist outlook; in the present chapter, we attempt an introductory overview of Tekinalp's general concept of Turkish nationalism.

One of his earliest (although by no means the first) exposition of his views on nationalism was the above-mentioned French article. Like most of his works, it dealt largely in abstractions and generalities with the obvious intention of proposing practical recommendations regarding attainable goals. Although the then oft-repeated question 'What should be done in order to save the State?' was not asked explicitly, it does appear to pervade much of his work, as proved by his view of the overall situation. As he saw it,[4] the Turks –backbone of the Ottoman Empire – were largely discouraged and demoralised and in an unenviable economic and educational situation. This was rendered all the more evident by comparison with the lot of non-Turks in the Empire, who were not only more prosperous than the Turks but also hostile to them under their own nationalist banners and goaded to revolt by interested European powers. The Turkish ruling class was rootless in its own Empire and increasingly on the defensive; they lacked a national conscience, which was provided by the political leadership only as late as the July 1908 Revolution. Initial feelings of euphoria passed, however, as the Turks soon found out that the exclusive particularism of the various ethnic and religious groups and their disparate aspirations continued much as beforehand. They discovered that a nation cannot be improvised, especially under prevailing geographic conditions of that time. The concept of Ottomanism was thus phased out for all practical pruposes.[5]

Nor were other solutions more useful for the Ottoman Empire and its Turkish population. Efforts at ensuring solidarity on the basis of Islamic sentiment failed to minimise in any meaningful way nationalist aspirations of a centrifugal character among non-Turk Muslim groups within the Ottoman Empire. As indicated by revolts in Albania, Yemen and Hawran, Pan-Islamism had as little success as Ottomanism[6] in awakening common national awareness. On the contrary, it constituted a danger for the Turks, who were isolated everywhere amongst more compact, self-contained communities. Tekinalp, whose clearly secularist approach is almost continuously in evidence (possibly enhanced by the fact that he was a Jew preaching, in large measure, to non-Jews), consistently adopted strong reservations towards politically-inclined Islamism and even more so towards Pan-Islamism.

In consequence, since approximately 1911 (i.e. for the last fifty years of his life), Tekinalp preached his own version of Turkism, which he interpreted to mean primarily an appeal to the Turks to turn unto themselves and employ ancient potential for creating their own brand of nationalism. He was indeed a fervent partisan of Turkification in all domains. He argued that the then current Turkish language, a mixture of such dissimilar components as Turkish, Arabic and Persian, somehow reflected the mixed population of the Ottoman Empire; Tekinalp estimated that about 70 per cent of the words in an average Turkish magazine[7] were of Arabic origin and sided energetically with Turks who advocated the purification of their language. To regenerate the Turks, he called for reforms based upon imitating the good in European civilisation, but only if associated with the revival of local traditions. In other words, he appealed for a forward look based not only upon the best in European technology but upon a renaissance of Turkish ancient history and literature as well. In his own words, "On ressuscitera le passé et on extraira la règle de la vie nationale."[8] In Tekinalp's opinion, this was much more than a mere matter of form and emphasis. It involved a change in style, which indicated a drive towards a new mentality, aiming at considerably broader horizons; contacts and cooperation with millions of co-nationals – people of Turkic origins living beyond the frontiers of the Ottoman Empire. Pan-Turkism was essentially "an exaggeration of nationalism."[9] According to Tekinalp, however, Turkism – together with its Pan-Turk extension – should be the main basis for a national ideal which is to be propagated amongst the Turkish masses.

It is this traditional type of nationalism that Tekinalp preached with certain variations, immediately before and during the First World War. He argued that the Turks had actually discovered their own national conscience[10] in it: first the *intelligentsia* themselves espoused the idea; later they would serve as much-needed cadres to spread it among peasant masses and assist in the formation of a Turkish nation. Aware of the Ottoman Empire's sad experience in the Balkan Wars and of the challenges facing it during the early part of the First World War, he preached the cause of Turkish nationalism even more forcefully in his 1914 book *Türkler bu muharabede ne kazanabilirler*? This may have been due primarily to the war in progress, but perhaps also to the fact that he was writing for a Turkish audience; his style, however, remained unaltered in the book's expanded translations into German and English. Tekinalp's message was loud and clear:

the situation showed the Turks "in crude and painful fact that they could count on no one's assistance but their own, and that their existence depended solely upon their political, social, intellectual, and economic power and unity."[11] Tekinalp especially hailed manifestations of patriotism among Turkish women and youth,[12] as well as its numerical increase and improving organisation.[13]

Tekinalp waxed lyrical in speaking of Turkish nationalism: "The Turkish national spirit has changed very greatly in a wonderfully short time. It is almost a miracle . . . The newly-awakened consciousness inspires in every part of the nation the will to gain for their fatherland a strong and favourable position among the nations."[14] However, he was perceptive enough to understand that, in addition to the change in spiritual values and political attitudes, the success of the new Turkish nationalism depended on radical improvement of the Ottoman Empire's economy. Tekinalp highly praised the efforts of the leaders of the Committee of Union and Progress, whom he regarded at the time as true patriots, in raising the economic situation of the Empire in general and that of the Turks in particular. Seeking to limit the financial stranglehold of foreign powers on the Empire, on the one hand, and the economic one of non-Turk groups, on the other, he noted that the Turks themselves were at long last beginning to organise: they opened their own shops and banks, boycotted others and preferred their own products.[15] Tekinalp not only approved of this phenomenon, but also did his patriotic duty in presenting several projects to the Government for promoting national economy,[16] writing regularly to the same end. In his *İktisadiyat Mecmuası*, as well as in lectures at the University of Istanbul, he constantly hammered home the ideas of national economy as patriotic duty to one's homeland, insisting on the principle of solidarity. A subsequent chapter will consider this subject at greater length. While Ziya Gökalp and his disciples were also keen on these same ideas during the First World War,[17] it was Tekinalp who phrased these national *desiderata* in economic terms.[18]

As a patriot, Tekinalp was undoubtedly chagrined at the defeat of the Ottoman Empire in the First World War and its subsequent dismemberment. Filled with admiration for Mustafa Kemal and his exploits in war and peace, Tekinalp soon became an ardent Kemalist. Now, two generations later, it is difficult to assess with any degree of certainty how Tekinalp's ideological make-up adjusted to the changed circumstances. While the failure of Pan-Turkism must have jolted him, his writings indicate that he found some solace in Turkism, the single major component common to both Pan-Turkism and Kemalism. Indeed, his first book to be published in the Republic of Turkey, following a long period of inactivity, was *Türkleştirme*, in which he elaborated his own interpretation of Turkism, i.e. that Turkification was a vital mission for strengthening Turkish society and preserving Turkish culture and awareness.[19] Every citizen who accepted Turkification thereby increased the power of both state and nation.[20] Consequently he called on all groups in Turkey – particularly on the minorities – to unite[21] and share in the Great Turkish Revolution.[22]

However, it was only years later, when he had fully adjusted to the new conditions and had grasped the essence of the regime's new ideology and reforms, that Tekinalp expressed his understanding of the new nationalism and his support thereof in two later books. In the first, *Kemalizm,*[23] Tekinalp introduced his subject by declaring that he was merely an observer "dans le milieu ou je vis et dont je partage naturellement les émotions et les réactions de toute sorte."[24] Tekinalp's identification with Kemalism and with this new version of Turkish nationalism as a whole is evident throughout his analysis. Tekinalp's views on Kemalism will be discussed below at greater length;[25] insofar as his general outlook is concerned, Tekinalp, who had already advocated change in the mentality of the Turks (as indicated above), considered Kemalism as having achieved this profound change.[26] In consequence, he regarded Kemalism as a successfully revolutionary form of nationalism.[27] Tekinalp noted the hope pervading all Turks during the Republican era[28] and his own patriotism throbbed with the surge of new hope for Turkey's future, in a mood strikingly different from that of his earlier writings. Following Ziya Gökalp, he argued that the Turkish people had always excelled when led by a hero-leader. Hence he was full of expectation from the results of Mustafa Kemal's leadership,[29] who had succeeded in arousing the best qualities of the Turks.[30] Mustafa Kemal's drive had created a different individual and a modern collectivity, expressed in a new state, a new fatherland and a new Turk.[31] However, Tekinalp considered the new Turkish nationalism, in its Kemalist version, as not only practical and activist but also imbued with humanitarianism and pacifism,[32] which appeared to suit Tekinalp's temper and private version of patriotism. He maintained that Turkish nationalism, unlike others, was anything but mystical; rather, it was characterised by a realistic feeling of self-preservation, providing means for saving land and nation.[33] Among these, Tekinalp singled out and emphasized common ideals, language and especially culture.[34]

Tekinalp's last book is equally relevant regarding views on Turkish nationalism. While earlier works discussed this subject in light of the time of their writing – with only brief incursions into the recent past – *Türk ruhu* aims at providing a broad analysis of the whole of Turkish history. It is a lengthy treatise, in the spirit of Turkism, if not the frowned-upon Pan-Turkism. Discussion commences with the ancestors of the Turks in Central Asia, covering many centuries and much territory. Of special interest is Tekinalp's intensive consideration of the Turkish Spirit, a subject upon which he had touched upon briefly in earlier works.[35] His main thesis was that the Turkish nation could not have set up a huge empire and achieved centuries-long greatness through mere physical strength; rather, spiritual force must have played a role as well. Tekinalp maintained that European historians had dealt at length with the Turks but had omitted due consideration of their moral qualities. It claimed that the Turks' spiritual force, in its different manifestations, was a constant factor in their history. For Tekinalp, 'Turks' are the descendants of the victorious tribes which swept down from Central Asia;[36] in true patriotic spirit,[37] Tekinalp discussed and highly praised the special characteristics which they acquired, namely dynamism, decisiveness, vigour, generosity and modesty – all of which remained unaffected by changing circumstances. He further argued that this ancestral spirit reawakened during Turkey's War of Independence, thanks to the merit of the Kemalists.[38] This spirit purportedly created and maintained the New Turkey[39] – a source of immense pride for

Tekinalp. His deep feelings for Turkey and the Turks may be gauged by recommendations to readers in the concluding chapter of *Türk ruhu,*[40] which may be paraphrased as follows: Know the exceptional spirit inherited from your Turanian ancestors and pride yourself on it; acquire the characteristics of progress to suit changing times; honour your national heroes; avoid foreign influence in the domains of society, morals and culture – imprint your own personality on these; do not slumber amidst your laurels; beware of the degenerate components of modernism; beware of the danger of individuality, the sickness of this generation; cling closely to national union; remember that nationalism is the cornerstone of New Turkey's ideology – but it is a nationalism based on realism and pervaded by humanitarianism.

This may be considered as Tekinalp's own credo regarding nationalism, which will be examined in further detail below.

5. OTTOMANISM AND TURKIFICATION ACCORDING TO TEKİNALP

Soon after the Young Turk revolution in 1908, Tekinalp became an ardent supporter of Ottomanist ideology, as indicated by references in the early part of his diaries[1] and by his above mentioned attempts at furthering this cause. This attitude was common (although by no means universal) in Salonica at that time, especially among minority groups, which were naturally excited by new prospects of equal rights and opportunities for all inhabitants of the Ottoman Empire. This remained so for some time, until it became clear that considerations motivating the Turks and others were apparently incompatible: some Turks were unwilling to relinquish their prerogatives, while members of the minorities aspired to full equality; the former wished to preserve the unity of the whole Empire, while some of the latter desired separation and even independent statehood.

Tekinalp's first detailed pronouncement in favour of Ottomanism was issued at the Ninth World Zionist Congress in Hamburg. He appears to have had some reservations about Zionism from the very beginning, voicing them frankly and directly in his speech at the plenary session of that Congress, on 30 December 1909.[2] Tekinalp's approach and arguments must have sounded rather odd in that milieu, advocating Ottomanist ideology before a gathering of confirmed Zionists. Firstly, he unhesitatingly introduced himself as 'a true Ottoman patriot'[3] then turned to the theme of his speech, Jewish immigration into Turkey. Claiming to speak for many of his coreligionists, Tekinalp praised the almost total absence of anti-Semitism in the Ottoman Empire and maintained that under such circumstances, it was no wonder that there were so many Turcophiles among the Jews[4] – thus reasserting the Ottoman Jews' commitment to the ideology of Ottomanism. He then argued that a massive wave of Jewish immigration into the Empire might alter this situation adversely. The national culture of all minority groups was respected in the Ottoman Empire; Jews there could maintain their national self-awareness, provided they were good Ottomans as well.[5] Consequently, the whole point of Jewish immigration into the Empire was for them to become devoted citizens of their adopted fatherland. It is inconceivable that a large number of Jews be allowed entry unless they became directly Ottomanised. Tekinalp insisted that Jewish immigration would serve the Ottoman Empire no less than the incoming Jews themselves, stressing that the interests of the Empire ought to be considered first and foremost.[6] From this perspective, the Jews could be directed to various parts of the Empire, particularly those requiring economic development, rather than settle in Palestine alone. A large number of Jews, loyal to the fatherland and non-supportive of separatism, would well serve as a counterbalance to insidious forces in the Ottoman Empire: the respective interests of the Jews and the Empire thus coincided.[7] All the above would obviously dictate a methodical distribution, organised by the Ottoman authorities, of the Jewish immigrants – all in the interests of the Empire.

The primacy of Ottoman interests (in contrast to the Zionist preference for all Jews to be gathered in one land – Palestine) characterised Tekinalp's approach; for a time he particularly emphasized the policies of Ottomanism, as frequently reflected in his writing. Articles published in the general Turkish and Jewish press reverted to the theme propounded at the Hamburg Congress, i.e. the need to encourage mass Jewish immigration into the Ottoman Empire for the sake of its economic rehabilitation. This was the main theme, for example, of the articles "Ebuzziya Tevfik Beye" (A reply to Tevfik Ebuzziya) in *Tesvir-i Efkâr*[8] (in Turkish) and "Una Explicación" (An explanation) in *La Epoca*[9] (in Judeo-Spanish). Tekinalp's own account of the Young Turk revolution and of the general enthusiasm which Ottomanism brought about provides an inkling of his own feelings in the matter. In his own words: "On discourut à tout propos sur la vie nouvelle que commençait pour la nation maintenant une et indivisible . . . . Il n'y avait plus qu'affection et que concorde. C'était si bon de vivre en frères, de communier dans les mêmes sentiments, d'entretenir le même idéal! . . . Il est indéniable que tous les éléments ethniques firent d'abord un généreux effort pour répondre à cette aspiration des Turcs vers une unité patriotique. Il y eut dans tous les milieux un entrain considérable pour les nouvelles idées, un élan ingénu, mais vigoureux, vers l'ottomanisme."[10]

Writing on the same topic, Tekinalp compared the Ottoman Empire to a huge hall in which various non-Turkish groups were feasting jovially as the owner of the place stood by the door, bayonet in hand, ensuring that nobody disturbed the festivities.[11] Ottomanism was supposed to alter this situation by inducing a better sense of equality and brotherhood. Tekinalp's own contribution to the short-lived Ottomanism, in addition to his writing, lay in his modest role in promoting various patriotic associations for furthering the cause.[12] He most frequently expounded on Turkification in all areas of life, with emphasis upon language purification.[13] Tekinalp focussed his propaganda primarily towards ethnic minorities and especially the Jews (whom he of course knew best). This trend is unmistakably evident in his speech at Hamburg and in articles written during the early Young Turk era in both Jewish and general newspapers. Tekinalp continued these efforts in later years as well, most probably considering them a cornerstone of his public activity during both the Ottoman and Republican eras.

Türkleştirme is entirely dedicated to the proposition that all efforts should be exerted in order to Turkify the ethnic minorities in Turkey, thus enabling them to identify completely with the destiny of their fatherland.[14] Citing numerous quotations from Mustafa Kemal and İsmet İnönü, Tekinalp elaborated his own interpretation of Turkism in detail. One of the basic tenets (according to Tekinalp) was "Be a Turk and love the non-Turk;"[15] hence Turkification was a vital task for strengthening Turkish society and preserving Turkish culture and awareness.[16] Every citizen who accepted Turkification thereby increased the power of both state and nation.[17] In consequence, he maintained, all members of minority groups living in Turkey should strive for total Turkification, a relatively simple task, considering their common past and ambience with the majority, as well as joint interests.[18] The majority should likewise do everything within its power to assist the minorities in this worthwhile intention – not by violent pressure but rather by persuasion[19] and creation of appropriate conditions for facilitating smooth Turkification.[20] As nationalism was largely dependent on mentality, a suitable mental attitude ought to be instilled.[21] Tekinalp essentially argued that anyone who declared himself a Turk should be accepted as such in principle.[22] However, he warned, only those who felt that they were Turks within their souls could be allowed to assume this title.[23] Turkey's strength lay in its population, which ought to digest the minorities who, without renouncing their ethnic origins, had to become a part of the nation (*millileştirme*[24]). As overall unity in Turkey,[25] expressed in national solidarity,[26] could be achieved only through Turkification of the minorities, Tekinalp set down the following ten imperatives: 1. Turkify [personal] names! 2. Speak Turkish! 3. Pray (at least partly) in Turkish! 4. Turkify your schools! 5. Send your children to state schools! 6. Become involved in state affairs! 7. Mingle with Turks! 8. Uproot the spirit of separation! 9. Do your share for the national economy! 10. Know your rights![27]

In the same vein, Tekinalp returned to the subject of Turkification in his book on Kemalism as well.[28] He argued for a responsive attitude towards Turkification by Turkey's minorities, especially considering the hospitality demonstrated towards them by the Muslim Turk majority. As he understood it, minority groups could become true Turks by adopting Turkish culture without necessarily renouncing their particularism and sentiments of solidarity.[29] Tekinalp applauded the laws introducing secularism as yet another factor in lowering the barriers between the various religious groups [30] and providing yet another impetus towards the Turkification of the minorities. Nevertheless, he had to acknowledge that these barriers still existed, largely due to the legacy of the past influencing those minorities. Even so, the passage of time and universal schooling in Turkish language and culture were already contributing visibly to Turkification of the minorities.[31] Tekinalp did his best, both during his youth and in his later years, to hasten this process. In so doing, he defied opposition and criticism within the Jewish community in Turkey – as observed at the time by the French Ambassador to Istanbul.[32]

6. THE PAN-TURK IDEOLOGUE

As noted earlier, Ottomanism did not prove a great success as state policy. Equality among all the Empire's inhabitants, proclaimed in the euphoria of the 1908 revolution, proved difficult – if not impossible – to put into practice. Both Muslim Turks and Christian communities displayed varying degrees of reluctance at relinquishing their special privilages and aspirations for the sake of the Empire's welfare. Consequently, Ottomanism as an ideology and state policy hardly prevented dismemberment of the Empire. During the years immediately preceding the First World War, a number of important leaders of the Committee of Union and Progress – Enver, in particular – gradually shifted towards a new policy, Pan-Turkism (although both Ottomanism and Pan-Islamism, still required occasionally for tactical purposes, were not discarded altogether).

Tekinalp soon followed suit: less well-known than either Yusuf Akçura or Ziya Gökalp – both of whom he greatly admired – Tekinalp soon became an ardent supporter of Pan-Turkism, playing a major role in its systematisation and in the exposition of its principles both in the Ottoman Empire and abroad. Most of his political-literary activity on behalf of Pan-Turkism took place between 1911 and 1916, i.e. during the very period that Pan-Turkism was becoming truly significant as the official policy of decision-makers in the Ottoman Empire's top political leadership.

While Tekinalp was neither the first nor the only proponent of a 'Greater Turkey', he did gain renown for these views in the Ottoman Empire and even more so abroad;[1] some even considered him to be the initiator of Pan-Turkism.[2] However, in the aforementioned 1912 article (in French), he added little original material to the debates on Pan-Turkism then taking place within intellectual circles in Ottoman Salonica.[3] That was not the case, however, regarding his two somewhat complementary books on the subject.

Turan, a fairly long treatise on the ideas of Pan-Turkism, focused upon the happy lands of Turan, allegedly the homeland of all peoples of Turkic origins and the symbol of their future reunification into a large, powerful state. Certain elitist circles in Istanbul then considered Turan to be far more than a mere ancient geographic term; Tekinalp who had moved to the capital two years earlier – soon after the fall of Salonica – contributed his share to these views, commencing his book with a fairly detailed survey, attributing Turkishness to several ancient empires and concluding that the Turks had remained alive even though their early states were destroyed. Turks were understood to have a common origin, history, language, tradition, customs, social institutions, literature and sentiments.[4] As Tekinalp perceived it, Turan was not merely an historical concept, just as Italy had not been merely a geographic one, despite Metternich's definition.[5] Rather, it was a living reality of 10,800,000 square kilometers and 43 million Turks and several million others,[6] many of them ruled by Russia and China – against whom the thrust of this book is directed. To bring Turan into fruition, he formulated a conception parellel but not identical to that of Gökalp, proposing both a 'minimum' and a 'maximum' plan.[7] The former, a first step towards the latter, would consist of setting up a relatively easy-to-achieve 'small Turan,' from Istanbul to Lake Baykal (which the author Turkicises to Bay-Göl) and from Kazan to Mongolia, while the latter, a second stage, would involve the establishment of 'Great Turan', from the frontiers of Japan to the Scandinavian mountains and from the Arctic Ocean to the Tibetan Plateau. This would be achieved through wars, by a 'New Genghizism' (*Yeni Cengizlik*),[8] to be carried out via a simultaneous national awakening of Turks everywhere, who would unite as Italy and Germany had done, using science and the sword, in a Holy War joined by all Turks and led by the Ottomans.[9] Turan, essentially rich although sparsely inhabited,[10] belongs to the 70 million Turks, a 'Golden Race' (*altın soy*), close to, but not identical with,[11] the yellow race – the Japanese, natural allies of the Turks[12] – probably due to common anti-Russian and anti-Chinese interests. Istanbul would be the capital of this 'Golden Fatherland' (*altın yurt*),[13] the New Turan stretching over an area ten times larger than Anatolia.[14]

Turan had a definitely Turanist character, aiming at a broad alliance of ethnic groups assumed to be racially close to the Turks. Many Pan-Turkists, however, had somewhat more limited plans. Soon after its publication, Tekinalp's *Türkler bu muharebede ne kazanabilirler*? was issued, to be subsequently expanded and published in German and English as well. Here, he attempted to synthesise the ideology of Pan-Turkism, which he then considered to be the most recent and finite stage of Turkish nationalism. He began with an historical introduction of the failure – through inadequacy – of both Ottomanism and Pan-Islamism,[15] then went on to describe the genesis of Turkish nationalism before, during and after the Balkan War[16] – an event which was traumatic for the author (as he had become an exile from Salonica) and the Empire (which had lost lands close to its very heart). According to Tekinalp, this defeat galvanized Turkish nationalism into Pan-Turkism. Opposition, in turn, only led Pan-Turkism to organise culturally, politically and economically.[17] To the best of our knowlegde, Tekinalp was the first Ottoman patriot to declare that Pan-Turkism was a complete political, economic, social and cultural system which could solve the Empire's immediate problems and save it from ever-increasing dangers. He also pinpointed the one enemy which constituted the greatest obstacle to achievement of Pan-Turkism's visions – the Russians (in ***Turan*** it had been Russia and China). Hence the historical partnerships between Turks and Germans[18] – for whose readership, after all, this book had been written in the first place. The second part of the book is an elaboration of the first, focusing upon an examination of Pan-Turkism as compared with other nationalist ideologies and movements of the time.[19] According to Tekinalp, the pivot of Pan-Turkism was the assistance offered by the Ottoman Empire, uniting all Turks living under foreign rule. In this context, he discussed irredentism at some length,[20] having covered the topic briefly in ***Turan*** as well. His methodical description and analysis of this subject may well be the very first such study in Ottoman political writing. Tekinalp praised irredentism highly, adducing examples of success which he ascribed chiefly to perseverance. He dwelled in particular upon Romanian irredentism, focussing upon Wallachians in Macedonia although they shared no common frontier with Romania. While irredentism was not an absolutely necessary policy for the Italians, Romanians, Bulgarians and Serbs, it was definitely vital for the Turks: "The Irredenta . . . is a political and social necessity for the Turks."[21] It meant liberation of Turks living in areas contiguous to the Ottoman Empire and cultural and moral support for all others. This was the essential duty of Turks in the Ottoman Empire if they did not wish to limit Turkish culture and spirit to Turkey alone. The Ottoman Empire did not need territorial aggrandisement,[22] but rather an influx of Turks and relations with Turks living abroad.[23] This, in brief, was Tekinalp's message to all Idealists – as he called nationalist Turks imbued with Pan-Turk sentiments.

Under the Republic, Tekinalp's Pan-Turk sentiments, which undoubtedly had suffered a rude shock upon the Ottoman Empire's defeat and dismemberment, were toned down considerably. As an active Kemalist, he could hardly write in favour of Pan-Turkism, an ideology officially supplanted by Kemalism. Moreover, it is quite conceivable that he had renounced Pan-Turkism; he never indicated the book *Turan* in his *curriculum vitae* and hardly mentioned his other Pan-Turk works in later writings. *Türk ruhu*, however, does revert to discussing Pan-Turkism. Tekinalp spoke admiringly of Ziya Gökalp[24] and maintained that the latter consistently considered Pan-Turkism as a means, not an aim – as a spiritual ideal to draw Turks together.[25] Tekinalp then repudiated Pan-Turkism, opting for Turkish patriotism (which he termed *Türkiyacılık*) instead.[25] However, he laid most of the blame for the failure of Pan-Turkism not upon its ideology – as he himself had aided in its formulation and propagation – but rather upon its leaders, who had erred badly in their estimates and decisions.[27] Thus, even at the age of sixty, Tekinalp did not completely renege on the principles which had been so close to his heart during his youth – despite the fact that Kemalism had long been his guiding light by then.

7. TEKİNALP'S ANALYSIS OF KEMALISM

As noted above[1], Tekinalp's analysis of Kemalism was neither the first nor the best-known of its genre; nevertheless it was indeed the most detailed and penetrating of its time. Tekinalp's numerous articles on Kemalism, which were chiefly concerned with economic problems, will be considered subsequently.[2] Most of his views on Kemalism itself were propounded in the book *Kemalizm*, published shortly before Mustafa Kemal's death and constituting a lengthy and intensive assessment of this ideology and of its achievements, written with *élan*, but adopting a rational viewpoint which serves to demystify the subject.[3]

Tekinalp's basic argument was that most previous works on the innovations of Mustafa Kemal had focused upon material achievements. These, he argued, did have their obvious merit, but Kemalism's most lasting success was its transformation of the Turkish spirit and mentality, a change particularly well-adapted to the character of the Turks. Examining Kemalism in its historical context, he concluded that it was not merely another link in the long chain of Turkish history, but rather a revolution, a severing of ties with the past.[4] Kemalism's greatest moral contribution was its victory over theocracy and its provision of an alternative godhead, nationalism.[5] Kemalism had turned Ankara into a true *Kızıl Elma*, the next best thing to a terrestrial Paradise for the Turks, replete with new achievements in science, art and industry, as well as in literature and language (essentially nationalist and secular in nature).[6]

Tekinalp highly praised Kemalists for their systematic and not unduly impulsive advance toward their goal.[7] He perceived several stages in Kemalism's methodical pursuit of these objectives:[8] recruitment of popular forces in the war of liberation, confirmation of independence and territorial integrity by the Treaty of Lausanne and maintenance of the struggle on the internal front for the regeneration of Turkey. According to Tekinalp, the success of all these stages was due to the moral qualities of Kemalism and to the combination of revolutionary zeal, courage and intrepidity, together with circumspect self-possession and lucid realism concerning the importance of power [9] – what today's political scientists would perhaps call successful *Realpolitik*. On several occasions, Mustafa Kemal did yield to rivals on tactical points, although he never lost sight of his main objectives, timing each reform subtly and undertaking it after due preparation.[10]

Tekinalp considered Kemalism essentially as a break with the past,[11] intended to establish a new state and create a new Turk with as little delay as possible. The formation of new cadres, for which Anakara served as a highly suitable training ground,[12] was a precondition for achievement of these objectives. According to Tekinalp, Kemalism's main efforts were then directed toward limiting theocracy – which he considered as its archenemy – and fostering secular nationalism.[13] In Tekinalp's view, Turkish nationalism, conceived during the War of Independence, was not at all mystical, as were foreign types of nationalism, but rather a pre-condition for survival.[14] This new approach characterised the Kemalist concept of a nation based upon a common language, culture and ideal, rather than upon religion, as was the case previously.[15] Mustafa Kemal's views on Turkish history and the books he commissioned were considered as merely one facet of this approach.[16] Secularisation was followed by speedy modernisation – identified in this book with Westernisation – especially since 1928,[17] as manifested both materially and spiritually in the emancipation of women, language reform, encouragement of the arts and music, adoption of family names, etc. All of these measures, argued Tekinalp, were effected continuously in a spirit of undiminished revolutionarism; any slowdown in the *élan* of Kemalism would divert it from its objectives.[18]

More than a third of this volume is devoted to close scrutiny of the Kemalist doctrine, which Tekinalp examined according to the "Six Arrows." He began by conceding that there are apparent contradictions in this ideology, such as the proclamation of democracy while government maintained authoritarian control or the declaration of liberalism as the authorities intervened in all individual activities.[19] Consequently, Tekinalp proposed to examine Kemalism against the background of realitiy, i.e. the existing conditions in Turkey at that time. In advocating Kemalism, he frequently argued that its adherents took steps which were best for the Turks. For example, he claimed that Kemalism was never anti-democratic; rather, it opposed some of the degenerate forms of democracy, adopting instead certain autocratic measures which were then imperative in Turkey in order to better safeguard the sovereignty of the nation and improve the collective mentality of the Turks.[20] Similarly, Tekinalp explained the etatist policies of the Kemalists in terms of Turkey's situation and needs. He believed that etatism was the best method of protecting Turkey's economy against foreign capitalism;[21] in fact, he maintained that it was probably the only way to save Turkey from renewed economic slavery. He evaluated Turkish etatism as *sui generis*, as it recognised private property and allowed the activity of private enterprise, even though it coordinated the latter, in contradistinction to Moscow's etatism.[22] This "directed economy" was said to be the shortest road to Turkey's economic recovery.[23] Etatism, as understood by Tekinalp, meant that the People's Party would not only control Turkey's economy, but its politics and culture as well,[24] assisted by the People's Homes.[25]

In analysing Kemalist methods, Tekinalp astutely concluded that they would wait patiently for the most opportune moment, constantly employing persuasion and personal examples[26] – as did Mustafa Kemal himself – all generally followed by legal decrees and by tireless and dynamic work towards pre-determined objectives.[27]Tekinalp considered Kemalism not only as a realistic policy, however, but also an ideology supportive of a humanitarian and pacifistic approach,[28] as in its limiting the cultivation and sale of opium, for example.[29]

All in all, the book provides a highly perceptive summary of Kemalism during Mustafa Kemal's lifetime. As Tekinalp himself wrote, "Nous voilà en 1935. Nous avons bien vu que, dans l'espace d'une douzaine d'années, le nouveau Turc s'est forgé une nouvelle âme, une nouvelle morale, une nouvelle histoire et je dirai même un nouveau Dieu, puisque celui-ci ne s'appelle plus Allah, mais Tanrı. Le nouveau Turc a maintenant une autre tête et un nouveau couvre-chef, un autre alphabet, un autre Etat, une économie différente et, finalement, une nouvelle langue."[30]

Tekinalp appeared certain not only of Kemalism's past and present, but of its future as well, concluding "le passé est le miroir de l'avenir."[32] He was to have the opportunity of verifying his image of Kemalism's future in his next book, *Türk ruhu*. The greater part of this volume is a study of the past history and literature of the Turks, although the last few chapters do deal with the Kemalist period,[32] repeating and elaborating upon several of the arguments Tekinalp had raised in earlier works.

Tekinalp understood the Kemalist Revolution as a continuing process, guarding Turkey from the encroachments of the Ottoman past.[33] Mustafa Kemal and Ismet Inönü preserved and "purified" the positive elements of Turkey's ancient (i.e. pre-Ottoman) past, striving to apply them in Republican Turkey. One basic characteristic of their reform was its all-embracing nature, from the Presidential Palace down to rank and file Turks.[34] Although possessing two different personalities, Mustafa Kemal and Inönü had acted as one in spirit and would be so considered by history.[35] While clearly oriented towards, the Occident, both were true representatives of the Turkish past, single-mindedly dedicated to the State in all their activities.[36] Thus, both were great leaders,[37] having created a new entity which defied simple comparisons to either democracies or authoritarian regimes and which aimed at surpassing the level of Western Civilisation, as Mustafa Kemal himself stated: "Garb medeniyeti seviyesinin üstüne yükselmelisin,"[38] a phrase which Tekinalp considered to be a pithy summary of Kemalism's main objective. A close translation would read, "You must rise above the level of Western civilisation."

It is not easy to evaluate precisely Tekinalp's contribution to the study of Kemalism. Now that so much has been written on the subject of Mustafa Kemal and his movement, there is a wholy unjustified tendency to belittle Tekinalp's own share in this area. Nevertheless, it is clear that he had largely concentrated upon Kemalism as an ideology, an aspect which no scholars had considered before his books were published (and only a few since).

Tekinalp's studies of Kemalism were undoubtedly influenced by his earlier politics and personal views, as is often true of writers. In his own case, this is most evident in his approach to the evaluation of nationalism and secularism in the Turkish Republic. With respect to the former, considering Tekinalp's earlier writings in favour of Pan-Turkism, it is hardly surprising that his estimate of Kemalism's position on Turkish nationalism primarily dwells upon its emphasis on past culture and Turkism's contribution to civilisation, while completely neglecting the other, more innovative facet of Kemalism's contribution to nationalism, namely its insistence upon a Turkey-centered (rather than all-Turk) approach. With regard to the latter, Tekinalp's Jewish origin and rabbinic training may possibly explain his frequent tirades against theocracy and constant praise of Kemalism's secularist policies; without being anti-religious himself, he sensed only too well that his chances of political equality and socio-cultural activity in an Islamic theocracy would be markedly less than in a secular democracy.

Such over-emphasis notwithstanding, Tekinalp's studies of Kemalist ideology do display several obvious merits:

Tekinalp was the very first (or at least the first 'insider') to write and publish a serious, systematic study of Kemalist ideology against the dual background of Turkish history and of the political regimes and economics of other states. Furthermore, he was the first to attempt an intensive analytical study of Kemalism, minutely examining the ideology and checking its validity, in every single aspect, against the day-to-day performance of its proponents. Finally, Tekinalp was one of the very few to approach the subject as a dedicated humanist; while granting the need for a strong Turkey, in a spirit of *Realpolitik*, he highlighted Kemalism as a response not only to the material needs of the new Turkey, but to its moral requirements as well.

Contemporary critics may find fault with Tekinalp's uncritical and somewhat excessively laudatory view of Kemalism. However, he did live during an era of great enthusiasm and it was only natural for him to have been impressed and excited by Kemalism's truly great achievements. While the present state of our knowledge renders it rather difficult to assess accurately the degree of his influence on the subsequent analysis of Kemalism, one may confidently assert that he was a pioneer in this domain too.

8. TEKİNALP'S VIEWS ON NATIONAL ECONOMY AND ECONOMIC NATIONALISM

Tekinalp's formal higher education consisted of legal studies alone. In Salonica Ziya Gökalp had urged him to study sociology and psychology,[1] advice which apparently was not followed. Nevertheless, from youth to old age, Tekinalp was always very interested in economic problems in general and in those of the Ottoman Empire (later, of Turkey) in particular. He read many works on economics – most of which were in German – not necessarily because he himself was involved in business; more often than not, he displayed greater concern about the overall economic situation than about his personal one.[2] Even in his Salonica days, he watched national economic and financial developments quite closely. For example, in his 1912 French article,[3] he applauded the establishment of the *Şirket*, commercial societies set up to assist the Turks economically. In Istanbul, particularly during the First World War, his comments on the economy of the Empire soon became more emphatic, both in his lectures at the University of Istanbul and in his frequent contributions to the *İktisadiyat Mecmuası* and the *Yeni Mecmua.*

It was doubtlessly not fortuitous that the very first article Tekinalp contributed to the first issue of *İktisadiyat Mecmuası* weekly was entitled "Millî iktisada doğru," translated in the same issue as "Notre programme: Vers l'économie nationale" and "Der Zweck unserer Zeitschrift: Unsere Volkswirtschaft."[4] Many such articles were published in two languages (generally Turkish and French), but this was one of the few instances in which an article was published in three – perhaps an indication of the importance Tekinalp attached to it.[5] In it, he argued that although the Ottoman Empire badly needed an improved economy of its own, most of its intellectuals and politicians were busy with other matters. He promised that the weekly would strive to discover the scientific bases of economic life in the Empire and would provide information, offer commentary and draw attention to all phenomena having an impact on the country's economic future: economic resources, national wealth, imports and exports, mines and forests, agriculture, labour, railways, ports, banking, insurance, and cooperatives. Several of these points were re-emphasized by Tekinalp in later issues.[6]

Tekinalp's articles continuously reverted to problems of national economy. In "Tütün meselesi"[7] (The tobacco problem) he appealed for an overall national approach to increase and improve tobacco-growing in Anatolia, while in "İki usul-ü istismar"[8] (Two systems of exploitation), he called for 'the economic education of the Turkish people,' which he saw as a precondition for 'economic renaissance.' As he understood it, the 'national economists' of the Turks would first have to devise a definite system for approaching pressing economic problems. Basing himself upon recent economic studies published in Germany, he much preferred a 'scientific approach' to the solution of those problems – which would educate the Turks to take care of their own economic needs – over a 'mercantile approach' which would bring about only quick profits. Settling this issue, he called for a determination of the scientific approach best suited to the conditions of the Ottoman Empire.

Furthermore, in "Ticaret-i hariciyemiz"[9] (Our foreign commerce), he pointed out the damage to the Empire's national wealth resulting from a deficit in the balance-of-payments, caused by import of too many consumer goods. In "Artırma sandıkları"[10] (Savings banks), he warmly supported the project of founding savings banks throughout the Empire, praising their future role in increasing national savings. A series of articles, entitled "Ziraat bankası"[11] (The Agriculture Bank), praised the new law creating a bank which would offer credit to peasants on a nationwide basis, calling upon the Government to increase tenfold the capital of that bank. His "Adana ovasının irva ve iskası"[12] (Irrigation of the Adana plain) pointed out that vast fertile areas were among the Ottoman Empire's main assests; combining this potential with German and Austrian knowhow would provide a real service to the national economies of all concerned. "Bu seneki mahsulümüz"[13] (Our harvest this year) emphasized the crucial importance of agricultural havests for the national economy of the Ottoman Empire. "Ziraat müze ve sergileri"[14] (The agricultural museum and its exhibitions) received high marks from Tekinalp for stimulating a desire to catch up with contemporary development. "Konya millî iktisad bankası"[15] (The Konya bank of national economy) was lauded by him for diversification of its activities in a region that was essentially Turkish.

Tekinalp applauded the establishment of an "İktisad derneği"[16] (Association for economics), set up by a distinguished gathering at Istanbul University's Faculty of Law. He particularly approved of theoreticians' joining forces with practicaly-minded people. He fully supported the ruling party's economic policies in "İttihad ve Terakki fırkasının iktisadî faaliyeti"[17] (The conomic activity of the Party of Union and Progress), in which his main argument was that the party had succeeded in consolidating the Empire's various types of economy with the aim of amassing the large capital required. In the same vein, he campaigned for heavy industry in his "Memleketimizde büyük sanai"[18] (Large industry in our country). He referred in particular to the industrial plants at Izmit and praised the Governement for developing them, even in time of war, for the sake of national economy. As national economy was all-important in his thinking at the time, he wrote approvingly of all measures liable to influence it favourably in such articles as "Millî iktisad nasıl vucuda gelir"[19] (How National Economy came into being), "Ticaret kanununun tadil ve ıslahı"[20] (The reform of the Commercial Code), or "İktisadiyat Meclisi"[21] (The Council for Economic Affairs). The last article, for example, expressed satifaction with the prospect of a projected high-level Council for research and co-ordination of economic life for the sake of the Empire's progress. He later reverted to lend his support to the projected establishment of an "İktisadiyat Nezareti" (Ministry of Economics).[22] Similarly, he hailed the establishment of an Ottoman credit bank in "İtibar-ı millî bankası"[23] (The National Credit Bank), arguing that this bank would have a triple role in the Empire's national economy: increasing confidence of all capitalists, serving as a centre of gravity for increasing national wealth and assisting the authorities in all their projected reforms for raising national productivity.

In "Madenlerimiz"[24] (Our mines), Tekinalp maintained that the discovery and exploitation of mines was a task of prime importance for the Empire's national economy; he therefore called for serious efforts in that direction. Because of his concern with the future, he devoted a lengthy article to "İstikbal-ı iktisadımız"[25] (The future of our economy), in which he argued against too liberal an economic policy and for moderate protectionism to safeguard the Ottoman Empire's developing economy and national production in particular ("İstihsalat-i milliye-yi artırmak meselesi"[26] – The problem of augmenting national production). He reverted to this topic later, considering the relative emphasis on industry and agriculture, in his "İstihsalat-ı milliye-yi artırmak meselesi – ziraat mı sanai mi?"[27] (The problem of augmenting national production – agriculture or industry?).

In his view, the optimal solution for the Empire's national economy lay in finding and practising the most suitable combination between Government supervision and private initiative during wartime and transition to peace alike. Thus, his article "Harbten sulha intikal iktisadiyatı"[28] (The economy of transition from war to peace) held that the controls so necessary in time of war should gradually give way to private initiative. Indeed, as Tekinalp perceived it in late 1917, in an article entitled "İktisadî inkılap"[29] (The economic revolution), the rapidly spreading individual initiatives were nothing less than a revolution in economic activity. This revolution, at least in the Ottoman context, he defined as "Kapitalizm devresi başlıyor"[30] (The capitalist era commences); his main evidence for this claim was the constant flow of local capital into many enterprises, large and small alike.

Obviously, not all of Tekinalp's economic writing was original. He had read a great number of foreign publications, which during the war were perforce mostly German ones. He acknowledges this debt frequently, telling his own readers about German economic theories, such as *Die neue Orientierung,*[31] which he rendered into Turkish as *Yeni istikamet.*[32] His own contribution, however, was an analysis of the Ottoman Empire's national economy and his well-considered suggestions for its development and improvement. Perhaps the most important of these was the concept of solidarity (*tesanütçülük*), about which he wrote a series of articles in 1918[33] in the Istanbul weekly *Yeni Mecmua*, edited by his mentor, Ziya Gökalp (who himself wrote on the subject in Tekinalp's journal *İktisadiyat Mecmuası*). Without attempting to decide which of the two originated the concept – it was very probably worked out between them – it suffices to say that Tekinalp rejected the idea of class-struggle and instead upheld socio-economic solidarity between professional groups, based upon reciprocal conciliation and aiming at national unity.[34] Much later, Tekinalp reverted to this topic in what may well have been his very last article, published in August 1959 and entitled "Ziya Gökalp'de tesânütçülük"[35] (Solidarity according to Ziya Gökalp), which appeared, appropriately enough, in a special issue of the Turkish Teachers Union's official organ, commemorating the thirty-fifth anniversary of Gökalp's death. In this essay, Tekinalp demonstrated the relevance of Gökalp's teachings for the advancement of social justice in Turkey.

Much of Tekinalp's writing during the First World War on the subject of national economy was influenced by his strongly patriotic views – truly an expression of what might be termed his own brand of 'economic nationalism.' This became all the more relevant in his study of Kemalism, which devoted a long chapter to etatism.[36] As already indicated by Dr. William Hale[37] and others, this was one of the most controversial principles of the Kemalist reforms; indeed, Tekinalp considered it the most contentious one, even for convinced Kemalists.[38] Tekinalp, a liberal generally tending to favour private initiative in economics,[39] had considerable difficulty in reconciling these views with state policy, particularly during the 1930s, when state controls and economic guidance were universally imposed. To justify this apparent contradiction, Tekinalp reminded his readers that the Republic of Turkey had inherited a lamentable economic situation from the Ottoman Empire:[40] agriculture was non-mechanised, the balance of trade was unfavourable, industry was nearly non-existent and commerce and finance were in the hands of foreigners. Under such conditions, free rein to individual activity would have resulted in handing over the whole economy to wealthier, more industrialised foreign powers. Mustafa Kemal and his collaborators knew well that only a collective enthusiasm, directed by the state, could bring about the required economic revolution in Turkey. Tekinalp then enumerated Kemalist achievements in the national economy: railways, savings accounts, national banks, sugar and textile plants, a stabilised currency and a favourable balance of payments. He argued that all the above, and most particularly progress in industry, could have been brought about only by state intervention and guidance of the national economy; he noted that agriculture had benefited as well. Etatism, moreover, was the only expedient adopted for accomplishing this goal rapidly.[41] Furthermore, measures were taken to encourage – under state guidance – private initiative,[42] wherever consonant with the interests of national economy. These were also safeguarded by state regulation of labour and relations between employers and workers, thus avoiding dangerous antagonisms.[43]

This apology of etatism does reveal some doubt on the part of a man whose ideological make-up had an evident component of liberal economic thinking. This was revealed in later years, when etatism ceased to be accepted unquestionably. After the Second World War, Tekinalp advocated a less authoritarian and more liberal type of etatism. Hè remained a loyal member of the People's Party and therefore had to watch his step. However, even members of the party began to speak of a mixed economy for Turkey – some combination of state guidance with individual initiative. Tekinalp's approach was that state supervision should continue wherever necessary, but those enterprises which had proven their economic viability should adopt the standards of private initiative; in other words, market economy should dictate all economic decisions and the state should adapt to it, rather than replace it. Tekinalp returned to these views in his frequent contributions to ***Türkiye İktisat Mecmuası***, between 1948 and 1956, as well as in articles published in other periodicals and newspapers.[44] One example is "Iktisadi demokrasiye doğru"[45] (Towards economic democray), in which he roundly attacked bureaucracy and plutocracy as sworn foes of national economic interests. Others include: "Mithat Pàşa ve millî iktisat"[46] (Midhat Pasha and national economy), in which he attempted to demonstrate Midhat's initiatives for the national economy of the Empire in instituting savings banks; "Türkiyenin iktisadî kalkınması"[47] (The economic progress of Turkey); or "Kemalizm ve devletçilik" (Kemalism and etatism).[48] In this work as in so many of Tekinalp's writings, the interests of national economy were given precedence.

One aspect of Tekinalp's writing on national economy was his constant reference to the individual, whom he always bore in mind when writing on more general issues. Tekinalp's partisanship for social reform was in accord with his affection for the poor. He may have been motivated by his own modest background, although it is no less likely that these views constituted yet another manifestation of his humanist and humanitarian approach.

It should be indicated, however, that Tekinalp's interest in social reform was merely secondary to his passionate advocacy of political achievement and economic progress. Indeed, the two topics were often considered jointly, as if their simultaneous application would bring about social improvement. Nevertheless, Tekinalp's favouring of the Empire's (then, Turkey's) national economy increased his concern for the poor, who constituted most of the population. During the First World War, for example, he frequently called for general measures by the authorities to halt rising prices, chiefly insofar as the basic commodities were involved; another remedy he suggested was the formation of consumers' cooperatives.[49] He returned to this same topic in a series of articles in *Tan*[50] in 1945 and, later, in *Türkiye İktisat Mecmuası*,[51] such as "İktisadi kalkınmamız ve sosyal tepkileri"[52] (Our economic progress and its social effects), in which he called public attention – and particularly that of Parliament – to the connection between economic development and social reform. Another article, "İnkılap rejimimiz ve sosyal inkılap"[53] (Our revolutionary regime and social revolution), appealed for rapid reform for Turkey's underprivileged. Consequently, it was hardly unexpected to find Tekinalp writing, in 1948, a detailed report entitled "Ucuz evler hakkında bir teklif"[54] (A proposal concerning inexpensive homes). The project emphasized its author's view that this was a necessary public service; Tekinalp's membership in Istanbul's Municipal Council at that time lent it additional relevance. It was characteristic of Tekinalp to work and write for causes of public significance. Hence it is hardly surprising that his analysis of Kemalist achievements rated measures which combat poverty among the most forceful and lasting accomplishments.[55]

9. TEKİNALP'S VISION OF CULTURE

A further area of great interest and concern to Tekinalp – in addition to politics and economics – was Turkish culture and history, the former primarily expressed in terms of language. Tekinalp himself was not too involved in *belles-lettres*; his closest approach to this genre is most probably the 1916 translations from Ottoman Turkish into German,[1] which show a remarkable sensitivity. In his youth, Tekinalp wrote an article in French on the Turkish theatre;[2] although his frequent reviews of "*Kitaplar ve mecmualar*" (books and magazines) in the *İktisadiyat Mecmuası*,[3] during the First World War, were usually devoted to works on politics and economics. Nevertheless, Tekinalp's writings more closely reflected his views on Turkish culture than did his day-to-day activities. As early as April 1911, he had attempted to establish an association in Salonica, called *Société de Culture Nationale*[4] or, in Turkish, *Millî hars birliği*.[5] It had only a very limited impact, however, as Tekinalp was more a man of the pen than of action.

In his younger days, Tekinalp participated heatedly in debates among Ottoman intellectuals regarding the Turkish language. Later on, he recalls clearly how revolted he was by language 'snobism'[6] as well as by the excessive use of Arabic and Persian words in Turkish.[7] He himself then supported preference for natural expression in simple Turkish, although not so exaggeratedly purified as to be vulgarly inadequate.[8] Tekinalp would have preferred Turkifying both Arabic and Persian words, simplifying syntax and adopting the language spoken in Istanbul.[9] In this respect, as acknowledged in another work,[10] he was at least partly influenced by Ziya Gökalp.

For Tekinalp, however, the public debate on the Turkish language was merely part of a larger one on the essence of Turkish culture.[11] Although he had previously touched on various aspects of this culture in his writings, it appears that the first detailed discussion constituted part of his analysis of Kemalism.[12] In keeping with his general approach to politics and economics, Tekinalp started from the premise that culture had a national basis.[13] He considered that 'the community of culture' represented the principal characteristic of nationality, as it was the basis for national solidarity. Following Gökalp, he called this national culture *hars*, defining its natural, popular and democratic character – a product of popular traditions and customs, literature, language, music, religion, morals, aesthetics and economy. Tekinalp went on to explain old Turkish *hars* as comprising the above components in a spirit of original and harmonious simplicity.[14]

He argued further that "culture is the product of history."[15] True to this conception, *Türk ruhu* – essentially an essay on Turkish history, old and new – constitutes an attempt to understand Turkish culture through the ages. Commencing with the assumption that the same essential spirit has motivated Turks from the most ancient times to our own days, he strove to identify the cultural milieu in which it was ever-present. This approach was evidently largely influenced by the official Kemalist view of history which, without any of Pan-Turkism's irredentist claims had still adopted a maximalist attitude and considered a number of peoples, throughout a long period of time, to be Turks.

Tekinalp adopted the above premise as a starting point for a lengthy exposition of his own conception of Turkish culture and history. In his opinion, although the Turks were mainly known abroad for their physical sturdiness, in reality their greatness was chiefly due to a spiritual strength based upon moral values.[16] This important aspect of Turkish history, he claimed, had been virtually neglected by European scholars; *Türk ruhu* was to fill some of this void. Tekinalp perceived four major stages in the crystallisation of the Turkish spirit: a. Ancestors (*atalar merhalesi*) starting in the Ural-Altay steppes and extending over a time period of thousands of years, with Mete and Atila as its great heroes. b. Islam (*İslamiyet merhalesi*): an era of eclipse in the ancestors' spirit, which was replaced by a synthetic one; the major figure of this stage was Namık Kemal. c. Constitution (*meşrutiyet devri*): from 1908 on, giving birth to modern Turkey; its most prominent personality was Ziya Gökalp. d. Kemalism, well represented by Mustafa Kemal and İsmet İnönü.[17] True to this approach, the book's cover featured photographs: Namık Kemal, Ziya Gökalp, Mustafa Kemal and İsmet İnönü.

Accordingly, Tekinalp considered all descendants of the original Central Asian Turkish tribes[18] to be Turks who had not lost the Turkish spirit. Again, his frame of reference is cultural rather than ethnic: Turks, Huns, Tatars and Mongols were all included. Assuming that nations differ from one another in their spiritual characteristics,[19] Tekinalp attempted to uncover those of the Turks. He maintained that nomads had spiritual qualities superior to those of sedentary groups; these virtues enabled them, as conquerors, to institute an exemplary system of government, later inherited by the Kemalists. Turkish determination during their equestrian period (*beygir devri*) was manifested in the resolute attempts of the Kemalists to introduce rapid modernisation in the industrial age.[20] The Turkish spirit bore the imprints of the pre-Islamic, Islamic and Western eras; the Kemalist revolution, according to Tekinalp, freed it from the vestiges of the Islamic era, restored the characteristics of the ancestors and directed it towards Western civilisation.[21]

As Tekinalp perceived it, one of the merits of Kemalism was its sponsorship and encouragement of research on the national spirit of the Turkish ancestors.[22] Tekinalp himself believed that much of their dynamism was inherited by the Turks who had ruled the Ottoman Empire and, later, by the creators of modern Turkey.[23] The hardship of steppe life imposed on the ancestors of contemporary Turks led to sentiments of solidarity and unity, discipline and order, adherence to rules for the public good, equality, respect for tradition, sharing, freedom of conscience, bravery, generosity and hospitality.[24] Contrasting these with the peculiarities of the 'synthetic spirit' introduced by Islam, he dismissed the latter in that Turks remained unaffected,[25] while several other nations were corrupted in spirit.[25] Indeed, the long existence of the Ottoman Empire may be explained by the ancestral spirit (*atalar ruhu*), which preserved it even while it was overshadowed by Islam,[27] an eclectic civilisation which is not in consonance with Turkish culture.[28] Turkish culture held its own against the Arab and Iranian;[29] it began to decline only after ties to the ancestral spirit had slackened.[30] During the era of the *Tanzimat*, Namık Kemal represented a return to this spirit and its renaissance.[31] Later, the Young Turks brought about a revolution; 'Young Turk' meant 'revolutionary,' indeed, as Tekinalp pointed out elsewhere;[32] but their revolution was hardly a spiritual one. Ziya Gökalp, a complex personality and a sponsor of several ideals, laid the foundation for impactful reawakening of the ancestral spirit during Turkey's War of Independence.[33]

As the 'synthetic spirit' had not disappeared in Turkey and was still encouraging the forces of evil, the Kemalist movement saw itself in perpetual revolution; the resuscitated ancestral spirit continued to predominate, so that the New Turk was essentially not very different from the ancient one.[34] Even the constitution of the Turkish Republic and the *yasa* laid down by Genghiz, Atila, Mete and others were drawn up along the same lines: the national tie was the strongest bond in all cases.[35] On this level and others, Mustafa Kemal and İnönü complemented one another; they were not only state leaders but spiritual guides as well, a contemporary manifestation of the ancestral spirit.[36] In conclusion, Tekinalp warned against an arbitrary return to the past, emphasising the dangers of individualism and appealing for a collective effort to graft Western civilisation unto Turkish culture, in keeping with the ancestral spirit.[37]

10. IN CONCLUSION

A careful examination of Tekinalp's career indicates the predominance of one overriding factor: an almost ceaseless effort to serve the common cause. In practical terms, he himself succeeded in attaining only modest positions, such as membership in the Salonica Provincial Council, the Istanbul Municipal Council and the boards of several scholarly and professional associations, of which the most notable was the *Tücar Derneği*. He did carry out these tasks with a considerable drive, zealously promoting Turkification of local Jews in both Salonica and Istanbul. In all these activities – and most particularly the last – he devoted himself to what he considered a service to the general public. Early in life, Tekinalp had written in his diary: "Je trouve qu'il faut travailler toujours pour le bien commun."[1] This evidently applied equally to his writings, for which he will very probably be best remembered. It seems that he initially regarded himself chiefly as spokesman of the Ottoman Empire – and later of Turkey – to the outside world. Later on, however, he appears to have adopted the view that the fate of the Turkish Republic would be decided ultimately within its own borders. Indeed, throughout all the years of the Republic he published only one book in France, and even this was a translation from Turkish. All his other books, as well as his numerous articles, were published in Turkey.

It should be re-emphasized that nearly all of Tekinalp's published works (as well as much of his manuscript diaries and letters), expressed his enthusiastic commitment to Turkish nationalism. His Jewishness, which he reasserted in his later years, always remained subordinate. Whether he edited periodicals or wrote himself on Ottomanism, Turkification, Pan-Turkism, Kemalism, national economy, or culture – and of course, whenever he dealt with nationalism – he was always the patriot, arguing for the national cause. Over the years, there were certain variations in his approach. In his youth, he conceived of the nation as an historic and emotional entity with which all Ottomans, then all Turks, had to identify. Although he would have unhesitatingly qualified himself as a hard-headed realist, his conception included a strong romantic streak, particularly during his Pan-Turk days. Romanticism, after all, is no stranger to the young. In later years, it was equally natural for him to adopt and support the *Realpolitik* nationalism of the Kemalists, with all their practical achievements.

What Tekinalp desired most was a powerful and modern Turkey – politically, economically, socially and culturally, based on a strong, united nation. While it is difficult to assess Tekinalp's precise impact towards achievement of the above, we may surmise that he did influence intellectuals and others amongst the reading public to some extent. Following Gökalp, he once defined a Turk as anyone who felt that he was one. If so, Moiz Cohen of Serres, *alias* Munis Tekinalp, certainly was one of the best of them.

MOÏSE COHEN, REFERAT ÜBER DIE EINWANDERUNG IN DIE TÜRKEI

Delegierter Moïse Cohen: Wir sind hier herzlich begrüsst worden, aber wir sind nicht gekommen, um Begrüssungen zu erhalten. Unsere junge Erfahrung in zionistischen Sachen verhindert uns, in die Debatte direkt einzugreifen. Wir sind gekommen, um Sympathie und Erklärungen gegenüber unserer Regierung und unserm Vaterlande zu provozieren. Glücklicherweise hat dies unser geehrter Präsident in seinem geschätzten Vortrage und auch andere Redner offenherzig getan. Man hat wiederholt gesagt, dass der Zionismus keinen politischen Zweck verfolgt. Diese Erklärung war für uns ottomanische Zionisten unbedingt notwendig, weil das ottomanische Gesetz national-politische Vereine nicht gestattet, und als ottomanische Patrioten sind wir gezwungen, national-politische Vereine energisch zu bekämpfen. Jetzt, meine geehrten Brüder, können wir kraft der ehrlichen Erklärung, die hier abgegeben wurde, ruhig weiter-arbeiten, nicht nur als Juden, sondern auch als echte ottomanische Patrioten; kraft dieser Erklärung können unsere Vereine seitens der Regierung anerkannt werden, und wir können dies als eines der besten Resultate dieses Kongresses betrachten. (Lebhafter Beifall und Händeklatschen). (Redner setzt seine Rede französisch fort[1]):

Geehrte Versammlung! Das unselige Gespenst des Despotismus ist in zu weite Ferne gerückt, als dass wir ottomanischen Staatsangehörigen es noch nötig hätten, eine furchtsame Zurückhaltung zu beobachten angesichts von Problemen, die unser Vaterland unmittelbar berühen. Es ist uns nicht länger gestattet, zu schweigen, wenn die Interessen der Türkei, unseres Vaterlandes, auf dem Spiele stehen.

Unter den verschiedenen Fragen, die gegenwärtig in der Presse und den leitenden politischen Kreisen unserer Heimat behandelt werden, gibt es eine, die die Aufmerksamkeit der ottomanischen Vaterlandsfreunde, insbesondere aber der ottomanischen Juden, sehr lebhaft in Anspruch nimmt. Sie ist für Tausende unglücklicher Juden von überaus grosser Wichtigkeit, und auch ihre Bedeutung für das ottomanische Reich darf nicht unterschätzt werden. Ich trete hier an diese Frage in meiner Doppeleigenschaft als ottomanischer Jude heran, an die Frage, die für die Juden der ganzen Welt recht einfach erscheint, die aber für die ottomanischen Juden überaus kompliziert ist; den wir müssen sie von zwei verschiedenen Gesichtspunkten aus betrachten vom ottomanischen und vom jüdischen Gesichtspunkte.

Die ottomanische Judenheit hatte sich hierüber schon längst geäussert und sich mit diesem Problem sehr eingehend befasst, wenn das neue Regime uns nicht in einem Zustande der vollendeten Desorganisation gefunden hätte. Ich erhebe also keinen Anspruch, ihnen hier ein Spiegelbild der öffentlichen Meinung der ottomanischen Judenheit zu geben, denn es gibt heute noch kein derartige öffentliche Meinung. Ich werde mich darauf beschränken, unsere persönliche Meinung auszusprechen, die von einem grossen Teil unserer Mitbürger geteilt wird.

Die Frage der Einwanderung von Juden in die Türkei wurde unmittelbar nach der Julirevolution aufs Tapet gebracht. Die Begeisterung und der Überschwang, die damals herrschten, die Freudenstimmung, in die wir durch unsere plötzliche Befreiung versetzt wurden, brachten es mit sich, dass wir die Hoffnung nährten, die konstitutionelle Türkei recht bald in ein gesichertes Asyl für unsere verfolgten Brüder verwandelt zu sehen. Die Türkei, das einzige Land, das von der Plage des Antisemitismus verschont geblieben ist, erschien uns als das neuzeitliche Kanaan, als das gelobte Land für die heutigen Israeliten, die die modernen Länder Mizraim, die Stätten der Knechtschaft und der Trübsal verlassen. Wir stellten uns vor, dass Tausende Juden kommen würden, um unsere Einöden in froher Arbeit mit dem Schweisse ihres Angesichts zu netzen, anstatt wie bisher die Steppen und Eiswüsten Sibiriens mit ihrem Blute zu tränken. Der Plan schien uns der Verwirklichung sehr nahe gerückt, auf dem geraden Wege der schönen Träume. Die Fieberstimmung und die naive Zuversicht jener Zeit der politischen Befreiung hinderte uns, die Wirklichkeit klar zu sehen. Später fingen wir an, die Vorteile und Nachteile einer Auswanderung der russischen, rumänischen und sonstigen Juden in die gastliche Türkei deutlicher zu unterscheiden. Gegenwärtig ist es sehr wohl möglich – obgleich die Lage in unserm Vaterlande noch wenig geklärt ist – an die Untersuchung dieses Problems mit einer gewissen kritischen Strenge heranzutreten; wir können mit einer genügenden Kenntnis der Bestandteile, aus denen es sich zusammensetzt, studieren.

Die legendäre Toleranz der Türken ist überall bekannt, sie ist zu einem Gemeinplatz geworden. Aus ihr schöpfe ich mein erstes und entscheidendstes Argument zugunsten der jüdischen Einwanderung in die Türkei. Jawohl, diese Toleranz der Osmanen und die festen Bande der Freundschaft zwischen den Muselmanen und den Juden bilden für unsere Auswanderer den verlockendsten Anreiz. Was veranlasst denn die Juden, ihr Geburtsland zu verlassen? Doch die Unduldsamkeit ihrer Bedrücker, die Geissel des Antisemitismus. Nun denn, da der Antisemitsmus und die Intoleranz bei uns unbekannt sind, können die Juden vertrauensvoll zu uns kommen in der sichern Erwartung, dass sie hier Ruhe finden werden. Die Türkei hat Beweise ihrer musterhaften Duldsamkeit selbst in den alten Zeiten, zur Zeit der allmächtigen Kalifen geliefert, die den Christen ausserordentliche Privilegien gewährten. Für die Juden war die Türkei mehr als tolerant; sie war ihr Schutzengel in den kritischen Zeiten unserer Geschichte, als der Geist der Inquisition, dessen Gifthauch ganz Europa erfüllte, Hunderttausende von Juden obdachlos machte.

In den christlichen Ländern, mag das gutmütigste Volk seine Sanftmut vergessen, wenn es sich um Juden handelt. Diese traurige Erfahrung haben wir im Verlaufe unserer Geschichte oft genug gemacht. Allein in den moslemischen Ländern, insbesondere in der Türkei, ist das Gegenteil der Fall. In der ganzen Christenheit sind die unwissenden Schichten der Bevölkerung allzu leicht geneigt, den Anstiftungen gewissenloser Judenfeinde Gehör zu geben, weil sie seit Jahrhunderten gewöhnt sind, in uns die Mörder des Stifters ihrer Religion zu sehen. Ein ebenso plumper und unsinniger Aberglaube hat die

Wahnvorstellung eines Ritualmordes erzeugt. Dem ungebildeten Mann aus dem Volke gilt der Jude noch heute häufig genug als der Mann, der die kleinen Kinder zu religiösen Zwecken tötet. Derartiges ist in den Ländern des Islam undenkbar. Hier hat man uns niemals beschuldigt, Mohammed gekreuzigt zu haben. Niemals wurde hier die wahnwitzige Beschuldigung ausgesprochen, dass das Blut der Moslems zur Erzeugung unserer Mazzoth dienen könne. Est is also unmöglich, dass sich in den Tiefen der moslemischen Volksseele die Keime eines Hasses gegen die Juden eingenistet hätten. Das antisemitische Gift findet hier keinen günstigen Nährboden.

Überdies gibt es mannigfache historische moralische und religiöse Bande, eine Verwandtschaft der Sitten und Bräuche zwischen den Juden und Türken, die uns vor dem Antisemitismus schützen. Dies wird durch zahlreiche Tatsachen bekräftigt, von denen ich nur eine anführe, die sich jüngst abgespielt hat, nämlich die wertvolle Hilfe, die die ausländischen Juden in Saloniki den Jungtürken in ihrem Kampfe gegen den Absolutismus angedeihen liessen. Ein albanesischer Geschichtsschreiber, der die Geschichte des Komitees "Einheit und Fortschritt" geschrieben hat, verzeichnet sehr eingehend die wirksame Mithilfe der fremden Israeliten in diesem Kampfe, die ja gar kein Interesse an der Befreiung der Türkei vom europäischen Joche hatten.

Nach Einführung der Verfassung begrüsste die ganze jüdische Welt mit grosser Freude den Anbruch der neuen Ära in der Türkei. Unsere moslemischen Mitbürger wissen sehr wohl, wie viele Juden aller Länder Turkophilen sind, genau wie auch wir wissen, wie viele Türken Philosemiten sind.

Allerdings, all dies ist recht schön in der Theorie. Wenn wir es aber in die Praxis umsetzen wollen, können wir Zweifel und Besorgnisse nicht unterdrücken. Und dann sehen wir kleine Wolken den Horizont unserer Zukunft verdunkeln. Fürwahr, das jüdische Volk wurde oft genug durch die bizarren Überraschungen des Antisemitismus enttäuscht. Unsere Feinde haben uns allzu oft selbst unsere Tugenden, die uns ihre Bewunderung und ihre Wertschätzung hätten zuziehen sollen, als Verbrechen angerechnet. Die Betriebsamkeit, die Intelligenz, die treue Anhänglichkeit an das Vaterland, die bei andern Völkern Ruhmestitel bilden, sind uns gegenüber Motive des Hasses und der Verachtung. Die dehnbare Moral gewisser Kreise verdammt die Vivisektion, duldet aber gleichmütig die Niedermetzelung Tausender von unschuldigen Juden. Der Entrüstungsschrei der zivilisierten Welt machte die Mächtigen zittern und stürzte Ministerien wegen der als ungerecht empfundenen Verurteilung eines Ferrer. Und diesselbe zivilisierte Welt bleibt unbeweglich angesichts der entsetzlichen Pogrome und der ungezählten Hekatomben, die der Judenhass alljährlich fordert. Alle Ungerechtigkeiten, alle Roheiten sind gerechtfertigt, wenn sie gegen menschliche Geschöpfe gerichtet sind, die den Namen Jude tragen. Wir machen ja oft genug die Wahrnehmung, dass unsere eignen Brüder die schrecklichsten Antisemiten sind. Welcher Nichtjude könnte uns also die Gewähr bieten, dass er dem Übel des Antisemitismus gegenüber gefeit sei? Gibt es nicht auch im Mond Antisemiten? fragte einst ein Humorist. Wie können wir nun eine grosse, jüdische Einwanderungsaktion unternehmen, sei es auch nach der Türkei? Wer kann uns dafür bürgen, dass unter den verschiedenen

Errungenschaften der Zivilisation, die die Türkei fortgesetzt aus Europa enführt, sich nicht auch die systematische Feindseligkeit gegen die Juden einschleichen wird, die von der europäischen Zivilisation unzertrennlich zu sein scheint? Zangwill stellt die Behauptung auf, dass der Antisemitismus der ständige Begleiter des Juden sei, dem Schatten vergleichbar, der einem überallhin folgt. In der Tat, sehen wir bereits in der Türkei Leute, die das Schreckbild einer "jüdischen Gefahr" zeichnen, die sie fern am Horizont als düstere Wolke heranziehen sehen. Und man appelliert bereits an die niedrigen Instinkte der Massen, um das Volk gegen die Ansiedlüng unserer Brüder aufzustacheln. Sollten wir für immer dazu verurteilt sein, auf völlige Ruhe und Sicherheit verzichten zu müssen und uns mit einer relativen Sicherheit zu begnügen? Unsere Vergangenheit und unsere Gegenwart scheinen dies zu bekräftigen. Es bleibt uns also nichts übrig, als uns jener relativen Sicherheit anzupassen. Dieser Grundsatz muss uns auch als Ausgangspunkt dienen bei der Untersuchung der Frage einer jüdischen Einwanderung in die Türkei.

Wenn also auch nicht anzunehmen ist, dass der Antisemitismus in unserm Lande stets unbekannt bleiben wird, so ist es doch ziemlich sicher, dass er niemals einen allgemeinen und dauerhaften Charakter wird erlangen können. Von Zeit zu Zeit wird er vielleicht in einzelnen Teilen des Reiches aufflammen, um alsbald wie ein Strohfeuer zu verglimmen. Wie ein hervorragender moderner Denker nachgewiesen hat, ist der Antisemitismus eine sehr natürliche psychologische Erscheinung; er ist die Reaktion der Mehrheit gegen die Minderheit, der sie alle Übelstände und alle Missetaten in die Schuhe schiebt. Wenn die jüdische Minorität in allen Ländern durch die blosse Tatsache ihrer zahlenmässigen Schwäche zu leiden hat, so fällt dies bei uns aus dem einfachen Grunde fort, weil es in der Türkei eine nationale Mehrheit nicht gibt. Zwanzig verschiedene Nationalitäten bewohnen das Reich. Keine erhebt sich durch ihre numerische Überlegenheit merklich über die andere. Die Reaktion der Majorität gegen eine Minorität ist also nicht zu befürchten. Das türkische oder, besser gesagt, moslemische Element, das als das beherrschende angesehen werden kann, ist von der antisemitischen Seuche ziemlich geschützt, da es sich im grossen und ganzen nicht mit dem Handel befasst. Seine Interessen kollidieren nirgends mit denen der Juden. Ausserdem gibt es, wie wir bereits ausgeführt haben, zahlreiche Berührungspunkte und verwandte Wesenszüge zwischen den Muselmanen und Israeliten. Nichts trennt sie feindlich; wohl aber gibt es eine Menge Dinge, die eine Annäherung zwischen ihnen bewirken und sie gegenseitig zu Brüdern und Gesinnungsgenossen machen. Sollten von Zeit zu Zeit in der Türkei wirtschaftliche Streitigkeiten ausbrechen und zu einem nationalen Kampfe ausarten, so werden sie niemals die Reaktion der Mehrheit gegen die Minderheit darstellen, vielmehr werden sie im Grunde stets reine wirtschaftliche Kämpfe bleiben und auf die politischen und gesellschaftlichen Beziehungen der einzelnen Völkerschaften keinen Einfluss ausüben. Im öffentlichen Leben und in der Gesellschaft wird der Jude, wenn ein Bevölkerungsteil gegen ihn mit den Waffen des Antisemitismus ankämpfen sollte, von den andern Nationalitäten, die seine Bundesgenossenschaft suchen, auf das nachdrücklichste in Schutz genommen werden. Auf diese Weise werden sich die Kämpfe mit gleichen Waffen, unter gleichen Bedingungen und bei gleichen Chancen abspielen; in jedem Falle aber wird die Regierung, die Staatsgewalt, die Allgemeinheit niemals antisemitisch sein.

Es gibt auch noch eine andere geheime Kraft, die eine eventuelle antisemitische Bewegung in der Türkei von vornherein zur Ohnmacht verurteilen würde. Und diese geheime Kraft ist nichts anderes als die jüdische Solidarität. Jawohl, eine grosse jüdische Siedelung in der Türkei kann eine defensive Kraft haben, wie sie anderswo nicht denkbar ist. In der Türkei wird der Jude in kultureller und moralischer Beziehung seinen nationalen Charakter stets rein erhalten, weil der Einwanderer bei uns keine höhere Kultur antrifft, die seinen Geist beherrschen und in ihren Bann zwingen könnte. Weder die albanesische noch die armenische Kultur z.B. werden den Juden zu assimilieren und ihm seinen jüdischen Charakter und sein jüdisches Geistesleben zu rauben vermögen. Die Juden, die nach Deutschland, England oder Frankreich auswandern, werden mit der Zeit in kultureller und moralischer Hinsicht zu Deutschen, Franzosen oder Engländern. Sie denken, empfinden und handeln als Deutsche, Franzosen oder Engländer, mit einem Worte, sie assimilieren sich völlig, verlieren ihren jüdischen Charakter und erregen sehr oft die Verachtung der wirklichen Autochthonen ihres Adoptivvaterlandes, die in diesen Juden, die sich ihres Ursprungs schämen, mit Recht Fremdlinge ohne Selbstachtung sehen, bereit, ihr eigenes Ich, ihre Persönlichkeit zu verleugnen und preiszugeben, ungeschickte und verächtliche Schüler, die sie sklavisch, oft in kleinlicher Weise nachahmen. Bei uns kann von alledem nicht die Rede sein. In unserm Lande wird der Jude, so sehr er seinem innersten Wesen nach ottomanischer Staatsbürger werden wird, niemals Veranlassung und Neigung haben, sich in kultureller Hinsicht zu hellenisieren. Er wird nicht leicht in Versuchung geraten, seine Nationalität gegen die arabische oder kurdische zu vertauschen. Er wird in nationaler Beziehung immer Jude bleiben.

In der Türkei hat man von alters her die nationale Kultur als eine geheiligte Sache angesehen. Sie galt hier immer als Privatsache, die den Staat nichts angeht. In den regierenden ottomanischen Kreisen weiss man sehr wohl, dass das Vaterland bei einer freien Entwicklung der nationalen Geisteskräfte der einzelnen Völkerschaften nur zu gewinnen hat, und dass das Reich, wenn die Juden in der Lage sein werden, sich frei zu entfalten, von ihrer Intelligenz, ihrem sittlichen Adel, ihrer treuen Anhänglichkeit und allen den vorzüglichen Eigenschaften, die den Schatz der jüdischen Volksseele ausmachen, den grössten Nutzen ziehen kann.

Wenn nun die jüdische Bevölkerung immer jüdisch bleiben wird, wenn die Assimilation ihr nichts anhaben kann, wenn sie nicht durch Parteiungen zerklüftet sein wird und die Bande der Brüderlichkeit in ihrer Mitte erhalten bleiben, kurz, wenn die jüdische Solidarität unverbrüchlich bestehen bleibt, wird der Antisemitismus zum Aussterben verurteilt sein. Und wenn es ein Land gibt, wo die jüdische Selbsthilfe nach dem Wunsche unseres verstorbenen Herzl wirksam sein wird, so ist dies die Türkei, denn die jüdischen Bewohner des türkischen Reichs können einen einheitlichen und unteilbaren Block bilden, der für das ganze jüdische Volk eine grosse moralische Stärkung bedeuten wird.

Dies hindert freilich nicht, dass der wahre, national selbst-bewusste Jude zu gleicher Zeit auch ein guter Ottomane sei, ein Ottomane in der vollen Bedeutung dieses Wortes. Der ruhelose, ewige Jude, der sich solange auf der Suche nach einem gastlichen Heim befindet, wird sicherlich, sobald er den belebenden Hauch der Freiheit einatmet, mit aller Kraft bestrebt sein, dieses Land zu seinem Vaterlande zu machen, den Boden, der ihn liebevoll aufnimmt, mit kindlicher Liebe zu umfassen. Die Geschichte aller Völker beweist, wie sehr der Jude zu allen Zeiten seinem Adoptivvaterlande treue Liebe und rührende Anhänglichkeit bewahrt hat. Gibt es ein Land auf dem weiten Erdenrunde, das nicht mit dem Blute jüdischer Vaterlandsfreunde getränkt wäre? Wurde jemals ein Kampf für die Güter der Zivilisation ausgefochten, zu dem die Juden nicht Mitkämpfer und Helden geliefert hätten? Um nur die allerjüngsten Begebenheiten anzuführen, so waren die Juden in der Türkei das einzige nicht moslemische Element, das sich mit den Jungtürken verband, um das hamidische Regiment, d.h. die Herrschaft des Terrors und der Tyrannei, zu bekämpfen. Es wäre ganz überflüssig, von den jüdischen Einwanderern erst zu fordern, dass sie gute ottomanische Vaterlandsfreunde werden sollten. Sie würden es ohne jede Aufforderung sein. Ohne die aufrichtige Ottomanisierung würde die ganze Einwanderungsbewegung im höchsten Grade sinnlos sein, da ja in diesem Falle der Jude, der sein Geburtsland verlässt, um eine neue Zufluchtsstätte zu finden, weiter ohne Vaterland bliebe und die Verleumdungen der Judenfeinde rechtfertigte, die uns als vaterlandslos verschreien.

Die zahllosen Anstrengungen und namenlosen Opfer, die die Wanderung der jüdischen Volksmassen im Gefolge haben, zielen ja bloss dahin, dem ewigen Juden endlich einen geschützten Erdenwinkel zu geben, auf dem er sich heimisch fühlen kann und wo er das Gefühl hat, dass ihn niemand als Fremden und Eindringling behandelt. Wie wäre es nun möglich, dieses Ziel in der Türkei zu erreichen, ohne die unmittelbare und aufrichtige Ottomanisierung der einwandernden Juden?

Meine Herren! Wenn ich bisher einige Vorbehalte machen musste, weil ich in meiner Eigenschaft als Jude zu Ihnen sprach, so ist ein Vorbehalt nicht angebracht, wenn man die Frage der jüdischen Einwanderung vom ottomanischen Gesichtspunkte prüft. Wenn ich in dieser Einwanderung den geringsten Nachteil für die Türkei erblicken könnte, so würde ich, der ich die Interessen meines Vaterlandes über alle andern Interessen setze, sprechen: Meine Brüder, ich nehme von ganzem Herzen Anteil an euren Schmerzen und will gern eure Bemühungen unterstützen, aber – kommt nicht zu uns. Lasst uns gemeinsam anderwärts eine Zuflucht für unsere bedrückten Volksgenossen suchen. Allein, dies ist durchaus nicht der Fall. Im Gegenteil, als Ottomane betrachte ich es als meine Pflicht, die Tausende meiner Brüder, die nichts anderes als eine ruhige Stätte für ihre friedliche Arbeit suchen, zur Einwanderung in mein Vaterland einzuladen. Unser so geräumiges und so fruchtbares Land braucht nichts als emsige Arbeiter, kraftvolle Arme, denen es die unermesslichen Schätze anvertrauen könnte, welche unser Boden in seinem Schosse birgt. Wir brauchen Millionen Einwanderer, um unsere unbevölkerten Gebiete zu besiedeln, unsere unbebauten Ländereien urbar zu machen. Die Juden sind für die Türkei das ideale Menschenmaterial. Im Gegensatz zu manchen andern Elementen sind sie fähig, sich von allen nationalen Vorurteilen frei zu machen, um treue Bürger, aufrichtige Patrioten zu werden. Sie können als Gegengewicht gegenüber gewissen Elementen der Zwietracht und des Umsturzes dienen, die bei uns um sich greifen. Kein anderes Volk wie das jüdische kann sich so leicht den Lebensbedingungen, den Empfindungen und Bestrebungen der wirklichen Ottomanen anpassen. Und die einwandernden Juden werden auch, indem sie das Land durch ihre Tätigkeit neu beleben, gleichzeitig die Saat des Fortschritts ausstreuen, getreu der zivilisatorischen Mission, die dem jüdischen Volke von alters her eigen ist.

Es ist möglich, dass diejenigen, die die jüdische Volksseele nicht kennen, von Unruhe erfüllt werden angesichts des Wiedererwachens unseres nationalen Bewusstseins, und dass sie den zukünftigen jüdischen Einwanderern separatistische Tendenzen zumuten. Alle diejeningen aber, die den wahren Charakter des Juden kennen, werden diese pessimistischen Befürchtungen in keiner Weise teilen. Die jüdische Brüderlichkeit hat den bürgerlichen Pflichten der Juden niemals Eintrag getan. Wäre dies der Fall, so müsste man alle deutschen, französischen und englischen Juden, die für die Leiden ihrer verfolgten Brüder warmes Mitgefühl hegen und nach Kräften beflissen sind, deren Los zu verbessern, als Verräter gegen ihr Vaterland ansehen, kraft der blossen Tatsache, dass sie die jüdische Solidarität pflegen, die jüdische Brüderlichkeit betätigen. Die Geschichte lehrt uns jedoch, dass die jüdische Solidarität von den Angehörigen des jüdischen Volkes niemals etwas anderes forderte, als die gegenseitige Beihilfe, um den zerstreuten Gliedern der Jacobsfamilie nach Möglichkeit ein ruhiges Dasein und Wohlergehen zu sichern. Der Jude, der ja allgemein als ein Mensch gilt, der sich von der Vernunft und den Realitäten des Lebens leiten lässt, dessen Denkart im höchsten Sinne praktisch ist, wird sich niemals blindlings einem überspannten Idealismus hingeben, der ihn bestimmen könnte, gegen diejenigen treulos zu handeln, die ihn aus dem Abgrund errettet haben; nie wird er fähig sein, das Land zu verraten, das ihn gastlich aufgenommen hat, um nachher den gierigen Wölfen, von denen er umgeben ist, anheimzufallen. Er wird sich wohl in acht nehmen, den gerechten Zorn und die verdiente Strafe seiner verratenen Freunde und selbst seiner eigenen Brüder zwecklos wachzurufen.

Abgesehen davon kann keine revolutionäre und meuterische Bewegung von einiger Bedeutung entstehen, wenn sie auswärts keinen Stützpunkt hat. Der jüdische Einwanderer im ottomanischen Reiche, der nach Jahrhunderten töricht genug sein wird, dem Phantom einer Unabhängigkeit nachzujagen und die Loslösung vom ottomanischen Staatsverbande anzustreben, wo wird er eine Stütze finden können? Etwa bei seinen Brüdern in England, Deutschland oder Frankreich, die nichts anderes sind als französische, englische oder deutsche Staatsbürger, und die die ersten sein werden, ein derart schmachvolles Verhalten zu verdammen? Nein, der Jude – mag das Land, das er bewohnt, Chaldäa, Judäa oder Türkei heissen – wünscht nichts anderes, als frei zu sein, frei in allen seinen Handlungen und Bewegungen und im Vollbesitze aller seiner Bürgerrechte, um seine sittlichen und geistigen Eigenschaften frei entfalten zu können. Diese Bürgerrechte sind ihm aber durch die Verfassung vollständig gewährleistet, und wenn sie jemals den Bürgern des türkischen Reiches vorenthalten werden sollten, so werden es nicht die Juden allein sein, die sich erheben werden, sondern alle Ottomanen ohne Unterschied der Rasse und des Glaubensbekenntnisses.

Es mag auch bei uns beschränkte und kurzsichtige Leute geben, die, durch das Gespenst der Konkurrenz auf dem Gebiete des Handels und der Volkswirtschaft erschreckt, sich einer jüdischen Einwanderung widersetzen werden, ohne Rücksicht auf die wahren Interessen des Vaterlandes. Allein die guten ottomanischen Patrioten werden sich durch solche nichtigen und kleinlichen Befürchtungen nicht beirren lassen, vielmehr werden sie die neuen Ankömmlinge mit offenen Armen aufnehmen, die berufen sind, das türkische Land durch ihre emsige Arbeit fruchtbar zu machen. Die wirklichen Jungtürken, vorausgesetzt, dass sie über unsere Aspirationen richtig informiert sind, werden uns ihre Mithilfe nicht versagen. Frei von allen Vorurteilen, beseelt vom Geiste der Duldsamkeit, ehrlich bekümmert um das Gedeihen des von ihnen wiedereroberten Landes, werden sie in jedem Juden, der ihre Gastfreundschaft in Anspruch nimmt, ein Element des Reichtums, einen tätigen Sendboten der Zivilisation erblicken.

Die Interessen der jungen Türkei befinden sich also in völligem Einklang mit denen der Juden. Die Türkei kann in den Juden dasjenige finden, was sie am meisten nötig hat, nämlich betriebsame, intelligente, friedfertige Einwanderer, die über zahlreiche Hilfsquellen verfügen. Anderseits können auch die Juden in der Türkei finden, was sie so lange suchen: ein gastliches, unbebautes Land, wo sie vor dem Antisemitismus geborgen sind.

Besonders hervorgehoben zu werden verdient noch der Umstand, dass eine Interessengemeinschaft zwischen dem jüdischen Volke und dem türkischen Reiche nicht bloss im Prinzip, sondern auch in der Praxis, in der Art der Verwirklichung dieses Prinzips besteht. Es entspricht den Interessen der gegenwärtigen Bewohner der Türkei, dass die jüdische Einwanderung keineswegs eine sporadische sei, sondern sich in einem oder mehreren Gebieten konzentriere. Denn die Argumente derjenigen Partei in der moslemischen Presse, die sich gegen die Einwanderung ausspricht, lassen sich in folgenden Worten zusammenfassen: Die Juden sind auf dem Gebiete des Handels äusserst gewandt, sie sind imstande, den ganzen Handel und die ganze Industrie den Händen der eingeborenen Bevölkerung zu entreissen. Ihr geistiges Niveau ist viel höher als das der gegenwärtigen Bewohner. Es wird ihnen ein leichtes sein, das ganze Kapital an sich zu reissen und die Herren des Landes zu werden.

Wenn man diesen Ultrapatrioten begreiflich machen wird, dass die jüdischen Einwanderer sich auf unbebauten und unbevölkerten Landstrichen ansässig machen können, dass sie geschlossene Gruppen bilden sollen, die in keinen unmittelbaren wirtschaftlichen Beziehungen zu den Eingeborenen stehen, so werden sie, wenn sie ehrlich sind, ihre Gegnerschaft aufgeben und uns zurufen: "Bouyoursounlar" (Willkommen!), um mich des bekannten Ausdrucks zu bedienen, der die moslemische Gastfreundlichkeit kennzeichnet.

In der Tat kann eine sporadische Einwanderung für die Juden von keinerlei Nutzen sein; im Gegenteil, sie wäre geeignet, Antisemitismus zu züchten. Wenn wir jüdische Einwanderer ins Land ziehen wollen, so können wir nichts anderes tun, als das System der Kolonisation, das bisher in Palästina angewandt wurde, weiter auszubauen. Es gibt bei uns unzählige fruchtbare Gebiete von grosser Ausdehnung, wo zahlreiche jüdische

Städte, umgeben von jüdischen Dörfern, erstehen könnten. Im Bereiche dieser Ansiedlungen wird der Antisemitismus sich unmöglich entwickeln können, aus dem einfachen Grunde, weil es hier nur Semiten geben wird. Keiner wird den Juden ihr Wohlergehen missgönnen oder sich in seinen Interessen durch die Tätigkeit und die Fähigkeiten unserer Brüder verletzt fühlen. Im Gegenteil, jeder wird sie bewundern und sich bestreben, von dem guten Beispiel, das sie darbieten, zu profitieren. Die ottomanischen Vaterlandsfreunde, die in den Einöden plötzlich Städte voll Leben und Glanz auftauchen sehen werden, ausgestattet mit dem ganzen Rüstzeug der modernen Zivilisation, werden sich zu einer so guten Nachbarschaft beglückwünschen, die einen wirksamen Anreiz zum Fortschritt für sie bilden und ihnen den besten Weg dazu zeigen wird.

Wenn die Ottomanen im allgemeinen durch das frische Blut, das der jungen, freien und konstitutionellen Türkei auf diese Weise zuströmen wird, nur zu gewinnen haben werden, so werden die ottomanischen Juden sich ganz besonders glücklich schätzen, den Nutzen zu beobachten, den ihr Vaterland aus den Fähigkeiten ihrer Stammesbrüder zieht, die aus den Ländern der Bedrückung gekommen sind und nunmehr die Gastfreundschaft, die sie bei den Ottomanen gefunden haben, durch ihre segensreiche Regsamkeit vergelten. Sie werden hocherfreut sein, zu sehen, wie ihre Volksgenossen die moralische Kraft und das Ansehen des jüdischen Bevölkerungselement im türkischen Reich heben.

Es bliebe nur noch zu prüfen, auf welche Weise die Aktion einer methodischen Einwanderung zur Durchführung gelangen kann. Dies ist die heikelste Frage, von deren Lösung der Erfolg des ganzen Unternehmens abhängt. Man könnte auf gut Glück einzelne Vilajets anführen, in denen die Errichtung städtischer oder ländlicher Ansiedlungen am leichtesten zu bewerkstelligen wäre. Es ist jedoch nicht meine Sache, auf diesen Punkt näher einzugehen, der ein gründliches Studium erfordert, welches lediglich durch eine wissenschaftliche Kommission angestellt werden kann, die die fraglichen Gebiete mit aller erforderlichen Sorgfalt zu erforschen hätte.

Geehrte Versammlung! Das Werk, das der Zionismus, diese ideale Bewegung, die Tausenden unserer verfolgten Brüder Trost und Hoffnung spendet, bisher vollbracht hat, kann nur als ein bescheidener Anfang angesehen werden. Wir wünschen aus ganzem Herzen, dass die notwendige Einheit zwischen der zionistischen Organisation, die das jüdische Volk repräsentiert, und allen andern europäischen und amerikanischen Institutionen, die speziell die jüdische Finanzmacht vertreten, sich auf diesem Boden vollziehen möchte. Und wenn der Zionismus sich erst der Mithilfe aller grossen jüdischen Organisationen versichert hat, wird sich die jüdische Einwanderung auf diejenigen Teile des ottomanischen Reichs konzentrieren können, die, wie Palästina, die vorteilhaftesten Bedingungen bieten. Es muss jedoch betont werden, dass die Pläne sich nicht von heute auf morgen verwirklichen lassen, während die Notstände des jüdischen Volks sich von Tag zu Tag häufen. Es gibt unter unsern Brüdern unglückliche Entwurzelte, die sich verzweifelt auf jedes neu ankommende Schiff stürzen, ohne zu wissen, wohin sie gehen und was sie beginnen sollten. Für diese ist die sporadische Einwanderung eine Wohltat. Aber auch andere Kategorien von Einwanderern könnte die junge Türkei schon jetzt heranziehen.

Sie könnte die jüdischen Künstler, Ingenieure, Gelehrten und sonstige Intellektuelle ins Land ziehen, Elemente, an denen wir jetzt noch grossen Mangel leiden. Für diesen Zweck wäre natürlich die Schaffung einer grossen Organisation auf gesunden Grundlagen erforderlich. Zunächst wären überall eigene Lokalkomitees einzusetzen, die den Interessenten die nötigen Auskünfte zu erteilen hätten. Durch eine solche Einwanderung würde die gegenwärtige jüdische Bevölkerung in der Türkei in ihrer Position gefestigt, und sie würde dann sicherlich freudig mitarbeiten, um das Ideal eines jüdischen Kulturzentrums, wie es der Zionismus anstrebt, zu verwirklichen.

Was uns türkische Juden betrifft, so möchten wir in unserer glühenden Liebe zu unserem Vaterlande nur die Worte des Sultans Bajazed II, die er an die aus Spanien vertriebenen Juden gerichtet hat, mit einigen Änderungen wiederholen: Kommt, Brüder, ihr werdet vielleicht die undankbaren Länder, die euch zur Flucht gezwungen haben, durch euren Wegzug arm machen, ihr werdet aber das schöne und edle ottomanische Land bereichern. Kommt, und als gute Juden wollen wir auch die Einladung wiederholen, die die jüdische Gemeinde von Saloniki im XVI. Jahrhundert an die Israeliten der Provence und Isaak Sarfati im XV. Jahrhundert an die deutschen Juden ergehen liess: באו אחי, באו רעי Kommt, Brüder, kommt nach der Türkei. Hier lebt ein jeder von uns ruhig איש תחת גפנו ותחת תאנתו unter dem Schatten seines Weinstocks und seines Feigenbaums, ohne dass irgendeiner uns in unserer friedlichen Entwicklung stören würde. Kommt zu uns, um in diesem fruchtbaren — und wir am Anfange des zwanzigsten Jahrhunderts fügen hinzu: — in diesem freien Lande in Ruhe und Sicherheit zu leben. (Lebhafter, sich immer wieder erneuernder Beifall und Händeklatschen).

Stenographisches Protokoll der Verhandlungen des IX. Zionisten-Kongresses in Hamburg, pp. 267-278

אונה איקספליקאסייון

אונוראב׳לי סי׳ רידאקטור

אין ב׳ואיסטרו נומירו די איייר, אזיינדו איל קואינטו רינדידו די מי קונפ׳ירינסייה די שבת, ב׳וס דישיטיש, פור יירו, קי יו פרוב׳י קי איל ציוניסמו איס קונטראריו אל מואיסטרוס אינטיריסיס די אוטומאנוס, מיינטריס קי יו נון אבורדי דיל טודו לה קיסטייון ציוניסטה; ב׳ואיסטרו יירו פואידי סירב׳יר די פריטיקסטו אה אלגונוס ג׳ורנאליס ציוניסטאס פור אקודרארליס מי אטיטוד פאב׳וריב׳לי אל ציוניסמו די אטראס סירקה און אנייו. איס פור איסטו קי ב׳ייו איל מיניסטיר די דאר אונה איקספליקה ביין ניטה אי פראנקה.

טודוס ייה סאב׳ין קי מיינטריס און סיירטו טיימפו ייו מי קריאי ציוניסטה, מי דיקלארי אי אזיי קומו טאל, מה קומו מיס איסקריטוס, מיס נומירוזוס ארטיקולוס אין לוס ג׳ורנאליס טורקוס, מי פולימיקה קון איבראהים ניפ׳איק ביי אין איל טאסב׳יר-איפ׳קייאר, מי קונפ׳ירינסייה אין איל קונגריסו די האמבורג לו פרואב׳אן, יו קונסידירי סיימפרי איל ציוניסמו קומו און מוב׳ימיינטו די אימיגראסייון ג׳ודיאה אין טורקיאה אי די פרופ׳ידינסייה אין פאליסטינה, קומו פודיינדו סירב׳יר אונה ב׳ייזה פארה אטראקסייון איספיסיפ׳יקה פור לוס ג׳ודייוס.

אין קולאבוראסייון קון אוטרוס די מיס אמיגוס אי קולינגאס — קי אב׳אנסאב׳אן איגואלמינטי איל ציוניסמו — איל אב׳ורימוס אונה פ׳ורמולה ספיסייאל פור סירב׳יר די באזה אה לוס ג׳ודייוס אוטומאנוס. סיגון איסטה פ׳ורמולה אפרוב׳אדה פור אלגונוס קאפוס ציוניסטאס, איל ציוניסמו סיריאה און מוב׳ימיינטו די אימיגראסייון ג׳ודיאה אין טורקיאה קון סינטרו קולטורל אין פאליסטינה. מואיסטרוס קומבאטימוס סיימפרי קון אינירג׳יאה איל פרוגראם די באזל, מה מוס אסיגוראראן קי אין איל קונגריסו די האמבורג איסטה סיר מודיפ׳יקאדו אי נון סי איסטה אב׳לאר מאס די «קריאר אין פאליסטינה אונה פאטרייה ג׳ודיאה גאראנטידה פור איל דירישו פוב׳ליקו».

איס קון איסטה איספירנסה קי יו פ׳וי אל קונגריסו די האמבורג, אי די אונה קונפ׳ירינסייה דוקומינטאדה סוב׳רי לה אימיגראסייון ג׳ודיאה אין טורקיאה אי דימאנדי קי איל ציוניסמו סי מיטייה די אקודרו קון לאס אוטראס אוב׳ראס די אימיגראסייון ג׳ודיאס פור אורגאניזאר און פלאנו די אימיגראסייון אין טודה לה טורקיאה.

קואנדו איל קונגריסו די האמבורג דיקלארו איל פרוגראם די באזל קומו סאנטו אי אינאטאקאב׳לי, קואנדו מי רינדי אינזאקטאמינטי קואינטו די לאס ב׳יראס אספיראסייונים דיל ציוניסמו, יו דיקלארי אאיי מיזמו, אנטי קאפוס, קי נון טיניאה מאס קי איר קון לה אורגאניזאסייון ציוניסטה, אונו די איילייוס, קונוסידו פור איל פוב׳ליקו די סאלוניקו מי ריספונדייו קי יו נון פ׳וי נונקה ציוניסטה. סוב׳רי איסטו יו אב׳אנדוני איל קונגריסו אנטיס קי סי סיראדה.

ריאלמינטי דונקי קי סיגון לוס ציוניסטאס יו נון פ׳וי נונקה ציוניסטה; סיגון מי, יו פ׳וי, סו אי סירי סיימפרי ציוניסטה, קירי דיזיר פארטיזאנטי די אונה גראנדי אימיגראסייון ג׳ודיאה אין טורקיאה; אין מיס ארטיקולוס פוב׳ליקאדוס אין איל טאסב׳יר-איפ׳קייאר, אין איל זמאן אי אין

איל ייני אסיר איג׳, יו פאב׳וריזי סיימפרי קון מוג׳ה אינסיסטינסייה איסטה אימיגראסייון אל פונטו די ב׳יסטה אוטומאנו אנסי ביין קי אל פונטו די ב׳יסטה ג׳ודייו, סיינדו קונב׳ינסידו קי איסטה אימיגראסייון פואידי קונטריבואיר מוי מוג׳ו אל רילאב׳אמיינטו די מואיסטרו פאיז אי אה אסיגוראר איל ריפוזו די מיליס די מואיסטרוס דיסגראסייאדוס קוריליג׳ונאריוס. יו קונטינואארי סיימפרי מיס פוב׳ליקאסייונים אין לה פריסה טורקה אי ג׳ודיאה אין פאב׳ור די איסטה אימיגראסייון.

איסטו ביין סיגורו קי לוס ציוניסטאס די בואינה פ׳יי קון לוס קואלוס איסטוב׳י אין קונטאקטו אי קונוסידאן מיס אידיאס נון מאנקאראן די קונפ׳ירמאר לו קי ב׳ינגו די אב׳לאר.

מואיז כהן
אבוקאטו

SOME MANUSCRIPT LETTERS[1]

I

MOÏSE COHEN
Avocat
Représentant de
"l'Union Commerciale"
SALONIQUE

Salonique, le 26 Décembre 1910

Honorable et cher collègue,

J'ai communiqué à mes collègues du Cercle des Intimes le contenu de votre honorée du 15 ct. et de celle de l'illustre fondateur de l'"ITO."[2]

Comme Monsieur Zangwill vous fait très bien remarquer nous pensons qu'il est très difficile de s'entendre de loin sur la ligne de conduite à adopter pour mener notre entreprise et nous voyons la necessité d'une rencontre pour pouvoir échanger des idées verbalement. Cependant pour des raisons de tact nous avons cru inopportun d'entamer dès maintenant de pourparlers avec le comité Union & Progrès sur les divers points envisagés dans la lettre de Mr. Zangwill. Nous avons voulu néanmoins avoir avec eux une entrevue sur la question de l'immigration juive en général et à cet effet une délégation de notre Cercle[3] s'est rendue au Bureau du Comité Central et s'est entretenue longuement avec ses représentants. Voici quelques conclusions retirées de cet entretien:

1) Le Comité Central est en principe très favorable à l'immigration juive, qu'il croit très avantageuse pour le Pays au point de vue tant moral que matériel. Les membres du Comité Central Union & Progrès sont persuadés qu'en facilitant d'une façon générale l'établissement dans l'empire de l'élément israélite, le pays aurait des avantages considérables et la Turquie gagnerait aussi les sympathies de tous les juifs de l'occident qui, déclarent-ils, ont une très grande influence dans la presse, les finances et dans toutes les branches de la vie publique en Europe et en Amérique.

2) Le Comité serait disposé à applanir toutes les difficultés d'ordre politique, administratif, etc.

3) On reconnait sans aucune réserve que le juif est un élément de prosperité, de paix et de tranquillité, qu'il s'assimile facilement, et que le pays ne pourrait que profiter de son énergie, de son intelligence et de toutes les qualités dont il est doué.

4) Il constate avec regret que ces derniers temps le mouvement sioniste a produit parmi les dirigeants et dans l'opinion publique musulmane une certain malaise et quelque méfiance envers l'élément israélite. Le mouvement sioniste est en effet considéré comme un mouvement politique national juif lequel ajouté aux questions déjà existentes provoquées par les bulgares, les serbes, les grecs, les albanais, les arabes, les druses, etc. contribuerait sensiblement à l'affaiblissement de la Jeune-Turquie.

5) Vu la recrudescence de cette méfiance et la surexitation qui règne actuellement dans l'opinion publique à cause de l'attendue crise ministérielle et les derniers débats sensationnels au parlement il serait dangereux d'en parler publiquement dans les circonstances actuelles.

6) D'après le Comité Union & Progrès aux immigrés israélites on pourrait affecter les régions du Vardar, Cassandra ou de Catérine, en organisant la Colonisation de façon à s'établir en même temps des israélites et des musulmans qui se partageraient les champs. Les musulmans serviraient aussi de protecteurs des israélites dans les cas d'attaques éventuelles de la part des bandes grecques ou bulgares.

D'accord avec le Comité nous avons arrêtés certaines mesures très efficaces pour réagir contre les conséquences néfastes du mouvement sioniste en nous promettant réciproquement de nous rencontrer bientôt pour entamer des pourparlers plus positifs sur la question qui nous intéresse.

Je tiens en attendant à vous assurer que le Comité du Cercle des Intimes a pris cette question en sérieuse considération et étant donnée son influence auprès des sphères officielles on pourra s'attendre à des résultats favorables.

Vous pourrez répondre à Mr. Zangwill que nous sommes parfaitement de son avis pour nous rencontrer et nous entretenir verbalement de la question et que nous tâcherons de fixer un rendez-vous quand nous aurons déjà de bases plus solides pour la réalisation de notre projet.

En transmettant les détails que je vous communique à Mr. Zangwill vous pourriez lui assurer que le Cercle des Intimes de Salonique est à son entière disposition et prêt à lui prêter tout son concours dans n'importe quelle circonstance.

Dans l'attente de vous lire bientôt, agréez cher et honorable collègue, avec l'expression des meilleurs sentiments du Cercle des Intimes l'assurance de ma haute considération.

Dr. M. Cohen

II

MOÏSE COHEN
Avocat
Représentant de
"l'UNION COMMERCIALE"
SALONIQUE

Salonique, le 23 Janvier 1911

Très honorable collègue,

J'ai reçu votre honorée du 17 ct. et pris note de son contenu.

Mes collègues du Comité du Cercle des Intimes et moi sommes parfaitement d'accord avec vous que l'appréhension du fantôme sioniste ne doit pas empêcher les dirigeants de la Jeune Turquie de favoriser l'immigration juive et qu'au contraire notre entreprise peut servir aussi à contrebalancer et contrecarrer la propagande sioniste si redoutée par les Jeunes Turcs. Mais malheureusement certains dirigeants de la Jeune Turquie s'exagèrent l'influence et l'importance du mouvement sioniste le confondant avec la question d'immigration juive en général. Nous ferons tout notre possible pour fair disparaître ces malentendus très regrettables.

Pour avancer plus vite dans notre entreprise tout en continuant nos rapports avec le Comité Central de Salonique nous pensons envoyer aussi une délégation à Constantinople pour s'entretenir avec les chefs du parti unioniste parlementaire et avec quelques membres du Cabinet que nous connaissons personnellement. Dans notre séance de ce soir nous prendrons les décisions nécessaires à ce sujet et je ne manquerai pas de vous informer au plutôt.

En attendant veuillez bien cher collègue nous expliquer d'une façon plus détaillée la phrase suivante de la lettre de Monsieur Zangwill: "Das von der Türkei uns zu gewährende Minimum müsste jedenfalls eine separate Vormundschaft und Vertretung jüdischen Rassen Interessen einschliessen".

Qu'est ce que Mr. Zangwill entend par "représentation" des intérêts juifs? En qui consisterait cette représentation? Entend-il obtenir du Gouvernement constitutionnel ottoman de privilèges et concessions de caractères politiques? Il est vrai que comme je vous l'ai déjà écrit, avant d'avoir une entrevue avec Mr. Zangwill nous ne nous occuperons pas des détails, mais ici il s'agit d'une question de principe sur laquelle il convient de s'entendre avant tout. Nous connaissons bien les idées de Mr. Zangwill concernant le Territorialisme, mais nous supposons qu'il ne s'agit pas de leur application en Turquie.

Tout en poursuivant un échange de vues sur les principes qui serviront de base à l'immigration nous continuerons nos démarches auprès des dirigeants, sans nous occuper, pour le moment, des principes et de détails. Demain ou après demain je vous communiquerai les résultats de notre séance de ce soir et les dispositions que nous prendrons à cet effet.

Agréez cher et très honorable collègue mes plus sincères salutations confraternelles.

Votre devoué collègue

M. COHEN

III

Moïse Cohen
Avocat
Représentant de
"L'UNION COMMERCIALE"
SALONIQUE

Salonique, le 3 Février 1911

Très honorable et cher Collègue,

J'ai reçu votre honorée du 27 de l'écoulé. Vous voulez avoir encore un petit succès. Je suis sûr cher Collègue que grâce au dévouement et aux nobles sentiments qui vous caractérisent, vous aurez encore d'autres succès très importants qui viendront se joindre aux innombrables bienfaits dont votre vie est remplie.

Nous ne manquons pas de nous occuper sérieusement de la question que vous avez bien voulu nous confier. Le représentant du Comité Union & Progrès croit toujours le moment inopportun de soulever maintenant la question pour des raisons et circonstances d'ordres intérieurs.

D'autre part, nous avons appris qu'une loi sur l'immigration en général a été déjà transmise au Parlement. Nous pensons qu'il est indispensable d'envoyer une délégation à Constantinople, mais nous ne pourrons pas le faire avant que la température commence par s'adoucir. Entretemps, nous pourrons avoir la réponse de notre ami M. Zangwill.

Au plaisir de vous lire, agréez, cher Collègue, mes plus sincères salutations confraternelles.

M. Cohen

IV

Uebersetzung des Briefes Moise Cohen, Salonique

Lieber und sehr geehrter Herr Kollege!

Ich habe ihr Geehrte vom 7. ds. erhalten, welches Sie mir trotz Ihrer Unpässlichkeit geschrieben haben und ersehe darin wieder einen Beweis Ihrer Hingabe und Anhänglichkeit an unsere Sache. Ich hoffe dass Sie bereits wieder hergestellt sind.

Die im Briefe des Herrn Zangwill enthaltene Erklärung war zur Feststellung der Natur unseres Unternehmens notwendig.

Es erübrigt, Ihnen über das Resultat der zu unternehmenden neuen Schritte Bericht zu erstatten.

Eine Delegation ad hoc unserer Clubs hat sich vergangenen Samstag zum Sitz des Comités Central Union & Progrès begeben um mit dem General-Sekretär, S.E. Hadji Adil Bey, den man die Seele des Comités nennen kann, Rücksprache zu nehmen.

Hadji Adil Bey, sowie eine anderen Kollegen glaubt, dass der Augenblick nicht günstig gewählt sei, um der fraglichen Sache auf den Grund zu gehen und zwar in Anbetracht des Misstrauen und Verdachtes des türkischen Volkes gegen den Zionismus, welcher stets mit der allgemeinen Auswanderung verwechselt wird.

Die ministerielle Krise, die Frage des Yemen, sowie viele andere ernstliche Ereignisse gestatten übrigens unseren Führern nicht, die Angelegenheit in Erwägung zu ziehen.

Ein anderes Mitglied unseres Comités war übrigens letzthin vorübergehend in Konstantinopel und nahm diese Gelegenheit wahr, um diesbezgl. mit S.E. Halil Bey, den Präsidenten der Partei Union & Progrès in der Deputierten-Kammer und kürzlich ernannten Minister des Inneren über diese Angelegenheit Rücksprache zu pflegen. Halil Bey erblickt in jedem fremden Juden einen Zionisten d.i. einen Separatisten. Auf jeden Fall lagen sich Halil Bey und Hadji Adil Bey über die Wichtigkeit der Sache Rechenschaft ab und sind derselben im Prinzipe günstig gestimmt.

In Anbetracht der gegenwärtigen Umstände, der Nervosität, sowie des allgemeinen Pessimismus unserer Führer glauben wir, dass es nicht angebracht wäre, im gegebenen Augenblicke die Frage der Auswanderung zu diskutieren; dies könnte im Laufe einiger Monate, wenn die allgemeine Situation sich geändert haben wird, geschehen. Wenn es sich schliesslich nur darum handeln würde, einige einzige Kolonie zu gründen, indem man einige Dutzend Auswandererfamilien aus Rumänien kommen liess, so wäre der gegenwärtige Zeitpunkt viel günstiger. In diesem Falle würde die Sache nicht das Gepräge einer politischen Affaire haben.

Wir bitten Sie also, uns die nötigen Verhaltungsmassregeln in dieser Sache zu geben, sowie Ihre Ansicht über die Anzahl der Familien, die finanziellen Verhältnisse etc. damit wir uns mit dem massgebenden Personen ins Einvernehmen setzen und Ihnen einen detaillierten Vorschlag unterbreiten können. Indem wir auf diese Weise kleinweise anfangen, so ist es sehr wohl möglich, dass wir gleich jetzt die Unterstützung der Regierung erlangen. Die Verhältnisse werden sich unterdessen ändern, die Nervosität und allgemeine Aenglichkeit wird verschwinden und man könnte sich über die allgemeine und eigentliche Frage der Auswanderung verständigen.

Für die Gründung einer einzigen Kolonie hätte uns die Regierung keine Bedingungen aufzuerlegen. Wir würden im Gegenteil bestrebt sein, uns deren Hilfe und Unterstützung zu versichern.

Ihrer geschätzten Nachrichten gerne entgegensehend, zeichne ich, werter Kollege, mit aufrichtigen und kollegialen Grüssen

m.p. M. Cohen

CZA, A 36/64

موئز قوهن
دعوى وكيلى
هئت متحدهٔ تجاريه وكيل عموميسى
سلانيك

Moïse Cohen
Avocat
Représentant de
"L'UNION COMMERCIALE"
SALONIQUE

Salonique le 3 Février 1911 191

Très honorable & cher Collègue,

J'ai reçu votre honorée du 27 de l'écoulé.- Vous voulez avoir encore un petit succès.- Je suis sûr cher Collègue que grâce au dévouement & aux nobles sentiments qui vous caractérisent, vous aurez encore d'autres succès très importants qui viendront se joindr aux innombrables bienfaits dont v/ vie est remplie.-

Nous ne manquons pas de nous occuper sérieusement de la question que vous avez bien voulu nous confier.- Le représentant du Comité U.&P. croit toujours le moment inopportun de soulever mainten ant la question pour des raisons & circonstances d'ordres intérieurs

D'autre part, nous avons appris qu'une loi sur l'immigrati en general a été déja transmise au Parlement.- nous pensons qui'il est indispensable d'envoyer une délégation à Constantinople, mais, nous ne pourrons pas le faire avant que la température commence par s'adoucir .- Entretempts, nous pourrons avoir la réponse de n/ ami M. I. ZANGWIL.-

AU plaisir de vous lire, agréez, cher Collègue, mes plus sincères salutations confraternelles.-

M. Cohen

P. RISAL, LES TURCS A LA RECHERCHE D'UNE ÂME NATIONALE

I

Dans l'immense empire des Turcs osmanlis, l'éternel négligé est le prétendu dominateur. Il existe une littérature abondante sur les Grecs et les Bulgares de Thrace et de Macédoine, sur les Arméniens, les Albanais, etc.; mais l'on a fort peu écrit sur les Turcs, leur vie sociale, leurs tendances, leur activité économique et mentale. Des publications multiples, des sociétés, des congrès défendent les nationalités vivant sous le sceptre d'Osman, revendiquent leurs droits méconnus, protestent contre les exactions, les oppressions auxquelles, hélas! elles n'ont que trop souvent été en butte. Mais qui donc a élevé la voix en faveur de cette sempiternelle victime, de ce serf taillable et corvéable à merci, le paysan turc?

Une population d'origine turcomane, probe, patiente, dure à la tâche, resignée et silencieuse, est courbée sur la glèbe ingrate et traîtresse de plusieurs régions des Balkans et de l'Anatolie. Elle seule, pendant des siècles, a alimenté les casernes de l'empire. Son sang a coulé dans tous les sillons abandonnés par les cultivateurs macédoniens devenus *comitadjis*, [1] et dans tous les sentiers des provinces insoumises, depuis l'Albanie jusqu'au Hauran et au Yemen. De tout temps, ses enfants, à peine sortis de l'adolescence, ont été arrachés brutalement aux campagnes pour être relégués en des garnisons reculées, dans un lamentable abandon. Des années se passaient, quinze et même vingt-cinq années parfois, sans que l'ordre de licenciement vint délivrer ces hommes de leur servitude. Quand ils regagnaient leurs foyers, ils n'avaient plus aucune vigueur, aucun goût pour le travail. Ils étaient aigris, démoralisés. Souvent, les vieux parents étaient morts après avoir traîné une vie misérable; la terre familiale était obérée d'hypothèques ou même vendue par les soins des fermiers de la dîme, voraces et impitoyables.

Un morne découragement régnait dans les chaumières sur lesquelles planaient en outre le fatalisme coutumier aux races asiatiques et la navrante résignation de l'Islam.

Sur le plateau anatolien et sur les agglomérations turques disséminées à travers les possessions d'Europe, s'appesantissaient toutes les oppressions et toutes les misères: routine, incurie, concussion, délation, terrorisme.

La prison et l'exil imposaient silence aux meilleurs, aux plus hardis. Toute velléité de relèvement était punie comme un crime. Si les Turcs, comme les *ghiaours*, essayaient de s'insurger, d'ébranler les fondements du trône d'Osman, sur qui pourrait désormais compter le gouvernement? Leur loyalisme et leur discipline, leur fanatisme et leur ignorance semblaient devoir être les meilleurs garants de la stabilité du régime. Ils n'avaient ni clubs, ni journaux. Rien ne pouvait exciter chez eux le désir du mieux-être. Les écoles, rares d'ailleurs, étaient un trompe-l'oeil. On n'y enseignait rien de ce qui forme l'homme, trempe son caractère et l'initie à l'action. La vie en était bannie. Un vain psittacisme, favorisé par le rabâchement d'ouvrages ineptes soigneusement expurgés, y remplaçait toute culture. Après avoir consumé sa jeunesse en de stériles exercises, on pouvait, comme Clément Marot, dire des cuistres revêches qui régentaient les établissements d'instruction:

Jamais je n'entre en paradis,
S'ils ne m'ont perdu la jeunesse!

Aucun souffle de réveil ne semblait secouer ce peuple insoucieux du progrès, qui paraissait voué à un asservissement certain, sinon à une fin très proche.

Groupés autour de leurs solides organismes communaux, les non-musulmans, cependant, développaient avec intensité leurs institutions nationales, leurs oeuvres d'entr'aide, leurs écoles; ils rachetaient les terres, faisaient revivre les industries indigènes, entraient en contact avec l'Occident, se livraient au commerce. Ils parvenaient à une prospérité remarquable. Les privilèges religieux que les sultans dédaigneux leur avaient conférés constituaient pour eux un palladium. Les consuls des puissances balkaniques, les agents de l'Europe les guidaient, les soutenaient, les défendaient contre les fonctionnaires faméliques. Instruits, entreprenants, actifs, ils distancèrent bientôt leur maître turc.

A mesure que les chrétiens s'élèvent, les Turcs dépourvus de tout secours, abandonnés sans espoir à l'empire du despotisme, s'abaissent, perdent pied. Le conquérant redouté est refoulé même de ses domaines. Deux peuples partis de directions opposées l'obligent à se masser dans le centre de l'Anatolie. Les Grecs venus des îles lui enlèvent progressivement le littoral, le rejettent vers les steppes salines et les déserts incultes, tandis que les Arméniens, enrichis grâce à leurs relations commerciales avec les places britanniques et devenus des prêteurs d'argent, lui dressent une barrière infranchissable du côté de l'Orient, le contiennent, le repoussent.

En Europe, sa situation n'est guère plus heureuse. Campé au milieu de populations hostiles, turbulentes, impatientes du joug, pourchassé des régions qui, l'une après l'autre, se détachent de l'empire, il voit son existence même menacée. Nulle part, il n'est chez lui. Il est l'intrus, l'ennemi. Il n'a pas su achever, par l'assimilation, l'oeuvre de la conquête; il n'a pas absorbé le vaincu. Il ne s'est pas non plus assimilé à lui. Il a planté une tente hâtive dans la terre envahie, a vécu en étranger parmi les nations soumises. C'est un déraciné qui ne se souvient plus des plaines dont il est issu et qui n'a pas su se fixer dans les pays que lui a donnés son indomptable bravoure. Confiant dans sa force, il avait négligé de jeter des ponts entre les garnisons qu'il essaimait à travers les contrées, à travers les colonies laborieuses des turcomans qui marquaient les étapes des armées triomphantes. Garnisons et colonies restaient dispersées, sporadiques. Aucun lien ne les rattachait entre elles. Elles s'ignoraient. Les espaces les séparaient. Elles ne se sont pas senties vibrer à l'unisson. Les éléments d'une âme collective lui ont fait défaut. Le peuple turc n'eut point de conscience nationale. Il fut un organisme sans tête, sans cerveau.

D'ailleurs, l'Europe n'a point laissé de répit au Turc. Toute la chrétienté s'est liguée contre lui et l'a contraint d'être en permanence sur le qui-vive. Il n'a guère pu déposer les armes; l'épée a toujours ceint ses reins. Il n'a point eu le loisir de se recueillir, de jouir en paix de ses acquêts. Il n'a pu rien organiser. Une défensive incessante a épuisé ses forces, accaparé son attention. Il était heureux de se décharger sur les communautés religieuses des soins pénibles de l'administration des peuples vaincus. Il se contenta du titre de suzerain et des avantages matériels qui y étaient attachés.

Mais une élite suivait les progrès de l'Occident et constatait avec angoisse la décadence dans laquelle s'abîmait le pays. Elle voulut éviter la perte irrémédiable des Turcs et, dès la fin du dix-huitième siècle, tenta d'introduire des réformes dans l'armée, dans l'administration, dans la politique économique et sociale. Sous Mustafa III, Sélim III, Mahmoud II et Abdul Medjid, les hommes d'Etat ottomans, animés d'excellentes intentions, se mirent à l'école de l'Europe. A coups de lois libérales et hardiment novatrices, ils essayèrent de relever le prestige de la dynastie d'Osman et de faire le bonheur des peuples de l'empire. Ces réformateurs pressés voulurent, à bref délai, conquérir dans le concert des nations civilisées une place honorable à la Turquie de leurs rêves qu'ils avaient laborieusement édifiée sur le parchemin des chartes organiques.

Mais leurs tentatives ne donnèrent pas tout le résultat qu'ils en attendaient, non sans quelque candeur. Elles étaient trop prématurées, trop précipitées. Elles faisaient abstraction de la période indispensable d'évolution. Rien ne se construit de durable quand on veut se passer du temps, cet allié lent et sûr. Les réformes avortèrent et Abdul Hamid, après une comique parade de parlementarisme, ajourna, *sine die*, la tâche de rénovation dont avaient rêvé Midhat Pacha et les hommes du Tanzimat.

Les trente-deux années de despotisme hamidien augmentèrent la misère générale, accentuèrent le discrédit du régime et achevèrent de placer la Turquie sous la tutelle humiliante des grandes puissances. L'entrevue de Reval allait consommer la séparation d'avec la métropole d'une des plus riches provinces ottomanes, quand éclata la révolution de juillet 1908 qui proclamait l'égalité des sujets de l'empire et les conviait tous à collaborer à la consolidation de l'état et à son relèvement.

Les Turcs furent presque les uniques artisans de cette révolution. Ils ne voulaient pas se résigner à disparaître. Ils aspiraient eux aussi à la vie. Ils ne pensaient pas que la loi de dissolution et de désagrégation, qui paraissait présider aux destinées de leur malheureuse patrie, fût inflexible. Les choses ne sont pas seulement régies par un ordre nécessaire et éternel. La volonté humaine en peut changer la disposition; elle peut intervenir dans la succession des événements, y insérer des causes nouvelles, et favorables; elle peut, tout au moins, l'essayer. Elle le doit. On ne devait pas laisser la fatalité agir en maîtresse incontestée. L'énergie de quelques-uns pouvait à coup sûr en faire dévier le cours.

Leur audace magnifique eut pour quelque temps un triomphe inoui. Le monde entier admira les héros qui avaient renversé, comme par un pouvoir magique, l'édifice gigantesque et terrifiant de la tyrannie séculaire.

II

L'enthousiasme, dans toute la Turquie, fut immense. Les temps étaient révolus. C'était la fin d'un monde. Des cieux nouveaux et une terre nouvelle allaient naître. Le verbe libérateur des Jeunes-Turcs avait accompli un grand miracle: il avait rapproché les os desséchés épars à travers les plaines, avait soufflé en eux l'esprit des quatre vents dont parle Ezéchiel, les avait rappelés à la vie et en avait fait une fort grande armée. Suivant la prédiction d'Essaïe, les réchappés des nations s'étaient assemblés, étaient venus et s'étaient rapprochés.

On s'embrassait dans les rues, sur les places. Les prêtres, les imams, les rabbins fraternisaient, se montraient à la population bras-dessus bras-dessous. Les bandits grecs, roumains et serbes descendaient de leurs nids d'aigles et venaient mêler leurs barbes farouches sur la poitrine chamarrée des officiers turcs. Le Kurde accourait exprimer son bonheur au milieu des Arméniens. L'Albanais renonçait à ses vendettas traditionelles. Les prionniers brisaient les portes de leurs geôles et se mêlaient à l'allégresse générale. Rentrés en hâte, les citoyens de tout culte qu'avaient bannis du pays les sévérités de la police hamidienne[2] étaient attendus dans les gares et sur les quais par des milliers d'hommes. On les arrachait à leurs proches et on les promenait en triomphe. La liberté, l'égalité, l'union, la fraternité étaient glorifiées du haut de tous les balcons, aux clameurs frénétiques des foules débordantes de confiance et de bonheur. Il n'y avait plus ni Musulmans, ni Chrétiens, ni Serbes, ni Turcs, ni Bulgares, ni Arméniens, ni Grecs, ni Juifs, ni Albanais. Toutes les différences sociales et religieuses s'effaçaient. Il n'y avait plus que des Ottomans, tous frères, tous unis dans le même amour profond pour la patrie retrouvée.

Dans les villes et dans les campagnes, les fêtes se prolongèrent. On discourut à tout propos sur la vie nouvelle qui commençait pour la nation maintenant une et indivisible. Tout était prétexte à banquets en commun, à congratulations, à accolades épiques. On confessait publiquement ses torts passeés, on s'accusait de particularisme, d'égoïsme. On se connaissait enfin. L'ancien régime était le seul coupable. Lui seul avait empêché l'union sincère des coeurs. Et il était mort pour toujours. Les Jeunes-Turcs l'avaient à jamais tué. Et, comme par enchantement, toutes les haines étaient tombées, tous les ressentiments s'étaient dissipés. Il n'y avait plus qu'affection et que concorde. C'était si bon de vivre en frères, de communier dans les mêmes sentiments, d'entretenir le même idéal: Comment avait-on pu vivre sans se connaître jusque-là. Comment avait-on pu vivre en ennemis? La paix était faite. Le bonheur allait commencer pour tous dans une patrie unie et harmonieuse. Les sceptiques les plus pessimistes sont convaincus, espèrent. Dans l'emballement des premiers baisers, chacun pensait pouvoir faire table rase du passé, chacun croyait à la possibilité de se faire une âme neuve. Il n'y aurait plus qu'une âme, qu'une conscience, qu'un idéal. Ce fut un âge d'or.

Au bout de quelques jours, on s'aperçut bien qu'il y avait des difficultés, des obstacles. Les Grecs regimbaient un peu à propos de vétilles; les Bulgares paraissaient se ressaisir, les

Albanais ronchonnaient. Mais c'était, en définitive, peu de chose, pensaient les Turcs. Le passé était bien enterré. Il n'y aurait plus de *comitadjis*, il n'y aurait plus d'insurrections. Les inimitiés s'étaient volatilisées au feu ardent des fêtes de la Constitution.

Ils désiraient la fusion franche des races. Leur sincérité était hors de doute. Partout ils essayèrent de réagir contre l'esprit de particularisme renaissant, et ils voulurent, pour cela, employer la persuasion, faire appel à l'idéal, aux sentiments. Des ligues de paix et d'entente, destinées à faciliter cette fusion, à l'accélérer, se formèrent, conviant toutes les nationalités à se rapprocher, à abaisser les barrières qui les avaient séparées jusqu'alors. Ce fut la politique d'ottomanisme préconisée par le groupe jeune-turc de Paris, à la tête du quel se trouvait Ahmed Riza.

Il est indéniable que tous les éléments ethniques firent d'abord un généreux effort pour répondre à cette aspiration des Turcs vers une unité patriotique. Il y eut dans tous les milieux un entrain considérable pour les nouvelles idées, un élan ingénu, mais vigoureux, vers l'ottomanisme.

Mais, dès que l'on voulut préciser la notion d'ottomanisme, on se trouva devant deux définitions très différentes, inconciliables et presque contradictoires. Pour les nationalités qui étaient parvenues à un certain degré de culture, qui avaient déjà pris conscience d'elles-mêmes, l'ottomanisme, c'était la trêve définitive, la paix dans les campagnes, l'égalité de tous les éléments raciaux, la libre accession de tous aux fonctions publiques, l'abolition des privilèges du conquérant qui rentrait spontanément dans le droit commun, cessait de revendiquer les premières places dans l'Etat, dans l'armée et dans la magistrature et consentait à devenir un simple citoyen. C'était , en somme, une sorte de nuit du 4 août où les Turcs, aristocratie de robe et d'épée, renonçaient à leurs droits historiques de dominateurs. Chaque nationalité garderait ses institutions, son organisation, les améliorerait, les développerait en toute liberté et en toute quiétude. Elle n'avait rien à sacrifier. Point d'abdication. Il y aurait autant de vies sociales distinctes qu'il y a de communautés ethniques. On conviait les non-musulmans à participer aux droits civiques et politiques, dont on les avait exclus jusque-là. Voilà tout. Il y avait eu jusqu'alors des Grecs, des Albanais, des Bulgares sujets de sa majesté turque; il y aurait désormais des Grecs, des Albanais, des Bulgares, citoyens ottomans. Il n'y aurait plus des *rehaya*, des troupeaux, soumis au bon plaisir du maître. On octroyait le droit de cité à tous les habitants de l'empire. Tous étaient promus à la dignité d'électeurs, de législateurs. La loi serait l'expression de la volonté de tous et non plus celle d'une race ou d'une camarilla. La communauté restait l'organisme social par excellence; la patrie ottomane était la somme des communautés, un superorganisme créé non plus par la contrainte, mais par un *oui* unanime des parties contractantes. Chacun mènerait une vie en partie double, communale et civique. Il y aurait la petite patrie et la grande, le patriotisme de clocher et la loyalisme ottoman. La grande patrie existerait seulement pour favoriser l'essor de la petite, seule aimée d'instinct, à laquelle on vouerait le meilleur de son être. Le régionalisme serait le but. L'Etat sera confiné dans son rôle utile de gendarme. Il assumerait la mission exclusive d'assurer la paix aux frontières, le repos à l'intérieur.

Ce n'est pas ainsi que les Turcs entendaient l'ottomanisme. Ils avaient été les seuls vrais Ottomans jusqu'à la révolution et ils n'avaient été qu'Ottomans. Maintenant ils partageaient leur titre avec les autres. Les autres ne devaient plus être que des Ottomans. Ils devaient répudier tout particularisme. Il n'y avait plus ni Grecs, ni Israélites, ni Arméniens; il n'y avait que des Ottomans. Il n'y avait plus *des* nations, mais *la* nation. Pour communier dignement dans le sentiment d'ottomanisme, chacun devait dépouiller le vieil homme. Tout son coeur était dû à la patrie. La vie sociale devait se confondre avec la vie civique. La solidarité ethnique leur semblait dès lors une monstruosité, les institutions particulières à chaque nationalité, des anachronismes injurieux pour la patrie. La *Roumélie*, organe du Comité Union et Progrès, s'exprime avec douleur et amertume sur l'existence des clubs, des sociétés de bienfaisance des Grecs, des Israélites. Puisque nous sommes tous Ottomans, pourquoi persister à maintenir les subdivisions, les parcages? Abaissons les haies. Ayons des oeuvres communes, même caisse, même administration. Les pauvres – Musulmans, Chrétiens ou Juifs – sont *nos* pauvres, nos frères Ottomans sans ressources. Donnons-nous la main pour secourir les malheureux et combattre la misère. Point d'ostracisme. L'exclusivisme, voilà l'ennemi!

Les Turcs en parlaient à leur aise, mais il ne convenait point aux éléments allogènes de faire abstraction de leur passé, d'effacer les résultats acquis au prix d'énormes sacrifices, de laborieux efforts. Le voudraient-ils, d'ailleurs, qu'ils ne le pourraient guère. Une nationalité ne se suicide pas par persuasion. Elle est l'oeuvre des siècles. On ne peut pas la supprimer par une affirmation de la volonté. Elle plonge des racines vivaces dans les traditions, dans la coutume, dans les institutions, dans le fond subconscient et inaccessible des individus et résiste aux atteintes fugaces et superficielles du vouloir. Une fusion artificielle ne peut point s'opérer. Il n'y a point de miracle dans la séculaire élaboration de l'âme des peuples. Les hommes politiques, dans leur naïveté et leur simplisme, peuvent se proposer toutes les suppressions. L'influence ancestrale est plus forte que tous leurs moyens. Les morts commandent aux vivants et leur autorité ne se discute pas. La fusion des peuples n'est pas la tâche d'un jour. Elle s'opère imperceptiblement, sous l'influence de la vie en commun, des croisements, de la lente et mystérieuse intrication des moeurs, des institutions, des croyances, des intérêts.

Aussi, la lune de miel passée, chaque élément tira de son côté, chacun forma ses rangs, les serra, rallia ses forces et se prépara à l'action. Après la période des platoniques et vaines manifestations de fraternité, l'ère de recueillement, d'isolement. Les groupes ethniques profitèrent de la liberté pour devenir plus compacts, plus fortement solidaires.

La notion d'ottomanisme, estompée, indécise, perdait de plus en plus ses contours. Ce ne fut bientôt que le sentiment instable et vacillant d'une communauté de droits politiques, d'intérêts lointains très contestés. Elle devint précaire, prête à s'évanouir devant les antipathies séculaires, les tendances décentralisatrices ou séparatistes.

Les Turcs ne tardèrent pas à constater leur erreur. Les belles illusions se dissipèrent. Le *fiat* révolutionnaire n'avait pas opéré. D'ailleurs l'ottomanisme était pour eux un vrai marché de dupes. Ils ne pouvaient qu'y perdre. Jamais, ils ne pourraient se mettre au niveau de leurs concitoyens allogènes. Les distances étaient trop grandes, impossibles à franchir en une génération. Ils risquaient d'être des seconds peu brillants dans l'association qu'ils avaient proposée sous l'empire de l'enthousiasme des premières étreintes. Ils n'étaient pas encore de force. Mis brutalement en face de concurrents préparés de longue main à la lutte, ils étaient condamnés à disparaître. L'organisation leur manquait. L'âme naissante de la race devait irrémédiablement sombrer dans la tourmente de l'impossible fusion. Elle n'avait guère encore de vitalité, de cachet distinctif. L'anéantir serait sans profit pour personne et fatal pour eux. L'avenir n'était à la chimère qu'ils s'étaient plu à caresser.

Leur beau rêve n'avait duré. Ils ne pouvaient improviser une nation. Les éléments étaient trop dissemblables, trop disparates, absolument réfractaires à l'ottomanisation intégrale, trop attachés à leurs traditions, à leurs institutions. Pourquoi dresser le faible obstacle des illusions contre la force irrésistible des poussées ethniques?

Il fallait chercher ailleurs. Pourquoi la religion ne serait-elle pas un ciment national, comme elle l'avait été à l'époque de la foudroyante conquête arabe?

Le panislamisme fut dès lors en vogue. Hamid l'avait suscité; ses émissaires avaient éveillé de grands espoirs dans le vaste monde islamique. Au nom du Prophète, tous les vrais croyants s'uniraient, formeraient bloc.

Les méthodes d'Occident ne paraissaient pas convenir à la société islamique. De plus, la chrétienté serait hostile à un empire où l'élément musulman s'imposerait par le nombre. Il n'y avait pas à compter sur son amitié. On avait bien tenté d'adapter à la Turquie régénérée les procédés de gouvernement de l'Europe. Des Turcs candides avaient même voulu s'appuyer sur la franc-maçonnerie mondiale considérée comme le soutien puissant du libéralisme, de la tolérance et de la justice internationale et à l'ombre de laquelle s'était organisé le Comité révolutionnaire de Salonique. Les *frères*, répandus dans tout le monde civilisé, seraient des avocats ardents de la cause ottomane auprès des gouvernements et des parlements. Mais leur déception fut prompte. Le concours espéré ne vint pas. Les divers orients pensaient à leurs intérêts nationaux, quand ce n'était pas aux intérêts étroits de leur ordre. Et puis, même animés des meilleures volontés, les orients maçonniques ne pouvaient pas grand chose. Leur force était diffuse, dérisoire et, somme toute, fallacieuse. Quant aux diplomates, surpris d'abord par l'imprévu de manifestations qui emplissaient les rues des villes et des villages de Turquie, ils se ressaisirent sans retard et s'apprêtèrent à la curée. La bête était acculée. Elle serait achevée sans peine. Il fallait se tenir aux aguets. Compter sur leur bienveillance serait folie.

Le salut était donc dans la solidarité avec tous les peuples islamiques. C'était le meilleur moyen de se procurer des alliés sincères dans l'empire et des amis puissants au dehors. A la chrétienté liguée, on opposerait les 250 millions de musulmans du monde. Religion contre religion. Force contre force. On croyait pouvoir s'appuyer sur les chefs des confréries mystérieuses qui dominent tout l'Islam. Il fallait, pour cela, de l'esprit de suite, quelque méthode, des subsides habilement distribués au nom du souverain des Ottomans, Sultan et Khalife, empereur et pape à la fois. Et quel auxiliaire on aurait ainsi! "L'Islam, dit Ali Kémal, est l'instrument d'unification idéal. Il broie les volontés, supprime les nationalités, les cimente, passe sur elles le lourd niveau de l'égalitarisme."

Ses sectateurs ne pensent, n'agissent qu'en Musulmans. Religion et nation se confondent, se couvrent. Le culte envahit l'existence, l'absorbe, plie le croyant à des observances précises, ponctuelles, répétées. Depuis son apparition, la doctrine de Mahomet domine toute la vie politique, sociale et intellectuelle des peuples qu'elle a subjugués. Le Coran est le livre par excellence. Il est tout pour le croyant. Il a servi de loi organique, de charte constitutionnelle, en même temps que de guide pour la vie journalière. Il est la source unique de toute jurisprudence. Le Musulman se tient pour le premier des hommes. Sa philosophie est sûre autant que simple. Allah est Dieu. Le monde est son oeuvre. Il le gouverne de près; sans relâche, il en modifie les détails, les règle d'après les lois de sa sagesse impénétrable. Il est le maître. On ne discute point sa volonté. La résignation, la soumission sans phrases, voilà le devoir. Seul le Musulman en a la claire conscience. De là sa supériorité incontestable. Aussi, dans les heures de contrariété comme dans les moments de satisfaction, se répète-t-il avec complaisance le fameux: *El Hamd ul Allah, musslumanim:* Dieu soi loué, je suis Musulman. De toute façon le paradis lui est gagné.

Avant d'être turc, persan, marocain, on est musulman. L'islamisme est la grande patrie, la seule vraie. Le chef tout désigné de cette patrie serait le Sultan des Turcs.

Les Turcs seraient ainsi à l'avant-garde des peuples islamiques. Ils recueilleraient tous les bénéfices de l'important mouvement de concentration. Comme résultat immédiat, ils devaient obtenir l'adhésion franche à la dynastie turque de tous les musulmans de l'Empire, Albanais, Grecs, Bulgares, Valaques islamisés, Lazes, Kurdes, Druses, Arabes de l'Irak, Arabes du Yemen. Leur puissance en était décuplée. Car quel est le fidèle qui oserait se soustraire à ses obligations de solidarité islamique? Quel est celui qui persisterait à conserver des aspirations séparatistes? Il serait réputé traître à la patrie spirituelle, renégat.

On ferait même, d'une façon active, de l'ottomanisme à base d'Islam. Tous les musulmans de Turquie seraient des ottomans, les seuls ottomans véritables. L'unité rêvée serait réalisée entre coreligionnaires. Les mosquées seraient le centre de ralliement.

Imbus de ces idées, les Turcs se reprirent à espérer. Mais une nouvelle déception les attendait. Des défections se produisirent. Les musulmans de l'Empire eux-mêmes manifestèrent des tendances particularistes. Les Albanais s'agitèrent. Ils voulurent s'isoler du reste du pays. Certains d'entre eux proposaient l'abandon des caractères arabes, vêtement de la parole sacrée, pour adopter l'alphabet latin, sous le prétexte futile que la langue skippe est indo-européenne et ne s'accommode pas aisément des signes graphiques destinés à une langue sémitique. Des révolutions sanglantes eurent lieu. A deux reprises, l'Albanie leva l'étendard de la révolte. Les Yéménites, les Druses se soulevèrent. Les troupes turques durent aller se battre contre les musulmans des plateaux glacés et des déserts brûlants, contre ceux du septentrion et contre ceux du midi.

Une fois encore, les yeux des Turcs se dessillèrent. Non, on ne pouvait faire fond sur l'Islamisme, du moins pour s'attacher les musulmans du pays. Peut-être le pan-islamisme pourait servir contre l'étranger, comme il sert en ce moment contre l'envahisseur de la Tripolitaine. Mais, il était exclusivement une force d'opposition, un engin de défense; il ne pouvait pas devenir une force active, agissante, une arme d'attaque.

Ils comprirent que l'ottomanisme islamique était pour eux un danger. Vivant chez eux, à huis clos, l'Arabe, le Persan, l'Albanais ne redoutent pas leur dépersonification, leur dénationalisation par l'Islam. Ils constituent chacun dans son teritoire – dans son milieu presque fermé – des masses compactes, homogènes, sans mélange sensible. Grâce à la ségrégation, ils conservent leur langue, leurs us et coutumes, leurs caractères ethniques propres. Il n'en est pas de même du Turc. Il n'est qu'une poussière de peuple. Il vit disséminé parmi les nations de l'empire qui ont, pour la plupart, une culture avancée.

Les races allogènes de culte islamique, groupées sur le même habitat, progresseraient, prospéreraient et bientôt toutes le dépasseraient. Il resterait isolé, diminué. Cet islamisme ottomaniste non plus ne présentait pas la solution cherchée. Les intellectuels se rendirent compte que l'unité ne se ferait pas par la religion. Les notions de race et de nationalité étaient distinctes. Il fallait se garder de les confondre.

III

Force était au Turc de se réfugier dans un nationalisme étroit. Il voulut être lui-même. L'heure du recueillement sonna. Les Chrétiens ne voulaient pas d'une association franche, les Musulmans allogènes non plus. L'exclusivisme turkiste s'imposa comme une nécessité. Il se révéla simultanément sur plusieurs points. Le peuple turc parut sortir de sa torpeur. Il se vit dépouillé de tout bien, lamentable. Il mesura la profondeur de son mal, sonda ses plaies, constata sa désorganisation, sa misère. Il désira intensément se faire une vie nouvelle. L'élite résolut de puiser dans les traditions ancestrales les éléments d'un idéal que l'on ferait descendre par degrés dans l'âme inculte de la race. Elle chercha à s'organiser pour le grand oeuvre de la régénération nationaliste.

Le service du gouvernement, l'impôt du sang, l'abandon de toutes les professions lucratives avaient décimé la population turque et l'avaient appauvrie. Sauf quelques centaines de beys, propriétaires terriens, les Turcs vivent du prolétariat fonctionnariste ou militaire. Ils se contentent de traitements de famine, de maigres soldes. Ils sont d'ailleurs d'une sobriété et d'une frugalité étonnantes. Ils déjeunent d'une pomme, dînent d'un quignon de pain et de quelques olives. En Anatolie, les laitages et le blé bouilli sont la base de leur alimentation. Ils ne font guère de grandes dépenses somptuaires. Un costume par an, acheté régulièrement à *bayram* leur suffit. Ils l'endossent le premier jour de la fête et le portent toute l'année.

Avec des besoins aussi modiques, l'habitude de l'initiative et une grande activité resteraient sans objet. Aussi n'ont-ils qu'une vie économique restreinte. Ils ignorent presque le commerce. Un écrivain turc compare plaisamment l'empire à une immense salle de festin. Les divers éléments non turcs sont les convives. Ils mangent et boivent tout à leur aise, tandis que le maître de céans, paterne, se tient à la porte, baïonnette au canon, veillant à ce qu'aucun intrus ne vienne troubler la fête.

Conséquence inévitable, les Turcs n'ont pas de culture propre. Ils vivent d'emprunts. Ils sont, pour les choses de l'esprit, les débiteurs de tous et n'ont rien de *sui generis*. Ils sont aujourd'hui à la remorque de la France. Ils traduisent les romans français, adaptent en turc la poésie française contemporaine, imitent les Parnassiens, les Symbolistes, les Décadents. Beaucoup de jeunes gens qui aspirent à l'intellectualité et qui ont été instruits d'après des méthodes européennes ne trouvent rien à aimer dans les traditions de la race, dans les rites figés du culte, le guindé et le solennel des moeurs. Ils affichent un mépris souverain pour la foule turque, pour les usages turcs, pour tout ce qui sent le terroir. Ils détestent la musique turque et qualifient de barbares les innocents divertissements du Karagheuz. Ils fuient leurs congénères, recherchent la compagnie des étrangers. La suprême élégance à leurs yeux est de revêtir un smoking pour assister aux bals, aux soirées, aux représentations de gala données par les colonies étrangères. Ils se donnent des airs d'Occidentaux raffinés, imitent les manières des gens chics qu'ils admirent dans les salons où on les admet, farcissent leur langage de *mon cher* et d'une foule d'expressions françaises, s'habillent chez le bon faiseur, parlent de la dernière pièce jouée aux Variétés, et fredonnent la nouvelle scie du boulevard. De Paris, ils connaissent surtout le luxe, la légèreté, la blague. Les côtés peu sérieux de l'existence les séduisent et les fascinent. Ferrus de dandisme, de smart, de snobisme, ils sont d'une affectation puérile et grotesque.

Cette singerie déraisonnable de l'Occident est, à juste titre, abhorrée des Turcs vraiment éclairés. Ils la flétrissent de l'appellatif méprisant de *levantinisme*. Il ne peut en résulter aucun bien pour la race.

"Les divers éléments de la civilisation d'un peuple, dit avec raison Gustave Le Bon, n'étant que les signes extérieurs de sa constitution mentale, l'expression de certains modes de sentir et de penser spéciaux à ce peuple, ne sauraient se transmettre sans changement à des peuples de constitution mentale différente. Ce qui peut se transmettre, ce sont seulement les formes extérieures superficielles et sans importance."

Les *levantins*, les *zoubés*, comme les dénomme encore le populaire, ne se sentent pas en communion d'idées ni d'aspirations avec leur entourage. Ils sont les ennemis jurés du nationalisme qu'ils jugent stérilisant et vain, ils constituent, pour le mouvement qui se dessine, de redoutables agents de désagrégation et de ruine.

Mais l'écueil du levantinisme est difficile à éviter dans un pays où les traditions littéraires et scientifiques sont complètement en contradiction avec les disciplines de la culture moderne. La littérature turque, en effet, est toute nourrie d'arabe et de persan. Elle se confine dans l'imitation servile des écrivains de la grande époque des Omeyyades, des Abassides, ou tire son inspiration de la lecture de Ferdousi, d'Omar Keyam, de Sadi, de Hafiz, de Djami. Elle perd rapidement son caractère turc. Les lettrés l'inondent d'éléments empruntés à profusion à l'arabe et au persan. Les vocables turcs disparaissent. Ils sont chétifs, humbles, sans prestance.

On les élimine impitoyablement. Tous les mots sont arabes. Seule la construction, le moule de la phrase reste turc, avec le verbe à la fin. Plus d'un écrivain, incommodé par l'emploi des auxiliaires *olmak* (devenir) *etmek* (faire), seuls vestiges souvent de la langue maternelle, préfère écrire tout uniment en arabe.

Tous ceux qui n'ont pas pâli sur les divans archaïques, qui n'ont pas été initiés aux finesses de la syntaxe sémitique et aux souplesses élégantes de l'idiome iranien, tous ceux qui n'ont pas bourré leur mémoire d'interminables listes d'expressions exotiques, sont incapables de comprendre cette étrange littérature trilingue.

Le peuple est privé de lecture. Seuls les érudits, rares mandarins qui se recrutent dans l'aristocratie, peuvent aborder les livres. Les périodiques eux-mêmes sont rédigés en cette langue savante.

Les mots arabes y représentent les 70 pourcent du vocabulaire du journal le plus lu. Ils conservent tout leur appareil propre de flexion, de filiation. Ils sont autonomes. Fièrement drapés dans leur burnous, ils ne condescendent à figurer dans la phrase turque qu'à la condition de ne se plier à aucune compromission humiliante, à aucune déchéance. Brochant sur un fouillis de gutturales confuses, bruit d'appel des nomades que les immensités du désert séparent, de purs aryanismes, aux sons francs et clairs, apportent leurs gaies fulgurances de métal. Une division assez nette s'est opérée dans le travail d'emprunt. L'art apollinien, pour parler comme Nietzsche, celui qui se borne à la représentation, à l'analyse, à puisé sa terminologie dans l'idiome arabe; tandis que l'art dionysien, exprimant la volonté, la joie de vivre, a trouvé la sienne dans le persan. L'arabe fournit la langue du culte, de la piété, de la contemplation, de la philosophie, de l'administration; le persan, plus musical, plus vivant, plus alerte, prêta les magnifiques résonnances de sa libre poésie, apte à chanter le vin, l'amour, toutes les passions humaines.

Le turc, aujourd'hui, est exubérant, désordonné. Il déborde de richesses encombrantes qu'il ne s'est point appropriées. C'est un amas incohérent sans vie, sans nerf. Il n'a aucune sorte d'originalité. Il est fait à l'image du peuple osmanli fraîchement échappé de l'oppression, dépourvu de cohésion et de personnalité et à peine conscient de son existence.

La misère désolante de l'âme turque qui n'a même point de langue pour exhaler sa peine, l'absence de toute activité intellectuelle, de tout sentiment national intense, préoccupent de nos jours l'esprit en Turquie. La jeunesse s'est donné pour tâche d'éveiller le peuple de son sommeil séculaire, de le faire sortir du long oubli de soi-même.

"O Turcs, ô jeunes, s'écrie le poète Mehmed Emin, réveillez-vous ou s'en est fait de vous et de votre glorieux passé. Unissez-vous, enfants des Turcs, ou vous êtes à jamais perdus. Seul un peuple égoïste a droit à la vie. Considère l'état lamentable de la patrie, ô jeune patriote! Elle a été morcelée, partagée entre tes ennemis, et tu dors encore!

"Hélas! qui pouvait imaginer que le pays des grands conquérants deviendrait la proie des bêtes féroces; qui pouvait imaginer que le Turc, le glorieux triomphateur, serait condamné à languir misérablement dans un sombre coin de l'Anatolie?

"Voyez ce pauvre paysan turc, le vrai turc. Il n'a guère de bien. Il n'a que son âme. Et il l'offre volontiers sur l'autel de la nation. Imite-le, ô jeune intellectuel! Prends pitié de ce peuple infortuné auquel tu appartiens! Marche, ô jeune Turc! tu portes dans tes mains le sort de ton peuple!"

IV

De toutes parts, on s'attelle à la tâche avec entrain. La période de découragement est passée. On ne se complaît plus en un pessimisme inerte. On a aperçu la vigueur immense que confère la confiance en soi et l'on a donné la chasse à tous les semeurs de doute. On va puiser chez les penseurs d'Occident, les Nietzche, les Gobineau, les Fouillée, les Gustave Le Bon, les Bergson, les Durkheim, des motifs d'espérer, de vouloir.

"Rien de pire pour un peuple, s'écrient avec A. Fouillée les partisans de la vie nouvelle, rien de pire que l'auto-suggestion de sa déchéance; à force de se répéter qu'il va tomber, il se donne à-lui-même le vertige et tombe. Comme, sur le champ de bataille, la persuasion de la défaite rend la défaite certaine, ainsi le découragement national enlève aux caractères leur ressort et devient semblable à l'obsession du suicide. En se payant de mots absurdes, comme "fin de race," "fin de peuple," on prétexte son impuissance individuelle contre une destinée qui pèse sur tout un peuple et prend même l'aspect d'une fatalité physique."

"En réalité, cette fatalité n'existe pas," affirment-ils avec l'éminent penseur.

Il faut régénérer la race en lui inculquant les méthodes, les disciplines des peuples civilisés. Le principe d'évolution, voilà ce qu'il importe surtout de savoir faire sien.

"Nous n'avons pas d'autre ressource si nous voulons résister aux forces qui s'élèvent contre nous, écrit un publiciste turc. Ce n'est par la forme extérieure, par l'appparence et l'habit qu'il faut nous identifier à l'Europe, c'est par la mentalité. Ne perdons pas en projets un temps précieux. Ce serait trop périlleux au moment où la civilisation emporte toutes les créatures avec une force impétueuse et irrésistible. Oui, la civilisation a envahi l'Afrique et l'Australie et a étendu ses ramifications dans les centres asiatiques. Elle renverse ceux qui lui résistent et les brise. Elle asservit aux plus basses besognes ceux qui sont incapables de la comprendre; elle avance sur mer, elle avance à travers les airs. Il serait fatal de vouloir rester inerts sur le passage d'une telle puissance."

Et l'on cite Bergson:

"Tous les vivants se tiennent et tous cèdent à la même formidable poussée. L'humanité entière, dans l'espace et le temps, est une immense armée qui galope à côté de chacun de nous en avant et en arrière de nous, dans une charge entraînante capable de culbuter toutes les résistances."

Nous ne saurions échapper à la loi du progrès. Soumettons-nous-y de bonne grâce, avant qu'elle ne vienne saper nos fondements vermoulus.

"Nous ne devons pas périr ni être réduits à la servitude, dit Ali Kémal, leader de l'ancien parti Ahrar; nous avons un passé glorieux; nous avons fondé un état grand et puissant qui, durant six cents ans, s'est assuré une place honorable dans le monde. Des circonstances passagères ont étouffé notre essor, mais nous nous relèverons. Nous sommes aussi aptes que les peuples occidentaux au progrès moderne. O Turc, lève-toi et marche! Va en France, en Angleterre, en Amérique, instruis-toi, trompe ta volonté!"

Mais dans l'oeuvre de rééducation nécessaire, un danger est imminent: l'altération, la déperdition de l'âme de la race. Il ne faut pas donner dans le travers du sot levantinisme. L'Europe a du bon et elle a du mauvais. Prenons ce qui nous convient, choisissons avec sagesse et discernement. La morale européenne, par example, est détestable, affirme le *Yeni Felséfé*. Quand on la débarrasse de sa gangue de mensonge, de pharisaïsme et de *cant*, on s'aperçoit qu'elle n'admet qu'un Dieu, Mammon, à qui sont immolés les plus nobles sentiments. L'intérêt personnel annihile tout idéal dans le coeur de ces civilisés, qui, à côté d'immenses richesses sans emploi, laissent mourir soixante-dix millions de miséreux. L'union et la paix de la famille sont inconnues dans ces sociétés occidentales. Le malthusianisme pitoyable émascule la race. La débauche est reine; elle s'étale au grand jour, somptueuse et respectée. Nous avons de meilleurs modèles de désintéressement et de vertu familiale dans nos contrées. C'est à ces modèles qu'il faut ressembler.

A l'Europe, empruntons sa science objective, son ardente et indomptable énergie, son goût de l'initiative, son sens pratique. Ce sont là choses d'excellent aloi, bonnes à prendre et qui nous mettront vite en un rang envié parmi les nations.

Concilier les traditions avec les exigences du progrès, voilà le problème urgent qui se pose maintenant à l'élite turque avec une grande précision. Une pléiade de penseurs, de romanciers, de journalistes l'étudie avec diligence. Elle a élaboré un vaste programme de rénovation nationale. Elle a dressé une nouvelle table des valeurs qu'elle s'efforce de porter à la masse par une propagande active. Livres, brochures, journaux, conférences sèment partout la bonne graine. Des associations s'organisent pour grouper les jeunes, les catéchiser au nom du nouvel évangile.

A vrai dire, ce travail de régénération turkiste n'est pas entièrement nouveau. Il remonte aux premières années du Tanzimat.

Les hommes d'Etat, Reschid, Fuad, Ali, voulaient surtout rendre un peu de vie à la société musulmane, affaiblie par les charges militaires qui pesaient sur elle.

"Il faut que les musulmans imitent les chrétiens, disait Ali Pasha, ministre d'Abdul Aziz, dans son testament politique; qu'ils s'adonnent à l'agriculture, au commerce, à l'industrie, aux arts. Le travail seul est un capital durable. Mettons-nous au travail, sire! Là seulement nous trouverons le salut! Sire, il est temps encore de libérer la population musulmane des charges qui l'oppressent au profit des chrétiens qui prospèrent et se multiplient et tendent à la supplanter. Un homme qui s'appelle Stéfanovitch, Ralli,

Tubini, Camondo, Zarifi est-il vraiment un subordonné? Jouit-il d'une considération moindre que nos plus hauts fonctionnaires? Bon nombre de ces derniers ne sont-ils pas aujourd'hui tenus de s'incliner devant eux?"

Le gouvernement de Napoléon III lui-même, sentant que l'Empire ottoman risquait de se dépecer entre les diverses nationalités indigènes patronnées par la Russie, l'Autriche et l'Angleterre, témoignait toute sa sympathie à la nation turque, seule capable de retenir en un faisceau les races soumises prêtes à se séparer. Il voulut la relever par l'éducation et par un système de sages réformes, lui fournir des capitaux pour ses chemins de fer et ses écoles. Victor Duruy lui-même élabora le programme du lycée de Galata-Séraï. Mais il était difficile aux réformateurs d'élever trop la voix. La toute-puissance du souverain s'accommode mal des initiatives trop hardies, trop radicales. On n'osait pas secouer le joug des préjugés trop tenaces. Les ulémas n'avaient point perdu leur empire et ils ne permettaient pas qu'on touchât aux us et coutumes. Les esprits trop libres, trop indépendants, devaient s'imposer une prudente discrétion. Bientôt l'exil les dispersa.

La colonie turque de Paris et surtout le groupe de réfugiés d'Egypte préconisèrent un nationalisme turquiste intégral. Une revue turque, en Egypte, recruta une élite d'écrivains qui rompirent des lances en faveur de la régénération du peuple turc.

V

A l'intérieur, les novateurs se faisaient petits, modestes pour vivre. Ils circonscrivirent leur action au domaine littéraire et linguistique, tentèrent de vulgariser la science, de populariser la poésie, de hausser la foule aux jouissances de l'art afin d'avoir prise sur elle. Chinassi, qui avait vécu de longues années à Paris, fonda dans ce but le *Tasvir-i-efkiar*, périodique qui eut un grand succès. Il s'acharna contre le style fleuri, solennel, prétentieux, pédantesque et inextricable dans lequel étaient rédigés tous les documents officiels et presque tous les ouvrages en langue turque de l'époque et poursuivit de ses railleries tous les écrivassiers qui s'épuisaient dans la recherche d'une hypothétique harmonie imitative, d'une vague correspondance entre le rythme et l'idée et allaient déterrer, dans les divans caducs et les lexiques poudreux, les substantifs précieux et les épithètes rares qu'ils sertissaient dans la trame confuse de leurs élucubrations.

Il adopta une langue simple, claire, dans laquelle tous les mots sont du domaine commun, accessibles au public peu lettré. Son disciple Namik Kiémal se jeta dans la mêlée avec une ardeur entraînante, et, épris des qualités toutes françaises de clarté, de sobriété et de simplicité, il produisit coup sur coup des romans, des drames, des compositions poétiques débordantes de lyrisme. Vainement, les nababs de l'empire, les pachas, les courtisans, les hauts fonctionnaires tenants de l'ancienne littérature qui était comme leur apanage exclusif, leur chasse réservée, essayèrent-ils de contrecarrer les efforts des deux apôtres. Malgré l'indifférence de la foule, le triomphe de Chinassi et de Kiémal fut complet. La plupart des auteurs renoncent dès lors au langage docte, contourné et bizarre, aux redondances, à l'emphase et au verbiage favorisés par l'extrême abondance lexicologique. Dès lors, on commence à écrire pour dire sa pensée et non plus pour avoir l'occasion d'enfiler les périphrases pompeuses et les arabismes ronflants et nébuleux.

A la même époque, Chemseddin-Sami, lexicographe de grande érudition, établit le vocabulaire de la langue osmanlie; Djevdet-Pacha en compose la grammaire. Un peu plus tard, Tahir bey révèle l'existence d'une foule d'écrivains d'origine turque parmi les arabes et met ainsi en évidence les capacités littéraires des gens de sa race; Nedjib Assim et ses collègues étudient les idiomes ouralo-altaïques, et particulièrement tchagataï, le plus riche d'entre eux, ce qui leur permet de vivifier un peu le turc rachitique et dépenaillé que les nomades incultes avaient conservé à grand'peine à travers leurs migrations.

Mais la tyrannie hamidienne vient imposer silence aux intellectuels. Le maître prend ombrage de toute activité. Il ne souffre guère qu'on pense sous son règne et encore moins que l'on imprime. Les écrivains se taisent, les journaux se bornent à enregistrer les faveurs impériales, les sélamliks.[3] Toute littérature disparaît qui n'adule pas sa majesté. L'art du journaliste se réduit à une écoeurante mnémotechnie: il consiste à savoir retrouver instantanément le cliché phraséologique qui convient aux évènements insignifiants qu'il est permis à la presse de relater, ou le cortège d'épithètes laudatives qu'un usage constant et invariable a accolées à chaque titre et à chaque dignité.

Quelques années avant la révolution, certains publicistes croient pouvoir infuser une vie nouvelle à la littérature agonisante en renouvelant la querelle moderniste de l'Ecole Chinassi-Kiémal. L'amour de la simplicité s'exagère chez eux et s'exaspère. Ils veulent désarabiser et dépersaniser radicalement la langue et se mettent avec un beau zèle à donner la chasse à tous les mots sémitiques ou iraniens. Ce furent les puristes, les purificateurs, les *tasfiedjis*, comme on les désigna bientôt par un arabisme, faute d'un mot turc approprié. Leur ambition était de revenir au turc originel, tant prôné par Nedjib Assim. Mais, en fait, c'était un nouvel idiome qu'ils tentaient d'instaurer, le turc vulgaire étant singulièrement insuffisant. Il fallait créer de toutes pièces un vocabulaire ou l'emprunter aux populations qui vivent encore sur les flancs de l'Altaï, l'Altoun-dagh, berceau de la race. De plus, le turc, dépouillé de ses éléments exogènes, serait malaisément apte à exprimer des conceptions morales, métaphysiques et philosophiques tout à fait étrangères aux peuplades primitives auxquelles seules on voulait s'apparenter.

Le grand journal *Ikdam* publia quelque temps des articles en style puriste dus à la plume de son rédacteur en chef Djevdet bey. L'*Ahenk* et le *Hidmet*, de Smyrne, avec Nedjib Assim et l'officier Omer Seïf-Eldine, essayèrent aussi d'évincer totalement le turc trilingue. Des efforts analogues furent faits de divers côtés par des publicistes isolés, mais les maigres productions qui en résultèrent vinrent prouver combien était grande l'erreur des *tasfiedjis.* Il était impossible d'alimenter une littérature avec quelques centaines de mots et avec le petit nombre d'idées simples et naïves qu'ils pouvaient exprimer.

Devant la pauvreté du vocabulaire minable auquel ils devaient recourir, les plus intrépides capitulèrent. Pourtant, un poète de valeur, Mehmed-Emin, persévéra avec une opiniâtreté qui lui réussit encore aujourd'hui. Dans le fond et la forme, ses poésies sont tout à fait turques, et elles sont souvent d'une belle venue. Il y décrit, avec un art ému, la vieille vie nationale de son peuple. Son succès est très grand auprès de la jeunesse pour qui il est devenu, depuis la révolution, un maître écouté et vénéré.

VI

Depuis les journées mémorables de juillet 1908, le courant de rénovation nationale est sorti de sa période de formation. Latent et timide à l'excès jusque-là, il s'étale désormais au grand jour, envahit la presse, occupe les revues, absorbe les polémistes et les écrivains de tout ordre. Il est l'objet constant de la sollicitude des intellectuels, retient l'attention des hommes d'état et ne manque pas d'inquiéter les éléments non-turcs du pays.

Le nationalisme grammatical et linguistique des *tasfiedjis* n'avait joui d'aucune faveur auprès du grand public. C'est cependant sur lui que s'est greffé un mouvement parallèle à l'ottomanisme et au panislamisme, le panturquisme. Le protagoniste en est Youssouf Aktchoura, publiciste turc, originaire du Caucase. Dès 1909, Youssouf Aktchoura, flétrissant la politique ottomaniste ou panislamiste, préconise, dans la presse, l'union de tous les Turcs de l'univers. Il veut prolonger, dans le lointain passé et dans l'espace, l'âme de la race turque, il veut la retremper aux sources natales, la renforcer en lui donnant pour soutien les peuples congénères du Caucase, de Sibérie, du plateau du Touran.

"Les Turcs de l'empire ottoman, écrit-il, n'ont aujourd'hui qu'un faible lien entre eux: la religion. Par le panturquisme, ils se solidariseront davantage, ils auront le vrai lien national. Leur nation acquerra une vigueur inconnue jusqu'ici. Elle assimilera les divers éléments islamiques hétérogènes de l'empire. Dans le panturquisme qui unira les millions de Turcs de l'Asie et de l'Europe orientale, les Osmanlis joueront un rôle semblable à celui du Japon dans le monde jaune. Malgré les obstacles que ne manquera pas de lui susciter la Russie peu soucieuse de voir des millions de ses sujets subir une influence venue de Constantinople, cet idéal, qui aura pour lui les encouragements des puissances, désireuses de créer des difficultés à un rival redouté, peut parfaitement se réaliser. Les Turcs verront, par lui, leur horizon s'agrandir. Leur histoire ne se limitera plus aux Fatih, aux Sélim, aux Nefhi et aux Kiémal. Elle englobera les Ougouz, les Djenghiz, les Timour, les Farabi, les Ibn-Sina, etc."

Une association, le *Turc Dirneyi*, fondée à cette époque, sert indirectement les vues du panturquisme. Elle comprenait toutes les sommités de la nouvelle Turquie. Hommes d'état, députés et écrivains y étaient inscrits. Il ne lui manquait que le caractère officiel pour devenir une véritable académie. Son but était de faire un vaste travail de récension de tout ce qui a été écrit par les Turcs ou sur les Turcs.

Elle se mit à compulser les documents anciens et modernes, pour en tirer un tableau véridique de la vie nationale dans le passé, et pour dégager le vrai caractère du peuple turc, avec toutes ses qualités foncières. Elle voulut déterminer la direction qu'il convenait d'imprimer à la culture naissante de la nation.

Dans le revue volumineuse qui lui sert d'organe collaborent des savants tels que Nedjib Assim, Veled Tchélébi, Tahir de Brousse, Tangar, et des poètes tels que Mehmed Emin, Ahmed Hikmet.

Confié à des mains fatiguées, le sort du *Turc Dirneyi* fut précaire. Il a manqué à cette association du sang jeune, ardent, batailleur pour se frayer la voie jusqu'au grand public, pour s'imposer à l'attention. La violence, seule propice aux novateurs, lui a répugné.

Un autre groupement, celui de la revue *Turk Yourdou* (le foyer turc), paraît plus qualifié pour pénétrer dans la masse et y propager l'idéal panturquiste. Le *Turk Yourdou* est dirigé par Youssouf Aktchoura. Il a soulevé dans la presse et parmi la jeunesse universitaire un enthousiasme indescriptible. Il étudie la situation économique, l'histoire, les moeurs, la langue des peuples turcs. En des nouvelles où circule une vitalité vigoureuse, les sentiments simples, nobles et mâles de la race sont exaltés. Mehmed Emin et d'autres poètes y chantent la vie rustique, les moeurs chevaleresques du Turc. Ils évoquent les types originaires du Touran, les tentes patriarcales, auprès des rivières murmurantes et des forêts aux arbres rares, les lentes pérégrinations des tribus ancestrales à travers les prairies herbeuses où paissent les troupeaux de chevaux et de moutons, l'héroïsme indomptable, le dévouement de ces primitifs dont l'héritage unique consiste en un sabre reçu des mains du père mourant. Les Djenghiz, les Timour sont lavés des actes de barbarie qu'une histoire partiale se plaît à leur attribuer. Une partie de la revue est consacrée aux conationaux du Caucase, des bords de la Léna, du Turkestan, de Perse, aux sentiments de solidarité de qui on fait souvent appel. Tous les collaborateurs ont à coeur l'épuration de la langue; ils s'expriment en turc très pur, mettant à contribution le yakout, l'oïgour, le nogaïque, tous les idiomes ouralo-altaïques pour enrichir leur vocabulaire dépouillé avec soin de tout alliage hétérogène.

VII

Le panturquisme est une exagération d'un sentiment national fort légitime. Il constitue un programme maximum. Il permet d'orienter les efforts vers un but déterminé, et en cela il est très utile.

La véritable mesure a été donnée par les intellectuels de Salonique, dont le groupement qui porte la dénomination de *Yeni Hayat* (nouvelle vie), est doué d'une belle vitalité. Salonique, d'où était parti naguère, à deux reprises, le signal de l'affranchissement civique et politique, devait aussi sonner le tocsin contre la routine sociale et contre les errements littéraires. La charge contre la vieille forteresse des préjugés fut conduite par les *Yentch-Calemler* (les jeunes plumes), revue littéraire qui précisa l'oeuvre de Chinassi et de Kiémal et ne retint de l'effort avorté des tasfiedjis que le souci de désencombrer la langue. Mais il y a dans l'action de la revue salonicienne plus de méthode que dans la tentative des deux maîtres écrivains et moins d'étroit ostracisme que chez Nedjib Assim et Mehmed Emin à l'égard des provenances linguistiques étrangères. Les adhérents du *Yeni Hayat* ne sont point des utopistes; ils ne cherchent pas à accomplir d'impossibles tours de force. Ils ne répudient que les néologismes, les emprunts superflus. Les mots depuis longtemps en usage et dont on ne peut se passer ont tous acquis droit de cité. Mais il faut fermer les écluses par lesquelles l'arabe et le persan déversent sans cesse tout leur contenu dans la langue, ce qui met les osmanlis qui ne veulent pas passer pour illetrés dans la ridicule obligation de connaître à fond trois idiomes, les plus dissemblables du monde. On devra se contenter d'une langue sobre, où chaque vocable ait une fonction précise et où il n'y ait, autant que possible, qu'un mot pour exprimer une idée. De plus, les mots arabes ou persans devront se turquiser, abandonner les modes de filiation, de flexion, de déclinaison propres à la syntaxe des langues auxquelles ils appartiennent. Ils doivent se plier à la loi turque. Ainsi, la grammaire turque conservera sa belle simplicité et ne sera pas un objet de torture pour les étudiants qui ne parviennent jamais, à l'heure actuelle, à en posséder parfaitement les mystérieux et puérils arcanes. La littérature turque cessera de ressembler à l'alphabet chinois. Voici le programme du *Yeni-lissan* (la nouvelle langue), tel qu'il est exposé dans un manifeste distribué à profusion et reproduit par tout la presse.

I. – Abandonner les règles de composition grammaticale arabe et persane.
II. – Supprimer les affixes de ces langues.
III. – Employer, dans la mesure du possible, une orthographe phonétique.
IV. – Recourir de préférence aux vocables turcs quand ils existent.
V. – Considérer comme norme la langue parlée à Constantinople.

Par ces moyens, l'afflux extravagant de l'arabisme et de l'iranisme s'arrête. On cesse de parler arabe en turc. C'est, en somme, une oeuvre sage et nécessaire, analogue à celle qu'accomplit Malherbe à l'aurore du grand siècle, qu'ont entreprise les jeunes écrivains du *Yeni-Hayat*. Ils viennent régenter la langue comme ils vont tout à l'heure régenter les moeurs; ils satisfont à un besoin d'ordre et de discipline qui ne s'était fait que trop sentir.

En poésie, les *Yentch-Calemler* se montrent plus hardis. Ils brisent les vieux moules et tentent de créer un vers souple, vivant. Ils s'attaquent avec une fougue juvénile à toutes les gloires usurpées, dégonflent les ballons et crèvent les grosses caisses. Ali Djanib, rédacteur en chef de la revue, livre un assaut furieux à tous les écrivains de la vieille école. Il ne ménage même pas Tewfik Fikret, le plus grand poète vivant après Abdul-Hak-Hamid. Tous les partisans de l'*eski-tchiguir* (l'ancienne méthode) sont flétris en bloc du nom de *dounkilar,* ceux d'hier, tandis que les jeunes du *Yeni-Hayat* sont les *bouyounkilar*, ceux d'aujourd'hui.

Parmi les promoteurs du *yeni-lissan*, il faut citer, indépendemment d'Omer Seïf Eldine et Ali Djanib déjà nommés, Kiazim Nami, un des dix fondateurs du Comité Union et Progrès, écrivain et conférencier de grand talent. Des Donmehs, membres d'une secte judéo-musulmane, et des israélites collaborent activement avec les Turcs pour jeter les bases de la langue nouvelle.

Les adversaires n'ont pas manqué aux *bouyounkilar.* Le *Servet-i-Finoun,* la plus importante et la plus ancienne revue turque, déclare par la plume de Kiuprulu Zadé Mehmed Fuad que le *yeni-lissan* n'est pas viable. Le *Rebab*, revue de fondation récente, veut accabler les novateurs sous le sarcasme et le ridicule. Le philosophe Riza Tewfik, la tête la plus encyclopédique de la nouvelle Turquie, est aussi contre les modernistes.

Cette opposition constitue un stimulant précieux pour la nouvelle école qui déploie une activité inlassable. Les livres succèdent aux brochures. Les presses ne chôment guère.

La partie est gagnée, à l'heure actuelle. Une profusion d'ouvrages ont été publiés en *yeni-lissan.* Le dernier congrès pédagogique du vilayet de Salonique a adopté le programme grammatical des *bouyounkilar*, d'après lequel, d'ailleurs, sont rédigés divers périodiques, entre autres le *Yeni Felsefé,* le *Roumélie,* organe du Comité Union et Progrès, le *Yentch Fikirlar* de Monastir, le *Kioylou* de Smyrna, le *Yeni Edirné* d'Andrinople. Le *Hak*, le quotidien le plus important de la capitale, organe officiel du parti unioniste, a commencé la publication d'une revue hebdomadaire où il vulgarise le nouveau credo linguistique et littéraire avec beaucoup d'énergie et de méthode.

VIII

Mais la réforme de la langue ne représente qu'une faible partie du programme du *Yeni-Hayat*. Zia bey, le véritable directeur du mouvement, le philosophe tout pénétré des idées d'Alfred Fouillée, de Gustave Le Bon et de Durkheim, nourrit de grands espoirs et de vastes pensées. Il est plein de foi dans les idées forces, dans le pouvoir des influences obscures qui agissent sur l'inconscient mystérieux et dans l'action toute puissante de la conscience collective des peuples. Il s'appuie sur ses auteurs favoris pour démontrer la possibilité de reconstituer une âme au peuple turc. Il faudra, pour cela, propager un esprit public spécial par des publication multiples, par des écoles, des conférences, des réunions fréquentes dans les clubs, de façon à atteindre les couches sociales les plus profondes, à façonner les caractères, pétrir les cerveaux. On y arrivera par étapes successives, si l'on agit avec une persévérance et une continuité que tempéreront fortement la prudence, le souci de ne rien brusquer, le respect des institutions existantes, des traditions et même des préjugés. Il sera nécessaire de répéter aux Turcs, sans se lasser, qu'ils sont des Turcs, qu'ils ont un passé glorieux et un avenir riche de promesses; que l'essentiel est qu'ils soient unis, solidaires en tout. Peu importe que la race ne soit point pure, qu'elle soit hybride, bigarrée, que des mélanges constants aient brassé sans trêve le sang des Osmanlis. Ce qui constitue un peuple, ce n'est pas autant la communauté réelle, historique d'origine, que l'illusion de cette communauté. La formation des nations ne relève pas de l'anthropologie.

"Ce sont les croyances et les sentiments communs à la moyenne des membres d'une société, dit Durkheim, qui forment ce qu'on peut appeler la conscience collective. Cette conscience est diffuse dans toute l'étendue de la société. Les individus passent, et elle reste. Elle ne change pas à chaque génération, mais elle relie au contraire les unes aux autres les générations successives."

Il s'agira d'élaborer un idéal national et d'en propager dans la masse les préceptes impératifs, les disciplines, les consignes.

"Le petit nombre d'idées fondamentales qui ont toujours guidé les diverses civilisations, enseigne Gustave Le Bon, ne sauraient avoir d'action réelle sur l'âme des peuples sans descendre des régions mobiles de la pensée dans cette région stable et inconsciente des sentiments où s'élaborent les motifs de nos actions. Ces idées deviennent alors des éléments du caractère et peuvent agir sur la conduite. Leur puissance est alors considérable parce que la raison cesse d'avoir prise sur elles."

Quelques personnalités puissantes, imprégnées de la notion des nouvelles contraintes sociales, iront communiquer leurs idées-forces, leurs représentations, leurs émotions, leurs tendances à la multitude, qui, tout en réagissant vigoureusement sur ces personnalités et en les modifiant, sera toute portée à se laisser gagner, à laisser se réfracter en elle, suivant l'indice qui lui est propre, les influences individuelles des apôtres.

Le *Yeni Felsefé* (la Nouvelle Philosophie) s'emploie à développer le programme intégral du *Yeni Hayat* qui refera au peuple une nouvelle vie dans le domaine familial, économique, social, esthétique, philosophique, moral, judiciaire. Mais il se garde de préciser d'ores et déjà son idéal. Le définir, en arrêter les contours, serait une entreprise fort préjudiciable. Un idéal n'a jamais un but clair, évident. Son attrait est dans son vague même, dans la part qu'il laisse couverte du voile de l'inconnu. Ce caractère d'inexprimé en fait un précieux stimulant de progrès. Souvent, courant après un idéal, on réalise des conquêtes imprévisibles et qu'on n'avait pas désirées. Les chercheurs de la pierre philosophale trouvèrent la chimie; on jeta les fondements de l'astronomie en tentant d'arracher aux astres le secret de nos destinées.

Ainsi, de propos délibéré, le ***Yeni Hayat*** reste flottant. Il se complaît dans les formules ondoyantes et qui autorisent tous les écarts, toutes les fugues de l'imagination. On ne saurait prévoir où il aboutira. C'est, pour employer une formule bergsonienne, une oeuvre de vie, susceptible de variation, soumise à l'évolution créatrice, qu'on déflorerait en voulant soumettre aux rigueurs de la logique cet instrument incomplet de compréhension.

Quelques principes, cependant, s'en dégagent avec une grande netteté. Le conservatisme nationaliste d'abord. Il faut vouloir être turc et avoir le courage de remonter aux ancêtres, d'aller puiser au berceau de la race l'inspiration d'une vie idéale. Arrière vers le Touran! On reculera de quatre, de dix, de quarante siècles s'il le faut, pour découvrir les vraies tendances de l'âme turque. On ressuscitera le passé et on en extraira la règle de vie nationale. On ira consulter les reliques ancestrales dans les entrailles de l'Altoun-Dagh et sous les ruines de Kara-Kouroum.

Comme corollaire, le *Yeni Hayat* répudie les idées humanitaires. Gustave Le Bon est son patron et A. Fouillée lui fournit des armes. Il cite copieusement ces deux sociologues.

"L'humanitarisme, dit Gustave Le Bon, devient un des fléaux de la France moderne. Il ronge sans relâche les bases de l'édifice social. Quand la funeste race des philanthropes s'abat sur un peuple, il est près des grandes catastrophes. Il faut craindre la peste, mais il faut redouter plus encore les philanthropes. Les sociétés n'eurent jamais de pires ennemis. Le philanthrope n'est nullement l'homme du progrès, mais celui qui détruit toutes les initiatives, tous les progrès."

"La France, dit à son tour Fouillée, obéissant à certaines idées humanitaires, contribua à la formation du royaume d'Italie, et facilita l'oeuvre de Bismarck. Ainsi elle suscita deux grands ennemis. Ce sont là les tristes présents des idées humanitaires. Tous les malheurs de la France, depuis un siècle et demi, en découlent."

Et ailleurs:

"Les illusions ingénues sur la fraternité des peuples fermèrent les yeux de tous les Français sur les farouches rivalités qui préparèrent le choc des nations. Nous avons été dupes de l'Italie, dupes de l'Allemagne, de toutes les nations qui ne demandent qu'à nous laisser notre "humanitairerie", pour conserver, fonder ou étendre leur nationalisme plus ou moins jaloux. La politique de sentiment, qui a plusieurs fois compromis la destinée de la France, devait être vaincue dans la réalité par la politique d'intérêt nationaliste."

Voilà ce que disent des rêveries humanitaires les maîtres de la pensée contemporaine. C'est aux Turcs ottomans surtout que le leurre de la fraternité des nations serait fatal. Le peuple turc n'a que des ennemis, il n'a point de soutiens. Sa force réside en lui. Il est particulièrement urgent, au dire des jeunes novateurs, de soustraire les esprits aux influences déprimantes qui tendent à s'insinuer sous le couvert de la propaganda maçonnique, véhicule d'un cosmopolitisme décevant et malsain, force puissante de désagrégation et d'indiscipline sociale.

L'institution maçonnique qui détruit tout sentiment d'amour national et déclare une guerre sournoise au principe de patriotisme, disent-ils, est un instrument d'asservissement entre les mains des gouvernements européens qui font volontiers de l'internationalisme, du radicalisme et même de l'anticléricalisme d'exportation pour miner la résistance de la Turquie et assurer mieux leur entreprise déjà séculaire d'exploitation cynique et systématique. Il faut renoncer aussi d'un coeur léger à l'utopie humanitaire de l'ottomanisme intégral; on ne peut pas, sans danger grave, prétendre à former une nation une et indivisible avec des peuples que la volonté de vivre en commun n'englobe pas en un tout cohérent.

A bas donc l'affadissante humanitairerie, l'internationalisme lâche, l'hypocrite maçonnerie universelle! Patrie et Nation! voilà la devise du *Yeni Hayat*. Tout pour la Patrie!

Ces réformateurs de moeurs traitent le levantinisme avec une grande sévérité. Ils conseillent d'adopter les principes de l'Europe, ses procédés de travail, sa technique, mais poursuivent de leur haine toute singerie des Européens. Moderniser les institutions, l'esprit public, oui; les troquer, non. Ils sont pour le développement et le redressement rationnels des vieux usages. "Contractons, à l'instar des Anglais, des Suédois, le goût des exercices physiques, disent-ils, mais faisons du *binédjilik* (équitation), du *pehlivanlik* (lutte). Cultivons nos qualités ataviques de courage et de dévouement que chantent dans leurs *Zafernamés* (chants de victoire) tous les vieux poètes osmanlis. Là est notre salut. Les grandes puissances et les états balkaniques ont juré notre perte. Si nous voulons vivre, si nous voulons résister aux appétits voraces qui nous guettent, nous devons être des Turcs, c'est-à-dire des guerriers intrépides et résolus."

C'est dans le sein de la famille que les générations qui lèvent feront l'apprentissage des mâles vertus rédemptrices. Préparer la femme à son rôle d'éducatrice, la relever à ses propres yeux, lui inculquer un savoir utile et des sentiments d'ardent patriotisme, voilà un point fondamental du programme de la jeune école.

Le *Yeni Hayat* concilie, comme nous venons de le voir, le principe d'évolution avec les traditions nationales. Il est pour le progrès, ce qui lui vaut le concours des intellectuels; il est traditionnaliste: la sympathie, ou, du moins, la neutralité des éléments rétrogrades du peuple lui est tout acquise. De là son succès rapide dans tous les milieux turcs.

IX

Les Turcs ont enfin trouvé une âme nationale. Le domaine de leurs recherches et de leurs expériences est allé en se rétrécissant. Après avoir, au début, englobé tous les éléments de l'empire, sans distinction de confession, de race ni de langue avec l'ottomanisme, il s'est circonscrit aux seules populations musulmanes, avec l'ottomanisme islamique renforcé par le panislamisme; et en dernier lieu, se rapetissant encore, il s'est vu limité au turquisme, étayé par le panturquisme du *Turk yourdou*.

Désormais, le tourbillon turquiste entraîne tous les Turcs de l'empire. On ne lui résiste plus. Les fonctionnaires, du haut en bas de l'échelle hiérarchique, les hommes d'état, les riches beys, la jeunesse des écoles, tout ce qui dans le pays compte, pense, agit est gagné à cause du *Yeni Hayat*. C'est sans doute l'élite, l'*intelligentia*, qui jusqu'ici a pu seule être atteinte. La masse semble encore distante, indifférente. On a dit que les dirigeants du mouvement constituent comme un état-major sans soldats. Mais c'est déjà beaucoup que d'avoir créé un état-major. Les cadres ne sauraient tarder à être remplis. Le peuple sera conquis graduellement, par les écoles, les associations, les journaux, les revues, les conférences. Des groupes multiples se sont formés à travers tout le pays. Ils sont encore sans attaches, leur action manque de cohésion, d'ensemble. Mais l'oeuvre de concentration et de coordination se fera à brève échéance. Les publications populaires foisonnent; tous les jours, il paraît une revue nouvelle qui dure, une brochure qui s'enlève à plusieurs milliers d'exemplaires. Aktchoura, Agaïef, font des conférences de propagande auxquelles la presse donne le plus grand retentissement. Des sociétés commerciales, les *Chirket,* sont fondées un peu partout, quoique sans beaucoup de succès, pour le relèvement économique des Turcs. A Constantinople, un groupe bien organisé que dirige Sélim Serri, orthopédiste de valeur, et de Dr. Riza Tewfik, grand admirateur des Anglo-Saxons, jette les bases d'un système de gymnastique nationale. L'histoire, la philosophie, la littérature prennent un essor remarquable sous la poussée des idées nouvelles. Une activité intellectuelle, économique et sociale bienfaisante se manifeste dans le monde osmanli, naguère sommeillant et apathique.

Quoique le *Yeni Hayat* soit dépourvu de tendances assimilatrices, il conquiert peu à peu toutes les minorités musulmanes allogènes de Turquie. Les Kurdes nomades, les Lazes indociles au joug, les Valaques, les Grecs et les Bulgares islamisés de la Turquie d'Europe, dont la foi mahométane est très tiède, seront absorbés à brève échéance par les Turcs, si toutefois la conscience collective turque continue à se renforcer. Ces populations sont sans passé historique connu d'elles, sans culture ni élite. Jusqu'ici, les Turcs, désorganisés eux-mêmes, n'ont pas tenté de les assimiler. Dans les villes, où leurs représentants sont isolés, ces musulmans non turcs prennent tout à fait le caractère du conquérant, abandonnent leur idiome, leurs moeurs, tout comme les Albanais déracinés de leur terroir et devenus fonctionnaires ou commerçants. On ne peut les distinguer des Turcs. Mais dans les campagnes, le paysan n'a pas été entamé. Cependant il n'est pas réfractaire à l'influence turque. Il accepte volontiers les écoles de l'Etat et se rallie au mouvement nationaliste osmanli.

L'apport de ces minorités n'est pas négligeable. Il se chiffre par plus de trois millions d'âmes. C'est beaucoup pour les Turcs qui ne sont qu'au nombre de huit millions à peine dans tout l'empire.

Mais le turquisme saura-t-il s'imposer par sa continuité dans l'effort, par sa persistance? Ce qui manque surtout à l'Orient, c'est l'esprit de suite, la persévérance, la méthode dans l'action. On amorce bien des projets, mais faute de constance, on en mène bien peu à bout. Le nationalisme turc, d'ailleurs, se bute à une difficulté très grande: la dispersion des Osmanlis à travers le pays. On ne trouve des groupements de quelque importance qu'en Anatolie; mais l'Anatolie est précisément la région qui est le moins entamée pas les nouvelles idées. Les écoles y sont très rares; les journaux n'y sont pas lus. On n'y connaît aucune ambition intellectuelle. Il faudra de longues années pour que l'influence du *Yeni Hayat* y puisse pénétrer. Y pénétrera-t-elle jamais? On peu se le demander.

Cependant le gouvernement semble suivre d'un très bon oeil la propagande des réformistes. Le Comité Union et Progrès observe, en apparence, une prudente réserve. Par l'affirmation de principes trop étroitement nationalistes, il risquerait de s'aliéner la masse qui est panislamique, et les éléments non-turcs, dont le concours lui est indispensable. Mais ses secrètes sympathies, son appui certain, quoique discret, va aux promoteurs de la renaissance nationaliste. Ses membres les plus influents, Zia bey, de Diarbékir, le Dr. Husny, originaire du Caucase, le Dr. Nazim sont des apôtres convaincus du turquisme. Devant les tendances particularistes tous les jours plus accentuées des Albanais et des Arabes, il sera contraint de prendre ostensiblement position. Le sentiment turquiste supplantera alors définitivement l'ottomanisme avorté et deviendra le principal facteur de la politique intérieure.

La lutte sera alors âpre entre le dominateur et les nationalités soumises. Néanmoins il est juste d'indiquer que le mouvement n'affecte pas une allure chauviniste. Il n'émerge pas de la foule. Il est d'origine tout intellectualiste et aristocratique, nourri des philosophies occidentales, des principes évolutionnistes. Il n'a guère la politique comme mobile, ne tend pas à imposer son empire à l'ensemble du pays.

Les dirigeants ne sont point les maîtres de l'heure; ils n'ont point de fonctions dans l'Etat. Ce ne sont pas des ouvriers systématiquement conduits. Devant le triste spectacle que présente l'état social du Turc, chaqu'un d'eux, le coeur navré, obéissant à une impulsion spontanée et tout individuelle, essaye de réagir contre la ruine et la mort, prêtes à s'abattre sur la race. Ils font même preuve d'une certaine largeur de vues dans leurs spéculations nationalistes. Un recueil de nouvelles d'un jeune, paru ces temps derniers, le *Turc Kalbi* (le Coeur turc), qui a été un grand succès de librairie, répète à toutes les pages en guise de leit-motif: *Turk ol, ve olmayanlari sev* (sois Turc et aime ceux qui ne le sont pas). Parmi les héros du livre, on voit figurer des généraux de l'armée ottomane qui portent le nom de Casbarian (arménien), Hristaki (grec), Samuel (israélite).

Les diverses nationalités ne dissimulent pas leurs craintes, malgré ces assurances de bonhomie et de bienveillance. Elles se demandent si le mouvement ne renferme pas, en germe, la menace d'une intolérance future à leur égard.

"Aucune menace de ce genre n'est à redouter, affirme résolument Zia bey. D'abord, nous désolidarisons le patriotisme d'avec la religion. C'est un effort de laïcisation dont les esprits éclairés doivent nous tenir compte et c'est un grand bien pour les citoyens de ce pays qui ne professent pas le mahométisme. L'idéal religieux, qui remonte de la foule à l'élite et engendre le mysticisme, la superstition, cède le pas à l'idéal nationaliste, plus rationnel, plus conscient parce qu'il descend de l'élite à la foule. Nous conjurons ainsi le péril du Chériat qui peut conduire aux pires excès. Autre argument digne de remarque: Aujourd'hui, le Turc ne souffre pas que les Albanais, les Grecs aient leur culture, leurs sentiments, leurs institutions propres, lui n'ayant encore rien de semblable. Lorsqu'il développera sa vie sociale, il trouvera très naturel le particularisme des autres; il deviendra plus compréhensif, partant plus tolérant."

Quoi qu'en pensent les éléments non turcs de l'empire, le sentiment turquiste est légitime. Le peuple osmanli, qui sait se battre et qui sait mourir, aspire à la vie. Il veut compléter l'oeuvre de régénération entreprise jadis sous Mahmoud II. Après avoir détrôné les tyrans du Yildiz, il tente de devenir une nation. Il veut réaliser sa révolution sociale après sa révolution politique.

La tâche est lourde et difficultueuse, toute hérissée d'obstacles. Mais les artisans du *Yeni Hayat* paraissent résolus à surmonter tous les obstacles.

"Nous nous inspirerons de l'histoire glorieuse de nos ancêtres, s'écrie le *Yeni Felséfé,* nous ressusciterons toute la splendeur, toute la magnificence de notre vieux peuple. Et nous prouverons au monde que le Turc n'a perdu sa valeur, qu'il a encore une âme, un orgueil national. Notre race vivra avec ses vertus et son honneur. Et si nous, nous succombons, nos descendants sauront réaliser notre idéal. Nous sommes passagers et débiles, mais la race est éternelle et toute puissante."

Mercure de France, 16 August 1912, pp. 673-707

MOÏSE COHEN,[1] DIE JUDEN IN DEN BALKANLÄNDERN

Die bedeutsamen Veränderungen, welche der Krieg in den Balkanländern verursachte, fangen nunmehr an, sich zu konkretisieren und die Folgen des Krieges treten immer deutlicher hervor. Nachdem nun keine wichtige Begebenheit unter der Himmelskuppel vor sich geht, ohne einen Widerklang in den auf schwankem Boden errichteten Zelten Israels zu erwecken, so erscheint es von grossem Interesse, diese Veränderungen vom jüdischen Standpunkte aus zu beleuchten.

Drei Fragen sind ganz speziell zu erörtern: welche Stellung hatten eigentlich die Juden des Balkans vor dem Kriege eingenommen? Wie wird sich ihre Zukunft nach dem Kriege gestalten?

Die Juden des Balkans werden kurzweg als Sephardim oder Spagniolen, zum Unterschiede von den Aschkenazim, bezeichnet. Bedeutet diese Unterscheidung etwa, dass es zwei verschiedene Judenheiten gibt, wie dies einige christliche Schriftsteller immer wieder von neuem behaupten? Gewiss nicht! Wie aus den modernen soziologischen Arbeiten hervorgeht, besteht zwischen den Aschkenazim und Sephardim kein anderer, als nur ein einfacher geographischer Unterschied. Die Aschkenazim leben seit Jahrhunderten in der gemässigten Zone Mitteleuropas während die Sephardim sich an den wärmeren Küsten des Mittelmeeres niedergelassen haben; aber beide sind das Produkt der gleichen soziologischen Faktoren, insbesondere der grausamen Verfolgungen des Mittelalters. Die jahrhundertelangen Leiden, die Notwendigkeit, immer auf der Hut zu sein, haben bei Aschkenazim und Sephardim in gleicher Weise eine besondere Denkungsart, einen eigenen Charakter ausgebildet, der durch die systematische Abschliessung im Ghetto, die minutiöse Beibehaltung derselben rituellen Gebräuche, die konstante Ausübung desselben Gewerbes ausserordentlich gefestigt wurde. Die Thora, der Talmud und alle anderen heiligen Bücher der Juden, diese wunderbaren Schmelztiegel, in welchem die Intelligenz und die moralischen Qualitäten des jüdischen Volkes in eherne Formen gegossen wurden, haben bei den Aschkenazim, wie bei den Sephardim, die gleichen Wirkungen erzeugt.

Was nun die Juden des Balkans anbelangt, so muss hervorgehoben werden, dass wir nicht rein sephardisches oder spagniolisches Blut in uns haben. In unseren Adern fliesst auch eine bedeutende Menge aschkenazischen Blutes. Dies ist eine historische Tatsache, die wohl bisher nicht oft erwähnt wurde aber trotzdem richtig ist.

Die erste Niederlassung der Juden am Balkan erfolgte bereits vier vor Christus, durch die sogenannten Romanisten. Diese waren aber vollständig hellenisierte Juden, d.h. sie hatten sich der griechischen Kultur angepasst. Trotzdem waren sie den Verfolgungen der römischen und später der byzantinischen Regierungen ausgesetzt. Sie lebten in einem grossen Galous, um den Ausdruck des berühmten jüdischen Reisenden des 12. Jahrundert,

Benjamin de Tudel, zu gebrauchen. Ihre einzige Zufluchtsstäte war die Synagoge, nur hier an dieser heiligen Stätte fanden unsere Vorfahren das ungetrübte Glück, welches durch die Beschäftigung mit der Thora und mit der Auslegung der anderen heiligen Schriften verbunden war. Jede jüdische Gemeinde, ob gross, ob klein, wurde als eine einzige Familie angesehen, als deren gemeinschaftliches Heim die Synagoge galt, wo Freud und Leid gemeinschaftlich getragen wurde.

Erst die Eroberung des Landes durch die Türken im 14. und 15. Jahrhundert hat den moralischen Leiden dieser uralten jüdischen Gemeinden ein Ende bereitet. Ihr nunmehriger Reichtum, ihr Wohlleben, hat auf ihre Brüder im Norden eine unwiderstehliche Anziehungskraft ausgeübt. Die Folge hievon war, dass diese kleinen jüdischen Gemeinden des Ostens von einer grossen Menge aschkenazischer Juden überflutet wurden, die von den Ufern des Rheins vertrieben worden waren. Die Türkei war damals, wie in dem bekannten Appell des Rabbi Isak Sarfati im 15. Jahrhundert ausdrücklich beschrieben wurde, das irdische Paradies für die in der ganzen Welt verfolgten Juden. Auch aus den italienischen Republiken sind viele Juden eingewandert, doch haben die Aschkenazim durch ihre grössere Zahl und ihre talmudische Gelehrsamkeit die Oberhand gewonnen.

Zur Zeit der grossen Einwanderung der aus Spanien vertriebenen Juden gegen Ende des fünfzehnten Jahrhunderts war die bisher unbestrittene Hegemonie der Aschkenazim bereits eine vollendete Tatsache. Doch haben diese spagniolischen und portugiesischen Einwanderer die aschkenazische Hegemonie verdrängt und es erfolgte gleich im Anfang ein heftiger Zusammenstoss zwischen den sephardischen und aschkenazischen Juden. Die letzteren stammten aus Ländern, wo mittelalterliche Willkür in grausamster Weise waltete; sie versenkten sich wohl tief in das Studium von Thora und Talmud, aber ihr Geist war rückständig und beeinflusst von den beschränkten Ansichten jener Völker, welche bisher ihre Umgebung gebildet hatten. Durch die hundertjährigen Verfolgungen herabgewürdigt und niedergedrückt, jeder Kultur und Bildung bar, waren sie der Finsternis des Fanatismus preisgegeben. Die Sephardim dagegen kamen aus Ländern, die seit drei Jahrhunderten die westliche Kultur in sich aufgenommen hatten und zu deren Entwicklung die spanischen und portugiesischen Juden viel beigetragen haben. Die Verfolgungen Torquemada's und der anderen gleich gesinnten Inquisitoren waren erst vor kurzem eingetreten und hatten noch nicht jenen Stolz und Edelsinn, die spanische Juden den Hidalgos entlehnten, allzutief verletzt. Die Einwanderer aus Spanien, welche sich für Abkömmlinge des Königs David hielten, empfanden eine tiefe Verachtung gegen ihre unkultivierten und fanatischen Brüder, die Aschkenazim; und diese wieder hassten die Sephardim als Renegaten, welche, statt ihre Zeit mit dem Talmudstudium zu verbringen, sich weltlichen Freuden und Vergnügungen hingaben, philosphischen und wissenschaftlichen Studien widmeten. Dadurch war ein Zusammenstoss unvermeidlich und diese Feindseligkeiten währten lange Zeit. Erst zu Ende des 16. Jahrhunderts war das aschkenazische Element vollkommen überholt und fast verschlungen durch die Majorität, die kulturelle Ueberlegenheit und die moralischen Vorteile der Sephardim.

Seit der grossen Auswanderung im Jahre 1498 ist die Türkei die einzige und sichere

Zufluchtsstätte für das gesamte Judentum, welches in der ganzen Welt der fanatischen Unduldsamkeit ausgesetzt war. Es kamen unaufhörlich Scharen von Marannen, welche zum Judentum zurückkehren wollten. Aber nicht Elend und Armut, sondern Reichtum, Kultur und geistige Erhöhung haben diese Einwanderer mitgebracht. Sie waren der mächtigste und wirksamste Faktor für die ökonomische Entwicklung der Türkei. Der kluge Sultan Bajasd hatte vollkommen Recht, wenn er sagte, dass Kaiser Ferdinand, der die Juden aus seinen Ländern verwiesen hatte, kein verständiger Mensch sei, da er sein eigenes Land der Armut preisgebe, um das Kaiserreich der Padischa zu bereichern. Tatsächlich wurden auch alsbald die früher grossen und blühenden Städte in Spanien ärmlichen, und stillen Dörfern gleich, während in der frisch eroberten Türkei, die eben noch einem Trümmerhaufen geglichen hatte, die Städte rasch emporwuchsen. Das türkische Volk welches unaufhörlich von seinen Kriegen in Anspruch genommen war, hatte weder Zeit noch die Mittel, um die ökonomischen Ressourcen des Landes zu verwerten. Die besiegten Völker aber waren meist wieder aufs flache Land zurückgedrängt und befassten sich hauptsächlich mit Ackerbau. Die Vertreibung der Juden aus Spanien erfolgte gerade zur rechten Zeit, um die Lücken in der sozialen Schichtung der Türkei auszufüllen und den für Handel, Gewerbe und Industrie unentbehrlichen Stand zu bilden. Diese Masse neuer jüdischer Bewohner fungierte auch sehr bald als wichtigstes Moment für Kultur und Bildung in der ganzen Türkei. Nicolai, der berühmte französische Reisende, welcher im Jahre 1552 den französischen Botschafter nach Konstantinopel begleitete, jammert voll Bitterkeit über das ausserordentliche Emporblühen der Juden im türkischen Reiche. Er schreibt wörtlich: "Der ganze Reichtum ist in Händen der Juden, die meisten guten und berühmten Ärzte gehören diesem Volke an, selbst der Leibarzt des Khalifen, der ein kolossales Vermögen besitzt und einen unbegrenzten Einfluss bei Hofe ausübt, ist ein Jude. Ohne zu übertreiben kann man behaupten, dass der ganze Handel des Orients ausschliesslich in Händen der Juden sei, welche sich durch ihre Tüchtigkeit in allen Zweigen der Industrie auszeichnen. Sie sind es auch, welche zu unserem Unglück bei den Türken die Fabrikation aller Arten von Feuerwaffen, sowie die Buchdruckerkunst eingeführt haben."

Diese goldene Periode des Judentums hat bis zum 17. Jahrhundert gedauert. Der Verfall began erst mit der Periode Zewi, als dieser falsche Prophet die Aufmerksamkeit der Juden von dem praktischen Leben abgelenkt und ihre Tätigkeit durch die in nahe Aussicht gestellte Erfüllung der messianischen Hoffnung lahmgelegt hat. Ihr praktischer und kommerzieller Geist ging immer mehr und mehr in den dunkeln Irrwegen der Kabbala unter. Die letzten Spuren von Kultur und Zivilisation, welche die Juden aus Spanien mitgebracht hatten, waren schon seit langem verwischt. Der Zufluss der Marannen welcher den schwächer gewordenen Glanz des Judentums wieder aufgefrischt hatte, war schon längst beendet. So wurden die Juden die Sklaven des Milieus, in welchem sie lebten. Unwissenheit und religiöser Fanatismus traten immer mehr hervor und der leuchtende Stern des Judentums wurde vollständig verdunkelt. Gegen 1840 verschlimmerte sich die düstere Lage der Juden noch mehr. In dem entlegenen Damaskus waren sie unter dem Vorwande eines angeblichen Ritualmordes Gegenstand heftiger Verfolgungen und ganz Europa war erregt von dem Gedanken, dass die Schrecknisse des Mittelalters für einen grossen Teil der Menschheit wiederkehren sollten. Bei dieser Gelegenheit kam ein Komitee, bestehend aus den bedeutendsten Männern des westeuropäischen Judentums, nach der Türkei, und ermass die Tiefe des Abgrundes, in welchen unsere einst so blühenden Gemeinden versunken waren. Damals wurde der Plan gefasst, die Brüder im Orient durch Gründung von Schulen zu erheben und zu neuem Ansehen zu bringen. Zwanzig Jahre später wurde, beeinflusst von den grossen Ideen des Jahres 1848 die "Alliance Israélite" gegründet, welche alsbald ein dichtes Netz von Schulen über die ganze orientalische Welt spannte. Konstantinopel, Saloniki, Adrianopel und später alle Städte des Balkans, welche mehr als tausend jüdische Einwohner zählten, wurden mit solchen vorzüglich eingerichteten Schulen bedacht. Eine aufgeklärte Jugend, stark und kampfbereit, welche über die westeuropäischen Ideen und Methoden unterrichtet war, trug bald dazu bei, das Ansehen der Balkanjuden zu heben. Der Handel und die kleine lokale Industrie kamen wieder in jüdische Hände und eine Reihe von Ärzten, Advokaten, öffentlichen Funktionären, Journalisten usw. zog bald die allgemeine Aufmerksamkeit auf sich. Reichtum und Licht überfluteten nunmehr wieder das bisher düstere Ghetto. Inszwischen haben bedeutende politische Ereignisse auf der Balkanhalbinsel grosse Veränderungen hervorgerufen. Im ersten Viertel des 19. Jahrhunderts haben sich die Serben und Griechen und ein halbes Jahrhundert später die Bulgaren von der türkischen Oberherrschaft losgelöst, um unabhängige Staaten zu gründen. Jede dieser neuen politischen Organisationen entriss dem ottomanischen Judentum einen Teil seiner Kräfte und die abgesplitterten Teile schlugen verschiedene Richtungen ein. Alsbald hat auch ein Häuflein von etwa 4000 bis 5000 griechischen Juden die griechische Umgangssprache angenommen, aber ihre ökonomische Lage verschlechterte sich, ihr Reichtum nahm ab und sie drohten gänzlicher Armut zu verfallen. Die serbischen Juden, etwa 12000 bis 15000 an der Zahl, konnten, trotz des kulturellen und sprachlichen Einflusses ihrer christlichen Mitbürger, ihrer kommerziellen Beschäftigung nachgehen, da die Serben sich mehr dem Ackerbau zugewendet hatten. Die serbischen Juden gelangten zu einer bescheidenen Wohlhabenheit, viele aber konnten in diesem Lande, welchem der Antisemitismus fern war, in der intellektuellen und administrativen Atmosphäre einflussreiche Stellen erlangen. Auch Bulgarien hat seinen 40000 Juden mancherlei Ressourcen angeboten. Sofia, Rustschuk, Warna, Burgas, Philipopel, Tatar-Bazartschik, sahen ihre Judenviertel blühen und gedeihen, doch hat man ihnen ohne Zweifel weniger Freundschaft erwiesen als in Belgrad oder Nisch. Oft trübten Verleumdungen hässlichster Natur ihren Frieden, doch ist der energische Fleiss und die loyale Gesinnung unserer bulgarischen Brüder dieser vorübergehenden Verstimmungen Herr geworden. Während die serbischen und griechischen Juden zur vollkommenen Assimilierung hinneigten, haben die bulgarischen Juden, dank ihrer grossen Zahl und den vorübergehenden Misshelligkeiten, ihre Individualität bewahrt, manchmal sogar nationale Gefühle gezeigt, die sogar den kampfsüchtigen Zionismus streiften, welcher dem von den intellektuellen Mazedoniern in den Strassen Sofias akklimatisierten lockeren Sozialismus ähnlich war. Jeder der Balkanstaaten hat nunmehr seine Juden nach seiner besonderen Vorstellung umgemodelt. Der Jude von Wolo ist griechisch, chauvinistisch, Megalomane, der von den grossen hellenischen Ideen begeistert ist und von der Eroberung Konstantinopels träumt. Es fehlt nicht viel, so würde er die Patriarchen Abraham, Isak und Jakob vergessen und sich für seinen Abkömmling der Leonidas, Alkibiades und Themistokles halten. Er schwört auf Aristoteles und dessen anmutige Sprache und ruft das martialische Andenken an den

Bulgaroctonem Bali II. wach. Der Serbe israelitischer Konfession hatte oft Gelegenheit, mit der Tscheta, den Banden, zusammen gegen die Türken zu schiessen, um ihre slavischen Brüder von türkischen Joche zu befreien, denn sie hielten sich für echte Slaven, authentische Serben. Die glorreichen Schwerter Nomanic', Karageorgevic' und Duschan's haben sie verblendet.

Der bulgarische Jude war durchdrungen vom Geiste des jugoslavischen Dranges und ist fest überzeugt, dass der Tag kommen wird, an welchem der Zar von Tirnowo unbestritten über die spiegelnden Ufer des Wardar und über das fruchtbare Mündungsgebiet der Maritza gebieten wird, Soloun und Zarigrad, d.h. Saloniki und Konstantinopel die beiden Perlen des Mittelmeeres, die Stadt der Heiligen und die der Zaren, früher oder später, doch sicherlich eines Tages unter bulgarischer Herrschaft sein werden. Das ist est, was der bulgarische Jude aus voller Seele wünscht, das ist echt bulgarisch, echt bulgarisch-chauvinistisch. Der Zufall führte während des Waffenstillstandes im Balkankriege drei Reisende in einem Eisenbahnzuge zusammen, welche miteinander ins Gespräch kamen. Konstantinis, der Redselige, erinnerte unter grossartigen Gesten an grosse Namen und sagte, dass alles Land vom Balkan bis zum Aegäischen Meere, von der Donau bis zu den Quellen des Nils einmal griechisch war und eines Tages wieder griechisch sein werde, denn der Hellenismus sei ein idealer Teil der ganzen orientalischen Menschheit. Dawidoff, stämmig, mit konzentriertem Blick und raschen Bewegungen, trat selten aus seiner Schweigsamkeit heraus, um in rauher und strenger Weise etwas zu sagen. "Wir wollen," meinte er, "dass Mazedonien bulgarisch sei und es wird sein." Lewic, lachlustig, launenhaft, mischte sich stellenweise in die Konversation, um naiver Weise zu sagen, dass die serbische Seele in allen diesen Gegenden lache und dieselben belebe. "Warum wollen Sie nicht, dass Mazedonien serbisch sei?" Die Unterhaltung wurde immer erregter, und als der Zug in Saloniki hielt, hatte die gegenseitige Erbitterung der drei Reisenden den Höhepunkt erreicht und sie verabschiedeten sich kühl von einander. Jeder von ihnen erblickte in seinem Reisegenossen verhasste Feinde. Aber welche Überraschung! Nach einigen Tagen trafen sich die drei Reisenden im Salon des "Klub des Intimes", des Klubs der Israeliten in Saloniki. Lewic, Konstantinis und Dawidoff gafften einander an und riefen. "Wie? Wir sind Brüder und hatten hiervon keine Ahnung als wir unseren kleinlichen Patriotismus auskramten?" Über dem durch den Zufall der Geburt beeinflussten Patriotismus schwebte jetzt eine unbegrenzte und von allen im gleichen Masse empfundene Brüderlichkeit. Das Unglück Israels war jetzt ihr Gesprächsstoff.

Auf diese Weise erfüllte während des Balkankrieges jeder Jude seine Pflicht in den Reihen jenes Heeres, in welches er durch das Schicksal geraten war. Die Züge von Heldenhaftigkeit der jüdischen Mitkämpfer sind zahlreich. Mit der Zigarette im Munde trotzt ein jüdisch-bulgarischer Offizier den türkischen Geschossen und begeistert ein ganzes Bataillon durch seine souveräne Verachtung des Todes. Abramic, ein einfacher, aber kühner Soldat, entscheidet den Sieg von Kumanowo, indem er die zu Boden gefallene dreifarbige Fahne erhebt und den entschwundenen Elan wieder wachruft. Die ottomanischen Generäle bewunderten die Kühnheit der israelitischen Soldaten, welche, obwohl mit der Handhabung der Waffen nicht sehr vertraut, dennoch allen Strapazen widerstanden und immer nur vorrücken wollten.

Aber dieser unglückliche Krieg war verhängnisvoll für den ganzen Balkan und alle jüdischen Gemeinden Mazedoniens, Thraziens und Bulgariens wurden durch denselben in eine schreckliche Armut gestürzt.

Unsere Glaubensgenossen auf der Balkanhalbinsel sind alle von dem gleichen Schicksal betroffen worden. Die seit einem Jahre auf der Tagesordnung stehenden Feuerbrünste, Plünderungen und furchtbaren Blutbäder haben unsere Brüder nicht verschont. Tausende von ihnen stehen vor einer düsteren und ungewissen Zukunft, Vermögen und Erwerbsmöglichkeit hat ihnen der Krieg geraubt[2] und hunderte armer Familien leben nur von Unterstützungen, welche die jüdische Solidarität aufbringt.

Es ist wohl möglich, dass die Gemeinden kleinerer Städte mit der Zeit sich wieder erheben und zu Wohlhabenheit gelangen werden, aber eine Stadt der Balkanhalbinsel wird, nach der heutigen politischen Lage, ihre blühende und glanzende Judenschaft verfallen, vielleicht sogar untergehen sehen. Die Stadt ist keine andere als das grosse Emporium des Aegäischen Meeres, die seit Jahrhunderten als Mutter Israels, als betrachtet wird. Es ist Saloniki. Dieses moderne Zion des Balkans hat schon längst sein Szepter niedergelegt. Vielleicht wird die hellenische Regierung ihre gerechte und korrekte Handlung den Juden gegenüber auch nach der Annexion beibehalten, doch dürfte dies nicht verhindern, dass die Bevölkerung ihre alte Judäophobie wieder in den Vordergrund treten lässt, denn die kleineren Verwaltungsbeamten sind kaum imstande, den Antisemitismus zu verbergen, und so wird der Kampf zwischen jüdischen und griechischen Kaufleuten mit ungleichen Waffen geführt werden. Übrigens wird für Saloniki nach Abtretung des Epirus, Thraziens, Albaniens und des grössten Teiles Mazedoniens nur ein eng begrenztes Absatzgebiet bleiben, welches kaum ein Drittel seiner jetzigen Bevölkerung ernähren kann. Ein grosser Teil unserer Glaubensgenossen wird zum Wanderstabe greifen müssen, um unter anderen Himmelsstrichen seine Existenz und ein freiheitliches Leben zu suchen. Schon hat dieser traurige Auszug begonnen und bestimmte Formen angenommen. Zahlreiche Familien wandern bereits nach entfernten Ländern, nach Nord und Zentralamerika, Brasilien, Argentinien, Frankreich, die Schweiz usw. aus. So geht die Metropole des orientalischen Judentums unter, und nichts vermag dieses Unglück aufzuhalten. Das ganze sephardische Judentum wird die Folgen dieser Zerrüttung seiner Metropole schwer empfinden, welche die Wiege aller edlen und grossmütigen Bewegungen war, die im letzten Jahre alle jüdischen Gemeinden der Balkanhalbinsel belebt haben. Die prächtigen, glänzenden jüdischen Klubs waren es, aus welchen jeder Fortschritt im Orient hervorgegangen ist. Die Tatsache, dass die Hauptstadt Mazedoniens, die schönste und blühendste Stadt der europäischen Türkei, die den Anstoss zur jungtürkischen Revolution gab, einen unbestreitbaren echt jüdischen Charakter besitzt, hat zur Hebung des jüdischen Ansehens viel beigetragen. Die jüdische Gesamtheit darf jedoch angesichts dieser ernsten Sache nicht gleichgültig und ohnmächtig bleiben. Sie muss zugreifen, nicht um dem Einsturz zu verhindern, sondern um aus den Trümmern soviel als möglich zu retten. Der Kern der Saloniker Frage besteht in der Organisierung der Auswanderung. Es muss vor allem jede Verzettelung der Kräfte vermieden werden. Die Auswanderung muss auf einen oder auf einige bestimmte Punkte konzentriert werden.

Die Balkanländer selbst bieten für unsere jüdischen Emigranten ein weites und unbegrenztes Tätigkeitsgebiet. Serbien und Bulgarien bedürfen nach dieser Periode der Verwüstung frischer Kräfte, neuer Hilfsquellen, um sich wieder zu sammeln, zu ihrem normalen Leben zurückzukehren und die ökonomischen Hilfsquellen der mit so vielen Opfern an Blut und Geld eroberten neuen Gebiete zur Geltung zu bringen. Schon jetzt hat eine grosse Anzahl von Saloniker Kaufleuten in Üsküb, Kiewgeli, Köprülü und anderen den Serben zugefallenen Orten Filialen errichtet. Es wäre zu wünschen, dass diese Bewegung sich immer weiter entwickle, denn sie würde eine grosse Wohltat sowohl für Serbien und Bulgarien, als auch für die entwurzelten Juden bedeuten, die überallhin nur Fortschritt, Gedeihen und neuen Wohlstand bringen. Die Serben und Bulgaren sind der Mehrzahl nach Ackerbauer. Die segensreiche Tätigkeit der eingewanderten Juden kann demnach nicht ihren Neid und ihre Eifersucht erwecken.

Nur wenige Jahren würden hinreichen, um die neuen Elemente zu assimilieren und sie aus Fremden zu echten und ergebenen Patrioten zu machen. Mit diesen neuen Elementen wird die durch die Assimilation hart bedrohte serbische Judenschaft ein starker, solider und unerschütterlicher Körper werden, welcher dem gesamten orientalischen Judentum neuen Stolz und neue Kraft einflössen könnte.

Es gibt nun noch eine andere Bewegung, die, wenn sie gut geführt und gut organisiert würde, für den Verfall Salonikis einen teilweisen Ersatz bringen könnte. Es handelt sich um die Konzentrierung der jüdischen Einwanderung nach dem wichtigsten adriatischen Emporium: Smyrna. Dieser Markt bietet dem Handelsgeiste und dem Fleisse der Saloniker Kaufleute ein unerschöpfliches Aktionsfeld. Die Türken, welche nicht nur das herrschende Element, sondern auch die Produzenten und Konsumenten in Kleinasien sind, knüpfen an den Erfolg dieser Bewegung grosse Hoffnungen und wichtige politische Interessen. Die Mitwirkung der westeuropäischen Juden könnte hierbei sehr nützlich sein.

Was nun die Juden betrifft, die unter der griechischen Herrschaft in Saloniki, Kawalla, Serres usw. bleiben und trotz der eigenartigen Emigration eine Körperschaft von Hunderttausend bleiben werden, so sind ihre Aussichten keineswegs hoffnungslos. Sie werden gezwungen sein, die volle Zähigkeit und Hartnäckigkeit des alten Volkes Israel zur Geltung zu bringen, um in dem bevorstehenden erbitterten ökonomischen Kampfe nicht zu unterliegen. Israel ist ja durch vielhundertjährige Kämpfe gestählt und es verlässt niemals den Kampfplatz, solange es nicht vollständig verzweifelt. Vorläufig machen die griechischen Behörden alle möglichen Anstrengungen, um die Gleichberechtigung aufrechtzuerhalten, aber leider hat uns Juden der Antisemitismus nach dieser Richtung nur zu sehr Grund zu Misstrauen gegeben. Wir kennen nur zu genau die ungeheure Infektionskraft dieser Seuche, welche die grösste Schande des 20. Jahrhunderts bildet, und darum können wir nicht vorher bestimmen, bis zu welchem Grade die für die grossen Grundsätze der Gleichheit und Gerechtigkeit begeisterten hellenischen Behörden unparteiisch bleiben werden, wenn gewisse Elemente, welche den glorreichen Namen des edlen hellenischen Volkes beflecken, die Oberhand gewinnen würden. Glücklicherweise waren bisher die höheren griechischen Behörden unausgesetzt auf den Hut und haben ihr Möglichstes getan, um die beabsichtigten Hetzereien hintanzuhalten.

Unsere grösste Hoffnung setzen wir nun auf die Belebung der bulgarischen und serbischen Judenschaft durch den Zufluss neuer jüdischer Einwanderer, insbesondere aber auf die Konzentrierung der Einwanderung nach Smyrna. Wenn die grossen jüdischen Organisationen hierzu ihre Mithilfe leihen, so kann das weltliche Judentum sich über den Untergang des modernen Jerusalem auf dem Balkan trösten mit der sakramentalen Formel: "Le roi est mort, vive le roi!"

Monatsschrift der Österreichisch-Israelitischen Union, XXV/9-10 (September-October 1913), pp. 16-24

TEKİN, YENİ CENGİZLİK

Turan yaşıyor, fakat çinli pençesi ve rus çizmesi altında yaşıyor, Turan, esir ve mahkûm, Turan hakir ve mazlûm! Onu bu halde bırakmak, turanlık için en büyük zilettir. Gözünü açmış, milletini tanımış her türkün en birinci, en mübrem, en mukkades vazifesi, vazife-yi milliyesi onun imdadına koşmak ve onu Çin ejderi ile Rus kartalının kanlı tırnaklarından kurtarmaktır. Türk şahsiyetleri, Türk devletleri hep bu vazife ile mükelleftirler. Herkese kuvveti derecesinde azim bir vazife teveccüh eylemektedir: Ta Osmanlı saltanatından, İran şahlığından, Buhara, Hive emirlerine, Kaşgar derebeylerine kadar. Büyüğe büyük küçüğe küçük bu vazife, fakat, hepsine ayni vazife: vatanı esaretten kurtarmak için cihad, bir cihad-ı milli vazifesi! Cihadta her türk silahlanarak mevkiini almaya mecburdur.

Turanı kurtarmak, bütün türklüğün menafi-i icabatındandır. Esir türkler için iktisap-ı hürriyetin derece-yi ehemmiyetini söylemeye bile hacet yok. Lakin, henüz hürriyet ve istiklalini muhafaza edebilenler içinde bunun [bundan] daha nafi daha faydalı bir meslek-i siyasi olamıyacağını idrak lazım!

Afgan hanlığı, İran şahlığı, Osmanlı padişahlığı! Bu üç devlet, ayni vaziyet-i siyasiyenin mahkumu bulunuyorlar! her üçü iki ateş arasında! Şimalden Rus, cenuptan İngiliz istilası! Bu çenber günden güne daralıyor. Bu kıskaç günden güne kısılıyor. Bu devletlerin hariçte, ecnebi muhitlerde bulacakları müzaheretler, hatta kazanacakları dostluklarla idame-yi hayat etmeleri ihtimali yoktur. Bu dostluklar riyakardır, yalancıdır, her halde geçicidir. Bu devletler, ancak, ana vatana kavuşmak, onun ellerine yapışmak, onun sinesine yaslanmakla muhafaza-yı mevcudiyet edebilirler. Mücadele-yi azime-yi atiyede bu kuvvete dayanmaktan başka bir çaremiz olmıyacaktır.

Devrimiz milliyet ve ırk devridir. Hatta milliyet bile geçiyor, ırk devri geliyor. Küçük, küçük milletler yaşayamıyorlar, her ırk, aksamını tefrik eden hudutları yıkarak birleşmeye doğru yürüyor. Bu cihetle — böyle giderse — çok geçmiyecek latinler birleşip bir latin ittihadı, anglo saksonlar birleşerek bir sakson heyet-i müttehide, islavlar, hep toplanarak bir islav vahdeti vücuda getireceklerdir. İşte bunlara karşı koyabilmek için türklerin de bir türk ittihadı, bir türk düvel-i müttehidesi tesis etmeleri lazımdır. Turanın islav çarlığı ve Çin Cumhuriyeti ezilmemesi, ancak buna mutevekkiftir. Bu günkü çürük çarık müteferrik kuvvetlerle bu azim cemiyetlere mukabelenin imkanı olamaz. Demek ezilmemek ve yaşamak istiyorsak, biz, yani hür ve müstakil türkler de dakika fevt etmeden, Turanı ihya ve tesise teşebbüs etmeliyiz. Turan lazım! Esirlere de lazım, serbestlere de. Mahkumlara da lazım, müstakillere de!

Evet, Turan kurtulmalı, Turan kurtarımalı . . . Turan kurtarılacak!

— Fakat nasıl ve ne ile? . .

— Nasıl ve ne ile mi? Pek basit: Demir ile ve ateş ile! Turanı kılıçlarımızın demiri ve fikirlerimizin ateşi feth ve teshir edecektir. Tarih bize gösteriyor: Bir milletin vahdeti, istiklâli, ancak kılıç ile ve kalem ile temin olunabiliyor. Bütün islavlar, bu yolda meydana çıktılar. Hakir bir Moskova kenezliği bütün rusları estrafında topladı, sonra o "münci" edebiyatı ile, kılıcı ile Balkanlara yürüdü ve sırpları, dağlıları, bulgarları da kollarından tutup ayağa kaldırıverdi.

Almanya da yine vahdetini bu yolda kazandı : Alman medeniyeti, alman edebiyat-ı milliyesi almanları uyandırmıştı. Buna, Moltkenin kılıcı ilave olundu, ve alman azamet-i milliyesi teessüs etti.

İtalya da böyle! İtalyanlar, Dante gibi, bir milleti yalnız başına yaşatmağa kadir dahilere malik oldukları halde yine Napolyonlar ve Garibaldiler sayesinde vahdet-i saltanata nail oldular.

Siyaset ve medeniyet, demir ve ateş, kılıç ve çırağ! İşte bu iki kuvvetle onlar kurtuldular, biz de bu iki hazırlıkla milleti esaretten kurtaracağız.

Turan için kılıç kuvvetini, cenubî Turanda bulacağız. Cenup türkleri henüz kılıçlarını bellerinden çıkarmamışlardır. Garbtan şarka, Osmanlıdan Kaşgarlıya, bütün cenubî Turan, kılıcı belinde yaşıyor. Turan altın ordusu, burada son hat müdafaasındadır. Ve maksat onu oradan bir mukabil taarruza kaldırmaktır.

Bunun için, bütün türk saray ve hisarları müteşebbis ve durbin bir diplomasi vasıtasıyla mukaddes mefküre etrafında birleştirilmelidir. Vahdet-i milliye ve diniye bu mesaiyi pek ziyade teshil edecektir. Ufak ihtilaflar, mesela bunların büyüğü olan sünnilik ve şiilik bile asrımızda mani-i ittihad ve itilaf olamaz. Şimdi değil, bundan yüzelli sene evvel bile, mani-i ittifak olamamıştı.

1746'da akd olunan Kardan muahadesi bu ihtilafın terkini kabul ediyordu. Ve bunu da imzalıyan Nadir gibi muazzam bir Şah idi! Bundan yüz yetmiş sene evvel resmi bir akde konulan bu maddenin bu günden, hususi bir itilaf ile tekid ve itilaf-ı diniyenin temini kadar kolay bir şey yoktur. Din, vahdet-i milliyeyi tehir değil, belki temine vasıta olmalıdır.

İşte bu gibi ihtilaflar ortadan kalkınca, o zaman mesele yalnız, siyasi itilafta kalır. Bunun için de diplomatlar mükalemelerini bir devlet-i müttehide, bir konfederasyon zemini üzerinde sevk etmelidirler. Filhakika Almanya şeklinde bir türk heyet-i müttehidesi teklifi mevcut tacdarları hatta, daha küçük zadeganı büyük bir suhuletle mefküre etrafında celp ve cem eyler.

Ve bu da olursa, işte o zaman, dini ve milli türk ordusu askerleri, zabitleri ve kumanda heyetleriyle birlikte teşkil ve tanzim olunmuş demektir. İstanbul'dan Yarkente uzanan saf-fı harbin her bir ordusu, kendine ait bir hedef-i harekete maliktir. Türkiye, Kafkaskaya ve İdile, İran Aral ve Kaspi arasından Ural dağlarına, Afgan Hive ve Buhara, Balkaş üzerinden Altaya, Kaşgarlılar da Bay Göle! İşte demirin, kılıcın ve diplomasinin vazifesi!

Fikir ateşlerinin, meşalelerinin, terakki çırağının hizmetine gelince : öbürü bir harb-i müsellah hazırlığı ise, biriki bir hulul-u sulhperverane faaliyetidir. Vicdan-ı milliyi uyandırmak, vicdanları feth etmek demek olan bu hulul-u sulphervane iki cihete de lazımdır : bir, harb-i müsellahın zeminini hazırlamak, Turan ordusunun asker ve zabitlerini bulmak için, bir de bu gün Turanın maruz bulunduğu düşman istilasının önünü almak için.

Vaktiyle muhaceret-i Asyadan Avrupaya, şarktan garba idi. Bu sel şimdi Avrupadan Asyaya, garptan şarka yürüyor ve kuvvetsiz mukavemetsız akvamı bu garp öldürüyor. Muhaceret-i akvam bitmedi, eskiden daha şiddetli. Ve bundan muvaffakiyet ve hezimet de eskisinden daha müthiş! İşte Çinliler ve bilhassa ruslar bu gün Turana bu kuvvet ve bu şiddetle yürüyorlar. Onların Turana nüfuz ve hululları Turan emelini boğacak, öldürecek bir taarruzdur. Buna mukabele için Turanlıyı der akab milli vicdan zırhı ile teslih etmelidir ki bu da yine çırağ-ı medeniyet ile, hulul sulhpervane ile temin edilecektir.

Bunun vasıtaları ne dir? Bu cihetleri, hemen tesisi icab eden bir Turan Cemiyeti düşünecektir. Fikrimizce bu cemiyetin esas mesaisi kısaca : Turanlıya hüviyet-i milliyesini öğretmek ve kendisini muhafaza yolunu göstermek olmalıdır. Bu da Turan da tarihi, dini, edebi ve fenni neşriyat ile kabildir.

Coğrafya ve tarih millete mazisini öğretir, dostlarını düşmanlarını tanıtır. Din ve edebiyat, ona, temessüle mani, bir terbiye-yi hususiye verir. Ameli-nazari değil, ameli ilimlerde düşman unsurlara karşı rekabet kuvvetini yetiştirir, sıhhatını hıfz etmek, çalışmak, zengin olmak ve çoğalmak lüzum ve vasıtalarını öğretir. Bir ırkı saklıyacak, yükseltecek ve nihayet hür ve müstakil yapacak hassalar işte bunlardır.

Turan cemiyeti, Turanın bu husustaki ihtiyacat-ı mahalliyesini her şeyden evvel teşebbüs edeceği seyahat-ı tetkikiye ile meydana çıkardıktan sonra, tesis edeceği vasıtalarla, Turan muhabbetini, Turan ilim ve terbiyesini türklüğün dört köşesine yaymağa, Turanı bu ateş ile tutuşturmaya çalışmalıdır . . . Ateş ile ve demir ile! . . .

"Vaktiyle İlhan, bir büyük harpte ezilmiş, kendisi ve bütün türkleri ölmüş, ve sağ kalan yeğeni de evlat ve ahfadı ile beraber doluz göbek Ergenekonda mahsur ve esir kalmıştı. Bu esaret, dörtyüz sene devam etti. Ondan kurtulmak için türkler her taşa baş vurdular, lakin bir türlü yol bulamadılar. Nihayet Bozkurt han, bu ilk münci kurtulmanın çaresini, hürriyetin tılsımını keşf etti : demir ve ateş!. Ateş demiri oyanattı, dağlar eridi, hudutlar yıkıldı; ve büyük Turanın yolu açıldı."

Ateş ve demir! İşte Türkleri, bundan üç bin sene evvel ilk esaretten kurtaran kuvvet! Bu kuvvet, bu gün de türklüğü son esaretten kurtaracak ve Turan, ancak bu yolda "bir elde kılıç, bir elde çırağ!" feth olunacaktır.

Turan, pp. 136-143.

TEKIN ALP, THE TURKISH AND PAN-TURKISH IDEAL

PART I

NATURE AND HISTORICAL DEVELOPMENT OF THE TURKISH NATIONAL MOVEMENT

CHAPTER I. OTTOMANISM AND PAN-ISLAMISM

A close observer of the development of modern Turkey might have gained, during the last two years, an insight into the progress of a highly significant social revolution, whose very existence has been almost unsuspected by the world at large. This social revolution started with the awakening of Turkish Nationalism which is now growing into a Pan-Turkish movement.

Three years ago, the Ottoman Turks regarded themselves simply as Mohammedans, and never considered their nation as one having a separate existence. The Anatolian peasant took the word "Turk" as synonymous with "*Kisilbash*" (Redhead: with red fez). Even among educated classes there were persons who did not know that members of the Turkish race were living outside Turkey. It was a very curious thing that the Turks should have realized the necessity for starting a national movement. Under the old régime, it is true, faint glimmers of awakening appeared from time to time, but were quickly quenched. Later, in Paris and also in Egypt, a few Young Turkish spirits became inspired with the fire of national aspirations and blazed into prominence, only to sink back in a moment, leaving little or no impression on the political structure. In Constantinople too, learned men such as Nejib Asim, Brussali Tahir Bey, and others occupied their minds from time to time with questions exclusively connected with the old Turkish civilization. The poet Mehmet Emin Bey conceived the idea of writing his poetry only in pure Turkish, without making use of the borrowed Arabic and Persian words which form 95 percent of the Turkish language. His poetry had to be published in small provincial papers because the important newspapers of the towns would not accept it.

These were, however, but isolated cases, there were no signs anywhere of a prepared or organized movement.

The Young Turks who belonged to the "Committee of Union and Progress," to whom Turkey owes her constitution, worked entirely as members of the Ottoman Empire. Their leading idea was Ottomanism, which was also expressed in the word "Unity," meaning the unity of all Ottoman subjects regardless of differences of religion or nationality. Immediately after the establishment of the constitution, the Young Turks, true to their original plan, set about the foundation of a league, with other affiliated leagues, having the object of collecting together all the Ottoman elements. This league has been much talked about and has created a great deal of disturbance, but it must be admitted that it has accomplished nothing definite.

The enthusiasm of the first inspired hours of newly-won freedom began to wear off. The Greeks, Bulgarians and Serbians, who had laid down their arms and come down from the mountains in great exultation to celebrate the birth of the constitution with the young liberators in Salonica, began gradually, one by one, to return to their mountains and their arms, to resume their struggle against Turkish authority.

This was the Young Turks' first awakening from their dreams of Ottomanism, upon which all their best hopes and beliefs were based. The pillars of the proud building were shaken.

From time to time voices were heard advocating "Pan-Islamism." They preached the union of all the Mohammedan elements in the kingdom, which would form a strong and reliable power upon which the Government could unfailingly depend. But this was shortly followed by the rising of the Mohammedan Albanians and the revolts in Yemen and Hauran. The upholders of Pan-Islamism did not, however, allow their faith to be so easily shaken by these revolutionary movements, opposed as they were to the whole Pan-Islamitic ideal. They, like the Ottomanists, would not admit defeat. Far from giving up their policy, they struggled with undiminished enthusiasm and unquenched zeal against the difficulties of the time, with the firm conviction that they were only dealing with passing opposition.

CHAPTER II. THE TURKISH MOVEMENT BEFORE THE BALKAN WAR

There were, however, a number of people who were anxious to believe that the political ideas of the Ottomanists and Pan-Islamists had proved themselves to be empty dreams; these people regarded the Turkish element as the saviour of the Ottoman Empire; the Turkish movement was considered as the one hope of the nation. The weak and still tentative voices of these "saviours" were, however, shouted down by their antagonists, though the seed of the Turkish movement continued to grow underground. Unknown to the people, the ideals of this movement spread even to the heart of the Committee of Union and Progress, which was the supporter of the Government and at that time had its headquarters in Salonica.

The mainspring of the National movement must be sought in the Branch Committee of Union and Progress in Constantinople. The Secretary of this branch (the Central Committee was still established in Salonica) was Kemal Bey, who was one of the delegates to the Committee Congress in Salonica in 1909, and showed himself on that occasion most anxious to give the first impulse to the movement in the name of his Constantinople Association. During the debates he repeatedly attempted to make his opnions heard. His words: "Gentlemen, we must first decide upon our ultimate goal, we must be quite clear about its real object – our national progress" – fell upon deaf ears, and he was unable once to give proper expression to his ideas, being continually shouted down with cries of "Our goal is organization and nothing else, we know our goal." In spite of his inability to place his ideas before the congress, he got privately into touch with a quiet unassuming man, who proved to be a most energetic partisan of the national movement; this was Ziya Bey, who had been sent to Salonica as a delegate from the branch committee in Diarbekr. After the congress, Ziya Bey did not return to Diarbekr, but accompanied Kemal Bey to Constantinople in order to come into closer contact and communication with his adherents.

There he formed a separate Committee, which for months discussed the burning question of Turkish nationalism down to its smallest details, and finally drew up a carefully studied programme for the defence of their ideas. Ziya Bey was then chosen to be a member of the Central Committee, which, as we have already said, had its headquarters in Salonica at that time. Ziya Bey took up his position with the fixed idea, which almost amounted to a monomania, of working to the end for the triumph of Turkish nationalism. This modest man, who had neither a conspicuous past to recommend him, nor an impressive demeanour, nor an eloquent tongue, nevertheless showed a curious obstinacy in clinging to his monomania, wonderful stubbornness in defending his principle, calmness in fighting his political opponents, and firmness of purpose in managing and championing his cause.

He first gathered round him a group of young people who devoted themselves zealously and enthusiastically to his cause. They started a paper in Salonica called *Genj Kalemlar* (Young Writers), which from the moment of its first appearance carried on a revolutionary and offensive policy.

The *Genj Kalemlar* heralded the foundation of a new language, a new literature and a new purely Turkish civilization. It promised that the language should be purified of the borrowed Arabic and Persian words, opened a campaign against the expressions and ideas taken from the old literature of these two languages, and proclaimed a new literature and civilization which should be based entirely on the old Turkish traditions.

All the great and celebrated writers and poets such as Tevfik Fikret, Halid Ziya, Abdul Hak Hamid, and others were decried as *Dünkiler* (old-fashioned). Such men belonged to the past, and shoud be relegated to oblivion.

The new literature had, however, to be made. A carefully drawn up programme for the foundation of a new language was issued, and the union *Yeni Lisan* (New Language) was founded. This new language was to consist of purely Turkish words and those Arabic and Persian expressions which had already become part of the Turkish vocabulary.

Nearly the whole youth of Salonica took part in this movement. The *Yeni Lisan* group was soon followed by the *Yeni Hayat* (New Life) who took for their organ the *Yeni Felsefe* (New Philosophy). *Yeni Lisan* and *Yeni Hayat* soon amalgated. They made sharp attacks in their papers on the youth of Constantinople, and addressed them in somewhat unflattering terms such as "Levantines" and "Supbe" (coxcomb) and "persons devoid of any ideals, who had merely taken from Western civilization a dusty veneer and manners of the demi-monde, under which they cloaked their own inanity."

The leaders of the *Yeni Hayat* were more or less acquainted with Western literature through those books which seemed to share their political ideals: Alfred Fouillée, Gustav Lebon, Bergson, Durkheim, Gobineau, Nietzsche, and others. They probably built up their theories from these books, as may be seen from the following extract: "We must be ouselves, that is, we must build up our intellectual life on our national traditions and cultivate our own talents. We must only borrow from Europe method and technique. Our whole literature, which is not Turkish in any respect, must be reformed and founded on a new basis, it must become purely national in character. Down with men such as Ahmed Midhat, who are merely blind followers, and wish to propagate a misunderstood and badly assimilated version of Western civilization!"

In this manner, the youth of Salonica encouraged and inspired each other, with loud and excited debates and bitter quarrels with every one who disagreed with them.

In Constantinople, these young braggarts were simply laughed at at first, and the whole affair ridiculed, while no one even took the trouble to think of valid and logical arguments with which to ward off the Salonica attacks.

At the same time, the behaviour of the non-Turkish element in the kingdom became increasingly assertive; the other nations made no attempt to hide their own nationalism, ambitions, and narrow-minded particularism. For this reason, the Central Committee was induced to attach itself to the Turkish national movement. It is true that the downfall of Ottomanism had not yet taken place on tactical grounds, but in reality the new movement received all possible support.

Everything was done to extend the Turkish national movement of Salonica to Constantinople, and the poet Mehmed Emin Bey was summoned and entrusted with the mission of starting a source of propaganda for the new ideals in the capital. Mehmed Emin Bey ceased his activities after a considerable time with the conviction that the ground had been sufficiently prepared, and his place was filled by Enver Bey.[1] This period saw the foundation of the review *Turk Yurdu*, which, under the editorship of Yusuf Akshura, soon obtained a comparatively wide circulation, and was eagerly welcomed by an enthusiastic circle of readers.

Meanwhile the Central Committee for Unity and Progress moved its headquarters from Salonica to Constantinople. Ziya Bey and his Salonican adherents followed with the firm purpose of bringing about the outbreak of a social revolution for the *Yeni Hayat.* The efforts of this small group of intellectual pioneers succeeded in creating a circle deeply imbued with the ideas and principles of Turkish nationalism. But the social revolution did not come. The great public, the press and the classical writers still remained indifferent and took no notice whatever of the new movement.

But the ground was prepared, the seed sown, and it was soon to bear fruit.

CHAPTER III. THE BALKAN WAR PERIOD

It was at this time that the Balkan War broke out.

The false friends tore the smiling masks from their faces and revealed themselves in all their hateful ferocity.

The old attitude of the non-Turkish element, and the revolt of the Mohammedan Albanians, once and for all opened the Turks' eyes, which had hitherto been blinded by lies and deception, and showed them in crude and painful fact that they could count on no one's assistance but their own, and that their existence depended solely upon their political, social, intellectual, and economic power and unity.

While the Bulgarians, Serbians, and Greeks engaged the Turkish armies in strife, the revolt of the bad element among the people began, the revolt of former "friends," who now one by one left the poor desolated country and nation in the lurch.

Treachery was practised on all sides; many former Ottoman deputies and politicians suddenly went over to the enemy without the slightest qualms of conscience. The rats were leaving the sinking ship.

With a few insignificant exceptions the poor desolated nation had no trustworthy and sympathetic friend left, who would help her to endure this sudden overwhelming sorrow, or at least comfort her with words of friendship.

The only people who united themselves with the hardpressed Turks and tried to help them in these days of general mourning, bitter sorrow and pitiable misfortune, were those of whose existence she had practically known nothing – her compatriots in Russia, in the Crimea, in the Caucasus and in Hindustan, etc. Besides large gifts of money, they sent missions from the Red Crescent who did much to heal the wounds inflicted by the war.

At this time of depression several important persons came from those districts, among whom were Ismail Gasparinski, Fatih Kerimoff, Arif Kerimoff, who was anxious to heal wounds with his own hand and personally relieve the oppressed. Among these sympathetic persons were also a number of highly cultivated women, included Gülsüm Khanum, Miriam Patatshova, and others.

While the brave Turkish soldiers were fighting with the courage of despair in front of Chatalja, to save at least military honour and the last remaining piece of their country, these compatriots were streaming in from all corners of the world to stand by their brothers in the hour of distress, and to unite and ally themselves with them, thus forming the basis of a future union of all the Turks in the world.

At that time Khalide Edib Khanum expressed the ideal of the aspiring people in the following words: "What I most wish to see is a powerful and independent union in political and intellectual matters of all the Turks in the world."

Enver Bey and other important Young Turks became closely allied to their compatriots from abroad. He was often to be seen among his Russian and Hindu brothers and friends, and even among the women, who, though Mohammedans, were no longer under the stern and repressive yoke of the harem life. The Society of *Turk Ojaghi*, which was founded during the crisis with the object of raising all the Turkish elements in the kingdom by all possible means, arranged a dinner at their club in honour of the foreign guests. It was on this occasion that Professor Yusuf Akshura, editor of the *Turk Yurdu*, spoke the inspired words, which rang with a note of invincible hope: "I no longer wish that I had never been born, since I have seen the first day of the national and religious renaissance of the Turkish and Tartar peoples."

During this crisis, too, came the first awakening of the Turkish women, who had hitherto led an unnoticed existence behind the impenetrable harem bars and the yashmak which hides the eyes, the windows of the soul.

A great women's meeting was held in the University Hall at Stamboul. This was the first time that Turkish women appeared in public and gave a sign of life to the world at large. Many ladies of the aristocracy were present at this brilliantly attended meeting, including the Princess Ni'met Khanum, wife of the former Grand Vizier Ghazi Ahmed Mukhtar Pasha, Fatima Alie Khanum, a celebrated authoress, daughter of the great historian Jevdet Pasha and many other ladies of rank and importance.

Many inspired speeches were given, which stirred the highly-strung hearts of the women and caused their tears to flow. Khalide Edib Khanum spoke among others and gave a broad outline of the nature and principles of Turkish nationalism. Gülsüm Khanum spoke of the nature and principles of Turkish women in Russia.

This was the first shock of the great social earthquake, whose upheaval is still being felt; it was the inauguration of a great new period.

The short space of time during which the peace negotiations were being concluded was a really historic period, in which the social revolution, so eagerly desired by the small groups of intellectual pioneers, became an accomplished fact.

The youth of Constantinople flocked to join the movement. All those who had hitherto been branded as "Levantines" and "Supbe" became enthusiastic supporters of the nationalist idea. Even the classical authors, who had hitherto kept aloof, lent their eloquence to the steadily growing movement. Public opinion, the great public, the educated and even the learned classes, adopted the nationalist point of view. The Government, which had fallen into the hands of the Committee, through the *coup d'état* of Enver Bey and his suporters, no longer considered it necessary to veil the fact that its sympathies were with the nationalist movement.

Husein Jahid Bey, former editor of the *Tanin,* now Vice-President of the Chamber, has summed up the results of this crisis in the typical words: "The present war has at least had the effect of rousing all the Turks and Mohammedans in the world from their lethargy. It has put clearly before them the dangers to which they are exposed."

CHAPTER IV. AFTER THE BALKAN WAR

The end of the Balkan War found Turkey a much reduced nation.

The Congress of London took away from her the larger part of her already diminished European territory, namely Macedonia and Albania, which for fifty years had been demanding the blood of Anatolia's noblest sons in long and bitter struggles. But the Turks gained through the war their ideal fatherland, their Turania, the cradle of their nation and home of their race. With a significant gesture the Turkish nation turned aside their gaze from the lost territory, from Salonica, Uskub, Monastir, Janina, and looked instead upon Turania, the ideal country of the future.

Ziya Gök Alp, the great apostle of Turanianism, shows us this ideal in his rhythmic and poetically inspired verses: "The impressions which flow in my blood are the result of my history. I do not read the famous deeds of my ancestors in the dead faded dusty leaves of the history books, but in my own veins, in my own heart. My Attila, my Genghiz, these heroic figures, which stand for the proud fame of my race, appear in those dry pages to our malicious and slanderous age as covered with shame and disgrace, while in reality they are no less than Alexander and Caesar. Still better known to my heart is Oghuz Khan, a dark and enigmatic figure in history. In me he still lives in all his fame and greatness. Oghuz Khan delights and inspires my heart and causes me to sing psalms of gladness. The fatherland of the Turks is not Turkey or Turkestan, but the broad, eternal land of Turania."

Ziya Bey proves himself in these verses to be the true interpreter of the feelings of educated Turks.

So at last had come the final triumph of *Yeni Hayat*. It was a complete return to the beginnings, traditions and the cradle of the race. The Turks realized that in order to live they must become essentially Turkish, become a nation, be themselves. The *Yeni Hayat*, which had hitherto been limited to the small circle of its own supporters, now won for itself a place among the great public, the press, and the educated and learned classes. After the great blow, which had finally put an end to Turkey's "Balkan troubles," the papers wrote of nothing but the awakening, the Renaissance, the rising and restoration, just as though the nation were a person who had been cured of a long chronic illness, which had nearly proved fatal. Indeed, every one was filled with an indestructible hope in the future of Turanianism, and was firmly convinced that the Turkish nation had been restored by its own strength and effort.

Among others, Mehmed Ali Tevfik Bey, a young writer filled with the fiery spirit of exultation, showed himself in a long series of articles in the *Tanin*, entitled "Bir Turanlinin defteri" ("Diary of a Turanian"), to be the truest interpreter of the soul of his people. In one of his most brilliant articles, which has recently been published in book form, he expresses the belief of the nation in the following words: "Constantine Paleologus, who saw the downfall of the great Byzantine Empire, cried out to a group of friends, "We need a long period of misfortune and trial in order to raise ourselves again and behold the dawn of freedom and lo, four centuries later, another Constantine enters the capital of Macedonia; the Ottoman capital is still under the economic authority of Greece and the blue and white flag still flies in triumph over the waters of the Aegean Sea."

But after this period of trial, the time of restoration for the Turkish nation will surely come.

Khalide Edib Khanum, in a lecture delivered at the University to a large meeting of Turkish women, discoursed upon the same theme, and spoke of the decline and restoration of different nations in history, and of her firm confidence in the raising of her people.

For a few months the reawakening and return to Turanianism formed the subject of open discussion. Professors, scholars, writers and all who felt called upon to address the people, gave lectures and spoke at the meetings which took place once or twice a week in the University and the *Turk Ojaghi* Club, besides speaking daily in the theatres etc. Nearly all the books published at this time treat of the same subject. An inspired literature aroused the national feelings of the people. From time to time huge processions, consisting of members of all classes, were seen passing through the streets of the capital with the appearance of indescribable rejoicing. What had happened? Had the Turks regained Macedonia?

It was only the anniversary of the taking of Constantinople, or some similar memorial day. The procession of demonstrators, thousands strong, would repair to the grave of Fatih, the great conqueror of Constantinople, in order to appeal to his sacred spirit and thus gain strength and inspiration for the hard taks of the future. The public seemed to believe that Constantinople had been conquered once more. They had never had an opportunity of remembering the names of their heroes, such as Fatih, Sultan Suleiman Kanoni, and others. It was not until this time that they began proudly to recall these heroes and celebrate their memories – this time when the Turks first began to find themselves.

These demonstrations were far from being ordinary public gatherings; not only the people, but the Government took part in these memorial days, by issuing the proclamation that these festivals were in future to be observed in all schools and that deputations of school-children and students were to take part in the various ceremonies.

These celebrations, "Ihtifal-i milli" (national processions), as they were called in the official documents, were henceforward to be held every year and were to be taken as an opportunity for a revival of hero-worship, in which the heroes and glorious episodes of Turkish history, might live again to be a strength and example to the nation. Thus the nation, who had hitherto regarded its past with indifference, and remaining in utter ignorance of its great men, made up for the past years, and made reparation for its omissions in erecting in its heart a Pantheon of all its national heroes.

CHAPTER V. THE OPPOSITION

It must be admitted that discords arose from time to time in the harmonious development of the national movement. Opposing voices were heard protesting against its progress. These protests were often merely directed against a part of the *Yeni Hayat's* programme, but sometimes against the principles of the *Yeni Lisan,* and would not consent to give up a technique and style which they had created in the course of a few decades. Well-known authors, such as Jenab Shehab-Eddin, Suleiman Nazif, and others, continued to use the customary Persian and Arabic phrases which were so bitterly attacked by the *Yeni Lisan.*

For some time the partisans of the old school even attempted publicly to defend their theories. The loss of the great treasure of Arabic and Persian words would detract from the charm and poetry of the language and literature would become a dead thing without attraction, power or beauty. In spite of their former authority on literary subjects, the adherents of the old school were finally obliged to give way to the great majority of reformers, with the result that *Yeni Lisan* is today in possession of an unlimited and absolute authority. It is true that essays by Shehab-Eddin and his colleagues occasionally appear in some reviews and are still admired by the public in spite of their old-fashioned style, but they are merely regarded as costly relics of a past age. Turkish poetry, too, was subjected to important changes. The highly complicated rhythm which had been taken from the Arab and Persian poets and practised in Turkey was unhesitatingly condemned as un-Turkish by the *Yeni Lisan* and replaced by the syllabic system. The old rhythm was kept up for a time by a few poets, but they too were unable to resist the vigorous strength of the new movement, and were obliged to follow the general trend of feeling.

The Turanians met with serious opposition from obstinate men such as Akif Bey, Suleiman Nazif and others. The latter, especially, fought with extraordinary zeal against the Turkish movement and its principles.

He is a believer in a "political Trinity", and shows great stubbornness in the defence of his theory, which is that all three groups of ideas, Ottomanism, Islamism and the Turkish movement should work side by side and together.

He is by no means convinced of the correctness of the Turkish theory. According to him, Turkish history, from a national point of view, dates only from the foundation of the Ottoman Empire under the Sultan Osman, and from a religious standpoint from the foundation of Islam. He does not regard Attila, Chingiz or Oghuz as national heroes, though the Nationalists celebrate their memory as the greatest figures in history. Turkish history, he claims, cannot be traced back further than that; all that comes before belongs to the realms of fancy.

On account of his views, he carried on a bitter feud with Ahmed Oghlu (Ahmed Agayeff) who may be regarded as one of the Apostles of Turanianism. The unequal contest did not last long. While Suleiman Nazif and his followers had taken up the challenge from purely conservative motives and without any set programme or organization, his opponents attacked the defenders of the old ideas with all the energy and power of convinced revolutionaries who had a firm organization and countless resources at their disposal. It was therefore no difficult task for them to silence the "relics of the past".

Still more serious opposition was encountered from the clerical party. This party has no position in Turkish politics, but exerts considerable influence in literature and intellectual life. The "Islamji" would have nothing to do with Nationalism; the religion of Islam is the only thing they consider. Because it is written in the Koran that Islam knows no nations but only believers, they thought that to occupy one's self with national questions was to act against the interests and principles of Islam itself.

The clerical party is a dangerous foe, for it has at its disposal an organization and newspapers whose influence must not be underrated. The *Surat-i-Mustakim* and the *Sebil-ul-Reshad* are widely-read reviews, which offer a steady and determined opposition to the Turkish movement. The last named is an especially powerful enemy because it is the organ of the "Mellami" sect, which is one of the largest Mohammedan brotherhoods, with an organization somewhat similar to that of the Freemasons.

The Nationalists fought against the "Islamji," but wisely took care to avoid any appearance of anti-clerical views.

According to them, the Koran's declaration that only Mohammedans would be recognized was directed exclusively against the very frequent dissensions of the clans and parties in the various Arab races. Although they (the Turkish Nationalists) proclaim themselves the most zealous followers of Mohammed, they do not nevertheless conceal the fact that their interpretation of Islam is not the same as that of the Arabs. They maintain that the Turks cannot interpret the Koran in the same manner as the Arabs, for instance, and they support their assertion with the well-known principle of the Koran, "Wa'mur bi'l-urf" (. . . live each according to his customs). According to this, the national customs, or national spirit, should be the moral judge of right and wrong.

As the national life of the Turks is not only identical with, but even extremely dissimilar from that of the Arabs, it follows that the same interpretation of the religion of Islam cannot be accepted by both nations. It is quite clear that profound differences naturally exist between the social life of the Semitic Arabs and that of the Mongolian Turks.

The Nationalist theologians are most anxious to insist on the great difference existing between the philosophies of the different sects and brotherhoods, which were founded, some by the Arabs and some by the Turks. While the Arab sects carry humble submission to the extent of physical self-denial, indeed almost to asceticism, the Turkish sects are chiefly characterized by a contemplative piety. The "Mevlevi" and "Mellami," the two largest Dervish sects in Turkey, have noting of asceticism in their point of view, and in this they present a contrast to the Arab sects and brotherhoods. Their philosophy, on the contrary, is not far removed from Epicureanism.

The Turks' idea of God is also different from that of the Arabs.

The latter think of God in the same way as their ancestors the Jews; He is a God of Vengeance and worshipped because He is feared.

"Makhafat Allah", or God of Vengeance[2] is He whom the Arabs worship.

The God of the Turks is the God of Love, "Muhabbet Allah;" He is worshipped because He is loved.

This difference in the idea of God is probably based on race differences.

The Turkish Nationalists made great efforts to nationalize religion itself and give it the impress of the Turkish national spirit.

This idea was zealously supported by the fortnightly *Islam Majmu'asi* which has a wide circulation in Turkey and will be a great help to the Nationalists in attaining this end. It has many times been bitterly attacked by its opponents, the *Sebil-ul-Reshad* and the *Surat-i-Mustakim*, but every attack causes an increase in its popularity. One of the noblest tasks undertaken by the *Islam Majmu'asi* is the translation of the Koran into Turkish; this is a reform of the greatest importance. It is well known that the translation of the Koran has hitherto been considered as a sin. The Nationalists have cut themselves off from this superstitious prejudice and have had three translations made, the above-mentioned and two others.

Another recently instituted reform is the reading of the "Khutba" (Prayer for the Caliph) in the Turkish language, instead of in Arabic, of which all hearers and believers and ignorant.

CHAPTER VI. THE ORGANIZATION OF THE TURKISH MOVEMENT

The various movements which attained a certain importance in Turkey during the last few years have all either disappeared entirely or almost completely lost their influence on the minds of the people.

We may perhaps mention "Ottomanism", which was supreme after the setting up of the constitution. At that time Greek and Bulgarians embraced one another in the streets, stirring speeches were made on every side, and the lasting brotherhood of all nations in Turkey was celebrated. All should form together one body, one single inseparable nation. It is well known how this "Unity" ended.

During the Tripoli War, "Pan-Islamism" was the cry; this outlasted the Balkan War, but is still far removed from playing an important part in international politics.

The Turkish National movement does not exhibit the failings of the earlier movements. It is in every way adapted to the intellectual standard and feelings of the nation. It also keeps pace with the ideas of the age, which have for some decades centred around the principle of Nationality.

In adopting Turkish Nationalism as the basis of their national policy, the Turks have only abandoned an abnormal state of affairs and thereby placed themselves on a level with modern nations. The basis of the movement is so sound and firm, the movement itself is so widely spread and so much a part of the people, that it cannot now be eradicated, even by force.

The movement has also a good, all-embracing organization, which takes into consideration the different branches of the physical and psychical development of the race.

We may first mention the *Turk Ojaghi*, whose work is the education of all classes, and the *Turk Bilgi Derneyi*, whose aim is the creation of a new language, literature and civilization on a national basis. The most important of the organizations for raising the physical strength of the nation are the *Turk Güji* and *Izji.*

The *Turk Ojaghi* (The Home of the Turks) was founded on March 25, 1912, in Constantinople. This society which is only open to Turks and even excludes foreign Mohammedans, expresses its aims in the following statute, which has received the approval of the Government: "To work for the national education of the Turkish people which forms the most important division of Islam; to work for the raising of her intellectual, social and economic standard, and for the perfection of the Turkish language and race." The same statute declares that the means of action is to be the foundation of clubs, the institution of evening schools, public lectures, literary and artistic evenings, the foundation of schools, the publication of books and periodicals. In order to increase and protect the national wealth, the proper authorities will be approached with a view to encouraging those interested in social and economic questions, showing them the best way to work, and if necessary supporting them; all pains will be taken to make the suitable arrangements for the carrying on of this work.

It is easily understood that the *Turk Ojaghi's* activities were very limited during the first year of its production, but in the second it increased to an extraordinary extent.

The Union numbers today 1,800 members in Constantinople alone, among whom are 1,600 students and former university men. It has a large and fairly well-appointed meeting club in the centre of Stamboul, which is very well attended. The Turkish papers published abroad may be read here, and there is a well stocked library which already boasts a large collection of volumes, although the Union is only two years old. There is, moreover, a huge lecture-hall, seating several thousand people, with arrangements for lantern-slide illustrations. A lecture evening is held every Thursday, devoted to Literature and Nationalist propaganda. University professors and other influential persons speak at these evenings, either on interesting episodes in Turkish history, the Turkish heroes, ancient arts, such as Architecture and the art of Enamelling, now unhappily forgotten, or else on the life of the Turks abroad, and numerous other interesting subjects. The lectures are illustrated with lantern slides. Pictures are shown illustrating the old Turkish civilization; for instance, the ancient mosques built by Turkish architects, country pictures from Hindustan, Afghanistan, Turkestan etc. The *Turk Ojaghi* has a rich and interesting collection, consisting of several thousand of these pictures.

These literary meetings are repeated every Friday for the Turkish women, who are most frequent in their attendance. The *Turk Ojaghi* helps the women's movement in Turkey in every possible way. Not only do men give lectures to women, but the women, too, mount the platform and address the men. In spite of the very strict harem laws in Turkey, the non-observance of which may give rise to police interference, there are women, such as Khalide Edib Khanum, for instance, who may frequently be seen lecturing to an audience composed entirely of men.

She has her face covered with a yashmak, but the mere appearance of a Khanum in a company consisting of men, many of whom are Khoja (priests) constitutes an historical event of the greatest importance. At one of these lecture evenings, after Khalide Edib Khanum's lecture, Turkish ladies belonging to the most aristocratic circles sat down at the piano, still hidden under the yashmak, of course, and played and sang national and patriotic airs.

At the Friday meetings every opportunity is taken of declaring that the Turks will never be a truly modern nation until their women are no longer hidden behind the bars of the harem and the folds of the yashmak. The *Turk Ojaghi* loses no occasion of preaching women's emancipation, which forms an important part of the Nationalists' social revolutionary programme. The general opinion is that the liberation of women will take place in a comparatively short time.

The *Turk Ojaghi* works hard for the enlightenment of the scholars in the Medresse and clerical seminaries.

The pupils of these seminaries, who are called Softas, number a few thousands in Constantinople, and formed an important body of reactionaries in the time of Abdul Hamid. They now are either members of the Union or visitors to the regular meetings.

An important philanthropic task undertaken by the *Turk Ojaghi* is that of receiving poor students in the Union's home, procuring them free medical attendance and generally looking after their welfare in every way. The national principles advocated by the Union are thus carried out in practice, by awakening and strengthening the sense of firm reliability.

The *Turk Ojaghi* has sixteen branches in the Turkish towns of the Empire; these are managed quite independently of the central body.

The provincial *Turk Ojaghis* are animated by the same spirit as that of the metropolitan center.

Turkish students in France, Germany, Switzerland, etc. have founded a Union called *Turk Yurdu* (Turkish Home). This Union has no great influence on the people, but is nevertheless preparing for the future. It is occupied in convincing the hundreds of Turkish students in Europe, who will surely become in a few years the leaders of Turkish intellectual life, of the truth of Nationalist beliefs. This success will certainly make itself felt in the near future.

A most excellent Union is the *Turk Bilgi Derneyi* (Academy of Turkish Science). It is semi-official in character, being supported by the Government and under the patronage of the Central Committee for Union and Progress. Although but recently founded (Summer 1913) this union is clearly destined to lay the foundation stone of the intellectual revival and civilization of the Turkish nation. Emrullah Effendi, former Minister of Education, who was himself engaged in the production of a Turkish encyclopaedia, is president of the "Dernek", which counts among its members nearly all the famous scholars of Turkey. The "Dernek" publishes a large well-got-up monthly review, the *Bilgi Mejmu'asi*, which contains articles by all the important members on questions connected with the nation. This is the only scientific review in Turkey.

The "Dernek" is divided into different sections, of which the following may be noted:

1. The "Turkiat" (Turkological section). The president of this section is Nejib Asim, one of the oldest Turkish historical students and philologists. The members include the following: Brusali Tahir Bey, the well known historian, Akshura Oghlu Jusuff, Ahmed Refik, etc.

2. The "Islamiat" (section for the study of Islam). President: Musa Kazim Effendi, former Sheikh-ul-Islam; most important members, Riza Tevfik, the great philosopher and Sheikh Mahmud, the famous theologian.

3. The "Hayatiat" (section for biological sciences), among whose members are the greatest medical authorities in the capital, including Suleiman Numan Pasha, Director of Medical Services in the War Ministry, Kadir Rashid Pasha and Adnan Bey, who are all well known in European circles.

4. The "Felsefe we Ishtimaiat" (philosophical and sociological section) under Emrulla Effendi, whom we have mentioned before. Its members include the following men, also well known in Europe: Javid Bey, former Minister of Finance, Lutfi Fikri Bey, the famous leader of the Opposition, etc.

5. The "Reyaziayat we Madiat" (section for mathematical and natural sciences), under Salih Zeki, the Director of the Polytechnic High School in Stamboul.

6. The "Turkjilik" (Executive Council) to which is entrusted the study of practical means of carrying out the plans of the different sections, the study of the encouragement and management of all scientific, social and economic movements which might assist the progress of Nationalism.

This Council consists of the most zealous Nationalists and authorities on every subject, including Philology, Poetry, Architecture, Aesthetics, Pedagogy, Economics, Politics, Hygiene, etc.

All the sections are carrying out their work with the greatest enthusiasm.

One of the national unions for the raising of the physical standard of the Turkish nation is the Constantinople Sports Club, the *Turk Güji*, which is endeavouring to make a strong robust nation, like that of ancient times, out of the physically degenerate Turkish peoples.

An important union, which is capable of great development, is the "Boys' Club", *Izji* which is organized after a European pattern, but in a purely Turkish form. The "Scouts" club was founded by Enver Pasha, the president, or rather by the Ministries for War and Education, and is protected and managed by the authorities, being thus of an entirely official character. The different members assume ancient Turkish names; the union is, indeed, organized on purely ancient Turkish principles, adapted to modern life. The Scout movement was eagerly welcomed upon its introduction and immediately became popular. Deputies from the provinces are sent to the capital to fraternize with their comrades there. A great deal has already been accomplished. For instance, the *Izjis* performed on foot the journey from Smyrna to Constantinople. This organization will completely revolutionize the former position of youth in Turkey. The boys, who were almost entirely inactive in their young days and only grew up to a still more inactive manhood, will now receive new life and happiness, strength and movement. The leaders will therefore sow the seeds of national thought in the hearts of the young people, whose life is becoming daily fresher and stronger, and we may be certain that in that impressionable soil those seeds will quickly take root and be tended with loving care.

CHAPTER VII. THE ECONOMIC ORGANIZATION

The leaders of the Turkish movement realized at the very start that the first national reforms must be in the direction of improving Turkey's economic position.

They never lost an opportunity of declaring that as long as the Turks remained poor and allowed the people of other nations to swallow up their trade, industries and indeed all the economic resources of the country, as long as they preferred to live by officialdom to engaging in trade or any free career, so long would they remain weak, and foreigners be the masters in Turkey.

The Nationalists devoted their efforts from the very first moment to raising the economic life of the country. It is, however, interesting to note that they wisely refrained from lending the banner of pure Nationalism to economic agitators.

They sought after a judicious mingling of the religious and national impulses. They realized only too clearly that the still abstract ideals of Nationalism could not be expected to attract the masses, the lower classes, composed of uneducated and illiterate people. It was found more expedient to reach these classes under the flag of religion. Religion has a universal appeal, whereas Nationalism is a finer instrument which requires good training if it is to be properly handled.

When the right moment arrives, and the masses come to believe in the national idea, there need to be no hesitation in making use of the more delicate appeal of Nationalism, without, however, entirely discarding the religious element.

The economic organization created by the leaders of the movement is widely spreading but is not yet perfect.

We must first mention the Esnaf (the Corporations). Those of the Kaikji (boatmen), Arabaji (cab-drivers), Hammals (porters), Bakkals (grocers), Kasab (butchers) etc. are inseparable bodies whose members are bound by perfect discipline.

Each Corporation has its own rules, laws and customs, which unite the hundreds and thousands of men. The "Kehaya" (superintendent) has complete control over his people, and the leaders of the National movement use the influence of these "Kehayas" for the good of the nation.

The Corporation Union is very old, but its adaptation for idealistic aims and purposes is modern. The National leaders, who are themselves under the control of the Committee, have reorganized all the Corporations on a new basis, taken them under their leadership and added to them hitherto non-existent Corporations. Thus, these Corporations form today a powerful tool in the hands of the Turkish Nationalists.

Besides the Corporations which only include artisans and small tradesmen, the merchants have recently founded a Union of Turkish Merchants. This forms the so-called "intellectual party" among the merchants, and is concerned with Export and Import, Industry, etc. This Union is also the work of the Turkish Nationalist leaders. It is Mohammedan in spirit, and also admits foreign Mohammedans to its membership. There are various Consumers' Unions (Milli Istihlak), which unite and group together the Turkish consumers. These form a further source of power to the Nationalists. There is even a Consumers' Union for women which is managed and conducted by Turkish ladies.

The results of these efforts and organizations can easily be seen. In the course of a few months hundreds of new Turkish shops sprang up in the different parts and quarters of the town, the suburbs, and provinces, where formerly all the trade had been in the hands of Greeks and Armenians. This applies equally to purely Turkish quarters. Nearly all these new shops bore Turkish signs. Here a restaurant called "Turania," there a draper's shop called "Mussulman" Bazaar, or a barber claiming to be a "Turkish Barber", or a tailor declaring that he employs exlcusively "Turkish Labour." Some signs have their inscriptions borrowed from Turkish literature and poetry. Ziya Gök Alp's famous book *Kizil Elma* (The Red Apple) has given its name to a hotel. Stamboul is full of such inscriptions. The awakening of Turkey and her economic restoration began with a great upheaval, the shock of which was even felt, to a small degree, in European economic circles, which either directly or indirectly took a certain interest in Turkish affairs. During the period of the negotiations between Turkey and Greece on the subjects of the Islands, the Turks declared a boycott on the Greek element. The Turkish press openly advocated this boycott, which was pursued with obstinacy and endurance. The unaccomodating attitude of the Greek Government towards the Island question and the Greek's persecution of the Turks in Macedonia were sufficient excuse; the real motive was, however, the longing of the Turkish nation for economic independence in their own country. The boycott, which was at first solely directed against the Greeks, was then extended to the Armenians and other non-Mohammedan circles, and was carried out with undiminished energy.

This movement, which lasted in all its vigour for a few months, caused the ruin of hundreds of small Greek and Armenian tradesmen who had been living on Turkish custom and were entirely dependent upon it.

The systematic and rigorous boycott is now at an end, but the spirit it created in the people still persists. There are Turks who will not set foot in foreign shops unless they are certain that the same articles cannot be purchased under the same conditions in the shops of men of their own race, or at least of their own religion. This feeling of brotherhood has taken firm root in the hearts of the people all over the Empire.

In various important centres in Anatolia, special banks have been founded to support Turkish retail tradesmen. The National Bank of Aidin with a capital of 50,000 Turkish pounds, and that of Konia, with an equally large capital, are flourishing concerns, in spite of certain faults of management. It can now be asserted that the movement for restoring the economic life of Turkey is on the right road, and that, under better management, it will most probably develop still more widely and favourably. There are, too, many Turks who have large capital lying idle in European banks. A larger proportion of the real property, such as land and real estates, is in the hands of the Turks. The Government, too, does not withhold its support, and is indeed a powerful agent of the whole movement. It is true that the Turkish character is usually lacking in the qualities most essential to trade or economic undertakings, but these may be acquired by a reasonable and methodical training and organization.

CHAPTER VIII. THE GOVERNMENT'S PART

The Government has also adopted the Turkish Nationalist principles, and proves this fact in most of its dealings, without, however, doing anything to infringe upon the legal rights of its non-Turkish subjects. On the contrary, the National policy is strongly opposed to narrow-mindedness on the part of the Government, which is highly to its credit. One of the most powerful motives for the preservation of the absolute independence of the Arabs in their provinces, the recognition of their language as official and the nomination of Arab officials to their provinces, is precisely that principle of nationality which the Government applies to the Turkish nation. A principle which is recognized as applicable to the Turks must also be acted upon in the case of other non-Turkish nationalities.

In nearly every Government Ministry, traces can be seen of the working of this principle in different actions which all tend towards the same goal.

The Ministry of Education must be given the first place. A large proportion of the professors for the higher-grade schools are chosen from among the leaders of the Nationalist movement.

The various higher-grade schools have adopted a programme of education in the new branches of learning, such as Turkology, Turkish Sociology, etc. A special effort is being made to keep the system of education on a level with the development of the National question, in order that the National awakening may thus be encouraged in every phase of its growth.

The same idea is followed with varying enthusiasm by all the other schools and is shown either in the programme of education, the choice of professors or the composition of the school books.

The Ministry for Education, under the influence of the National movement has founded various new institutions, as, for instance, the *Istilah Enjumeni* (Academy of Terminology). Hitherto no one had troubled about the creation of technical expressions, but always made use of those current in Europe. Occasionally a few technical words were adapted from the Arabic, being expressly borrowed from one writer or another. The *Istilah Enjumeni* creates the proper terms for every branch of science and art, as well as for literature, taking great care to adhere as far as possible to the *Yeni Lisan*'s principle of employing only pure Turkish words. This is one of the most important anticipations of an emphatically Turkish intellectual life and civiliztion.

The latest institution, that of the *Dar Elbedai* (conservatoire), is based on the same principle.

The Ministry has also just nominated a *Teelif we Terjume Enjumeni* (Writing and Translation Committee) which is to undertake the translation or composition of books essential to the development of Turkish intellectual culture.

We spoke further back of the *Izji* or Scouts. These organizations have gradually been introduced by the Ministry of Education into all the schools under its control; this step will do much towards building up a strong, healthy and at the same time Nationalist spirit in the youth of Turkey.

The Ministry of the Interior is directed by Talaat Bey, the leading spirit of the Committee, who devotes all his influence and power to the progress of the Turkish movement.

This spirit, this national tendency, is the chief factor in the nominations of Town Prefects and Mayors, who in their turn carry out the ministerial duties and orders with the same idea.

Most interesting of all is the work of the Evkaf Ministry (Ministry of Religious Institutions), into whose treasury millions flow from the various pious foundations. The Ministry has now started to use these millions for the economic restoration of the nation.

It has just begun the foundation of a National Bank, with a capital of one million Turkish pounds. Part of the huge, hitherto untouched, fortune of the Religious Institutions Ministry, is in future to be devoted to the education of the Turkish people.

In future, therefore, besides the more or less "Ottoman" schools, managed by the Education Ministry, Evkaf schools will be founded, which will work on the lines of our Christian national schools, and provide the elementary education in Turkey.

The Evkaf Ministry has lately turned its attention to a thorough reform of the Medresses (clerical seminaries) which have hitherto been hotbeds of religious fanaticism. Hundreds of these seminaries, which have never taught anything but the most unenlightened scholastic divinity and the most hair-splitting sophistry, and were entirely out of touch with the requirements of modern life, have now been transformed into well-organized theological colleges. Profane sciences have been introduced, such as sociology, Turkology, history and other studies, which are all taught by leaders of the Turkish movement.

These reforms are not nearly completed, but in a few years the hundreds of Medresses will become theological schools in the modern sense of the word, and the Khojas who leave them will form a new progressive element in Turkey.

The Evkaf Ministry has also laid the basis of a new Turkish architecture, and has caused a large number of buildings to be erected in ancient Turkish style, and after old designs. The head of this branch is Chief Engineer Kemaleddin Bey, who studied in Germany and is recognized as an authority in Turkey. The Ministry's initiative is therefore bringing about the revival of the forgotten architecture of ancient Turkey, which is daily winning for itself new supporters and a wider popularity.

The Evkaf Ministry is also occupied with the foundation of a large general library of books dealing with Turkish life. The library of the late Russian Orientalist Katanoff has already passed into the hands of the Ministry, whose new collection consists of thousands of volumes, part of which are devoted to Turkology. An attempt is being made to unite all the valuable and neglected Turkish libraries which lie forgotten in different parts of the capital.

These are to be collected in a magnificent library building in the centre of Stamboul, and rendered accessible to the public.

Nearly all the Ministers declare their Nationalist sympathies. The Minister of Marine, Jemal Pasha, Talaat Bey, and others have declared at the *Turk Ojaghi* meetings before thousands of people, that "Biz da Ojakhjis" ("We too are supporters of the *Turk Ojaghi*").

The portfolio of the Minister of Trade and Agriculture, which has been in the hands of Greeks and Armenians since the time of the constitution, and was lately given to a Christian Arab, has at last been handed over to the Constantinople deputy, Ahmed Nesimi Bey, who joined with Ziya Gök Alp in laying the foundations of the Turkish movement immediately after the proclamation of the constitution. With one exception the members of the cabinet are all imbued with the same ideas and principles.

CHAPTER IX. THE PAN-TURKISH IDEAL AND GERMANISM

The fact that the Turks are today the allies of Germany is no mere whim of destiny, but the conscious expression of an unconscious brotherhood in arms which has existed between the two nations for a thousand years. For ten centuries, both nations have had one common enemy – the Slavs.

The Turkish conquerors from the East crushed the Slav peoples under their horses' hoofs; the German races from the West pressed the same nation back into her old territory with mailed fist. The Slavs then fought in century-long wars to prevent the union of the two dangerous powers, which in unconscious agreement were striving in opposite directions towards the same goal. This unsuspected community of purpose represents an alliance exacted by the very nature of things and events; it is an historical and geographical necessity. It bore rich fruit. A Russian historian writes as follows: "It is this unconscious Germano-Turkish alliance which prevents the development of the Slav Union in the Carpathians, the Danube country and the Balkans."

The Turkish nation of the Magyars is placed like a wedge between the Northern and Southern Slavs, which remain separated still after the efforts of a thousand years.

Ten centuries of history have brought about no change in the position of the Germans and Turks towards the Slavs. The two nations have always remained the common foe of the Slav power, and must both protect themselves from the menace of the Muscovite Empire. As long as the Russian colossus remains, Germanism is threatened with isolation, on account of her geographical position and ethnographical formation. In the same way, the Pan-Turkish aspirations cannot come to their full development and realization until the Muscovite monster is crushed, because the very districts which form the object of the Turkish Irrendenta, such as Siberia, Caucasus, the Crimea, Afghanistan, etc. are still directly or indirectly under Russian rule. Russia, who hinders the natural expansion of Germany and Turkey, is for her part stopped in her expansion by two strong nations, the Germans and the Turks: the Germans who have prevented the union between the Northern and Southern Slavs for which the Russians have striven in vain for ten centuries; the Turks who bar the way to the Mediterranean for Russia, and therefore for Pan-Slavism, and keep her shut up in the Black Sea. Russia, who is unable to overcome both these obstacles at once, first directed her attention to the smaller of the two, and chose to make her first attacks against the weaker and presumably more easily overcome of her two enemies.

Then began a period extending over hundreds of years, during which the Turks were obliged to resist endless attacks of every different kind. In spite of her great conquests, victories and successes, Turkey has never been able to remain strong outside, and was therefore not absolutely successful in repelling these long, stubborn attacks of the Russian tyrants, and the world saw the Russian bear gradually devouring one limb after another from its victim's body. So were lost the northern frontier provinces, and so, gradually, in the course of many terrible battles, the provinces on the northern, eastern and western coast of the Black Sea. The Russians attempted at the same time to free the Southern Slav races from the Turkish dominion, and give the separate nations their independence, thus forming in Turkey's very territory a number of small, but no less dangerous foes. In this they were successful, and the small Balkan kingdoms were founded. The last blow to the Turks and not the least disastrous, was the Balkan Union and consequent Balkan War, which was the grim and terrible forerunner of the present world war.

The Turks were almost entirely overwhelmed by Europe, and had it not been for the irony of fate which brought about the horrible discords among the Southern Slavs, causing them to attack each other like hungry wolves around their stolen prey, the Russian ideal would have approached realization more quickly. Russia would have been able to protect her free exit into the Mediterranean by means of the Southern Slav puppet-states.

Immediately after the Balkan War, Russia began to make preparations for a new blow, the reforms in Eastern Anatolia.

If Russia had been able then to realize her first ideal of free exit into the Mediterranean, her efforts would have immediately been directed against Germany in order to attain her second goal – union with the southern seas.

In her work of destruction, Russia found an unnatural ally, a degenerate branch of the Teuton race – England. Two monsters were united in the same purpose, the colossus of darkest barbarism and the cruellest oppression joined with the colossus of a degenerate civilization and shameless exploitation of his people. This England, whose Mohammedan subjects possessed a dangerous centre of attraction in the Caliphate, which might well wrest from here her authority over them, wished for this very reason to get possession of Arabia, and the coast of the Persian Gulf as far as Bombay, thus realizing her dream of making the Indian Ocean an English ocean, and setting up the well-known Gibraltar-Singapore line, which would give her the monopoly of the trade of the Old World.

"Treacherous Albion's" policy of robbery and her petty commercial spirit brought her into opposition with Germany on two points:

1. Germany's ideal, which she has followed since the time of Friedrich List, has been the creation of German expansion lines, starting from Hamburg and ending at Baghdad or perhaps Bassora; this scheme is seriously crippled by the above-mentioned English line.

2. By Germany's rise as a colonial and commercial power, whose irresistible expansion threatened seriously to damage English trade, and endangered England's command of the world by its ever-increasing development.

This war is merely the natural and expected conflict between the two different groups. Since Germany has always shown herself to be the natural protector of Islam, and therefore of Turkey, who recognized her (unfortunately, somewhat late) as her one true friend, it was therefore only logical and consistent that Turkey should place herself openly on the side of Germany against two common foes. Nothing shows better or more clearly the community of interests between the Pan-Turkish ideal and Pan-Germanism than the following extracts from a circular sent by the "Committee of Unity and Progress" to its branches in Turkey. This circular was sent out on the day following the declaration of war between Turkey and the Triple Entente powers:

"For two centuries, the outer powers of Europe have directed their expansion on land and sea against the Turkish and neighbouring Mohammedan countries. The Central Powers, who were being shut in and isolated by the outer nations, were obliged to confine their natural desire for expansion to themselves, being careful of course to watch the circle which was hemming them in. In consequence of this an enmity, having its origin in the very nature of things, grew up between the two groups of powers. This natural hostility of the Germanic, Turkish and Mohammedan nations towards the outer powers brought about a sort of moral alliance between the two first-named nations.

"In accordance with the last will of "Deli Peter" (Peter the Lunatic, i.e. Peter the Great) the Russians have been always attempting to bring about the destruction of Turkey. England and France, who until recent times thought it to their interest to allow Turkey to continue her existence, now see it as their duty to work with Russia for the downfall of Turkey, so that they may thus enjoy uninterrupted posession of Mohammedan countries such as India, Tunisia, Algeria, Morocco, etc., which they have grabbed with unexampled greed. These three powers have united against the Central powers and the world of Islam and formed a Triple Entente, which is nothing less than a twentieth century crusade. The first successes in this devilish crusade have been the conquest and snatching of Persia, Morocco and Turkish Rumelia. In order to seduce Italy from the Triple Alliance, the outer powers gave her Tripoli.

"If we seek the causes of all our misfortunes, both at home and abroad during the past century, we see clearly on every side the traces of the cruel and blood-stained hand of our greatest enemy – the Triple Entente. This Entente has led us into so much misery already, and now its predatory form rises once more before us to bar our road. With a dictatorial 'Halt!' it tried to stand in our way when our troops were advancing to our beloved Adrianople with cries of 'Allah! Allah!' It was this evil and pitiless Entente who recently forced us to give a special form to the East Anatolian provinces. When these wretches attempted to impose the same fate upon Germany and Austro-Hungary as had been meted out to us, and to lay the same trap for the two Central Powers, the great war broke out. In order that their atrocious crime agains the Central Powers should be successful, they decided upon a plan by means of which the Dardanelles should be forced from the Mediterranean side and Bosphorus from the Black Sea side simultaneously. The robbery of England of our two dreadnoughts, the *Reshadie* and *Sultan Osman*, is nothing but a direct result of this plan. It is quite obvious that if the Russians and English had gained possession of the straits, which are the key to the Caliphate, they would have forced us to take up arms against the Central Powers. Thus would the weapon for suicide have been forced into our hand. Fortunately, our Government acted with the greatest wisdom by ordering mobilization at the right moment and taking over the *Yavuz* and *Midilli* from Germany. In this way, our authority in the Black Sea and our possession of the straits were assured, and our position became one of armed neutrality. But are we to remain idle while our natural allies are at war with Russia – our sworn, irreconcilable, and eternal enemy? Will not victory for the Triple Entente be to us a sentence of death? Were it not madness if we refrain now from devoting all our moral and physical energy to meeting this danger?

"We must not forget that our participation in the world war would not take place solely to defend ourselves agains threatened ruin; it would also represent something far nearer to our hearts – the vindication of our national ideal.

"The national ideal of our nation and people leads us, on the one hand, towards the destruction of the Muscovite enemy, in order to obtain thereby a natural frontier to our empire, which should include and unite all branches of our race.

"On the other hand, our religious principles urge us to free the Mohammedan world from the power of the unbelievers, and to give independence to the followers of Mahomet. For these reasons we must sooner or later become involved in the world war. The enemy has already forced the obligation upon us by trying to mine the entrance to the Black Sea and to surround or disperse our fleet. Now we know why we are fighting. The goal shines before us and we can take up our arms with zeal and enthusiasm.

"We are fighting for our nation, our religion and our national ideal!"

This document, which is of great historical value, speaks for itself. It forms a convincing and concrete definition of the Pan-Turkish ideal. It shows still more clearly the close intimate bond which unites this ideal to that of Pan-Germanism.

Of especial importance is this sentence in the circular: "On the other hand, our religious principles urge us to free the Mohammedan world from the power of the unbelievers and to give independence to the followers of Mahomet."

A third ally is added to the Pan-Turkish and Pan-German ideals – that of Pan-Islam. It is true that the Turks are striving for the union of all Turks under the banner of Osman, but they are nevertheless determined upholders of Pan-Islamism.

The United Turks, they say, should form the centre of gravity of the world of Islam. The Arabs of Egypt, Morocco and Tunisia, the Persians and Afghans, etc, must enjoy complete independence in their own affairs, but outwardly the world of Islam must present a perfectly united front.

This conception of Pan-Islamism expressed by the upholders of the Pan-Turkish movement applies perfectly to Germany's policy towards Islam. Germany, whose sovereign declares himself the friend of Islam, is also anxious to preserve the complete independence of the Mohammedan world, in order to bring about her own economic expansion.

We need only add that as long as the Turks have an ideal, as long as they remain conscious of their mission in the world, so long will their destiny be bound up with that of Pan-Germanism.

We must not believe that the Russian, i.e. Slav peril will cease after the war. The defeat which the Russians will suffer in this war cannot render them harmless forever. It may, on the other hand, cause an awakening, an intellectual and moral renaissance of the Slav world. The Pan-Turkish and Pan-German ideals will therefore be united in their aims at least so long as the Slav peril exists.

The two Powers, Germany and Turkey, complete one another in a marvellous way. Turkey, as leader of the Mohammedan world, most urgently requires European science and the modern developments of European civilization and intellectual life in all branches of human activity, in intellectual, social, administrative, and especially in economic spheres. Germany is the only country to whom she can apply for this without endangering her national independence and territorial integrity. Germany's national ideal is economic expansion. Who could suggest a wider field for this than the inexhaustible regions of Anatolia, Asia Minor and all Turkish territory both before and after the war?

No power on earth can destroy such a bond which is welded out of a community of interests of such precious solid and substantial interests!

PART II

THOUGHTS ON THE NATURE AND PLAN OF A GREATER TURKEY

CHAPTER I. THE NATIONAL CONSCIOUSNESS

The Turkish army's defeat in the Balkan War was regarded with justifiable surprise throughout Europe. Various writers have taken pains to discover the causes of the complete overthrow of these armies which were once the wonder and terror of the Old World.

One of these essays interested me very much. "The Turkish soldier in that war was unable to see before him the figures of his ancient heroes. The noble cause of the other days was lacking and he had nothing to call forth his bravery. Once the feeling for 'Jihad' (Holy War) was firmly engrained in him. The soldier marching to war knew that he would either return as 'ghazi' (victor), covered with glory, or die, and enter the happy realms of Paradise as 'Shehid.'

"The nineteenth century brought with it the wholesale destruction of the religious ideal and placed in its stead the national idea.

"This took place in Turkey also, where the old 'Jihad' spirit was to be supplanted by nationalism. The old régime tended to crush all the interests and every manifestation of a national spirit in the people. The new régime at first placed the Turkish people in a vague and ill-defined position. Which aims should they follow? They hesitated between an unrealizable "Ottomanism" – the union of all the nations in the kingdom into one body – and "Pan-Islamism." Turkish national consciousness was not yet awakened. But a soldier who goes into battle without this national ideal cannot fight well."

I do not know to what extent this opinion is correct, but the final sentence seems to me most remarkable, in that it contains a bitter truth.

If the Turks had possessed a national consciousness in the Balkan War, they might perhaps have been spared many trials, not only in their war against their neighbours, but also in the "struggle for existence" – in their inner development.

Even before the Balkan War, this state of affairs had attracted the attention of European observers. I should like to draw attention to the following extracts from an article in the *Mercure de France* of August 16, 1912:[3]

"The Ottoman Turks – the real owners of the Empire – form an element in the population which is ignored and forgotten in its own country. The Turks, who belong to the

Turkoman race, have remarkably good traits of character, including uprightness, honesty, industry, modesty and patience. They struggle in vain with the hard soil of Anatolia, and do not even succeed in making enough to live on. They are everlasting slaves and prisoners, who waste their best strength in hard compulsory labour, while their very blood is sucked dry by the tax farmers. No one protects them. They form the one element of the people which has filled the barracks and garrisons of the empire for centuries past. Its blood has watered the furrows of the Macedonian fields, and has drenched the trackless plains of Hauran and Yemen. A pitiless despotism snatches the sons of this race, while still almost children, from their native soil, and banishes them to the distant barracks and garrisons on the frontiers of the Empire. They are left there forgotten – five, ten, fifteen years pass, and the discharge order never comes. If the poor man who has become a stranger to his home and his work has the good fortune to be sent home, he has no more energy or strength left to work. His father and mother have probably died in his absence, and he sees poverty staring him in the face. The field his father left him has been sold by the hard-hearted tax farmers. Misery such as this is common in the villages on the Anatolian plain and in the gorges of Rumelia. Every kind of misfortune assails them – poverty, pestilence, and the greatest evil of ancient Turkey, the horrors of spying and suspicion. The best sons of the race are in prison or banished. There are no newspapers worth mentioning, no clubs or unions. The schools only exist to teach devotion to the authorities. The Turkish people seem doomed to everlasting slavery.

On the other hand, the Christian population of Turkey has been consistently progressing, partly by means of privileges too easily granted, and partly by their own initiative, and they are ousting the real owner of the country more and more from their heritage. Two nations, pressing upon them from either side, have succeeded in driving the old 'conquerors' more and more into the interior of the country. The Greeks from the sea and the islands have taken possession of the harbours and coast towns of Anatolia, and pressed the Turks further and further back into the salt steppes of the interior. The Armenians, who, thanks to their friendly relations with England, have become very rich, have cut off their retreat. The Turk is such a miserable wretch that he has forgotten the plains of Turania, without even having been able to assure his footing in the country he has conquered. He was so convinced of his own power that he omitted to build bridges between his old and new homes, bridges between the different conquered territories. For centuries the conquerors have lived scattered over huge districts without any communication joining the separate settlements, and without any internal unity, which is of such vital necessity. Separated by enormous distances, they lived isolated lives and were lacking in community of spirit, and therefore in any national civilization. The Turks have always lived like an organism without a head or a brain."

This description applies of course to the old régime; and the coming of the new régime has not yet brought about any material improvement. The causes of this national evil have not yet disappeared, precisely because the Turks have not yet come to their national consciousness.

The efforts to awaken a national spirit have met with loud protests and violent opposition. People laboured at first under the delusion that a national movement meant opposition to religion. The few liberal-minded spirits who dared to identify themselves more closely with the movement were silenced. The true awakening of national consciousness did not take place until after the Balkan Wars.

CHAPTER II. THE AWAKENING

It is a well established historical fact that great political or social crises usually produce great social movements. The awakening of the German nation came at the time of its greatest misfortune. A large part of Germany was groaning under the Corsican's yoke, and her very existence was menaced. At that time, great poets, philosophers, and orators rose, summoned the youth of the nation to resist, and rallied the national thought by word and deed. The foreign yoke of France was shaken off in fierce battles, Germany's political independence was won, and the influence of the French language, literature and civilization was weakened and dispelled. The spirit of the German people received new life. When, therefore, French arrogance once more threatened the frontiers of Germany, the nation rose in a body against her hereditary foe. Sedan and other names bear witness to the successes of Germany's combined forces. Men such as Bismark, Moltke and others were the sons of this German national spirit. Forty-four years of peace, of quiet development outside and consistent progress inside the country, followed on this period. In a few decades Germany reached the front rank of the civilized nations, and the cowardly fear of being outstripped gave "faithless Albion" no peace until she could vent upon us the rate which is the heritage of the great German-hater Edward VII, and raise all Europe in a furious blow against the dangerous strength of Germany. This war is a brilliant proof of Germany's highly developed national consciousness. The number of her volunteers, who can be counted by millions, bears eloquent witness to her spirit. We are now seeing the results of organization and national strength.

The present awakening of Turkey may well be compared to that of Germany exactly a hundred years before, in that it followed upon a critical and unhappy period.

The Turkish national spirit has changed very greatly in a wonderfully short time. It is almost a miracle. It may be asserted without hesitation that the Turkish people, who up to two years ago were totally lacking in national consciousness, are now imbued with it. This new spirit filters like beneficent life-giving rain through all the strata of the nation, restoring the whole people. The great men in whose hands is placed the nation's destiny today are imbued with this spirit and are solving the national problems by its light. The newly-awakened consciousness inspires in every part of the nation the will to gain for their Fatherland a strong and favourable position among the nations. The "Academy of Turkish Sciences" (*Turk bilgi Derneyi)* strives to create an individual intellectual life. The "National Union" (*Turk Ojaghlari*) works at the awakening of a national idea and the union of all Turks by a strong bond of nationality. The Sports Unions do their best to give the nation a physical development equal to that of the old "Conquerors." The Turkish "Scout" movement provides a modern and patriotic education for the youth of the country, and attempts by bringing boys into direct contact with nature in their expeditions, to rouse in their impressionable hearts a love for their Homeland and their nation. The economic leagues and societies are founding firms and business houses in Stamboul and all over Anatolia, and are confident of fruitful development.

The word "Turk" has now taken on a new and improved significance. Two years ago, even liberal-minded Turks interpreted this word in the European sense, i.e. as meaning raw, anti-social, anti-national, uncivilized, reactionary. The number of Turks who were proud of their nationality was shamefully small. Now, however, "Turk" connotes honest, industrious, enduring, persevering, self-sacrificing and progressive. The dictionary of nations is obliged to accept this change of meaning. When the word "Turk" is mentioned now, it does not express the calumny so current in Western literature, but brings back the memory of the famous days of ancient Turkey, of noble help given freely to oppressed nations and toleration to foreign religions. To this is added a fine shade of meaning, implying the modern progressive and newly-awakened spirit of Turkey. People have also become accustomed to the fact that the words "Turk" and "Mohammedan" are not identical and are aware that now "Turk" is the expression of national and "Mohammedan" that of religious citizenship, just as Arabs and Albanians, for instance, must be called Arabs and Albanians in spite of their religious brotherhood, and not be designated under the common title of Mohammedans.

Today there is a Turkish nation; her subjects feel a Turkish heart beat in their breast, Turkish blood flow through their veins and Turkish feelings and ideas rule their life.

CHAPTER III. THE IDEAL

The awakening of the national consciousness, in itself a cause for rejoicing, is only a beginning, a preparation for the real goal. The way is clear but the end is still far away. What great distances must be covered by the people in order to reach this end! What developments from their good beginning! An ideal is needed to make the national consciousness bear fruit. A spur or a goad must urge on the nation, lest it weary before the goal is reached. Every class, every individual in the country should, through his consciousness of self, see this ideal shine before him, forming the end of all his desires, and making the goal still more worth striving for.

Every nation under the sun possesses such an ideal, be it great or small, powerful or uninspiring.

The Germans proclaim their ideal in their national songs: "Deutschland, Deutschland über alles . . . " Every German knows this song from his childhood, all through his life it rings in his ears and with those words on his lips he dies – "Deutschland, Deutschland über alles," and in very truth every German longs with his whole soul and will to see his nation "über alles." In striving for this ideal the Germans have become so great and powerful a nation that they are now able to defy a whole world of assailants and defeat them all.

The English have also an ideal, and as it is precisely identical with Germany's, the conflict between the two nations became inevitable.

The French ideal is in contradiction to the needs and conditions of the age.

Since the great Revolution, the nation has striven towards "liberty, equality, fraternity." The French philosophers have created a special term for this: "Humanitarianism." Gustave Lebon says:

"France's greatest misfortune is that humanitarianism has become her national ideal. Italy was created through this ideal, and she has always been among the enemies of France.

"In short the training of a Frenchman is not national but anti-national."

The Balkan peoples, Greeks, Bulgarians, Serbians and even populations who till yesterday were under the dominion of Turkey all possess a national ideal. From the statesman who is concerned with the hard questions of political and social life, down to the simple peasant who knows nothing but his cow and his sickle, all long to see a powerful Greece,

Bulgaria or Serbia. As the Turks have only today found their national consciousness, they cannot be expected to have a very well defined ideal yet, and, indeed, they have not got it. In order to imbue a people with such an ideal and make it take firm root, much time is needed.

To avoid misinterpretations, let us hasten to add that although the Turks had no such ideal up to quite recent times, there were nevertheless a large number of idealists in the country, who brought about the revolution of July 23 and warded off the danger of April 23; they too raised Turkey from the Balkan disaster. Had Turkey not possessed men such as Enver, Talaat, Jemal and others, during those hard and disastrous times, the Ottoman Empire would have disappeared entirely by to-day.

But even if a number of idealists are living and working in the country, it does not follow that the nation itself has an ideal.

It only proves that the nation is capable of developing ideals. In this fruitful soil the seeds of an ideal should be sown with loving care, and the young shoots carefully tended.

CHAPTER IV. THE TURKISH IDEAL

What is to be the ideal of the Turkish nation? What aims should it embrace? What feelings and desires should be inculcated in the babies in the kindergartens, the children in the schools, the young men in the universities and the full-grown men in their working life? Of course desires and feelings cannot be forced on a nation unless they are in harmony with its soul and individuality. A nation's ideal must rise from the spirit of tradition.

The thinkers who led the new movement in Turkey never lost this point of view for a moment. They went back to the origins of the nation and laid bare the Turanian question.

The adherents of the *Yeni Lisan* (new language) who undertook to reform the Turkish language, confine themselves to the ancient Turkish treasury of words and strive to purify the language from the foreign, i.e. Persian and Arab, elements.

In their literary reforms, they advocate the pure national impulse, and give preference to old national themes and subjects which express the genuine Turkish spirit.

Old, forgotten Turkish songs and tales are revived, and it is hoped and believed that the soul of the ancient people will be found in the old traditions.

All these efforts only show what method is being pursued and on what lines the founding of an ideal for Turkey is being based. Turanianism itself, which lately received frequent mention in the newspapers, cannot form the true substance of this ideal, as far as it connotes the Turkish race.

Community of this race is of extremely small importance in this modern age. The English and the Germans are of the same race, and yet they are the bitterest enemies in the world. The same thing may be noticed in our near neighbourhood; community of race does not prevent the Serbians and Bulgarians from nourishing the deepest hatred against each other; each longs for nothing more heartily than the downfall of the other.

Russia, of course, proclaims her hypocritical Pan-Slavism, but her policy is not really directed towards the union of all Slav nations, but the extension and glorification of Russian despotism by means of the Slav nations.

The only nation which is a true member of the "Order of the Knout" is Serbia who has had to realize the bitter truth that as far as she is concerned, "Slav" is synonymous with "Slave," and that the "Brother of Russia" comes to the same as the "Servant of Russia." Poles and Ukrainians, who live too near to their Russian "brother" to be taken in by "Pan-Slavism," hate the Russian authority with a whole-hearted and bitter hatred, and regard it as their greatest, worst and most dangerous enemy.

The Czech, Ruthenian, Polish, Slovenian and other Slav soldiers who are fighting in the Austrian Army are especially bitter against their "brothers" the Russians. This affords sufficient proof of the fact that the bond of racial relationship is nowadays a very slight one. If, therefore, an attempt is made to give the Turks a national ideal based on the principle of the Brotherhood of all Turkish nations, the attempt will certainly fail. This does not imply that the feeling of racial community is to be discouraged or opposed. This feeling is, on the contrary, of great value, and it is a matter of congratulation that the *rapprochement* between Magyars and Turks is being so well received here.

Yet once again: The Turks' national ideal cannot be the race theory, because the latter is really nothing but a Utopian dream. The natural ideal of the Turkish nation can only grow out of the national movement. Could anything be more worth striving after, more beautiful than the union of all the Turks in the world, and the ardent desire to give all these Turks a common soul, a common consciousness, and a common civilization? It must not be forgotten that the Ottoman Turks, who already possess a national consciousness, now only represent a tenth of the whole nation. There are now sixty to seventy million Turkish subjects who should succeed in giving the nation an important place among the other powers. Unfortunately there is no relationship between the separate groups, which are distributed over great tracts of land. Their aspirations and national institutions still divide them.

The Turks who live under foreign rule have one hope and strength – the Ottoman Turks – but, not yet being come to national consciousness, they do not realize the great danger to which they and their brothers have been exposed: now that the Ottoman Turks have awakened from their sleep of centuries, they do not only think of themselves but hasten to save the other parts of their race who are living in slavery or ignorance.

CHAPTER V. THE IDEALS OF THE NEW NATION

The history of recent times shows us that all nations on awakening to national consciousness think first of their brothers in neighbouring lands. This thought has then gradually risen to become their national ideal. This is seen for the first time in the case of Italy. Hardly had she won her national unity when she became eager to help her compatriots abroad. This movement to free her brothers in Southern Tyrol and neighbouring districts gave rise to the Irrendenta. Political considerations induced Italy to enter into an alliance with Austria, but the Irrendenta never lost sight of its goal for a moment. The reason for the fact that public opinion is against Austria in spite of the alliance is to be found only in the Irrendenta. In spite of the community of interests between Italy and Austria, a real friendship has never existed between the two States. They were even obliged to strengthen their common frontiers. Even in this war public opinion in Italy is against her allies. If this reaction were not heavily counterbalanced by the wise statesmanship of the leading personalities, the Italians too would have fallen into the clutches of hypocritical and self-seeking Albion at the beginning of the war.

The Irrendenta policy, which has its origin in Italy, is today one of the strongest and most remarkable factors in the policy of nations.

Roumania has long been regarded as the satellite of the Triple Alliance, or rather of Austria-Hungary. She is almost completely surrounded by Slav nations and has her only natural *point d'appui* in the Monarchy. It was, therefore, to be expected that she would openly declare herself to be a partisan of Austria and promptly fall upon Russia, the enemy of civilization. The latest events have unfortunately proved the contrary. Immediately after the outbreak of war, public opinion ranged against Austria and demanded that the Government should take the favourable opportunity of joining forces with Russia against Austria. An explanation of this strange and certainly unexpected fact is not far to seek. The Irrendenta movement has recently spread to Roumania and taken a firm hold on the nation. Its object is to free the Roumanians in Transylvania from the Austrian authority and unite them with their Fatherland. This movement has also extended to the Roumanians in Hungary, and the Hungarian Government found itself obliged to take the necessary steps. Russian money and intrigues could only have had so surprising an effect in Roumania for this reason, that the ground was amply prepared by the Irrendenta. Thus the Irendenta, regarded as a national ideal, almost succeeded in perverting Roumania to the extent of inducing her to take up arms against Austria in this great war.

The Roumanian Irrendenta is not only directed towards Transylvania but also to Macedonia, although Roumania has no common frontier with Macedonia, which is the home of a few hundreds of thousands of Kutzovlachs of Roumanian blood. Innumerable unions were founded in Roumania for the purpose of protecting these people from Greece's efforts to Hellenize them, and the Roumanian Government grants them a yearly subsidy of 700,000 – 900,000 francs. Up to the time of the Balkan War the position of the Kutzovlachs was an important factor in Roumania's foreign policy. By this policy Roumania became a friend of Turkey, broke off her relations with Greece for some time and drove thousands of Greeks out of the country.

The small Balkan States of Bulgaria, Serbia, etc, whose foundation dates from the last century, were also willing and eager to receive Irrendenta ideas. Hardly had their independence been won, when they began to think of their brothers in the frontier lands. Even their Governments were obliged to support this national idea.

Bulgaria had hardly become a principality before it took up the Eastern Roumelian question, and by dint of revolutions, robber bands, and other well-known Balkan methods, succeeded in annexing this province. After this lucky start Bulgaria used exactly the same means to bring the Bulgarians in Macedonia under her rule. It is only too well known what was the result of this policy in Macedonia.

Serbia likewise made use of the customary methods of murder and robbery for the same purpose in Macedonia, thus finally turning the poor country into a terrestrial hell. Macedonia is soaked in blood. Atrocities were committed there, the mere thought of which makes one's hair stand on end. Nevertheless, the leaders of robber bands and members of the terrible Irrendenta were not regarded by the public as wild robbers but as heroes fighting for the unity of the nation.

The Balkan peoples, who have fought in this terrible and grisly manner, but with all their best strength, for many years for the union of their compatriots, have really attained their ideal in their victory over Turkey in the last war.

CHAPTER VI. THE TURKISH IRRENDENTA

The ideal of the new nations, and the policy of their Governments as interpreters of the national ideal, show a strong tendency towards the liberation of their compatriots abroad from the foreign yoke, or at least the awakening of their national consciousness.

The newly-awakened Turks can have no other aim. The Turkish Irendenta may be directed towards material or moral reforms according to circumstances. If the geographical position favours the venture, the Turks can free their brothers from foreign rule. In the other case they can, like the Roumanians in Macedonia, carry on their Irrendenta on moral or intellectual lines.

While the Irrendenta did not come to the Italians, Roumanians, Bulgarians and Serbians at the bidding of actual necessity, it formed for Turkey an inevitable policy. The Italians and other nations could easily have carried on their national development without the help of an Irrendenta, because they have in their own country sufficient political, social and economic resources to give them the upper hand over any possible alien element. Their national integrity is therefore unthreatened.

This is unfortunately not the case in Turkey. The Turks have not got the actual mastery in their own country. If Turkish civilization, the Turkish spirit, the Turkish national aspirations, were to be confined solely to Turkey, they could only be ephemeral in their influence, because they would be continually exposed to strong opposing influences. The Ottoman Turks are indeed the only strength of their brothers abroad, but they themselves are dependent on the co-operation of the different parts of their nation in foreign lands, because their numbers in the Fatherland are too small, and they are thus constantly menaced by the danger of assimilation into their *milieu.*

The Irrendenta, which other nations may regard as a luxury – though often very terrible and costly – is a political and social necessity for the Turks. The motive of the Turkish Irrendenta is not, as with other nations, greed for conquest, because Turkey has no need of increased territory or conquests. The fruitful land of Anatolia would provide good homes and food for a population three times greater than the present number. The Turkish element at home not only requires material but moral expansion and strengthening. The Ottoman Turks have allowed themselves to be too greatly influenced by the mode of thought and conditions of life in their country, and have lost many of their national qualities, while Turks living abroad under different conditions have been better able to retain them. The Ottoman Turks have not, for instance, been able to preserve in all its strength the well-known warlike spirit of their forefathers. But the Kashkai peoples in Persia, the Afghans, and other Turkish elements have retained this material spirit to the full. The Ottoman Turks who have been under a political rule for centuries have always regarded officialdom and a bureaucratic career as the highest possible aim. The spirit of enterprise no longer lives within them. On the contrary, the Turks of Azerbaijan and in Russia have this quality to a very high degree.

The Ottoman Turks have however many other good and useful qualities to a greater extent than other Turks.

If all the Turks in the world were welded into one huge community, a strong nation would be formed, worthy to take an important place among the other nations of the world.

CHAPTER VII. THE IDEALISTS

It is indeed not easy (but therefore all the more noble) task to give a common spirit and common national soul to all Turks. An ideal is an idea which may come to fulfilment at any moment. The ideal is the most distant point on the mental horizon of a nation, and every step taken towards it means a very real progress.

The raising of a nation depends not only upon the presence of an ideal, but also upon the co-operation of idealists who are ready to devote all their strength, and even their lives and fortunes, to its attainment. As we have seen before, the Turkish Nation is in no wise lacking in such idealists. A convincing proof of this may be gained by a close study of the persons holding the highest positions in the Government. These men have never ceased for a moment to work with utter self-abnegation for the good of the nation. The life of these men is a shining and encouraging example to the youth of the country. Observers who, like myself, are Macedonians and, like myself, had ample opportunity of gaining an intimate knowledge of the Irrendentist propaganda of the Bulgarians, Greeks, Serbians and Vlachs, are able to judge the significance of this striving after a national ideal, and how sweet and inspiring it is to go through the greatest dangers for such a cause. This is best illustrated by a few living examples.

First let us take the case of a young Bulgarian. He came of a wealthy family and was therefore pampered and indulged in every possible way by his parents. Up to the age of 30 he studies at the University. Does he then move to a luxuriously appointed lawyer's office in Salonica, surrounded by all the most modern comforts? No! His office is in the mountains, his desk is a rock, his pen a gun and dagger, and his clients Turkish gendarmes and Greek robber bands upon whom he passes sentence of death without much ceremony.

Another illustration. The young man has studied medicine in a European University and returns home with his doctor's degree. Will he now declare war on the microbes and the thousands of diseases which assail human life? No, indeed! He wanders, armed to the teeth, from village to village, from mountain to mountain, dispensing out his only medicine, those death-dealing blue pills, to all the opponents of his ideal, and even to those of his own countrymen who do not share his ideas.

A third picture is afforded by a professor of the highest philosophical attainments. Does he establish a centre of training in Athens, Bucharest, Sofia or Belgrade? No, again! In secluded villages such as Grebena and Dikvesh, etc, he instills the Irrendenta principles into the minds of the village children, and prepares them to sacrifice life and fortune for this ideal.

During the last few years the prisons of Salonica and Monastir have been filled with a curious class of men. The dark dungeon cells do not hide thieves or ordinary criminals, but chiefly doctors, lawyers, professors, and similar idealists.

The mountains and fields of Macedonia hold hundreds of graves of such men as these. The rivers Vardar and Struma have been reddened by the blood of thousands of these idealists. The men may die but the ideal is immortal. It is ever brought closer to realization by the death of these men.

Will the Young Turks emulate the self-sacrifice of these men? Or will they rather, on leaving the University, seek as their one object in life an official or similar position in Constantinople or Smyrna or one of the larger towns in the kingdom, without troubling about the needs of their Fatherland, which demands so many young lives? They know the road, and the goal towards which it leads. They know also that this goal cannot be reached but by the sacrifice of blood and fortune. But they know best of all that the Fatherland needs them and that the nation is calling.

CHAPTER VIII. THE TURKS OF AZERBAIJAN

There are many different kinds of countries which form a fruitful ground for the development of the national ideal. In some places ordinary propaganda is sufficient, but in hotly contested territory recourse is made to the more violent measures which were used in Macedonia.

The neighbouring land of Persia is without doubt the best of all countries with Turkish population for spreading the new ideas, and it has been found that simple propaganda is amply sufficient to produce a satisfactory effect on this fruitful soil. One-third of the whole population of about ten millions is of Turkish blood.

It can quite clearly be seen to-day that the destiny of the Persian State is closely bound up with that of Turkey. Russia and England, who saw the decline of Turkey, and tried to bring about her final downfall as quickly as possible, were also united on the subject of the complete partition of Persia. They did not even take the trouble to hide this intention. A victory for the Triple Entente would seal Turkey's fate, and the inevitable result would be the fall of Persia.

The material interests of these two countries, which are exposed to the same danger, are therefore closely bound together; indeed, they are almost identical. The maintenance of Turkey is a guarantee for that of Persia, just as in the opposite case, the strengthening of Persia is a protection against a Russian invasion of Turkey.

These two Mohammedan States are obliged to defend their lives against Russian attack. It is true that this natural and indeed necessary *rapprochement* for purposes of resisting a common danger and of mutual protection is not yet an accomplished fact. Turkey has hitherto been far too occupied with internal and external disturbances, wars and crises, while Persia was cowering under the knout of the notorious Liakoff's Cossacks and those of his playmates. There is, however, no reason for postponing or hindering this *rapprochement* and union now. As soon as Iran is freed from Russian despotism, efforts will be made to form a strong and binding union between Turkey and Persia.

For this reason, the Turkish propaganda in Persia is by no means hostile to that nation, but will, on the contrary, be a strong factor in the internal and external progress of the country, especially as the Turks in Persia form the progressive element in the population.

The province of Azerbaijan, which is the richest, most active and most enlightened in Persia, is almost entirely inhabited by Turks. Two and a half millions are of pure Turkish blood, and think, speak and pray in Turkish.

The Turcoman and Kashkai population, who live outside this province, are also of pure Turkish descent. Even in the other parts of Turkey,[4] the progressive and internal power is mostly in the hands of the Turks. The national wealth of Persia belongs to the Turks, who in their turn fill the Persian Government's treasury. The warlike families in Persia are also Turks; they form the national army of the Government, whose one strong support they are.

The Kajar dynasty, which has ruled over Persia for centuries, is also of Turkish origin. Of the same descent are the Grand Vizier and other State dignitaries, in whose hands has hitherto been placed the welfare of the State. The majority of Persia's thinking men are Turks. The spirit of the administration is Turkish, as also the leading spirit of Persian civilization, even though these be clothed in Persian guise.

Unfortunately all these services rendered by Turks to Persia have been wasted for the former, because all those Turkish warriors and heroes, Shahs and Grand Viziers, thinkers and scholars have lost their Turkish consciousness and have become assimilated with the Persians in writing, speech and literature.

It has also been proved historically that Turks have always rendered great services to science, and especially to intellectual life; never, indeed, under Turkish names and designations, but under names taken from those nations with whom they are living. This is shown in the case of the Arabs, for instance. Men such as Farabi and Ibn Sina, who are famous as the protagonists of Arab civilization, belong to the Turkish race.

We needed however research students and historians such as Tahir Bey and Leon Kahun[5] to enlighten us about the nationality of those heroes of civilization, and to show the world, even the Turkish world, that it is absolutely false to believe that Turks had never cared for or helped civilization at any time or in any place.

First, these historical students had to fill many blank leaves of Turkish history books with the fame of their nation. It may be taken for granted that, if only the Turks' national consiousness had dawned upon them at an earlier period of their historical development, they could have looked back on an individual civilization in the same way as other nations, such as the Romans, Greeks, Arabs, etc.

The lack of a national idea has hitherto caused the Turks, even in the independent Ottoman Empire, to clothe all their scientific and intellectual work in Persian guise. The Turkish spirit feels itself too weak to dispense with the borrowed foreign cloak. If the Ottoman Turks do not become assimilated like their Persian brothers, the reason lies in the fact that in many places they form the majority of the population. Another reason is that a high barrier has been formed between the Turks and the Christian nations by various privileges granted by the different Sultans to the Patriarch. Close intercourse between the Turkish subjects and those of other faiths was practically impossible.

On the other hand, the Turks who poured into Persia and subdued her had once been subdued themselves. The Turkish subjects in Persia were therefore placed in a very curious position. They speak Turkish but always use Persian when writing, as though Turkish were forbidden. Even the simplest letter is always written in Persian. Although efforts have recently been made to introduce the use of Turkish in writing, they have not been very favourably received. An attempt was even made to publish newspapers printed in Turkish. The journals *Forad* and *Suhbet* both had a very limited circulation and a very short life.

In spite of all this, it does not seem too hard a task to win the Turks in Persia over to the national interest, and give them all a Turkish soul. It is sufficient that a few obstinate and persevering idealists should undertake this beneficent task.

To be convinced of this, it is only necessary to glance at the situation of the Kutzovlachs in Macedonia. The few hundreds of thousands of Vlachs in Macedonia have, until recent days, been in a far worse situation than the Turks in Persia. They are Roumanians and write and speak Roumanian. From a national point of view they regarded themselves, nevertheless, as Greeks, and never imagined that they could belong to any other nation than Greece. Their religious services were performed in the Greek church and they always made use of Greek priests. At the same time, the language, race customs, mode of life and even dress of the Greeks were different. And these Vlachs did not confine themselves to the mere consciousness of being Greeks, but they also opposed Greek propaganda to that of the Bulgarians.

During the second half of the nineteenth century the first signs of a national awakening were seen – not among the Vlachs in Macedonia, but among those living in Roumania and Hungary. Not until the end of the nineteenth century, when the Roumanians themselves rose to the occasion and started the arousing of the Vlach element, was there any real awakening. At that time, however, Vlach Nationalists started to build Vlach churches and schools, and the Roumanians organized an extensive propaganda. The Greeks tried, indeed, by robber bands and all kinds of forcible means to put down the new and unexpected movement; but the leaders who were sent from Roumania took up the challenge with the greatest decision and simply opposed the Greek gangs with Vlachs.

With the financial help of the Roumanian Government, just one decade saw the creation of a combined Vlach element of a few hundred thousand people.

It may be easily understood that a movement which was so succesfully started by a few Roumanian idealists could also be conducted in Persia and would have an assured success, in that the difficulties encountered by the Roumanian Nationalists would not have to be overcome by the Turkish idealists in Persia. There is no power in Persia to put down such a movement, because it could not do harm to anyone. The nationalization of the Persian Turks would even be a great and unexpected help to the Persian Government, because an enlightened element of three to four millions, thinking and acting in unison, would thus be formed in Persia. If the standard of civilization were raised in Persia by this movement, a strong internal union would thus be possible between the two countries.

Persia could be situated with regard to the Turkish Government as Bavaria towards Prussia, or Hungary towards Austria, i.e. Persia can live her internal life in absolute independence and liberty, while outwardly forming with Turkey one body and soul, one great united nation.

The idea that in helping the Turks in Persia, Turkey will lay hands on the country is foolish and unfounded. It has always been maintained that Turkey has no desire for territorial expansion. No one can be a better judge than the Turks themselves of the difficulties and disadvantages of ruling over heterogeneous elements of population. The future of Turkey lies only in the extension of her economic and progressive scope and in an increased number of hands and brains to work for the progress and development of the Turkish nation.

If Persia, as a Mohammedan power, accepts the idea of a Union, the Turkish population will be increased by three to four millions, but the Turkish Empire by about ten million souls.

It is without doubt that many Turks in Persia are eager for a Union, and would not hesitate to devote their lives to the realization of the project. For among the Persian Turks, too, the idealists and "Fedai" (Zealots) are numerous. They have repeatedly proved that they are willing to lay down their lives for an ideal. The Persian revolution, which was crushed under the heel of the Cossacks, and put down by the knout, was started by the Turks in Azerbaijan. The heroes who sacrificed their lives for the realization of their plan were mostly Turks, as also were the martyrs of the reaction. The parts played in the Turkish revolution by heroes such as Enver, Niazi and others, were played in Persia by men such as Sadar Chau, Bakir Chau, etc.

Those brave men who, during the reaction, made an heroic resistance for a year at the siege of Tabris, and went through the most terrible privations, were also Turks. That is to say that there is no lack in Persia of Turks who are worthy of fighting for an ideal, and even of dying.

If, therefore, a part of these many self sacrificing ideâlists could be won for the Turkish National movement in Persia, the cause is assured.

CHAPTER IX. THE CAUCASIAN TURKS

The greater part of the Turkish nation is in Russia, who is now at war with Turkey.

The Caucasus, the present goal of our doughty troops, is the home of a large number of these Turks. The country south of the Caucasus Range may really be regarded as Turkish territory. The Turkish element forms the chief part of the population (50 percent); in some provinces this figure is increased even to 80 percent of the whole population.

The alluvial plains of the Volga and the Kama, in European Russia, are inhabited by four or five milion Turks who are closely allied to the Ottoman Turks in language, institutions and civilization.

These, and their brothers in the Crimea and Caucasus, lead an independent life, cut off from one another, especially in the provinces of Kazan and Ufa, where the Turks are in the majority. The Northern Turks are not indeed superior to the Ottoman Turks, but must not therefore be underrated; they are indeed in the proud position of having come to national consciousness before the Ottoman Turks. Their progressive, economic and social organization is in every way a great help to the national movement.

The Ottoman Turks owe to their earlier despotic system of Government the peculiarity of being always Hukumetji, i.e. that they are always too much tied to their "mother" Government's apron-strings and will not be independent. If anything is to be done for the good of the people, the Government must start it. The Government, who has so much to bear, so many dangers to avert, so many cares assailing it, cannot always find time to deal with all the details, which are really the people's business. A people must make its future for itself; the Government can only help and advise, for the whole question is one of natural development. The Ottoman Turks have not yet obtained a common organization like that of the non-Mohammedan peoples.

This is not the case with the Northern and Causasian Turks, all progress among whom is the result of their own efforts. The Russian Government has given them no support but, on the contrary, suppressed them as much as possible. In spite of this, the schools, for instance, in these Turkish communities are in no wise inferior to those in Turkey proper. The scholars leaving these schools are equal to pupils of the Russian schools and are even superior to them to a certain extent. The Russian Turks have an absolutely independent common organization. In each district or community the people all rally around the Imam, who is regarded as their teacher and guide. These Imams are usually very enlightened and wise men, possessing a wide general knowledge which is naturally a great help to the progress of the community.

A sort of common council is formed under the presidency of the Imam, which deals with schools and other national institutions. The work, which, among the Ottoman Turks, is given out by the Patriarchates to the different Mejlis, is here carried out by the common council. The management and upkeep of the schools and national institutions have never been entrusted to the Government by the Russian Turks. The generosity of the members of the community, whose munificent gifts are ample for the upkeep of the various public institutions, has entirely obviated the need for a Government subsidy.

The Russian Turks have their own civilization and speech. They boast many writers, such as Tokai, Ajas, Fateh and others, who are also intellectual leaders. The Press does not discuss the political situation, but only questions directly connected with the national interests. In short, the intellectual standard and moral attainments of these Russian Turks is so high that they are in no need of the leadership of the Ottoman Turks. They only demand one thing of the Ottoman Empire – the strengthening and progress of the Turkish Government and the Turkish nation, for therein they see the one support of the whole Turkish people.

The development of national intellectual life and national civilization needs a strong and independent government.

If the Russian Despotism is, as we hope, to be destroyed by the brave German, Austrian and Turkish armies which oppose it, thirty to forty million Turks will receive their independence. Together with the ten million Ottoman Turks, this will form a nation of fifty millions, advancing towards a great civilization, which may perhaps be compared to that of Germany, in that it will have the strength and energy to rise ever higher. In some ways it will be even superior to the degenerate French and English civilizations.

All the desires of the Turkish nation are fixed on this goal – the building up of a new, national Turkish civilization, founded on the basis of the old sacred traditions.

The Turkish and Pan-Turkish ideal, pp. 7-48.[6]

TEKIN ALP, DEUX SYSTÈMES D'EXPLOITATION

Comment faut-il s'y prendre pour mettre en valeur les richesses naturelles de l'Anatolie qui restent inexploitées des siècles? Comment pourrait-on faire l'éducation économique du peuple turc qui jusqu'ici n'a pu s'occuper que des choses militaires, politiques et administratives? Quels sont les moyens les plus efficaces pour réaliser ses aspirations vers la Renaissance économique?

Nous ne prétendons pas résoudre ici en quelques lignes ces question d'une importance vitale. Cela demande un travail qui doit absorber pendant longtemps les recherches de nos économistes nationaux. Nous ne voulons insister ici que sur un seul point; d'adopter un système unique et inaltérable, grâce auquel les efforts de toute la nation seraient dirigés vers le même but et l'éparpillement des forces pourrait être évité. Les problèmes que nos économistes nationaux devront résoudre sont tellement nombreux et difficiles, que sans un système fixe et immuable, on ne pourra pas s'y retrouver. C'est ainsi que, avant de commencer le travail, nos économistes devront se mettre à la recherche de ce système.

Il faut ajouter que nous ne sommes pas seuls dans cette recherche. Ceux qui par la force des choses seront appelés à collaborer avec nous dans le rélèvement économique de notre pays, s'en occupent aussi sérieusement. Les économistes nationaux de nos alliés s'efforcent eux aussi de trouver le meilleur système pour l'exploitation des ressources économiques de l'Anatolie. A juger d'après les publications multiples qui ont eu lieu en Allemagne ces derniers temps, deux systèmes d'exploitation se dessinent à l'horizon: l'exploitation scientifique et l'exploitation mercantile.

Ceux qui préconisent l'application du système scientifique font complètement abstraction des profits immédiats résultant éventuellement de certaines entreprises isolées. Il sont d'avis qu'avant d'entreprendre quoi que ce soit en Turquie, il est nécessaire d'arrêter un plan d'ensemble pour que toutes les branches de l'activité économique se relèvent au fur et à mesure dans les mêmes proportions, afin que l'équilibre et l'harmonie ne soient pas atteints. Ils sont d'avis aussi que l'exploitation économique de la Turquie ne peut être utile et efficace sans que le peuple turc lui-même soit en mesure de la faire, naturellement avec les concours et la collaboration des européens qui lui apporteront les capitaux, la technique et l'expérience. Il faut exploiter les ressources de la Turquie, disent les partisans de systèmes scientifiques, mais il faut absolument éviter l'exploitation du peuple turc. Avant d'introduire dans l'Anatolie le système d'exploitation européen, il faut que les habitants du pays eux-mêmes soient en mesure d'y contribuer avec leur propre travail et d'en tirer les profits légitimes. Il ne faut pas que l'européen s'enrichit au dépens du peuple turc. Il faut que les intérêts de l'étranger soient en parfaite harmonie avec ceux de l'indigène.

Nous relatons dans la rubrique spéciale, les passages d'un livre très intéressant du Prof. Dr. Philippson, un des représentants les plus autorisés du système scientifique, où ce dernier défend ce point de vue avec la plus grande énergie.

L'orientaliste Reinhardt Junge, dans son dernier ouvrage dont nous relatons également les passages les plus intéressants dans la rubrique spéciale, est plus explicite encore et s'exprime avec plus de précision.

Plusieurs autres économistes allemands sont du même avis et préconisent avant tout l'adoption d'un système scientifique et d'un plan d'ensemble pour réformer d'une façon harmonieuse toutes les branches de l'activité économique et mettre le plus possible en valeur le travail du peuple turc lui-même.

Il y en a pourtant d'autres écrivains qui s'arrêtent au système mercantile, qui ne vise que les profits immédiats de l'entrepreneur, du capitaliste et du négociant sans se soucier des intérêts particuliers du peuple auquel ils ont à faire et sans suivre un plan d'ensemble destiné au relèvement intérieur du pays qu'ils exploitent.

Un écrivain allemand, qui se pique de connaître l'Orient, et qui a publié plusieurs œuvres sur la Turquie, recommande aux capitalistes de poursuivre en Turquie seulement des entreprises industrielles qui ne sont pas de nature à influencer l'exportation allemande.

Dans le même ordre d'idée, ce même auteur recommande aux maisons d'exportation de son pays de se faire représenter en Turquie par des jeunes allemands qui, dit-il, seraient capables de s'adapter facilement aux conditions de notre pays.

Heureusement les représentants du système mercantile sont seulement ceux qui nous connaissent le moins. Il n'y a pas de doute que le système scientifique représenté par les politiciens et les savants les plus autorisés, finira par dominer et ainsi nous pourrons jouir tranquillement de la collaboration et du concours de nos alliés dans nos efforts pour la Renaissance économique.

Mais l'essentiel pour nous n'est pas de connaître le système d'exploitation préconisé ailleurs, mais d'examiner le système et la méthode scientifique qui nous conviendraient le mieux.

Malheureusement notre gouvernement n'a pas pu suivre jusqu'ici une politique économique fixe et uniforme. Des écrivains tels que von Mackay et autres qui ont critiqué avec beaucoup de bienveillance la politique économique que nous avons suivi jusqu'ici, n'ont pas tenu compte des circonstances et nous ont adressé certaines critiques que nous ne méritons pas.

Mais il faut avouer qu'à l'avenir la politique opportuniste ne peut être justifiée. Nous avons besoin d'une politique ferme et définitive, basée sur des systèmes et des méthodes scientifiques.

S.E. Ahmed Nessimi Bey, ministre du Commerce et de l'agriculture, dans les déclarations importantes qu'il a faites dans le premier numéro de notre Revue, nous annonce la formation prochaine d'un conseil supérieur des affaires économiques qui sera chargé de fixer les lignes générales de notre programme économique. Nous sommes les premiers à applaudir cette mesure et reconnaître son importance et son efficacité. Mais nous devons ajouter que ce n'est pas suffisant. C'est à nos économistes nationaux qu'il incombe le devoir de faire des recherches scientifiques à ce sujet, éclairer l'opinion publique et fournir aux dirigeants les bases scientifiques sur lesquelles doit s'appuyer leur politique économique intérieure et extérieure.

İM, I/4 (20 March 1916)

TEKIN ALP, LES CAISSES D'ÉPARGNE

D'après nos informations particulières, le ministère des Postes et Telégraphes ouvrira bientôt des caisses d'épargne dans les bureaux des postes et télégraphes. Désormais ceux qui dans les villes et villages parviennent à réaliser la moindre économie pourront déposer leur argent dans les caisses d'épargne des bureaux de poste. Le projet de loi préparé à cet effet par le ministère en question après de longues recherches et études, a été approuvé par le conseil des ministres et envoyé à l'étude au conseil d'état. En même temps nous constatons avec plaisir, que d'après son nouveau règlement la banque agricole aussi aura le droit d'ouvrir des caisses d'épargne dans ses succursales.

Notre pays fait ainsi un premier pas en avant dans la question de l'épargne nationale.

L'expression de «question de l'épargne nationale» paraît un peu bizarre. Car on ignore généralement l'existence d'une pareille question sur laquelle la presse n'a jamais soufflé mot. Pourtant la question de l'épargne nationale constitue une des plus graves plaies sociales dont souffre notre pays. Et ce qu'il y a de plus regrettable encore c'est qu'on ne paraît pas apprécier l'importance de la chose. On entend souvent des lamentations sur le manque d'instruction, des routes etc., et ces lamentations produisent plus ou moins d'effet. Mais ils sont rares ceux qui remarquent que nous n'avons pas une épargne nationale. Notre opinion publique reste entièrement indifférente à cette question.

Or dans tous les pays du monde, l'épargne nationale constitue un des plus importants facteurs du bien être et de la richesse générale. L'aisance et la richesse d'une nation s'accroît dans la mesure de l'augmentation de ses économies et de l'emploi efficace qu'on en fait.

L'épargne présente deux genres d'avantages, l'un social et l'autre économique, c'est à dire que celui qui économise contribue d'abord à son bien être personnel et en même temps au développement de la force productive et par conséquence de l'économie nationale de son pays. Avec les petites économies de millions de personnes, on constitue de grands capitaux, grâce auxquels on est en mesure d'exploiter des entreprises de grande envergure d'ordre agricole, commercial et industriel. Le capital qui constitue la base de toute vie économique, provient principalement de l'épargne.

On ne peut pas dire cependant que l'épargne n'existe pas dans notre pays, quoique par rapport aux autres pays elle soit presque insignifiante. Une enquête superficielle faite deux années auparavant a établi que notre population possède dans les banques étrangères au moins 12 millions de Ltq. qui ne rapportent aucun intérêt quelquefois 1 ou 2 pourcent seulement. Mais l'argent déposé dans les banques chez nous ne constitue que le 10% à peine de l'épargne totale. Le reste est conservé et caché précieusement dans les bas de laine. La plus grande partie de la monnaie d'or mise en circulation a subi le même sort. Ainsi malheureusement toute cette épargne n'est d'aucun profit pour le pays. Les millions de Livres qui dorment dans les banques étrangères ou dans les bas de laine, n'exercent la moindre influence sur notre force productive.

L'importance des caisses d'épargne fut appréciée dans la plus part des pays civilisés depuis deux siècles. La première caisse d'épargne fut fondée en Allemagne en 1778 sous le nom de «Versorgungs Anstalt». L'utilité de cette institution ayant été vite constatée, l'example fut vite suivi par diverses villes d'Allemagne où les caisses d'épargne ne tardèrent pas à devenir le plus important facteur de la force productive et contribuèrent puissamment au développement de la vie économique de ce pays.

En Angleterre aussi les premières caisses d'épargne furent fondées en 1781. Quelques années plus tard le gouvernement intervint et promulga plusieurs lois et réglements sur ces établissements. Le système des caisses d'épargne commença peu à peu se répandre en France, en Italie et dans tous les pays civilisés. Dans tous ces pays ces caisses d'épargne sont considérées comme des établissements d'utilité publique de la plus haute importance. De temps à autre de nouvelles lois sont promulguées pour les rendre plus utiles et plus efficaces, et partout les conseils municipaux considèrent comme leur plus grand devoir de contrôler et faire progresser les caisses d'épargne par des subsides pécuniaires.

Les caisses d'épargne ne se contentent pas seulement de drainer l'argent du peuple et le faire fructifier, mais constituent aussi un puissant moyen pour répandre dans la population le goût de l'épargne. Il existe partout en Europe des caisses d'épargne où les jeunes écoliers confient les quelques sous qu'ils parviennent à économiser.

Quant à nous nous commençons il est vrai avec un siècle de retard. Mais si nous nous mettons sérieusement à l'oeuvre, il est hors de doute que nous réussirons à rattraper le temps perdu. La banque agricole et le ministère des postes et télégraphes ont assumé à ce point de vue une charge extraordinaire et, nous espérons, qu'ils parviendront à s'en acquitter dignement. Dans un prochain article nous entrerons dans les détails de la question.

İM, I/8 (17 April 1916)

TEKINE ALP, L'IKTISSAD DERNEGHI

Nous constatons avec plaisir que le projet de création d'une association économique dont le besoin se fait tellement sentir en notre pays, est près d'être réalisé. La séance qui eut lieu dimanche dernier au local de la faculté de droit pour jeter les fondements de la nouvelle société, s'est déroulée de façon très satisfaisante, ce qui est de bonne augure pour l'avenir de l'œuvre. Un grand nombre de personnalités des plus compétentes, s'empressèrent de répondre à l'invitation qui leur fut faite, et participèrent aux délibérations de l'assemblée qui furent très intéressantes et animées.

Un des points qui fut le plus discuté pendant la séance de dimanche, concerne le programme d'action de la société. Le projet des statuts présenté à l'approbation de l'assemblée, préconisait de donner à l'activité de la société un caractère purement théorique et scientifique. Par contre un certain nombre des personnalités présentes, montrèrent la nécessité d'un travail plutôt pratique, car disent-ils, si l'on s'en tient seulement à la théorie, on ne pourra pas obtenir des résultats sérieux.

Si l'on suppose que seulement cette société représentera l'activité de la vie économique du pays, les dicussions de la susdite réunion, sont réellement dignes d'être prises en considération. Mais il est certain que le manque d'organisation qui existe actuellement dans notre vie économique, ne pourra pas continuer longtemps encore. Pour peu qu'un pays commence à entrer dans la voie du développement économique, il ne peut pas échapper aux luttes et discussions entre les diverses classes. Naturellement des sociétés diverses se forment, les personnes d'une même classe, d'une même profession, s'unissent pour la protection de leurs intérêts. Ce sont donc ceux-ci qui s'occuperont du travail pratique basé sur l'intérêt. Mais il ne faut pas oublier qu'au dessus des différences sociales, de classes, de carrières et de professions, il y a un Etat et une nation. Les divers membres de la société doivent travailler aussi pour la collectivité.

L'«Iktissad Derneghi» pourra exprimer son opinion sans faire de différences de classes et de profession. S'il y a un champ d'activité où l'on a le plus besoin de l'éclairement de la science pour le progrès et le relèvement, c'est bien la vie économique. Les hommes du gouvernement, les fabricants, les agriculteurs, les négociants, soit individuellement, soit collectivement, ont besoin de l'assistance de la science et de la technique. Les hommes du gouvernement pour pouvoir déterminer leur ligne de conduite dans la politique économique intérieure, aussi bien qu'extérieure, ont besoin de suivre de systèmes et de méthodes scientifiques, faire des recherches, établir des statistiques, etc. Les fabricants, les mineurs et même les spéculateurs, ne peuvent pas également s'écarter des règles posées par les spécialistes dans les sciences économiques.

Si l'«Iktissad Derneghi» parvient à réunir quarante à cinquante personnes des plus éclairées du pays, dans le but de faire des études et recherches, se livrer à des discussions et délibérations purement scientifiques, elle aura rendu autant des services à la cause du développement économique du pays, que les grands établissements industriels travaillant avec de gros capitaux.

Nous félicitons chaleureusement les initiateurs de cette œuvre et leur souhaitons une complète réussite.

İM, I/27 (14 September 1916)

TEKIN ALP, L'ACTIVITÉ ÉCONOMIQUE DU PARTI «UNION & PROGRES»

> «Nous avons pris les mesures nécessaires
> en vue de contribuer au développement de
> l'économie nationale qui assure le solidarité
> et la réunion dans un centre unique des
> économies privée, domestique et urbaine . . . »

Le passage que nous venons de citer du rapport présenté par le siège général du parti «Union et Progrès» au congrès tenu dernièrement, et qui dans son ensemble constitue un véritable chef d'œuvre, résume d'une façon parfaite le programme économique du parti, tout en donnant une définition concise et claire de ce que signifie l'économie nationale.

Jusqu'à présent l'expression économie nationale a donné lieu chez nous à beaucoup de controverses entre les personnes s'occupant plus ou moins de la science économique. Plusieurs d'entre eux trouvent l'expression économie nationale vide de sens. D'après eux, il n'existerait pas une science ou un art portant le nom d'économie nationale, et que l'économie, de même que les autres sciences, possède un caractère d'ordre général. L'honourable Zia Gueuk Alp bey, professeur d'économie à la faculté, a déjà expliqué dans les numéros 1 et 7 de notre revue, la véritable signification de l'économie nationale et donné à ce sujet une réponse convaincante et catégorique aux économistes de la vieille école.

La définition contenue dans le passage ci dessus résout aussi complètement la question. Une science économique ayant un caractère général ne permet pas de réunir autour d'un centre unique les économies privée, domestique et urbaine. Pour y parvenir on a besoin du lien dénommé nation. Si les économies privée, domestique et urbaine, ne se solidarisent pas par le facteur puissant que constitue la nation, on ne pourra jamais créer une importante force économique. Les individus, groupes et communautés, travaillant économiquement, chacun pour son compte, séparément les uns des autres, sont condamnés à végéter dans un état d'impuissance. Tandis que grâce à la solidarité créée par le lien national, on parvient a créer par le travail commun réuni, une force imposante qui permet d'augmenter la production de la richesse et à renforcer le résistance contre l'étranger. Le lien et le facteur national n'est pas partout le même. D'après le caractère national, l'effet qu'il produit est tout à fait différent chez les Français, chez les Allemands, chez les Anglais ou chez les Turcs. Par conséquent l'économie n'est pas partout la même. Chaque nation a une économie nationale appropriée qui est soumise aux influences du sol, du climat, de la population ainsi que d'autres facteurs et éléments particuliers.

Afin d'éviter tout malentendu, nous ajouterons qu'il n'est question ici que de l'art économique, c'est à dire que l'on prend en considération les moyens et les remèdes employés pour l'amélioration de l'économie de la nation. Nous ne voulons pas parler des systèmes et règles qui doivent être appliqués pour les recherches et les investigations à faire sur l'état économique. Dans ce dernier cas il ne s'agit que de la science de l'économie, qui à peu de différence près est la même pour toutes les nations et peuples.

Il est naturel que dans le rapport présenté au congrès de l'Union et Progrès, on n'ait traité que seulement de la partie qui concerne l'art économique. En effet jusqu'à présent chaque fois que l'on traitait d'économie chez nous, c'est l'idée de science qui venait à l'ésprit. On traitait des règles et principes généraux de l'économie comme par exemple de celles sur l'offre et de la demande, du libre échange, du système protectionniste etc., tandis que personne ne s'intéressait aux études et investigations concernant les questions se rapportant directement au pays et à la nation. C'est à dire que l'on ne s'est occupé jusqu'ici chez nous de l'économie que seulement de la partie scientifique ou théorique, tandis que la partie art a été complètement négligée.

Nous avons maintenant enfin le ferme espoir que désormais, nos spécialistes laissant de côté la partie purement théorique de l'économie, c'est à dire le côté général, consacreront leurs efforts à la partie art, concernant l'économie nationale.

Revenant au programme de l'Union et Progrès, nous constatons avec satisfaction que dans le cercle de son activité, le parti ne s'est nullement départi du principe que nous venons d'exposer. D'après ce principe, le but principal de l'économie nationale, est d'assurer la solidarité des économies privée, domestique et urbaine. En effet les faits rapportés dans ce rapport démontrent que pour parvenir, le parti a eu recours aux moyens les plus efficaces et qui consistent dans l'accumulation des grands capitaux qui lui sont indispensable. Le capital est le plus important facteur pour emmener l'union des économies privée, domestique et urbaine. Grâce au capital, les diverses forces de la nation, les divers facteurs économiques, se réunissent dans un même centre, afin de servir ensemble au bien être et au bonheur de la nation. Partant de ce point de vue, nous ne pouvons que féliciter le siège central de l'«Union et Progrès» pour la création de la commission commerciale qui est parvenue à réaliser un capital de 300.000 Livres. Il est hors de doute qu'à l'avenir aussi, l'Union et Progrès considèrera comme une partie importante de sa mission, de continuer à créer des grands capitaux pour le progrès de notre économie nationale.

Le parti a fait preuve d'un grand savoir faire dans le placement des capitaux recueillis jusqu'à présent. On a d'abord créé avec ces capitaux trois grandes sociétés: La société anonyme ottomane des produits nationaux, la société anonyme d'importation d'articles coloniaux et la société des boulangers. Il est vrai que pour la création de ces sociétés le capital disponible dut être employé, mais une fois le succès assuré, ce capital ne sera plus nécessaire, car les actions seront payées par ceux qui les détiennent, et ainsi le capital inutilisé deviendra libre.

Dans la dernière réunion du congrès de l'Union et Progrès, le capital initial a été affecté pour la création d'une banque nationale. Par cette décision, le congrès touche à un des points des plus délicats et des plus importants de notre économie nationale.

Nous exprimerons notre opinion à ce sujet dans un autre article.

İM, I/30 (19 October 1916)

TEKINE ALP, LA GRANDE INDUSTRIE DANS NOTRE PAYS

Les coups de sifflets retentissants du train spécial qui partait vendredi dernier à huit heures du matin, emportant vers l'intérieur de l'Anatolie, S.E. Enver pacha ainsi qu'un grand nombre d'autres haut dignitaires civils et militaires, et le bruissement des machines mises en mouvement trois heures plus tard, de la main propre de S.E. Enver pacha, dans les ateliers de la nouvelle fabrique, invitaient une fois de plus au réveil la population de l'Anatolie et proclamaient partout le commencement d'une nouvelle ère de régénération.

Pour très important que soit l'inauguration d'une fabrique, il est probable que dans d'autres lieux et dans d'autres temps, un pareil événement aurait passé presque inaperçu, et ne donnerait lieu à aucune manifestation publique. Mais la cérémonie d'inauguration qui a eu lieu aux environs d'Ismidt est arrivée dans des moments tout-à-fait extraordinaires. Depuis deux années, la nation, dans la lutte pour la défense de son indépendance et de son existence, verse le sang de ses plus chers enfants et se soumet aux plus durs sacrifices. Les héros de l'Anatolie se dirigent en toute hâte vers les frontières, la plus fidèle incarnation de notre nouvelle vie militaire, S.E. Enver pacha, convaincu que le salut de notre pays ne peut être obtenu que par la victoire de nos armes, tâche de transformer la nation ottomane en une nation armée; en un mot une importante révolution s'accomplit qui va créer une ligne de démarcation entre le passé et l'avenir. En examinant les événements extraordinaires qui se suivent avec une rapidité vertigineuse, tout le monde cherche à comprendre où cela va aboutir et quel sera le résultat de tous les efforts deployés jusqu'ici.

C'est juste en ce moment que S.E. le ministre de la guerre et vice-généralissime, laissant de côté les troubles de la guerre, et accompagné des dirigeants les plus respectés de la nation, ainsi que des membres les plus en vue de la presse, partit pour procéder à l'inauguration d'une fabrique installée dans un coin de l'Anatolie. Par cette façon d'agir, S.E. le ministre de la guerre, a montré à l'évidence quel est pour nous le véritable but de la guerre.

Le vice-généralissime a voulu prouver une fois de plus aux amis comme aux ennemis que le militarisme, la guerre, ne constituent pas des buts directes, et qu'ils ne tendent qu'à assurer le bonheur et le bien être de la nation en rendant possible son relèvement économique.

Dans cet ordre d'idées on peut dire que l'inauguration de vendredi dernier, ne concerne pas telle ou telle fabrique, mais directement la nouvelle ère de réveil économique. Le réveil est marqué par ce fait que cette grande et puissante fabrique a pu être créée comme entreprise privée, en pleine guerre.

Le nouvel établissement créé sous le nom de société anonyme ottomane pour la fabrication d'objets en fer et en bois, possède une grande importance au point de vue historique. En effet cette fabrique qui a été créée comme un établissement purement national, qui travaillera avec un capital purement national, constitue dans le véritable sens du mot le premier modèle de la grande industrie dans notre pays. Auparavant il existait déjà chez nous quelques établissements importants pour la fabrication du ciment, de la bière, des soieries, des briques etc., mais aucun de ces établissements ne pouvait, ni par ses fondateurs, ni par ses capitaux, ni par sa grandeur et importance servir à se faire une idée des propriétés et des capacités d'expansion économique de notre nation et de notre pays. Tandis que la nouvelle fabrique, soit par son système, et par son organisation, soit aussi par la qualité de ses fondateurs, constitue le premier produit des forces économiques de la nation, dans le terrain de la grande industrie.

Ce n'est pas nous qui nierons que notre pays est avant tout un pays agricole et que par conséquent, ce dont il a le plus besoin, c'est de travailler à la réforme et au progrès de l'agriculture. Mais nous croyons que ce n'est pas là une raison pour se résigner à la dure nécessité de faire venir d'Europe les produits industriels les plus élémentaires. Si nous continuons à nous fournir à l'étranger des articles industriels et dont nous possédons amplement les matières les plus indispensables, nous ne pourrons jamais profiter de la richesse et de la fertilité de nos terres. Comment pourrons nous nous émanciper de l'esclavage économique, lorsque nous continuons à brûler le bois de nos forêts, tandis que l'Europe en fabrique des objets précieux de premier ordre. Tandis qu'en Europe le travail des centaines des milliers et même de millions d'hommes, est fait par ces morceaux de métal qu'on appelle machines, chez nous tout se fait encore par les bras humains, par l'effort personnel de nos ouvriers. Si nous continuons dans ce sytème, nous ne pourrons jamais nous élever au même niveau que les nations européennes au milieu desquelles nous vivons.

C'est pourquoi nous sommes- d'avis que l'on ne peut obtenir que par les progrès de l'industrie, le salut et le relèvement de notre économie nationale. Par une seule machine on peut obtenir le même travail que celui fourni par des milliers des personnes. Par exemple une machine mûe par un moteur de 400 chevaux peut faire le même travail que 8.000 personnes et contribuer dans une égale proportion à l'augmentation de la richesse nationale.

La cérémonie de vendredi dernier constitue à un autre point de vue aussi, un indice favorable pour le futur développement de notre économie nationale: c'est le fait que le ministère de la guerre se trouve à la tête de cette œuvre. Nous sommes de cet avis que le premier facteur qui peut aider au développement et au progrès de la grande industrie dans notre pays, n'est autre que le ministère de la guerre. Déjà avant la guerre, lorsque notre force militaire n'avait pas encore atteint le degré de perfection voulu, le ministère de la guerre faisait importer annuellement pour environ six millions de livres d'objets manufacturés. Maintenant enfin le ministère de la guerre s'est convaincu d'une façon catégorique que continuer à s'adresser à l'étranger pour se procurer les articles nécessaires à l'armée, cause des préjudices à notre économie nationale.

C'est justement à ce point de vue, que la cérémonie de vendredi dernier constitue un indice favorable pour la politique qui sera suivie à l'avenir par les autorités militaires, dans le but de contribuer au relèvement de l'économie nationale; l'appui qu'elle accorde aujourd'hui à cette initiative privée pour la fabrication d'objets en bois, elle l'accordera demain aux fabriques qui seront établies pour produire des articles en fer et en cuir, des conserves, de comestibles, et toute sorte d'équipements militaires, et ainsi en peu de temps une grande industrie nationale pourra être créée chez nous grâce à la protection des autorités militaires.

Nous croyons inutile de nous étendre davantage sur ce point. S'il y a quelque chose à ajouter, ce sont les paroles prononcées par S.E. Enver pacha devant la mission qui participa à la cérémonie d'inauguration.

«A l'avenir pour notre relèvement économique, nous serons forcés de déployer dans une seule année, les même efforts que l'Europe a déployé en vingt années.»

Ces paroles sont très edifiantes sur les fermes intentions de nos dirigeants et constituent un puissant stimulant pour tous les membres de la nation dans l'accomplissement de leur tâche.

İM, I/33 (16 November 1916)

TEKINE ALP, LE CONSEIL DES AFFAIRES ÉCONOMIQUES

Comme on le verra dans la rubrique des nouvelles de notre revue, le ministère du commerce et de l'agriculture vient d'organiser un conseil économique qui a tenu déjà sa première réunion.

C'est là certainement une institution des plus utiles. Mais nous tenons à faire relever ceci que ce qui nous cause le plus de satisfaction dans cette affaire, est moins le fait en lui même, que l'esprit qui a poussé à la création d'une pareille institution, ainsi que l'espoir de son développement dans l'avenir.

Ce serait nous illusioner que de fonder des espoirs exagérés sur les résultats qui seront donnés par l'activité du conseil économique. Il a plutôt le caractère d'une assemblée consultative, dépourvu de toute influence sur la ligne de conduite générale de notre politique économique. Mais l'esprit qui a présidé à la fondation de cette institution, est des plus encourageants. En effet nous constatons avec plaisir que depuis un certain temps, un désir irrésistible de progrès, domine dans notre vie économique, qui fait acheminer vers un même but toutes les actions officielles aussi bien que privées. C'est sous l'influence de cet état d'esprit que l'on est parvenu à la création d'une pareille assemblée consultative, dont on ne rencontre d'exemple dans aucun autre département de l'état, et qui au point de vue du résultat, ne répond pas à aucun besoin absolu. C'est à ce point de vue que nous trouvons inutile d'examiner les critiques formulées par certains juristes et économistes qui prétendent que cette institution est privée de compétence et de fonction et mettent en doute les résultats pratiques qu'elle pourra donner. A notre point de vue, toute organisation propre à augmenter l'intérêt général pour les affaires économiques et permettant surtout un échange de vue entre les personnes intéressées, est digne d'intérêt et doit être encouragée.

Nous avons déjà exprimé dernièrement dans notre revue, lorsque la création de cette institution n'était encore qu'un simple projet, notre opinion sur ce qu'elle devait être et sur le caractère qu'elle devait avoir. Nous avions émis alors l'avis de voir ce conseil rester sous forme de commission. L'organisation actuelle quoique n'ayant pas tout à fait le caractère d'une commission n'en est pourtant moins éloignée de ce que nous nous imaginons. Elle n'a aucune personnalité propre. Elle aura simplement à émettre ses opinions sur les questions qui lui seront soumises par le ministre. Mais nous aimons à espérer qu'elle ne restera pas dans cet état et qu'elle prendra un grand développement qui donnera plus d'importance et de poids à son action. Le développement de notre vie économique, ne peut pas être obtenu par de consultations, mais plutôt par l'étude approfondie et par les recherches minutieuses. Les questions économiques ne ressemblent nullement aux autres questions administratives.

Ces questions ne peuvent pas être réglées seulement par l'intelligence et la pratique, ou le savoir faire. Leur solution nécessite plutôt des faits, des chiffres, et l'étude de ces faits et chiffres ne peut se faire qu'avec méthode et système. Naturellement un conseil composé de 24 personnes, ne peut s'occuper des études et des recherches; tout au plus, par l'échange d'idées, peut il aider à l'éclaircissement de certaines questions. Mais si l'on veut que ce conseil rende au pays un service dont il a réellement besoin, il doit adopter une ligne d'activité autre que celle indiquée dans le réglement.

Nous ne demandons pas que le conseil aie un caractère tout à fait indépendant et que les résultats de ces délibérations soient exécutoires. Car la Constitution ne reconnaît comme responsable dans les affaires exécutives, que seulement le ministre, et en dehors de lui ne reconnaît pas d'autre force exécutive. Mais comme nous l'avons expliqué plus haut, si au lieu de se consacrer aux discussions et consultations, il s'adonne aux études et recherches pratiques, son activité sera plus féconde pour le pays, et en même temps il pourra avoir un caractère plus indépendant. Le conseil, tout en s'occupant de la discussion des questions qui lui seront soumises par le ministre, peut s'occuper également des recherches et de l'étude des questions qui lui paraissent avoir le plus d'intérêt pour le pays et exprimer là-dessus son opinion sur les moyens à employer pour leur application. Le ministère du commerce et de l'agriculture se trouve aujourd'hui en présence de plusieurs problèmes importants, qui ne peuvent être jamais résolus sans de recherches techniques approfondies, des statistiques comparatives, etc. Ainsi il y a chez nous par exemple une question d'émigration pour laquelle on dépense chaque annéee des centaines de milliers de Livres. Or, est ce que le pays en tire le maximum de profits possibles, si non quelles en sont les causes? Pour pouvoir régler une pareille question, il y a lieu de prendre en considération une série des détails sur les terres, les conditions climatériques, les caractères et les capacités des immigrants etc. C'est là une question qui quoique touchant de très prés à l'économie, est en dehors de la compétence du ministère du commerce et de l'agriculture. Il y a de nombreuses autres questions sur les chemins de fer, les douanes qui sont exclues de la sphère d'action du susdit département.

Dans la branche de recherches, il est bon de laisser au conseil toute liberté d'action en lui donnant la faculté de fixer lui même son ordre du jour. Dans ce cas le conseil fixe les lignes générales de son rayon d'action et fixe une récompense de quelques centaines de Livres à celui qui lui présente le meilleur ouvrage sur les questions qui doivent être examinées.

Dans tous les cas nous sommes d'avis que la création de ce conseil constitue un pas en avant dans la voie du progrès. Cette institution se développera de plus en plus et pourra devenir un des plus importants facteurs de notre relèvement économique.

İM, I/38 (14 January 1917)

TEKINE ALP, NOTRE AVENIR ÉCONOMIQUE

Nous ne croyons pas exagérer en disant que cette question est celle qui occupe le plus actuellement non seulement toute la classe intellectuelle, mais même toute l'opinion publique de notre pays. Car on s'est généralement convaincu que l'existence et le développement de l'état et de la nation, sont intimement attachés à l'avenir économique.

Nous devons avouer que tout le monde n'est pas optimiste à ce sujet. Il y en a qui craignent que notre émancipation financière et économique ne soit pas arrivée trop tard, et qui ne sont pas sûrs si nous arriverons à temps à nous élever au niveau économique désiré. Un des économistes allemands très au courant de la situation économique de notre pays, dit dans un ouvrage qu'il vient de publier que pour que la Turquie puisse occuper une place convenable dans le concert des nations, elle doit s'élever économiquement avec une rapidité extraordinaire, et qu'autrement elle serait exposée à des graves dangers. Allant plus loin encore le susdit économiste dit que la Turquie est obligée d'attendre en peu d'années le succès économique que les autres nations ont obtenu pendant des dizaines d'années, et ajoute qu'il ne voit aucun motif spécial qui l'autorise à croire que la Turquie pourra facilement accomplir cette besogne.

Ce pessimisme qui règne également dans certains classes de notre pays, ne manque pas d'exercer son effet sur notre vie économique. La baisse de nos papiers monnaies est une des conséquences naturelles de ce pessimisme. Car les économistes les plus autorisés sont d'accord pour affirmer que la confiance est le facteur le plus efficace dans la valeur des papiers monnaies dans tout le pays. Plus la confiance dans la force financière et économique du pays est grande, plus le crédit des papiers monnaies augmente. Il est incontestable que si chez nous aussi les porteurs des papiers monnaies acquèrent la conviction de la fermeté de notre force financière et de l'avenir économique du pays, ils ne s'en presseront pas à changer leur papier monnaie contre de la monnaie en or ou contre toutes sortes d'objets nécessaires ou inutiles, en consentant de sacrifices énormes.

C'est justement à ce point de vue que S.E. Djavid bey, ministre des finances, dans les déclarations qu'il fit dernièrement à la chambre, ne s'est pas contenté de parler seulement de la valeur que le papier monnaie possède déjà par lui même, mais a trouvé nécessaire de parler aussi de l'avenir économique du pays. Car la conviction de la solidité de notre avenir économique peut faire augmenter la confiance, et partant la valeur des papiers monnaies.

S.E. Djavid bey a fait en effet à cet égard des déclarations très catégoriques et dignes d'attirer toute notre attention. D'ailleurs depuis la proclamation de la constitution, le nouveau ministre des finances n'a jamais cessé de nourrir une confiance inébranlable dans l'avenir économique du pays et toutes les fois que l'occasion se présente il ne manque pas d'exprimer publiquement cette confiance et communiquer sa foi aux membres de la nation. Toutes les crises qui se sont produites depuis la constitution n'ont porté et ne pouvaient porter la moindre atteinte à cette confiance, car elle est le résultat non pas des sentiments, mais des faits, des réalités et de l'étude calme et réfléchie des événements. Et maintenant avec sa vaste compétence dans la science économique en général et surtout dans les affaires économiques et financières du pays, il fait les intéressantes déclarations suivantes:

«La Turquie se trouvera dans une situation financière telle qu'elle lui permettra de payer dans dix années, non seulement les intérêts, mais encore le capital de ses dépenses ordinaires ainsi que des dettes contractées pendant la guerre et celles existant d'avant la guerre.»

Plus loin dans son discours, il se montre plus catégorique encore. «Dans cinq ou dix années, dit-il, il sera possible de délivrer le pays des malheurs et des ennuis auxquels il s'est trouvé en butte.»

Il est vrai que ce n'est pas sans condition que Djavid bey formule cette convinction. Mais les conditions qu'il pose, loin d'affaiblir cette conviction, ne font que la renforcer et la confirmer. Ainsi dans ces déclarations il nous dit à ce sujet: Notre alliance conclue avec l'Allemagne pendant la guerre, devra continuer après la guerre. Cet accord ne peut nullement être comparé à l'accord offensif des puissances de l'Entente, qui poursuit le but de détruire économiquement les Puissances Centrales. Le nôtre n'est qu'un accord fait dans le but de protéger nos intérêts réciproques, c'est pour ainsi dire, une sorte d'association d'intérêts. Notre apport constituera dans nos richesses naturelles, et l'apport de l'Allemagne dans ses capitaux et sa technique, et avec ces moyens nous tâcherons de développer nos richesses nationales. L'Allemagne a besoin de nos trésors naturels, car elle ne peut pas se les procurer ailleurs sans difficultés et sans obstacles. De notre côté nous avons besoin des capitaux et de la technique de l'Allemagne, car c'est à peine maintenant que nous venons nous débarasser d'un esclavage économique et financier datant depuis des siècles.

Nous ne voyons pas la nécessité d'expliquer le sérieux, la fermeté et la sincérité d'un pareil accord conclu sur la base des intérêts réciproques. Se basant sur cette vérité, Djavid bey assure que les hommes d'état allemands sont décidés à fournir, avec un système et un programme bien établi, les capitaux nécessaires à la régénération et le développement de la Turquie.

Le succès de cette association des intérêts réciproques est soumis à une autre condition, qui plus que la première, est digne d'attirer notre attention.

«Pour suivre une politique économique et financière, droite, solide et libre, il est nécessaire d'agir d'une façon ferme et catégorique et non pas en marchant d'une façon hésitante, tantôt à droite tantôt à gauche.»

Eh bien, c'est là le problème: Est ce que nous parviendrons facilement à acquérir cette marche ferme et décidée, est ce que les restes d'un passé funeste n'entraveront pas notre marche en avant?

Ils nous faudra accomplir toute une révolution dans notre système économique et financier pour y parvenir. Tant que notre population rurale est chargée du 80 au 90% des impôts, tant que ces impôts sont de nature non pas à augmenter notre protection, mais à la faire diminuer, tant que nous suivrons envers les hommes d'initiative et les capitalistes, une politique de méfiance nous ne pourrons jamais établir une politique droite et ferme. Heureusement le gouvernement actuel est fermement décidé sur ce point à reformer de fond en comble notre système politique et financier.

Dans le programme du cabinet lu à la chambre des députés, par S.A. le Grand Vizir Talaat pacha, il est dit qu'une politique à larges vues sera suivie dans les questions économiques. Quel est le but de cette politique à larges vues? Le programme du cabinet nous fournit aussi une explication là-dessus: Les importantes entreprises industrielles et des travaux publics qui seront projetés par les capitalistes et les industriels rencontreront de notre part de l'encouragement et le gouvernement accordera toutes les facilités et l'assistance nécessaires pour faire aboutir rapidement ces entreprises.

Malheureusement dans le passé, nous n'avons pas suivi toujours une pareille politique et c'est justement ce qui a empêché notre rapide extension économique. Il est hors de doute que la politique économique à large vue qui sera suivie par le cabinet Talaat pacha obtiendra un complet succès.

Djavid Bey parla dans son discours d'une politique économique libre.

On ne comprend pas bien en quoi consiste cette politique libre. Nous ne croyons pas que la politique libre consiste dans le principe de la non intervention préconisée par Adam Smith et ses partisans. L'économie nationale ne s'accorde nullement avec l'économie politique libre, surtout lorsqu'il s'agit d'une nation qui est obligée maintenant de vivre parmi des peuples et des nations infiniment plus avancés qu'elle dans le domaine économique. Appliquer le principe de la liberté économique parmi une pareille nation, c'est la condamner à vivre éternellement dans l'esclavage. Comme nous l'avons déjà dit à maintes reprises, pour que notre nation puisse progresser dans le domaine économique, elle a besoin d'une protection matérielle et morale. Et cette tâche ne peut être remplie que seulement par le gouvernement.

Seulement, en adoptant le principe protectionniste nous devons bien nous garder d'aller trop loin, de ne pas empêcher le libre jeu de l'initiative privée sans laquelle il n'y a point de progrès possible. La mission du gouvernement à cet égard doit consister à contribuer à la juste répartition de la richesse par son système financier et faire tout son possible pour le relèvement de certaines classes de la population qui sont privées de la force du capital.

S.E. Djavid bey, nous montre aussi les chemins qu'il y a lieu de suivre pour assurer notre avenir économique et même donne à ce sujet quelques chiffres édifiants.

«Il nous faudra importer dans le pays cent à cent cinquante millions de livres pour notre agriculture, nos travaux publics, nos chemins de fer et autres travaux d'utilité publique.»

Ces paroles constituent un brillant démenti aux auteurs étrangers qui nous accusent de «nativisme.» Ainsi donc le plus important de nos économistes et celui qui est appelé à jouer un rôle des plus importants dans notre avenir économique, proclame du haut de la tribune de l'assemblée nationale, qu'il nous faudra importer cent cinquante millions de Livres pour la réforme de notre agriculture, de notre industrie et de nos voies de communication. De la sorte S.E. Djavid bey tout en nous donnant des assurances sur notre avenir économique, encourage les capitalistes étrangers à venir dans notre pays.

Comme on le voit, les déclarations de S.E. Djavid Bey poursuivent deux buts différents: Raffermir à l'intérieur notre confiance dans l'avenir économique et encourager les capitalistes étrangers à venir collaborer avec nous.

S'il est vrai que les capitaux étrangers rendront des services inappréciables à notre vie économique, il n'est pas moins vrai que nous nous rapprocherons plus de notre but par la confiance et l'optimisme bien réfléchi en ce qui concerne notre avenir économique.

İM, I/42 (22 February 1917)

À NOS LECTEURS

Notre revue entre dans la seconde année de son existence. Nous trouvons inutile d'expliquer les grandes difficultés que nous avons eu à surmonter pour pouvoir faire vivre notre publication, venue au monde au milieu de la crise universelle que nous traversons et qui est sans exemple dans l'histoire. Malgré toutes ces difficultés, notre revue n'a pas manqué un seul instant de persévérer dans la voie qu'elle s'est tracée dans le domaine de l'économie nationale. Au moment où l'expression d'économie nationale sonnait comme quelque chose d'étrange parmi nous, notre revue s'est efforcée de propager les principes de l'économie nationale et à continuer avec persévérance et fermeté dans la tâche qu'elle s'est imposée d'éclairer l'opinion publique sur la matière.

Pendant la première année de la vie de notre publication, une profonde et heureuse révolution s'est accomplie dans la vie économique de notre pays. Le réveil économique qui dès le début a constitué le but de notre programme, est devenu finalement un fait accompli. Les manifestations de ce réveil apparaissent de jour en jour avec plus d'évidence et l'idée du progrès et du développement de notre économie nationale, domine maintenant tous nos autres désirs et idéaux.

Comme on l'a constaté à la lecture des importants articles publiés dans notre dernier numéro, notre revue a mis toujours sur le tapis de la discussion, par les plumes les plus autorisées, un grand nombre des questions ayant rapport avec notre réveil économique, et a cherché à attirer sur la matière l'attention des intéressés, des hommes dirigeants et de l'opinion publique, et ainsi notre revue est devenue le miroir des idées et opinions de nos intellectuels et des économistes les plus compétents et les plus capables.

Nous basant sur l'expérience d'une année, nous comptons introduire quelques améliorations dans les publications de notre revue:

1. Nous nous efforcerons d'être autant que possible l'interprète des opinions, des désirs et des plaintes des intéressés dans le domaine de l'agriculture, du commerce et de l'industrie. Mais notre réussite dans cette tâche dépend de la collaboration et de l'assistance des cercles directement intéressés.

2. Nous suivrons avec grand soin la situation et les événements économiques des provinces. A cet effet des mesures ont été prises pour nous procurer des correspondants particuliers dans les centres des vilayets les plus importants.

3. Nous nous efforcerons d'être les interprètes non seulement d'une seule classe détermineée d'intellectuels, mais de mettre en lumière les idées et les opinions de tous les cercles, de toutes les classes, de tous les partis intellectuels. A cet effet de nouveaux noms seront joints à la liste de nos collaborateurs.

4. Tout en continuant à éclairer l'opinion publique sur la politique économique du gouvernement et sur ses efforts régénérateurs, nous ne manquerons pas, toutes les fois que l'occasion se présente, d'exprimer librement notre opinion et nos convictions au point de vue de la critique. Nos colonnes seront largement ouvertes aux observations justes et raisonnées tendant à attirer l'attention des départements officiels sur toutes sortes des questions.

En un mot, nous ferons tout notre possible pour accomplir convenablement la tâche qui nous incombe dans cette période historique de réveil économique. Le succès dépend seulement du concours et de l'assistance des lecteurs et des intéressés.

LA RÉDACTION

İM, II/49 (15 March 1917)

TEKINE ALP, LA RÉVOLUTION ÉCONOMIQUE

Plusieurs indices démontrent qu'une révolution économique s'est produite ces derniers temps dans notre pays. L'initiative individuelle s'est réveillée dans toutes les parties du pays et parmi toutes les classes de la population, ce qui fait que nous voyons chaque jour se former de nouvelles sociétés, de nouvelles institutions. Notre jeunesse qui courait jusqu'à présent derrière des postes calmes et tranquilles dans les bureaux du gouvernement, préfère maintenant chercher son avenir dans le commerce et dans les entreprises personnelles. De nombreuses entreprises de nature à contribuer au relèvement économique du pays sont créées, soit par le gouvernement, soit par la nation. On remarque partout dans l'opinion publique un réveil incontestable. Mais toutes ces manifestations pour trop satisfaisantes qu'elles soient, sont encore loin de former une véritable révolution dans notre vie économique. Car leur effet se fait sentir non pas directement sur le système de la vie économique, mais sur les individus seulement. On travaille toujours avec les mêmes moyens dans le monde commercial, et sauf quelques modifications, l'agriculture et l'industrie se trouvent toujours dans le même état. L'introduction des nouveaux éléments de travail dans le domaine commercial, constitue pour sûr un important signe de progrès, mais ceci est loin d'avoir le caractère d'une révolution. On peut croire à la révolution économique lorsqu'un pays, de riche devient pauvre, d'agricole devient industriel, ou se trouvant sous le régime de petits capitaux, passe à celui du capitalisme moderne. Aucune de ces situations ne s'est produite encore chez nous. Cependant nous n'exagérons nullement en disant que durant ces trois dernières années, une ère d'heureuse révolution économique, dans la véritable acception du mot, a commencé pour notre pays. Les héros de cette révolution ne sont pas les nouveaux riches connus sous le nom de commerçants de 1332. Peut être ceux-ci, en administrant convenablement leur fortune, pourront à l'avenir contribuer au développement de cette révolution. Les véritables héros de la révolution économique sont les agriculteurs, ces humbles travailleurs de la terre que nous considérons avec indifférence, qui se tiennent loin des centres d'activité et qui nous nourrissent par leurs récoltes et par leurs impôts.

Il est inutile d'expliquer dans quel état se trouvaient jusqu'à présent chez nous les cultivateurs. Le commerçant, le professionnel ou plutôt le citadin, travaillant dans les conditions les plus calmes et les plus reposées, gagne aisément des centaines et des milliers de Livres, et par contre, il ne paye comme impôt que quelques dizaines de livres qui, au maximum n'atteignent même pas le 2% de ses revenus. Quant à l'agriculteur il travaille toute l'année durant aux durs travaux de champs, et de la récolte qu'il obtient de la terre à la sueur de son front, il donne le 12,50 pour 100, de sorte, que seulement avec la dîme, le pauvre agriculteur paye cinque à dix fois plus d'impôts que le citadin.

Par suite du système de perception de la dîme qui était employé jusqu'à présent, la situation de l'agriculteur était encore plus digne de pitié. Les fermiers de la dîme se servant de toutes sortes de ruse, parvenaient à lui arracher la 30 à 40 pour 100 de récolte à la place de 12,50 pour 100; de sorte que l'agriculteur ne voyait aucun profit du reste de sa récolte. Il s'en débarrassait en la cédant aux usuriers à un prix de 30 à 40 pour 100 au moins inférieur à celui du prix réel. De sorte que les quelques piastres qui lui tombaient ainsi sous la main, lui permettaient à peine de manger un pain sec. Pour satisfaire ses besoins les plus urgents, il était obligé de s'adresser à droite et à gauche pour se procurer un peu d'argent et tombait ainsi de plus en plus sous les griffes des usuriers, d'où il lui était difficile de se sauver ensuite. Il était impossible au cultivateur vivant dans ces conditions d'améliorer son système agricole qui était encore des plus primitifs. Le nouveau système de travailler la terre, ne peut se faire qu'avec des capitaux plus ou moins abondants. C'est seulement avec de l'argent qu'on peut se procurer les instruments aratoires perfectionnés, les engrais chimiques, les semences de bonne qualité, etc. C'est pourquoi le malheureux cultivateur manquant de tout capital, ne pouvait lever la tête et était condamné à vivre misérablement au jour le jour.

Ce n'était pas seulement de misère qu'avait à souffrir le cultivateur; il était assailli encore par beaucoup d'autres calamités. L'ignorance empoisonne sa vie et le manque d'école dans le village l'empêche d'améliorer un peu sa situation à ce point de vue. Il n'y a pas de routes régulières rattachant son village au reste de la patrie, ce qui l'empêche de profiter des acquisitions de la civilisation. Parfois par suite de ce manque de communications, il ne peut pas même faire écouler ses marchandises au marché, ce qui fait que les récoltes pourrissent sur place. Les marais qui entourent le village détruisent sa santé, le font tomber victime des impitoyables fièvres paludéennes et ses enfants viennent au monde dans un état de débilité lamentable.

En un mot le cultivateur donnait son travail, sa vie, ses biens à la nation, ne recevant en échange que peu d'avantages de la part de cette dernière.

Le cultivateur se trouvant dans un pareil état de misère, c'était oiseux de nous attendre au relèvement de l'économie nationale. Lorsque le fermier ne produit pas en quantité suffisante la récolte et les matières premières, l'industriel ne peut pas créer ses produits, ni le commerçant gagner de l'argent par son commerce. Le gouvernement a pris jusqu'à présent beaucoup de mesures sérieuses dans le but de relever l'économie nationale, d'améliorer notre situation financière. Mais il est naturel que sans que l'un eut porté remède à la situation déplorable des cultivateurs, ces mesures ne pouvaient pas donner le résultat désiré.

Nous constatons avec plaisir qu'à la suite du nouvel état des choses résultant de la guerre, la situation des agriculteurs est entrée franchement dans la voie du progrès et de l'amélioration. La nation étant tombée sous l'obligation de se procurer à l'intérieur tous les articles de nutrition, et même une partie des articles d'habillement, le cultivateur se mit à l'œuvre pour faire face à la nouvelle situation. En même temps le gouvernement s'occupait sérieusement de lui, en lui fournissant une quantité suffisante des semences, des instruments aratoires perfectionnés, en dépensant des centaines des milliers des Livres

Turques pour le sauver des ravages des sauterelles, en faisant travailler dans les champs les femmes et les enfants, en promulguant des lois et réglements en faveur de l'agriculture, en faisant donner une plus grande impulsion à l'activité de la Banque Agricole, en un mot en faisant tout ce qui était possible dans le but d'améliorer sa situation si précaire auparavant. Par suite des circonstances actuelles, le cultivateur parvint à vendre sa récolte à des prix des plus convenables et à acquérir aussi plus ou moins de capital.

Il y a certaines organes de province qui prétendent que le cultivateur qui ne possédait pas auparavant une seule Livre dans sa poche, est aujourd'hui propriétaire de milliers des Livres. Un de nos confrères, entrant dans les plus amples détails, dit:

«Avant la guerre, le cultivateur était criblé de dettes qu'il renouvelait chaque année. Or, maintenant il n'a plus aucune dette. Et non seulement il a acquitté toutes ses dettes, mais encore il est devenu propriétaire de grands capitaux. N'importe quel villageois que nous rencontrons aujourd'hui, est possesseur de quelques milliers de Livres. La meilleure preuve de cet enrichissement du cultivateur, est qu'un terrain qui valait auparavant cent Livres, se vend aujourd'hui mille Livres. Les registres du cadastre sont pleins d'achats et ventes de cette nature.»

Cette assurance de notre confrère ne s'applique évidemment qu'à quelques parties seulement du villayet d'Aïdine. En tous cas il ne faut pas perdre non plus de vue que la valeur de l'argent est aujourd'hui moindre, surtout aux yeux des cultivateurs. Les prix des bœufs, chevaux et autres moyens de production est monté de cinq à dix fois; par conséquent, les milliers des Livres se trouvant entre les mains des cultivateurs, doivent être considérées comme des centaines des Livres seulement.

Quoi que ce soit, il est incontestable qu'une ère d'évolution vient de commencer pour l'agriculteur. Ce dernier, tout en devenant propriétaire de capitaux plus ou moins importants, a commencé aussi à appliquer dans ses champs un système de culture relativement plus perfectionné. Dans les lieux où les circonstances leur sont favorables, les cultivateurs se sont réunis entre eux, formant des coopératives. Ils créent ainsi peu à peu des organisations de nature à protéger leurs intérêts communs.

Le cultivateur tout en s'éveillant lui même, est parvenu à attirer sur lui l'attention du gouvernement. Il est incontestable que le gouvernement s'occupe aujourd'hui sérieusement de la situation de l'agriculteur. Quoiqu'il n'ait pas trouvé moyen encore de supprimer la dîme, il cherche au moins à en améliorer le système.

Ainsi donc nous pouvons soutenir sans hésitation, qu'une révolution a commencé chez les agriculteurs, d'où elle ne manquera pas de s'étendre à toute notre vie économique. C'est à nous d'être vigilants pour faire marcher cette révolution dans la voie du développement voulue.

İM, II/66 (11 October 1917)

TEKINE ALP, LE COMMENCEMENT DU RÉGIME CAPITALISTE

Avant la guerre la question qui préoccupait le plus le monde civilisé était celle concernant la lutte entre le capital et le travail. Les courants sociaux se produisant dans la politique intérieure de chaque pays, avaient directement ou indirectement, trait à cette question d'importance vitale. Et même la politique extérieure de chaque Etat se trouvait sous l'influence de cette lutte. Dans les pays belligérants, les socialistes attribuent à la classe capitaliste la responsabilité de la guerre. On peut dire aussi que les courants qui se produisent actuellement dans ces pays, soit pour la continuation de la guerre, soit en faveur de la paix, ne sont autre chose que la manifestation de la lutte latente entre ces deux classes.

Quoique le progrès social de la classe ouvrière augmente et se développe de jour en jour, le pouvoir se trouve toujours entre les mains de la classe capitaliste. Dans tous les pays, à mesure que la grande industrie se développe, le capital se condense entre quelques mains, des centaines des milliers et même des millions d'ouvriers entrent sous la domination de quelques capitalistes. D'un côté l'influence et là prépondérance de la classe ouvrière dans la vie générale et politique augmente de jour en jour, et de l'autre les suppôts de la classe capitaliste ne cessent de renforcer les organisations pouvant contribuer à l'augmentation de leurs richesses.

S'il y a un pays qui est resté jusqu'à présent à un certain point à l'écart de ces luttes des classes, c'est bien le nôtre. Et cela parce que le régime capitaliste n'a pas encore commencé chez nous et que l'industrie n'est pas encore assez développée ici pour prendre sous son joug toute la classe ouvrière. Mais la guerre générale qui a provoqué une révolution tellement profonde dans notre pays, a contribué également à faire commencer chez nous le régime capitaliste. En effet, il n'y a pas de doute que le régime capitaliste vient de commencer chez nous et qu'il ira en se développant toujours. Les petits capitaux qui se trouvaient jusqu'à présent entre les mains des classes moyennes sont en train de passer entre les mains des nouveaux riches, de ceux que l'opinion publique qualifie des commerçants de la guerre, accapareurs, spéculateurs. Le capital ainsi réuni entre quelques mains ira toujours en se développant, et permettra à leurs propriétaires de se livrer à la grande industrie, de fonder d'importantes entreprises commerciales. Les petits capitaux iront en disparaissant et c'est le capitalisme qui restera maître absolu dans le monde économique. Cet état de choses ne manquera pas de provoquer chez nous également la lutte entre le capitalisme et la classe ouvrière.

S'il y a besoin de preuves pour démontrer le commencement du régime capitaliste chez nous, il nous suffit de jeter un coup d'oeil à la formation des sociétés anonymes dans notre pays. Il résulte des statistiques élaborées par le département compétent, que pendant l'année 1332 il a été fondé dans notre pays une banque de crédit national au capital de quatre millions de Livres et plus de 45 sociétés anonymes avec un capital total de sept à huit millions de Livres. Quoique nous ne possédons pas des statistiques sur le nombre des sociétés annonymes fondées en temps de paix, il est certain qu'alors les entreprises créées par des capitaux indigènes, non pas pendant une année, mais même pendant cinquante années, ne disposaient pas du dixième de cette somme. Pour la plus petite entreprise, nous étions obligés d'avoir recours au capital étranger. Tandis qu'aujourd'hui, c'est le capital indigène qui domine dans notre vie économique. Les phénomènes qui se sont produits ces derniers temps à la bourse des fonds servent aussi à démontrer le commencement du régime capitaliste dans notre pays. Notre public qui était habitué jusqu'à présent à ne montrer que la méfiance à l'égard des actions et obligations des sociétés anonymes, montre une grande inclination maintenant pour des pareilles valeurs et les cours quotidiens de la bourse montrent que les prix des actions vont en augmentant considérablement.

Tous ces indices et plusieurs autres encore démontrent que le régime capitaliste vient de commencer chez nous et que peu à peu il atteindra le même degré de développement auquel il est parvenu dans les autres pays.

Au point de vue économique nous saluons avec satisfaction cet événement, car plus le capitalisme se développe, plus la force productive du capital va en augmentant. D'un autre côté il y a lieu d'appréhender les conséquences d'un pareil état de choses au point de vue social. Dans les pays occidentaux et particulièrement en Allemagne, à la suite des luttes continuelles entre le capital et le travail, le gouvernement s'est vu obligé d'adopter une série de lois et de créer de nombreuses organisations dans le but d'assurer le bien être de la classe ouvrière et de la protéger des manœuvres du capitalisme. Chez nous aussi on pourra prendre exemple sur ce qui se passe dans les autres pays pour adopter à temps les mesures propres à empêcher la classe ouvrière d'être lésée par le capitalisme débutant.

İM, II/67 (26 October 1917)

TEKİN ALP, TÜRKLEŞTİRME

Millileştirme Usulü

Türk Ocakları içinde bulundukları milliyetler için birer menba-yı feyz olmaya başlamalıdır.
(Ağaoğlu Ahmed)

Türkiyede tatbik edilmesi lazım gelen millileştirme usulü hakkında şek ve tereddüde mehal yoktur. Türk hükumeti uzun müddet Rumelide, Bulgar, Rum, Ulah, Arnavut gibi anasır-ı muhtelife arasında cereyan eden hun harane mücadelelerde jandarmalık vazifesini ifa etmiş ve görmüştür ki hiç bir yerde millileştirme cebir ve şiddet ile kabul ve infaz ettirilmemiştir. Rumelide anasır-ı muhtelifenin yek diğerine karşı takip ettikleri bomba ve dinamit siyaseti her yerde aksi tesir hasıl etmiştir. Harpten evvel bomba ve dinamite rağmen milliyetlerine dört elle sarılmış olan anasırlar harpten sonra bazı hükümetler tarafından tatbik edilen telkin ve tetyib usulüne mukavemet edemiyerek muhite tabi olmuşlar, ve içinde yaşadıkları millete intibaka şitap etmişlerdi.

Fil vakı Bulgaristan, Yunanistan, Romanya gibi bütün Balkan memalikinde "intibak" için pek parlak ve mukni misaller bulunuyor. Yunanistanda en asıl Ulah, Bulgar veya Arnavut olan bizzat pek çok zevat bilirim ki millileştirme suretiyle büsbütün rumlaşmışlar. Kendileri rumcayı ana dil olmak üzere konuşuyor ve fakat evlerinde ihtiyar anaları veya babaları olan ulahça veya bulgarcadan başka bir dil konuşmazlar. Bu gibi adamlara müessesat-ı maliye ve iktisadiye rüesası ve hatta devlet ricalı meyanında pek çok tesadüf olunuyor. Muhitlerinde bunların şecerelerini bilenler çoktur. Fakat hiç bir kimse onlara yan gözle bakmaz. Kendileride şecelerini de ketm ve ihfaya asla lüzum görmezler.

Millileştirme mesaisinde rehberlik vazifesi ile mükellef olan Türk Ocaklarına Ağa Oğlu Ahmed Bey[1] şu usulü gösteriyor :

"Artık birleşmiş ve istikrar peyda etmiş olan ocaklar muhitlerini nurlandırmaya gayelerini etrafa saçmağa, içinde bulundukları milliyetler için bir menba feyz olmaya başlamalıdır."

Filvakı inkilap hareketi sayesinde Türklük yükselmiştir, ve gittikçe yükselecektir. Türklük muhiti içinde yaşayan anasırlar bundan sonra artık kuvve-yi cazibesine mukavemet edemezler, Türklük cazibesine teslim-i ruh etmekten başka bir şey yapamazlar.

Türkleştirme, pp. 10-11

Türk Kimdir?

Akide itibarıyla türküm diyen her ferdi türk tanımalıdır.

O halde yanlış zan ve zehaplara meydan vermemek için merhum üstadın[2] vaz ettiği umdeyi şu yolda tadil ve tesbit etmek lazım gelir : "Akide itibarıyla türküm diyen her ferdi türk tanımalıdır."

Benim gibi merhumun en eski mukarribinden olmak şerefine nail olanlar pek ala bilirler ki merhum en ziyade akideye atf-ı ehemmiyet ederdi. Her hususta ferdin akidesini, kanaat-ı deruniye ve samimiyesini arardı. Akide ise arzu ve irade ile icab-ı zaman ve menfaat sevkiyle peyda olmaz. Muhit ve terbiye mahsulüdür, kan ve şecere itibarıyla şu veya bu zümreye mensubiyet akideye haiz-i tesir olamaz.

Türküm diyen bir arnavut, bir acem, bir arap veya bir musevinin karşısında bulunulduğu zaman mazisine, icinde yasşadığı muhite, telakki ettiği terbiyeye, menafi-i maddiye ve manevisinin sevaik-i daimesine bakılır. Bütün bu amiller Türk akidesinin mevcudiyetine delalet ederse Türklük iddiası şayan-ı kabul ad olunmalıdır.

Akidenin ehemmiyet-i fevkaladesini iraye ve isbat etmek üzere burada profesör Leger'in İslav alemi, Monde Slave nam eserinde münteşir bir türk zabitinin neferiyle cereyan eden enmuzeci bir muhaveresini buraya nakl etmeden vazgeçemiyeceğim :

— Nerelisin?
— Bosnalıyım.
— Hangi millettensin?
— Türküm.
— Türkçe konuşuyor musun?
— Hayır!
— Türkçe konuşmadığın halde kendine nasıl Türk diyebiliyorsun?
— Bilmem bana, Türksün dediler, bende kendimi öyle bilirim.
— Benimle ne dil konuşuyorsun?
— Bilmem.
— Ben seninle sırpça konuşuyorum, sen de bana sırpça cevap veriyorsun. O halde ikimiz Sırbız.
— Hayır sen sırpça konuşuyorsun. Ben Boşnakça cevap veriyorum. Binaenaleyh sen Sırpsın ben Türküm.

Şüphesiz ki bu yolda konuşan Boşnak neferinde bu günkü telakkiye nazaran Türkluk namına bir şey yoktu. Dili, harsı, terbiyesi, ırkı, muhiti Türkten büsbütün başka idi. Öyle olduğu halde adamcağız samimi bir ifade ile la tezelzül bir katiyet ile kendine Türk diyordu. Çünkü Müslümanlık rabıtasından dolayı akidesi Türk idi.

Bu cümleden olarak harb-i umumiden evvel "Epir" (Bizim eski Yanya Vilayeti) kıtasında bütün şideteyile cari olan anasır mücadelesini hal ve fasl etmek için o zamanki tabir-i mahsusası ile "düvel-i muazzama" tarafından teşkil olunan tahkikat komisyonunun tecrübelerini zikr etmek mümkündür.

Malüm olduğu vechiyle Epirdeki hristiyan ahalinin çoğu Arnavut oldukları halde ötedenberi kendilerine rumluk akidesi ilka ve telkin olunmuştu. Tahkikat komisyonunun bir takım azaları evlere kapıdan giriyorlardı. Kendilerine sümmettedarik rumca olarak biz rumuz diye cevap veriyorlardı. Halbuki bir takım azalar arkadaki pencereden içeri girerler müstahzir olmıyan evdekileri isticvap ederlerdi. Evdekiler arnavutça konuşarak rum olduklarını iddia ederlerdi. Herifler arnavutça konuştukları ve tek bir kelime rumca bilmedikleri halde kendilerine ötedenberi telkin olunan akideden dolayı kemal-i samimiyetle rumluk iddiasında bulunuyorlardı.

Yukarıda zikr olunan boşnak neferi veya türk akidesini besleyen her hangi birisi tabii tahtında türk muhitinde yaşarsa bittabi yalnız akide itibarıyla değil ana dil, hars ve terbiye itibarıyla dahi türk olur. Akide bazan terbiyenin mahsulü olur, türk terbiyesi ile büyüyen, türk muhitinde yaşayan bir gayr-ı türk, terbiyenin tesiri neticesi olarak bittabi "ben türküm" der, ve bu suretle kendisinde türk akidesi peyda olur.

Bazan keyfiyet bir akis olabilir. Kalb-ı incizab, mevhum veya hakiki bir menfaat saikasıyla ve "Hükm-ü bilnefs" auto suggestion tesiriyle insan kendini türk telakki eder. Ben türküm diyerek türk muhitine kavuşur, türk camiasının emel ve matalibine, bütün duygularına, maddi manevi mukadderatına iştirak eder. Çocuklarını dahi ayni yola sevk eder ve bilnetice yalnız akide ile başlıyan türklük, hars ve terbiye ile takamül etmiş olur.

Netice itibarıyla şuna kanıyım ki Türkiyede yapılacak en birinci iş Türk olmak arzusunda olan fertlerde veya zümrelerde türklük akidesini vücuda getirmekten, yani menafi-i maddiye ve maneviyesi türklüğe merbut olan ve bu vaziyette yaşamak isteyen kimsenin ben türküm demesine imkan ve zemin hazırlamaktan ibarettir.

Binaenaleyh türkleştirme mesaisinde bütün vatandaşların içtimai uzviyetimizin ecza-yı mütemmimesinden olmalarını, Osmanlılık devrinden arta kalan mütekabil tüfeylilik vaziyet almasının tedrici surette ortadan kalkmasını cidden arzu edersen hiç bir vakit hakiki gayeyi nazar-ı dikkatten dur tutmamalıyız.

Yukarıda izah ettiğimiz esasata nazaran hakiki gaye ise "bila fark-ı ırk ve şecere" bütün vatandaşlara türk akidesini ilka ve telkin etmekten ibarettir. Akidenin ilka ve telkini ise ancak mantık ve irade kuvvetiyle hissiyatımıza galebe çalmakla mümkün olabilir. Vatanın menafi-i aliyesi mevzu-u bahs olduğu zaman hissiyatı susturmak, yalnız akıl ve fikre, mantık ve iradeye söz vermek inkilabımızın ruhuna muvafık bir harekettir.

Şu ciheti de nazar-ı dikkatten dur tutmamalıdır ki henüz türkleşmemiş olan vatandaşlara türklük akidesinin ilka ve telkini amak-ı ruh ile alakadar pek nazik bir keyfiyettir. Binaenaleyh bu günden yarına temin ve ikmal olunabilecek bir vazife değildir. Bazan kabil-i iktiham gibi görünen müşkülata da tesadüf olunabilir. Fakat şuna emin olmalıdır ki türklerde türklük mefküresi baki kaldıça diğer vatandaşların intibaka mukavemet etmesi imkan haricindendir. Ara sıra zuhur edebilecek olan müşkülat netice-yi katiyeyi tehir edebilir, muvaffakiyete mani olamaz.

Türkleştirme, pp. 25-28

Müşterek Vicdan

"Irk, din, dil, bütün bu prensipler müşterek vicdana dahil iseler, milliyet prensiplerini teşkil ederler aksi takdirde hükümsüz kalırlar."

Görülüyor ki vatandaşların türkleştirilmesi zor zor bir iş değildir. Bundan onyedi sene evvel türkçülük yani türkleri türkleştirmek cereyanı baş gösterdiği zaman zayıf ruhlu olanlar türkçülerin hayal-ı muhal ile uğraştıkları zehabına düşmüşlerdi. Selanikte çıkan "Genç Kalemler" o vakitki tabir-i mahsusile bu günkülerin dünkülerle mücadelesi cüce "David" in devasa Golyata hücumu hükmünde telakki olunmuştu. Bu muazzam işi başarmış olan türkçülük gayr-ı türkleri millileştirme mesaisinde daha ziyade sühuletle gayeye vasıl olabilir. Çünkü türkleri türkleştirmek mevzu-u bahs olduğu zaman ortada bir vicdan-ı milli mevcut değildi. Vicdan-ı milliyi yoktan yaratmak veyahut amak-ı ruhdan bulup çıkarmak icap etmişti. Şimdi ortada güneş gibi parlak ve şaşaadar bir vicdan-ı milli mevcuttur ki ona ısınmak istiyenlere nur ve hayat bahş eder. Ona lakayd kalanları sinesinden def edip atar. Bu günkü türklük bütün muhiti için gayr-ı kabil-i mukavemet bir mıknatısı kuvvet-i cazibe haline gelmiştir. Bu memlekette sakin olan gayr-ı türk unsurları bu kuvvet-ı mıknatısıyeden tefrik eden kuvvetli hailler bulunmazsa cazibe-i mıknatısıyenin hükmünü icra etmemesi gayr-ı mümkündür!

Evet! Maateessüf bazı gayr-ı türk unsurları türklükten uzaklaştıran kuvvetli bir hail mevcuttur. Bu da mazi hem de uzak bir mazi değil dünkü mazidir.

Dünkü mazinin neden ibaret olduğunu izaha lüzum görmüyorum. Bir meşum mazinin feci safhalarını gözden kaybetmiş hatırdan çıkarmış olan bir vatandaş tasavvur edemem. Binaenaleyh bu maziyi örtecek kafi bir zaman geçmeyince millileşme cereyanının daha şimdiden umumu şamil olabileceğine inanmak doğrusu safderunluk olur. Fakat bu meşum mazi ile alakadar olmıyan unsurlar yok mudur? Ancak yarın veya öbür gün ikmali mümkün olan bir işe bu günden başlamak kar-ı akıl değil midir? Bir kere bu mazi ile alakadar olmıyan müslim unsurlar vardır. Bunların şimdiden türkleştirilmesine hiç bir mani yoktur. Onlar dil, din, menfaat ve muhit-i içtimai itibarıyla esasen türktür. Türklüklerine mani olan bir kuvvet varsa o da etrafındaki adamların kendilerine sen lazsın, kürtsün, arapsın, arnavutsun, boşnaksın, dönmesin demelerinden ve bu zan ve zehabın ara sıra görülen bazı tezahüratla teyid eder gibi görünmesinden başka bir şey değildir. Halbuki milliyetperverliği ferdi hodperestlik hissinden tecride muvaffak olanların en mukkades vazifesi tüfeyliler, arttırmak suretiyle uzviyet-i içtimaiyemizi zayıflatmak değil, tüfeylileri anasır-ı asliyeye istihale ettirmek suretiyle kuvvetlendirmekten, ben türküm diyenlere sen arnavutsun veya lazsın demek değil ben lazım arnavutum diyenlere sen türksün demelerinden ibarettir.

İşte bu suretle ve ancak bu suretledir ki bu vatanda sakin olan muhtelif unsurlarda müşterek vicdan hasıl olur. Müşterek vicdan ise vahdet-i milliyenin üs elesasıdır.

İntibak yolunda uzak ve yakın bir mazi gibi bir haile maruz bulunmıyan bir unsur da musevilerdir. Museviler İspanyada hristiyan taassubunun, enkizisyon ruhunun kemal-ı şiddetle hükümferma olup, binlerce, yüzbinlerce müslüman ve museviyi diri diri yakdığı bir hengamede felaket kardeşleri olan ümmet-i Muhammediyenin kalemrev hükümeti olan Türkiyeye iltica etmişlerdi. Müslümanlar hemdertlerine, felaket kardeşlerine kapılarını dört açmışlar, fakat o vakit türklerde şuur-u milli uyanık bulunmadığı için bu mültecileri dil ve akide itibarıyla uzviyet-i içtimaiyeye intibak ettirmek çaresi düşünülmemiştir. Ve bu suretledir ki bu güne kadar Türkiyedeki museviler maateessüf dünyanın hiç bir yerinde mevcut olmıyan bir garibe halinde kalmışlardır. Dünyada mevcut on beş milyon musevi, bulundukları memleketin dilini ana dili ittihaz etmişler vatandaşlarından yalnız mezhep ve tarihi anane itibarıyla ayrılırlar. Hatta daha dün Türkiyenin eczasından bulunan arap illerinde bile araplığa intibak etmişler, yalnız Türkiyede olan enkizisyoncuların dilini muhafazaya devam ediyorlar. Türklerin vicdan-ı milliden mahrum bulundukları müddetçe bu vaziyet-i garibeye göz yummak mümkün idi. Fakat bu gün ortada güçlü kuvvetli bir türklük mevcut iken museviler için türkçeyi ana dil ittihaz etmemek akıl ve mantık, maddi ve manevi menfaat sevaikiyle kabil-i telif bir vaziyet değildir. Mazide museviler türklerden, ve türkleri musevilerden uzaklaştıracak hiç bir hal hiç bir hadise yoktur. İsmet Paşa Hazretleri tarafından Lozan konferansının hal-ı inikatta bulunduğu sırada irat olunan bir nutukta izah olunduğu vechiyle "Türklerle musevileri birbirine bağlayan rabıtalar bu gün eskiden daha kuvvetlidir. Her yerde olduğu gibi Türkiyede dahi museviler her vakit say ve ikdamın, nizam ve intizamın, terraki ve müsalemetin mümessilleri bulundular, Türkiyede museviler kemal-ı sükun ve refah ile çalışıyorlar. Ve memleketimizde türkler gibi iğvaat tezvirata asla kulak asmıyorlar. Bu vatanı her vakit kendi vatanları ad ve telakki etmişlerdir. Herkes musevileri numune-yi imtisal ittihaz etmelidir."

Binaenaleyh Fransada fransız, İngilterede ingiliz, İtalyada italyan olan bir musevinin Türkiyede hemen türk olmaması için hiç bir sebep yoktur.

Türkiyedeki musevilerin başka memleketlerdeki mezhepdaşlarından daha çabuk ve daha kolay bir surette millileşmeleri için bir çok saikler vardır. Bunların başlıcalarına atf-ı nazar etmek faydadan hali değildir.

Bu amillerin en mühimi yukarıda bilmünasebet zikr olunduğu vechile müslümanlarla museviler arasında ötedenberi bir nevi dini tesanüdün mevcudiyetidir. Kurun-u vustada hristiyan alemine hakim olan ve mahut ehl-i salip muharebelerine meydan vermiş olan taassup-u dininin tek bir hedefi vardı müslümanlığı ve museviliği mahv ve ifna etmek. Arz-ı mukaddese doğru akın akın hücum eden ehl-i salip kafileleri silahlı müslümanlara kılıç sallamağa fırsat bulmadan evvel vehgüzarlarında tesadüf ettikleri silahsız musevi cemaatlarını ayni hiss-i taassubun sevkiyle perişan etmekten hali kalmazlardı. Yüzbinlerce müslüman ve museviyi diri diri yakan "Turkemado" ların müslüman ve museviliğe karşı husumet-i taasupkaranesi kurun-u vusta ile hitam pezir olmamış ta zamanımıza kadar temadi etmiştir. Daha düne kadar Türkiyenin mukasaması için en ziyade ileri sürülen sebepler meyanında hristiyan anasırın esaretten kurtarılması, müslüman hakimiyetinin Avrupadan tay ve rafı gibi umdeler görünmüyor muydu? Eski Türkiyeye karşı çevrilen siyasi entrikaların en büyük saiki hristiyan taassubundan ibaretti. Avrupanın muhtelif memleketlerinde sık sık hadisata meydan veren antisemitizm dahi, ister içtimai, ister iktisadi kisvelere bürünsün bütün bu hareketlerin arkasında hristiyan ruhunda meknuz olup Hazret-i İsanın çarmıha vurulmasıyla başlıyan husumet-i diniyenin meşur ve gayr-ı meşur tezahüratından başka bir şey değildir.

İşte halkın taht elşuurunda olan yaşıyan bu dini tesanüt bu hemdertlik hissi saikasıdır ki Sultan Beyazıt hristiyan taassubunun kurbanlarına memleketin kapılarını dört açmıştır, o vakittenberi museviler Türkiyede intibak etmedikleri halde kemal-ı aman ve refah ile vakit geçirdiler. Ne resmi ne gayr-ı resmi mehafilde hiç bir vakit gayr-ı müslim mefhumuna dahil olmamışlardı.

İntibakı kolaylaştıran diğer bir amil de Türkiyedeki musevilerin münhasıran "sefaradi" yani İspanyol zümresine dahil olmalarıdır. Anatole Leroy Beaulieu tarafından ispat olunduğu vechiyle sefaradi musevilerinin intibaka kabiliyet ve istidatları pek kuvvetlidir.

Ve bunun içindir ki bütün Avrupada en kolay, en çabuk ve en mükemmel surette intibak eden museviler ekseriyet itibarıyla "sefaradi" olan İtalya musevileridir.

Musevilerin intibak edebilmesi için atideki evamir-i aşaraya tevrattaki evamir-i aşara kadar riayet etmeleri lazım gelir :

Evamir-i Aşara

1. İsimlerini türkleştir
2. Türkçe konuş
3. Havralarda duaların hiç olmazsa bir kısmını türkçe oku
4. Mekteplerini türkleştir
5. Çocuklarını memleket mekteplerine gönder
6. Memleket işlerine karış
7. Türklerle düşüp kalk
8. Cemaat ruhunu kökünden sök
9. Milli iktisat sahasında vazife-yi mahsusanı yap
10. Hakkını bil

1. İsimlerini türkleştir — Türk olmak için türk adını taşımak şarttır. Başka memleketlerdeki mezheptaşların dahi bu vecibeyi takdir ederek isimleri millileştirmişlerdir. Frenklik daiyesiyle Moize inkilap eden Mişonun Musa esasen Avram olan Alber İbrahim, Şelomo olan Salamonun Selim veya Süleyman olmasına ne mani vardır? Bundan sonra doğacak çocuklarına doğrudan doğruya halis türk isimleri ver.

2. Türkçe konuş — Umumi yerlerde Türkçe bilenlerle türkçe konuş. Bu türkçe konuşma, yalnız yabancılara karşı bir nümayiş teşkil etmez, bizzat kendi üzerine pek derin bir tesir-i ruhi icar eder, yavaş nümayiş bir ittiyat bir tabiat-ı saniye haline gelir.

3. Havralarda duaların hiç olmazsa bir kısmını türkçe oku. Türkçe duasını bir taraftan allaha diğer taraftan vatana yaklaştırır.

4. Mekteplerini türkleştir — Kanun ve kanunları tatbike memur olan hükümet sana mekteptleri türkleştirmek için yolu açtı. Usul-ü tedriste muallimlerin hüsn-ü intihabında bazı noksanlar varsa sükut edip lakayt kalma. Noksanları islah boşlukları ikmal için uğraş çabala.

5. Çocuklarını memleket mekteplerine gönder — Mezheptaşların başka memleketlerde çocuklarını cemaat mekteplerine göndermezler. Memleket mektepleri derece-yi kifayede olduğu dakikada bunların hikmet-i vücutları kalmıyacaktır. O zamana kadar sen mevcuttan istifade etmeye çalış. Çocukların için mektep kapılarını kapayan olursa uğraşmaktan mafevke müracaattan üşenme. Bu memleketin bir hak ve fünun memlekti olduğunu unutma.

6. Memleket işlerine karış — Memlekette umuma taallük eden hususta lakayt kalma, alakanı her vechile izhar et. Senin cidden hizmet edebileceğin mesai sahaları az değildir. Şunun bunun seni yabancı telakki etmelerine ehemmiyet verme. Teşkilat-ı esasiye kanunu seni türk tanıyor. Sen de türk gibi hareket et. Şunun bunun yanlış hareketi payıdar olamaz. Sen sağa sola bakmıyarak türklük yolunda ilerlemeğe devam et. Memleket işlerinde rehberliği deruhte etmiş olan ricalin umdeleriyle sana çizdikleri hatt-ı hareketten katiyen şaşma.

7. Türklerle düşüp kalk — Cemiyet ve salon hayatında, içtimai ve iktisadi münasabatta, türklere yanaş, turklerle kaynaş, ruhun mefküreye, gıda-yı ruhiye muhtaçtır. Onsuz yaşayamazsın. Bu ruh gıdasını memleket alakasında, memleket muhitlerinde bulacaksın. Emin ol ki bazı geçici ve aldatıcı zevahire rağmen bu muhitler sana pek sıcak bir ağuş-u kabul açmağa hazırdır.

8. Cemaat ruhunu kökünden sök — Bu gün cemaat ruhu muhitine hakim ise kabahat senin değil. Bütün bu evlad-ı vatanı bedbaht eden meşum mazinindir. Fakat inkilap

ruhuna dikkat et, bu inkilap ruhu mazi ile kat-ı alaka etmeğe azm etmiştir. Ve merhale merhale gayeye doğru ilerliyor. Sen de inkilap ruhuna imtisalen mazinin bu meşum yadigârını ruhundan sökmeğe memleketin müşterek vicdanına bir an evvel kavuşmağa gayret et.

9. Milli iktisat sahasında vazife-yi mahsusanı yap — Her vatandaş memlekete karşı olan vazifesi vesait-i maddiyesine, müktesebat-ı ilmiyesine, evsaf ve mezaya-yı mahsusesine göre taayun eder. Senin rolün en ziyade iktisat sahasındadır. Milli iktisada alelade kolay ve hafif işlerle değil memleketin istihsalatını milli servetini artıracak umur-u ticariye ve sanaiye ve bu gibi iktisadi teşebbüslerle hizmet olunabilir. Senin harici münasebetlerin, Avrupa ve Amerikadaki temasların sayesinde bu memleketin menabi-i servetini istismara medar olabilecek bir çok teşebbüsler vücude gelebilir. Ciddi mesainle bu günkü türklük her nokta-yı nazardan haricte hakiki renk ve mahiyetiyle tanıttırılabilir. Ancak sen kendini bu memleketin ezeli ve ebedi evladı ad ve işlerini hayatını ona göre tanzim et.

10. Hakkını bil — Teşkilat-ı esasiye kanunu sana türk namını bahş etmiştir. Bu bir hak, bir imtiyazdır ki akide, ruh ve vicdan itibarıyla türk olmadan layıkıyla istismar olunamaz. Akide itibarıyla türk olduğuna ve yahut yakında olacağına kanaat getirirsen hakkını bil, hiç bir kimse tarafından bu hakka tecavüz olunmasına tahammül etme türk namının bahş ettiği hukuk ve imtiyazatı husudane bir azim ve metanetle kanun kuvvetiyle müdafaa et.

Şunu da ilave edelim ki burada intibak için musevileri misal olarak gösteriyoruz. Diğer anasırın peyderpey intibakına mani olacak hiç bir kuvvet mutasavver değildir. Mazinin asar-ı meşumesi ortadan kalkıncaya kadar beş on senelik fazla bir zaman geçmesi bir milletin tarih ve mukadderatı üzerine haiz-i tesir olamaz. Yeter ki intibak alakadaran yani türklerle gayr-ı türkler tarafından cidden arzu olunsun, er geç gayeye ermek üzere şimdiden azm-ı kati ile işe mubaşaret olunsun!

Türkleştirme, pp. 60-68

TEKIN ALP, LE KEMALISME

L'ESPRIT KEMALISTE

Peut-on brosser une esquisse du Kemalisme? Peut-on le définir en le plaçant dans le cadre des idées générales qui ont régi les peuples pendant ces siècles derniers, et qui continuent à les guider encore?

Au premier abord, rien de plus simple. Puisque le mot d'ordre de Kamal Atatürk c'est l'acheminement vers la civilisation occidentale, son œuvre ne peut qu'être calquée sur certaines idées générales de cette civilisation même.

Mais en réalité, tel n'est pas le cas. On se ferait une fausse idée du Kemalisme en tant qu'idéologie en se basant sur les termes et les expressions dont se servent ses adeptes pour expliquer leurs idées et leurs directives. Les dirigeants du Kemalisme n'ont pas inventé une terminologie originale pour exprimer leurs idées spéciales. Ils se servent des formules classiques employées par tous les peuples depuis des siècles, mais ces formules ne sont que des enveloppes, l'esprit et les principes qu'ils renferment sont tout à fait différents.

C'est ce que Chukru Kaya, ministre de l'Intérieur, dans un discours prononcé au Congrès de la Presse, réuni récemment à Ankara sous sa présidence, a voulu dire en s'écriant:

«Le Kemalisme ne peut pas être renfermé dans les formules étroites de 'droite ou de gauche'.»

De son côté, Receb Peker, le secrétaire général du Parti du Peuple, dans un discours prononcé devant le IVe Congrès du Parti pour en analyser le nouveau programme, a fait entre autres le procès des dogmes démocratiques et a dit à ce propos:

«La démocratie, ce n'est pas un dogme ou un précepte religieux, c'est un esprit, une âme et un sens. Ce que l'on fait ne peut être utile et durable que si on le fait passer par le tamis qui a nom cerveau, et si on le met en harmonie avec le milieu. On ne plante pas des orangers sur le mont Zigana. Nous ne sommes pas de ceux qui disent: Telle nation a fait ceci, faisons de même. Nous en faisons que ce qui est conforme à la situation de notre pays et ce qui convient à notre nation. Dans les affaires nationales, nous préférons suivre les chemins qui conviennent à notre peuple, plutôt que d'imiter les autres et tâcher de plaire à ceux qui nous voient du dehors.»

Plus loin, dans le même discours, l'éminent orateur ajoute:

«Nous ne sommes pas de ceux qui barbouillent du papier avant de se mettre à l'œuvre.

Nous préférons produire l'œuvre d'abord. Des personnes superficielles nous reprochent de travailler sans plan ni programme, mais elles ont perdu de vue que les meilleurs plans et les meilleurs programmes ne sont pas toujours écrits; le plan cardinal, la source, le point de départ de tous nos programmes, c'est l'énergie, la perspicacité condensées dans le cerveau et dans l'âme des dirigeants spirituels. L'humanité a vu beaucoup de plans écrits. Mais le grand plan cardinal n'est pas griffonné sur du papier. L'idée de la création de la nouvelle Turquie a germé dans le Grand Cerveau (celui d'Atatürk). C'était une nouvelle étoile qui, au moment de son apparition, a produit une lumière, une colonne de feu qui indiquait avec une clarté éclatante les directives définitives de tout ce qui a été fait jusqu'ici, de ce qui se fait actuellement et de ce qui sera fait dans l'avenir. C'est là le plan dont émanent tous les autres.»

On ne peut pas être plus clair et plus précis. Le Kemalisme ne réside pas dans des devises, des formules transmises d'une génération à une autre, que les différents pays et les différents peuples copient les uns des autres, que chaque politicien et chaque homme d'État interprète et applique à sa façon et au nom desquelles on élabore et on met en application des plans et des programmes diamétralement opposés et qui présentent des aspects différents, à travers des périodes différentes. La nouvelle Turquie n'est pas créée par des formules caduques et surannées, qui ont vu le jour dans des circonstances et dans des périodes différentes, mais par un cerveau, par un génie vivant qui sait ce qu'il veut et qui, dès le premier moment, a arrêté son plan, a fixé la voie à suivre, l'déal vers lequel convergent désormais les aspirations et les efforts du peuple turc tout entier.

Voilà pourquoi le régime, le système de la nouvelle Turquie ne peut être défini par aucune formule, mais simplement par le nom de son créateur et son réalisateur. Le terme Kemalisme renferme donc toute l'histoire de la nouvelle Turquie d'après-guerre, le programme d'action de l'État et les aspirations du peuple turc vers son idéal, tel que son chef le lui a fixé.

Peut-on comprendre ce qu'est le Kemalisme, en tant que régime ou système spécial, en lisant les dizaines d'ouvrages qui ont été publiés jusqu'ici sur les différents aspects de la révolution turque et sur les progrès énormes qu'elle a réalisés?

Malheureusement, non. Parce que tout ce qui a été dit et écrit jusqu'ici sur la révolution kemaliste ne se réfère qu'aux faits matériels, à la chronique et à l'histoire des événements, ce qui est naturellement très intéressant; mais l'esprit nouveau, qui a donné successivement naissance aux élans impétueux vers le progrès et la civilisation, les réactions de l'âme nationale qui ont affranchi le peuple d'une oppression séculaire, n'ont pas été mis suffisamment en relief.

Ainsi, par exemple, en parcourant la littérature relative à la révolution kemaliste, on a l'impression que le plus important, dans cette révolution, c'est la suppression du fez et du voile et d'autres réformes saillantes de ce genre. Le changement de mentalité et d'état d'âme de tout un peuple passe souvent inaperçu. On parle bien de l'émancipation de la femme, mais l'émancipation de l'homme échappe à la description. On constate bien que les fantômes voilés qui circulaient dans la rue et lui imprimaient un air triste et mystérieux, se sont mués d'un coup en fées gracieuses, répandant charme et gaîté sur leur passage; mais on ne remarque pas que des millions d'hommes qui, jusqu'ici, marchaient dans la vie d'un air resigné et indolent, ont changé du jour au lendemain de physionomie.

Plus de trace de l'expression fataliste de ces yeux sans éclat, tournés vers l'au delà. Les rues d'Istanbul ne sont sillonnées que par des physionomies exprimant l'énergie et la vitalité, des yeux reflétant la joie de vivre, l'aspiration vers le progrès, le bonheur et le bien-être. Ceux qui veulent bien se rendre compte du changement qui s'est opéré dans la nouvelle Turquie, ne doivent pas regarder simplement le chapeau qui a remplacé le fez traditionnel. Le changement du couvre-chef ne peut avoir que la valeur et l'importance d'un symbole. Il faut fixer son regard quelques centimètres plus bas que le couvre-chef. Les yeux, protégés par la visière du couvre-chef occidental, ne sont plus les mêmes qu'il y a trois lustres. La vivacité a succédé à la résignation et au fatalisme oriental. L'expression générale de la physionomie aussi est tout à fait différente. L'expression d'indolence a cédé la place à l'énergie, à la gaîté et à la bonne humeur.

Ainsi donc, les écrivains étrangers qui caractérisent principalement le Kemalisme, par l'émancipation de la femme, se trompent énormément. Avant l'émancipation de la femme, il faut faire cas de l'émancipation de l'homme. La première n'est autre chose que la conséquence naturelle de la seconde. Un homme obsédé par des préjugés pseudo-religieux, par une mentalié obscurantiste qui domine tous les faits et gestes de sa vie publique et privée, pouvait bien s'accommoder d'une femme sans culture, sans individualité, bonne seulement pour ses fonctions charnelles et les travaux de ménage. Un homme émancipé, conscient de sa dignité individuelle ne peut avoir pour compagne qu'une femme ayant le même niveau culturel et intellectuel, la même mentalité, les mêmes aspirations et les mêmes façons de vivre, de sentir, de penser et d'agir.[1]

Ce n'est la qu'un exemple entre mille, prouvant la nécessité d'analyser le Kemalisme, non pas sous sa forme apparente et superficielle, mais en prenant comme base l'esprit qui a présidé à la création de son œuvre. C'est à la lumière de l'analyse de cet esprit du Kemalisme qui s'est déjà transformé en réalités, que nous pourrons comprendre d'une façon plus claire et plus précise les aspirations réelles de la nouvelle Turquie et prévoir ses réalisations futures.

Le Kemalisme, pp. 14-18.

LA CLÉ DE L'ÉNIGME

Toutes les fois qu'on cherche à voir de près et à comprendre l'essence de ce qu'on appelle communément le miracle turc, on se demande avec raison: «Puisque le peuple turc était capable de tant d'héroïsme, puisqu'il renfermait en lui tant de forces dynamiques, pourquoi donc s'est-il laissé piétiner pendant des siècles par des dictateurs et des usurpateurs de tout acabit, pourquoi s'est-il laissé traîner jusqu'au bord de l'abîme sans réagir. Qu'a-t-il attendu pour mettre en mouvement les mêmes qualités et les mêmes facteurs moraux qui ont rendu possible la révolution kemaliste? Atatürk lui-même n'a-t-il proclamé, à différentes reprises – ainsi que nous l'avons relevé plus haut – que les idées et les principes dont lui et son Parti poursuivent la réalisation, constituent la quintessence des idéals et des aspirations de la nation turque?»

Ce n'est un secret pour personne que pour bien comprendre le véritable caractère et les destinées réelles d'une nation il faut avoir toujours recours à son histoire. Donc, c'est en tournant les pages de l'histoire turque qu'on pourrait comprendre les causes profondes qui ont determiné ses destinées dans les derniers siècles de décadence qu'Atatürk qualifie avec raison de période «non nationale.» Mais une histoire turque proprement dite n'existait pas jusqu'ici. Il y avait bien une histoire ottomane qui constituait une intime partie de l'histoire turque et où on ne trouvait que la chronique mal interprétée de certains événements guerriers ou autres. Une histoire turque conçue sous un point de vue national, s'occupant de façon objective de la vie sociale et culturelle du peuple, n'a jamais été écrite, et, comme nous le verrons plus loin, c'est toujours à la révolution kemaliste que revient le mérite d'avoir reconstitué l'histoire de la Nation turque.

Zia Gök Alp, qui comme nous l'avons vu, a eu le mérite de prophétiser ou de rêver l'avènement du kemalisme, a essayé il est vrai d'esquisser l'histoire de la civilisation turque. Mais la mort l'ayant enlevé en pleine période d'épanouissement il n'en a pu écrire que le premier volume. C'est dans ce volume que nous trouvons la clé de l'énigme qui nous préoccupe.

Voici ce que nous y lisons:

«La Nation turque ne ressemble pas aux autres nations. Lorsqu'elle avait à sa tête un héros, elle brillait toujours d'un coup, soit en politique, soit en culture et son niveau politique et culturel s'élevait subitement. Lorsqu'elle n'avait pas un héros à sa tête, elle commençait à se disloquer rapidement.»

Ces paroles de Zia Gök Alp peuvent donner lieu à une fausse interprétation lorsqu'on ne connaît pas les idées du grand philosophe sur le nationalisme en général et le nationalisme turc en particulier. Pour lui, nationalisme signifie l'union culturelle de tous les membres composant une collectivité. Une des devises à laquelle il tenait le plus et qu'il aimait répéter toujours, c'était: «L'individu ne compte pas, il n'y a que la société qui compte.» Or, il est évident qu'on ne peut obtenir l'union absolue des membres composant une collectivité que grâce à l'autorité d'un chef ayant les qualités d'un héros.

Il n'y a pas de doute que Zia Gök Alp emploie le terme de héros dans le sens employé par Carlyle. Un héros, c'est l'homme qui symbolise les qualités de la société et de la collectivité à laquelle il appartient. C'est la synthèse personnifiée des forces vivantes de la nation. Sans ce symbole et cette synthèse personnifiée, la nation demeure désagrégée, sans tête et sans liaison.

Tous les peuples n'ont pas besoin d'un héros à leur tête. Cela dépend du caractère national. La route crée le type social, dit Desmoulins, l'histoire crée le type social, dirons-nous. En effet, la principale caractéristique de la Nation turque est sans contredit sa qualité de conquérant. Conquérant, l'est-il depuis qu'il a quitté les hauts plateaux de l'Asie Centrale, conquérant, l'est-il depuis qu'Oguz Han, d'après la légende, a distribué le globe terrestre entre ses six fils et les a envoyés à la conquête des territoires qu'il leur a affectés en les armant de flèches et des arcs magiques. Or, peut-on être conquérant sans avoir à sa tête un chef ayant l'autorité absolue d'un commandant sur le champ de bataille? Un peuple qui, pendant des millénaires, l'épée à la main, a toujours poussé son cheval de bataille vers de nouvelles conquêtes, vers de nouveaux horizons de gloire, pouvait-il progresser sans la discipline militaire, sans l'autorité absolue d'un chef héros? C'est donc cette histoire millénaire de conquérant qui a forgé le caractère national du peuple turc et lui a inculqué dans le tréfonds de son âme la caractéristique collectiviste qui implique un esprit de discipline absolue envers le chef. C'est donc là la principale source de la grandeur du peuple turc lorsqu'il a le bonheur d'avoir comme chef un héros – comme dit Zia Gök Alp – et c'est en même temps la raison principale de sa décadence lorsqu'un pareil héros lui fait défaut.

Étant donné son caractère disciplinaire, la dictature, l'usurpation du pouvoir peut avoir, dans certaines circonstances, une prise sur lui, mais ce n'est que momentanément. Abdul Hamid, qui était un dictateur des plus redoutables, a opprimé le peuple turc de la façon la plus abominable. Mais on ne peut pas dire que le peuple turc, représenté naturellement par les intellectuels, par l'élite de la Nation marchait de plein gré derrière lui. Le peuple souffrait et attendait son heure ou plutôt son héros.

Il ne faut pas oublier que le «Baykouche du Yildiz» (le hibou du Yildiz) – c'est le nom par lequel le désignaient les intellectuels turcs qui le détestaient – n'a pu se maintenir que parce qu'il s'est entouré d'un ramassis d'intrus hétérogènes, d'aventuriers non turcs, arabes, kurdes, albanais, tcherkesses ou autres. C'était pour ainsi dire une domination étrangère. Le peuple turc gémissait sous le joug d'usurpateurs étrangers dont le chef Abdul Hamid lui-même, s'il n'était pas tout à fait étranger de race et de sang, était étranger par l'esprit et par la culture théocratique dont il s'est servi pour subjuguer le peuple.

Les Jeunes-Turcs ont bien renversé la dictature d'Abdul Hamid. Ils ont bien établi la Constitution, mais ils n'ont pas produit un héros capable de réunir tous les membres de la nation sous son autorité morale. C'est pour cette raison que, faut d'un héros qualifié, les libertés contitutionnelles se sont confondues souvent avec des mouvements anarchiques de toutes sortes.

La thèse idéologique mise en avant par Zia Gök Alp sous une forme abstraite et générale a été concrétisée par Atatürk lui-même dans son discours historique:

«L'histoire prouve d'une façon irréfutable que pour réussir dans les grandes questions il faut la présence d'un chef dont le pouvoir et la capacité sont inébranlables. Dans les moments pathétiques, est-il possible d'arriver au but en marchant d'un pas ferme et résolu quand on se résigne à se soumettre à des consultations, à certains égards et certaines influences? Peut-on montrer à travers l'histoire une collectivité quelconque qui a réussi en procédant de la sorte?»

Voilà donc la clé de l'énigme. Il faut la présence d'un chef. C'est naturellement par modestie que K. Atatürk n'a pas ajouté que ce chef doit avoir comme lui le caractère d'un héros. C'est en rapprochant ses paroles de celles de Zia Gök Alp que nous pourrons comprendre leur véritable sens et c'est ainsi que nous pourrons trouver la clé de l'énigme.

Dès qu'Atatürk a debarqué à Samsoun le 19 mai 1919, le peuple turc a eu l'intuition que c'était bien lui le héros national qu'il attendait depuis des siècles qu'il est arrivé juste au moment suprême où l'ombre de la mort planait sur sa tête. C'est grâce à cette intuition que toute la Nation l'a suivi comme un seul homme à travers toutes les péripéties de la lutte pour l'indépendance matérielle et morale.

Le Kemalisme, pp. 29-33

PATRIE RENOVÉE ET NOUVELLE NATION

La suppression du Califat ouvre une nouvelle étape au Kemalisme. Jusqu'ici, nous n'avons assisté qu'à des travaux de déblaiement. il fallait en effet déblayer le terrain encombré par des obstacles redoutables, tels que le Sultanat et le Califat, avant de commencer l'œuvre constructive: la création d'une patrie renovée et d'une nouvelle Nation.

Désormais, il n'y a plus de secret national qu'Atatürk doive garder dans son cœur. Le moment de commander la construction du nouvel édifice est venu. Il est temps d'entreprendre finalement la création du nouvel État, de la nouvelle Patrie et du nouveau Turc.

Un nouvel État, une organisation, des cadres; voilà ce qu'il était urgent de créer. Le legs du passé n'était guère alléchant. Le réformateur s'empressa de le répudier. Le nouvel ordre des choses ne devait pas se présenter comme une suite, une succession du vieil édifice politique vermoulu et branlant. Que pouvait-il emprunter au passé? Le cadre des fonctionnaires, les ministres et dignitaires élevés dans l'atmosphère viciée de l'ancien régime? On n'avait pas versé des torrents de sang pour confier les destinées de la Nation aux mêmes individus qui l'avaient laissée traîner aux bords de l'abîme. Emprunter l'élite soi-disant intellectuelle qui se complaisait dans les vains artifices verbaux, dans les phrases creuses et emphatiques, bourrées de formules pompeuses en arabe et en persan? Non, la génération du feu avait d'autres soucis que les futiles recherches d'une rhétorique verbeuse dénuée de sens. S'annexer les milliers de religieux ignorants qui ne faisaient que répandre dans leur entourage la mentalité que nous appelons «Kismet,» faite de nonchalance contemplative? Non! Le dynamisme irrésistible de cette génération kemaliste ne pouvait plus tolérer dans son sein de pareils éléments de pourriture. Ce qu'on appelle la plèbe n'était plus une masse d'esclaves sans dignité et sans volonté, mais une collectivité de personnes libres et avides de progrès.

Le nouvel État répudia même le qualificatif d'Osmanli provenant du nom du chef de tribu qui en fut le fondateur. Mais pourquoi désigner par le nom d'un chef de tribu un grand peuple qui, à travers les âges, fonda des empires immenses dont le souvenir embellit encore l'histoire de l'humanité.

L'Empire faisait reculer les frontières de la patrie jusqu'aux confins de régions telles que l'Albanie, la Syrie, la Mésopotamie qui n'avaient d'autres attaches avec la Patrie turque que d'attirer vers elles des milliers de paysans d'Anatolie, venus pour combattre au sacrifice de leur vie les émeutes et les révoltes sans fin de ces contrées turbulentes. Très souvent la notion de Patrie était confondue avec la conscience islamique et perdait complètement son véritable sens. La nouvelle Patrie, dans le sens kemaliste, ne renfermait plus dans son sein que des compatriotes ayant les mêmes intérêts et les mêmes aspirations et formant une collectivité une et indivisible.

Avec le Kemalisme, non seulement la collectivité a changé de physionomie, ce qui n'est pas sans précédent dans l'histoire, mais l'individu même a changé d'allure, de moralité et de mentalité, ce qui n'est guère commun dans l'histoire des peuples.

Ainsi donc, la nouvelle étape de la révolution kemaliste avait comme tâche de créer, d'organiser, de former ce nouveau Turc, cette nouvelle Patrie et ce nouvel État sur des nouvelles bases. Cette tâche était difficile parce que le terrain sur lequel on devait construire était encombré des ruines du passé. Le fantôme d'un passé néfaste rôdait toujours sur les ruines de l'ancien édifice écroulé. Kamal Atatürk n'a reculé devant l'immensité de cette tâche. Il a tenu seulement à choisir la meilleure méthode pour arriver au but par le plus court chemin et dans le plus bref délai possible. Le nouveau Turc qui, sous l'impulsion du grand chef, s'était acheminé vers la culture occidentale, devait rattraper en très peu de temps l'avance de quelques siècles des autres peuples civilisés.

Le Kemalisme, pp. 57-59

HUMANITARISME ET PACIFISME

Ainsi que nous le verrons plus bas, dans un chapitre spécial, le nationalisme turc repose sur des bases tout à fait réalistes. Il n'est altéré par aucune influence ou infiltration mystique, comme c'est le cas pour les nationalismes de bien des pays. Voilà pourquoi la nouvelle Turquie, qui a fait du nationalisme la base principale de sa doctrine et de son idéologie, a pu concilier la doctrine nationaliste avec les principes éthiques de l'humanitarisme et du pacifisme, qui ailleurs, sont considérés comme incompatibles avec le mouvement nationaliste. L'humanitarisme, qui est un facteur important dans la politique intérieure des peuples, ainsi que dans la vie privée des individus, ne joue aucun rôle dans les relations internationales. L'égoïsme sévèrement condamné dans la vie individuelle devient «égoïsme sacré», quand il s'agit des intérêts nationaux. Ce point de la morale machiavélique est devenue un axiome incontestable dans la politique internationale. Eh bien, sur ce point aussi, la nouvelle Turquie fait exception à la règle générale. Atatürk a tenu à incorporer l'humanitarisme dans sons régime gouvernemental. C'est ce qu'Ismet Inönü a fait ressortir très nettement dans son discours d'inauguration du cours sur la Révolution à l'Université:[2]

«Dans le domaine moral et social aussi, le sens de notre révolution mérite d'être examiné de près. La Révolution turque poursuit l'idéal humanitaire. Les sociétés humaines possèdent toutes les possibilités et tous les moyens nécessaires pour assurer le travail en commun dans l'univers et grâce à ce travail en commun augmenter leur bonheur et leur bien-être. Poursuivre le sublime idéal humanitaire est un devoir, le seul moyen pratique pour atteindre cet idéal est de se soumettre aux dures réalités. Le but de notre révolution, c'est de vivre en tant que nation turque comme une société particulière de la grande famille humaine. Mais, en même temps, notre révolution considère de son devoir de contribuer au bonheur de cette famille.»

L'exemple le plus typique de cette haute morale, nous le trouvons dans le règlement de la question de l'opium. La Turquie est un des principaux pays qui produisent l'opium. Une grande partie de cette production était transformée sur place en drogues stupéfiantes qui étaient exportées en contrebande et qui rapportaient des millions à l'économie turque. Mais, contre ces millions de livres turques, des millions d'être humains étaient empoisonnés dans le monde entier. Atatürk décida de contribuer à la tâche de la S.D.N.[3] Il réunit le Conseil des Ministres, sous sa présidence, et fit prendre toutes les mesures nécessaires pour enrayer la fabrication dans le pays de ces drogues et leur exportation en contrebande. Pour rendre ces mesures vraiment efficaces, on dut même restreindre, réglementer la culture de l'opium et faire de son exportation un monopole d'État. A la suite de ces mesures, la production et l'exportation de l'opium turc a sensiblement diminué au profit de certains pays qui se sont empressés d'exploiter la situation. N'empêche que la police turque continue à poursuivre avec une extrême rigueur les contrebandiers internationaux de ces drogues. Un grand nombre d'individus appartenant à la haute pègre internationale se trouvent actuellement sous les verrous dans les prisons d'Istanbul et d'ailleurs en Turquie.

Un autre point saillant de ce réalisme positif du régime kemaliste, c'est sa politique pacifiste qui pourrait servir d'exemple aux puissances occidentales petites et grandes.

Dès qu'il a assumé la présidence du Conseil après sa rentrée de Lausanne, Ismet Inönü a proclamé du haut de la tribune de la Grande Assemblée Nationale, que le but principal de son Gouvernement consisterait dans l'affermissement de la paix: «Nous tâcherons par tous nos moyens et avec toute notre force, proclame-t-il, de consolider nos liens d'amitié sincère avec tous nos voisins, avec tous les pays avec lesquels nous avons échangé des traités, ainsi qu'avec ceux qui n'ont pas encore conclu des traités avec nous.»

Ismet Inönü a tenu sa promesse. Les traités d'amitié, de solidarité ou de neutralité se sont succédé. Après le renouvellement et le renforcement du Traité de solidarité avec les Soviets, il y a lieu de citer le traité d'amitié et de neutralité avec l'Italie en mai 1928. Ainsi que l'a fait ressortir M. Grandi à Ankara, ce pacte de neutralité et d'arbitrage constitue un événement dont les répercurssions sur le terrain de la paix et de la concorde internationale ne se limitent pas au bassin de la Méditerranée. Le traité conclu avec la Perse met fin à un passé d'inimitié, résultant de l'antagonisme entre les sectes chiite et sunnite, et marque une nouvelle ère de fraternité sincère. Les parties contractantes s'engagent à défendre leur neutralité par les armes et à ne tolérer sur leurs territoires aucune agitation contre l'autre partie. Dans le traité échangé avec l'Afghanistan, les parties s'engagent à se concerter et à s'entraider si l'une d'elles est l'objet d'un acte hostile de la part d'une tierce puissance. La Turquie fournira à l'Afghanistan les techniciens, les professeurs, les ingénieurs et les instructeurs militaires dont il aura besoin. En octobre 1928, 115 élèves afghans, dont 15 jeunes filles, sont arrivés à Istanbul et ont été répartis entre différentes écoles d'Istanbul et d'Ankara.

Qui aurait pu s'imaginer, il y a quelques années, que la Turquie et la Grèce se tendraient une main fraternelle et sincère par-dessus les centaines de milliers de cadavres qui, hier encore, ont ensanglanté le sol de l'Anatolie. Des millions de Turcs et de Grecs, victimes d'une hostilité séculaire, qui ont dû abandonner leur pays natal, pour vivre en réfugiés parmi leurs co-nationaux, sont encore vivants et traînent derrière eux la nostalgie du coin de terre qui les a vu naître. Comment donc aurait-ont pensé qu'il devînt possible d'oublier un passé si proche et si sanglant? Eh bien, aujourd'hui, ce rapprochement considéré impossible est une réalité. La Turquie et la Grèce sont devenues, non seulement des amies mais des alliées sincères. Le passé d'hier est mort et enterré à jamais. On dirait qu'il ne s'est jamais rien produit entre ces deux peuples, hier encore considérés comme ennemis séculaires et inexorables.

Inutile de rappeler que la pierre angulaire de l'entente balkanique, qui constitue un des meilleurs éléments de la Paix mondiale, c'est toujours cette fraternité turco-grecque, érigée sur la tombe des inimitiés séculaires, et sur celles de centaines de milliers de cadavres. Les passages suivants du message d'Atatürk communiqué par téléphone à Ismet Inönü, au cours du banquet donné le 25 mai 1937 à Athènes en son honneur constitue une garantie inébranlable pour la paix dans les Balkans: «Les frontières des États balkaniques amis constituent une frontière unique, et ceux qui ont des visées sur ces frontières seront atteints comme par les rayons brûlants du soleil. Je conseillerai à ceux-là de tâcher de se prévenir eux-mêmes.»

La paix mondiale gagnerait beaucoup si certaines puissances occidentales de haute culture prenaient exemple sur la Turquie et sur la Grèce, et basaient leur politique sur des facteurs réalistes, en abandonnant à tout jamais certains éléments sentimentaux mystiques et ombrageux.

Le Kemalisme, pp. 148-153

LE PARTI ET L'ÉTAT

Le nouveau programme du Parti prévoit, pour la prochaine période quaternaire, une autre réalisation des plus importantes: c'est la stabilisation du régime kemaliste et l'intégration du régime dans l'État.

Comme nous l'avons vu, le régime kemaliste est basé sur six principes: républicanisme, nationalisme, populisme ou démocratie, étatisme, laïcisme et révolutionnarisme. Mais ces principes, sauf le principe de républicanisme, ne figurent nulle part dans la loi fondamentale, de sorte que le Parti lui-même, ou bien un autre Parti qui lui succéderait, peut les modifier à la première occasion.

Dans son dernier Congrès, le Parti a décidé de mettre fin à cette situation peu stable. Ces principes mis à l'épreuve pendant douze ans se sont avérés les mieux adaptés à la structure sociale et économique du pays. Les résultats déjà obtenus attirent l'admiration de tous ceux qui ont eu l'occasion de les examiner. Pourquoi donc permettre qu'ils soient exposés à des attaques inopinées? Les principes sur lesquels s'appuient les destinées d'une nation ne peuvent assurer son bonheur et son bien-être que s'ils sont stabilisés. Imaginez la situation d'un pays qui, après avoir organisé ses institutions, élaboré ses lois d'après le principe étatiste, devient le théâtre d'expériences d'ordre individuel et libéral? Imaginez aussi des expériences théocratiques dans un pays qui en a été purifié et s'est organisé sur des bases tout à fait laïques. C'est là un danger aussi évident que sérieux, surtout pour un pays comme le nôtre qui se trouve en voie de reconstruction et de relèvement. Le IVe Congrès du Parti a voulu garantir les générations futures contre un pareil danger, contre une offensive inopinée du passé, contre les infiltrations possibles de courants d'idées qui prédominent déjà aujourd'hui dans d'autres pays européens et ceux qui pourraient se produire à l'avenir, comme suite de ce bouillonnement d'idées et d'intérêts de l'après-guèrre, qui est encore loin de se calmer. Dans ce but, il a décidé d'introduire ces devises dans la Constitution. Par conséquent, les Gouvernements qui se succéderont au Pouvoir ne pourront pas se départir de ces principes. Les élus de la Nation ne pourront pas voter des lois non conformes à ces principes, ni accorder leur vote de confiance à un cabinet qui s'en écarterait.

L'article 3 du nouveau programme est donc ainsi conçu:

«Lois fondamentales de l'État: La Turquie est une République nationaliste, populiste-démocratique, étatiste, laïque et révolutionnaire (radicale).»

C'est donc dans ce sens que devra être modifié l'article premier de la loi fondamentale qui stipule tout simplement que l'État turc est une République.[4] Cet article premier de la loi fondamentale, d'après le dernier paragraphe de l'article 102 de la même loi, échappe à toute proposition de modification.

Il en résulte que tant que le régime lui-même ne sera pas renversé par une révolution, aucune Assemblée nationale ni aucun cabinet n'auront le droit ni le pouvoir d'agir contrairement aux principes qui forment la base du Kemalisme.

Reste à savoir si, après la modification de l'article premier, on ne jugera pas opportun de modifier aussi l'article 102 qui interdit toute modification ou proposition de modification de l'article premier. Il est fort possible que cette interdiction de modification de la loi fondamentale demeure toujours réservée seulement au républicanisme.

Après la stabilisation du régime, il y aura a réaliser l'intégration du Parti avec l'État. Il est vrai que les organes du Parti dans tout le pays ont été toujours en contact direct avec les organes de l'État. Une collaboration permanente s'était déjà établie entre les fonctionnaires de l'État et les représentants autorisés du Parti du Peuple, mais cette collaboration n'était appuyée sur aucun règlement et n'était basée sur aucun texte de loi, ce qui pourrait donner lieu de temps à autre à des malentendus ou même à des conflits. Maintenant, par les articles 35, 36 et 97 nouvellement introduits dans les statuts du Parti, celui-ci devient une partie intégrante de l'État. Désormais, Parti et Gouvernement formeront un corps un et indivisible. Le Gouvernement aura comme mission de gouverner d'après les directives et les principes du Parti et l'organisation du Parti se fera un devoir d'aider par tous les moyens dont il dispose à la réussite du Gouvernement dans l'accomplissement de sa mission. Ainsi donc, le travail des fonctionnaires du Gouvernement sera complété par le concours effectif des organes du Parti qui a de vastes ramifications hiérarchiquement organisées dans toutes les parties du pays. Tous les membres du Parti doivent aide et collaboration au Gouvernement.

Les statuts du Parti prévoient les dispositions nécessaires pour que le contact entre ces deux forces, qui se complètent l'une par l'autre, se fasse dans les meilleures conditions possibles. Ainsi, par exemple, d'après les status, seulement les chefs représentatifs de ces deux forces peuvent prendre contact entre eux. À Ankara, c'est seulement le secrétaire général du Parti qui peut s'aboucher ou correspondre avec les membres du Cabinet, chacun de ces derniers ayant à harmoniser avec le Parti ce qui concerne les affaires ressortissant de son ministère. Dans les provinces, le contact a lieu seulement entre le Gouverneur général et le Président du Conseil d'administration du Parti.

Il est bien évident que chacune des réalisations prévues pour la période quaternaire prochaine constitue une révolution en elle-même et on pourrait peut-être croire qu'il sera difficile d'en venir à bout dans un laps de temps si court. Mais ceux qui connaissent les méthodes de travail d'Atatürk et des lieutenants formés à son image, ceux qui savent que le Parti n'inscrit dans son programme que des choses dont l'exécution est préparée et assurée d'avance, ne doutent pas que ces articles du nouveau programme seront bientôt transformés comme par enchantement en réalités vivantes.

Le Kemalisme, pp. 164-167

À LA LUMIÈRE DES RÉALITÉS

Maintenant que nous avons vu comment le Kemalisme s'est développé pendant quinze ans, que nous avons vu la réalité, que nous avons passé en revue les différentes révolutions qu'il a accomplies, les divers états de métamorphoses par lesquels il est passé, il ne nous sera pas du tout difficile d'en dégager la doctrine et l'idéologie qui l'animent. Nous tenons à souligner tout spécialement ce point: la doctrine et l'idéologie kemalistes ne peuvent être définies qu'à la lumière des faits et des réalités précises. Car, comme nous avons eu l'occasion de l'expliquer, les idées et les principes kemalistes ne peuvent pas être condensés dans des mots et des formules classiques. Si l'on fait cas de ces formules que l'on emploie pourtant faute de mieux et à titre simplement indicatif, on sera porté à croire que le Kemalisme est plein de contrastes. Citons, à titre d'exemple, quelques cas typiques: Le Kemalisme est-il démocratique? Oui, puisque l'affirmation de la démocratie est l'une des six devises du Parti. Pourtant, nous voyons très souvent qu'il ne l'est pas. Ses porte-parole les plus autorisés n'hésitent pas à dénigrer publiquement la démocratie toutes les fois que l'occasion se présente. Ce n'est un secret pour personne que le Kemalisme est un régime autoritaire et partisan d'une discipline très rigoureuse, ce qui est précisément le contraire des principes démocratiques envisagés selon la conception classique. Le Kemalisme est-il libéral? Oui, puisqu'il est républicain jusqu'à la moelle des os et qu'il a comme principe fondamental le bien-être et la prospérité du peuple. Pourtant, dans la pratique, la liberté de l'individu est limitée. L'intervention de l'État s'étend à toutes les branches de l'activité nationale. Le Kemalisme est-il nationaliste? Oui, et farouchement. Le nationalisme constitue même une des principales devises du Parti. Pourtant, toutes les traditions considérées comme nationales s'écroulent ou se volatilisent, les institutions les plus profondément enracinées chez le peuple sont démolies les unes après les autres sans aucun scrupule. Ainsi donc, le Kemalisme ne serait fait que de contrastes, d'incompatibilités entre la réalité et l'idéologie.

Voilà pourquoi nous ne pouvons parler de la doctrine et de l'idéologie kemalistes qu'en ayant la réalité en vue et en prenant en considération que les mots et les formules classiques dans la bouche des dirigeants kemalistes ont un sens et une signification tout à fait différents de ceux employés ailleurs. C'est là une des raisons pour lesquelles le Kemalisme s'est abstenu de publier un programme défini, ayant des contours précis, avant de se mettre à l'œuvre. Un programme ne peut être exprimé que par des mots qui sont, pour la plupart, trompeurs et fallacieux. L'illusion des mots, le mirage des formules fallacieuses, ce sont là des pièges que les dirigeants kemalistes ont réussi toujours à éviter.

Le Parti du Peuple a tracé, dès le premier moment, un programme minimum dans lequel figurent entre autres les six devises, les six flèches symboliques qui constituent la base du Kemalisme, à savoir:

1) Républicanisme; 2) Nationalisme; 3) Laïcisme; 4) Étatisme; 5) Démocratie; 6) Révolutionnarisme.

Chacune de ces formules exprime un esprit qui est plus ou moins analogue à celui qui est employé ailleurs, mais la conception, la procédure, les moyens d'action employés sont tout à fait différents.

A ce propos, il est utile de rappeler ici l'importance qu'il faut attribuer à la juste désignation des mots et des formules. Cette question qui a fait l'objet de longues dissertations dans le Congrès sur l'avenir de l'esprit européen, à Paris en 1933, revêt une importance spéciale lorsqu'on examine la façon dont les formules classiques sont appliquées dans la nouvelle Turquie. Le comte Keyserling, dans son livre sur *La Révolution mondiale*, cite à ce propos le passage suivant d'un auteur chinois du IIIe siècle av. J.-C.:

«Si les désignations sont justes, l'ordre règne, mais si les désignations sont troublées, le désordre. Celui qui provoque la confusion des désignations corrompt la langue. Alors les choses permises prennent la place des choses défendues, l'exactitude de l'inexactitude, la justesse de la non-justesse et la fausseté de la non-fausseté. Lorsque les maîtres des hommes sont de la basse espèce et que pourtant ils appliquent des mesures nobles en apparence, lorsqu'ils semblent donner audience au bien et faire ce qui est permis, tout le mal vient de ce fait: ce qu'ils appellent noble correspond à la bassesse, ce qui est bien à leurs yeux correspond à la dépravation et ce qu'ils nomment permis est en réalité ce qui contredit à l'ordre.»

L'auteur chinois d'il y a vingt-trois siècles exprime ici une vérité profonde, dont l'importance n'a pu qu'augmenter depuis lors au fur et à mesure que les relations entre les peuples se sont développées, que la culture a pris un caractère universel et international et que les expressions employées dans un pays donné, passent à l'usage d'autres pays et d'autres nations qui vivent dans des circonstances différentes, et doivent tenir compte de conditions et de réalités spéciales. Plus la culture devient universelle, plus l'interdépendance des peuples, par la fréquence des relations, se généralise, plus encore les formules classiques et générales deviennent autant de sources de confusion et d'incompréhension parmi les peuples.

Ainsi donc, répétons-le, en cherchant à comprendre ce que les idéologues kemalistes entendent par nationalisme, démocratie, libéralisme, nous devons faire abstraction du sens que les autres nations attribuent à ces termes et chercher à comprendre le sens que les idéologues kemalistes lui attribuent.

Le Kemalisme, pp. 171-174

L'ÉTATISME

Nous abordons à présent un sujet des plus délicats et en même temps des plus importants. Le Parti du Peuple se proclame étatiste. Dans le programme du Parti, la flèche symbolique de l'étatisme, voisine avec celle de la démocratie. Comment ces deux ennemis réputés mortels et implacables arrivent-ils à faire bon ménage sous le même toit?

La clé de l'énigme, nous la trouvons toujours dans la structure spéciale du peuple et du pays, telle que nous l'avons exposée dans le chapitre précédent, ainsi que dans le principe du régime kemaliste:

«Mieux vaut prévenir que guérir.»

Il n'y a pas de doute que c'est le libéralisme inhérent au régime démocratique, la liberté de l'individu, l'initiative privée qui ont assuré les énormes progrès réalisés dans le monde occidental dans tous les domaines de l'activité humaine, depuis la Renaissance.

La Révolution française, ainsi que les autres qui l'ont suivie dans différents autres pays, ont proclamé «Les Droits de l'Homme,» abolissant les privilèges des castes qui avaient entre leurs mains la force de l'État. L'homme, l'individu, le citoyen, grâce à la liberté et à l'égalité qui lui ont été assurées par le régime démocratique, a pu développer toutes ses facultés morales et intellectuelles et, dans l'espace de moins d'un siècle, a réalisé dans tous les domaines, dans les sciences, dans les arts, dans l'agriculture, dans l'industrie et dans toutes les branches de l'activité humaine, des progrès immenses, en créant ce que nous appelons la culture moderne. Mais, comme il n'y a pas de principe, fut-ce le meilleur, qui ne renferme dans son sein le germe de sa propre destruction, le libre épanouissement de l'individu et l'égalité des droits, ont abouti aux inégalités sociales qui constituent le plus grand malheur dont pâtit l'humanité, à l'heure actuelle: accumulation de fortunes d'un côté et aggravation du paupérisme de l'autre.

Le Kemalisme, en s'acheminant vers l'Occident, en s'appropriant le régime démocratique, n'a pas voulu avancer les yeux fermés. Il a bien vu le triste spectacle du capitalisme se dressant comme un vampire contre le paupérisme. A quoi bon, s'est-il dit, sauver la Nation de l'esclavage politique, pour la laisser tomber dans l'esclavage capitaliste?

C'est pour cette raison qu'Atatürk lui-même, en défendant la nouvelle loi fondamentale de 1er janvier 1920, devant la Grande Assemblée Nationale, s'est écrié:

«Nous sommes de ceux qui tiennent à lutter en tant que collectivité nationale contre le capitalisme qui veut nous engloutir.»

Il s'agissait justement des libertés démocratiques et c'est précisément alors qu'Atatürk a vu le danger inhérent a toute démocratie et lui a déclaré la guerre au nom de la collectivité nationale.

Empressons-nous d'ajouter que la lutte contre le capitalisme se poursuit d'ordinaire à l'intérieur des frontières du pays. Divisé en deux camps adverses, le peuple est en proie à une guerre civile perpétuelle. Les prolétaires qui se croient exploités par les patrons, ne cessent pas d'attaquer avec plus ou moins de violence le bastion du capitalisme. L'État qui a comme mission de protéger l'ordre social établi s'érige le plus souvent en protecteur des patrons et, au besoin, emploie la force contre les assaillants. S'agissant d'une lutte interne entre citoyens, la neutralité de l'État peut se défendre selon le point de vue où l'on se place. Garantir l'épanouissement de l'individu, laisser libre jeu à l'initiative individuelle, défendre la légalité, l'ordre social et économique existant, garder sa neutralité dans la lutte entre adversaires d'un même pays, ce sont des points de vues qui peuvent se justifier dans un régime démocratique libéral. Mais tel n'est pas le cas en ce qui concerne la nouvelle Turquie. Le capitalisme contre lequel la nouvelle Turquie a dû déclarer la guerre, contre lequel elle a dû se dresser de toutes ses forces morales et matérielles, avait le caractère d'un ennemi étranger. C'est contre le capitalisme étranger qui s'apprêtait à s'implanter dans le pays qu'Atatürk a dû se défendre, en lui opposant la force de l'État organisé et toutes les ressources de la collectivité.

Nous n'avons pas besoin de rappeler une fois de plus, que la situation économique léguée à la nouvelle Turquie par l'Empire ottoman démembré, était des plus lamentables. L'agriculture dont vivaient les quatre-cinquièmes de la population était à l'état primitif. Presque tous les pays agricoles en Europe, dans les Balkans, dans l'Amérique du Nord et dans l'Amérique du Sud, pratiquaient la culture intensive, la culture mécanisée. Seul, le cultivateur turc continuait à gratter la terre avec son antique charrue, et n'obtenait après un dur labeur, que le tiers ou le quart des produits que l'on pouvait obtenir ailleurs d'un même lopin de terre. La Turquie qui possédait des terres arables et pouvait produire assez de céréales pour toute l'Europe, était très souvent obligée d'en importer pour nourrir sa population. Le cultivateur n'obtenant jamais une contre-valeur suffisante de ses produits agricoles pour payer les produits industriels qu'il achetait à la ville, et qui étaient presque tous importés de l'étranger, ne pouvait que s'endetter auprès des usuriers. Ainsi, la misère de la grande majorité du peuple ne faisait qu'augmenter de jour en jour. La balance commerciale du pays accusait depuis longtemps un passif annuel considérable qui était, sous l'Empire, couvert par des emprunts à jet continu. Ainsi, l'appauvrissement du pays, l'asservissement vis-à-vis de l'étranger ne pouvaient que s'accentuer.

La marche du pays vers l'occidentalisme ne pouvait qu'accroître les besoins du peuple. Plus une population est éclairée, plus ses besoins sont grands. L'industrie étant presque inexistante dans le pays, l'importation des produits industriels de l'étranger ne pouvait qu'augmenter et, par conséquent, le passif de la balance commerciale ne pouvait que s'accentuer.

Le commerce et la finance étaient aussi, pour la plupart, entre les mains des étrangers ou des élements non-turcs. L'épargne était inexistante ou s'était réfugiée à l'étranger par l'entremise des banques étrangères qui avaient un monopole de fait.

Le Traité de Lausanne avait beau rendre à la Turquie son indépendance économique sur le papier. Par quels moyens la réaliser? Avec quels capitaux? Où étaient les forces et les ressources de technique avancée dont disposent les pays occidentaux? Où étaient les personnes capables de créer les grandes entreprises industrielles et économiques, les grands travaux de technique avancée dont le pays avait grandement besoin pour se relever et échapper au joug économique de l'étranger? Peut-on recruter des capitaines d'industrie, des jongleurs de millions, des Ford et des Citroën dans une population, qui, pendant des siècles, n'a pu produire que des fonctionnaires, des gendarmes ou des rentiers? Il va sans dire que, dans ces conditions, si la nouvelle Turquie laissait le champ libre au libéralisme et à l'individualisme qui font partie intégrantes de la démocratie classique, cela n'aurait pu l'être qu'au profit du capitalisme étranger. Déjà pendant la Conférence de Lausanne, le délégué d'une Grande Puissance qui ne voulait pas se résigner à passer l'éponge sur le Traité de Sèvres, n'a pas pu se retenir de laisser tomber de ses lèvres ces paroles édifiantes, tout en redressant son monocle sur son oeil narquois:

«Vous, les Turcs, vous pouvez supprimer les capitulations, mais sachez qu'il ne se passera pas longtemps, elles seront rétablies sur votre demande.»

Ce délégué avec lequel Ismet Pacha a eu continuellement maille à partir n'avait pas tort. La situation financière et économique était si lamentable qu'on ne pouvait pas espérer que la Turquie pourrait se relever sans le concours le plus large de l'Europe. Le prix de ce concours aurait été certainement le rétablissement des fameuses capitulations, en d'autres termes de l'esclavage économique et financier, tel que nous l'avons connu du temps de l'Empire.

Ces paroles sarcastiques n'ont provoqué le moindre effet sur celui qui représentait la volonté et le dynamisme de 15 millions de Néo-Turcs, incarnés par leur chef Kamal Atatürk. Comme le personnage de la Bible qui est monté sur la montagne pour proférer des malédictions, ne put prononcer que des bénédictions; le délégué ennemi le plus têtu, en voulant décourager le délégué turc ainsi que le peuple qu'il représentait, n'a fait que renforcer et exalter l'élan impétueux du Néo-Turc vers la lutte pour l'indépendance morale et matérielle qui a commencé immédiatement après le Traité de Lausanne. Ces paroles gravées dans la mémoire du Néo-Turc, attiraient continuellement son attention sur la profondeur de l'abîme dans lequel il devait tomber s'il trébuchait dans sa marche en avant vers l'indépendance.

Mais, diront les individualistes, dans tous les pays démocrates d'Europe et d'Amérique, qui a créé la technique avancée, les grandes entreprises, la grande industrie et tout ce qui fait la force de l'économie moderne? C'est toujours l'initiative privée. L'initiative privée a accumulé les capitaux, a réalisé des inventions techniques. A-t-on jamais eu besoin d'une intervention de l'État pour créer les richesses dont sont inondés aujourd'hui les pays occidentaux? Pourquoi voulez-vous qu'en Turquie les choses se passent autrement?

Les individualistes perdent de vue le point le plus essentiel: autres temps, autres moeurs, dit la sagesse des nations, et on peut ajouter: «Autres temps, autres lois, autres principes et autres politiques.» Le développement de l'économie moderne par l'initiative privée a mis plus d'un siècle pour arriver au niveau actuel. Le monde entier se trouvant alors au même niveau arriéré, il n'y avait pas de raison pour précipiter la marche et brûler les étapes. L'initiative privée pouvait prendre son temps et suivre l'évolution naturelle des choses.

Or, ce n'est pas le cas pour la nouvelle Turquie. Elle avait souffert pendant des siècles d'un sommeil léthargique. Elle s'est réveillée brusquement au milieu d'un monde complètement mécanisé. Tout, autour d'elle, des colosses en fer et en acier produisent des richesses immenses. Fallait-il faire comme les autres nations, attendre un siècle pour que l'initiative privée accumulât des capitaux, préparât le matériel humain et les conditions économiques nécessaires pour la création des richesses? Entre temps, l'esclavage économique se serait implanté dans la nouvelle Turquie avec plus de force que dans l'ancienne. Sous le joug du capitalisme étranger, l'initiative privée turque aurait-elle pu jamais lever la tête et aspirer a l'indépendance?

L'esprit réaliste et positif de Tchan-Kaya[5] ne pouvait pas s'abandonner à de pareilles chimères. Il n'a pas hésité un seul moment à reconnaître que la Turquie nouvelle avait besoin d'une révolution économique et une révolution ne se fait pas par l'initiative privée, par l'individu matérialiste, égoïste et calculateur. La révolution économique ne pouvait s'effectuer que par la même force impétueuse qui avait réalisé la révolution politique et la révolution sociale: La Nation, la collectivité.

Cette force qui a réalisé des miracles dans le domaine politique et social, pourquoi ne ferait-elle pas preuve, dans le domaine économique du même esprit d'abnégation, du même dynamisme créateur? Les individus d'élite et bien doués ne seraient certainement pas poussés par l'aiguillon de l'intérêt privé, mais par le dynamisme de la révolution, l'enthousiasme collectif qui est mille fois plus fort et plus efficace que l'intérêt privé, qui pousse des millions d'individus vers les champs de bataille pour affronter la mort. Il n'y a que l'enthousiasme collectif qui est capable de changer l'individu matérialiste et égoïste en homme d'idéal, d'abnégation et d'héroïsme. Cet esprit d'idéalisme et d'abnégation qui se manifeste sur le champ de bataille grâce à l'enthousiasme collectif, pourquoi se déroberait-il lorsqu'il s'agit de sauver la Nation de l'esclavage économique et du joug étranger?

Voilà en quoi consiste le miracle réalisé dans ce domaine par Atatürk et ses collaborateurs. L'enthousiasme collectif des temps de guerre qui, d'ordinaire, s'éteint et s'épuise aussitôt que l'on met bas les armes, a été canalisé avec une habileté remarquable vers la vie civile, vers le champ de bataille de la vie sociale et de la vie économique.

Après la guerre mondiale, après que les canons eurent cessé de tonner et que la vie quotidienne eut repris, Lloyd George avait déclaré:

«En pleine paix, l'union sacrée, l'enthousiasme collectif pour faire de la patrie un pays digne de ses héros, c'est un miracle encore inconnu.»

Eh bien, ce miracle qui était encore inconnu lorsque Lloyd George prononça ces justes paroles, s'est produit dans la Turquie nouvelle. L'enthousiasme collectif de Doumlou-Pounar et de Sakaria a survécu à la paix. Il s'est transformé en héroïsme sans armes, en une providence panthéiste, toujours présente là où son intervention était utile.

Ce serait sortir du cadre de ce travail que d'énumérer ici tout ce que le Kemalisme a pu réaliser dans le domaine économique grâce à l'intervention de l'État. Cela peut faire l'objet d'un volume spécial. La construction en quelques années de milliers de kilomètres de voies ferrées, la création d'une épargne nationale de plusieurs dizaines de millions – chose qui n'avait jamais existé en Turquie – la substitution des banques nationales aux banques étrangères qui avaient le monopole de la finance, la tranformation en balance active de la balance commerciale avec l'étranger, la création, en une dizaine d'années, de trois fabriques de sucre qui produisent tout le sucre dont le pays a besoin, de fabriques textiles dont la production a quintuplé en dix ans; le maintien d'une monnaie saine stabilisée de fait depuis sept ans, sans avoir recours à la contrainte légale, etc., ce sont autant de succès remarquables qui ne pouvaient pas être obtenus sans le dynamisme collectif inspiré par l'esprit Kemaliste.

Nous devons cependant faire une mention spéciale des réalisations de l'Étatisme kemaliste dans le domaine industriel où il prend la forme d'un véritable socialisme d'État. Là, nous voyons l'État faire le capitaliste, l'entrepreneur et le commerçant.

La nouvelle Turquie a aussi son plan quinquennal qui se trouve en voie de réalisation depuis quatre ans. Le plan quinquennal kemaliste diffère essentiellement de celui des Soviets par le fait qu'il est appliqué sous la forme d'économie privée. Les industries créées par l'État sont gérées par des sociétés anonymes soumises exactement comme toutes les autres sociétés similaires en économie privée, aux dispositions y relatives du Code de Commerce. Le contrôle et la surveillance exercés dans les autres sociétés par les actionnaires, sont exercés par l'État, non pas en tant qu'État, mais en sa qualité d'actionnaire.

Ainsi donc, les organes chargés de l'application du plan quinquennal jouissent de la liberté d'action et de tous les avantages qu'on attribue d'ordinaire à l'économie privée, tout en étant contrôlés et surveillés non pas par une foule d'actionnaires très souvent inconsciente, incohérente et, disons le mot, oligarchique, mais par une force parfaitement organisée, consciente et vigilante, qui a nom: État.

Le Kemalisme, pp. 190-198

La seule controverse possible en ce qui concerne notre Étatisme ne pourrait se référer, comme nous l'avons vu, qu'au monde d'application du régime étatiste, aux proportions et à la mesure de son étendue. Le principe en lui-même ne peut nullement être l'objet d'une controverse quelconque, ni au point de vue théorique, ni au point de vue pratique.

Mais, avant d'entrer dans le fond de la question, nous devons faire ressortir que, lorsqu'il est question chez nous d'Étatisme, nous n'entendons pas seulement l'Étatisme économique, qui est certainement le principal, nous entendons aussi l'Étatisme social et culturel, chose presque inconnue dans les autres pays. C'est grâce à l'intervention et au concours de l'État, surtout à celui de son chef, – pour ne citer que quelques exemples typiques – que l'histoire turque a été reconstituée, que la langue et l'alphabet turcs ont été rénovés, que la société turque tout entière a été régénérée. Ailleurs, toute intervention de l'autorité de l'État, dans le domaine culturel et scientifique, soulèverait de violentes protestations. L'histoire, la langue, la culture en général – dirait-on – sont des matières qui relèvent de la compétence et de l'autorité scientifiques. C'est l'affaire des spécialistes. L'autorité de l'État, incompétent en la matière, n'y peut être que nuisible.

En effet, ce sont là des idées qui, en théorie, sont très justes et dont on tient parfaitement compte dans tous les pays libres ou libéraux. Mais chez nous, les choses se passent autrement. Chez nous, les compétences sont incorporées dans les cadres de l'État.

Nous sommes en période de révolution. Cette révolution est dirigée par l'État, c'est-a-dire par le chef de l'État et les cadres dont il est entouré. Les savants, les spécialistes et les compétences les plus en vue font partie des cadres. Ainsi donc, l'État n'est pas modelé à l'image de la Nation, mais la Nation est modelée à l'image de l'État.

Pour expliquer l'Étatisme kemaliste, il ne suffit pas de mettre en avant des formules classiques, telles que socialisme d'État, économie dirigée, etc., car la Nouvelle Turquie entend par Étatisme, diriger non seulement l'économie, mais aussi la société et la vie culturelle. Rien ne doit être laissé au hasard. L'État n'est pas là pour faire seulement la police, comme l'entendent les partisans du libéralisme classique, mais pour organiser de haut en bas toute la vie de la Nation. Il doit suivre de près toutes les pulsations de son cœur et déterminer en conséquence la conduite de sa vie. L'individu n'est pas le centre de la vie, comme le prétendent les anthropocentristes en régime libéral. La liberté individuelle ne peut jouer que dans le cadre de la société, en l'espèce l'État.

Le trait d'union entre l'État et la Nation, c'est le Parti. Après une longue période d'expériences, le Kemalisme a adopté le système du Parti unique et c'est le peuple tout entier qui s'est prononcé pour ce système. On a pendant longtemps, laissé le champ libre à l'activité d'autres partis politiques. Lors de la formation du «Parti Libéral,» sous l'oeil indulgent d'Atatürk lui-même, le Parti gouvernemental et le nouveau Parti d'opposition entrèrent tous les deux dans la bataille électorale, en se mettant sous l'égide d'Atatürk. Les électeurs ont voté pour l'un ou pour l'autre Parti, selon qu'ils croyaient qu'Atatürk était d'un côté ou de l'autre. Ce faisant, le peuple s'est prononcé pour le Parti unique, le Parti d'Atatürk, le Parti dont le chef et l'animateur est Atatürk lui-même.

Depuis lors, le Parti du Peuple a été intégré de fait à l'État. Depuis lors, Parti et État ne font plus qu'un. Ils ont des attributions et des devoirs qui se complètent les uns les autres. L'État a entre ses mains le gouvernail du navire, mais le Parti en a la boussole. Le Parti, qui renferme dans son sein des centaines de milliers de membres sélectionnés, répartis en cellules, par lesquelles il est en contact intime et permanent avec toutes les couches de la Société turque, observe et stabilise les aspirations de la Nation et se rend compte de ses besoins. Les vœux émis par les plus humbles citoyens auprès du Parti, qui a des sections bien organisées dans chaque secteur administratif, sont examinés à la loupe par les dirigeants du Parti, distillés un à un par des commissions spéciales et ceux qui sont retenus, comme dignes d'être pris en considération, sont portés officiellement à l'attention des ministres responsables qui donnent suite ou rejettent en expliquant les motifs de leur décision.

Cette activité du Parti est très avantageusement complétée par celle des Maisons du Peuple qui se trouvent sous l'égide et sous le contrôle du Parti.

Les plus petites localités en Anatolie possèdent aujourd'hui leurs Maisons du Peuple confortablement installées et solidement organisées. L'accès de ces Maisons est libre et gratuit pour tous les citoyens affiliés ou non au Parti. Les plus humbles citoyens peuvent les fréquenter pour entendre les conférences, les concerts populaires, lire les journaux et les livres et assister à des représentations théâtrales, données par des amateurs, discuter librement avec leurs amis et connaissances les questions d'actualité d'ordre politique, social ou économique. Les dirigeants du Parti y frayent librement avec toutes les classes de la population, entendent leurs doléances, se rendent compte de leurs mentalités et profitent de toutes les occasions pour leur inculquer les idées et les principes kemalistes et entretenir chez eux toujours vivant l'esprit et le dynamisme de la révolution.

Dans les villes plus ou moins importantes, les Maisons du Peuple publient même des périodiques destinés à la vulgarisation de toutes sortes de connaissances utiles et instructives et à la propagation des idées et des principes kemalistes.

Les passages suivants du discours d'ouverture de la première Maison du Peuple à Ankara, prononcé le 19 février 1932 par le secrétaire général du Parti du Peuple, suffisent pour nous faire comprendre dans quel esprit et vers quel but évolue l'activité des 80 Maisons du Peuple qui se trouvent en plein développement dans toutes les parties du pays:

«Le but poursuivi par le Parti en fondant les Maisons du Peuple, c'est d'organiser la Nation et d'en faire une société d'hommes conscients, liés par l'amitié et la compréhension réciproque et qui poursuivent le même idéal. Nos concitoyens qui ont eu les moyens et la possibilité de s'instruire, de s'éclairer et de se former y pourront servir de guide à ceux des nôtres qui n'ont pas eu ce bonheur. L'élite de notre peuple n'est pas encore habituée à consacrer une partie de son temps à l'activité sociale pour le bien de la collectivité. Un maître d'école, lorqu'il remplit consciencieusement sa fonction, pense qu'il ne doit plus rien à la société, au milieu dans lequel il vit. Nous voulons mettre fin à cette mentalité bizarre et nuisible et nous habituer à travailler en commun pour le bien de la société. Sous les toits des Maisons du Peuple imbues de l'atmosphère vivifiante de la camaraderie, nous cesserons de vivre en individus isolés pour nous former en masses compactes, unies et cohérentes, marchant vers un but et un idéal commun.»

Lors du 3e anniversaire de la fondation des Maisons du Peuple, le ministre-président Ismet Inönü s'est exprimé en ces termes:

«Ce dont notre patrie a été privée depuis des siècles, c'est la possibilité de réunir ses concitoyens comme les membres de la même famille pour travailler en commun aux œuvres destinées au relèvement de la collectivité. Nos Maisons du Peuple comblent cette lacune séculaire de notre patrie. Aujourd'hui, après trois années d'activité, nous pouvons affirmer avec certitude que les Maisons du Peuple s'acquittent avec un parfait succès de la mission éducative qui leur est confiée.»

Necip Ali, chef de la section culturelle du Parti du Peuple, a été en mesure de déclarer en mars 1934 dans un discours de circonstance que, dans l'espace d'une année, 915 conférences publiques ont été données dans les Maisons du Peuple. Les représentations théâtrales, pendant la même période, s'élèvent à 511 et le nombre d'assistants a été de 478,000. Il y a eu, en outre, 375 concerts musicaux auxquels ont assisté 500,000 personnes. La plupart des Maisons du Peuple ont leurs bibliothèques populaires possédant ensemble 60,000 volumes lus régulièrement par 150,000 lecteurs enregistrés.

Les aspirations et les besoins du peuple ne sont pas notés seulement par les organes du Parti, ils sont très fréquemment l'objet des observations directes d'Atatürk, du Premier ministre, Ismet Inönü, et de tous les ministres, qui font aussi souvent que possible des tournées d'étude en Anatolie et prennent directement contact avec le peuple, notent ses doléances et tâchent d'y donner suite dans la mesure du possible. C'est là une forme de démocratie dont on trouve rarement l'exemple dans les pays démocratiques et qui s'adapte parfaitement à la structure économique et sociale du pays.

Les candidats pour les élections administratives sont désignés par la même méthode sélective. Les membres du Parti votent librement pour les candidats qu'ils croient les plus dignes; la présidence du Parti désigne les candidats définitifs parmi les membres qui ont eu la majorité des voix et qui ont été considérés aptes par les Conseils hiérarchiques du Parti.

Les candidats pour les élections législatives aussi sont choisis par les sphères hiérarchiques et désignés définitivement par la présidence du Parti sur base de cette sélection.

Ce système fonctionnerait peut-être mal ailleurs et donnerait de piètres résultats, mais il fonctionne admirablement bien en Turquie. Voici ce qu'en dit un observateur objectif et impartial, comme le général Sherrill, déjà cité:

«Les Parlements ont généralement mauvaise presse, parce qu'ils deviennent des assemblées de discussions, ou parce que la crainte de n'être pas réélus semble aux parlementaires plus importante que les intérêts de la Nation entière. C'est donc un plaisir de certifier que l'Assemblée turque semble composée de tourte autre manière; elle comprend des hommes choisis pour leur valeur dans toutes les branches, l'industrie et la banque, les professions scientifiques et libérales.»

Le Kemalisme, pp. 219-225

LE NATIONALISME TURC

Maintenant que nous avons vu plus ou moins ce que signifie le nationalisme chez les différentes Nations et que nous avons obtenu ainsi des points de comparaison intéressants, nous pouvons examiner avec plus de clarté le nationalisme turc qui est à la base du Kemalisme et qui en constitue l'élément dynamique.

Pour commencer, hâtons-nous de le dire, le nationalisme kemaliste n'a rien de commun avec les autres movements similaires. Il n'est pas comparable à celui des Français, des Italiens, des Anglais, etc. Il est d'une nature différente, d'un caractère tout autre.

Comme nous l'avons vu plus haut, le ferment le plus puissant des principaux mouvements nationalistes, c'est le mysticisme qui se manifeste sous des formes et des couleurs différentes. Or, le mysticisme n'a pas le moindre prise sur le mouvement kemaliste. Celui-ci n'a jamais eu besoin de pareils excitants. Il suffit de suivre les différentes phases de son développement depuis sa naissance, pour nous convaincre que le nationalisme kemaliste n'a rien de factice ou de surnaturel et qu'il ne représente que l'épanouissement de l'instinct de conservation, ce qui est la chose la plus naturelle chez tous les hommes et même, en général, chez tous les êtres vivants.

Pour pouvoir suivre depuis le début l'épanouissement de cet instinct de conservation, nous devons rappeler avant tout qu'Atatürk est originaire de Salonique, qu'il a passé les premières années de sa jeunesse en Macédoine, et que les premiers remous du réveil de l'âme nationale chez les Turcs ont vu le jour dans cette région. Or, que se passait-il à cette époque-là en Macédoine?

C'était un champ de batailles perpétuelles, où des Grecs, des Bulgares, des Serbes, des Koutzo-Valaques, etc., s'entre-tuaient continuellement. Obéissant à un nationalisme acharné, et de plus en plus exalté, ces nationalités voulaient s'assurer la prédominance ethnique dans tel ou tel secteur de la Macédoine au moment du partage de la succession de «l'Homme Malade» dont on attendait la fin d'un moment à l'autre. Toutes ces nationalités ennemies avaient cependant un front commun contre les Turcs. Le Turc n'etait le maître que de nom. En réalité, il ne faisait que fonction de gendarme pour le compte de ses héritiers présomptifs. Ces derniers étaient les uns à la solde de la monarchie dualiste qui poursuivait sa politique traditionnelle de «Drang nach Osten,» et les autres à la solde de la Russie, championne de la politique panslaviste. Les meilleures forces de l'armée ottomane, les officiers les plus énergiques et les plus éclairés étaient affectés à la poursuite et à la répression des bandes terroristes chrétiennes qui fourmillaient un peu partout en Macédoine, terrorisaient la population et tâchaient d'exterminer les Turcs. La plupart des dirigeants actuels de la Turquie kemaliste ont passé les meilleures années de leur jeunesse à accomplir consciencieusement cette tâche ingrate et périlleuse. Ils ont vu plusieurs de leurs camarades tomber sous les balles ou les bombes perfides de ces bandes nationalistes.

L'activité des bandes terroristes dirigées par des comités nationalistes grecs, bulgares, serbes, koutzo-valaques, etc., n'a cessé que pendant un laps de temps très court, après l'établissement de la Constitution en 1908. Les premiers moments d'ivresse écoulés, la lutte contre les bandes terroristes reprit de plus belle. À l'activité terroriste des nationalistes chrétiens vint s'ajouter celle des nationalistes musulmans en Albanie, en Syrie, en Arabie et au Kurdistan. Pour ce qui concerne la Macédoine, ou plutôt la Turquie d'Europe, il faut citer en premier lieu le mouvement nationaliste albanais sous l'instigation du comité Bachkim dont les dirigeants se recrutaient en partie parmi les fonctionnaires et les dignitaires civils et militaires de la Turquie constitutionnelle, appartenant à la race albanaise.

Parmi toutes ces nationalités chrétiennes et musulmanes, il n'y avait que le maître nominal du pays, le Turc, qui n'eut pas encore sa conscience nationale suffisamment éveillée, et qui, de ce fait, fût condamné à succomber tôt ou tard dans la lutte des nationalités. Sa situation était d'autant plus précaire qu'il ne possédait même pas les éléments nécessaires pour pouvoir espérer le réveil définitif de sa conscience nationale. Sa langue ne contenait que très peu de mots essentiellement turcs, sa littérature se composait de pastiches de littérature arabe et persane et, vers les derniers temps, des plagiats des littératures occidentales. Son histoire, ce n'était que l'histoire de guerres, d'intrigues et de révolutions de Sérail. Les intellectuels et l'élite du peuple, ceux qui devaient être l'avant-garde du réveil national, étaient en grande partie subjugués par l'esprit théocratique et éparpillés dans différents milieux parmi lesquels figuraient les confréries religieuses qui, par leur essence même, étaient antinationales, non pas seulement à cause de leur credo théocratique, mais à cause de leur particularisme de clocher.

Le peuple turc dépourvu d'idéal national, s'est trouvé dans la situation d'un soldat sans armes au milieu d'une foule d'ennemis armés jusqu'aux dents. On voyait très bien que ce corps inerte au milieu de tant de nationalismes ardents pourrait être mis en morceaux dès que ses ennemis, héritiers présomptifs de l'Homme Malade, arriveraient à se mettre d'accord sur le partage de la succession. Une première fois, un accord éphémère intervint entre eux et il en résulta la Guerre Balkanique avec ses conséquences désastreuses pour la Turquie. Le Traité de Sèvres, c'était le coup de grâce, le dénouement fatal de cette tragédie qui n'avait que trop duré. Un peuple millénaire de conquérants était condamné à l'esclavage sous le joug de ceux qui furent ses propres sujets.

C'en était assez pour secouer, une fois pour toutes, l'apathie séculaire. On assiste au réveil explosif de l'instinct de conservation d'un peuple de conquérants. Le mot de ralliement: «L'indépendance ou la mort,» lancé par Atatürk dès qu'il eut débarqué à Samsoun en 1919, tomba comme une étincelle dans une poudrière. L'indépendance ou la mort, répétaient à l'unisson, toutes les classes de la population turque.

L'indépendance? Il y avait des Turcs patriotes qui n'en voulaient pas. Après l'occupation de Constantinople par les Alliés, en proie à un désarroi indescriptible, ils se faisaient le raisonnement suivant:

«Nous sommes incapables de nous gouverner nous-mêmes. Notre passé séculaire le prouve. Nous sommes criblés de dettes et nous n'avons pas les moyens d'exploiter et de mettre en valeur les ressources naturelles dont nous disposons. Plaçons-nous donc sous le protectorat de l'Amérique, ainsi nous serons sauvés des griffes des puissances victorieuses qui sont en train de se partager la succession de l'empire en déconfiture. On mettra à notre disposition des millions de dollars pour exploiter nos resources naturelles, etc.»

Atatürk laissa passer les premiers moments de désarroi et se mit sans perdre de temps à organiser les forces nationales, les seules sur lesquelles on pouvait compter pour avoir l'indépendance intégrale. Ses fidèles collaborateurs finirent par comprendre qu'il avait parfaitement raison, que si on n'obtenait pas l'indépendance complète grâce aux forces nationales, c'était la mort.

La devise pathétique: l'indépendance ou la mort, très souvent répétée par Atatürk aux moments les plus critiques de l'histoire, resonne encore dans les oreilles du peuple turc, et c'est pour cela que ce peuple sent d'instinct, pour ainsi dire, qu'à l'avenir aussi, s'il n'assure pas son indépendance nationale, appuyé uniquement sur des forces nationales morales et matérielles, il va à la mort: c'est là le véritable sens du nationalisme turc.

La mort, le peuple turc l'a vue venir. Il en a même senti les griffes hideuses qui ont effleuré sa peau. Les étranges sensations qui l'ont envahi à ce moment tragique sont encore toutes fraîches dans sa mémoires.

Un peuple qui a d'un passé récent de si tragiques souvenirs, a-t-il besoin de recourir à des forces mystiques et à des sentiments de vanité nationale, à des exaltations artificielles et autres éléments de ce genre pour alimenter et ranimer son nationalisme? L'instinct de conservation auquel il doit son indépendance actuelle lui suffit amplement pour comprendre le sens de profond réalisme qui caractérise son sentiment national. Ce réalisme est une réaction contre la mystique religieuse qui avait traîné la Nation jusqu'au bord de l'âbîme.

S'il faut donner un nom caractéristique au nationalisme turc, on peut bien l'appeler le nationalisme de réaction. Du reste, chacune des six devises du Parti du Peuple est le résultat d'une réaction:

La nouvelle Turquie est laïque par réaction contre l'ancien régime, contre le passé néfaste qui était obscurantiste et théocratique. Elle ne peut pas perdre de vue que, si le Turc avait perdu sa conscience nationale, c'était parce que celle-ci était subjuguée et obstruée par la conscience religieuse qui l'avait maintenu à l'écart de la culture et de la civilisation occidentales, que c'était au nom de certains prejugés d'ordre religieux que la femme turque, la moitié du contingent national, était condamnée à se morfondre derrière les grilles du harem, a pâtir dans l'ignorance et à passer sa vie dans la soumission et l'esclavage.

La Nouvelle Turquie est democratique. Elle est pour l'égalité sociale parce qu'une des plaies principales de l'ancien régime, c'était justement l'inégalité sociale.

S'il est vrai qu'il n'y avait pas sous l'ancien régime une aristocratie de naissance, comme c'était le cas lors de la renaissance occidentale, il n'en est pas moins vrai que la société turque subissait l'oppression d'une double aristocratie: l'aristocratie théocratique et l'aristocratie économico-sociale.

L'aristocratie théocratique était composée des représentants du culte et de la religion de tous grades et de toutes catégories. C'étaient pour la plupart des ignorants et des incapables, mais ils parlaient au nom d'Allah et avaient sur le peuple une espèce d'influence occulte. Les représentants de la religion, c'étaient les patriciens et le reste du peuple, c'etait la plèbe. Une grande partie de cette plèbe était enrégimentée dans les confréries religieuses qui comptaient des milliers d'adeptes, se soumettant aveuglément aux ordres et aux volontés des chefs, les Chéikhs.

L'aristocratie économico-sociale était composée des grands propriétaires des terres, des affermeurs des dîmes, etc., qui se comportaient en féodaux et étaient désignés sous le nom de «Mutégalibés,» c'est-à-dire oppresseurs.

Il faut avoir suivi la campagne intense menée par toute la presse turque contre ces Mutégalibés, dès que la constitution de 1908 eût assuré la liberté de la presse, pour comprendre jusqu'à quel point la Nation était opprimée par cette classe privilégiée.

Exception faite de quelques grandes ville comme Istanbul et Izmir, presque dans toutes les villes de province, ils étaient les maîtres. Ils puisaient leurs forces soit dans leur situation de grands propriétaires de terres, soit dans leurs accointances avec les hauts fonctionnaires. Plusieurs d'entre eux s'imposaient par leur intelligence, flanquée d'un tempérament audacieux et remuant. Avant l'abolition de la dîme, c'étaient toujours ces Mutégalibés qui s'en faisaient affermer la perception. S'agissant d'un système de perception qui laissait le champ libre à l'arbitraire pratiqué sur une grande échelle, le producteur devait toujours passer sous les fourches caudines de cette espèce de féodaux qui s'arrangeaient pour en percevoir très souvent jusqu'au double et même jusqu'au triple de ce qu'ils devaient verser au fisc. Ainsi, très souvent, plus de la moité de la récolte passait entre leurs mains. Une fois leur fortune acquise et leur influence établie, rien ne se faisait sans eux. Les représentants de la force publique les laissaient faire, soit par vénalité, soit pour des raisons de commodités personnelles.

Intuile d'ajouter que ce «Mutégalibéisme» était une conséquence naturelle de l'absolutisme de l'ancien régime. On sait très bien que, dans un régime absolutiste, la tyrannie est toujours exercée par degrés hiérarchiques. Il y a la tyrannie d'en haut et la tyrannie d'en bas, des grands et des petits tyrans. Là où il n'y a pas la protection de la légalité, c'est naturellement la loi du plus fort qui règne.

La constitution de 1908 a aboli, il est vrai, le régime absolutiste, mais elle n'a pas eu le temps ni la force de supprimer le «Mutégalibéisme.» La structure sociale et économique cristallisée petit à petit pendant plusieurs siècles d'absolutisme, ne pouvait être modifiée que par le dynamisme révolutionnaire, et c'est précisément ce qui faisait défaut au régime constitutionnel.

Le nationalisme kemaliste constitue donc une réaction vigoureuse contre cet état de choses, contre une structure sociale qui divisait la peuple en différentes castes et en diverses catégories.

La nouvelle Turquie est étatiste parce que l'ancienne était par trop libérale, si libérale, qu'elle a livré complètement l'économie du pays entre les mains des étrangers. Il n'y a que l'État qui pouvait reconquérir ces domaines occupés par l'étranger. L'individu turc, sans capital, sans compétence et sans expérience, n'aurait pu faire le moindre pas en avant dans ces domaines occupés par d'autres.

Le Kemalisme est révolutionnariste, parce que le régime constitutionnel de la Jeune Turquie, qui a voulu être évolutionniste, n'a fait qu'aggraver la situation au lieu de l'améliorer. La Jeune Turquie a eu plus d'une fois l'ennemi entre ses mains, elle aurait pu l'assomer d'un coup, mais elle a préféré s'en débarrasser graduellement, et ainsi, elle lui a laissé le temps de se ressaisir et de rebondir avec plus de vigueur qu'auparavant.

Enfin, inutile de relever que le Kemalisme est républicain par réaction contre l'ancien régime autocratique qui a été la principale cause de la décadence de l'Empire ottoman.

Le Kemalisme, pp. 243-250

CONCEPTION KEMALISTE DE LA NATION

Pour mieux saisir le sens profond du nationalisme turc, nous devons voir avant tout ce que les Kemalistes entendent par Nation. Nous ne nous occuperons pas des définitions données à ce terme par un grand nombre d'auteurs célèbres, nous ne parlerons pas des longues études qui lui ont été consacrées par Renan, Lévi-Brühl et autres sociologues, ceci nous mènerait trop loin. Nous nous contenterons d'examiner seulement le point de vue du Parti du Peuple à ce sujet.

Voici la définition de la Nation dans le programme de ce Parti:

«La Nation, c'est une formation sociale et politique renfermant les concitoyens liés les uns aux autres par la communauté de langue, de culture et d'idéal.»

Cette définition est différente, et nous dirons même diamétralement opposée à la notion de Nation avant la période kemaliste. Au temps d'Abdul Hamid appartenaient à la même Nation des individus qui n'étaient même pas des concitoyens, qui ne parlaient même pas la même langue, qui avaient, au point de vue social et culturel, des tendances même opposées, mais qui appartenaient à la même religion. Un musulman d'Algérie ou des Indes avait, au palais du Sultan Calife et à la Sublime-Porte, le même accueil et la même place que l'autochtone de Konia ou d'Istanbul. Les facteurs moraux qui liaient entre eux les membres de la Communauté n'étaient pas d'ordre séculier, mais d'ordre religieux. Les co-nationaux devaient prier Dieu de la même façon, libre à eux de parler des langues différentes, comme s'il s'agissait d'une communauté céleste n'ayant rien à faire avec ce bas monde.

La vie en société, même pendant la période constitutionnelle, était partagée en communautés. Différence de religion signifiait en même temps différence de culture et d'idéal. Dans la société aussi bien que dans les relations officielles, la population de l'Empire était toujours divisée en deux catégories, musulmane et non-musulmane. Zia Gök Alp même, l'apôtre du mouvement turquiste, a cru devoir inclure le facteur «religion» dans la définition de la Nation. Ainsi que je le fais ressortir dans mon livre en turc, *Türkleştirme*, Zia Gök Alp, qui a vécu à une époque où régnait la théocratie, ne pouvait pas concevoir une définition différente. Sous le régime théocratique, la culture, l'idéal et même la langue étaient imprégnés de l'esprit religieux. Tandis que sous un régime laïque comme le nôtre, la religion peut faire partie de la culture individuelle, mais n'a rien à faire avec la culture nationale.

C'est ainsi que la loi constitutionnelle ne stipule plus que l'Islamisme est la religion de l'État. Les privilèges culturels dont jouissaient autrefois les éléments non-musulmans n'existent plus.

Mais, dira-t-on, le particularisme religieux enraciné en Turquie depuis des siècles peut-il disparaître du jour au lendemain comme par enchantement? Empressons-nous de le dire, il n'en est pas question. Le fait que le facteur religion n'entre pas dans la définition de la Nation ne signifie pas que ce facteur n'existe pas. Les adeptes de chaque religion conservent plus ou moins leur particularisme séculaire. Mais n'oublions pas que le Kemalisme ne se base pas seulement sur ce qui est, sur la réalité actuelle, mais sur ce qui doit être, ou ce qui, tôt ou tard, sera, d'après le credo et les principes kemalistes. Il s'agit d'un régime qui a comme devise le révolutionnarisme, la suppression de tout ce qui n'est pas conforme aux intérêts moraux et matériels de la Nation. Combien d'institutions sociales enracinées depuis des siècles ont été déjà jetées par-dessus bord au moment propice? Puisque le credo kemaliste l'exige, il n'y a pas de doute que, tôt ou tard, le particularisme des communautés religieuses aussi s'en ira, le moment venu, rejoindre dans l'histoire tant d'autres survivances du passé.

Il y a lieu de remarquer tout particulièrement que le facteur race aussi est éliminé de la définition de la Nation dans le programme du Parti. Voici ce que dit Recep Peker à ce sujet dans une causerie faite dans la salle des conférences de l'Université en octobre 1931:

«D'après notre conception, le nationalisme n'a aucun rapport avec les masses dont les destinées politiques sont séparées des nôtres. Nous conservons un intérêt chaleureux et affectueux pour les Turcs qui vivent hors de nos frontières, soit comme État indépendant, soit comme ressortissants d'autres États. Nous considérons comme un sujet d'ordre scientifique, la parenté de sang et la parenté historique entre les susdites masses turques dont le nombre augmente de jour en jour au fur et à mesure que se développent les vérités historiques.

«Dans cet ordre d'idées, nous considérons comme des nôtres ceux de nos concitoyens qui vivent parmi nous, qui, politiquement et socialement, appartiennent à la Nation turque et auxquels on a inculqué des idées et des sentiments tels que le «Kurdisme», le «Circassianisme» et même le «Lazisme» et le «Pomakisme.» Nous considérons comme de notre devoir de mettre fin, par des efforts sincères, à ces fausses conceptions, léguées par le régime absolutiste, et qui sont le produit de longues oppressions historiques. Les vérités scientifiques d'aujourd'hui n'admettent pas la possibilité d'existence indépendante pour une Nation de quelques centaines de milliers ni même d'un million d'individus.

«Les liens qui nous attachent à ces concitoyens n'ont rien de commun avec la politique panislamique poursuivi par l'État ottoman disparu. Nos liens sont d'ordre purement national.»

Recep Peker, poursuivant son exposé, ajoute:

«Nous tenons à exprimer avec la même franchise et avec la même sincerité notre opinion en ce qui concerne nos concitoyens juifs et chrétiens. Notre Parti reconnaît complètement comme Turcs, ces concitoyens pour autant qu'ils rentrent dans notre communauté de langue et d'idéal. Il est inutile d'ajouter que, dans cette façon de voir et d'agir de notre Parti, il n'y a pas même trace de la mentalité de «Raya» qui régnait dans la période d'absolutisme. Dans ces paroles sincères, il faut voir un sens réel conforme à nos principes et qui n'a rien de commun avec les manifestations factices de compatriotisme qui ont eu lieu pendant les tumultes constitutionnels des dernières années de l'Empire.»

Le vice-président du Parti, Ismet Inönü, s'est exprimé à ce sujet dans un de ses discours avec plus de franchise et de clarté:

«Est Turk, a-t-il dit, celui qui désire et aime l'être.»

Il va sans dire qu'il ne faut pas déduire de ces mots laconiques d'Ismet Inönü qu'il n'est pas besoin d'une communauté de langue, de culture et d'idéal, comme l'exige la définition de Nation dans le programme du Parti du Peuple. Car, au fond, peut-on sincèrement désirer et aimer être Turc sans s'en approprier la langue, l'idéal et la culture nationaux? Il est évident qu'entre la définition scientifique du programme du Parti et la devise laconique d'Ismet Inönü, homme d'État pratique et réaliste, il y a parfaite identité.

Ainsi donc, la communauté de race et de religion ne signifie plus, pour la nouvelle Turquie, communauté nationale. Pour appartenir à la même Nation, il n'est pas indispensable d'appartenir à la même race et à la même religion, mais parler la même langue, avoir la même culture et le même idéal.

Il ne faut pas croire cependant que le Kemalisme n'a plus aucun intérêt pour les frères de race ou de religion. Déjà, dans les déclarations de Recep Peker, nous voyons l'intérêt sincère porté à la solidarité raciale, à la voix du sang.

Comme le Kemalisme ne se paie pas de mots, il faut bien comprendre que l'intérêt pour les frères de race manifesté dans les déclarations du secrétaire général du Parti du Peuple ne signifie pas amour platonique, et qu'à l'occasion, il peut donner des résultats concrets et positifs dans le cadre des principes généraux posés par le Kemalisme.

Dans la politique démographique du Gouvernement turc et dans les mesures pratiques prises par ce dernier en vue d'augmenter la population du pays, le facteur race occupe la première place. Les portes de la Turquie sont grandement ouvertes aux immigrants de race turque et le Gouvernement leur accorde toute aide et tout concours matériel et moral dans la mesure du possible.

A ce propos, nous croyons utile de citer ici les déclarations du ministre de l'Intérieur Chukru Kaya, devant le IVe Congrès du Parti du Peuple:

«Notre population en Thrace se compose aujourd'hui de 610 a 650,000 habitants éparpillés sur une superficie de 22,000,000 de kilomètres carrés, ce qui revient à 26 habitants par kilomètre carré. Avant la guerre, il y en avait 28. Dans les régions voisines, la densité est de 50 en Bulgarie et de 60 en Roumanie. Dans la partie de la Thrace appartenant à la Grèce, la densité est de 102 habitants. Chez nous, la région la plus dense, c'est le littoral de la Mer Noire, où l'on trouve dans certaines parties 200 habitants au kilomètre carré. Il n'y a pas de raison pour que nous n'ayons pas, dans toute la Turquie, 50 et même 100 habitants par kilomètre carré.

«Une de nos ressources pour arriver à ce but, c'est l'affluence des immigrants. Il en arrive continuellement de Roumanie, de Bulgarie et de Yougoslavie en grand nombre. Ils forment un contingent de 1,200,000 habitants. N'étant pas encore bien preparés pour leur installation, nous avons dû endiguer leur affluence. Nous aurons la possibilité d'en installer en Thrace, y compris la région des Dardanelles, dans l'espace de cinq à six ans, 600,000. Cette année, nous espérons pouvoir en installer 35 a 50,000.»

Il y a lieu de remarquer que la Turquie kemaliste compte ouvrir ses portes, non seulement aux Turcs musulmans de Roumanie, mais aux Turcs chrétiens appelés «les Kara Oguz» et qui vivent en Bessarabie en masses compactes. On évalue leur nombre de 250 à 300,000.

Examinons maintenant ce que le Kemalisme met en avant à la place de la race et de la religion, comme éléments constitutifs de la nationalité. Langue, culture et idéal, dit le programme du Parti du Peuple. La communauté d'idéal, c'est naturel et compréhensible. On ne peut pas vivre et fraterniser dans la même patrie quand on a des aspirations différentes. Pour s'en convaincre, nous n'avons qu'à rafraîchir notre mémoire en reculant d'une trentaine d'années, à l'époque où les nationalités chrétiennes de l'Empire avaient les yeux tournés hors des frontières du pays et nourrissaient des aspirations identiques à celles de leurs co-nationaux de Sofia, d'Athènes, de Belgrade, etc. La communauté de langue est aussi un facteur indispensable. La vie en commun devient insupportable quand on parle des langues différentes.

Le seul élément qui mérite un examen spécial et approfondi, c'est la culture. La langue elle-même fait partie de la culture. Raison de plus pour nous arrêter davantage à l'examen de ce point.

Une loi spéciale a été promulguée sur l'installation des immigrés et le déplacement des agglomérations non encore assimilées à la culture turque. Cette loi autorise le Gouvernement à déplacer certaines populations allogènes, pour les installer au milieu des populations turques où elles pourront s'assimiler à la culture turque. Elle ne prévoit comme élément de nationalisation que la culture. S'il n'y est pas question de langue et d'idéal, c'est que la langue est l'élément principal de la culture et on ne peut s'inféoder à une culture, sans s'en approprier la langue au point d'en faire sa langue maternelle; quant à l'idéal, c'est une conséquence naturelle de la communauté de culture. Quand on est enfant de la même mère et qu'on parle la même langue et qu'on a la même culture, on ne peut pas avoir des aspirations nationales différentes. Ainsi donc, la nationalité s'exprime par la culture. C'est par elle, par la culture nationale que l'on est Français, Italien, Grec ou Bulgare.

Qu'est-ce que c'est que la culture? Nous connaissons tous, plus ou moins, le sens de ce vocable. Mais le sens que lui attribue chacun de nous n'est pas toujours le même. Pour ce qui nous concerne, nous ne prétendons pas pouvoir donner ici une définition acceptable pour tout le monde. C'est là une tâche dans laquelle ont échoué les savants les plus compétents dans la matière. Il y a trois ans, s'est réuni, à Madrid, sous l'égide de l'«Institut de coopération intellectuelle de la S.D.N.,» un Congrès auquel ont pris part des savants et des philosophes du monde entier et où on a longuement discuté sur la définition de la culture. Des orateurs éminents y ont étudié et analysé la culture sous différents aspects, individuel, national et international, mais ils ne sont pas parvenus à se mettre d'accord sur une définition universelle.

Voici, à titre d'exemple, quelque citations typiques: le délégué des États-Unis d'Amérique, Mr. Edwin M. Gay, a commencé son discours par ces mots: «Quand j'ai vu le programme de cette importante réunion, je me suis demandé quel sens on attribuait à ce mot; je me suis rendu compte que ce mot avait toutes sortes de significations et je m'aperçois qu'ici même, à cette réunion, on ne semble pas s'être mis d'accord sur le sens que l'on veut attacher au mot culture. Quand nous parlons de culture, tout au moins en anglais, je crois que nous avons tendance à employer ce mot dans un sens un peu différent de celui que nos amis allemands donnent au mot Kultur. Pour eux, il a un sens beaucoup plus large, plus étendu.»

Mr. Gay aurait pu ajouter que les amis français et les amis italiens et ceux des autres Nations aussi ont, sur la culture, des conceptions différentes.

Le délégué espagnol, le Pr Unamuno, a commencé sa conférence en disant: «Je dois vous avouer qu'après plus de quarante ans de professorat, j'en suis venu à ne pas savoir ce qu'est la culture. Ce que je sais, c'est qu'elle m'écrase un peu.»

Après s'être livré, tout au long, à des épanchements personnels – pour employer son propre terme – le délégué espagnol a terminé en disant: «Toutefois, je crois que c'est une question qu'il ne faut pas trop éclaircir. Trop de lumière, ce n'est guère bon.»

Ces paroles n'ont pas eu l'air de plaire au délégué italien, le Pr Arestano, qui s'est écrie: «Les orateurs qui m'ont précédés, et spécialement M. Unamuno, ont pensé qu'il n'est pas nécessaire de définir la culture. Je m'excuse donc de déclarer que je pense, au contraire, qu'il est nécessaire de commencer par s'entendre sur ce que nous appelons la culture.»

M. Arestano, après avoir dit ce qu'il pense des aspects individuel, national et international de la question, a donné, de la culture, une définition qui me paraît des plus complètes. «La culture, dit-il, commence avec la production, c'est-à-dire, avec la création de valeurs humaines. Ce monde, tout constitué de valeurs humaines, ce monde de l'homme de plus en plus civilisé est quelque chose d'ajouté au monde donné, d'ajouté à la nature. Même si l'on puise des moyens et des inspirations dans la nature, c'est toujours une nature refaite par l'homme, cette nouvelle nature qui sort des labeurs de la culture humaine; c'est un monde créé, augmenté, croissant, qui se développe au fur et à mesure que croît la puissance de l'homme sur le monde et sur soi-même, que se développe son esprit d'invention, son génie de création.

«Dans ce domaine, les peuples se distinguent et se graduent dans une échelle de volonté et de pouvoir, selon leur capacité d'accroître et de transfigurer la réalité donnée, par voie d'invention de réalités, valeurs nouvelles conçues dans un style original.

«Voilà pourquoi il est aussi facile de distinguer, dans le monde de la culture, *grosso modo*, des peuples créateurs et des peuples tributaires de valeurs humaines.»

Après avoir entendu les différentes sommités scientifiques qui se sont succédées à la tribune pendant cinq jours, le président du Congrès, Mme Curie, célèbre par sa découverte du radium, a résumé les débats et a dit, entre autres:

«Je n'insisterai pas sur la définition de la culture. Certains d'entre nous ont tenté de donner cette définition et ont présenté des vues intéressantes. C'est une raison de plus pour que je m'abstienne et que je me rallie à l'opinion de Mr. de Madariaga qu'on peut parler de ces problèmes sans les définir. Les définitions en sciences sont difficiles, à plus forte raison dans le cas présent. Peut-être n'arriverons-nous pas à nous mettre d'accord, quel que soit le temps consacré à cette tâche.»

Pour ce qui nous concerne, nous ne nous attarderons pas non plus à passer en revue tout ce qui a été dit et ce qui pourrait être dit concernant la définition de la culture, cela nous mènerait trop loin et peut-être hors de notre sujet. Ce qui nous intéresse dans cette question, c'est l'aspect national de la culture. Mme Curie, dans son allocation précitée, s'est arrêtée spécialement sur l'aspect national de la culture et a relevé, entre autres, «comme il est toujours agréable et désirable, dans toute réunion tenue sous les auspices de la S.D.N., que l'on dégage les opinions communes aux membres du Comité, je constate qu'il y a ici un élément d'entente évident. Tous les aspects de la culture sont jugés importants et nécessaires, tous nous pensons que le sol, l'ambiance et les facteurs naturels exercent une influence sur elle.

«Nous sommes d'accord qu'il existe un élément national à la base de toute culture, et nous sommes tous d'accord aussi sur ce point fondamental qu'une culture universelle doit être superposée à toute culture à base nationale et que le développement de l'individu est une obligation dans toute culture nationale ou internationale.»

Ainsi donc, répétons-le avec le président du Congrès, Mme Curie:

1) Tout le monde est d'accord qu'il existe un élément national à la base de toute culture;
2) Tout le monde admet que le sol, l'ambiance et les facteurs naturels exercent une influence sur elle.

C'est là, naturellement, le point qui nous intéresse le plus dans cette question, puisque la communauté de culture constitue la principale caractéristique de la nationalité, puisque c'est cet élément qui est à la base de la solidarité et de la fraternité nationales.

Une fois arrivés à ce point, nous devons abandonner le domaine international des Congrès et de la S.D.N., pour chercher une définition de la culture au point de vue national.

La plus précieuse définition de la culture nationale nous a été fournie par l'inoubliable pionnier du Turquisme, Zia Gök Alp. Zia Gök Alp, – comme l'ont fait d'ailleurs la plupart des orateurs du Congrès précité, – sépare la culture en deux catégories: la culture, pour ainsi dire, «démocratique,» qu'il appelle «hars» et à laquelle il attribue un caractère national et la culture, pour ainsi dire «aristocratique,» à laquelle il reconnaît un caractère international.

Voici ce que Zia Gök Alp entend par «hars»: «hars, c'est la quintessence harmonieuse de la vie religieuse, éthique, esthétique, juridique, linguistique, économique et technique d'une Nation.

«Ce qui rentre dans le cadre du «hars» ne sont pas des choses qui se produisent par la volonté des individus, suivant une règle et une méthode appropriées, c'est-à-dire, ce ne sont pas des éléments artificiels. Elles se forment et se développent d'une façon naturelle et biologique.

«Le «hars» populaire par essence, est le produit des traditions populaires, des us et coutumes, des littératures orale et écrite, de la langue, de la musique, de la religion, de la morale, de l'esthétique et de l'économie. Comme la source de ces belles choses et dans le peuple, le hars est, de ce fait, populaire.

«Il y a quinze ans, deux langues vivaient côte à côte dans notre pays: l'une était la langue ottomane, composée de turc, d'arabe et de persan; l'autre n'était qu'un dialecte que parlaient entre eux les gens du peuple. On l'appelait aussi, par dérision, le turc, le considérant comme un argot vulgaire. Or, c'était justement cet idiome qui était notre langue véritable, la langue de notre hars, de notre culture. Dans la poésie, également, la mesure n'était pas celle du turc ordinaire. Les poètes populaires composaient des pièces lyriques sans se douter qu'ils observaient le rythme. Il s'ensuit que ce rythme faisait partie du hars turc.

«Dans notre pays, outre la musique ottomane, des chants populaires avaient vu le jour sous l'inspiration de la masse. C'était cela la musique de notre hars.

«Le hars est fait de sentiments qui ne reposent sur aucune règle et qui ne sont pas copiés des autres peuples. La musique turque est faite de chansons qui jaillissent de l'âme populaire, de mélodies que n'ont ni règles ni méthodes, ni aucune science de la musique. En littérature aussi, il y a à côté de la littérature ottomane, une littérature populaire. Celle-ci est faite de proverbes, de dictons, de charades, d'allégories, de récits épiques, d'anecdotes et de farces. Les proverbes ne sont que l'expression du bon sens populaire.

«Les anecdotes, les histoires de fées, n'ont pas été inventées par des individus, elles ont été transmises, depuis l'âge mythologique, de génération en génération par tradition orale jusqu'à notre epoque.

«Les fables que nous trouvons dans le livre de «Dédé Korkout» sont également de transmission orale et elles n'ont été écrites qu'il y a quelques siècles seulement. Les livres de Chah Ismail, Achik Kerem, Achik Garip, Koroglou, ne sont que des légendes populaires enregistrées par la suite. Dans l'histoire et l'ethnographie turques, les légendes et les épopées font les éléments de la littérature turque. Les poètes tels qu'Achik Omer, Dertli, Karadjaoglan, étaient des troubadours chéris du peuple. Les poésies de Younous Imre et des cyniques Bektachis appartiennent à la même catégorie. Nasreddine Hodja, Indjili Tchaouch, Bekir Mustafa et Bektachi Baba, sont les idoles du peuple. Le «Karagheuz»[6] et l'«Orta Oyounou», qui sont des spectacles populaires, forment, pour ainsi dire, le théâtre traditionnel.

«Il y a encore une morale qui fait partie du hars turc. Dans l'ancien dictionnaire de Mahmoud Kachgeri, il est dit au mot turc: «Le Turc n'a ni de l'ostentation ni de l'orgueil. Lorsqu'un Turc accomplit un acte d'héroïsme ou de dévouement, il ignore avoir fait quelque chose d'exceptionnel.»

«Il y a aussi des ulémas (savants religieux) qui appartiennent au hars populaire. Ils n'ont pas de grades, comme ceux des Ottomans, ils sont plutôt empiriques. Chez eux, il existe une religion dont certains côtés sont en rapport avec le hars populaire. Ainsi, par exemple, ils conservent encore l'expression «Gheuktanri» antérieure à l'Islamisme. Ce Dieu est celui des récompenses. Il ne se mêle pas de punir. Il passait aux yeux des Turcs pour l'Être magnanime; les anciens Turcs n'aimaient que lui et n'avaient devant lui aucune espèce de crainte. Après l'avènement de l'Islamisme chez les Turcs, le «Mouhhabbetoulah» (l'amour de Dieu) est resté intact par tradition de l'ancien Tanri, à l'encontre des Arabes à qui Allah inspirait la peur, le «Muhafetullah.»

«Dans l'ancienne religion des Turcs, il n'y avait pas d'ascétisme.

«Les cérémonies spirituelles et les fêtes joyeuses étaient, par contre, plus nombreuses. Le fait que les Turcs font une place dans les Mosquées à la Mythologie, qu'ils lisent le mevloudou chérif et qu'ils admettent la poésie et la musique dans les tekkés (les oratoires), prouve qu'ils ont une prédilection pour la religion esthétique.

«Dans toutes les branches de l'art, nos ancêtres se distinguaient par leur goût du naturel, de la simplicité et de l'originalité. Leurs tapis, leurs porcelaines, leur architecture, leur calligraphie en sont autant de témoignages édifiants. Comme dans les beaux-arts, les Turcs manifestaient les mêmes particularités dans les choses de la religion et de la morale.

«Dans la vie sociale, qui constitue le hars turc, on remarque surtout une harmonie intime. La simplicité qui caractérise sa langue se retrouve aussi dans sa religion, sa morale, ses arts, sa politique, son économie et sa vie domestique.

«La courtoisie des manières, l'originalité que l'on voit dans la vie du Turc ne sont que les manifestations de ce caractère national.»

Le caractère naturel et, pour ainsi dire, biologique, de la culture dont parle Zia Gök Alp, ressort aussi de la définition suivante de Meyer: «La culture est le produit de l'histoire, on ne peut la créer à volonté. Elle s'est formée et se forme d'elle-même. Aussi, malgré la multiplicité des rapports internationaux, cette culture reste ce qu'elle est; elle ne vieillit, ni ne s'use. C'est le noyau indestructible de notre entité. Certes, sous l'effet des relations internationales, ce noyau peut être limé ou peut revêtir un aspect étranger, mais tant que la nation reste debout, il n'est pas possible qu'il soit écrasé et réduit en poussière.»

Quant au caractère démocratique de la culture nationale sur lequel Zia Gök Alp appuie tout spécialement, il a été relevé, à plusieurs reprises, dans le Congrès de Madrid, notamment par le Pr Unamuno, qui a dit entre autres:

«Je suis un Espagnol, foncièrement Espagnol; vous êtes dans un pays qui, je crois, a une grande, une profonde culture, les illettrés, les analphabets en ont peut-être même plus que les autres, ils ont sur leur âme de longs siècles, pas seulement de pensée et de foi. Socrate allait dans les rues d'Athènes en parlant avec tout le monde, c'est cela la culture. Il y a ici en Espagne une culture populaire de profondes sources, qui s'est faite par tradition dans la grande Université populaire de l'Espagne, que sont les cafés.»

Mr. Unamuno a exprimé, sous forme de boutades, dont il a la spécialité, les mêmes vérités que Zia Gök Alp a analysées sous une forme scientifique.

Le régime kemaliste aussi, dès le début, a reconnu la caractère populaire de la culture nationale et c'est pour cette raison que, sous l'impulsion d'Atatürk, les chansons populaires, les proverbes, les anecdotes et, surtout, les vocables et les expressions inconnus par les lettrés, mais employés toujours dans les humbles coins de l'Anatolie, ont été recherchés soigneusement par des centaines de Maisons du Peuple, par des milliers de profeseurs et par tous les fonctionnaires civils et militaires de toutes catégories. C'est une mobilisation générale, unique dans son genre, qui, au début, a commencé par des recherches se référant au folklore et qui, ces derniers temps, s'est consacrée à des recherches plutôt linguistiques. Mais il n'y a pas de doute qu'une fois la tâche linguistique achevée, on reprendra les recherches relatives au folklore pour mettre en valeur les trésors de culture cachés dans les couches profondes du peuple à travers l'immense étendue du pays.

«Causez et faites causer», aiment à répéter souvent Recep Peker et les autres chefs du Parti du Peuple, formés à l'école de Tchan-Kaya.[7] On veut faire parler le peuple pour que les trésors culturels que l'âme nationale renferme depuis de longs siècles et qui, pendant la période osmanlie, sont restés abandonnés dans le subconscient, puissent être mis en valeur.

Nous ne voulons pas clore ce chapitre sur le nationalisme turc sans traiter de la situation des colonies étrangères et des minorités nationales sous le régime kemaliste.

A première vue, on est porté à croire qu'un régime qui se proclame ostensiblement nationaliste ne peut pas adopter vis-à-vis des étrangers et des éléments minoritaires une politique très généreuse. D'autant plus qu'il s'agit, dans notre cas, d'un pays où le souvenir du régime des capitulations, de triste mémoire, n'est pas encore oublié. Une réaction contre les bénéficiaires de ces iniquités paraîtrait, sinon justifiable, du moins bien compréhensible. Or, tous ceux qui sont plus ou moins au courant de la situation, savent parfaitement que tel n'est pas le cas. Le Nouveau Turc met un point d'honneur à faire comprendre au monde entier que les capitulations ont été supprimées, non pas à la suite d'une victoire ou à la suite d'une manœuvre diplomatique, mais parce qu'elles n'avaient plus leur raison d'être, parce que l'étranger n'avait plus besoin de protection, parce que la loi commune, l'ordre et la légalité suffisent amplement désormais à assurer à l'étranger, au même titre qu'à l'indigène, toute la securité à laquelle tout civilisé est en droit de prétendre lorsqu'il est en pays civilisé.

En outre, il ne faut pas perdre de vue que la nouvelle Turquie est toujours habitée par un peuple connu pour son caractère hospitalier et chevaleresque. Depuis de longs siècles, l'hospitalité a été toujours une des vertus cardinales du peuple turc, même au temps où il était dénigré sous toute espèce de prétextes. La révolution kemaliste a bien fait table rase du passeé, elle a balayé tout ce qui handicapait sa marche en avant, mais ce qui est essentiellement turc, ce qui est dans le sang, dans la race, reste intact. Or, qu'y a-t-il de plus traditionnel chez le Turc que l'hospitalité?

On est souvent tenté de voir une tendance chauviniste dans certains faits et gestes de la nouvelle Turquie. Mais, peut-on parler de chauvinisme lorsque presque dans tous les ministères, dans toutes les administrations et les entreprises économiques de l'État, dans toutes les écoles, les facultés et les universités, les spécialistes étrangers se comptent par dizaines? Des centaines d'étudiants sont envoyés chaque année dans divers pays d'Europe parfaire leurs études. On a beau exalter l'amour propre et l'orgueil national, on n'a jamais perdu contact avec la réalité des faits. Le bon sens n'a jamais perdu ses droits. On n'a jamais perdu l'équilibre et la mesure. Des fougueux, des exaltés, il en surgit toujours, comme partout ailleurs, qui veulent singer tel dictateur des temps modernes, qui prêchent l'ostracisme économique contre les sociétés, la fermeture pure et simple des écoles étrangères, etc., mais ces excès de paroles n'ont pas dépassé le cercle d'une petite clique, qui n'a jamais réussi à influencer les principes immuables du Kemalisme. Ce dernier ne se départit jamais de l'esprit réaliste et de la politique strictement utilitaire, sans jamais se payer de mots, de phrases et de formules creuses.

Quant à la question des minorités nationales, la Turquie kemaliste n'en a jamais admis le principe. La nouvelle Turquie ne reconnaît dans ses citoyens que des turcs. Ceux qui ne le sont pas de race peuvent l'être ou le devenir en adoptant sa culture. Si aujourd'hui, la nouvelle Turquie, comme survivance du passé, compte quelques centaines de milliers de citoyens qui ne se sont pas encore approprié la culture turque, il est certain qu'il n'y en aura plus dans quelques dizaines d'années. Le régime kemaliste est basé sur l'unité nationale. Ceux qui ne veulent pas s'excclure eux-mêmes des bénéfices de la communauté et de l'unité nationales ne peuvent pas manquer de s'y inféoder en s'en appropriant la culture.

Adopter la culture nationale turque ne signifie pas renoncer au particularisme kurde, laze, arménien ou juif. Toutes les Nations occidentales comptent dans leur sein des éléments ethniques ayant des particularismes assez prononcés, mais qui ne pensent pas un seul instant à revendiquer un traitement minoritaire.

Ainsi, par exemple, les grands pays occidentaux, comme la France, l'Angleterre et l'Italie, se sont débarrassés depuis longtemps de la mentalité minoritaire, grâce a une assimilation sincère et profonde. Il y a en Grand-Bretagne des Écossais, des Gallois, etc., en France des Bretons, des Corses, etc., qui conservent jalousement leurs particularités nationales plus ou moins prononcées. Certaines de ces nationalités ont tout ce qu'il faut pour avoir une existence nationale indépendante, mais jamais il n'est venu à l'esprit d'un politicien quelconque de considérer ces nationalités comme des minorités nationales. Puisque tous les Français ont la même culture, le même idéal et la même langue, quel mal y a-t-il si certains d'entre eux conservent leur patois, leurs us et coutumes et d'autres particularités? Il peut y avoir entre ces éléments ethniques certains sentiments de solidarité comme il y en a dans tous les pays entre personnes originaires de la même région. Ceci ne porte pas ombrage a l'unité nationale. Considérer, par exemple, un Breton comme un élément minoritaire parce qu'il a son patois, parce qu'il a un intérêt spécial pour ses co-régionaux, parce qu'il conserve certaines particularités traditionnelles, ce serait une hérésie qui ne traverse pas l'esprit d'un Français ou d'un Anglais.

Il est évident que nulle part en Occident, il n'existe une question de minorités telle qu'elle apparaît en Orient et dans certains nouveaux pays où elle forme la pierre angulaire de la politique intérieure et extérieure. Les traités de paix, où l'on a intercalé des chapitres spéciaux concernant la protection des minorités, n'ont pas apporté une solution quelconque à cette question, mais, au contraire, ils l'ont aggravée et envenimée.

A l'instar des autres traités de paix, le Traité de Lausanne aussi comporte un chapitre spécial contenant un grand nombre de clauses consacrées à la protection des minorités. Ismet Inönü s'est declaré disposé à signer des deux mains ces paragraphes parce qu'il savait très bien qu'ils seraient restés lettre morte, que la révolution kemaliste les rendrait caducs et inopérants.

En effet, les minorités ethniques elles-mêmes n'ont pas tardé à reconnaître l'inopportunité de ce chapitre relatif aux minorités et l'ont déclarés caduc par des déclarations signées des représentants des conseils communaux.

De son côté, le Gouvernement, pas ses lois laïques, a unifié la législation sur le statut personnel et supprimé toute différence entre éléments musulmans et non-musulmans. La loi fondamentale a reconnu comme Turcs tous les citoyens du pays sans distinction de race ou de religion, et a préparé le terrain pour une intégration complète des éléments minoritaires au turquisme.

Nous devons avouer, cependant, que la fusion des éléments visée par la loi fondamentale n'est pas encore sortie de son stade idéologique. Les Grecs, les Arméniens et les Juifs qui sont des Turcs d'après la loi fondamentale et d'après les principes idéologiques du Kemalisme ne le sont pas encore en réalité. Les cloisons étanches qui les séparaient avant le Kemalisme ne sont pas encore complètement renversées.

Il y en a qui se demandent comment se fait-il que le Kemalisme tolère encore ce dualisme entre son idéologie et la réalité. Le Kemalisme, qui a fait de l'Osmanli oriental un Turc occidental ayant une autre langue, une autre mentalité et une autre façon de vivre, de penser et d'agir, serait-il incapable d'assimiler quelques centaines de milliers de concitoyens qui ne demandent pas mieux que de vivre dans leur propre pays, dans les mêmes conditions matérielles et morales que leurs concitoyens pour ainsi dire majoritaires?

C'est là vraiment une situation anormale, dont on ne peut attribuer la faute ni au Kemalisme, dont les principes idéologiques sont imprégnés de la plus parfaite sincérité, ni aux éléments minoritaires parfaitement conscients de leurs intérêts au point de vue moral, aussi bien qu'au point de vue matériel. La faute ne peut être attribuée qu'à l'ombre, au fantôme du chapitre du Traité de Lausanne sur la protection des minorités.

Ainsi que nous l'avons souvent dit et répété, le Kemalisme est un mouvement qui ne tient aucun compte des réalités existantes, fussent-elles même séculaires, si ces réalités semblent pernicieuses. Il remplace d'un trait de plume ce qui est par ce qui doit être dans l'intérêt suprême de la collectivité. Il emploie à cet effet toutes les ressources de l'État et le dynamisme de la révolution. Mais, dans cette question des minorités, l'État turc ne peut employer ni la loi, ni le prestige de ses chefs, ni aucune mesure coercitive ou éducative. L'esprit qui a présidé à l'élaboration du chapitre fantôme sur les minorités dans le Traité de Lausanne l'en empêche.

Obliger, par la force, un Grec, un Arménien ou un Juif à devenir Turc, serait une violation des règles et des lois internationales.

Voilà l'ancienne Turquie tyrannique ressuscitée! clameraient les démagogues de tous les pays.

Quand aux minorités elles-mêmes, elles ne disposent d'aucune force pour lutter contre les faits. Elles sont subjuguées par le passé séculaire, par ce qui est enraciné au fond de leur conscience, elles sont les esclaves des institutions et des mentalités léguées par la période pré-kemaliste. Elles voudraient bien s'en affranchir, mais elles ne disposent d'aucune autorité, ni morale ni matérielle pour changer les mentalités des masses populaires.

Il n'y a pas de doute que le temps fera le nécessaire pour trancher aussi cette question restée nécessairement en marge de la réalité kemaliste. Comme nous l'avons dit plus haut, une ou deux générations suffiront pour que la turquisation des minorités passe du stade idéologique au stade de la réalité vivante. Déjà aujourd'hui, la langue et la culture turques constituent la base de l'enseignement dans toutes les écoles minoritaires. Un grand nombre d'enfants minoritaires reçoivent leur éducation directement dans les écoles turques, officielles ou privées.

Avec le temps, l'unité nationale, l'assimilation des éléments allogènes deviendra une réalité et ceci constituera la seule réalisation que le Kemalisme révolutionnaire aura obtenu par voie d'évolution.

Le Kemalisme, pp. 251-271

LE RAYONNEMENT DU KEMALISME

Il n'y a pas de doute que le désir de contribuer au relèvement moral et matériel des peuples et des pays d'Orient n'est pas étranger a l'idéal kemaliste. Mais, comme nous l'avons vu souvent dans les différentes chapitres de cet ouvrage, la Turquie kemaliste aime toujours suivre l'ordre logique des choses et n'entreprend la réalisation de ses désirs qu'à son heure et au moment opportun. Son esprit foncièrement réaliste ne lui permet pas de donner libre cours aux épanchements idéalistes, que tant qu'ils sont compatibles avec les intérêts réels de la nation. C'est dans cet ordre d'idées que nous voyons un des hommes les plus représentatifs du régime parler du rayonnement kemaliste auprès des pays et des peuples voisins.

Dans sons discours prononcé à l'occasion de l'inauguration de la ligne de chemin de fer d'Ergani-Diyarbékir, Ali Tchétinkaya, ministre des Travaux publics, a dit entre autres:

«Cette ligne ne s'arrêtera certainement pas à Diyarbékir. Elle sera reliée aux lignes de chemin de fer des pays voisins, nos frères et nos amis de la Perse et de l'Irak. Diyarbékir et ses environs ne sera plus comme il a été au cours du XVe et du XVIe siècle, le centre de ralliement des caravanes qui transportaient les produits de l'Orient, traversant la mer Indienne, la baie de Bassorah et les eaux du Tigre vers Mossoul, mais le centre de ralliement pour le rayonnement de la civilisation occidentale vers l'Orient. Plus de caravane, mais des voies ferrées qui, à travers ce pays, colporteront vers l'Orient la culture, la technique et les progrès du XXe siècle.»

La jonction des voies ferrées dont parle Ali Tchétinkaya se trouve être en même temps la jonction de l'idéalisme et le réalisme kemalistes. Le relèvement moral et matériel des pays voisins habités par des peuples frères et amis, répond naturellement aux intérêts supérieurs sociaux et économiques de la Turquie nouvelle.

Les extrémistes dont nous avons eu l'occasion de parler plus haut croient au rayonnement du Kemalisme non seulement dans le monde musulman, mais dans tous les pays et les peuples d'Orient. Ce rayonnement s'exercerait, d'après eux, non seulement dans le domaine social, mais surtout dans le domaine économique. A titre documentaire, nous croyons intéressant de résumer ici les idées d'un de leurs principaux représentants en ayant soin d'ajouter que ce ne sont là que des idées personnelles de l'auteur:

«Le régime libéral actuellement en vigueur en Europe a eu comme résultat l'asservissement des pays agricoles à technique arriérée, aux métropoles industrielles à technique avancée. Ces pays à technique arriérée sont tombés au niveau de colonies ou semi-colonies, tributaires des susdites métropoles. Le mouvement d'indépendance nationale doit mettre fin à cet état de choses intolérable. Chaque pays doit être une entité économique indépendante. Pour y arriver, l'autarchie absolue n'est pas nécessaire. On peut établir un régime d'échanges, basé sur l'égalité des droits et l'égalité des conditions.

«La Turquie sera le premier type de pays émancipé, jouissant d'une indépendance complète et absolue. Avec son industrie nationale développée et réglementée d'après sa capacité de production et de consommation, avec son crédit national et sa circulation des marchandises se suffisant à soi-même, avec son surplus de productions en produits spécifiques et grâce aux conditions climatériques extraordinairement favorables, elle pourra prendre part aux échanges de marchandises dans le monde, à titre de Nation complètement indépendante. C'est là le véritable sens de la révolution turque au point de vue mondial et cela non seulement pour la Turquie, mais pour tous les autres pays qui lui ressemblent.

«Tous les événements, le développement de la crise mondiale, ou plutôt les changements de structure économique s'effectuent d'une façon à confirmer de plus en plus notre mission efficace et significatrice d'importance mondiale. Le bonheur d'être le prototype le plus complet et le plus caractéristique de l'émancipation nationale constitue un précieux présent de l'histoire pour notre peuple. Nous considérons comme un devoir de nous approprier ce rôle et nous considérons qu'il est très utile que la génération de cette période révolutionnaire soit tout a fait consciente de ce rôle.

«Les peuples de colonies ou semi-colonies, en poursuivant leur lutte nationale, ne peuvent manquer de profiter de notre stage et de notre expérience historique sur cette question. Du reste, à notre époque, il est très difficile de s'imaginer et de faire perpétuer une grande révolution dont l'effet reste limité à l'intérieur des frontières nationales. La victoire de la Révolution française a fait propager ses principes dans tous les pays similaires. Les auteurs des révolutions qui ont éclaté en Europe après la guerre se considèrent obligés de maintenir leur prestige hors de leurs frontières nationales aussi. Notre mouvement d'émancipation nationale également doit s'assurer un champ d'action moral ayant pour objectif l'indépendance de toutes les Nations, la suppression des déséquilibres économiques entre les peuples et les inégalités irrationnelles entre les différentes classes des Nations respectives. Nous devons être conscients du sens universel de notre révolution. Nous vivons dans une telle période de l'histoire, dans un point de globe tellement délicat, dans un tel cours d'événements, que pour qu'elle puisse se maintenir en tant que Nation, la Nation turque est obligée d'assurer le triomphe de l'indépendance nationale dans tous les points du monde.»

A ce propos, il est intéressant de citer les déclarations caractéristique du général chinois Ho-Yao-Tsu, ambassadeur de la République chinoise à Ankara:

«La Révolution turque jouera, dans le relèvement et le progrès de tout l'Orient, le même rôle important et aura les mêmes effets profonds que la révolution française a eu dans le relèvement et la marche en avant de l'Occident vers la culture et la civilisation modernes.

Ne croyez pas qu'en prononçant ces paroles je me base sur des suppositions fantaisistes, je ne fais que répéter une vérité évidente, qui peut être remarquée par tous ceux qui ont des yeux pour voir. Les étincelles de votre grande révolution ont envahi déjà l'atmosphère de tout l'Orient. Le feu qui sortira de ces étincelles apportera la véritable lumière qui éclairera et éblouira tous les peuples de l'Orient.»

Le Kemalisme, pp. 279-282

RÉVOLUTIONNARISME

On se demande souvent avec étonnement, puisque le Kemalisme a réalisé déjà ses buts et ses objectifs, puisqu'il a stabilisé le régime et s'est identifié lui-même avec l'État, pourquoi se proclame-t-il toujours révolutionnaire? Désormais, le Parti devrait se proclamer conservateur. Il aura à conserver et a consolider les acquisitions de tant de révolutions. Il doit préserver son laïcisme, son républicanisme, son étatisme, son populisme, etc., contre toute velléité révolutionnaire quelconque. Pour y arriver, le Parti doit être farouchement conservateur.

Ce raisonnement n'est juste qu'en apparence. Ceux qui s'y cramponnent pour faire des critiques trahissent qu'ils n'ont rien compris de l'esprit kemaliste. Ils sont victimes de l'illusion, du mirage des mots, comme dirait Keyserling.

On traduit toujours, il est vrai, le «Inkilab» qui figure dans le programme du Parti, par «révolution». Les quatre professeurs qui enseignent à l'université les cours de l'Inkilab ont traduit eux aussi ce mot par «révolution» et ont donné à ce sujet de longues définitions et d'amples explications. Mais il ne faut pas oublier que les mots n'ont pas toujours un sens fixe et immuable. Leur sens change et évolue avec le temps. Il n'y a que l'esprit qui ne change pas. Dans des périodes normales, le sens des mots n'évolue qu'après des générations ou, du moins, après plusieurs dizaines d'années. Mais, dans une période de métamorphose profonde comme la nôtre, dans une période où on voit toute une Nation faire peau neuve du jour au lendemain, le sens de certains mots, malgré qu'ils sont des institutions séculaires, ne peut pas rester le même. Puisque le Turc de 1935 n'est pas le même que celui de 1919, certains mots employés par le premier ne peuvent pas avoir le même sens dans la bouche de son prédécesseur. Nous pourrions citer des centaines d'exemples à l'appui de notre thèse. Pour le moment, nous nous contenterons de citer un seul mot qui nous paraît des plus typiques: le mot «Millet» (Nation). Dans la bouche de l'Osmanli, ce mot signifie plutôt la plèbe, la populace, tout ce qui ne fait pas partie de l'élite; mais, depuis que le Kemalisme a adopté comme leitmotiv la souveraineté de la Nation, depuis qu'Atatürk a proclamé que le véritable maître du pays devant lequel tout le monde doit s'incliner avec respect et vénération, c'est le paysan, depuis que la République turque est allée jusqu'à supprimer les titres de pacha, bey, etc., le mot «Millet» évoque un sens, une conception tout à fait différente. «Millet,» c'est aujourd'hui la personnalité morale de la société superposée à l'individu. Ce mot a acquis dans l'espace d'une dizaine d'années un caractère de noblesse digne de respect. Surtout depuis que la nouvelle langue turque l'a remplacé par celui d'«Ulus,» qui n'a pas un passé pour ainsi dire dégradant, ce caractère de noblesse est devenu plus saillant, la conception pleine d'élévation en est plus accentuée.

Pour en revenir au mot Inkilab, il n'y a pas de doute que, lorsqu'il a été lancé au début, il signifiait bel et bien révolution, toujours par rapport au résultat comme nous l'avons déjà expliqué. C'était le mot d'ordre donné par Atatürk en faveur de la révolution sociale, qui a fait acheminer le peuple vers l'Occident, vers la culture et la mentalité occidentales. La marche en avant dans cette voie continue et continuera éternellement, mais le mot d'ordre qui a constitué le point de départ n'aura pas le même sens qu'au début. On n'a plus à faire peau neuve, à changer de culture et de mentalité, mais l'esprit qui l'anime reste toujours le même, on continuera toujours à aller de l'avant, non pas par une marche normale, mais par sauts, par des pas de géants.

S'il faut absolument trouver en langue étrangère une formule pouvant rendre jusqu'à un certain point le nouveau sens de l'Inkilab, on pourrait peut-être le représenter par radicalisme, mais empressons-nous d'ajouter que nous employons ce mot au sens étymologique et pas au sens employé couramment dans la terminologie politique. Au point de vue étymologique, radical signifie au sens figuré «ce qui a rapport aux principes, à l'essence des choses.»

En effet, le Kemalisme, dans son élan réformateur, n'admet jamais les demi-mesures et de tactiques opportunistes. Il procède toujours par chambardements, si on nous permet ce mot, comme l'indique le sens étymologique du mot Inkilab. Quand il veut supprimer une tradition, une institution sociale qui a fait son temps, le Kemalisme ne s'embarrasse pas des ménagements, des susceptibilités de tel ou tel élément ou de telle ou telle classe dont les intérêts se trouveraient en cause. En effet, on ne peut agir autrement quand on est obligé de rattraper le temps perdu en réalisant dans une année, les progrès obtenus par d'autres dans un siècles seulement. C'est pour cela que le radicalisme turc signifie:

«Agir avec la plus grande célérité possible, en brûlant les étapes et en faisant des sauts à travers le temps.»

Ainsi que le font ressortir à toute occasion les personnes les plus autorisées du Parti et du Gouvernement, l'Inkilab doit veiller à ce que le dynamisme, l'élan pris depuis le début, ne se relâche pas avec le temps. Le moteur doit être continuellement sous pression.

Pour le Kemalisme, arrêter sa marche en avant signifie reculer ou plutôt s'exposer aux influences retrogrades, à des offensives dangereuses du passé comme celles qui se sont produites presque dans tous les mouvements révolutionnaires de l'histoire.

Pour résumer, nous devons dire que la devise Inkilab, qui figure toujours dans le programme du Parti, se réfère à la mentalité, à l'esprit, à la méthode plutôt qu'à l'action. A l'avenir, on n'aura peut-être pas besoin d'action révolutionnaire proprement dite, mais on aura toujours besoin de l'esprit, de la mentalité et de la façon d'agir de l'Inkilab.

Le Kemalisme, pp. 283-286

ANTICIPATIONS

Avant de prendre congé de nos lecteurs, nous voudrions bien hasarder quelques anticipations sur l'avenir du Kemalisme. Les anticipations sont très faciles dans le domaine de l'évolution. On peut imaginer et deviner les résultats ou les réalisations futures en suivant l'enchaînement logique des événements. Mais, quand on a affaire à un régime révolutionnaire comme celui du Kemalisme, les anticipations deviennent difficiles. On est obligé d'avoir plus ou moins recours à la fiction. C'est ce que nous ferons pour entrevoir l'avenir, sans cependant nous aventurer trop loin. Nous nous arrêtons au 15 septembre 1942.

C'est le 20e anniversaire de la République turque. Nous sommes heureux d'y assister, du moins par l'imagination, grâce au roman *Ankara* de Yakoup Kadri, actuellement ministre de la Légation turque à Prague, dont toutes les œuvres sont empreintes d'un réalisme captivant. Nous y voyons sur la scène des personnages, des types d'hommes idéalistes qui représentent vraiment le nouveau Turc tel qu'il a été façonné par la métamorphose kemaliste. Relevons en passant que les personnages créés par d'autre romanciers qui ont essayé de refléter dans leurs livres la vie de la nouvelle Turquie, sont très loin de représenter le type du nouveau Turc. Un type de jeune fille dégénérée, de bonne famille, comme Leyla[8] qui passe sa vie dans des milieux de débauche, et finit par se jeter par la fenêtre après s'être donnée par vice à un vieil homme, cela se rencontre un peu partout, en marge de la société moderne. Ce n'est pas la peine de venir le chercher à Istanbul où on le rencontre plus rarement qu'ailleurs. Quant aux trois dames d'Ankara de Cl. Farrère, aucune d'elles ne constitue un type représentatif de la société moderne turque. Yakoup Kadri a pu nous représenter de véritables types représentatifs de la nouvelle Turquie, parce qu'il est un des ouvriers de la première heure et connaît parfaitement la psychologie de son propre milieu.

Dans le susdit roman, *Ankara*, publié en 1934, Yakoup Kadri nous décrit le développement du milieu d'Ankara, et de la nouvelle société turque depuis 1919 jusqu'en 1942, le 20e anniversaire de la République. A l'occasion des fêtes et cérémonies de cet anniversaire, nous voyons se dérouler sous nos yeux des tableaux représentant les progrès réalisés jusqu'alors et des scènes où se reflètent la véritable psychologie, le milieu idéologique où évolue le nouveau Turc.

Donnons maintenant la parole a Yakoup Kadri:

«La physionomie d'Ankara, ainsi que la vie de toute la Turquie nouvelle, n'a pas changé d'un coup, comme le croyait Selma Hanoum.[9] Ce changement avait commencé d'un côté par le réveil idéologique et scientifique représenté par la révolution de l'alphabet de 1928 et les mouvements de rénovation de la langue et de l'histoire qui l'ont suivi et, de l'autre côté, par la lutte pour le relèvement économique qui est une conséquence naturelle de la lutte pour l'indépendance. Ce changement a pris sa forme définitive après 1935. L'Institut de la langue et celui de l'histoire ont fusionné et l'Académie turque d'aujourd'hui est le résultat de cette fusion. A partir de 1935, l'organisation de la «Conscription sociale» qui prend ses directives de l'Institut économique ainsi que des Maisons du Peuple affiliées au Parti se sont mises à l'œuvre. C'est grâce à ces deux organisations dont l'une d'ordre matériel et l'autre d'ordre spirituel, que les aspirations relatives au relèvement économique et culturel sont sorties du domaine de la théorie et sont devenues des réalisations d'ordre national, s'étendant à tout le pays et à la Nation elle-même. La notion d'histoire pour la nouvelle génération n'est plus la simple connaissance du passé, mais la base de la conscience nationale du peuple turc. La lutte pour l'épanouissement économique a puisé sa force et son dynamisme dans l'instinct de conquérant qui est la caractéristique principale de la Nation. Les mœurs sociales et économiques ont changé de fond en comble. Celui qui s'écarte des principes généraux établis pour le bien de la collectivité est cloué au pilori par l'opinion publique, comme un déserteur détestable. Les «profiteurs» sont relégués par l'opinion en général au ban de la société. La presse est devenue un des principaux facteurs de l'ordre, de la discipline et de l'élan de la Nation vers le progrès. Ceux qui s'écartent des buts et des principes nationaux sont punis par devant l'opinion publique par la raillerie et le sarcasme qui constituent les armes les plus efficaces de l'intelligence. C'est ainsi que certains courants sociaux fréquents en Occident qui sont peu conformes à l'idéal national, les éléments de réaction et de dégénérescence ont été éliminés de la nouvelle société turque. Les types de snobs cosmopolites, ainsi que les affairistes rapaces, sont devenues la risée de tout le monde. Les cinémas ne montrent plus ces films vulgaires et sans goût, qui flattent les bas instincts de la foule. Celle-ci préfère toujours les films épiques et satiriques utiles à la cause nationale. Le public afflue vers ces films avec intérêt et empressement et se laisse entraîner aux rires et aux pleurs, autant que par les pleurs de Greta Garbo envers ses amants et les gestes comiques d'un Charlie Chaplin. Les applaudissements de la foule atteignent leur comble chaque fois que le journal d'actualités montre l'assèchement d'un marais dans un coin quelconque de l'Anatolie, l'inauguration d'une nouvelle ligne de chemin de fer, la tranformation en tissu dans la fabrique de Césarée, du coton produit dans la région d'Adana.»

Néchet Sabit, le héros idéaliste du roman, s'exprime en ces termes sur la situation de la classe ouvrière turque en 1942:

«Les ouvriers, les hommes de peine et les techniciens turcs ne sont pas malheureux comme le sont leurs congénères dans presque tous les pays de l'Europe. Il n'y a pas de traces, en Turquie, des misères et des malheurs du pauperisme qui accablent le prolétariat européen dont les meilleures vertus sont détruites par l'alcohol ou la famine. Il n'y a pas chez nous de malheureux ouvriers soumis à toute sorte de peine, comme l'étaient les galériens dans l'ancienne Rome. L'ouvrier en Turquie a la dignité d'un fonctionnaire. Il a la conscience d'être un serviteur de la collectivité. Il sait que la sueur qui coule de son front fait l'effet de la pluie qui vivifie et fertilise le sol de sa patrie. Il se considère comme le brave soldat qui défend héroïquement sa patrie sur le champ de bataille.»

La paysannerie est aussi heureuse que le prolétariat. Grâce à l'organisation de la «Conscription sociale,» la plus grande partie des paysans sont enrégimentés dans des coopératives solidement organisées. Les échanges entre la ville et la campagne ont été rationalisés. Cela fait vraiment plaisir de voir les groupes de paysans, hommes et femmes, petits et grands, rentrer du marché en chantant joyeusement à pleine gorge. Il n'existe plus un seul de ces paysans d'autrefois, chétif ou invalide, affublés de haillons et ayant l'air de mendiants. De jeunes médecins attachés à la «Conscription sociale» contrôlent soigneusement leur régime alimentaire et leurs conditions d'habitation et les soumettent à des examens médicaux très fréquents. Leurs effets vestimentaires sont fournis par les coopératives spéciales de consommation, qui s'approvisionnent auprès des fabriques gouvernementales à des prix très modiques.

Pour terminer, donnons de nouveau la parole à l'auteur même du roman:

«Les mœurs publiques ont complètement changé. La vie sociale a pris des formes tout à fait nouvelles. Tout le monde, et particulièrement Néchet Sabit et tous ceux qui appartiennent au même milieu idéaliste, trouvent leur bonheur dans celui de la collectivité. On est tellement habitué à vivre et à sentir à l'unisson, avec les rires et les pleurs, les besoins et les aspirations de la collectivité, que personne ne trouve le loisir et ne sent pas le besoin de s'occuper de soi-même et de s'abandonner à des vices ou des plaisirs individuels.»

Il y a lieu de remarquer que, dans ce tableau, l'auteur attribue la plus grande importance à la révolution de la morale et des mœurs publiques. C'est le point sur lequel presque tous ceux qui ont publié des études et des livres sur la nouvelle Turquie ont fait des réserves expresses.

Jusqu'à quel point le nouveau régime kemaliste a-t-il pu enrayer les vices de l'administration, le règne du fameux bakchiche, la vénalité des fonctionnaires du haut en bas de l'échelle et surtout le manque de sentiment du devoir social chez tous les citoyens en général? Certains écrivains étrangers, comme Paul Gentizon, font ressortir que «la grande majorité des fonctionnaires d'aujourd'hui, sont encore ceux d'autrefois, de l'époque de l'empire, que la seule vertu du nouveau régime ne pouvait en aucune façon changer leurs mœurs, leurs habitudes et leur psychologie que, dans ces conditions, le règne du bakchiche a tendance à se maintenir sous les mêmes formes que jadis et que le nouveau régime n'est donc pas indemne de ce mal».[10]

Paul Gentizon ne peut pas être taxé d'esprit de malveillance. Ses écrits sur la nouvelle Turquie sont empreints d'une sincerité et d'une objectivité incontestables. Il a perdu de vue cependant que, s'il est vrai qu'il y a encore dans l'administration une partie des fonctionnaires de l'ancien régime, les postes de commandes se trouvent presque tous entre les mains des jeunes, de cette génération pétrie dans la lutte pour l'indépendance, tout imprégnée de l'esprit kemaliste et profondément animée du dynamisme révolutionnaire. L'auteur a relevé lui-même la sévérité extrême avec laquelle les dirigeants de la nouvelle Turquie sévissent contre ceux qui trahissent la cause nationale, en se laissant aller à la corruption.

Yakoup Kadri qui connaît mieux que quiconque les aspirations du régime kemaliste et le but vers lequel convergent tous les efforts de ses dirigeants, ne pouvait pas manquer de constater comment la morale et les mœurs publiques évoluent sous l'impulsion de l'esprit kemaliste et faire des anticipations en conséquence.

Ces anticipations sont-elles flattées et jusqu'à quel point? C'est le secret de l'avenir. Ce que la réalité nous montre, c'est que le Kemalisme s'est orienté vers cet idéal et que le dynamisme initial, qui a donné jusqu'ici des résultats miraculeux, n'a rien perdu de sa force. Le passé est le miroir de l'avenir.

Le Kemalisme, pp. 287-292

MUNİS TEKİNALP, HAL TERCÜMESİ[1]

1883 tarihinde Serezde doğum. Babamın adı İshak'tır. Tahsilimi Selanikte Aliyans ve bilahara Hukuk Mekteplerinde yaptım.

Fikriyat sahasında 1906 senesinde Selanikte "Yeni Asır" gazetesinde muharrirlikle başladım. O tarihten Selaniğin sukutuna yani 1912 tarihine kadar yine Selanik'te : 1) İktisadî ve içtimaî mevzular üzerine muhtelif eserler neşr ettim. 2) Tamimi Lisanı Osmanî Cemiyetini tesis ve reisliğini der'uhte etmekle daha o zamandanberi Millî birliğe hizmet etmeğe çalıştım. 3) Meclisi Umumiyi Vilayet ve encümeni Vilayet azası ve umumî kâtibi sıfatile umumî hayatın bütün safhalarında faaliyette bulundum. 4) Ziya Gök Alp'ın ilham ve irşadile resmî makamların direktiflerini takip ederek hars ve kültür sahalarında mühim vazifeler der'uhte ve bu cümleden olarak millî intibahın ilk hamlesi olan Türkçülük, Yeni Hayat, ve Yeni Lisan ceryanlarına büyük bir gayretle iştirak ettim.

1910 senesinden 1937 senesine kadar Türk Millî intibahının takip ettiği muhtelif safhaları ilmî esaslarla dairesinde sistemleştirerek Türk milliyetperverliğini Türkçe ve ecnebî lisanlarda neşrettiğim eserlerle bütün dünyaya tanıttırmağı kendim için vazife saydım. Bu cümleden olarak 1910 senesinde[2] Türkçe ve Fransızca olarak "Türkler bir ruhu millî arıyorlar" 1914 senesinde Almanca, İngilizce ve kısmen Türkçe "Türkizm ve Pantürkizm" ve 1937 senesinde muhterem partinin tasvibile ve Fransız parlamentosu reisi Mr. Herriot'nun pek sitayışkâr mukaddimesile Fransızca ve Türkçe ve Prag Üniversitesi rektörünün mukkadimesile Çekçe olarak "Kemalizm" namlarile birbirini tamamlıyan üç eser neşr ettim. Türk Milliyetçiliğinin muhtelif safhalarını sistemleştiren ve canlandıran bu üç eser Avrupa ilmî mahafilinde büyük bir rağbete mazhar oldu ve Avrupa muharrirleri tarafından bu mevzuu üzerine muhtelif lisanlarda neşr olunan yüzlerce eser için esas ve mehaz ittihaz olunmuştur.

1912 senesinde İstanbula hicret ettikten sonra dahi en mühim ticaret müesseselerinin umum müdürlüğünü der'uhte etmek suretile hayatımı serbest surette kazanmağa devam etmekle beraber yine Ziya Gök Alp'ın ilham ve irşadile resmî makamların direktifleri dairesinde hars ve kültür sahalarında çalışmağa ve bu itibarla Türk Yurdu, Türk Derneği, Yeni Mecmua gibi mecmualarda muntazam surette millî intibaha hadım yazılar neşr etmekten geri kalmadım.

1916 tarihinde Türkiye'de o zamana kadar münteşir olmıyan Millî İktisat fikrini memlekete sokmak ve yaymak maksadile ve memleketin en maruf iktisatçılarının iştirakile İktisat Derneği namı altında bir cemiyet kurdum ve bu cemiyetin organı olmak üzere Türkçe, Fransızca ve Almanca olarak merhum Celal Sahir'le beraber ve Hükûmetin maddî ve manevî muzahereti ile İktisadiyat mecmuası namı altında bir haftalık mecmua neşir ve ayni zamanda Hukuk Fakültesinde İlmî Mali müderris muavinliğini der'uhte ederek Ali Kemalin Maarif Nazırlığına kadar vazife ifasına devam ettim.

Selanikte Tamimi Lisanı Osmanî Cemiyetini tesis etmek suretile daha o zaman takip ettiğim Millî Birlik gayesine matuf mesaıme İstanbulda dahi büyük bir gayretle devam ve bu itibarla hars birliği ve Türk Birliği namındaki Cemiyetleri tesis ve bu Cemiyetlerin reisliğinde uzun seneler faaliyette bulundum. Millî Birlik hususundaki fikir ve kanaatlerimi 1928 senesinde neşr ettiğim "Türkleşdirme" nam eserimde evamiri aşere şeklinde toplıyarak neşr ettim. Bu eser en güzide mütefekkirlerinin takdirkâr mütalealarını havi olduğu gibi gerek Türk ve gerek ecnebi matbuatında büyük bir alaka ile karşılaşmıştır.

Ticarî ve İktisadî faaliyetimde ihtisasa büyük ehemmiyet atf ederek memleketimizin en mühim ihraç maddesi olan tütün üzerine ihtisas peyda ettim. 1916 senesinden 1922 senesine kadar Duhan Türk Anonim Şirketinin ve 1922 senesindenberi Herman Spierer ve Şürekâsı müessesesinin umum müdürlüğünü ifa etmek suretile memleketimizden senede hiç olmazsa 4-5 milyon kilo tütün ihracına hizmet etmekteyim. 1936 senesinde Ankarada İktisat Vekaletinde in'ikad eden tütün kongresinin umumî kâtipliğini ifa ettiğim gibi elyevm de Türk Tütüncüler Birliğinin umumî kâtipliği uhdemde bulunmaktadır.

Ecnebi lisan olarak Fransızca ve Almancayı eserler yazabilecek kadar iyi bilirim. Rumca, İtalyanca ve İngilızceye vukufum vardır.

MUNİS TEKİNALP, HAL TERCÜMESİ (1939)[1]

Fikrî ve Umumî Hayatım Hakkında : Fikriyat faaliyetine Selanikte intibak eden Yeni Asır gazetesinde iktisadî ve içtimaî mevzular üzerinde 1908 senesinde muntazam neşriyat yapmak suretile başladım. Bu yanda muhtelif içtimaî ve iktisadî mevzular üzerine ayrıca bazı eserler neşrettim.

Selanikte İttehat ve Terraki cemiyetinin içtimaî ve harsî faaliyetine pek yakından alakadar oldum. "Tamimi lisanı Osmanî" namile bir cemiyet tesis ederek reisliğini deruhte ettim. Maarif müdiriyetinin resmî takdirnamesi sureti merbuttur. 1910 senesinde Selanik meclisi umumî vilayet azalığına ve bilahara encümeni vilâyet azalığına intihap olundum ve Selaniğin sukutun kadar bu vazifeyi ifaya devam ettim.

Selanikte İttihat ve Terakki umumî merkezinde Ziya Gök Alpın idaresi altında başlayan *"Türkçülük"*, *"Yeni Hayat"*, ve *"Yeni Lisan"* cereyanlarına büyük bir gayretle iştirak ettim. Ziya Gök Alpın ilhamı ile "Türkçülük" hakkındaki dağınık fikirleri ilk defa olarak sistemleyerek 1912 tarihinde "Türkler bir ruhu millî arıyorlar" namı altında Paris'in en maruf mecmuası olan Mercure de France mecmuasında neşrettim. Bu teşebbüs merhum Yusuf Akçora tarafından Türkçeye tercüme olunarak Türk yurdunda Türkçüluğün ilk esasları olmak üzere neşrolunmuş ve bundan sonra bu mevzu üzerine Avrupa müellifleri tarafından neşrolunan bütün eserlerde dahi bu tettebü yegane mehaz teşkil etmiştir.

Aynı devrede diğer Fransız ilmî mecmualarında Türk tiyatrosu Türk matbuatı ve bu gibi mevzular üzerine uzun tetebbüler neşrettim. (memleketimizde tanınmış kalem sahipleri bu faaliyetimden malumat sahibidirler).

Selânigin sukutu üzerine İstanbula hicret ettim. Zaten Yunanlılar Türk millî ve vatanî vazifelere olan alakalarımı, bu husustaki faaliyetlerimi ve ezcümle Girit hakkındaki bütün mitinglerdeki nutuklarımı bilirlerdi.

İstanbulda yerleşdikden sonra dahi hayatımı serbest surette kazanmağa devam etmekle beraber fikrî ve umumî hayat sahalarındaki faaliyetime aynı suretle devam ederek Ziya Gökalp'ın ilham ve idaresi altında azamî gayretle hizmet ifasına çalıştım. Falih Rıfkı, Necmeddin Sadık, Köprülü Fuat gibi kalem erbabile beraber "Büyük Mecmua"nın daimi muharrirlerinden olarak senelerce çalışdığım gibi merhum Celal Sahirin iştirakı ile İttehad ve Terraki umumî merkezinin maddî ve manevî yardımı ile Türkçe, Fransızca ve Almanca olarak "İktisadiyat Mecmuası". namı altında haftalık bir mecmua neşrettim. Bu mecmuanın şiarı Türkiyede o zamana kadar meçhul kalmış olan "millî iktisat" fikirlerini sokmak ve yaymakdı. Aynı zamanda yine bu maksadla teşebbüsüm üzerine "İktisadiyat Derneği" namile bir cemiyet kuruldu. İktisadiyat mecmuası bu derneğin organı olarak iki sene müddetle neşriyata devam etti. İttehat ve Terakki hars şubesinin yardımı ile intişar eden Türk Derneği, Türk Yurdu gibi gazete ve mecmualarda dahi tahriri muavenette bulundum.

1914 senesinde yine Ziya Gök Alpın ilham ve teşvikîle Almanca olarak "Türkismus und Pantürkismus" namile bir eser neşrettim. Bu eser İngilizceyede tercüme olundu. Her iki edisyon dünyanın her tarafında fevkalade rağbete mazhar oldu. René Pinon gibi maruf müverrihler[2] bu kitabı o zamanki Türk milliyetçiliğinin "kitabı mukaddesi" olarak telekki ve ilân etmişlerdir. Bu eserin mühim fasılları kitap halinde Türkçe dahi neşrolunmuştur.

Serbest mesleğimden ayrılmamakla beraber harbi umumî ve mütareke senelerinde İstanbul hukuk fakültesinde "İlmi Malî" müderris muavinliğinde bulundum. Ali Kemalin maarif vekilliği zamanında ittehatçılık şaibesile vazifeme nihayet verildi.

1928 senesinde Türkiyede bulunan bütün vatandaşların türkleşdirilmesi mevzuu üzerine "Türkleşdirme" namile bir kitap neşrettim. Bu kitap Necmeddin Sadık, Köprülü Fuat, Celal Sahir, Yunus Nadi, Ağaoğlu Ahmet gibi mütefekkirlerimizin bu eser ve eserin mevzu olan mesele hakkındaki mütalaalarını dahi muhtevi bulunuyor. Bu Türkleşdirme meselesi hakkında Türkiyede müteaddid neşriyatım ve konferanslarım olduğu gibi işim için sık sık yaptığım Avrupa seyahatlarından istifade ederek Avrupa'nın muhtelif yerlerinde Türkiye hakkında Fransız ve Almanca olarak bir çok konferanslarım vardır.

Fikriyat sahasında en son eserim Kemalizm mevzuu üzerine olup muhterem partinin tensip ve tasvibile aynı zamanda Türkçe ve Fransızca intişar etmiştir.

Türkçe edisyon Türkiyede büyük bir rağbete mazhar olduğu gibi Fransızca edisyon dahi Avrupa ve Amerikada umumî takdir kazanmıştır. Fransızca edisyon Fransız parlamento reisi Herriotnın pek sitayışkâr bir mukaddimesini havidir. Bu kitap ahiren Prag üniversitesi rektörünün mukaddimesile Çekçe neşrolunduğu gibi yakında Romence dahi neşrolunacaktır.

İş Faaliyetim Hakkında: İş sahasında dahi 35 senelik faaliyetim vardır. Bu müddet zarfında umuru hukukiye müdiri veya ticarî müdür sıfatile en mühim ticarî ve iktisadî müesseselerin başında bulunduğumdan ticaret ve iktisadın bütün sahalarında ilmî tetkik ve tetebbülerim olduğu gibi amelî tecrübelerim pek çoktur.

Uzun müddetten beri Türkiye'nin en mühim tütün müesseselerinden birinin başında bulunduğumdan ezcümle tütüncülükte ihtisasım vardir, ve bu itibarla 1935 senesinde Ankarada İktisat Vekâletinde akdolunan tütün kongresinde umumî kâtiplik vazifesini ifa ettiğim gibi ahiren teşekkül eden Türkiye tütüncüler birliğinin umum kâtipliği dahi öhdemde bulunuyor. Bu itibarla memleketi alakadar eden malî ve iktisadî hususatta dahi haddim olmayarak az çok nafi olabileceğimi ümid ediyorum.

TEKİN ALP, TÜRK RUHU

Türk Ruhu ve Millî Kahramanlar

Bütün cihan, Türkü, ancak bedenî kudreti ve gürbüzlüğü ile tanır. (Türk gibi kuvvetli) sözü, asırlardanberi bütün dünyanın tasdik ettiği tarihî bir hakitatın ifadesidir.

Fakat Türk milleti, yalnız bedeni kuvvetile teferrüt etmez. O, bunca kuvvetli devleti, bunca mühim imparatorluğu, yalnız bedenî kuvvetile yaratmış değildir. Türk milletinin asırlar süren azamet ve ihtişamı, daha ziyade, ruh kuvvetinin neticesidir. Orta Asyanın yaylalarından ve steplerinden taşan bu millet, gerçi beraberinde, eşsiz bir beden kuvveti getirmiş ve bu kuvvet, iklimin ve yeni hayat şartlarının icap ettirdiği değişikliklere maruz kalmıştır. Fakat, bu millet, bundan başka, iklimlerin ve hayat şartlarının değişikliklerinden pek az müteessir olan, tartıya gelmez bir şey daha getirmiştir: Ruhunun kuvveti. Türk, harp menkibelerini ve şanlı zaferlerini, herşeyden evvel, manevî âmille kıyas edilince ikinci derecede bir unsur vazifesi gören beden kuvvetinden ziyade, bu tartılmaz kuvvetine borcludur.

Bu eserin gayesi de, işte, nice sağlam ve kudretli imparatorluğun yaratılmasını mümkün kılan o türk ruhunun ahlakî ve manevî vasıflarını belirtmcktir.

Avrupalı âlimler ve tarihçiler Türklerle çok meşgul olmuşlardır. Türklerin tarihi menkıbelerine dair yüzlerce eser yazılmış ve kendilerine barbar vasfı verilmesi unutulmamıştır. Fakat, bu milletin ruhunu tetkik eden ve onun, cihan tarihinde bu derece mühim mühim bir rol oynamağa nasıl muvaffak olduğunu anlamak gayretini gösterenler nadirdir,

Biz, bu muazzam boşluğu doldurmak kabiliyetinde olduğumuzu iddia etmiyoruz; bununla beraber, umuyoruz ki, bu mütevazi eser, o hedefe doğru atılmış bir adım olabilecektir. Giriştiğimiz işin son derece muğlak olduğunu, gözden uzak tutmuyoruz. Bizzat Türk ruhunun, tarih boyunca değişmez bir mahiyet arzetmemesi de, bu işi daha fazla güçleştiriyor. Ata yurdlarından göçen Türkler, çeşitli kültürler ve medeniyetler ortasında gelişmişler, bunlara az çok uymak zaruretinde kalmışlardır. O sebeple, eserimizi, herbiri Türk ruhunu başka başka şekillerde gösteren muhtelif devrelere ayırmak mecburiyetindeyiz. Bunu yaparken, bu devreleri birbirine bağlayan, çıplak gözle seçilmesi imkânsız bağları da belirtmeyi ihmal etmiyeceğiz. Bu devrelerden her birinin hususiyetini teşkil eden noktaları daha iyi belli etmek için, bu devreleri şahıslandıran kahramanları tetkik edeceğiz. Şuna kaniiz ki, Türk ruhunu kavrayabilmek için en iyi çare, onun, inkişafının muhtelif devrelerinde timsalini teşkil eden şahısları tetkik ve tahlil etmektir. Bundan evvel de bir münasebetle diğer bir eserimizde söylediğimiz gibi, türk milleti, ancak, başında, onun özünü, ruhunu ve milli emellerini şahıslandıran bir başkan bulunduğu zaman kuvvetini ve hayatiyetini gösterir.

Türk ruhunun tebellürü, dört merhaleye ayrılabilir. Başta, atalar merhalesi gelir ki, binlerce yıl süren bu merhalede, atalar ruhu Ural-Altay steplerinin potasında yoğrulmuştur. Bu devreyi, millî kahraman olan Mete ve Atila şahıslandırılar. Bu, İslâmiyetten önceki devredir. İkinci merhale İslâmiyet merhalesidir ki, devamı müddetince, atalar ruhu uzun bir küsuf geçirmiştir. Onun yerine, milletin manevi hayatı üzerinde, sentetik yahut islâmlararası adını vereceğimiz ruh hâkim olmuştur. Bu merhaleyi, o ruhun son timsali, tanzimat devrinin kahramanı olan Namık Kemal şahıslandırır. Namık Kemal hürriyete susamış bir kahramandır. Vatanı hürriyete kavuşturmak istiyordu : fakat, milleti hürriyete kavuşturmak için, sentetik ve islâmlararası ruhun esiri olan Türkün atalar ruhuna hürriyet bahşetmek lâzım geldiğini idrak etmemişti.

Tanzimat devrinde, Namık Kemal'le çağdaşlarının feryat ederek millet için hürriyet istediklerini görüyoruz. Namık Kemale göre, millet, padişahın meşrutiyeti vermesile hürriyete kavuşmuş olacaktı. Namık Kemal, Türk ruhunu, asırlık esaretinden kurtarmayı hiçbir zaman düşünmedi. Onun kanaatince, Türkiye 400 çadırlık bir müslüman aşiretinin yarattığı bir müslüman devletti. Namık Kemal, sürgünde ve zindanda istisnaî bir muameleye kavuştuğu zaman, dostlarına "Bakın müslümanlığın kuvvetine" diye yazıyordu. Namık Kemal, garptan, vatan mefhumunu getirdi, fakat asrî manada milliyet mefhumu, kendisinde, şuurlu bir tarzda henüz tebellür etmemişti. Milliyet prensibi müteyakkız gümrükçülerin gözleri önünden geçerek, Osmanlı İmparatorluğu hududunu aşmışsa da, bu hal, müslim ve gayri müslim, Türkten gayri milletlere mahsustu; öyle bir modern silahtı ki, ona sahip olmıyan türklere karşı kullanılıyordu.

Üçüncü merhale meşrutiyet devridir ki, gebelik devri diye vasıflandırılabilir. Bu gebelik, yeni Türkiyeyi doğurmuştur. Jöntürk ihtilâlı, 1908 de, milleti esaretten kurtardı, fakat atalar ruhu, zincire vurulmuş olarak kaldı.

Türk askeri, Makedonya dağlarında, Arnavutluk yaylalarında, Suriye ve Irak çöllerinde, imparatorluğun muhafızlığı olan ezelî vazifesini hakkiyle başarmak için, halâ kanını dökmeye mecburdu. Fakat pek çok aydın Türk, acı acı şöyle diyordu : "Bu komıtacılar, türk jandarmanın kurşunu ile ölen bu müslim ve gayri müslim asiler ne istiyorlar? Yunanlı, Arnavut, Bulgar, Arap olduklarını söylemeğe, kendi dillerini konuşmağa, kendi edebiyatlarına ve kendi kültürlerine sahip olmağa hak iddia ediyorlar. Daha doğrusu, milletin kanını dökmesini intaç eden zahirî ideal budur. Pekâlâ, türk jandarmasının kendisi bu hakka sahip midir? Hiçbir yabancı onun bu tabii hakkını inkâr edemez, fakat bir türk, jandarma rolünü oynamak hakkına sahip olmak için, asla türk değil, osmanlı veya islâm olduğunu söylemek mecburiyetindedir. Onun özdili, bayağı köylünün, yahut rençberin konuştuğu kaba dil olmaktan başka işe yaramıyor. Fikrinin gıdası olan edebiyatı, ancak kendi kaba dilinden, birkaç kelime karşılık olarak, yabancı bir dilde buluyor. Karısı halâ haremin kafesi arkasında kapalı oturmağa mecburdur. Milletin büyük çokluğunu teşkil eden türk köylüsü, türk rençberi, bütün sene dolap beygiri gibi çalıştıktan sonra, ya, türk olduğunu söylemeğe utanan İstanbuldaki padişahı, ya, kendisini istismardan başka bir şey düşünmeyen âşâr mültezimini, yahut, İstanbuldaki, İzmirdeki veyahut imparatorluğun diğer büyük şehirlerindeki reayadan olan madrabazı, bezirgânı beslemek zorundadır. Camide, bir tek türkçe kelime işitmez. Sırf türkçe konuşan ve yazan, arapça ve farsça cümleler ve formüllerle hünerler göstermesini bilmeyenler, ümmî, cahil, hülâsa "Türk" oldukları için istihkar edilirler.

Aydın Türkler, eski rejimin açtığı yaraları sarmak, bunca fedakârlıklar bahasına kazanılan hürriyeti istifade mevkiine koymak çarelerini araştırırlarken, devrin bazı nüfuzlu kimseleri, her şeyden evvel, imparatorluktaki bütün unsurların ittihadını tahakkuk ettirmek lâzım geldiğini ileri sürüyorlar. Bir takım politikacılar ise memleketin ancak bütün islâm unsurlarının birleşmesile yükselebileceğini iddia ediyorlardı. Hiç kimse, işe başından başlamağa, türk unsurunu öteki unsurların bulundukları vaziyete getirmeye cesaret edemiyordu.

Şuradan buradan, Türklerin türkleştirilmesini isteyen hafif sesler işitiliyordu. Fakat bu sesler, yalnız çok hafif olduklarından değil, tebellür etmiş bir ideal ifade etmediklerinden çabucak susturuluyordu.

İşte, o zaman Ziya Gökalp, ilmî ve sistemli türkçülüğü ve yorulmaz dinamizmi ile, hükumeti elinde tutan İttihad ve Terakki fırkası komitasındaki bütün meslektaşları üzerinde kazandığı inkâr kabul edilmez nüfuzu ile, ortaya çıktı.

Binaenaleyh, Ziya Gökalp'ı, yeni Türkiyenin bu gebelik devresini hakkile temsil eden "şahıslanma" (incarnation) telâkki ediyoruz. O, parmağı yaraya batırmış, tam teşhisi koymuş ve takdire değer bir enerji ile işe girişmiştir.

Fakat İsmet İnönü'nün de nutuklarının birinde belirttikleri gibi :

"Osmanlı devrini görmüş olanlar bu fikirlerden (inkılâp rejimimizin esasları) herhangi birinin üzerine konmasına osmanlı nizamının asla mütehammil olmadığını iyice hatırlarlar. Osmanlı nizamı son asırların fennî ve içtimaî terakkilerine karşı bünyesini terdricî olarak değişen ve yükselen tekâmülden uzak tutmak gayretile dört duvarı kalın bir hücre içinde çalıştılar. Bu çırpınmalar türk milletinin kurtuluş davasiyle münasebettar olamazdı."

Demek oluyor ki, milletin, yeni Türkiyeyi doğuran tam hürriyeti, Kemal Atatürk'ün ve İsmet İnönü'nün şahıslandırdıkları Kemalist inkılâbın eseridir.

Türk ruhu, pp. 1-5.

TÜRK RUHUNUN YAPISI NEDİR?

Birçok âlimler, umumî surette millî ruhun tahlili ile uğraşmışlardır. Alman, Fransız, İtalyan, Rus, İspanyol ilh, ruhunun tahliline çalışılmıştır. Fakat hepsinin muvaffak olduğunu kabul etmek rastgele bir iddia olur.

Başka milletler hakkında güç olan bu tahlil işi, mukadderatı ve tarihi diğer Şark ve Garp milletlerinki ile mukayese mümkün olmayan türk milleti hakkında büsbütün güçtür. Hergangi bir milletin, ortaya çıktığı andan itibaren bugüne kadar olan inkişafını tarih boyunca takip ediniz, gelişiminin muhtelif merhalelerini, melezleşme hareketlerini, onun kati teşekkülüne yardım eden ve bugünkü çehresini kendisine veren bütün âmilleri kavrayabilirsiniz. Meselâ biliyoruz ki, İngiliz milleti, şimalli ve Normandiyalı milletlerin bir halitasıdır. Alman milleti, tarih boyunca Slav ahalinin karıştığı Cermen milletlerden mürekkeptir; ve bu Slavlar, Töton kabilelerinin içinde erimiş, tamamile kaybolmuştur. Fransız milleti, Lâtin ve cermen milletlerin bir halitasından vücude gelmiştir, ilh. Fakat şu veya bu milletin halitasına, bidayette girmiş olan muhtelif ahalinin ırk seciyesi ne olursa olsun muhtelif unsurların bir tek pota içinde izabesi keyfiyeti, tam ve kat'i surette vuku bulmuştur. Bazı milletlerde azçok bariz, bazılarında belirsiz olan bu gibi halitalardan öyle mütecanis milletler çıkmıştır ki, terekküp ettiği unsurları ayırdetmek imkânsızdır. Yalnız, dilini, edebiyatını, kültürünü diğerlerine zorla kabul ettiren hâkim unsuru ötekilerden tefrik edebiliyoruz. Diğer unsurlar, iz bırakmadan kaybolmuştur. Tarihin potasından, bütün efradı ayni dili konuşan, ayni edebiyatı işleyen ve ayni kültürden feyiz alan, ekseriya ayni dinin saliki milletler çıkmıştır. Milletin teşekkülü için vücudü elzem bütün unsurlar ayni cemiyet içinde birleşmiş bulunuyorlar ve ilk anından bugüne kadar milletin birliğini hiç bir sebep ihlâl etmemiştir.

Türk milleti için vaziyet böyle midir? Türkün ilk ataları Orta Asyanın yüksek yaylalarında yetişmiş bir insan tipidir. Binlerce yıl, orada, oturduğu yerin iklimine, toprağına, muhitine ve hayat şartlarına uygun bir yaşayış, hareket ve fikir tarzı edinmiştir. Bu yüksek yaylaların milyonlarca ve milyonlarca sakini, Milâttan evvel ikinci asırdan beri birbirini takip eden muazzam dalgalar halinde Avrupaya ve Asyaya akmaya başlamışlar ve orada, fatih sıfatile yerleşmişlerdir. Bu müstevliler, çetin, gürbüz, cesur, binlerce yıllık kökleşmiş geleneklere, adeta insiyakı mahiyette, atalar mirası temayüllere uyan insanlardır. Hâkimiyetleri altına aldıkları milletlerin yaşayış tarziyle, kültürü ile hiçbir surette bağdaşmıyan, kendilerine has kültürleri vardı. Bu fatihler, sade ve mütevazı, fakat iyi nizam altına alınmış, iptidaî fakat kuvvetli teşkilâta sahip göçebelerdi. Buna mukabil, zaptedilen memleketlerin ahalisi, azçok incelmiş bir kültüre sahip yerlilerdi. Fakat, içtimaî bünyeleri, fatih milletlerin içtimaî bünyeleri kadar sağlam değildi. Bu fatihlerin yazılı olmayan kanunları, ihlâl edilemez gelenekleri, nizam ve asayiş kaideleri, yüksek ahlâk prensipleri, yerli milletlerin, inceliklerinden, medeniyetinden, yazılı kanunlarından ve edebî eserlerinden çok daha tesirli bir kuvvet teşkil ediyordu.

Fatih göçebelerle yerli ahali arasındaki bu kültür ve medeniyet tezatları, milletlerin yaptıkları bütün diğer göçlerde olduğu gibi, çeşitli unsurların imtizacına ve milletler arasında kaynaşmaya bittabi mâni olmuştur. Stepin mağrur silahşorları, mağlup memleketlere yerleşince, kendi âlemlerine çekilip kapanıyorlar, muhteşem infirad usulü tatbik ediyorlar, bir yandan da askerlik mesleklerine devam ve, icabeden teşkilâtla, efendilik mevkilerini muhafaza ediyorlardı. Onların hakimiyetine boyun eğen yerli halk, kendi idarî, kültürel ve dinî muhtariyetine sahip kalıyordu. Zaptedilen bütün memleketlerde, birbirinden tamamen ayrı iki cemiyet vardı ki, ayrı ayrı yaşamakta devam ediyor, aralarında hiçbir çarpışma, hiçbir imtizaç olmuyordu. Fatihlerin cemiyeti, steplerden gelen yeni yeni kütlelerle mütemadiyen artıyor, stepler, fazla gelen nüfuzlarını, zaman zaman komşu memleketlere, tercihan, hemcinslerinin daha evvel yerleşmiş bulundukları bölgelere taşırıyorlardı.

İşte, esas itibariyle türk olan kültür, ata yurdun uzaklığına, ve yabancı milletlerle müşterek hayata rağmen, böylece sapsağlam kalmıştır.

Türk fatihlerin İslâmiyeti kabulünden sonra, her iki cemiyeti yani fatihlerle mağlupları birbirinden ayıran şu sızmazlık hali, ortadan kalktı. Artık, ayrılık, müminlerle kâfirler, müslümanlarla dinsizler arasında idi. Türk fatihler, artık kendi âlemlerinde sıkı sıkı kapalı değillerdi. Ayni dine salik başka milletlerle yaşayışta ortakdılar. Zamanla, Milletin kendi bünyesinde bir ayrılık oldu. İslâmiyeti kendilerinden evvel kabul eden milletlerin dilile Allaha ibadet etmek, peygamberinin izinde yürümek zarureti, türk okur yazarlarını arapça ve farsça öğrenmeğe mecbur ediyordu. Yalnız din bilgileri değil, arap ve fars dilleri ve edebiyatları fatih Türkler tarafından, geniş ölçüde okunup öğrenilmek icap etti.

Bu suretle, aydın Türkler, arap ve fars diline, şiirine ve kültürüne tamamen bağlandılar; Türk dilini, atalar kültürünü, ancak halk muhafaza etmişti. Fütuhata kadar fatih unsurla yerli halk arasında mevcut ikiliğin mahiyeti başkalaşmıştı. Ayrılık yer değiştirdi, şimdi, fatihlerle mağluplar arasında değil, bizzat fatihler arasında, güzide sınıfla halk tabakası arasında kendini gösteriyordu. Güzide sınıfla aydın insanlar, yerli halkın, kendilerile ayni dinden olan araplarla İranlıların kültürlerini benimsedikleri halde, halk kendi dilini, kendi geleneklerini, kendi ırk ve adetlerini ve kendi kültürünü muhafaza ediyordu.

Galiplerle mağluplar arasındaki din birliğinin, güzide sınıf mensuplarında bariz bir şekilde, halk tabakasında mutedil bir ölçüde kültürel ve içtimaî bir yakınlık hasıl etmekte kalmadığını, bir ırk melezliğine de sebebiyet verdiğini ilâveye hacet yoktur. O tarihde, fertleri ayırd etmek hususunda yegâne kıstas olan din birliği sayesinde, içlerinde, hayli çok miktarda mühtedi bizanslı da bulunan muhtelif islâm unsurlar arasında evlenmeler tabiî ve sık sık vuku bulan bir işti. Bu melezleşme, güzelliklerile şöhret bulmuş Gürcü, Kafkas ilâh . . . kadınlarıyle dolu saraylarda oturan sultanlar başta olmak üzere, bilhassa yüksek tabakada fazla idi. Binaenaleyh, bir yandan kan yakınlığı, bir yandan kültür yakınlığı, milletin güzide sınıfını, türkün millî geleneğinden ve millî şahsiyetinden, gitgide daha fazla uzaklaştırıyordu. Bu vaziyet, asırlar uzunluğunca, son zamanlara kadar, kâh artarak kâh eksilerek devam edegeldi.

Binaenaleyh, bugünkü türk ruhunun, evvelâ Ural-Altay yaylalarındaki binlerce yıllık hayatla yoğrulmuş İslâmiyetten önceki devrin öz türkünün, sonraki, dinî hayatın silinmez tesirlerine tabi İslâmiyet devri türkünün, en nihayet de modern ve garplı kültürün tesirlerini benimsemiş modern türkün hususiyetlerini taşıyan bir halitadan yapılmış olduğunu kabul etmek mecburiyetindeyiz. 1908 jöntürk inkılâbından sonra başlayan türkçülük hareketinin öncüleri, türkçülükle islâmcılığı birbirinden ayırmamakta pek haklı idiler. Türk millî ruhunun Ural-Altay âlemile islâm âleminin bir araya gelmiş şeklinden yoğurulduğunu, onlar iyiden iyiye biliyorlardı. Kemalist inkılâbı, türk ruhunun esas terkibini hiç bir zaman inkâr etmemiş, ancak, Muhammed'in hakikî şeriatile hiç alâkası olmıyan sözümona dini, kara taassubun tesirlerini, keza, umumiyet itibariyle şark ruhu veya zihniyeti adı verilen izleri, milletin hayatından kat'i surette uzaklaştırmak istemiştir. Kemalist inkılâbı, bu sahada yalnız mazinin döküntülerini süpürmekle iktifa etmemiş, asırlık esaretinden kurtulan atalar ruhunun inkişafına tam bir serbestî vermek suretile, bu süpürülüp temizlenmiş saha üzerinde, garp medeniyeti nimetlerinin gelişmesine yol açmıştır.

Türk ruhu, pp. 20-24.

NETİCE : İNHİTAT VE SATVET

Roma, Bizans, Endülüs, İran İmparatorlukarı gibi büyük imparatorluklar tarihile meşgul olmuş birçok müellilflerin kullandıkları "satvet ve inhitat" formülü yerine bu faslın başına "inhitat ve satvet" tabirini koymamız dikkatsizlik eseri değildir. Osmanlı İmparatorluğunun tarihini yazanlar da "Türkiyenin satveti ve inhitatı" tabirini kullanmışlardır. Fakat tarihî olaylar, onlara; aldandıklarını, ve bizim bu fasıl da yaptığımız gibi, kelimelerin yerlerini değiştirmek gerektiğini ispat etmiştir. Bu münasebetle kendime ait bir hatırayı burada zikretmek isterim.

Müteveffa Gustave Lebon, *Bibliothèque philosophique* direktörü sıfatile, felsefe kitapları serisinde "Osmanlı imparatorluğunun satveti ve inhitatı" adlı bir eser neşrettirmeği pek istiyordu. 1912 senesi idi. Türkiye, Trablus harbinden sonra patlak veren Balkan harbi neticesinde, yeniden, mühim toprak kayıplarına uğramıştı. Jön Türk inkılâbına rağmen, Türkiye halâ "Hasta adam"di. Hem eskisinden daha hasta idi. Gustave Lebon, daha nice kimseler gibi, Türkiyenin inhitatını kat'i ve şifasız sandığı için, kendi *Bibliothèque Philosophique* serisine girecek hususî bir eserde, büyük bir satvet devrinden sonra gelen bu inhitatın sebeplerini izah etmekliğim teklifinde bulundu. Seçkin feylosofun teklifini, tabiî, redettim; çünkü, bilhassa, koca imparatorluğun bir başından öteki başına kadar, Türk milleti bir hayat hamlesile sarsıldığı anda, Türkiyenin inhitatına inanmak istemiyordum. Bence bu inhitat Türkiye tarihinde, geçici bir safhadan ibaretti, ve kendi tahminlerime göre, sonradan Kemalist inkılâpla neticelenen Türkçülük uyanışı, bu safhaya nihayet verecekti. O tarihte, "Türkler millî bir ruh arıyorlar"[1] başlığı altında, muhtelif dillerde bir etüd neşretmiştim. Bu etüdde, Türkiyenin inhitatı, haddi zatında mukadder bir şey olmadığını ve millî şuurun uyanması sayesinde Türk milletinin; kendisine gelmeğe ve kalkınmağa başladığını anlatıyordum. Iki sene sonra 1913[2] umumî harbi patladı. Türkiye dört yol ağzında bulunuyordu. O sırada vereceği karar onun akıbetini kat'i surette tayin edecekti. Devletin ve milletin hayatı veya ölümü, bu karara bağlı idi. O zaman iktidar mevkiinde bulunan ve hepsi yeni millî rönesans ruhu ile meşbu olan jön Türkler, bir an tereddüt etmediler. Millî istiklâli başlı başına inkâr eden kapitülasyonların ilga edildiğini ilân ettiler. Türk milletini iki asırdan beri tazyik eden çarlık tehdidinden ebediyen kurtulmak imkânlarını, bu harbin vereceğini kuvvetle umuyorlardı. O devir jön Türk idarecilerinden bazıları, istenilen hedefe ulaşmak için en iyi çarenin, çarlar tarafından ayni tehdide maruz bulunan Almanlarla ittifak etmek olduğu kanaatini beslediler. Türk milliyetçilik hareketine dayanan dinamik bazı zevat tarafından, söz gelişi kaçak suretiyle içeri sokulan Türk-Cermen ittifakının esası budur.

1912 de[3] neşredilen "Türkçülük ve Pantürkizm" adlı kitabımda bilmünasebe bu meseleden bahsetmiştim. Churchill, umumî harbe dair olan kitabında, eserimin bu kısmından bahsederek, İstanbulda vazife gören müttefik diplomatlarının, ortaya döktüğüm âmilleri hesaba katmamış olmalarına hayret etmektedir.

Sonraki hadiseler Pantürkizm ideolojisinin ateşli önderlerinin, tahminlerinde ve takdirlerinde yanıldıklarını ispat etmiştir. Fakat Türk milleti, mağlubiyete boyun eğmekten imtina etmekte yanılmamıştır. Irkın insiyakı uyanmış, kanın sesi duyulmuş, millî ruhun tahteşşuurunda bulunan kahramanlık zihniyeti galip gelmiş ve millete hep bir ağızdan ya "istiklâl ya ölüm" avazesini yükselttirmişti. İçerideki düşmana, Türkiyenin henüz bir çok müteaddid vilâyetlerini işgal etmekte bulunan İtilâf Devletlerine Anadoluyu işgal eden Yunan kıtalarına, nihayet, Türkiyenin hakikî inhitatına sebep olan manevî kara kuvvetlere karşı istiklâl savaşı, bu intihaba davet avazesile başladı.

İstiklâl uğrunda yapılan bu savaş, Avrupanın, Türk mucizesi adı verdiği mesut şekilde bitti. Türk mucizesi, ancak bir zâf âmili olabilen imparatorluğu diriltmemiş, Türk milletinin ittihadını, kuvvetini ve kudretini ihya etmiş ve Türk milleti, satvetine tekrar erişmiştir. Bu satvet, saha satveti değil, imparatorluk satveti değil, derinliğine bir satvet, bir ruh satveti idi ve Türk milletinin birkaç sene içinde, medeniyetin bütün sahalarında, başka milletlerin ancak asırlar devamınca tahakkuk ettirebildikleri terakkileri vücude getirmesine imkân vermiştir.

Bununla beraber artık bundan sonra zafer ilân edip gaflet uykusuna dalmak tehlikeli olduğunu belirtmeğe lüzum görmüyorum. Şimdilik elde edilen netice Atalardan miras kalan manevî kuvvetlerin dirilişinden ibarettir. Bu da ancak bir başlangıç teşkil edebilir. Hakikî satvet Türkün yeni mefkûresi olması lâzım gelen netice henüz elde edilmemiştir. Atatürk'ün "Asrî medeniyetin seviyesi üstüne yükselmeliyiz" parolasının tahakkukundan henüz uzak bulunuyoruz.

Milletin şefleri, bukadar asırlık şaşkınlıktan sonra yeniden elde edilen manevî kuvvetleri titizlikle korumak mecburiyetindedirler. Onlar pek iyi biliyorlar ki mazide Atalar ruhunu uyuşukluğa mahkum eden sinsi kuvvetler henüz büsbütün ortadan kalkmamıştır. İlk fırsatta yeniden saldırmağa hazır bir vaziyette pusuda duruyorlar. Bilhassa manevî ölçüleri altüst eden umumî harp buhranları zamanında bu sinsi düşmana karşı milleti korumak başlıca vazifelerimizden biridir.

Temas ettiğimiz manevî tehlikeleri burada saymak uzun olur. Fakat, biri şark tarafından, diğeri garp tarafından tehdit gösteren belli başlı iki tehlikeyi sükutla geçiştirmemize imkân yoktur.

Bu eserin ikinci kısmında izah ettiğimiz gibi, Türk milletinin takriben on asır taşıdığı sentetik ruh, şarktan gelme yabancı nüfuzların bir halitasıdır. Binaenaleyh, şark tarafından bizi tehdit eden tehlike, şark ve Bizans esaslı sentetik ruhun hiç beklenmiyen bir aksülâmeli, bir uyanışı ihtimalidir. Eğer şeflerimizin uyanıklığı mâni olmasaydı, sahnede tekrar hangi âmiller gözükecekti, bunu iyice biliyoruz. Bunlar, son asırlar zarfında, Türk milletinin manevî sukutuna ve Osmanlı İmparatorluğunun inhitatına sebebiyet veren ayni âmillerdir. Bu âmiller arasında, en başta, şarklı tevekkülü, hafiyelik, iki yüzlülük, dalkavukluk, hırs ve tamah ve eski Türklerin ruh kuvveti ve feragat duygusu ile telifi kabil olmayan daha nice hususiyetler gelir.

Bu tehlikeyi önlemek içindir ki, Kemalist inkılâbın esas umdelerinden birini teşkil eden ve çeyrek asıra yakın bir zamandanberi tetikte duran "devamlı inkılâp", hızını gevşetmek şöyle dursun, yalnız siyasî ve idarî sahada değil, daha ziyade, kültürel ve içtimaî sahada, yapıcı icraatını arttırmağa çalışmaktadır.

Bilhassa şarktan gelen tehlikeye müteveccih bu devamlı inkılâp, bizi, garpten gelen öteki tehlikeden de vikaye etmelidir. Atatürkün verdiği ve kendi adını taşıyan rejimin mümessillerinin o zamandanberi tekrar etmekten geri durmadıkları ilk parola "Garba doğru" parolasıdır. Gerçek, Türk milleti, garba doğru dolu dizgin koşmak sayesindedir ki dirilmiş ve kara cehaletle sözde dinin nüfuzu altında kaybettiği asırları kazanmıştır. Amma, garbin kendisi tahrip tohumlarından büsbütün azade değildir. Herşeyde olduğu gibi, bu işte de madalyanın ters tarafı vardır. Kemalist inkılâp tarafından tekrar kazanılan atalar yadigârı manevî kuvvetler, bazı garp memleketlerini son zamanlarda istilâ eden bir takım tereddi âmillerinin tehdidi altındadır.

Garpta, ilmin ve fennin terakkileri, manevî terakkilerle daima at başı beraber gitmez.

Ahlâkî ve manevî kıymetlerin inkişafı, her zaman, ilmî ve fennî kalkınma seviyesinde bulunmaz. Meselâ, modern medeniyetin öncüsü olan mutlakıyetçi bazı memleketlerde devlet otoritesinin tatbiki şekli eski hakanların, halkçı otorite zihniyetine uymaz. Buna mukabil; bir takım garp memleketlerindeki demokrasi hürriyetlerinin bazı görünüşleri, taşkın serbestlik, anarşi, oligarşi ve ayni nev'iden daha başka içtimaî tefessüh unsurlarile karışacak derecede terreddi alâmetleri gösterir. Bu unsurlar, Türk ve ata ruhunun derin surette meşbu bulunduğu türe ve yasanın feragat ve itaat zihniyetile telif edilemez. Kemalizm önderleri, bu vaziyeti, baştan beri mükemmel surette gördüler; onun içindir ki garbın siyasî ve içtimaî müesseselerini aynen almaktan, daha doğrusu taklitten içtinap etmişlerdir. Garpten, sırf modern medeniyet ve terakki zihniyeti iktibas edilmek istenildi. Siyasî ve kültürel müesseselere gelince, bunlar, dirilen Türk millî kültürüne intibak ettirildi.

Fakat, alınan bütün tedbirlere rağmen, sirayet tehlikesi tamamile zail olmuş değildir. Modernleştirilen Türk cemiyeti, tıpkı diğer garp milletlerinin cemiyetleri gibi, tereddi mikrobundan tamamile masun sayılamaz.

Bu cümleden olarak mütemadiyen tetikte durulmasını icabettiren tehlike, ferdiyetçilik adını vereceğimiz modern içtimaî âfettir.

İlâveye hacet yoktur ki, ferdiyetçilikten anladığımız mana ne ferdlerin cemiyet içindeki tecerrütleri sistemi; ne, ferdî teşebbüsün devlet teşebbüsüne üstünlüğü, ne de umumiyet itibariyle bu isimle gösterilen felsefe ve sosyoloji sistemlerinden herhangi birisidir. Bu tabirden kastettiğimiz mana, ferdin, âmme menfaatine karşı duyduğu alâkasızlık ve bağsızlıktır. Bu nevi ferdiyetçilik, bugün öyle bir içtimai âfettir ki, en medenî memleketlerde, ezcümle en gıptaya lâyık demokrat cumhuriyet idarelerinde hesapsız tahribat yapmaktadır. Bazı demokrasi memleketlerinde siyasî partilerin ve sınıfların hususî menfaatleri koruyan hakikî zümreler haline bu sınıfların birer entrika yuvası şekline gelmiş olması; umumî reylerin, çok zaman, kepazece manevralara ve dolaplara mevzu teşkil etmesi, irtişanın, irtikâbın, selâhiyetleri ve nüfuzları suiistimal hareketlerinin, korkulacak derecede artması, bu içtimaî afetin meş'um neticesidir. Bazı anlarda ve bazı muhitlerde, siyasî hürriyetlerin bu şekilde yoldan çıkışları, devleti, resmî vazifeleri ve siyasî mevkileri, pervasız insanların hırslarını kendisine çeken hakikî bir yağma sofrası haline getirmiştir.

Bu nevi ferdiyetçilik, Kemalizmden evvelki Türk cemiyetinde büsbütün meçhul olmadığı icin, bu modern içtimaî afetten, daha ziyade korkmalıyız; uzun mutlakiyet asırlarında, bu ferdiyetçilik, Türkiyede, hakimi mutlak sıfatile hüküm sürmüştür. Amme işlerinin sevk ve idaresi, câmianın menfaatleri hesaba katılamıyordu. İdare makamlarının bütün derecelerini işgal eden, âmme salâhiyetlerine sahip kimseler, milleti ve devlet hazinesini, kendi menfaatleri için ve müşterilerinin, yani kendilerine en fazla dalkavukluk etmesini ve en becerikli şekilde el etek öpmesini bilenlerin menfaatine istismar için en mükemmel yolu aramaktan başkabir kaygu gütmiyorlardı. Tanzimat devrinin en seçkin insanları arasında bulunan şair ve devlet adamı Ziya Paşa, tercii bendinin büyük bir kısmını, çağdaşlarının, bu bakımdan, içinde bocaladıkları manevî sukutu, büyük bir cesaretle takibe hasretmiştir. Pek meşhur olan "çaldımsa da miri malı çaldım" mısraı, o devrin, âmme menfaatı bakımından taşıdığı zihniyeti ve sahip olduğu ahlâk derecesini aynen gösterir.

Amme menfaatı mefhumu, bizde, ancak tanzımattan sonra kendini gösterebilmiş, meşrutiyet devrinde tebellür etmiş ve istiklâl savaşında tam hızını almıştır. Ziya Gökalp'ın meşhur "Fert yok, cemiyet var" vecizesi, o zaman elle tutulur ve tesirli bir realite haline gelmiştir. Bu sayede Osmanli İmparatorluğunu kökünden süpüren korkunç âfetin vehameti anlaşılmıştır. Zaferle bitirdiğimiz istiklâl savaşından sonra gelen Kemalist rejim, tabiatile, kaynağı yine Altay yaylalarında bulunan ayni feragat zihniyetile meşbudur.

Fakat mücadele devresi çoktan geçti. Yeni rejim istikrar kazandı ve bütün millet, başardığı "Turk mucizesi" sayesinde huzur ve refah seviyesine yükseldi. İşte asıl tehlike, bu huzur ve refah durumundadır. Ferdiyetçilik âfeti, refah havası içinde gitgide daha fazla gelişebilir.

Bu eserin muhtelif yerlerinde de belirttiğimiz gibi, ideal, doğmak, yaşamak ve gelişmek için, bu buhran ve kaynama havasına muhtaçtır. Huzurla, refahla ve bereketle meşbu bir muhit ideale müsait değildir. Hattâ, bu muhitin, ideal üzerinde meşum tesirleri olabilir. Cihan tarihi, ezcümle Türk tarihi, bize, kendi menkıbelerinin kurbanı olan cüretkâr muharipleri, şanlı fatihleri gösteren örneklerle doludur. Umumiyet itibariyle, bir iki nesil süren refah ve huzur, kuvvetli muharip kabileleri gevşetmeğe, onların akıncılık hamlelerini dindirmeğe, geçmişteki zaferlerini borçlu oldukları feragat ve kahramanlık zihniyetini ruhlarında söndürmeğe yol açabilir.

Bu tehlikenin vehametini ilk gören ve değerini takdir eden Cengiz han olmuş ve tehlikeyi, tam, şan ve kudretin en üstün derecesine yükseldiği zaman görmüştür. Şan ve şerefin son kademesine vardık, diye düşünüyordu, Fakat oğullarımızla torunlarımız, şimdi, kuvvetimizin kaynağı olan mütevazi yurtlarımızı bırakıp muhteşem saraylara yerleşecekler, ipekli esvaplar giyecekler, yumuşak ve mutedil iklimlerde yaşamağı tercih edecekler; güzel kadınlar etraflarını alacak, çeşit çeşit zevkler içinde vakit geçirecekler ve bu imparatorluğu kurmak için bizim kendi isteğimizle çektiğimiz hesapsız mahrumiyetleri, yaptığımız fedakârlıkları maruz kaldığımız zahmetleri çabucak unutacaklar. Bu şartlar içinde, bu imparatorluk, benden sonra uzun zaman yaşıyabilir mi?

Cengiz, yüreğine dert olan bu endişenin tesirile, oğluna, imparatorluk merkezini, çorak, kuş uçmaz, kervan geçmez, step ortasında bir konak yeri olan Karakurumdan katiyen başka yere götürmemesini tavsiye etmek ihtiyatkârlığında bulunmuştu. Fakat, Cengiz, bu gibi tedbirlerin katiyen kâfi gelmediğini pek âlâ biliyordu.

Gerçek, torunu Kubilây, muhteşem Pekin'in cazibesine dayanamadı ve sema imparatorluğunda imparator olmak için, mütevazi Karakurum yerine, ikame etti. Bu imparatorluğu zapt eden kuvvetli ve ateşli mogollar, o andan itibaren, gevşek ve rahata düşkün mahluklar haline geldiler ve hükümleri altına aldıkları çinlilerle bir seviyeye indiler.

Şurasını derhal ilâve edelim ki, ferdiyetçilik dediğimiz tehlike, modern Türk cemiyetinde gözden kaçmış değildir. Evvelce de söylediğimiz gibi, milletin manevî terbiyesine ötedenberi büyük bir ehemiyet veren İsmet İnönü, sık sık söylediği nutuklarda, milleti muhtelif şekillerde tesanüde, camianın faydası ve müşterek dava uğrunda feragat zihniyetine teşvik etmeği hiç ihmal etmez. Türk mütefekkirlerile Türk muharrirleri de bu vadide, millî şefi örnek tutmakta kusur etmiyorlar ve her fırsattan istifade ederek milleti, ferdiyetçilik tehlikesine karşı uyanık durmağa davet ediyorlar.

Fakat, Türk hükûmetinin, manevî sahadaki kuvvetlerin işlemesini temin için ceza tedbirlerine baş vurmağa ihtiyacı olmadığını unutmamak lâzımdır. Kemalist hükûmet, manevî nüfuz bakımından, demokratik ve mutlakiyetçi hiç bir hükumetle mukayese edilemez. Onun, bütün milleti arkasından yürüterek hakikat sahasına çıkardığı mucizeler zecri tedbirlerle, yasaklarla, şiddetli kanunlar ve kararnamelerle veya bu nevi daha başka tedbirlerle elde edilmiş değildir. Bu mucizeler, sırf, iktidar mevkiindeki önderlerin, büyük milletin idealizmini ve manevî emellerini şahıslandırmaları sayesinde imkân dairesine girmiştir. Hâkimiyetin millette olduğu ilân edilmiş ve bu hâkimiyet, açık ve sarih anayasa kanunlarile tasdik edilmiştir; fakat millet, belki de, atalar yadigârı ayni yasa ruhundan mülhem olarak, bu hakimiyet hakını, hiç bir zaman, önderinin kendi timsalinden başka bir şey olmayan modern hakanın vasıtasından gayri şekilde kullanılmamıştır. Kemalizme dair olan eserimizde de uzun uzadıya izah ettiğimiz gibi, Atatürk, prensip olarak, inkilâp eserlerini, tazyikle değil, ikna ve terbiye yoluyle tatbik etmek şeklini kabul etmişti. Serpuşun değiştirilmesi, kadına serbestî verilmesi, dil ve harf inkılâbı, devletin laikleştirilmesi ilh, bunlara müteallik olan kanunların kabulünden evvel Atatürkün ikna ve terbiye edici icraatı sayesinde birer emri vaki olmuştur. Başka memleketlerde normal olarak vukua gelen halin hilâfına, Kemalist Türkiyede, icraat daima sözden evvel gelmiştir. Seçkinler sınıfı, milletin mütefekkirler kadrosu önderler tarafından itina ile yetiştirilmiştir. Daima şefinin ruhundan ve zihniyetinden ilham alan halk partisi, büyük bir medenî bilgiler mektebinden başka birşey değildir. Sağlam temeller üzerine kurulan ve Anadolunun en ücra köşelerinde kuvvetli bir teşkilâtla vücude getirilen yüzlerce halkevi, filiz veren fikirlerin ve duyguların, önder tarafından ileri sürülüp halkın her tabakasına, görünür görünmez sayısız kanallar vasıtasiyle yayılmağı temin eden yüzlerce halk terbiye mektebidir. Bilkuvve var olan basının bütün organları üzerindeki hükûmet nüfuzu eşsizdir. Basın, devlet işlerinin idareciler tarafından sevk ve idare tarzını pervasızca tenkit eder, fakat bu tenkitleri acı bir lisanla yaparken hiç bir vakit âmme menfaatini gözönünden ayırmaz.

Nevi şahsına münhasır olan bu manevî kuvvet sayesindedir ki milletin çok saygı gösterdiği önderler, yalnız ferdiyetçiliği değil, herhangi nevi içtimaî hastalığı, telkin ve terbiye yolu ile tedavi etmek ve onun önüne geçmek imkânına sahiptirler.

İsmet İnönünün nutuklarını ve halk arasındaki tezahürlerini bu bakımdan mütalâa ve muhakeme etmek lâzımdır.

Netice olarak şunu söyleyelim ki, eğer iyi anlamışsak, bu eserde izah ettiğimiz Türk millî ruhunun özü, Yeni Türkiyenin Amentüsü, aşağıdaki yasada hulâsa edilebilir :

1 — Turanlı atalarından sana miras kalan müstesna ruh kuvvetini bil ve onunla övün.

Cihan, yalnız, senin efsanevî hale gelen beden kuvvetini biliyor. Senin, asıl manevî kuvvetinle mücehhez olduğunu, bilhassa, atalarının, onun sayesinde muhteşem cihan imparatorlukları kurduklarını anlamalıdır. Atalarının sayısız şanlı menkıbelerinin başlıca sebebi, milletin bütün diri kuvvetlerini bir araya toplayan ve ayni ideale doğru götüren "türe ile yasa" dır. Bu tek ideal "timsali hakan olan milletin kudreti ve refahı" idi. O sebeple, millî müdafaaya ehemmiyet verdiğinden fazla olamazsa bile, ayni nisbette, bu manevî kuvveti korumağa, gece gündüz gayret et. Dinamizm, camianın faydası uğrunda feragat ve fedakârlık duygusu, kahramanlık, geleneğe saygı ve binlerce yıldanberi damarlarındaki kanda mevcut daha nice manevî hasletler, senin en kıymetli millî mirasındır. Bu kıyemtli mirasın en küçük zerresini kaybetme.

Kof ve manasız düsturlarla gözlerin kamaşmasın. Avrupalı, ari garplı ilh, adı takınmağa yeltenme. Asyali ve Şarklı milletler arasında sayılmaktan korkma. Avrupalı, ârî, yahut garplı sınıfına girmiş milletlere tabiat hiç bir imtiyaz bahşetmemiştir; Asyalı veya Şarklı milletler de, hilkatın üveyi evlâtları değildir. Terakki ve medeniyet, tarihin bir devresiyle öteki devresi arasında yer değiştirirler. Avrupa ve Garp, orta çağ karanlıklarına gömülü iken, arasında senin ataların da bulunan bazı Asyalı milletler, medeniyetlerinin şa'şaasını saçıyorlardı. İster Avrupalı ister Asyalı ol, ister Şarklı ister Garplı ol, yine, Turan steplerinden taşan ve bütün cihanda, uzun asırlarca, muhteşem ve kudretli devletler, imparatorluklar ve mamureler kuran o efendi ve fatih milletin evlâdısın. Senin en büyük asalet unvanın budur.

II — Hayat, ezelî ve ebedi bir tekâmüldür. Zaman değiştikçe, âdetler de değişir. Zamanla beraber yürüyecek, yeni hayat şartlarına uyacak; kaynakları ne olursa olsun, bütün terakki eserlerini benimsiyeceksin. Onun için, muhitin ve zamanın icaplarına göre tekâmül et;

fakat bu tekâmülün, etrafında döneceği mihver, millî gelenek ve millî kültür olmalıdır. Medeniyetin ve terakkinin, senin türeni yutmasına müsaade etmemelisin; bilâkis, medeniyet ve terakki, senin türene uymalıdır.

III — İctimaî hayatta olduğu gibi ferdî hayatta da bütün hareketlerinin ve işlerinin rehberi, millî kahramanlara saygı olmalıdır. Kilisenin, din tarafından resmen kabul edilmiş azizleri vardır. Dini bütün hristiyanlar, her işlerinde ve hareketlerinde, dünya hayatından ziyade ahret hayatını temsil eden azizlere uymağa gayret ederler. Senin, işleri ve hareketleri, destanlarda ve oğuznamelerde görülen millî kahramanların var. Senin kahramanların, ahretin değil, bizzat senin, senin ruhunun ve emellerinin timsalidir. Hareketini bu kahramanlara uyduracaksın. Onların manevî ve maddî menkıbeleri, senin takip etmen gereken örnekler olmalıdır. Senin eskı ve yeni tarihine şeref veren birçok kahramanlar arasında, Mete ve Atilla, Namık Kemal ve Ziya Gökalp, Fatih ve Kanunî Süleyman, Gültekin ve Alp Arslan, Atatürk ve İnönü, nurlu yüzlerile yükseliyorlar. Senin kahramanlarının gösterdikleri yiğitlik feragat ve ruh asaleti örnekleri, hayatının her anında sana rehber olmalıdır.

IV — Her şeyın, senin kendi damganı ve kendi şahsiyetinin izini taşımalıdır. Cemiyet, ahlâk ve kültür sahalarında yabancı tesirlerden kaçın. Hele, çekici şekiller ve renkler altında ve sinsi bazı propagandalar arkasına sığınarak bazı garp memleketlerine sokulan fakat senin içtimaî bünyende izleri mevcut manevî kuvvetlere hiç uygun olmayan bazı ideolojilerden sakın. Unutma ki, manevî kuvvetlerini kökünden yıkan ve seni inhitata doğru sürükleyen şey, dışardan gelen seciyene.uymıyan yabancı tesirler, ezcümle Bizans tesirleri, yabancı mistiklik tesirleri, sözde dinin tesirleridir. Kemalist inkılâbı sayesinde tahakkuk ettirebildiğin manevî kuvvetleri tekrar bulduğun zamandır ki, o yabancı tesirlerın boyunduruğunu silkip atabildin. Kültür ve medeniyet seviyesi ne olursa olsun, hiçbir yabancı milleti taklit etme. Etrafında gördüğün her iyiden ve her doğrudan ilham al, hiç bir şeyi taklit etme.

V — Zafer eklilleri arasında uykuya yatma. Bir zamanlar mucizeler yarattın; bütün dünyanın hayranlığını kazandın. Refah ve saadet yolu üzerindesin. Meş'um mazi, pek uzakta değildir. Hortlayabilir. Seni ondan koruyacak olan, önderlerin, başından beri ilân ettikleri daimi inkılâptır. Bu parola, daima hatırında kalmalıdır.

VI — Modernizmin tereddisinden kendini sakın. Önderlerin, sana, "Garba doğru" parolasını verdiler. Onları, sadakatle takip ettin. Modernleştin, rönesanstanberi, daha doğrusu, senin, uzun süren inhitatının başındanberi garpta tahakkuk ettirilen terakkileri benimsedin. Fakat, garp medeniyetinde yalnız iyi şey yoktur, bunun aksi de vardır. Bazı garp memleketlerinde, modern medeniyet tereddi etmiş, ezcümle, asırlardan beri kurulmuş manevî kıymetleri altüst eden bazı ideolojilere vücut vermiştir. Önderlerin, garba doğru ilk adımlarını atar atmaz, sirayet tehlikesine karşı tedbir almaktan geri durmamışlar ve herşeyden evvel, adalet ve insanlık prensiplerine, ferdin inkâr edilmez hakkına, millî hâkimiyete, vicdan hürriyetine karşı olan mutlak saygılarına, senin atalarına şeref veren geniş müsamaha zihniyetine olan bağlılıklarını ilân etmişlerdir. Etrafında kaynaşan tereddi tohumlarından sakınarak bu manevî kıymetlere sıkı sıkıya sarıl.

VII — Bu asrın hastalığı haline gelmek üzere bulunan ferdiyetçiliğin vahim tehlikesinden kendini sakın. Bu hastalıktan kaçınırsan hayatın hakikî zevklerinden katiyen mahrum olmazsın. Camianın menfaatlerini feda etmeden de hayattan istifade etmek mümkündür. Sulh halinde iken, toylarda ve şölenlerde vakit geçiren ataların, örnek olmağa lâyık idealistlerdi. Ferd, hayatın zevklerini, ancak, camia ile birlikte tadardı. Cemiyetin menfaatine sadakat, onun en büyük zevki idi. Kemalist inkılâbi, ancak, müşterek dava ve âmme menfaatı uğrundaki bu topyekun feragat sayesinde tahakkuk ettirebilmiştin. Eğer bir dalgınlık anında, asrın hastalığına yakalanacak olursan, manevî kuvvetin, ruh kuvvetin mahvolur; o zaman, yakın mazi nükseder ve dünkü düşmanlar, bugünkü ve yarınki düşmanlarınla birleşmek ve Kemalist inkılâbın akıllara durgunluk veren neticelerinden seni mahrum etmek için, ellerini uzatsalar yeter.

VIII — Millî birliğine sıkı sıkı sarıl. O birlik, senin önderlerin tarafından, beşer kuvveti üstünde sarfedilen gayretler bahasına vücut bulmuştur. Artık, senin memleketinde, ne sınıf, ne zümre, ne parti, ne sıra, ne de herhangi nevi taksim vardır. Bütün millet Kemalizmin bayrağı altında bir araya toplanmıştır. Unutma ki binlerce yıllık tarihinin boyunca, kuvvetli ve sağlam olduğun devirler, bütün ulusun, milletin emellerini temsil eden bir tek başkan, bir tek han veya hakan bayrağı altında toplanmış bulunduğu devirlerdir. Millî birlik kaybolunca, ulusun, anarşiye ve düzensizliğe mahkum olmuştur. Senin başlıca kuvvetin, başkanınırr otoritesinde ve milletin disiplinindedir. Belki başka milletler, iktidar ve salâhiyet mevkiinin suiistimallerinden kurtulmak için kuvvet muvazenesine ve partilerin oyununa muhtaçtırlar. Kemalist Türkiye vatandaşı olan sen, bundan müstağni kalabilir ve dirilen yasana tam itimad besleyebilirsin. Mazide senin mensup olduğu milletin satvetini temin edenler, kuvvet muvazenesinin, idare edenlerle idare edilenler arasında karşılıklı itimad ve feragatle tahakkuk ettirmişlerdir. Hakan, Kurultay, tekinler ve o derin bütün ileri gelen devlet adamları daima milletin satvet ve şevket bulması için çalışmışlardır. Seni idare edenler, kuvvetlerini ve otoritelerini hiçbir zaman partilerin ve zümrelerin muvazenesinden almamışlar, senin atalar mirası ruhunun esasını teşkil eden nizam, otorite ve disiplin zihniyetinden almışlardır. Ataların, başkanların otoritelerini, daima, millete danışmak, prensipi ile uzlaştırmak yolunu bulmuşlardır. Yeni Türkiyeyi yaratan önderler, bu siyaset mucizesini, millî hakimiyete zerre kadar halel vermeden, yirminci asrın ortasında tahakkuk ettirdiler. Atalarından miras kalan manevî kuvvetler seni terketmedikçe, senin bin yıllık kuvvet ve kudretinin kaynağı olan millî birliği, olduğu gibi muhafazaya daima muvaffak olacaksın.

IX — Unutma ki, beşercilik dahi senin binlerce yıllık tarihini süsleyen manevî kuvvetler arasında yer tutar. Gerçi milliyetçilik, yeni Türkiyenin akidesinin ve ideolojisinin temelini teşkil eder. Ancak, bu milliyetçilik, gayet realist esaslara dayanır, her türlü mistik nüfuzdan ve tesirden azadedır. Onun içindir ki, yeni Türkiye, ateşîn milliyetçiliğini, en temiz ve en samimî beşercilik ideali ile uzlaştırmak yolunu bulmuştur. Yeni Türk, bunda da, atalar mirası ruhunun meyelânlarına uymaktan başka bir şey yapamaz. Turanlı ateşîn fatihlerin, zaptettikleri memleketler halkına karşı, ne dereceye kadar şefkatlı, müsamahakâr, insanca ve alicenab davrandıklarını, bu kitabın bundan evvelki kısımlarında görmüş; silahsız, müdafaasız ve himayesiz insanlara ve ahaliye karşı, son derece civanmert durumlarını kaydetmiştik. Yeni Türkiye, sulhu tesis edecek duruma gelir gelmez, garp milletlerinin bazınsında henüz itibarda olan "mukaddes hodbinlik"i, Machiavelin meşhur beynelmilel düsturunu açıktan açığa reddetmekten geri durmadı. Yaptığı hareketler ve icraat bu noktada da samimî olduğunu isbat etti. Atatürk ve İnönü, daima, her fırsattan istifade ederek, beşercilik ve barışçılık prensiplerinin sarsılmazlığını bütün cihan karşısında ilân ve teyit etmişlerdir. Nutuklarının çoğunda, bu prensipleri mütemadiyen tekrarlıyan İsmet İnönü, beşercilik idealini, yeni Kemalist rejimin başlıca esasları arasına katmakta tereddüt etmemiştir. Üniversite gençliği karşısında, kemalist akidesi ve ideolojisi hakkında söylediği nutukta, yeni Türkiyenin beşercilik ideali hakkındaki emellerini uzun uzadıya anlattı ve muhtelif vesilelerle şu vecizeleri söyledi :

"Yüksek isaniyet ülküsünü takip etmek bir vazifedir. İnkılâbımızın gayesi büyük insan ailesinin bir cüzü mahiyetinde yaşamaktır.

Türk milletinin sahai esasiyesi sulh ve musalemet vadisinin de unsuru terakki ve medeniyet olmaktır. Türk milleti insaniyet ailesinde kıymetli bir varlık vaziyetini almıştır".

Türk milliyetçiliğinin birinci nazariyatçısı olan Ziya Gök Alp dahi eski Türklerde ahlâk prensiplerinin, mağlup milletlere karşı gösterdikleri uluvvücenabı uzun uzadıya izah ettikten sonra şu neticeye varıyor. "Büyük milletlerin her biri medeniyet sahasının bir şubesiinde temeyyüz etmiştir. Eski Yunanlılar bediiyatta, Romalılar hukukta, Beni İsrail ve Araplar dinde, Fransızlar edebiyatta, Anglo-Saksonlar iktisadiyatta, Almanlar mafevkaltabiiyede, Türkler ahlâkiyat ve insaniyetçilikte birinciliği kazandılar.

Ayni ideolog Malta sürgününde en büyük eza ve cefalara maruz bulunduğu sıralarda hep bütün insaniyetin refah ve saadeti rüyasile vakit geçirir, ve oradan küçük kızına gönderdiği mektuplarda hep bundan bahsederdi. Bu mektupların birini bu sözlerle bitirmiştir: "Bir gün gelecek bütün insan ailesi sulh ve refah havası içinde bahtiyar olacaktır".

Demek oluyor ki beşercilik ideali, şeflerini örnek alarak ve onların nasihatlarını tutarak, kıskanç bir itina ile muhafaza etmekliğin gereken millî mirasa dahildir.

Ebedi şef Atatürk'ün şu yüksek tavsiyesini asla gözden uzak tutmamalısın:

"Garp medeniyeti seviyesinin üstüne yükselmelisin."

Çok kısa bir zaman içinde tahakkuk ettirdiğin muazzam terakkilere rağmen, bu en son hedeften henüz çok uzakta bulunuyorsun. Atalar yadigârı dinamizminin timsali olan ebedi şefinin, rehavetten nefret ettiğine, bu bir misal daha teşkil eder. Rahavetin, düşkünlüğe ve inhitata doğru ilk merhaleyi teşkil ettiğini, o, çok iyi biliyordu. Türk milletini, feyizli her câmianın bu can düşmanına karşı korumak için, Atatürk birbirini tamamlayan iki parola verdi. Bu iki paroladan birincisi, bizi; mazinin herhangi bir hortalyışına ve irticaın hain kuvvetlerine karşı koruyan daimî inkılâptır. Fakat daimî inkılâp, bizi, ancak gerideki düşmandan korur. Bir de öndeki düşman vardır ki, ona karşı da, gayet büyük bir enerji ile konrunmak lâzımdır. Öndeki düşman da gevşekliğin tâ kendisidir. Eğer en son hedefe vardığını sanarak garp medeniyetinin seviyesinde duracak olursan, bunun neticesi, bütün diri kuvvetlerinin gevşemesi ve uyuşması olacaktır. Dirilen atalar yardigârı ruhunun meşbu bulunduğu dinamik kuvvetler seni, sukuttan artık kurtaramaz. İşte, seni gevşeklik denilen o can düşmanına karşı korumak içindir ki, Atatürk, sana, medeniyet seviyesinin fevkine yükselmek emri verdi. Seviyenin fevkine çıkmağa çalışmak, yukarı doğru daimî harekettir. Sonsuz ve sınırsız bir yapıcılık hareketidir. Sırf, bu ebedî yükselme zihniyeti sayesindedir ki, sen, o koca Cengizin bile, şan ve şeref şahikasına ulaştığı demde, karşısında titrediği müthiş gevşeme tehlikesine karşı kendini koruyabilirsin.

Garp medeniyeti seviyesinin fevkine yükselmek, senin için, alelâde bir emel değil kendi nefsine karşı mukaddes bir vazifedir. Asaletin bunu icabettirir. Binlerce sene efendi millet olarak, "herrenvolk" olarak yaşadın. Şimdi, zamanlar değiştikten sonra, kendini gevşekliğe bırakarak seviyede kalırsan, efendiliğini kaybetmek, bayalığa düşmek tehlikesine maruz kalırsın.

Türk ruhu, pp. 273-287.

M. TEKİN ALP NOUS PARLE DU SIONISME ET DU JUDAÏSME TURC

La question de savoir si un citoyen turc de confession mosaïque peut nourrir et manifester des sympathies à l'égard du mouvement sioniste ou du nouvel État d'Israël, a éveillé un vif intérêt parmi le public. Nous avons donc été demander à M. Tekin Alp, conseiller municipal et ancien professeur de Sciences Financières, dont l'autorité en la matière est incontestable son opinion sur cet intéressant cas de conscience. L'éminent économiste, auteur de plusieurs ouvrages dont nous mentionnerons les plus connus: «Kemalisme,» «Turquisation,» «L'Âme Turque,» a bien voulu répondre aux questions que nous lui avons posées.

Le Congrès de Hambourg

Q. – Croyez-vous qu'un bon citoyen turc puisse être en même temps sioniste?

R. – L'amour de la nation et de la patrie, à mon avis, n'implique aucune exclusivité. Un bon citoyen, dans tous les pays, peut nourrir des sentiments et des sympathies particuliers de caractère régional, traditionnel, racial, confessionel, etc. Autrement, il faudrait admettre qu'il n'y a pas de bons citoyens en Amérique puisque presque tous les citoyens américains ont des sentiments particularistes. Les uns ont des sympathies pour le Germanisme, les autres originaires d'Italie, d'Irlande, etc., nourrissent des sympathies à l'égard de leur patrie d'origine, sans parler des millions des Juifs qui sont restés attachés à leurs traditions. Ils ne voient aucun inconvénient à organiser des manifestations et même à intervenir politiquement en faveur de ce mouvement. En Grande-Bretagne qui est un Royaume-Uni, les sentiments particularistes écossais et gallois se manifestent très souvent dans la vie politique. En France, les bons Français se divisent en Provençals, Bretons et tant d'autres nationalités qui ont chacune leurs propres idiomes, leurs us et coutumes, leurs folklores et autres particularismes de ce genre. Dans notre pays aussi on remarque des particularismes régionaux très prononcés. Les originaires de la Mer Noire, c'est-à-dire les compatriotes du Premier Ministre Hasan Saka, ceux des régions de la Mer Egée, les natifs de Rumeli, ceux des Vilâyets Orientaux, ne cachent pas leurs sentiments de solidarité envers leurs compatriotes.

Ainsi donc les bons citoyens turcs fidèles à leurs traditions ataviques et à leurs attaches confessionnelles peuvent très bien nourrir des sympathies pour le Sionisme tant que ce mouvement ne va pas à l'encontre des intérêts du pays.

La question du Foyer Juif

Q. – Pourquoi donc cette dernière réserve? Pensez-vous qu'une pareille éventualité peut se produire?

R – Dans l'état actuel il n'y a pas lieu d'envisager une éventualité de ce genre mais il ne faudrait pas oublier que cette éventualité a joué un certain rôle dans le passé. Je saisis cette occasion pour évoquer un épisode historique très intéressant.

C'était en 1908, l'année où la Constitution fut proclamée en Turquie, grâce au triomphe de la Révolution des Jeunes Turcs. M. le Dr. Jacobson, alors membre du Comité d'action sioniste, qui était de passage à Salonique me proposa de me rendre au Congrès Sioniste de Hambourg en qualité de délégué. Je lui fis savoir que je ne pouvais accepter cette charge que seulement dans le cas où il trouverait une formule qui permettrait aux Juifs de Turquie d'y participer, sans que leurs sentiments et devoirs patriotiques aient à en soufrir. Il me proposa de préparer moi-même cette formule et de la lui soumettre. C'est ce que je fis en demandant de supprimer du programme élaboré au Congrès de Bâle la clause relative à la garantie du Foyer National par le Droit Public. Je lui fis remarquer que la Constitution turque suffisait déjà à garantir le Foyer National pourvu que le Gouvernement turc y consentît. Je lui proposai aussi de ne pas limiter l'immigration juive au seul territoire palestinien, mais de l'étendre à toute la Turquie. Juste à cette époque j'étais en train de mener une campagne dans les journaux turcs en faveur de cette immigration, campagne qui avait trouvé un très bon accueil auprès des dirigeants de l'Union et Progrès. Le Dr. Jacobson m'avisa que le Congrès de Hambourg offrait déjà une occasion propice pour mettre en avant officiellement ma proposition. Je me rendis à Hambourg et fis une conférence en pleine séance du Congrès sur l'opportunité d'étendre l'immigration juive dans toute la Turquie, attendu que celle-ci avait grandement besoin à cette époque d'éléments actifs et loyaux. Après avoir pris contact avec le Comité Permanent du Congrès, j'eus l'impression que ma proposition tendant à l'abrogation de la clause relative au Foyer National n'avait pas grande chance d'aboutir. Là-dessus, je quittai le Congrès et rentrai à Salonique cessant ainsi toute relation avec le mouvement sioniste. Cependant la question de l'immigration juive dans toute la Turquie me tenait toujours à cœur. Obéissant à ce sentiment et sur l'intervention du Dr. Gustav Kohn, Président de la J.T.O. (Jewish Territorial Organisation) j'entrai en correspondance avec Israël Sangwill, Président de cette organisation mondiale. Le célèbre écrivain juif s'intéressa beaucoup à cette question, mais exprima le désir de demander aux autorités turques l'affection d'un territoire déterminé où on créerait un centre culturel où les immigrants trouveraient la possibilité de développer leurs cultures et traditions nationales. Je me suis rendu compte alors que ce désir du Dr. Sangwill n'était pas conforme aux intérêts des communautés juives établies en Turquie.

A cette époque nous avions plutôt besoin de faire tout notre possible pour nous assimiler la langue et la culture turques dont nous nous étions éloignés pendant la période de l'ottomanisme. C'est depuis lors que j'ai acquis la conviction que notre premier devoir, à nous Juifs de Turquie, était de nous assimiler complètement la culture, la langue et l'idéal du pays dans lequel nous vivions et où nous jouissons aujourd'hui de tous nos droits civiques grâce à la Constitution. Dès lors je me suis voué à cette tâche. Vous connaissez certainement mon livre et mes nombreux écrits sur cette question. Pendant des dizaines d'années je n'ai cessé de déployer une activité intense dans ce but et maintenant je suis heureux de constater que, malgré les erreurs fatales commises par certains politiciens au pouvoir, l'idée de l'assimilation a triomphé et la nouvelle génération se trouve élevée dans des écoles turques et a fini par s'assimiler la langue, la culture et l'idéal turcs.

L'assimilation

Q. – Ne croyez-vous pas que le mouvement sioniste puisse entraver le développement de cette assimilation?

R. – Je suis convaincu qu'une fois l'assimilation accomplie, les Juifs de Turquie pourront donner libre cours aux sentiments et sympathies en faveur de ce mouvement sans que ceci puisse porter le moindre ombrage à leurs sentiments patriotiques comme c'est le cas chez tous les Juifs du monde entier.

L'Etoile du Levant, I/5 (20 August 1948)

MUNİS TEKİNALP, A PETITION TO THE TURKISH MINISTRY OF FOREIGN AFFAIRS

Munis Tekinalp
Taksim Sarayı Kat 3 No : 10
P.K. 15 Beyoğlu
İstanbul

Dış İşleri Bakanlığı Yüksek Makamına

ANKARA

Uzun Senelerden Beri her sene ikişer ay süren tatil devrini öteden beri orada yerleşmiş bulunan ailemin nezdinde Nis şehrinde geçirmeğe devam ettiğimden Göz renk (Cote D'azur) mıntıkasında memleketimizi alâkadar eden hususatı yakından tetkike fırsat buldum. Ve bu tetkiklerime dayanarak aşağıdaki mazuratta bulunmayı faideli görürüm.

Montekarlo, Kann, Juan les Pins gibi mühim Turizm merkezlerini muhtevi olan bu mıntıkanın baş şehri olan Nis'te ikinci Umumi harbin sonuna kadar vazifeli bir şehbenderlik makamı mevcuttu. Bu makamın lağvından sonra "Gök renk sahilleri" mıntıksasının coğrafı ehemiyeti her bakımdan artmış ve Türk vatandaşlarının bu mıntıkaya alâkaları ziyadeleşmiş bulunmaktadır.

Son zamanlarda dünyanın en maruf turizm merkezlerinden biri olarak, her sene, Ağa Hanlar, Çörçiller, Krallar, İmparatorlar ve milyonlarca turiste cevelângâh olan bu mıntıka ayrıca moda, itriyat gibi lüks sanayi için mühim bir merkez halina gelmiş bulunmaktadır. Orada yerleşmiş bulunan ve bazıları villalar oteller iktisap eden ve ezcümle ziyaret maksadile her sene Gök Renk mıntıkasına giden Türk vatandaşlarının adedi günden güne çoğalmaktadır. Bu itibarla bu mıntıkada vazifeli bir Şehbenderlik makamının yeniden ihdası mümkün olmasa bile, Memleketimizin orada Fahrî bir Konsolosluk ile temsili yüksek makamınızca münasip görüleceği kannaâtındayım. Bu senenin nihayetine doğru yeniden Nis'e giderek orada Fikrî faaliyetime devam etmek azmile yerleşmek kararında bulunduğumdan, Yüksek Vekâletinizce Fahrî Konsolosluk şerefi benim için münasip görüldüğü takdirde kendimi bahtiyar addedeceğimi derin saygılarımla arz ederim.

İşbu hizmet arzımın Hüsnü kabule mazhar olacağı ümidi ile tercümenin bir hülâsası ilişik olarak takdim kılınmıştır.[1]

Copy of Tekinalp's petition to the Turkish Ministry for Foreign Affairs, undated (probably written in 1955-1956)

MUNİS TEKİNALP, HAL TERCÜMEÎ HÜLASASI[1]

Selânik'te Aliance İzraelite hukuk mektebi ve Musevi Darül muallimin mekteplerinde yüksek tahsilimi ikmâl ettikten sonra 1906 tarihinde Selânik'te Muharrirlik ve Avukatlıkla hayata atıldım. Orada İttihat ve Terraki ve Ziya Gökalp'ın idaresi altında bulunan kültür mahafilinde muhtelif vazifelerde bulundum. Beş sene müddetle Yeni Asır gazetesinde daimi muharrirlik yaptım. 1908 senesinde "Teşebbüsü Şahsi ve tevsii Mezuniyet" mevzulu bir kitap neşrettim.

Meşrutieytin ilânını müteakip Selânik Vilâyeti meclisi Umumi ve bu meclis tarafından Encümeni Vilâyet azalıklarına intihap olundum. Ve 1912 senesine kadar bu vazifelere devam ettim.

1912 senesinde Selânik'in sukutu üzerine Selânik'ten hicret edip İstanbul'a yerleşerek Muharrirlik ve Avukatlık mesleklerine devam ettim. 1914 senesinden itibaren İstanbul'da muhtelif ticaret şirketlerinde Müdürlük ve hukuk müşaviri sıfatile faaliyetime devam etmekle beraber, Fikri ve umumi hayat sahalarında mesaime hız verdim ve vermekteyim.

Bu cümleden olarak :

a) İstanbul'da yerleştiğim 1912 tarihinden beri Yeni mecmua Türk Yurdu, Türkiye İktisat Mecmuası gibi mecmualarla Akşam, Cumhuriyet, Vatan, Hürriyet, Son Posta gibi muhtelif Yevmî gazetelerde İktisadi ve Sosyolojik mevzular hakkında kitap şeklinde Türkçe ve ecnebi lisanlarda muhtelif eserler neşrettim, ve etmeğe devam etmekteyim. 1916 dan 1918 senesine kadar İttihat ve Terraki kültür merkezinin organı olarak Türkçe, Fransızca ve Almanca olarak "Milli İktisat" fikrini yaymak maksadile (İktisadiyat Mecmuası) namı ile bir haftalık mecmua nesşrettim.

b) 1914 senesinden 1918 senesine kadar İstanbul Hukuk Fakültesi Müderris muavinliğinde bulundum.

c) 1945 senesinden 1950 senesine kadar Belediye meclisi azası sıfatile hizmet ifa ettim.

d) Ayrıca hususi ve serbest sektörde dahi fikri ve umumi hayat faaliyetine devam ederek İstanbul Tüccar derneğinin on sene evvelki kuruluşuna iştirak ettim ve o tarihten beri memlekette İktisadi demokrasinin gelişmesine hizmet etmiş olan bu teşekkülün, sırası ile, Reis vekilliğinde, Umumi katipliğinde, ve İdare meclisi azası sıfatile fasılasız olarak çalıştım ve çalışmaktayım.

e) Kitap şeklinde Türkçe ve muhtelif ecnebi lisanlarında neşrettiğim başlıca eserler şunlardır :

I) Kemalizm (1937) Türkçe, Fransızca, Çekçe ve diğer ecnebi lisanlarda edisyonları vardır. Fransızca edisyonda Fransa eski Baş vekillerinden ve Parlemento reislerinden Mösyö Eduard Herriot'un Türkçe edisyonunda Köprülü Fuat'ın sitayışkâr mukaddemeleri vardır.

II) Türk Ruhu (1944) Sabık Baş vekillerinden Tarih Kurumu başkanı Şamsettin Günaltay'ın mukkademesi vardır. Fransızca edisyonu yakında Pariste intişar edecektir.

III) Türkleştirme (1928) Necmettin Sadık, Köprülü Fuat, Celâl Sahir, Yunus Nadi, Ağaoğlu Ahmet'in mütalânameleri vardır.

IV) Türkizm ve Pantürkizm (1914) Almanca intişar etmiştir. Bilâhare İngilizce ve diğer ecnebi lisanlara tercüme olunmuştur.

V) Elli seneden beri basın alemine hizmet etmiş olan zevatın şerefine 2 Ekim 1948 tarihinde İstanbul Üniversitesi salonunda tertip olunan jübileye iştirak etmek saadetine mazhur oldum.

VI) 1955 senesinde "Türkiye Harsi ve İçtimai araştırmalar derneği'nin" şeref azalığına hey'eti umumiye kararı ile intihap olundum.

Tekinalp's typewritten *curriculum vitae*, undated (probably written in 1955-1956)

TEKİNALP, ZİYA GÖKALP'DE TESÂNÜTÇÜLÜK

Evvelemirde ilmî ve felsefî bir mefhumu olan tesânütçülük tâbiriyle amiyâne bir tâbir olan "gecekondu milyonerleri" kelimesini yan yana buluşdurmak mecburiyetinde bulunduğumdan dolayı özür dilerim. Fakat, meramimi daha veciz bir şekilde ifade etmek için başka çare bulamadım.

Tesânütçülük, Ziya Gökalp devrinde sık sık bahis mevzuu olan iktisadî ve içtimaî bir mezhebin adıdır. Fransızca mukabili solidarizmdir.

Merhum üstad bu içtimaî mezhebe senelerce müddet pek büyük bir bağlılık göstermiştir. 35 sene evvel cuma günleri evinde öğle yemeğinde topladığı yakınları ve mesaî arkadaşları, İttihat ve Terakki merkezinin kültür seksiyonunun müdavimleriyle, Hamdullah Suphi'ler, Köprülü Fuat'lar, Celâl Sahir'ler ve Halim Sabit'lerle başbaşa kaldığı zaman bu meseleyi ele alır. Berkson'lardan, Durkaym'lardan dem vurarak saatlerce müddet konuşur, beşer cemiyetinde tesânüt müesseselerini iyice sağlama bağlamadan huzur ve sükûna, refah ve saadete kavuşmak mümkün olmadığını ve bu itibarla cemiyetin hayır ve selâmetini hedef ve gaye ittihaz eden güzîde ve münevverlerin ilk vazifesi ezcümle iktisadî ve içtimaî sahalarda yardımlaşma ve tesânüt müesseselerini inkişaf ettirmekten ibaret olduğunu belirtmeye çalışırdı. Meşrutiyet zamanında yeni hayat ve daha doğrusu Ziya Gökalp devrinin mâruf sloganları olan (Ferd yok, cemiyet var. Hak yok; vazife var) gibi içtimaî dövizler bu felsefî mezhebe dayanırdı. Ancak Ziya Gökalp zamanından bu yana cemiyetimizde bir çok devreler oldu. İdeale dayanan devirleri bazı muhitlerde maddeyi ve şahsî menfaatleri esas tutan devirler takip etti. Ve bu gün bazı muhitlerde maddeyi idealden üstün tutan gecekondu milyonerleri devrine ulaşmış bulunuyoruz. İşte bundan dolayıdır ki 40 sene evvel yaşadığımız ve ideale dayanan tesânütçülük müesseselerini hatırlatmayı bu münasebetle faydalı gördüm. Şunu da ilâve etmek gerektir ki; o zaman maaşerî vicdana hâkim olan bu gibi mânevî ve ahlâkî görüşler tarihe karışmış olmasaydı bugünkü gecekondu milyonerleri âfetine meydan kalmıyacaktı.

İzah edelim :

40 sene evvel Ziya Gökalp muhitinde hâkim olan felsefî görüşlerden ilham alarak Yeni Mecmuada tesânütçülük bahsi hakkında neşrettiğim makalelerde belirttiğim veçhile tesânütçülük mezhebinin en mühim esaslarından biri iktisadî sahada kıymet artışı ve ilmî tâbiriyle plusvalue meselesine teallûk eder. Ziya Gökalp'ın tesânütçülük bahsinde ileri sürdüğü kanaate göre :

(Ferdin emeği sebketmeden, ferdin iradesine tâbi olmayan ahvâl ve hâdisatın tesiri altında menkul ve gayri menkul envâl üzerine hasıl olan kıymet artışları ferdin hakkı addolunamaz. Bu kıymet artışları cemiyete, yani devlete aittir. Bu itibarla cemiyetin idaresine, cemiyet içinde servetin adalet ve hakkaniyet devresinde tanzimine teallûk eden kanunlar, nizamlar ve idarî tedbirler bu temel prensibin çerçevesinde ayarlanmalıdır).

Ziya Gökalp, senelerce müddet yakınları arasında bu mealde konuştu. Kâfi derecede izahat verdi. Fakat, bu husustaki fikirleri ve görüşleri hakkında uzun boylu yazı yazmaya, tesânüt müessesesini tahakkuk ettirmek için tatbiki lâzım gelen kanunları, nizamları ve idarî tedbirleri formülleştirmeye imkân ve fırsat bulamamış. O zaman bu mesele günün mevzuu değildi. O zaman iktisat âleminde ferdin emeği sebketmeden belli başlı kıymet artışları dikkat nazarına çarpmazdı. Bu gün herkesin mâlûmu olduğu veçhile gecekondu milyonerleri meselesi bahs mevzuudur. Büyük çaptaki kıymet artışları bu günden yarına teallûk ediyor. Aklû hayâle gelmiyen spekülâsyon hamleleriyle mahdut kimselerin elinde milyonların yığıldığına şahit oluyoruz.

Herkesin mâlûmu olan bu vaziyetin en mükemmel tasvir ve tarifini tesadüf olarak bu günlerde dinlemek fırsatına mazhar oldum. Ve bunun içindir ki bu meseleyi aktüel, günün mevzuu olarak ele almıya ve 35 sene evvel yaşadığımız tesânütçülük devrini hatırlatmayı faydalı gördüm :

Martın 14 cü Çarşamba günü[1] şehrimizin en mâruf, en muteber 500 müessesesini sînesinde toplayan İstanbul Tüccar Derneğinin senelik umumî heyet toplantısında hazır bulunuyordum. Toplantıda okunan ve muhtelif hatipler tarafından tartışma mevzuu olan senelik faaliyet raporunda bugün ticaret âlemimizin içinde bocalamakta bulunduğu iktisadî müşküller birer birer sert ve tenkitkâr ifadelerle gözden geçirilmiştir. Günün en mühim mevzuları olan hayat pahalılığı, ihtikâr, karaborsa, Millî paranın kıymetinin düşmesi ve millî korunma hükümlerinin şiddetlendirilmesi gibi meseleler üzerinde uzun uzun duruldu. Bu sırada fevrî olarak heyecana gelen yaşlı ve muhterem bir zat ayağa kalktı. Heyecanlı bir eda ile şu meâlde sözler sarfetti :

"Burada saatlerce heyecanlı konuştuk. Bir çok acı hakikatler açıkladık. Fakat, hiç birimiz bünyemizi kemiren en vahim bir yaramıza parmak dokundurmadık. Bu yaraya, arsa ve binalar üzerine görülen nispetsiz, sebepsiz ve âyarsız fiat artışlarıdır. Bu fiat artışları spekülasyondan başka bir şey değildir. Son zamanlarda büyük şehirlerimizde ve bilhassa İstanbul'u baştanbaşa sarmış olan bu âfet millî paramızın iştira kuvvetini müthiş nispetlerde düşürüyor. Bu yüzden bir taraftan halk kitleleri fakrü sefalete mahkum olurken, diğer taraftan her gün yeni yeni gecekondu milyonerleri peydah oluyor ve binnetice hayat günden güne pahalılaşıyor. Meselâ; 10.000 liralık bir arsa veya bina bü günden yarına sebepsiz olarak 100.000 liraya çıkıyor. Bu suretle nice milyonlar durup dururken şunun bunun ceplerine akıyor. Bu gecekondu milyonerlerinin paraları haketmeleri için ne gibi hizmetlere sevketmiştir? Alın teri dökmeden, hiç bir emek sarfetmeden, hiç bir hizmet yapmadan kazanılan paralar milleti soymaktan başka bir mana ifade etmez. Amiyâne tabiriyle haram sayılması lâzım gelen bu kazançlara kanunî yollar ve nizamlarla bir an evvel son vermek lâzımdır."

Bilmem berlirtmeye lüzum var mı? Bu muhterem vatandaşın ateşli sözleri ayni hakikattir. Gecekondu milyonerlerini yaratan ahvâl ve şerait cemiyet için bir musibettir.

Hatip, bu meselenin ilmî ve içtimaî cephesine dokunmamıştır. Fakat, kanaatimce yukarda izah ettiğim veçhile içtimaî bünyemizi, iktisadî uzviyetimizi kemiren bu âfete karşı en müessir çare tesânütçülük prensibidir. Emek mukabili olmayan kıymet artışları kanunî yollar ve nizamlarla cemiyete mal edilmelidir. Ingiltere gibi en müterakki garp memleketleri veraset vergisini %80 - 90 a çıkarmak suretiyle mirasyedilik âfetine sed çekmiye muvaffak olmuşlardır. Haksız, emeksiz ve nispetsiz kıymet artışlarını bu gibi kanunî yollara başvurmak suretiyle sed çekmek, bu suretle içtimaî adaleti sağlamak pek âlâ mümkündür.

Bilgi, 149 (Aug. 1959)

APPENDIX

ENGLISH TRANSLATION OF JUDEO-SPANISH AND TURKISH SELECTIONS

MOISE COHEN, AN EXPLANATION

Honourable Editor,

In yesterday's edition, which reported on my Saturday lecture, you erroneously stated that I maintained that Zionism contradicts our interests as Ottomans – although I did not at all touch upon the Zionist question. Your error may serve as a pretext for certain Zionist newspapers to recall my favourable attitude to Zionism one year ago. I therefore consider it necessary to provide a clear and candid explanation.

Everyone knows that I had considered myself a Zionist at one time, declaring myself to be one and acting accordingly; however, as my writings, numerous articles in the Turkish newspapers, polemics with Ebuzziya Tevfik Bey in *Tasvir-i Efkâr,*[1] and lectures at the Hamburg Congress[2] prove, I always considered Zionism as a movement of Jewish immigration into Turkey and preferably into Palestine, which holds a certain historical attraction for the Jews.

In collaboration with one of my friends and colleagues – who equally abandoned Zionism – I worked out a special formula to serve as a basis for Ottoman Jews. According to this formula, approved by certain Zionist leaders, Zionism would be a movement of Jewish immigration into Turkey with a cultural centre in Palestine. We were always energetically opposed to the Basle Programme, but they[3] assured us at the Hamburg Congress that this Programme would be modified and would no longer be understood as ' creating in Palestine a Jewish homeland guaranteed by public law.'

It was with this hope that I went to the Hamburg Congress, delivered a documented lecture about Jewish immigration into Turkey and urged that Zionism come into an agreement with the other societies for Jewish immigration, in order to organise a plan of immigration into all of Turkey.

When the Hamburg Congress adopted the Basle Programme as sacred and unimpeachable, whereupon I realised precisely the true aspirations of Zionism, I informed its leaders there that I had nothing more to do with the Zionist Organisation; one of them, known to the Salonica population, replied that I had never been a Zionist. At this point, I left the Congress prior to its conclusion.

Consequently, according to the Zionists, I have never been a Zionist; according to me, I have been, am and shall always be a Zionist, which means a partisan of a large Jewish immigration into Turkey; in my articles, published in *Tasvir-i Efkâr,* in *Zeman* and in *Yeni Asır*, etc., I have always favoured, with great insistence, this immigration – from an Ottoman as well as from a Jewish point of view – since I am convinced that it may contribute very much to the progress of our country and guarantee the security of thousands of our unfortunate coreligionists. I shall always continue publishing articles in the Turkish and Jewish press in favour of this immigration.

I am quite certain that the Zionists of good faith, with whom I have been in contact and who have been aware of my ideas, will not fail to confirm what I have stated.

Translated from Judeo-Spanish

TEKIN, THE NEW GENGHIZISM

Turan is alive but lives under the Chinese claw and the Russian boot – Turan the captive and condemned, Turan the humiliated and oppressed! For it to remain in this condition is Turanism's greatest shame. The first, most urgent and sacred duty of any Turk who is conscious and aware of his nation is to run to its assistance and deliver it from the bloody claws of the Chinese dragon and the Russian vulture. Turkish personalities and states are all charged with this task; all are obligated in this great mission according to their abilities – from the Ottoman Sultanate and the Empire of Iran to the Emirs of Bukhara and Khiva and the Lords of Kashgar. A mighty task for the great and a lesser one for the small, but the same duty for all: a jihad to save the homeland from captivity, a jihad of national obligation! A jihad in which every Turk must arm himself and take up his position.

Saving Turan is the obligatory interest of all Turkdom. We need not mention how important it is for the captive Turks to gain liberty. However, those who can still preserve their liberty and independence must understand that there is no political means more useful and advantageous!

The Afghan Khanate, Iranian Empire and Ottoman Sultanate are all condemned to the same political situation; all three are between two fires; the Russian invasion from the north and the English from the south. This encirclement grows tighter daily as the pincers are squeezed. It is impossible for these states to continue to exist on the basis of help found abroad in foreign environments, or even thanks to the friendship they can win. Such friendships are hypocritical, deceptive and in all cases transitory. These states may preserve their existence only through reaching the fatherland, clinging to its hands and pressing against its bosom. In the great coming struggle, our salvation will arise only through our reliance upon this strength.

The current period is one of nationality and race; even nationality passes on, however, and the era of race is imminent. Tiny nationalities are unable to survive. Every race, destroying the frontiers which separate its components, marches towards unification. If matters proceed in this way, the Latins will soon unite and set up their own union, as will the Anglo-Saxons and Slavs. In order to stand against them, the Turks must likewise establish a Turkish union, a Turkish United States. Only thus will Turan not be crushed by the Slav Empire and the Chinese Republic. Confronting these huge societies is impossible with today's corrupt and divided forces. If we desire to live and not to be crushed, then we – that is, the free and independent Turks – must immediately initiate the revival and establishment of Turan. Turan is vital for the captive as well as the free, for the condemned as well as the independent!

Yes, Turan must be delivered, must be saved – Turan will be saved!

But how and with what? The answer is very simple: with iron and fire! Turan will be conquered and freed by the iron of our swords and the fire of our thoughts.

History has shown us that a nation's union and independence can be ensured solely by the sword and the pen. All the Slavs came into being in this way. A humble Moscow princedom rallied all Russians around it; then, with its 'saviour' literature and its sword, it marched into the Balkans and raised the Serbs, Montenegrins and Bulgarians to their feet.

Germany, too, won its unity in this manner: German civilisation and national literature awakened the Germans. To this, the sword of Moltke was added and German national grandeur was established.

And Italy as well: The Italians – although possessing geniuses such as Dante, who could sustain the nation all by himself – won the unity of their kingdom thanks to the likes of Napoleon and Garibaldi.

Politics and civilisation, iron and fire, sword and torch! Just as others were saved by these two forces, so we too, with this dual preparedness, will save the nation from captivity.

We will find the force of the sword for Turan's sake in South Turan: the southern Turks have not yet unsheathed their swords. From west to east, from the Ottoman to the Kashgari, all of southern Turan lives with sword at waist. Here is the last defense line of Turan's Golden Horde. There we shall prepare for the counteroffensive.

For this, all Turkish palaces and fortresses must unite around the sacred ideal, via an enterprising and far-sighted diplomacy. National and religious unity will greatly facilitate these efforts. Small differences – of which the major is Sunnism and Shiism – cannot be an obstacle to unity and alliances in our own era, just as this could not have prevented an agreement even a hundred and fifty years ago.

The [Ottoman-Iranian] treaty of 1746, signed by a great Shah, like Nadir, agreed to abandon this difference. Nothing is easier than reaffirmation of this principle, which was put into an official treaty a hundred and seventy years ago, by a special agreement today, thereby securing our religious union. Religion does not hinder national unity; rather it may be the means of ensuring it.

After removing such differences, the question will be solely one of political alliance. In this respect, diplomats should direct their discussions towards a united state, a confederation. Truly, the proposal of a Turkish united entity, on the model of Germany, will very easily attract and rally crowned heads and even lower aristocracy.

Achievement of this [goal] means that the religious and national Turkish army, with its soldiers, officers, and commanding cadres will then be formed and organised. Every single army of this line-of-battle, stretching from Istanbul to Yarkent, possesses its own objective: to Turkey, towards the Caucasus and the Volga; to Iran, towards the Ural Mountains between Aral and the Caspian; to Afghanistan, towards Khiva and Bukhara; to the Altay, towards Balkaş; to the Kashgaris, towards Baykal! This is the task of iron, sword and diplomacy!

As to the tasks of the fires and torches of ideas and the lights of progress: if the former mission was to prepare for an armed war, the latter's role is to prepare a peaceful infiltration, i.e. to awaken the national conscience and to conquer people's minds. This is necessary for two reasons: on the one hand, to prepare the ground for an armed war and find soldiers and officers for Turan's army and, on the other hand, to prevent the enemy invasion to which Turan is exposed today.

Once, people migrated from Asia to Europe and from east to west. This torrent now flows from Europe to Asia and from west to east; the west is murdering powerless unresisting peoples. Migration of peoples has not ended; it is stronger than ever and more terrible in victory and defeat! The Chinese – and, even more so, the Russians – are marching today with these forces and power against Turan. Their penetration and infiltration into Turan is an aggression [intended] to strangle and kill Turan's aspirations. In order to counteract this, Turanians should arm themselves at once with the armour of national conscience, which will be ensured through peaceful infiltration by the torch of civilisation.

What are the means to be employed? A 'Turan Association', which should be set up immediately, will take care of these matters. Briefly stated, we believe that the basic mission of this association should be to teach national identity to the Turanian and show him the way to [ensure] his own preservation. This may be accomplished through [distribution of] historical, religious, literary and scientific publications in Turan. Geography and history instruct a nation in its past and point out its friends and enemies, while religion and literature endow it with a specific culture which will prevent it from assimilating. The applied, non-theoretical sciences provide strength for combatting alien elements and for informing the race of the need and the means for protecting its own health, work, wealth and continuity. These, then, are the qualities which preserve the race, elevate it and ultimately render it free and independent.

Above all, the Turan Association should despatch a field exploration mission to undertake the study of Turan's local needs. Then it will be concerned with disseminating to the four corners of Turkdom the love, knowledge and education of Turan – utilising the means it will institute – and kindle Turan with this fire . . . with fire and iron!

«Once upon a time, İlhan was pressed in a great battle; he and [almost] all Turks were killed. His surviving nephew, together with his children and grandchildren, lived besieged in Ergenekon for nine generations, a captivity of four hundred years. The Turks looked for a means of escape, but found no solution of any kind. Finally, Bozkurt Khan, the first saviour, discovered the way out – a talisman for liberty: iron and fire! The fire removed the iron; mountains melted, frontiers collapsed and the way of Great Turan was inaugurated.»

Fire and iron! This is the very force which saved the Turks from their captivity three thousand years ago! Today, too, this force wil save Turkdom from its last captivity, and Turan will be conquered only with «a sword in one hand, a torch in the other!»

Turan, pp. 136-143. Translated from the Turkish

TEKIN ALP, TURKIFICATION

THE METHODS FOR NATIONALISATION[1]

«The Turkish Hearths must commence becoming a source of enlightenment for the nations around them.»

Ahmed Ağaoğlu

There is no room for doubt and hesitation about the methods for nationalisation which must be applied in Turkey. For a long while, the Turkish government has played the role of gendarme in the cruel struggles which occurred in Rumelia among various elements, such as the Bulgarians, Greeks, Wallachians and Albanians, ensuring that nationalisation would nowhere be carried out in an oppressive or violent manner. The policy of bombing and dynamiting, pursued by the various elements in Rumelia against each other was universally counterproductive. Elements which held tenaciously to their nationalism before the [First World] War, despite bombs and dynamite, could not oppose the post-war methods of persuasion and conciliation applied by certain governments; they assimilated to their milieu and hastened to adapt to the nations among which they were living.

In fact, very perspicuous and persuasive examples may be found for 'adaptation' in all Balkan countries, such as Bulgaria, Greece and Romania. I personally know very many personalities in Bulgaria, originally Wallachians, Bulgarians or Albanians who, in consequence of nationalising, became Greeks. They speak Greek as their own mother tongue and Wallachian or Bulgarian only in conversation with their old parents at home – [otherwise] employing no other language. Such people are frequently encountered among the heads of financial and economic enterprises and even among statesmen. Many people in their milieus are aware of their genealogical trees, but absolutely nobody looks at them askance. They themselves see no definite reason for concealing their genealogical trees.

Ahmed Ağaoğlu Bey prescribes this method to the Turkish Hearths,[2] which are charged with a pioneering task in the efforts of [spreading the idea of] nationalisation:

«The hearths, already united and stable, must illuminate their milieus, propagate their aims and commence to enlighten the nations which live within.»

In fact, thanks to the revolutionary movement, Turkism has risen and will rise continuously. Elements living in a milieu of Turkism will be unable to resist the force of gravity and will have no choice but submit in spirit to the attraction of Turkism.

Türkleştirme, pp. 10-11. Translated from the Turkish

WHO IS A TURK?

«Any individual who declares as his belief:
'I am a Turk', should be recognised as such.»

In order to prevent erroneous thoughts and suspicions, we must accept and modify the principle laid down by my late Master [Gökalp]: «Any individual, who declares as his belief: 'I am a Turk,' should be recognised as such.»

Those who have had, like myself, the privilege of being among the oldest associates of the late Master, know very well that he attibuted the utmost importance to belief. In every case, he searched for an individual's beliefs, intrinsic convictions and sincerity. As to belief, it cannot be produced at will or by force of circumstances and the urge of interests. It is the product of milieu and education; belonging to one group or another through blood and lineage cannot influence belief.

An Albanian, Iranian, Arab or Jew, saying: 'I am a Turk,' has to be considered in accordance with his past, the milieu in which he has lived, the education he has received, and the permanent factors of his material and spiritual interests. If all these factors indicate the existence of a Turkish belief, the claim of Turkishness must be accepted.

In order to demonstrate and confirm the extraordinary importance of belief, I cannot refrain from repeating herein a sample conversation, held between a Turkish officer and one of his soldiers, published in a book by Professor Léger, entitled *Monde slave*:

- Where are you from?
- I am a Bosnian.
- Of what nation are you?
- I am a Turk.
- Do you speak Turkish?
- No!
- If you do not speak Turkish, how can you call yourself a Turk?
- I do not know; I was told that I was a Turk, so I know myself as such.
- What language are you speaking with me?
- I do not know.
- I am speaking to you in Serbian and you ar answering me in Serbian as well. In that case, we are both Serbs.
- No, you speak Serbian. I reply in Bosnian. Consequently, you are a Serb and I am a Turk.

Undoubtedly, the Bosnian soldier speaking in this manner has nothing of Turkishness in its currently-understood sense. His language, civilisation, education, race and milieu were entirely different from the Turkish ones. Despite this, our poor fellow defined himself a Turk with a statement of unshakable definitiveness – because his belief, owing to his Islamic connection, said that he was Turkish.

In this context, one may mention the experience of a committee of inquiry established by what was then termed 'The Great Powers', to resolve and put an end to the violent struggle among all factions in the Epirus sector (our former province of Yanya) before the [First] World War.

As we know, although the majority of the Christian inhabitants of Epirus were Albanians, they have long been prompted and inspired by a belief in Greekness. Some members of a committee of this commission of inquiry entered [people's] homes through the door. The inhabitants replied in Greek, without preparation: [We are Greeks.] Meanwhile [other] members of the committee entered [the same house] through the rear window to question the unprepared residents. The latter, while talking Albanian, claimed to be Greeks. These people spoke Albanian and, although not knowing one single word of Greek, claimed with complete candour to be Greeks, on account of their belief of having long been so inspired.

The aforementioned Bosnian soldier, or anyone nurturing the Turkish belief – provided he lives in a Turkish milieu under natural conditions – naturally becomes a Turk not only regarding belief, but also in terms of mother tongue, culture, and education. Belief is sometimes the product of education; growing up with Turkish education and living in a Turkish milieu, any non-Turk – thanks to the influence of [his] education – says, as a matter of course: 'I am a Turk.' In this manner, the Turkish belief is produced within him.

Sometimes, the reverse may be true; a man may consider himself a Turk with the motive of gaining an imaginary or true advantage or under the influence of auto-suggestion. Saying: 'I am a Turk,' he joins the Turkish milieu and shares the aspirations and wishes of the Turkish community, all its feelings, material and spiritual values. He guides his children in the same way and, in consequence, Turkism, which began only as a belief develops with culture and education.

In conclusion, I am convinced that the very first thing to be done in Turkey consists of instilling the ideology of Turkism among individuals and groups desiring to be Turks and preparing opportunities and grounds, for saying: 'I am a Turk' among all who wish to live under such conditions, i.e. with their material and spiritual interests linked with Turkism.

Therefore, if we seriously wish that all compatriots become part of the social organism in the task of Turkification and in the gradual disappearance of the mutual parasitism remaining from the Ottoman era, then we must never neglect paying attention to the true goal.

According to the basic rules we have explained above, the true objective is to prompt and inspire the Turkish belief in all compatriots, 'Without distinction of race and lineage.' In this respect, we may overcome our sentiments only through logic and will. To silence our sentiments – and let only mind and thought, logic and will speak when the fatherland's supreme interests are at stake – is an act which conforms to the spirit of our revolution.

We must never forget that the prompting and inspiration of Turkish belief to our not-yet-Turkified compatriots is a very delicate matter connected with the depths of the spirit. Consquently, it is not a task which can be ensured and completed from one day to the next. Sometimes, difficulties which are perceived as insurmountable may be encountered. However, it is certain that, as long as the Turkish ideal survives among the Turks, it is impossible for other compatriots to oppose adaptation. Difficulties which emerge from time to time may delay the final result but cannot prevent success.

Türkleştirme, pp. 25-28. Translated from the Turkish

THE COLLECTIVE CONSCIENCE

> «Race, religion, language – if all these principles are included in the collective conscience, they form the nation's principles; in the opposite case, they remain null and void.»

It appears that Turkification of the compatriots is not a very difficult matter. Seventeen years ago, at the time when Turkism – that is, the trend of Turkifying the Turks – arose, those weak in spirit sank into conjecturing that Turkists were wearying themselves with absurd chimeras. The *Genç Kalemler,*[3] published in Salonica, was considered, to use the expression of that time, as [leading] the struggle of today's people against yesterday's – the attack of David the dwarf on Goliath the giant. Turkism, successful in this vast mission, may attain with greater ease its aim of having the non-Turks nationalised. As there was no national conscience in this respect, one had to be devised *creatio ex nihilo* or discovered and extracted from the depths of the soul. Now, national conscience does exist, bright and shining like the sun, bestowing light and life on those who wish to sympathise with it. It wards off and drives away from its bosom those who remain indifferent towards it. Today's Turkism has become a magnetic force of gravity, irresistible to its entire milieu. If there are no powerful obstacles separating non-Turk elements in this country from this magnetic power, then it is impossible for this law of magnetic gravity not to work!

Yes! Regrettably, there is a powerful obstacle which drives off from Turkism some non-Turk elements: the past; moreover, it is not remote but recent.

I see no need to clarify the elements of the recent past; I cannot imagine that any single compatriot has forgotten the awful pages of this inauspicious era. Consequently, as not enough time has passed to obscure this period, it would honestly be naive to believe henceforth that the trend towards nationalisation may become comprehensive. However, are there not elements which were not involved in this inauspicious past? Is it not reasonable to commence today a task to be completed only tomorrow or on the following day? We may say that certain Muslim elements were uninvolved in this past; hence there is no impediment whatsoever in Turkifying these henceforth. They are essentially Turks, from the point of view of language, religion, interests and social milieu. If there is a force hindering their Turkism, it consists of nothing but people around them saying: «You are a Laz, a Kurd, an Arab, an Albanian, a Bosnian, a Dönme!»[4] and nothing but some conjectures and guesses occasionally appearing to confirm these beliefs and suspicions. Nevertheless, the most sacred task of those who have succeeded in ridding their nationalism of selfish sentiments is not to weaken our social organism by increasing the parasites, but to strengthen it, transforming parasites to real elements; not to say 'You are an Albanian, you are a Laz, to those who say 'I am a Turk,' – but to say 'You are a Turk' to those who say 'I am a Laz, I am an Albanian.'

In this manner – and only in this manner – will a collective conscience, the fundamental base of national union, be formed among the various elements residing in this country.

The Jews constitute another element unexposed on the road of adaptation to an obstacle such as the remote or recent past. They found refuge in Turkey, a sovereign government of the Muslim *ümmet*, and were brethren-in-misfortune in a crowd of Muslims and Jews, burnt alive in their thousands and hundreds of thousands in Spain, where Christians fanaticism and the spirit of the Inquisition prevailed in violence. The Muslims opened wide their doors to their fellow-sufferers and brethren-in-misfortune; however, as national sentiment had not yet awakened then among the Turks, no solution was devised for those refugees to adapt to the social organism in terms of language and faith. And so it happened that, until today, the Jews in Turkey have regrettably remained in an abnormal situation, unparallelled elsewhere in the world. There are fifteen million Jews in the world; they have adopted the language of their country-of-residence as their mother tongue and differ from their compatriots solely in their religion and historical tradition. Even in the Arab provinces, until recently part of Turkey, they adapted to Arabism; only in Turkey do they continue to use the language of the agents of the Inquisition. For a while, it was possible to close an eye to this peculiar situation, so long as Turks were deprived of national conscience. Today, however, as a powerful Turkism exists, for the Jews not to adopt Turkish as a mother tongue is a situation incompatible with the norms of mind and logic, of material and spiritual interests. In the past, there had been no causes and no incidents whatsoever to drive Jews from Turks and Turks from Jews. The honourable İsmet Pasha clarified this in a speech delivered during his presence at the Lausanne Conference: «The ties linking Turks and Jews are stronger than ever today. In Turkey, as elsewhere, the Jews have always exemplified exertion and perseverance, security and order, progress and tranquility; in Turkey, too, the Jews have worked in utmost calm and prosperity. In our country, like the Turks, they have paid no heed to temptations and intrigues. They have always counted and considered this fatherland as their own. Everyone should consider the Jews as models.»

Consequently, a Jew who is a Frenchman in France, an Englishman in England and an Italian in Italy, has no reason not to be at once a Turk in Turkey.

The Jews in Turkey have many motives for being nationalised in a speedier and easier manner than their coreligionists in other countries. It would be useful to review some of the more important of these factors:

The main motive, already mentioned above, is the long-term existence of a sort of religious solidarity between Muslims and Jews. During the Middle Ages, the unique goal of the religious fanaticism which reigned in the Christian world and which caused the notorious Crusades was to destroy and annihilate Islam and Judaism. Convoys of Crusaders, rushing *en masse* towards the Holy Land, driven by the same feeling of fanaticism, left the unarmed Jewish communities which they encountered on their way in a state of ruin prior to finding the opportunity of crossing swords with the armed Muslims. The hostility of the curse of fanaticism against Islam and Judaism by the likes of Torquemada, who burned alive hundreds of thousands of Muslims and Jews, has not ended with the Middle Ages; it continues up to our own times. Even recently, arguments for saving the Christian elements and removing Muslim rule from Europe have been heard among the most frequently adduced reasons for dividing Turkey. Christian fanaticism was the most important driving factor in the political intrigues woven against Old Turkey. Even if Antisemitism, which causes frequent troubles in various European countries, covers itself either with social or economic pretexts, the Christian spirit remains concealed behind these movements; it is nothing but a conscious and unconscious manifestation of religious hostility, beginning with the crucifixion of Jesus.

It is because of this sentimental *motif* of religious solidarity and co-suffering, which still exists in the subconscious minds of the people, that Sultan Bayezid opened wide the doors of his country to the victims of Christian fanaticism and, since then, the Jews – although they have not integrated in Turkey – have lived there in absolute security and prosperity. At no time have they been included, by either official or unofficial circles, among the non-Muslims.

Another factor facilitating adaptation is that the Jews in Turkey are exclusively those of the Sephardic or Spanish group. Anatole Leroy-Beaulieu[5] has proved that Sephardim have a powerful capacity and aptitude for adaptation. Of all European Jews, those who have integrated in the easiest, speediest and most accomplished manner are the Italian Jews, who are mostly Sephardic.

In order to integrate, the Jews must keep the following ten commandments like the Ten Commandments of the Bible.

The Ten Commandments:

1. Turkify your names.
2. Speak Turkish.
3. In prayers at the Synagogue, pray – at least partly – in Turkish.
4. Turkify your schools.
5. Send your children to the public schools.
6. Become involved in public affairs.
7. Maintain close relations with the Turks.
8. Uproot the spirit of the religious community.
9. Perform your specific task in the domain of national economy.
10. Know your rights.

1. Turkify your names: Bearing a Turkish name is a condition for being Turk. Your coreligionists in other countries, too, have nationalised their names, deeming this to be their duty. What is to prevent Mişon – already turned into Moïse with the intention of Europeanisation – from becoming Musa, Alber (originally Avram) from becoming İbrahim and Salamon (originally Shelomo) from becoming Selim or Süleyman? Give pure Turkish names at once to children born henceforth.

2. Speak Turkish: Speak Turkish in public places with those who know it. It is not merely a demonstration against foreigners but will have a very strong spiritual impact upon yourselves; gradually it becomes a habit, second nature.

3. In prayers at the synagogue, pray – at least partly – in Turkish: Praying in Turkish brings one closer to God, on the one hand, and to the fatherland, on the other.

4. Turkify your schools: The laws and the Government charged with applying them have opened the road to Turkifying your schools. If there are certain deficiencies in methods of instruction selected by teachers, do not remain silent and indifferent. Apply your efforts to mend the deficiencies and fill the gaps.

5. Send your children to the public schools: In other countries, our coreligionists do not send their children to [the Jewish] community schools. Once public schools reach an adequate level, there would be no *raison d'être* for community schools. Until that time, try to benefit from whatever is available. Do not be too lazy to employ superhuman efforts if the school doors are closed to children. Do not forget this is a country of justice and science.

6. Become involved in public affairs: Do not remain indifferent to matters pertaining to the general public in the country; display your interest in every way. There are many areas in which your efforts can render serious service. Do not pay attention if some people consider you as a foreigner. The Constitution recognises you as a Turk. You, too, behave as a Turk. An error in this or that cannot be lasting. Continue to march forward on the road of Turkism, without looking left and right. Never go astray from the course of action mapped out for you by the statesmen who have undertaken leadership of national affairs and their principles.

7. Maintain close relations with the Turks: Approach the Turks and mix with them in social life and in social and economic relations. Your soul needs ideals, spiritual food. You cannot live without it. You will find this spiritual food in relating to the country and in its various milieus: Trust that – some transient misleading appearances nothwithstanding – these milieus are ready to open up and welcome you warmly.

8. Uproot the spirit of the religious community: It is not your fault if the religious community spirit reigns today in your milieu. It is the unfortunate past which is to blame

for causing unhappiness to all compatriots. However, do pay attention to the spirit of revolution which has determined a definite break with the past. It is progressing, step by step, towards this goal. You too, in complying with the spirit of the revolution, must exert yourself to uproot from your soul this inauspicious relic of the past and to join the collective conscience as soon as possible.

9. Perform your specific task in the domain of national economy: The duty of every compatriot towards his country is defined in his material means, intellectual attainments, and personal characteristics and virtues. Your role is mostly in the economic domain. National economy can be served not by ordinary, simple and light matters, but by economic enterprises in commercial and industrial affairs and their like, intended to increase the country's production and national wealth. Thanks to your foreign connections and contacts in Europe and America, many enterprises can arise for exploiting this country's resources. Thanks to your serious efforts, today's Turkism, in every aspect, can be recognised abroad in its true character and essence. You, however, should count yourself as a perpetual and eternal son of this country and organise your affairs and life accordingly.

10. Know your rights: The Constitution has granted you the title 'Turk.' This is a right and a privilege which one is not fit to use without being a Turk by belief, spirit and conscience. If you are persuaded, on the basis of your belief, that you are a Turk or going to become one soon, know your rights and do not allow anyone to violate them; defend the laws and privileges which have bestowed upon you the name of 'Turk' with jealous determination and tenacity, and with the force of law.

Let us add that we indicate the Jews here as one example for integration. No force preventing the gradual adaptation of other elements is to be imagined. The passing of another five or ten years until the inauspicious traces of the past are removed will not have any impact upon the history and fate of a nation, providing that integration is earnestly desired by the two interested parties, that is Turks and non-Turks, and providing that they commence to work on it immediately, with resolute determination, in order to attain the goal ultimately!

Türkleştirme, pp. 60-68. Translated from the Turkish

M. TEKINALP, CURRICULUM VITAE (1939)

Concerning intellectual and public life: I began my intellectual life by writing regularly – since 1908 – on economic and social subjects for the *Yeni Asır* newspaper, published in Salonica. In addition, I also published separately several works on various social and economic topics.

Between 1908 and 1912. I was closely linked with the social and cultural activities of the Committee of Union and Progress in Salonica. I founded and assumed the presidency of the Society for Propagation of the Ottoman Language. I enclose an official letter of appreciation from the Director of Education. In 1910 I was elected in Salonica as member of the Provincial General Council and subsequently of the Provincial Association, continuing in these [posts] until the fall of Salonica.

I participated with great enthusiasm in the currents of Pan-Turkism, New Life and New Language which began under the guidance of Ziya Gök Alp at the Committee of Union and Progress general Centre in Salonica. Under Gök Alp's inspiration, I systemised for the first time the diverse ideas of Pan-Turkism and published [them] in 1912, in an article entitled «Les Turcs à la recherche d'une âme nationale,» for the *Mercure de France,* the most renowned periodical of Paris. This study was translated into Turkish by the late Yusuf Akçora and was published in *Türk Yurdu,* serving as initial foundations of Pan-Turkism; it subsequently constituted the sole authority for all works published by European writers concerning this subject.

During the same period, I published lengthy studies in other French scholarly periodicals about the Turkish theatre, the Turkish press and similar topics (Known writers in our country are aware of this activity of mine).

After 1912. Upon the fall of Salonica, I migrated to Istanbul. The Greeks already knew of my interest in the Turkish national and patriotic services and of my activities in this respect, particularly my speeches at meetings concerning Crete.

After settling in Istanbul, I continued to make my living in the free professions, but simultaneously continued my activities in the fields of intellectual and overall life, serving with the utmost enthusiasm under the inspiration and guidance of Ziya Gök Alp. For many years, I was one of the permanent journalists of the *Büyük Mecmua,* together with such distinguished writers as Falih Rıfkı, Sadık Necmeddin and Fuat Köprülü. In collaboration with the late Celâl Sahir, I edited a weekly, with the material and moral assistance of the Committee of Union and Progress general Centre. The aim of this periodical was to introduce and disseminate the ideas of National Economy which had been ignored in Turkey until then. At the same time, again by my initiative, a society was established with the same intention, called The Economics Association. The *İktisadiyat*

Mecmuasi, organ of this association, continued publication for two years. I also aided in writing for such newspapers and periodicals as *Türk Derneği* and *Türk Yurdu,* published with the assistance of the cultural division of the Committee of Union and Progress.

In 1914, again under the inspiration and encouragement of Ziya Gök Alp, I published a book in German entitled *Türkismus und Pantürkismus,* which was also translated into English. Both editions enjoyed unusual favour throughout the world. Renowned historians such as René Pinon considered and proclaimed this work to be 'The Bible of contemporary Turkish nationalism.' The most important chapters of this work were published as a book in Turkish as well.

Without leaving my liberal profession, I simultaneously worked at the Law Faculty in Istanbul as a Teaching Assistant in economics. I was dismissed on suspicion of being a supporter of the Committee of Union and Progress during the time that Ali Kemal was Minister of Education.

In 1928, I published a book entitled *Türkleştirme,* concerning the Turkification of all peoples living in Turkey. It comprised comments on this mission and subject by [some of] our own thinkers, such as Sadık Necmeddin, Fuat Köprülü, Celâl Sahir, Yunus Nadi and Ahmet Ağaoğlu. In addition to my numerous publications and conferences in Turkey on the question of Turkification. I used my frequent business trips to Europe in order to deliver, in various places in Europe, numerous lectures – in French and German – about New Turkey.

My most recent book in the intellectual sphere concerns the subject of *Kemalism*, published simultaneously in Turkish and French with the approval and authorisation of the esteemed party. The Turkish edition enjoyed great favour in Turkey, while the French one gained wide appreciation in Europe and America. This latter edition includes a highly laudatory preface by Herriot, President of the French parliament. This book, which has recently appeared in Czech, with a preface by the Rector of Prague University, will soon be published in Romanian as well.

Concerning my business activity: I have been active in business for 35 years. During this period, I was at the head of the most important commercial and economic enterprises, as director of legal affairs. I have undertaken many scientific studies concerning all areas of commerce and economics and have much practical experience [in these fields].

I specialise particularly in tobacco-related affairs, as I have long headed one of Turkey's most important tobacco enterprises. Consequently I served as secretary-general of the tobacco congress, convened at the Ministry of Economics in Ankara in 1935; I am in charge of the recently-established general secretariat of the Union of Tobacco Dealers in Turkey. Considering this, I venture in all modesty to express the hope that I may be very useful in financial and economic matters pertaining to our country.

Translated from Turkish

TEKIN ALP, THE SPIRIT OF THE TURKS

THE SPIRIT OF THE TURKS AND NATIONAL HEROES

The entire universe knows the Turk solely for his physical strength and robustness: 'Fort comme un Turc' expresses an historical truth which the whole world has affirmed for centuries.

However, the Turkish nation is not distinguished by physical force alone. It could not have created such a powerful state and such an important empire solely through brute strength. The age-old greatness and splendour of the Turkish nation results more from spiritual power. This nation, flowing over from the plateaus and steppes of Central Asia, indeed bore an unrivalled physical strength, exposed to the changes which the climate and new life conditions required. In addition, however, this nation indisputably brought along something else which was very little influenced by such changes – spiritual strength. Taking the moral factor into account, the Turks owe their war exploits and glorious victories firstly and foremostly to this indisputable force rather than to physical strength, which is regarded as a secondary element.

The aim of this work, then, is to determine the moral and spiritual characteristics of that Turkish spirit which enabled the creation of many a sound and powerful empire.

European scholars and historians have busied themselves very much with the Turks. Hundreds of works have been written about the historical exploits of the Turks and none have omitted characterising them as barbarians. Rarely, however, did they research the soul of this nation and endeavour to understand how it had succeeded in playing such a significant role in universal history.

We do not pretend to be able to fill this enormous void; still, we hope that this modest work may be a step towards that goal. We are not unaware that the labour we have embarked upon is complex in the utmost degree. The fact that the Turkish spirit has not remained an unaltered essence throughout history enhances the difficulties of this work. Turks emigrating from their fatherland developed among various cultures and civilisations, adapting but little to them. Because of this, our work must sort out the different periods, each of which bears upon the Turkish spirit in a distinct manner. In doing so, we cannot neglect determination of the ties linking the periods to one another – ties which cannot be discerned with the naked eye. In order to better clarify the points which comprise the characteristics of each of these periods, we shall study the heroes representing them. In this respect, it is our view that the best means for comprehension of the Turkish spirit are study and analysis of the personalities who have symbolised its incarnation in various periods. As we have previously had an occasion to say in another of our works, the Turkish nation demonstrates its strength and vitality only when headed by a leader – incarnating its soul, spirit and national hopes.

We may distinguish four stages in the crystallisation of the Turkish spirit: First, the ancestors' stage, the pre-Islamic period: in this stage, stretching over thousands of years, the spirit of the ancestors was forged in the crucible of the Ural-Altay steppes. In this period, Mete and Atila personified national heroes. The second stage is that of Islam: during its duration, the ancestors' spirit underwent a long eclipse. In its stead, a soul which we shall call synthetic or inter-Islamic predominated over the nation's spiritual life. The last symbol of that soul, Namık Kemal – hero of the Tanzimat era – incarnates this period. Namık Kemal is a hero who longed for liberty. He thought to link fatherland and liberty; however, he did not comprehend that in order to do so, it was necessary to bestow liberty on the ancestral spirit of the Turks, which was a prisoner of the synthetic and inter-Islamic spirit.

We have seen that in the Tanzimat era, Namık Kemal's contemporaries lamented together with him and desired freedom for the nation. According to Namık Kemal, the nation attained liberty with the Padishah's proclaiming the constitutional regime. At no time did Namık Kemal think of freeing the Turkish spirit from its centuries-old captivity. According to him, Turkey was a Muslim state, created by a Muslim tribe of 400 tents. When Namık Kemal enjoyed exceptional treatment, in exile and in prison, he wrote his friends as follows: «Behold the power of Islam.» Namık Kemal had adopted the Western concept of fatherland, but his own idea of nationality, in the modern sense, had not yet been formulated in any conscious manner. Even if the principle of nationality did pass before the eyes of alert customs officials and cross into the boundaries of the Ottoman Empire, it was particular to non-Turks – both Muslims and non-Muslims; thus it was a modern weapon, employed against the Turks who lacked it.

The third stage is that of the constitutional regime, which may be qualified as the stage of pregnancy preceding the birth of the New Turkey. The Young Turk revolution, in 1908, saved the nation from captivity, but the ancestors' spirit remained fettered in chains.

In order to achieve total success in its eternal duty of preserving the Ottoman Empire, Turkish soldiers always had to shed their blood in the mountains of Macedonia, the plateaus of Albania and the deserts of Syria and Irak. However, very many enlightened Turks were bitterly saying as follows: «These brigands and rebels – Muslims and non-Muslims – who are killed by the bullets of Turkish gendarmes, what do they want? They claim the right to say that they are Greeks, Albanians, Bulgarians, or Arabs; to speak their own languages and to possess their own literatures and cultures. This is truly an apparent ideal resulting in the nation's shedding its blood. Very well, does the Turkish gendarme himself possess this right? No foreigner can deny him this natural right; but in order to maintain the right of playing the gendarme's role, a Turk must never say that he is a Turk, only that he is an Ottoman or a Muslim. His own language serves no purpose except that of vulgar speech, as spoken by common villagers or peasants. The Turk finds his literature, which nourishes his ideas, in a foreign language which comprises only few words from his own coarse language. His wife still must sit locked up behind the harem lattice-work. After having worked the whole year like treadmill horses, Turkish villagers and peasants, who constitute the large majority of the nation, are forced to fatten up an Istanbul-based Padishah who is ashamed to say that he is a Turk, farmers-of-public revenues who think of nothing but exploiting them, or cheats from among the non-Muslim subjects residing in Istanbul, Izmir or the Empire's other large cities. He cannot hear a single word of Turkish in the mosques. Those who speak and write pure Turkish, who do not know how to use phrases, formulas and artifices in Arabic and Persian, are scorned as illiterate, ignorant, or 'Turks', in short.»

Enlightened Turks are seeking remedies to heal the wounds of the *ancien régime* and to instal in its stead the benefits of the liberty obtained at the cost of so many sacrifices. Several influential people of the period maintain that, first and foremost, it is necessary to bring about a union of all elements in the Empire. However, a number of politicians claimed that only by uniting all Muslim elements could one improve the country's situation. No one dared start from the beginning and bring the Turkish element to the level of the others.

Soft voices were heard sporadically, opining for the Turkification of the Turks. However, they were soon silenced, not merely because they were very soft, but also because they did not express a well-formulated ideal.

At that time, Ziya Gökalp became prominent for his scientific and systematic Turkism and his tireless dynamism. He exerted an undeniable impact over all his colleagues in the Committee of Union and Progress Party which held the government in its power.

Consequently, we consider Ziya Gökalp as the incarnation rightly representing this pregnant period of New Turkey. He plunged his finger into the wound, made a perfect diagnosis and started to work on the case with considerable energy.

As İsmet İnönü asserted in one of his speeches, «Those who have seen the Ottoman period remember well that the Ottoman regime could never be based upon 'The foundations of our revolutionary regime'. The Ottoman regime tried, within a cell of four thick walls, to protect its structure from gradual progress [induced] by the scientific and social developments of the last centuries. These convulsive struggles could not be related to the cause of saving the Turkish nation.»

Thus the nation's perfect liberty, which has given birth to New Turkey, is the product of the Kemalist revolution, incarnated by Mustafa Kemal and İsmet İnönü.

Türk ruhu, pp. 1-5. Translated from the Turkish

WHAT IS THE STRUCTURE OF THE TURKISH SPIRIT?

Numerous scholars have applied themselves to general analysis of the national spirit; the German, French, Italian, Russian and Spanish spirits were so analysed. To assert that they have all succeeded, however, is a risky pretence.

Such analysis is difficult for other nations and all the more so for the Turkish nation, whose fate and history are not comparable to those of other eastern and western nations. Follow the advance of any nation, from its emergence to the present day, throughout history and you will be able to comprehend the various stages of its development, its mingling (with others), and all factors which aid in its finite formation and mark it with its own current features. For example, we know that the English nation is a mixture of the northern and Norman nations, while the German nation is made up of German peoples which have mixed with a Slav population throughout history; those Slavs fused into the Teutonic tribes and were totally lost. The French nation came into being out of a mixture of the Latin and German nations, and so forth. But whatever the character of the race of the various populations which first entered the mixture of one nation or another, whatever the nature of the fusion of various elements within a single crucible, all (such activity) took place in a complete and finite manner. Of mixtures like these – which in some nations are very evident and in others unnoticeable – such homogeneous nations have emerged that it is impossible to distinguish the elements which shaped them. We may distinguish only the dominant element which has forcibly imposed upon the others its language, literature and culture. Other elements have been lost, without leaving a trace. Nations have emerged from the crucible of history: all members of each speak the same language, labour at the same literature, learn from the same culture and usually follow the same religion. All elements which are indispensable for the formation of a nation find themselves united within the same society and nothing prejudices the unity of the nation from its earliest times up to the present.

Is this the situation concerning the Turkish nation? The earliest ancestors of the Turks are types raised on the high plateaus of Central Asia. Over thousands of years, a style of life, activity and thinking – appropriate to the conditions of climate, soil and environment of the place they inhabited – took form there. From the second century B.C. on, the many millions of inhabitants of these high plateaus started pouring into Europe and Asia in huge successive waves, settling there as conquerors. These invaders were tough, robust, courageous people who conformed almost instinctively to traditions thousands of years old and inclinations inherited from their ancestors. They had their own special culture which would not mix with the culture and life style of the nations they had subjugated. These conquerors were simple and modest nomads who had a primitive but powerful organisation with positive mores. On the other hand, the population of the conquered countries comprised natives whose cultures were more or less refined, but whose social structures were not as sound as those of the conquering nations. The unwritten laws of the conquerors, their inviolable traditions, rules of order and security, and high moral principles formed a much more effective organisation than the refinements, civilisation, written laws and literary works of the native nations.

These contrasts of culture and civilisation between the nomad conquerors and the native population – as in all other national migrations – prevented the harmonious blending of various elements and the combining of nations. The proud armed knights of the steppes, upon settling in the vanquished countries, retreated into their own world, pursued their own separate magnificent customs, and, on the other hand, continued their military careers and, with the necessary organisation, preserved their ruling positions. The local population, bowing to their domination, retained its own administrative, cultural and religious autonomy. In all captured countries, there were two societies, completely separate from one another, which continued to live apart; there was no overlap and no blending whatsoever between them. The conquerors' society incessantly grew as new masses arrived from the steppe; [as] the steppes, from time to time, would send their surplus population to neighbouring countries, preferably to areas where their brethren had settled earlier.

A culture which was basically Turkish, despite its remoteness from the ancestors' home and its common life with foreign nations, thus remained perfectly sound.

After the Turkish conquerors converted to Islam, the reciprocal isolation of both societies – that is, conquerors and vanquished – disappeared. Henceforth the separation was between Believers and non-believers, Muslims and atheists; henceforth, the Turkish conquerors were no longer tightly closed in into their own world. They were partners in life-style with the other nations following the same religion. In time, a change occurred in the nation's own structure. The need to worship God in the language of the nations which had previously embraced Islam and to tread in the steps of the Prophet compelled the Turkish literates to learn Arabic and Persian. It was required that the conquering Turks read and learn not only religious works, but the Arabic and Persian languages and literatures as well.

In this way, educated Turks became totally attached to the Arabic and Persian languages, poetry and culture; the common people alone preserved the Turkish language and the ancestors' culture. There was a change in the nature of the prevailing duality between the conquering element and the local conquered population, as distinctions became displaced: no longer between conquerors and vanquished, but rather among the conquerors themselves – between the elite class and the popular masses. While educated people and the elite class appropriated the cultures of the native residents, those of the Arabs and Iranians having the same religion as themselves, the masses preserved their own traditions, race, customs and culture.

There is no need to add that the unity of religion between victors and vanquished produced no cultural and social proximity – clearly so amongst the elite class and moderately so amongst the popular masses – although it did cause racial mingling. At that time, marriages between different Muslim elements, among whom were very many Byzantinian converts to Islam, were natural and very frequent events, due to religious union, the unique criterion to discriminating among individuals. This mingling occurred mostly in the upper class, particularly among the Sultans, whose palaces were filled with Georgian, Caucasian and other women of renowned beauty. Consquently, kinship of blood, on the one hand, and proximity of culture, on the other, increasingly drove the nation's elite class away from Turkish national tradition and personality. This situation continued over generations, up to recent times, increasing and decreasing periodically.

Consequently, we must agree that today's Turkish spirit is a mixture comprising, first of all, the characteristics of the pure Turk during the pre-Islamic period – kneaded by thousands of years of life in the plateaus of Ural-Altay, then, of the Turk in the Islamic period – dependent on the indelible impact of religious life and, lastly, of the modern Turk – who has appropriated the effects of modern Western culture.

The leaders of the incipient Pan-Turk movement, after the Young Turk revolution of 1908, were perfectly right in not separating Pan-Turkism and Islamism from one another. They knew well that the Turkish national spirit had been kneaded in a form devised in the worlds of Ural-Altay and of Islam. The Kemalist revolution never denied the basic make-up of the Turkish spirit, but determinedly wished to remove from national life the effects of black fanaticism – the so-called religion which had no relation whatsoever with the real religious law of Muhammad – and, likewise, the traces generally called 'eastern soul and mentality.' The Kemalist revolution did not content itself in this respect merely with sweeping away the vestiges of the past; [rather,] by granting complete freedom to the development of the ancestral spirit, liberated from generations-long captivity, it opened the way for western civilisation's blessings to flourish in this swept-clean area.

Türk ruhu, pp. 20-24. Translated from the Turkish

CONCLUSION: DECLINE AND RISE

It is not through oversight that we have entitled this chapter with the expression 'Decline and Rise' instead of the formula 'Rise and Decline' employed by numerous authors dealing with the history of large empires, such as Rome, Byzantium, Muslim Spain and Iran. Historians of the Ottoman Empire have also used the expression 'Rise and Decline of Turkey.' However, historical events demonstrate that they were mistaken and that we must exchange the words as we have done in this chapter. On this occasion I wish to recall a personal memory.

The late Gustave Lebon, in his capacity as director of the series 'Bibliothèque Philosophique', much desired to publish a work entitled 'The Rise and Decline of the Ottoman Empire'. The year was 1912: Turkey had again suffered great territorial losses in the Balkan war which had broken out after the fighting in Tripoli. Notwithstanding the Young Turk revolution, Turkey was still 'the Sick Man', even sicker than in the past. Because Gustave Lebon, like many others, thought Turkey's decline to be final and incurable, he requested that I elaborate the causes of this decline – which followed a period of great rise – in a special work to be included in the 'Bibliothèque Philosophique' series. Naturally, I rejected the outstanding philosopher's offer, refusing to believe in Turkey's decline at a time when the Turkish nation was vibrant with *élan* from one end of the vast empire to the other. I maintained that this decline expressed a temporary page in Turkey's history and estimated that the Turkist awakening (resulting later in the Kemalist revolution) would put an end to it. I have published a study of that history, in various languages, entitled 'The Turks seek a national spirit'. In it, I explained that Turkey's decline was not essentially a matter decreed by Providence and that the Turkish nation would recover and progress thanks to the revival of national sentiment. Two years later, in 1913, the World War broke out. Turkey was at the crossroads: Decisions taken at that time would determine its future definitively. The life and death of state and nation were linked with these decisions. The Young Turks, who were then in power and filled with the new spirit of national renaissance, did not hesitate an instant: they proclaimed the abrogation of the capitulations which denied national independence, strongly hoping that this war would provide the means to save the Turkish nation forever from the threats of Czardom which had been pressuring it for two centuries. Several of the Young Turk higher officials of that period cherished the conviction that the best means to arrive at the desired goal was to reach agreement with the Germans, who were exposed to the same threat by the Czars. This is the basis of the Turco-German agreement, promoted in a clandestine manner by several dynamic personalities supporting the movement of Turkish nationalism.

In this connection, I dealt with this question in my book, entitled *Türkismus und Pantürkismus,* published in 1912. Churchill – in his book on the world war – discussed this part of my work and wondered why the Allied diplomats in Istanbul did not take the factors I had mentioned into account.

Later events confirmed that the enthusiastic leaders of the Pan-Turk ideology were mistaken in their evaluations and estimates. The Turkish nation, however, was not mistaken in refusing to bow to defeat. Race instinct was aroused, and the voice of blood was heard; the mentality of heroism – found in the subconscious of the national spirit – triumphed and led all people to declare 'Independence or Death.' The war of independence against internal enemies – the Allied Powers, which still occupied numerous provinces of Turkey, the Greek troops occupying Anatolia and, lastly, the black spiritual forces which were the true reason for Turkey's decline – commenced with this slogan calling for an awakening.

This war, carried out for the sake of independence, ended happily; Europeans called it 'The Turkish Miracle.' The Turkish Miracle did not restore an empire which could have proved to be a weakening factor; it revived the unity of the Turkish nation, its strength and capability. The Turkish nation rose again. Its rise was neither regional nor imperial; it was profound and spiritual, enabling the Turkish nation to attain progress in all areas of civilisation within a few years; other nations had taken centuries to achieve the same.

Nevertheless, it is needless to mention the dangers of proclaiming victory and sinking into a sleep of heedlessness. As yet, the result obtained is only the revival of spiritual forces inherited from the ancestors. This too may be only a beginning. The result which must be the new Turkish ideal, true revival, is not yet in hand. We are still far from attaining Atatürk's declared objective: 'We must rise above the level of modern civilisation.'

The heads of the nation must guard punctiliously the spiritual forces, which are again at hand after eons of confusion. They know very well that the insidious forces, which in the past had condemned the ancestors' spirit to torpor, have not yet been totally removed. They remain in ambush, in a state of readiness to pounce anew at the first opportunity. One of our main duties is to guard the nation against these insidious enemies, particularly during the crises of large-scale wars, which overturn spiritual standards. Enumeration herein of the spiritual risks upon which we have touched will be a lengthy process. Nevertheless, there are two significant dangers which cannot be ignored silently: one threatens us from the east, the other from the west.

As we have explained in the second part of this work, the synthetic spirit which the Turkish nation has borne for nearly ten centuries is a mixture of foreign influences coming from the east. Consequently, the danger threatening us from the east is a totally unexpected reaction and probable awakening of the synthetic spirit which is substantially eastern and Byzantinian. We well know which elements will re-appear on the scene, if our leaders' vigilance does not prevent them [from doing so]: the very same elements which over the past centuries have caused the spiritual downfall of the Turkish nation and the decline of the Ottoman Empire. Among these elements are, first and foremost: eastern fatalism, denunciation, hypocrisy, flattery, greediness, covetousness and so many other characteristics which are incompatible with the spiritual strength of the ancient Turks and with their sentiment of self-sacrifice. In order to oppose this danger, 'the perpetual revolution' – which forms one of the basic principles of the Kemalist revolution – has remained on the alert for nearly one-quarter of a century; far from slowing up its tempo, it is busily increasing creative activities not only in the political and administrative areas, but even more so in the cultural and social spheres.

This perpetual revolution, chiefly directed towards the danger from the east, ought to protect us as well from the other danger, which comes from the west. The first watchword proclaimed by Atatürk to the regime bearing his name is: 'Towards the West;' it has become representative of this regime and has been repeated incessantly since then. Thanks to its running full-gallop towards the west, the reborn Turkish nation has truly regained the centuries lost under the impact of would-be religion and black ignorance. However, the west itself is not wholly free of the seeds of destruction. As in all other matters, here, too, the coin has an obverse side. The spiritual forces – relics of the ancestors – regained by the Kemalist revolution are being threatened by a set of elements of degeneration which have recently invaded several western countries.

In the west, scientific and technological advancement does not always go hand-in-hand with moral progress. Development of moral and spiritual values is not always at the level of scientific and technological progress. For example, in several absolutist countries, which are in the vanguard of modern civilisation, the method of applying state authority does not conform with mentality of the ancient *Hakans*.[1] On the other hand, certain aspects of the democratic freedoms in a number of western countries display degenerative signs to a degree interchangeable with excessive licence, anarchy, oligarchy and other, similar elements of social decay. These elements cannot be compatible with the mentality of self-sacrifice and discipline pertaining to the customs and code of laws with which the spirit of the Turks and of the ancestors is deeply saturated. The leaders of Kemalism perfectly understood this situation from the very start; hence they refrained from taking over or – more correctly – from imitating a replica of the political and social institutions of the west. They desired that only modern civilisation and the mentality of progress be borrowed from the west. As for political and cultural institutions, these were adapted to the revived Turkish national culture.

However, despite all the measures taken, the danger of contamination did not vanish completely. The modernising Turkish society, just like those of other western nations, cannot be considered immune to the microbe of degeneration.

Included in this is a modern social calamity which we have called 'individualism,' a danger which could force the cessation of continuous preparedness.

There is no need to add that our understanding of individualism does not imply a system of secluding individuals within society, nor the superiority of state over private initiative, nor, generally speaking, any of the philosophical and sociological systems which go by this name. The meaning we intend by this expression is that of the indifference and disengagement an individual feels towards the public interest. This type of individualism is today such a social calamity that it unaccountably destroys the most civilised countries, in particular the administrations of the most enviable secular democratic republics. In certain democratic countries, the inauspicious consequences of this social calamity have been: the creation of nests of intrigue in each of the social classes and their becoming real groups defending personal interests of political parties and classes alike; the molding of public opinion, a practice which often involves ignominious maneuvres and tricks and a frightening increase in bribery, corruption and misuse of authority and influence by various movements. At certain times and in several milieus, diversion of political freedoms in this manner turned the state, public offices and political positions into a real division of spoils which attracted the greed of unscrupulous people. As this type of individualism was not entirely unknown in pre-Kemalist Turkish society, we should fear this modern social calamity even more; during the long centuries of absolutism, this individualism dominated Turkey single-handedly. The interests of the community were not taken into account in public affairs. Those occupying all ranks of administrative offices and those possessing public competence did not cherish any interests except to seek the most accomplished way to exploit the Treasury of the nation and state to their own profit and that of their clients, i.e., those who knew how to flatter them best and kiss their hands and robes. Ziya Pasha, poet and statesman, one of the most distinguished among the personalities of the Tanzimat period, devoted a large portion of a poem to this subject, reproving – with great courage – the moral downfall inherent in his contemporaries' sly behaviour. The very well-known hemistich of this poem, «If I stole, it was public property I stole,» indicates precisely the mentality of that period regarding public interest, as well as its moral degree.

In our environment, the concept of public interest could present itself only after the Tanzimat crystallised in the era of the constitutional regime and accelerated during the war of independence. Ziya Gökalp's famous maxim, 'There is no individual, there is society,' became tangible at that time and turned into an impactful reality. Thus there became manifest the gravity of this calamity which was sweeping the Ottoman Empire from its foundations. The Kemalist regime, coming after our victoriously-concluded war of independence, naturally had its sources once again saturated with the same mentality of self-sacrifice found in the Altay Plateaus. However, the period of struggle has long since passed. The new regime became stable and the whole nation progressed in tranquility and prosperity, due to 'the Turkish miracle' which it had accomplished. Now, the main danger lies in this very situation of tranquility and prosperity. The calamity of individualism can develop even more within an atmosphere of prosperity.

As we have asserted throughout this work, an ideal requires an atmosphere of crisis and agitation in order to be born and to live and develop. A milieu suffused with tranquility, prosperity and abundance is not favourable to ideals; it may even have an inauspicious impact upon them. World history, and particularly Turkish history, is replete with examples of brave fighters and glorious conquerors sacrificing themselves in their heroic exploits. Generally speaking, prosperity and tranquility, lasting for one or two generations, may open the way to weakening tribes of strong fighters, stopping their raids and extinguishing in their spirit the mentality of self-sacrifice and heroism which was responsible for their past victories.

The first to note the gravity of this danger and evaluate its worth was Genghiz Han; he perceived it well when elevated to the highest degree of glory and power. He pondered, «We have been at the highest echelon of glory and honour. However, our children and grandchildren will leave our modest homeland, which is the source of our power now, to settle in luxurious palaces, wear silken clothes, prefer to live in soft and temperate climates, take beautiful women, pass the time with various kinds of pleasures and forget quickly our self-imposed deprivations, self-sacrifices and the troubles to which we were exposed in order to establish this empire. Under these conditions, can this empire outlive me for long?»

Under the impact of this heart-rending anxiety, Genghiz prudently recommended that his son not transfer the centre of the empire away from Karakum, where the camp was situated – a barren site in the midst of the steppes over which no bird flew and past which no caravan crossed. However, Genghiz knew perfectly well that such measures were definitely insufficient.

Indeed, his grandson Kublay could not resist the splendid attractions of Peking and, in order to become emperor of the Heavenly Empire, settled there instead of modest Karakum. The powerful and fiery Mongols, who subsequently took possession of this empire, became languid, weak creatures and descended to the level of the Chinese whom they had taken under their domination.

Here we should immediately add that the danger of individualism, which we have mentioned, was not overlooked by modern Turkish society. As noted above, İsmet İnönü, who has long since attached great importance to the spiritual education of the nation, never neglected in his frequent lectures to urge the nation, in different ways, towards solidarity, thereby encouraging the mentality of self-sacrifice for the benefit of the community and the common cause. Turkish thinkers and writers did not fail to follow the example of the national leader[2] on this subject, using every opportunity to call upon the nation to remain alert against the danger of individualism.

However, we should remember that the Turkish Government need not have recourse to punishments in order to ensure employment of spiritual forces. The Kemalist Government may by no means be compared to democratic and absolutist governments insofar as moral influence is concerned. The miracles which it has achieved, surpassing those of all other nations, were not carried out through compulsory means, prohibitions, strong laws and regulations or [other] measures of that type. These miracles have entered the realm of the possible thanks to the leaders in the positions of power, who have incarnated the great idealism of the nation and its spiritual aspirations. It has been proclaimed that sovereignty belongs to the nation, as confirmed with open, clear constitutional laws; however, the nation, perhaps inspired by the spirit of the same code of laws – a relic of the ancestors – never employed this right of sovereignty in any way other than representation by its leader, who is nothing more than a modern *hakan*. As we have explained at length in our work on Kemalism, Atatürk's revolutionary works were accepted, in principle, not through pressure but rather through persuasion and education. The change in headgear, emancipation of women, reform of language and alphabet, secularisation of the state, etc. – all became facts before laws relating to them were passed, thanks to Atatürk's persuasive and educational activities. Contrary to conditions normally occuring in other countries, in Kemalist Turkey actions always preceded words. The elite class, the cadre of the nation's thinkers, has always been cultivated with consideration by the leaders. The People's Party, always inspired by the leader's spirit and mentality, is nothing but a large school for civic sciences. People's homes in the hundreds, set up on sound bases and brought into existence with a powerful organisation in the most remote corners of Anatolia, are schools in the hundreds for the education of the masses, ensuring by means of countless channels – visible or invisible – the dissemination of the leader's thoughts and sentiments, striking roots among all classes of the people. Government influence on all organs of the press is virtually matchless. The press dauntlessly criticises high officials' methods of managing and administering affairs of state; these criticisms, however, although sharp, never ignore public interest.

Because of this *sui generis* spiritual power, the leaders, to whom the nation shows considerable respect, have the possibility to cure and even prevent – through suggestion and education – not only individualism, but all kinds of social diseases as well.

The speeches of İsmet İnönü and his appearances among the people must be perused and evaluated from this point of view.

In conclusion, it may be said that if we well understand the essence of the Turkish national spirit, as explained in this work, the Manifesto of New Turkey may be summarised in the following code of laws.

1. Know and take pride in the exceptional spiritual strength bequeathed to you by your Turanian ancestors.

The world knows only of your physical strength, which has reached legendary proportions. It must grasp that you are equipped with spiritual strength and particularly that, thanks to it, your ancestors succeeded in establishing magnificent world empires. The main reason for the countless glorious exploits of the ancestors is the customs and code of laws which have assembled all the living forces of the nation and led them towards the same ideal. This unique ideal was the power and prosperity of the nation, whose sovereign was its symbol. Because of this, without underestimating the importance of national defense, do your best – in the same manner – to defend this spiritual strength day and night. Your most valuable national heritage is dynamism, a sentiment of self-sacrifice for the benefit of the community, heroism, respect for tradition and so many other spiritual qualities found in the blood of your veins for thousands of years. Do not lose the minutest particle of this valuable heritage.

Do not let your eyes be dazzled by hollow and meaningless slogans. Do not venture to assume lables such as 'European,' 'Aryan,' 'Western,' and so forth. Do not be afraid to be counted among Asian and eastern nations. Nature has not bestowed any privilege upon nations in the categories of European, Aryan or western; Asian or eastern nations, too, are not the stepchildren of creation. Progress and civilisation change places from one historical period to another. While Europe and the west were buried in the darkness of the Middle Ages, certain Asian nations – which included your ancestors – spread forth the splendour of their civilisations. Whether European or Asiatic, Western or Eastern, you are still the descendants of that masterful and conquering nation which had poured out of the steppes of Turan, and, over long centuries, had set up through the whole world magnificent and powerful states, empires and flourishing countries. This is your greatest title of nobility.

2. Life is an eternal evolution. As times change so do customs. Move with the times, conform to new conditions of life; adopt all the achievements of progress, whatever their source, thus evolving according to the requirements of place and time. However, the axis around which this evolution turns must be national tradition and national culture. You should not allow civilisation and progress to swallow up your ancient customs; on the contrary, civilisation and progress ought to conform to them.

3. Respect for national heroes ought to guide all movement and activity in social and individual life. The Christian Church has saints, officially approved by religion. All religious Christians do their best, in their activities and movements, to conform to these saints, who symbolise life in the next world more than in this one. You have your heroes, whose activities and movements are to be observed in epic poems and fabulous tales. Your heroes do not belong to the next world – they are symbols of your very self, in person, of your spirit and aspirations. Conform your action to these heroes. Their spiritual and material exploits should serve as necessary models for you to follow. Among many heroes honouring your ancient and recent history, there rise the luminous faces of Mete, Atilla, Namık Kemal, Ziya Gökalp, Mehmed the Conqueror, Süleyman the Magnificent, Gültekin, Alp Arslan, Atatürk and İnönü. The examples of courage, self-sacrifice and nobility of spirit displayed by your heroes ought to guide your life at all times.

4. Everything should bear traces of your own mark and personality. Avoid foreign influences in the areas of society, morals and culture. Beware especially certain ideologies – incompatible with the spiritual forces which mark your social structure – which have penetrated several western countries, under cover of attractive forms and colours and of a certain insidious propaganda. Do not forget the things which destroy spiritual forces from

their roots and drag you towards decline: foreign influences, coming from abroad and unsuited to your character, especially the influences of Byzantium and of foreign mysticism and the so-called influences of religion. You succeeded in overthrowing the domination of foreign influences only when you could find the spiritual forces that you required thanks to the Kemalist revolution. Do not imitate any foreign nation, whatever the level of its culture and civilisation. Find inspiration in everything good and right which you have seen around you; do not imitate anything.

5. Do not rest upon your laurels of victory. Once upon a time, you achieved miracles; you won the admiration of the entire world. You are on the way to prosperity and happiness. The inauspicious past is not very far away. It may arise from the dead. What will protect you from it is perpetual revolution, proclaimed by the leaders from the outset. You must always remember this watchword.

6. Beware the degeneration of modernism. The leaders have given you the watchword 'Towards the West.' Follow them loyally. You have modernised and appropriated as your own the progress achieved in the west since the Renaissance or, more correctly, since the beginning of your long-continuing decline. However, not only good things are found in western civilisation; there is the opposite as well. In certain western countries, modern civilisation has degenerated; in particular, it has created several ideologies which have upset spiritual values instituted long ago. Your leaders, as soon as they took their first steps toward the west, did not refrain from taking measures against the danger of contamination; above all, they proclaimed their attachment to the principles of justice and humanitarianism, the undeniable rights of the individual, unconditional feelings towards national sovereignty, absolute respect towards freedom of conscience and a mentality of wide tolerance honouring your ancestors. Beware the seeds of degeneration abounding around you and cling tightly to these spiritual values.

7. Beware the grave danger of individualism which has become the disease of this century. If you avoid this disease, you will surely not be deprived of the real pleasures of life. It is possible to profit from life without sacrificing the benefits of the community. In days of peace, our ancestors were exemplary idealists who spent their time in feasts and banquets. The individual enjoyed the pleasures of life only with the community. His greatest pleasure was loyalty to the benefit of the community. You may carry out the Kemalist revolution only through collective altruism for the sake of the joint cause and the public good. If, in a moment of torpor, you are seized by the disease of the century, your moral and spiritual strength will perish; then the recent past would return, and the enemies of yesterday would need only to extend their hands in order to coalesce with your enemies of today and tomorrow, depriving you of the wonderful results of the Kemalist revolution.

8. Cling tightly to national unity, which came into being through the superhuman efforts by your leaders. Now your country has neither classes, nor groups, nor parties, nor hierarchies, nor any division whatsoever. The whole nation was assembled together under the

banner of Kemalism. Do not forget that over a history of thousands of years, the powerful and sound periods were those in which the entire people gathered under the banner of a single chief – a single Han or sovereign – symbolising the hopes of the nation. Upon losing national unity, your nation was sentenced to anarchy and disorder. Your main strength is in the authority of the chief and the discipline of the nation. Perhaps other nations need a balance of power and a game of parties in order to prevent misuse of positions of power and authority. You who are a compatriot in Kemalist Turkey do not need all of this; you may keep on relying upon our revived code of laws. Those who had previously assured the rise of the nation to which you belong achieved a balance of power through altruism and mutual trust between rulers and ruled. The *hakan,* assembly, princes and all important statesmen of that era always worked to promote the potential and might of the nation. Your rulers have never taken their strength and authority from a balance of power between parties and groups, but from a mentality of authority and discipline which had formed the spiritual basis of your ancestors' heritage. Your ancestors have always found a way to reconcile the chief's authority with the principle of consulting the nation. The leaders who have created New Turkey achieved this political miracle at mid-twentieth century without prejudicing national sovereignty even one iota. Without relinquishing the spiritual forces left to you by your ancestors' heritage, you will always succeed to preserve national unity as it was – a unity which is your thousand year long source of power and might.

9. Do not forget that humanitarianism, too, has a place among the spiritual forces adorning your millenia of history. Nationalism indeed constitutes the foundation of New Turkey's credo and ideology. However, this nationalism rests upon strictly realistic bases, free from all kinds of mystical influences and effects. This is why New Turkey has found a way to reconcile ardent nationalism with the purest and most sincere humanitarianism. In this respect, the New Turk needs only to conform to the spiritual inclinations of the ancestors' heritage. Earlier in this book, we noted the degree to which the Turanian ardent conquerors behaved compassionately, tolerantly, humanely and magnanimously towards the people in the countries they had captured; we observed their generous attitude, to the utmost degree, towards the unarmed, defenceless and unprotected population. New Turkey, as soon as it reached a position to make peace, did not fail to reject openly Machiavelli's famous international maxim of 'sacred egoism,' still esteemed among certain western nations. The performance and activities it carried out proved its sincerity in this respect. Atatürk and İnönü utilised every opportunity to proclaim and emphasise before the entire world that their principles of humanitarianism and peace policies never wavered. İsmet İnönü, continuously repeating these principles in most of his speeches, did not hesitate to add the ideal of humanitarianism among the main bases of the new Kemalist regime. In a speech before university students about the Kemalist credo and ideology, he explained at great length the aspirations of New Turkey regarding the ideal of humanitarianism and, in various contexts, proposed the following maxims:

«It is a duty to pursue the high ideal of humanitarianism.

The goal of the revolution is to live as a part of the large family of man.

The fundamental policy of the Turkish nation is peace and, in the course of its implementation – progress and civilisation.

The Turkish nation has acquired an important place in the family of mankind.»

After explaining at length the moral principles of the ancient Turks and the magnanimity they had displayed towards the vanquished nations, Ziya Gökalp, the first theoretician of Turkish nationalism, reaches the following conclusion, «Each of the great nations distinguished itself in one area of civilisation. The ancient Greeks won their first place in aesthetics, the Romans in law, the Jews and Arabs in religion, the French in literature, the Anglo-Saxons in economics, the Germans in metaphysics and the Turks in morals and humanitarianism.»

This same ideologue, while exposed to the greatest pain and suffering in his Malta exile, passed his time envisioning the prosperity and happiness of all mankind; he discussed all this in the letters sent to his young daughter, one of which ends with these words, «A day will come when the whole family of man will rejoice in an atmosphere of peace and prosperity.»

That is to say that the ideal of humanitarianism is included within the national heritage which must be guarded jealously, taking the leaders as models and following their advice.

You should never stray from this eminent recommendation of Atatürk, the eternal leader, «Rise above the level of western civilisation.»

Despite the enormous progress you have achieved in a very short while, you are still very far from this final goal. Your eternal leader's aversion to lethargy, symbolising the dynamism which is a relic of the ancestors, constitutes an example as well. He knew very well that lethargy constitutes the first step toward misery and decline. In order to protect the Turkish nation from the mortal enemy of all flourishing communities, Atatürk proclaimed two complementary watchwords. The first was that «perpetual revolution defends us against any sort of revival of the past and against the traitorous forces of fanaticism. Nevertheless, it protects us solely from the enemy behind us. But there is also an enemy facing us, against whom we should defend ourselves with the very greatest energy. The enemy facing us is slackness itself. If you remain at the level of western civilisation, considering its attainment as the ultimate aim, the result will be a slackening and numbing of all vital forces. The dynamic forces, suffused with the revived spirit – a legacy of the ancestors – would be unable to save you from downfall then. Thus, Atatürk commanded you to rise above the level of civilisation, in order to defend you against that mortal enemy called slackness. Efforts at rising above this level imply a continuous movement upwards, an endless and unlimited movement of creativity. Only through this mentality of eternal rising will you be able to defend yourself against the terrible danger of slackness, before which even Genghiz quivered as he reached the climax of his glory and honour.

To rise above the level of western civilisation is for you not an ordinary aspiration but a sacred duty toward yourself. *Noblesse oblige!* For thousands of years, you lived as a nation of masters, as a *Herrenvolk*. Now, once the times have changed, if you remain at [this] level, entrusting yourself to slackness, you will remain exposed to the danger of losing superiority and of falling into inferiority.

Türk ruhu, pp. 273-287. Translated from the Turkish

MUNIS TEKINALP,
A PETITION TO THE TURKISH MINISTRY OF FOREIGN AFFAIRS

To the exalted Ministry for Foreign Affairs, Ankara.

Having spent an annual two months' vacation in Nice with my family (settled there long ago), for many years, I had the opportunity to study closely affairs in the Côte d'Azur region, which related to our country. Basing myself on these studies, I consider it useful to present the following suggestions.

Until the end of the Second World War, there was a consul in Nice, capital of a region which comprises such important centres of tourism as Monte Carlo, Cannes and Juan les Pins. After the elimination of this post, the geographic importance of the Côte d'Azur increased in every respect and relations of Turkish compatriots with the region acquired greater significance.

This region, in recent years one of the world's best-known centres of tourism, annually an arena for the likes of the Aga Khan, Churchill, kings, emperors and millions of tourists, has also become an important centre for fashions and luxury goods such as perfumes. The number of Turkish compatriots – those who settled there, acquired villas and hotels, and particularly those who visit the Côte d'Azur each year – increases daily. Consequently, even if the re-establishment of an active consular office in this region is impossible, I am convinced that you will deem appropriate representation by an honorary consulate of our country. Since I have decided to go to Nice once again towards the end of this year, with the intention of continuing my intellectual activity and settling there, I present my profound respects and shall consider myself fortunate in case the dignity of an honorary consulate would be deemed suitable for me by your exalted Ministry.

Along with the favoured hope that this my petition for service will be well received, a summary of my *curriculum vitae* is presented herewith.

Translated from the Turkish

CURRICULUM VITAE (1955/6)

In 1906, having completed my higher education in Salonica – at the Alliance Israëlite School, the Law College and the Jewish [Rabbinical] Seminary – I began a life of journalism and law practice in Salonica, where I worked in various capacities in the cultural circles of the Committee of Union and Progress, led by Ziya Gökalp. For five years, I continuously wrote for the *Yeni Asır* newspaper and in 1908 I published a book entitled *Teşebbüsü şahsi ve tevsii mezuniyet*.

Following the proclamation of the constitution, I was elected member of the Provincial General Council and chosen by this Council as representative to the Provincial Association of Minorities, duties which I continued to fulfil up to 1912.

In 1912, upon the fall of Salonica, I migrated to Istanbul and settled there, continuing in my professions as journalist and lawyer. From 1914 on, while continuing my activity as director and legal adviser for various commercial companies in Istanbul, I have intensified my efforts in [various] areas of intellectual and public life, as I do still.

These comprise:

a. Since 1912, when I settled in Istanbul, I wrote on economic and sociological topics for periodicals such as *Yeni Mecmua, Türk Yurdu, Türkiye İktisat Mecmuası* and dailies such as *Akşam, Cumhuriyet, Vatan, Hürriyet* and *Son Posta*; I also published various books in Turkish and foreign languages – activities which I am still engaged in to this day. Between 1916 and 1918, I edited a Turkish, French and German weekly, entitled *İktisadiyat Mecmuası*, organ of the cultural centre of the Committee of Union and Progress, with the intension of disseminating the idea of National Economy.

b. Between 1914 and 1918, I was a Teaching Assistant at Istanbul's Law Faculty.

c. Between 1945 and 1950, I served as a member of the Municipal Council.

d. In addition, continuing my activity in the intellectual and public life of the private and free [enterprise] sector, I participated in the establishment of Istanbul's Merchant Association ten years ago; since then I have strived to serve the development of economic democracy in our country; since the Association's establishment, I have been involved continuously as its vice-president, secretary-general and member of its administrative board.

e. My principal published works, in Turkish and various foreign languages, are the following:

I. *Kemalizm* (1937), in Turkish, French, Czech and other foreign languages. Monsieur Edouard Herriot, former Prime Minister of France and one of the leaders of [its] parliament, wrote a preface for the French edition and Fuat Köprülü a laudatory foreword for the Turkish edition.

II. *Türk ruhu* (1944), whose preface was written by Şamsettin Günaltay, former Prime Minister and [now] chairman of the [Turkish] Historical Association. A French edition will soon be published in Paris.

III. *Türkleştirme* (1928), with comments by Necmettin Sadık, Fuat Köprülü, Celâl Sahir, Yunus Nadi and Ahmet Ağaoğlu.

IV. *Türkismus und Pantürkismus* (1914), published in German and later translated into English and other foreign languages.

V. I enjoyed the bliss of participating in a jubilee held in the [main] hall of Istanbul University, on 2 October 1948, in honour of personalities serving the press for fifty years.

VI. In 1955 I was elected honorary member of the Association for the Cultural and Social Studies of Turkey, by a decision of its general board.

Translated from the Turkish

TEKINALP, SOLIDARITY ACCORDING TO GÖKALP

I commence with an apology for mentioning such a vulgar term as «slum millionaires» together with a scholarly and philosophical term like «solidarity». However, I found no more concise way to express my thoughts.

Solidarity is a socio-economic system which was a very frequent subject of discussion in Ziya Gökalp's time. Its French equivalent is «solidarisme.»

For a number of years, the late Master displayed a very great attachment to this social system. Thirty-five years ago, people like Hamdullah Suphi, Fuat Köprülü, Celâl Sahir and Halim Sabit – close colleagues and permanent members of the cultural section in the centre of Union and Progress, who met at his home for lunch on Fridays – discussed this question in private. They argued for hours about the likes of Bergson and Dürkheim and worked together to emphasise that, without properly securing the institutions of solidarity within human society, it was impossible to reach peace and tranquility, prosperity and happiness; therefore, the first duty of the elite and intellectuals who aim at the good and safety of society is to develop institutions of mutual aid and solidarity, particularly in the economic and social areas. New life in the Constitutional Era,[1] or more correctly such social mottos as 'There is no individual, only society,' 'There are no rights, only duties' – known slogans of Ziya Gökalp's time – were based on such a philosophical system. However [several] epochs have passed in our society since Ziya Gökalp's day. Eras focussing upon material and individual interests, in certain circles, have followed eras inclined to ideals. And today we find ourselves having reached the period of slum millionaires who, in certain milieus, consider the material superior to the ideal. Because of this I considered it useful, on this occasion, to mention the institutions of solidarity based on ideals, with which we lived forty years ago. It is also necessary to add the following: if the spiritual and moral views predominant in the collective conscience at that time had not become obsolete, the catastrophe of contemporary slum millionaires would not have occurred.

Let us explain: Forty years ago, inspired by the philosophical views prevalent in Ziya Gökalp's circle, I opined – in articles published in *Yeni Mecmua* concerning discussions on solidarity – that one of the most important principles in the system of solidarity was value-increase in the economic domain or, more scientifically stated, 'plus-value.' Ziya Gökalp propounded the following in discussions on solidarity:

«Value-increases in movable and immovable property, due to conditions and developments external to the individual's will and with no effect upon him, cannot be accepted as his right. Such value-increases pertain to society, i.e. to the state. Consequently, laws, ordinances and regulations connected with the administration of society and with regulating wealth within it in a period of justice and equity should be enacted according to this basic principle.»

For years, Ziya Gökalp spoke to this end among those close to him, clarifying his view appropriately. However, he was unable to write long articles about his thoughts and views in this respect, nor could he formalise laws, ordinances and administrative regulations for setting up the institutions of solidarity. At that time, it was not considered a topic of the day; value-increases occurring without any labour on the part of the individual did not attract attention in the world of economics. Today, however, as everyone knows, the question of slum millionaires is a topic of discussion. Great value-increases occur from one day to the next. We witness how millions are collected in the hands of a few people, with the mind-boggling thrust of speculation.

I recently had a chance opportunity to hear the most perfect description and definition of this universally-recognised situation. As the issue is not considered timely today, I believe it is useful to recall the era of solidarity through which we lived thirty-five years ago.

On Wednesday, 14 March, I found myself at a meeting of the general annual assembly of the Merchants' Association of Istanbul, which encompassed the 500 best-known and most respected establishments. The economic problems of our current commercial world, [recorded] in the annual report of activities – which was read at the meeting and was the subject of debate by the various speakers – were successively scrutinised severely and critically. Problems like the cost-of-living, profiteering, the black market, a decline in the value of the national currency, tightening-up of the law on national defence – all most important topics of the day – were clarified. Then, an elderly and respectable person stood up impulsively and excitedly declared:

«We have discussed matters heatedly for hours. We have uncovered many bitter truths. However, none of us has pointed a finger at our gravest sore, one which is gnawing at our very structure – the above-mentioned disproportionate, unreasonable and uncalibrated increases in the price of lands and buildings, which are nothing but speculation. Lately, this calamity – which has plagued our large cities and most particularly Istanbul – has excessively decreased the buying power of our national money. As a result, on the one hand, the popular masses are condemned to extreme poverty, while, on the other, brand-new slum millionaires crop up daily; consequently, the cost-of-living rises from day to day. For example, the price of a plot of land or building worth 10,000 Turkish pounds may increase in one day to 100,000 without any reason. In this manner, many a million pours into the pockets of various individuals. What kind of services have these slum millionaires rendered in order to earn their money? Money earned without sweat, without perfotming any work or rendering any service, may only be considered as stolen from the nation. Commonly expressed, it ought to count as theft; legal means and regulations should be found, without delay, to put an end to these profits.»

I do not know whether [further] comments are required; the passionate words of this respectable compatriot are truth itself. The circumstances and conditions which create slum millionaires constitute a disaster for society.

The speaker did not touch upon the scientific and social aspects of this problem. However, as I have explained above, I believe that the principle of solidarity is the most effective remedy against this calamity which corrodes our social structure and economic organism. Legal means and regulations should be instituted by society against price increases without a labour equivalent. By raising the inheritance tax to 80%-90%, England – the most advanced country in the West – has succeeded in building a barrier against the calamity of extreme wealth through inheritance. In this manner, it is quite possible to build a legal barrier against illegal, labourless and disproportionate value-increases, thus ensuring social justice.

Translated from the Turkish

NOTES

NOTES TO CH. 1: INTRODUCING THE SUBJECT

[1] Turkish spelling for the French name Moïse.

[2] E.g., Zehra Önder, "Panturanismus in Geschichte und Gegenwart," *Oesterreichische Osthefte* (Vienna), XIX/2 (May 1977), p. 95: "der türkische Schriftsteller Tekin Alp."

[3] Niyazi Berkes, *The development of secularism in Turkey*, Montreal, McGill University Press, 1964, p. 344.

[4] See below, appendix, 'Preliminary List of Tekinalp's Writings.'

[5] I am most grateful, for pertinent information, to Tekinalp's three children: Mr. Isaac Tekinalp, Istanbul; Mrs. Thérèse Negrin, New York; and Mr. Guillaume Tekinalp, London. All three graciously granted me long interviews.

[6] Mr. Isaac Tekinalp permitted me to read his late father's manuscript diaries in French, covering the years 1907 to 1911. Mr. Guillaume Tekinalp allowed me to read his late father's diaries in Turkish, covering the years 1946 to 1959.

NOTES TO CH. 2: TEKİNALP'S LIFE

[1] The following account of Tekinalp's life is based on a brief typewritten *hal tercümesi* ('curriculum vitae'), prepared by him in his later years (see also in my 'Selections from Tekinalp's works') and on the scanty data supplied in several of his books, checked against, and amplified by, information provided by his three children and some of his friends, such as Mr. Elie Bourla, a Jewish Industrialist; Dr. Salvatore Zekeriya, Tekinalp's dentist; Mr. Cihat İren, a business associate of his; Mr. Sylvio S. Hatem, a businessman; and Mr. Jetvart Beyaz, an Armenian industrialist and businessman who had been politically close to Tekinalp – all residents of Istanbul. My thanks go to them all.

[2] Most were murdered in Greece by the Nazis during the Holocaust of the Second World War.

[3] There is a vast body of source materials on Salonica at the time, including memoirs (in Hebrew) by David Benveniste and others. Still worth reading is J. Nehama's monograph *La ville convoitée, Salonique,* Paris, Perrin, 1914. See also P. Dumont, "La

structure sociale de la communauté juive de Salonique à la fin du dix-neuvième siècle," *Revue Historique* (Paris), CCLXIII/2 (Apr.-June 1980), pp. 351-393 and "Une organisation socialiste ottomane: la fédération ouvrière de Salonique," *Etudes Balkaniques* (Sofia), XI/1 (1975), pp. 76-88 and the numerous references in the footnotes of both articles.

[4] Public Record Office, London (further: PRO), Foreign Office series (further: FO) 295/18, Consul General H. H. Lamb's no. 128, dated Salonica, 13 Dec. 1907. Lamb enclosed the school's curriculum.

[5] *Diaries,* 3 Oct. 1907.

[6] Cf. Avram Galanti, *Türk harsı ve Türk Yahudisi: tarihî, siyasî, içtimaî tetkik,* Istanbul, Fakülteler Matbaası, 1953, p. 16.

[7] *Diaries,* 2 Feb. 1909. Cf. *ibid.,* 17 Aug. and 3 Nov. 1909, and 23 Aug. 1910.

[8] *Ibid.,* 27 Mar. 1910. Cf. *ibid.,* 8 May and 20 Dec. 1910, and 17 Mar. 1911.

[9] He was to continue his freemasonic activity for many years, until it was banned in the Republic of Turkey. However, the claim by İ.H. Pirzade, *Türkiye ve Yahudiler,* Istanbul, 1968, p. 33, to which no evidence is adduced, that Tekinalp founded the local lodge, is farfetched. See also "Farmāsūniyya," in the *Encyclopaedia of Islam,* 2nd ed., Supplement to vols. I-II-III, *s.v.*

[10] See in my 'Selections from Tekinalp's works.'

[11] *Ibid.* His manuscript letters may be found in the Central Zionist Archives, Jerusalem (further: CZA), file A 36/64.

[12] Cf. David Farhi, in the annual *Sefunot* (Jerusalem, in Hebrew), XVI (1981), p. 141.

[13] According to an interview with Mr. David Benveniste (who had lived in Salonica in those years), in Jerusalem, on 4 October 1981.

[14] For instance, in 1910, see the Club's circular, summarized in the manuscript "Brief aus Konstantinopel," in CZA, file Z 2/10.

[15] See N.J. Mandel, *The Arabs and Zionism before World War I,* Berkeley, University of California, 1976, p. 95.

[16] *Diaries*, 30 July 1908.

[17] *Ibid.*, 22 June 1911.

[18] *Ibid.*, 18 May 1910 and subsequently, esp. 23 Nov. 1910 and 3 Apr. 1911.

[19] *Ibid.*, 17 Sep. 1910.

[20] *Ibid.*, 21 and 22 Mar. 1911.

[21] Based on the retail prices of 26 basic commodities, see ***İstatistik Yıllığı*** (Ankara), VIII (1935-36), p. 341. For inflationary trends before the war, see Tekinalp's *Diaries*, 5 June 1911.

[22] Evidently, Tekinalp was never an 'evil genius' inspiring Gökalp, as suggested, without any proof, by H. Mustafa Genç, ***İslâmî açıdan Ziya Gökalp ve Türkçüler***, Istanbul, Tek Yol Yayınları, n.d. (1978), pp. 27, 34-37.

[23] Abraham Galante, *Histoire des Juifs d'Istanbul,* Istanbul, Imprimerie Hüsnütabiat, 1942, II, pp. 68-69; cf. *ibid.*, pp. 99, 224.

[24] Information obtained in an interview with Mr. Cihat İren, in Istanbul, on 21 July 1980. Iren had served together with Tekinalp on the Administrative Board of the ***Tüccar Derneği.***

[25] ***İkdam*** (Istanbul), 10 Mar. 1928, reported in *Oriente Moderno* (Rome), VIII/5 (May 1928),pp. 220-221.

[26] Galante, ***Türk harsı ve Türk Yahudisi, op. cit.***, p. 16.

[27] FO 424/279, E 4806/877/44, Sir P. Loraine's no. 381, to Sir Samuel Hoare, dated Istanbul, 2 Aug. 1935.

[28] Abraham Galante, *Turcs et Juifs: étude historique, politique,* Istanbul, Haim Rozio & Co., 1932; 160 pp. *Cf.* id., ***Türkler ve Yahudiler : tarihî siyasî tetkik,*** Istanbul, 1928; 216 pp.

[29] Id. (signed Avram Galanti), ***Vatandaş, Türkçe konuş! Yahut Türkçenin tamimi meselesi, tarihî, içtimaî, siyasî tetkik,*** Istanbul, Hüsnütabiat Matbaası, 1928; 68 pp.

[30] For the manuscript text of this petition, see in my 'Selections from Tekinalp's works.'

[31] At least according to C.J. Walker, *Armenia: the survival of a nation,* London, Croom Helm, 1980, p. 190.

[32] His Jewishness was emphasized by several antisemitic journalists in Turkey, such as the

above Pirzade, or Ziya Uygur, *Tarih boyunca inkilâplar ve Siyonizm*, Istanbul, *Kardeşler Basımevi,* 1952, I, pp. 6-8, and more recently, Sadık Albayrak, *Devrim çakıl taşları,* Istanbul,Medrese Yayınları, 1979, pp. 137-141.

Notes to ch. 3: INTELLECTUAL ACTIVITY AND WRITINGS

[1] Partly based on my interview with a close associate of his, Mr. Cihat İren, in Istanbul, on 21 July 1980.

[2] *Diaries,* 7 Nov. 1907.

[3] See below, Bibliography.

[4] See below, Appendix.

[5] According to C.O. Tütengil, in *Kitap Belleten* (Istanbul), II/13-14 (Nov.-Dec. 1961), p. 13. See also id., "Sosyoloji tarihimizde Tekinalp," *Varlık* (Istanbul), 575 (1 June 1962), p. 7.

[6] I have as yet been unable to find a complete set of *Yeni Asır*; the issues I have seen at various libraries (chiefly at the Tarık Üs Library in Istanbul) comprised few signed articles by Tekinalp.

[7] I have been unable to locate this work, published in 1909 or 1912 – see below, appendix, 'Preliminary list of Tekinalp's writings,' where details may be found about his writings mentioned below.

[8] See below, appendix, 'Preliminary List of Tekinalp's writings.'

[9] *La Epoca* (Salonica), 20 Dec. 1910, p. 1. See also below, in my 'Selections from his works.'

[9a] Cf. *ibid.*

[10] In his *op. cit., La Ville convoitée, Salonique,* published in 1914.

[11] *Türk Yurdu* (Istanbul), II (1328/1912), pp. 656-657.

[12] See also Hilmi Ziya Ülken, *Türkiye'de çağdaş düşünce tarihi,* Istanbul, Ülken Yayınları, 1979, p. 368.

[13] Moïse Cohen, "Die Juden in den Balkanländern," *Monatsschrift der Oesterreichisch-Israelitischen Union,* XX/9-10 (Sept.-Oct. 1913), pp. 16-24. See also above, in my 'Selections from his works.'

[14] On his activities and importance as a Pan-Turkist, see my *Pan-Turkism in Turkey: A study of irredentism,* pp. 33-34, 51, 74.

[15] For which see C.W. Hostler, *Turkism and the Soviets: the Turks of the world and their political objectives,* London, Allen & Unwin, 1957, p. 115. E.Yu. Gasanova. *O kontsyeptsii Turkizma v idyeologii Mladoturok,* repr. from *Premier Congrès des Etudes Balkanique (Sofia, 1966), Communications de la Délegation Soviétique,* Moscow, 1966, p. 3.

[16] But *not* into French, despite Ülken's assertion, in his *op. cit.,* p. 368.

[17] See *Report on the Pan-Turanian movement* (anonymously authored by A. J. Toynbee), London, Intelligence Bureau – Department of Information, October 1917, p. 6. The *Report*, p. 4, errs however in giving the author's name as Albert Cohen (it was, of course, Moïse Cohen).

[18] Copies may be consulted in the British Library, London, and in the PRO, under FO 395/15, file 204719. See also below, my 'Selections from his works.'

[19] FO 396/139, file 15725, no. 70477.

[20] *The Round Table* (London), especially June 1917, pp. 515 ff., and Dec. 1917, pp. 107, 112.

[21] *Turkey: a past and a future* (according to the FO files in the PRO, anonymously authored by A. J. Toynbee), London, Hodder and Stoughton, 1917; 79 pp. Another edition was published in New York by George H. Doran, 1917; v, 85 pp.

[22] Such as that of C.O. Tütengil, *op.cit.* in *Kitap Belleten,* II/13-14 (Nov.-Dec. 1961), p. 13. For the book itself, see extracts below, in my 'Selections from his works.'

[23] Like François Georgeon, *Aux origines du nationalisme turc,* Paris, Editions ADPF, 1980, p. 30.

[24] About this translation see Otto Hachtmann, *Die türkische Literatur des zwanzigsten Jahrhunderts,* Leipzig, Amelangs Verlag, 1916, pp. 51, 54, 60.

[25] I have been unable to find the *Wirtschaftszeitung der Centralmächte* and base my information on Galante, *Histoire des Juifs d'Istanbul,* vol. II, p. 69.

[26] These views will be discussed below. See also Zafer Toprak, "II. Meşrutiyet'te solidarist düşünce : halkçılık," *Toplum ve Bilim* (Istanbul), 1 (Spring 1977), pp. 92-123.

[27] *Büyük Mecmua* (Istanbul), 1 (6 Mar. 1919), p. 3; 2 (13 Mar. 1919), p. 20.

28 I have found no articles of his for that period, but there may well be several I have missed, for example in the daily press.

29 *La Epoca*, 1712 (6 Sept. 1908), p. 1, letter on "Lingua Turca."

30 According to *Stamboul* (Istanbul), 10 Mar. 1928, reported in *Oriente Moderno,* VIII/5 (May 1928), p. 221. See extracts from this book below, 'Selections from his works.'

31 According to the back-cover of Tekinalp's *Türk ruhu*. For extracts from *Le Kemalisme,* see below, 'Selections from his works.'

32 Elie Kedourie, *Nationalism in Asia and Africa,* N.Y. and Cleveland, Meridian Books, 1970, pp. 207-224.

33 Berthe Georges-Gaulis, *Le nationalisme turc,* Paris, Plon, 1921; 145 pp.

34 Mediha Muzaffer, ***İnkilâbın ruhu,*** Istanbul, Devlet Matbaası, 1933; 79 pp.

35 **Ömer Barkan, in** ***Ülkü Halkevleri Dergisi*** (Ankara), VIII/43 (Sep. 1936), pp. 62-64.

36 E.g., M. Saffet Engin, ***Kemalizm inkilâbının prensipleri,*** Istanbul, Cumhuriyet Matbaası, 1938; 348 pp. Mahmut Esat Bozkurt, ***Atatürk ihtilâlı,*** Istanbul, 1940; 500 pp.

38 Tekinalp, *Le Kemalisme,* p. 292.

39 For extracts, see below, 'Selections from his works.'

Cf. *ibid.*

Notes to ch. 4: TEKİNALP THE PATRIOT

1 FO 395/47, file 98089, no. 214716, cover-page, dated 25 Oct. 1916, to "Articles on Turkish Nationalism."

2 "Band-ı mahsus," ***İttihad ve Terakki*** (Salonica), 1/70 (15 Dec. 1908), p. 4.

3 *Mercure de France,* 16 Aug. 1912, p. 673.

4 *Ibid.*, pp. 673 ff.

5 For further details, see below in my chapter on Ottomanism and Turkification.

[6] Tekinalp reverted to this in his *The Turkish and Pan-Turkish ideal, op. cit.*, p. 8.

[7] Cf. his *op.cit.* in *Mercure de France,* 16 Aug. 1912, p. 688. Elsewhere, he estimated that Arabic and Persian loanwords formed about 95 percent of the vocabulary of Turkish. See his *The Turkish and Pan-Turkish ideal,* p. 7.

[8] Cf. his *op.cit.* in *Mercure de France,* 16 Aug. 1912, p. 701.

[9] *Ibid.*, p. 697. For further details, see below in my chapter on the Pan-Turk ideologue.

[10] Or, in his own words, "a national soul" – "une âme nationale (*op.cit.,* in *Mercure de France,* p. 703).

[11] *The Turkish and Pan-Turkish ideal,* p. 11.

[12] *Ibid.*, pp. 12-14.

[13] *Ibid.*, p. 18.

[14] *Ibid.*, p. 35.

[15] *Ibid.*, pp. 22-24.

[16] Galante, *Histoire des Juifs d'Istanbul, op.cit.*, II, pp. 68-69.

[17] See Zafer Toprak's above article in *Toplum ve Bilim.*

[18] See also below, in my chapter on National Economy and Economic Nationalism, for further details.

[19] *Türkleştirme, p. 8.*

[20] *Ibid.*, p. 16.

[21] *Ibid.*, Introduction.

[22] *Ibid.*, p. 8. See also below, in my chapter on Ottomanism and Turkification.

[23] I shall quote according to the French translation, *Le Kemalisme.*

[24] *Le Kemalisme,* p. 1.

[25] See below, in my chapter on Tekinalp's analysis of Kemalism.

26 *Le Kemalisme*, pp. 3, 9 ff.

27 *Ibid.*, p. 7.

28 *Ibid.*, pp. 17-18.

29 *Ibid.*, pp. 29-33.

30 *Ibid.*, pp. 46 ff.

31 *Ibid.*, pp. 57-59.

32 *Ibid.*, pp. 149 ff.

33 *Ibid.*, pp. 243-249.

34 *Ibid.*, pp. 256-265. For his views on culture, in more detail, see below, in my chapter on Tekinalp's vision of culture.

35 *Türk ruhu*, esp. pp. 1 ff.

36 *Ibid.*, pp. 6 ff.

37 *Ibid.*, pp. 20 ff.

38 *Ibid.*, pp. 19, 24, 232 ff.

39 *Ibid.*, pp. 233-241.

40 *Ibid.*, pp. 281-287.

Notes to ch. 5: OTTOMANISM AND TURKIFICATION ACCORDING TO TEKİNALP

1 E.g., *Diaries*, 14 July and 8 Nov. 1910.

2 *Stenographisches Protokoll der Verhandlungen des IX. Zionisten-Kongresses in Hamburg.* Köln & Leipzig, Juedischer Verlag, 1910, pp. 267-278. See also in my 'Selections from his works.'

3 *Ibid.*, p. 267.

4 *Ibid.*, p. 270.

[5] *Ibid.*, pp. 271-273.

[6] *Ibid.*, pp. 273-274.

[7] *Ibid.*, pp. 275-276.

[8] *Tesvir-i Efkâr* (Istanbul), 155 (22 Oct. 1909), pp. 1-2.

[9] *La Epoca* (Salonica), 20 Dec. 1910, p. 1. See also in my 'Selections from his works,' below.

[10] See his *op.cit.* in *Mercure de France*, pp. 678-679.

[11] *Ibid.*, p. 686.

[12] See above, in my ch. 2 ('Tekinalp's Life'). Cf. his *The Turkish and Pan-Turkish ideal*, pp. 7-8.

[13] Among his works concerned with this, see his *op.cit.* in *Mercure de France*, esp. pp. 686-688.

[14] For this work, see above, in my ch. 3 ('Intellectual Activity and Writings'). Cf. my "Tekinalp: Portrait of a Kemalist," in **Boğaziçi Üniversitesi**, *Proceedings of International Conference on Atatürk, November 9-13, 1981*, vol. III, no. 47, p. 2.

[15] *Türkleştirme*, p. 3.

[16] *Ibid.*, pp. 4, 8.

[17] *Ibid.*, p. 16.

[18] *Ibid.*, pp. 50 ff, 60 ff.

[19] *Ibid.*, pp. 9-11.

[20] *Ibid.*, pp. 27-28.

[21] *Ibid.*, p. 46.

[22] *Ibid.*, pp. 25 ff.

[23] *Ibid.*, pp. 67-68.

[24] *Ibid.*, pp. 10-22.

25 *Ibid.* p. 8.

26 *Ibid.*, pp. 30 ff.

27 *Ibid.*, p. 65. These are further elaborated on pp. 65-68.

28 *Le Kemalisme,* pp. 266-271.

29 *Ibid.*, pp. 267-268.

30 *Ibid.*, p. 269.

31 *Ibid.*, pp. 269-271.

32 France, Ministère des Affaires Etrangères, Archives, E - LEVANT, vol. 112, fos 212-213, report no. 126, by French Ambassador E. Daeschner to the Minister for Foreign Affairs, Aristide Briand, dated Constantinople, 20 Mar. 1928.

Notes to ch. 6: THE PAN-TURK IDEOLOGUE

1 See, e.g., the comments in FO 395/47, file 99089, no. 214716, "Articles on Turkish nationalism."

2 Cf. René Pinon, "L'offensive de l'Asie," *Revue des Deux Mondes* (Paris), XC (15 Apr. 1920), p. 813: "Le pantouranisme fut inventé par un Juif de Salonique, Cohen dit Tekinalp."

3 See his *op.cit.* in the *Mercure de France,* esp. pp. 695-696.

4 *Turan,* p. 10.

5 *Ibid.*, p. 3.

6 *Ibid.*, p. 127. Cf. different figures *ibid.*, pp. 76 ff.

7 *Ibid.*, pp. 113 ff.

8 *Ibid.*, pp. 8-9, 136-143. Cf. also A. J. Tvyeritinova, "Mladotyurki i Pantyurkizm," *Kratkiye Soobshchyeniya Instituta Vostokovyedyeniya* (Moscow), XXII (1956), pp. 68-69.

9 *Turan,* pp. 136-137. Elsewhere, on p. 138, the author writes "with sword and fire." See also below, my 'Selections from his works.'

10 *Turan*, pp. 93 ff.

11 *Ibid.*, p. 65. The arguments are largely of a linguistic character.

12 *Ibid.*, pp. 67 ff. Race is a dominant consideration in this book; see, e.g., p. 138.

13 *Ibid.*, pp. 76 ff.

14 *Ibid.*, pp. 127 ff.

15 *The Turkish and Pan-Turkish ideal*, pp. 7-8.

16 *Ibid.*, p. 8 ff.

17 *Ibid.*, pp. 15-18.

18 *Ibid.*, pp. 27 ff.

19 *Ibid.*, pp. 32 ff.

20 *Ibid.*, pp. 39-41.

21 *Ibid.*, p. 41.

22 In this, Tekinalp seems to veer away from his more extreme stand in *Turan*. He reiterated this more moderate position later, in *Türkleştirme*, p. 16.

23 *The Turkish and Pan-Turkish ideal*, p. 41.

24 *Türk ruhu*, pp. 217-229.

25 *Ibid.*, pp. 217-218.

26 *Ibid.*, p. 217.

27 *Ibid.*, p. 275. On this overall role in formulating and fostering the Pan-Turk ideology, see also my *Pan-Turkism in Turkey: a study of irredentism*, pp. 33-34, 51, 74.

Notes to ch. 7: TEKİNALP'S ANALYSIS OF KEMALISM

1 See above, ch. 3 of my study, 'Intellectual Activity and Writings.'

[2] See below, ch. 8 of my study, "His Views on National Economy and Economic Nationalism."

[3] As already noted by Ömer Barkan, in his review of this book in *Ülkü Halkevleri Dergisi* (Ankara), VIII/43 (Sep. 1936), esp. p. 64.

[4] *Le Kemalisme,* pp. 22-23.

[5] *Ibid.*, p. 24.

[6] *Ibid.*, p. 28.

[7] *Ibid.*, pp. 38-39.

[8] *Ibid.*, pp. 39 ff.

[9] *Ibid.*, p. 48.

[10] *Ibid.*, pp. 54-55.

[11] *Ibid.*, pp. 57-59.

[12] *Ibid.*, pp. 79-80.

[13] *Ibid.*, pp. 80 ff.

[14] *Ibid.*, pp. 243-250.

[15] *Ibid.*, pp. 251 ff.

[16] *Ibid.*, pp. 112-113.

[17] *Ibid.*, pp. 91 ff.

[18] *Ibid.*, pp. 283-286.

[19] *Ibid.* pp. 171-172.

[20] *Ibid.*, pp. 176-189.

[21] *Ibid.*, pp. 190 ff.

[22] *Ibid.*, pp. 208-209.

[23] *Ibid.*, pp. 211-212.

[24] *Ibid.*, pp. 219 ff.

[25] *Ibid.*, pp. 221-224.

[26] *Ibid.*, pp. 84 ff.

[27] *Ibid.*, p. 285.

[28] *Ibid.*, pp. 149 ff.

[29] *Ibid.*, pp. 150-151.

[30] *Ibid.*, p. 145.

[31] *Ibid.* p. 292. See also my paper, *op.cit.* in Boğaziçi Üniversitesi, *Proceedings of International Conference on Atatürk.*

[32] *Türk ruhu,* esp. ch. 30.

[33] *Ibid.*, pp. 232-233.

[34] *Ibid.*, pp. 234-236, 255 ff.

[35] *Ibid.*, pp. 258 ff.

[36] *Ibid.*, pp. 260-263.

[37] *Ibid.*, p. 272.

[38] *Ibid.*, pp. 275, 286.

Notes to ch. 8: HIS VIEWS ON NATIONAL ECONOMY AND ECONOMIC NATIONALISM

[1] See Tekinalp's *Diaries,* 28 Apr. 1911.

[2] As attested by a business associate of his, Cihat İren, in my interview with him, in Istanbul, on 21 July 1980.

[3] *Op.cit.*, in *Mercure de France,* esp. p. 704.

[4] *İktisadiyat Mecmuası,* 1 (21 Feb. 1916), pp. 1-2.

[5] See it in my 'Selections from his works'.

[6] See, e.g., "A nos lecteurs," *İktisadiyat Mecmuası,* 49 (15 Mar. 1917),p. 1.

[7] *Ibid.*, 2 (22 Feb. 1916), pp. 1-3.

[8] *Ibid.*, 4 (7 Mar. 1916), pp. 1-2.

[9] *Ibid.*, 5 (14 Mar. 1916), pp. 1-2.

[10] *Ibid.*, 7 (7 Apr. 1916), pp. 1-2.

[11] *Ibid.*, 9 (14 Apr. 1916) to 15 (26 May 1916).

[12] *Ibid.*, 20 (30 June 1916), pp. 1-3.

[13] *Ibid.*, 21 (14 July 1916), pp. 1-2.

[14] *Ibid.*, 25 (18 Aug. 1916), pp. 1-3.

[15] *Ibid.*, 24 (7 Aug. 1916), pp. 5-6.

[16] *Ibid.*, 23 (28 July 1916), pp. 1-2.

[17] *Ibid.*, 30 (6 Oct. 1916), pp. 1-2.

[18] *Ibid.*, 33 (3 Nov. 1916), pp. 1-2.

[19] *Ibid.*, 35 (24 Nov. 1916), pp. 1-3.

[20] *Ibid.*, 37 (15 Dec. 1916), pp. 1-3.

[21] *Ibid.*, 38 (29 Dec. 1916), pp. 1-2.

[22] *Ibid.*, 68 (22 Oct. 1917), pp. 1-3.

[23] *Ibid.*, 40 (19 Jan. 1917), pp. 1-2.

[24] *Ibid.*, 41 (26 Jan. 1917), pp. 1-2.

[25] *Ibid.*, 42 (9 Feb. 1917), pp. 1-2.

26 *Ibid.*, 43 (10 Mar. 1917), pp. 1-2; 49 (15 Mar. 1917), pp. 2-3.

27 *Ibid.*, 61 (2 Aug. 1917), pp. 1-2.

28 *Ibid.*, 62 (16 Aug. 1917), pp. 1-3; 63 (30 Aug. 1917), pp. 1-2.

29 *Ibid.*, 64 (14 Sept. 1917), pp. 1-3.

30 *Ibid.*, 67 (8 Oct. 1917), pp. 1-2. Repr. in *Toplum ve Bilim* (Istanbul), I/1 (Spring 1977), pp. 121-123.

31 See also Toprak, *op.cit.* in *Toplum ve Bilim*, pp. 116-117. Cf. Toprak's *Türkiye'de "Milli iktisat" (1908-1918)*, passim.

32 See, e.g., Tekinalp's article "Yeni istikamet istikrazı" (The 'new orientation' loan), *Yeni Mecmua,* 40 (18 Apr. 1918), pp. 263-264.

33 See below, Preliminary List of Tekinalp's writings.

34 See above Toprak, *op.cit.* and Fr. Georgeon, *Aux origines du nationalisme turc, op.cit.*, esp. pp. 59, 60, 72.

35 *Bilgi* (Istanbul), 149 (Aug. 1959), pp. 7-9. See also below, in my 'Selections from his works.'

36 See his *Le Kemalisme,* pp. 190-225.

37 William Hale, *Assessment, origins and objectives of etatism,* Istanbul, Türkiye İş Bankası International Symposium on Atatürk, 1981, pp. 1 ff.

38 *Le Kemalisme,* p. 209.

39 See, e.g., *ibid.*, p. 191.

40 *Ibid.*, pp. 193 ff.

41 *Ibid.*, pp. 211-212.

42 *Ibid.*, pp. 212 ff.

43 *Ibid.*, pp. 215 ff.

44 See below, Preliminary List of Tekinalp's writings.

[45] *Türkiye İktisat Mecmuası,* 2 (Feb. 1948), pp. 22-26. Another article of his, bearing the same title, was published *ibid.,* 88 (Feb. 1956), pp. 2265-2269.

[46] *Ibid.,* 36 (July 1951), pp. 1-4.

[47] *Ibid.,* 50 (Sep. 1952), pp. 11-14.

[48] *Ibid.,* 77 (Dec. 1954), pp. 1693-1696.

[49*] "Gala-yı esara karşı mücadele," *İktisadiyat Mecmuası,* 56 (24 May 1917), pp. 1-3 and other articles in the same periodical.

[50] See below, Preliminary List of Tekinalp's writings.

[51] Cf. *ibid.*

[52] *Türkiye İktisat Mecmuası,* 74 (Sept. 1954), pp. 1467-1471.

[53] *Ibid.,* 86 (Dec. 1955), pp. 2219-2222.

[54] *İller ve Belediyeler Dergisi* (Ankara), 30 (Mar. 1948), pp. 983-986.

[55] *Le Kemalisme,* p. 189.

Notes to ch. 9: TEKİNALP'S VISION OF CULTURE

[1] "Aus dem Osmanenreiche," *Oesterreichische Rundschau,* XLVI/6 (15 Mar. 1916). See below, in my Preliminary List of Tekinalp's writings.

[2] This is mentioned in his *hal tercümesi.* I have been unable to consult it, however.

[3] Cf. Preliminary List, below.

[4] See his *Diaries,* 16 Apr. 1911.

[5] Cf. Tütengil, *op.cit.* in *Varlık*, 575 (1 June 1962), p. 7.

[6] In his *op.cit.* in *Mercure de France,* pp. 686-687.

[7] *Ibid.,* pp. 687-688.

[8] *Ibid.,* pp. 692-694, 697 ff.

[9] *Ibid.*, pp. 697-698.

[10] *The Turkish and Pan-Turkish ideal,* esp. pp. 9-10.

[11] Cf. *op.cit.* in *Mercure de France,* pp. 699 ff.

[12] *Le Kemalisme,* esp. pp. 256-265.

[13] *Ibid.*, pp. 260-261.

[14] *Ibid.*, pp. 261 ff.

[15] *Ibid.*, p. 264.

[16] *Türk ruhu,* pp. 1 ff.

[17] *Ibid.*, pp. 2-5.

[18] *Ibid.*, pp. 6 ff.

[19] *Ibid.*, pp. 11 ff.

[20] *Ibid.*, pp. 13-19.

[21] *Ibid.*, pp. 20-24.

[22] *Ibid.*, pp. 25 ff.

[23] *Ibid.*, p. 42.

[24] *Ibid.*, pp. 43-103.

[25] *Ibid.*, pp. 107-112.

[26] *Ibid.*, pp. 113-120.

[27] *Ibid.*, pp. 121 ff.

[28] *Ibid.*, pp. 127 ff.

[29] *Ibid.*, p. 134.

[30] *Ibid.*, pp. 155-156.

[31] *Ibid.*, pp. 173 ff.

[32] "Genç Türk ruh ve zihniyeti" (The Young Turk spirit and mentality), ***Türkiye İktisat Mecmuası***, 68 (Mar. 1954), pp. 957-960.

[33] ***Türk ruhu***, pp. 209 ff. Tekinalp returned to discuss Gökalp's special role in his "Ziya Gökalp'de tesânütçülük," *Bilgi*, 149 (Aug. 1959), pp. 7-9. See also below, 'Selections from Tekinalp's Works.'

[34] ***Türk ruhu***, pp. 232-241.

[35] *Ibid.*, pp. 254-257.

[36] *Ibid.*, pp. 258-270.

[37] *Ibid.*, pp. 276-285.

Notes to ch. 10: IN CONCLUSION

[1] *Diaries*, 8 Jan. 1909.

Notes to REFERAT ÜBER DIE EINWANDERUNG IN DER TÜRKEI

[1] The French version has not been preserved. We have this speech only in a German translation.

Notes to SOME MANUSCRIPT LETTERS

[1] These four letters, all signed M. Cohen or Moïse Cohen, were sent, between December 1910 and February 1911, to the Secretary General of the Jewish Territorial Organization, an association based in London, which was trying to secure a territory for the settlement of Jewish refugees (not necessarily in Palestine). The first three letters are in the original French, the fourth is in a German translation.

[2] That is, the Jewish Territorial Organization. The reference is to Israel Zangwill.

[3] Obviously, the *Cercle des Intimes* (or *Club des Intimes*) in Salonica.

Notes to LES TURCS A LA RECHERCHE D'UNE ÂME NATIONALE

[1] Rebels, members of revolutionary societies.

[2] This refers, evidently, to the police (and secret agents) of the Sultan Abdul Hamid II.

[3] The public procession of the Sultan to the mosque, for the Friday-noon prayer.

Notes to DIE JUDEN IN DER BALKANLÄNDERN

[1] The author defined himself as "Ehemaliger Landtagsabgeordneter in Salonika, derzeit Advokat in Konstantinopel."

[2] All of this had happened to Tekinalp himself; his presentation of the events and their consequences, as well as the following exposé of the ensuing decline of Salonica's Jewish community, are poignant.

Notes to THE TURKISH AND PAN-TURKISH IDEAL

[1] Better known later as Enver Pasha, one of the Triumvirate ruling the Ottoman Empire.

[2] Actually, the fear of God (author's footnote).

[2] Here he quoted from his own article, without specifying this.

[4] "Turkey" is here, obviously, a misprint for "Persia."

[5] More correctly, Léon Cahun.

[6] This comprises the whole of Tekinalp's booklet, as translated by the Admiralty War Staff's Intelligence Division; pp. 1-6 consist of the Division's foreword.

Notes to **TÜRKLEŞTİRME**

[1] **Ahmet Ağaoğlu** (1869-1939), an Azeri who was an active proponent of Pan-Turkism

in the Czarist Empire, then in Turkey itself during the Young Turk era.

[2] A reference to Ziya Gökalp.

Notes on LE KEMALISME

[1] This might well reflect Tekinalp's own personal tragedy: the Jewish girl from Seres, which he had married as a young man, displayed little interest in intellectual activities.

[2] Courses on the Kemalist revolution have been given at the University of Istanbul since 1931, by four ex-Ministers: Recep Peker, Hikmet (Bayur), Mahmud Esad and Yusuf Kemal (author's footnote).

[3] Société des Nations.

[4] This amendment was passed by the Grand National Assembly in Ankara, in March 1937 (author's footnote).

[5] Çankaya, the Ankara suburb comprising the palace of the President of the Republic. An obvious reference to Mustafa Kemal.

[6] The Turkish *guignol* (author's footnote).

[7] That is, at Mustafa Kemal's own table, where, during long dinners, matters of state, culture and socio-economics were debated.

[8] Heroine of Simenon's novel, *Les Clients d'Avrenos* (author's footnote).

[9] Heroine of the novel *Ankara* (author's footnote).

[10] Paul Gentizon, *Mustafa Kemal ou l'Orient en marche* (author's footnote).

Notes to HAL TERCÜMESİ (1939)

[1] Dated February 1939, this typewritten *curriculum vitae* is similar to, but not identical with, another, undated, seemingly from the late 1930s.

[2] This is an obvious exaggeration. René Pinon was a journalist (albeit a successful one).

Notes to TÜRK RUHU

[1] This is a reference to his article in *Türk Yurdu*, previously published in French in the *Mercure de France*. See below, 'Preliminary List of Tekinalp's Writings.'

[2] The correct date should be, obviously, 1914.

[3] The date should be corrected to 1915.

Notes to A PETITION TO THE TURKISH MINISTRY FOR FOREIGN AFFAIRS

[1] I have been unable to locate the official reply to this petition, but I understand from Munis Tekinalp's son, Isaac, that it was rejected.

Notes to HAL TERCÜMEÎ HÜLASASI

[1] This undated *curriculum vitae*, typewritten, appears to be an updated version of the one Tekinalp had prepared in 1939. Enclosed in his 1955-1956 petition to the Turkish Ministry for Foreign Affairs, it was probably written at that time.

Notes to ZİYA GÖKALP'DE TESÂNÜTÇÜLÜK

[1] Since Tekinalp was abroad in 1959, he could not have witnessed this then. It seems that he must have written the article a short time before leaving Turkey definitely in 1956, rewriting it several years later for the commemoration of thirty-five years to Gökalp's death. The atmosphere described, also, fits the mid-1950s.

Notes to AN EXPLANATION

[1] This refers to Ebuzziya Tevfik's article "**Türkiyede müstemleke tesisi ve Siyonist meselesinin teceddüdü**" (The foundation of colonies in Turkey and the renewal of the Zionist Question), ***Tesvir-i Efkâr***,, 145 (12 Oct. 1909), p. 1; and to his own answer, *ibid.*, 155 (22 Oct. 1909), pp. 1-2.

[2] For which see above, in my 'Selections from his works.'

[3] I.e., the Zionists.

Notes to TURKIFICATION

[1] The term 'Nationalisation,' the closest I could find to the Turkish *Millileştirme*, means, in this context, 'Inducing someone to become a complete (Turkish) national.' See also my notes to **TÜRKLEŞTİRME**, above.

[2] An association, set up by **Ağaoğlu** and others in 1911 to promote Turkism (and Pan-Turkism); it continued its activities until 1931. See details in my *Pan-Turkism in Turkey*, pp. 40 ff, 73-5.

[3] *Genç Kalemler* (Young Pens) was one of the Turkish periodicals in Salonica, before the First World War, in which intellectual views found frequent expression.

[4] *Dönme* (convert) is the Turkish appellation for the crypto-Jews, descendants of Shabbetai Tsevi. Early in the twentieth century, there was a sizable *Dönme* community in Salonica. See "Dönme" in *The Encyclopaedia of Islam*, 2nd edition, *s.v.*

[5] French historian and journalist (1842-1912), noted for his support of liberalism.

Notes to THE SPIRIT OF THE TURKS

[1] Rulers of the ancient Turks.

[2] İnönü. See also my notes to **TÜRK RUHU**, above.

Notes to **SOLIDARITY ACCORDING TO ZİYA GÖKALP**

[1] I.e., in the days of the Young Turks, when Abdul Hamid II's constitution was restored. See also my notes to **ZİYA GÖKALP'DE TESÂNÜTÇÜLÜK**, above.

PRELIMINARY LIST OF TEKİNALP'S WRITINGS

a. In Manuscript

i. Books

Diaries, 4 Mar. 1907-18 June 1911. 154 pp., French. In the possession of his son, Isaac Tekinalp, Istanbul.

The Turkish and Pan-Turkish Ideal. N.p. [London], Admiralty War Staff – Intelligence Division, March 1917; 48 pp. (No. C.B. 1293).

Diaries, 1 Dec. 1946- 4 Mar. 1959. 2 vols. (146, 54 pp.) Ottoman Turkish, in the possession of his son Guillaume Tekinalp, London.

L'âme turque. A French translation, prepared by Munis Tekinalp, of his *Türk ruhu,* during the later years of his life. Discarded by the family during the late 1970s and lost.

ii. Letters, Documents, Essays and Lectures

Four handwritten letters of his, signed Cohen, to the Jewish Territorial Organization, between December 1910 and February 1911 – all in the Central Zionist Archives, Jerusalem.

"Hal Tercümesi," 2 typewritten pages of Tekinalp's own *curriculum vitae,* dated February 1939. Modern Turkish. In the possession of his son, Isaac Tekinalp, Istanbul. Two versions have survived.

"Hal Tercümeî hülâsası," 2 typewritten pages of Tekinalp's own *curriculum vitae.* Another version of the preceding item, dating from 1955-6, apparently. Modern Turkish. In the possession of his son Isaac Tekinalp, Istanbul.

"Israel et la Diaspora." 8 typewritten pages, with Tekinalp's own handwritten corrections. Full text of a lecture in French, delivered in Nice, in December 1954 or January 1955. A brief summary was published in *L'Etoile du Levant,* 331 (14 Jan. 1955), p. 2. In the possession of his son, Isaac Tekinalp, Istanbul.

Petition to the Turkish Ministry for Foreign Affairs. 1 typewritten page, undated, probably written in 1955-1956. In the possession of his son, Isaac Tekinalp, Istanbul.

"Israel chez les nations." 29 typewritten pages with Tekinalp's own handwritten corrections. Lecture delivered in French in the 1950s. In the possession of his son, Isaac Tekinalp, Istanbul.

b. Published works

i. Books

Teşebbüs-ü şahsi ve tevsi-i mezuniyet. Salonica, 1909, 96 pp. Ottoman Turkish. This legal work, which I was unable to consult, was published in 1909 according to its author, in 1328 (1912) according to C.O. Tütengil, in *Yeni Yayınlar* (Ankara) VII/4 (Apr. 1962), p. 133.

Turan. Istanbul, Türk Yurdu Kitaphanesi, 1330 (1914); 143 pp. Ottoman Turkish.

Türkler bu muharebede ne kazanabilirler. Büyük Türklük: en meşhur Türkçülerin mütalaatı. Istanbul, Kader Matbaası, 1330 (1914); 42 pp. Ottoman Turkish.

Türkismus und Pantürkismus. Weimar, Gustav Kiepenheuer, 1915; xi, 112 pp.

Türkleştirme. Istanbul, Resimli Ay Matbaası, 1928; 99 pp. Ottoman Turkish.

Kemalizm. Istanbul, Cumhuriyet Basımevi, 1936; 347, x pp. Modern Turkish. Some extracts have recently been reprinted by Nissim Benbanaste, in his *Bir dehanın analizi: Atatürk,* Istanbul, 1982, pp. 123-154.

Le Kemalisme. Paris, Felix Alcan, 1937; 8, 298 pp. Ch. XV of this work (pp. 109-129) has been translated into English and published by Elie Kedourie, in his *Nationalism in Asia and Africa,* N.Y. and Cleveland, Meridian Books, 1970, pp. 207-224.

Türk Ruhu. Istanbul, Remzi Kitabevi, 1944; xiii, 287 pp.

ii. Articles

"Elli sene sonra," *Asır* (Salonica), 1019 (19 Oct. 1905), p. 3; 1020 (23 Oct. 1905), p. 3. Signed M. Cohen.

"Maxim Gorki," *ibid.,* 1025 (9 Nov. 1905), p. 3.

"Mezar kaçkını," *ibid.,* p. 3; 1026 (13 Nov. 1905), p. 3.

"La presse Turque," *La Revue* (Paris), LXI/23 (1 Dec. 1905), pp.373-384. Signed P. Risal.

"Semere-yi gayret," *Asır,* 1044 (18 Jan. 1906), p. 3.

"Islâmiyet ve Museviler," *ibid.*, 1058 (12 Mar. 1906), p. 3.

"Olympyad oyunları," *ibid.*, 1071 (26 Apr. 1906), p. 3.

"Amerika garaibi," *ibid.*, 1073 (3 May 1906), p. 3; 1089 (28 May 1906), p. 3; 1098 (30 July 1906), pp. 3-4; 1140 (27 Dec. 1906), p. 4.

"Kadınlar ve elbiseleri," *ibid.*, 1094 (16 July 1906), p. 3.

"Band-ı mahsus,"*İttihad ve Terakki* (Salonica), I/70 (15 Dec. 1908), p. 4.

"Ebuzziya Tevfik Beye," *Tesvir-i Efkâr* (Istanbul), 155 (22 Oct. 1909), pp. 1-2. Also in *Le Jeune Turc,* prob. between 22 Oct. and 8 Nov. 1909.

"Referat über die Einwanderung in der Türkei," *Stenographisches Protokoll der Verhandlungen des IX. Zionisten-Kongresses in Hamburg,* Köln und Leipzig, Juedischer Verlag, 1910, pp. 267-278.

"Una eksplicacion," *La Epoca* (Salonica), 20 Dec. 1910, p. 1.

"Les Turcs à la recherche d'une âme nationale," *Mercure de France* (Paris), 16 Aug. 1912, pp. 673-707. Signed P. Risal. Also in Turkish, as "Tükler bir ruh-u millî arıyorlar," *Türk Yurdu* (Istanbul), II (1328/1912), pp. 656-661, 684-690, 725-727, 773-779.

"Die Juden in den Balkanländern," *Monatsschrift der Oesterreichisch-Israelitischen Union* (Vienna), XXV/9-10 (Sept.-Oct. 1913), pp. 16-24.

"Alman müteallimerinin yaşayışı," *Bilgi Mecmuasi* (Istanbul), I/3 (Jan. 1329/1914), pp. 311-323.

"Almanlarda içtimaî hayat : askerî yaşayışı," *ibid.*, I/4 (Feb. 1329/1914), pp. 418-425.

"İngiltere-Almanya rekabet iktisadiyesi," *İçtihad* (Istanbul), 118 (25 Sep. 1330/1914), pp. 329-331.

"Alsace-Lorraine meseleyi tarihiyesi," *ibid.*, 119 (9 Oct. 1330/1914), pp. 343-344.

"Avrupa hükümet müttefikası," *ibid.*, 120 (23 Oct. 1330/1914), pp. 359-361.

"İgilizlerin sebeb-i felaketi," *ibid.*, 121 (6 Nov. 1330/1914) pp. 377-379.

"Muharebe nasıl bitecek?" *ibid.*, 122 (20 Nov. 1330/1914), pp. 391-393.

"Avusturya-Macarıstan meselesi," *ibid.*, 124 (11 Dec. 1330/1914), pp. 423-424.

Millî İktisada doğru," ***İktisadiyat Mecmuası*** **(İstanbul),** I/1 (8 Feb. 1331/1916), pp. 1-2. Also in French and German translations.

"Tütün meselesi," *ibid.*, I/2 (22 Feb. 1331/1916), pp. 1-3. Also in French translation.

"Meskukat meselesi," *ibid.*, I/3 (29 Feb. 1331/1916), pp. 1-3.

"İki usul-ü istismar," *ibid.*, I/4 (7 Mar. 1332/1916), pp. 1-2. Also in French translation.

"Yeni Kitaplar," *ibid.*, pp. 3-5. Also in French translation, signed T.A.

"Ticaret-i hariciyemiz," *ibid.*, I/5 (14 Mar. 1916), pp. 1-2. Also in French translation.

"Aus dem Osmanenreiche: literarische Beiträge gesammelt von Dschelal-Sahir ins Deutsche übertragen von Tekin Alp, mit einer Einleitung von Universitätsprofessor Dr. Friedrich von Kraelitz-Greisenhorst," *Oesterreichische Rundschau* (Vienna), XLVI/6, (15 Mar. 1916), pp. 243-298.

"Yeni iktisadî müesselerimiz," ***İktisadiyat Mecmuası***, I/6 (21 Mar. 1332/1916), pp. 1-3.

"Millet nedir, millî iktisad nereden ibarettir?" *ibid.*, I/7 (28 Mar. 1332/1916), pp. 1-2.

"Artırma sandıkları," *ibid.*, I/8 (7 Apr. 1332/1916), pp. 1-2. Also in French translation.

"Ziraat bankası," *ibid.*, I/9 (14 Apr. 1332/1916), pp. 1-2; I/10 (21 Apr. 1332/1916), pp. 1-2; I/11 (28 Apr. 1332/1916), pp. 1-2; I/12 (5 May 1332/1916), pp. 1-3; I/13 (12 May 1332/1916), pp. 1-3; I/15 (26 May 1332/1916), pp. 1-3. Also in French translation.

"Kitaplar ve Mecmular," *ibid.*, I/12 (5 May 1332/1916), pp. 6-7. Also in French translation, signed T.A.

"Kitaplar ve mecmualar," *ibid.*, I/13 (12 May 1332/1916), pp. 4-6. Also in French translation, signed T.A.

"Yeni ticaret muahadesi," *ibid.*, I/16 (2 June 1332/1916), pp. 1-2. Also in French translation.

"Türkiye-Almanya ticaret muahadesi," *ibid.*, I/18 (16 June 1332/1916), pp. 1-3; I/19 (23 June 1332/ 1916), pp. 1-4. Also in French translation.

"Adana ovasının irva ve iskası," *ibid.*, I/20 (30 June 1332/1916), pp. 1-3. Also in French translation.

"Bu seneki mahsulümüz," *ibid.*, I/21 (14 July 1332/1916), pp. 1-2. Also in French translation.

"**Ticaret muahadeleri — Merkezî Avrupa ve biz,**" *ibid.*, I/22 (21 July 1332/1916), pp. 1-2. Also in French translation.

"**İktisad derneği,**" *ibid.*, I/23 (28 July 1332/1916), pp. 1-2. Also in French translation.

"**Konya millî iktisat bankası,**" *ibid.*, I/24 (7 Aug. 1332/1916), pp. 5-6. Also in French translation. The date on this issue was mistakenly written down as 28 July 1332.

"**Ziraat müze ve sergileri,**" *ibid.*, I/25 (18 Aug. 1332/1916), pp. 1-3. Also in French translation.

"**İktisat nokta-ı nazarından terbiye ve talim,**" *ibid.*, I/26 (25 Aug. 1332/1916), pp. 1-3. Also in French translation.

"**İktisat Derneği,**" *ibid,* I/27 (1 Sep. 1332/1916), p. 4.

"**Yeni gümrük tarifesi,**" *ibid.*, I/28 (15 Sep. 1332/1916) pp. 1-2. Also in French translation.

"**İhracat kanunu,**" *ibid.*, I/29 (21 Sep. 1332/1916), pp. 1-2. Also in French translation.

"**İttihad ve Terakki fırkasının iktisadî faaliyeti,**" *ibid.*, I/30, (6 Oct. 1332/1916), pp. 1-2. Also in French translation.

"**329 senesine ziraat istatistiği,**" *ibid.*, I/31 (13 Oct. 1332/1916), pp. 1-3. Also in French translation.

"**Memleketimizde büyük sanayi,**" *ibid.*, I/33 (3 Nov. 1332/1916), pp. 1-2. Also in French translation.

"**Türkiyede bankalar,**" *ibid.*, I/34 (10 Nov. 1332/1916), pp. 1-2. Also in French translation.

"**Millî iktisad nasıl vücuda gelir?**" *ibid.*, I/35 (24 Nov. 1332/1916), pp. 1-3.

"**Kitaplar ve mecmualar,**" *ibid.*, I/36 (1 Dec. 1332/1916), pp. 3-4.

"**Ticaret kanunun tadil ve ıslahı,**" *ibid.*, I/37 (15 Dec. 1332/1916), pp. 1-3. Also in French translation.

"**İktisadiyat meclisi,**" *ibid.*, I/38 (29 Dec. 1332/1916), pp. 1-2. Also in French translation.

"**İtibar-ı millî bankası,**" *ibid.*, I/40 (19 Jan. 1332/1917), pp. 1-2. Also in French translation.

"**Madenlerimiz,**" *ibid.*, I/41 (26 Jan. 1332/1917), pp. 1-2. Also in French translation.

"**İstikbal-ı iktisadımız,**" *ibid.*, I/42 (9 Feb. 1332/1917), pp. 1-2. Also in French translation.

"**İstihsalat-ı milliyeyi artımak meselesi,**" *ibid.*, I/43 (10 Mar. 1333/1917), pp. 1-2; II/49 (15 Mar. 1333/1917), pp. 2-3. Also in French translation.

"**İktisadî teşkilât,**" *ibid.*, II/52 (19 Apr. 1333/1917), pp. 1-2. Also in French translation.

"**Ecnebî sermayesine karşı siyaset-i iktisadiyemiz,**" *ibid.*, II/53 (26 Apr. 1333/1917), pp. 1-3. Also in French translation.

"**Gala-yı esara karşı mücadele,**" *ibid.*, II/56 (24 May 1333/1917), pp. 1-3. Also in French translation.

"**Kitaplar ve mecmualar,**" *ibid.*, pp. 5-6.

"**Tütün zürraı kooperatif şirketi,**" *ibid.*, II/59 (5 July 1333/1917), pp. 7-8. Also in French translation.

"**İstihsalat-ı milliyeyi artırmak meselesi — ziraat mı sanai mi?**" *ibid.*, II/61 (2 Aug. 1333/1917), pp. 1-2. Also in French translation.

"**Memleketimizde iş bölümü,**" *Yeni Mecmua* (Istanbul), I/6 (16 Aug. 1917), pp. 117-118.

"**Harbten sulha intikal iktisadiyatı,**" *İktisadiyat Mecmuası*, II/62 (16 Aug. 1333/1917), pp. 1-3; II/63 (30 Aug. 1333/1917), pp. 1-2. Also in French translation.

"**İktisadî inkılap,**" *ibid.*, (II/64 (14 Sep. 1333/1917), pp. 1-3. Also in French translation.

"**Kapitalizm devresi başlıyor,**" *ibid.*, II/67 (8 Oct. 1333/1917), pp. 1-2. Also in French translation. Reprinted in *Toplum ve Bilim* (Istanbul), I/1 (Spring 1977), pp. 121-123.

"**İktisadiyat nezareti,**" *ibid.*, II/68 (22 Oct. 1333/1917), pp. 1-3. Also in French translation.

"**Islahat-ı maliye,**" *ibid.*, II/69 (Nov. 1333/1917), pp. 1-3.

"**Tesanütçülük ve solidarizm,**" *Yeni Mecmua*, I/26 (3 Jan. 1918), pp. 517-519.

"**Tesanütçülük, içtimaî siyaset,**" *ibid.*, II/28 (17 Jan. 1918), pp. 21-23; II/30 (31 Jan. 1918), pp. 61-63.

"Tesanütçülük, yeni istikamet," *ibid.*, II/37 (28 Mar. 1918), pp. 205-207.

"Tesanütçülük, yeni istikamet istikrazı," *ibid.*, II/40 (18 Apr. 1918), pp. 263-264.

"Tesanütçülük, harp zenginleri meselesi," *ibid.*, II/42 (2 May 1918), pp. 313-314.

"Tesanütçülük gayesi," *ibid.*, II/43 (9 May 1918), pp. 335-337.

"İnkilâbın son perdesi," *ibid.*, II/44 (16 May 1918), p. 358.

"Tesanütçülük, içtimaî siyaset için zemin müsait mi?" *ibid.*, II/45 (23 May 1918), pp. 363-364.

"Tesanütçülük, Almanyada içtimaî faaliyet," *ibid.*, II/47 (6 June 1918), pp. 406-408.

"Tesanütçülük, içtimaî duygu," *ibid.*, III/55 (1 Aug. 1918), pp. 45-46.

"Tesanütçülük, demokrasinin gayesi," *ibid.*, III/56 (8 Aug. 1918), pp. 67-68.

"Harp ve iktisad, millî iktisad," *ibid.*, III/59 (29 Aug. 1918), pp. 133-134.

"Tesanütçülük, zevaid vergileri," *ibid.*, III/60 (5 Sep. 1918), pp. 154-155.

"Tesanütçülük, harp ve iktisad, memurin ve mustahdamının adısı," *ibid.*, III/61 (12 Sep. 1918), pp. 178-179.

"Yeni Osmanlılık," *Büyük Mecmua* (Istanbul), 1 (6 Mar. 1919), p. 3; 2 (13 Mar. 1919), p. 20.

"Yahudiler Türkleşmelidir! Kohen-Tekinalp Beyin muharririmizde beyanatı," *Vakıt* (Istanbul), 22 Oct. 1930, pp. 1-2.

"Harp sonrası ekonomisi : iki iktisatçı arasında konuşmalar," *Tan* (Istanbul), 12 Apr. 1945, pp. 3-4.

"Hayat pahalılığı : iki iktisatçı arasında konuşmalar," *ibid.*, 17 Apr. 1945, pp. 3-4.

"Harpten sonra hayat pahalılığı : iki iktisatçı arasında konuşmalar," *ibid.*, 25 Apr. 1945, p. 3.

"Yine hayat pahalılığı ve devlet iktisadiyatı," *ibid.*, 30 Apr. 1945, pp. 3-4.

"Ofisler ve birlikler," *ibid.*, 24 May 1945, p. 3.

"Klering ve takas rejimleri," *ibid.*, 30 May 1945, p. 3.

"Türk-İngliliz ticaret ve tediye anlaşması," *ibid.*, 1 June 1945, p. 3.

"Tekin Alp'ın cevabı : 'Harp sonrası meseleleri' tanınmış iktisatçı ve sanayicilerin 6 suale cevapları," *ibid.*, 11 June 1945, p. 3.

"Halkımızın yaşayış seviyesi," *ibid.*, 24 Aug. 1945, pp. 3-4.

"Hayat pahalılığı ve enflasyon," *ibid.*, 25 Aug. 1945, p. 3.

"Hayat pahalılığına konulan teşhis," *ibid.*, 29 Aug. 1945, pp. 3-4.

"Kürsü ve hayat," *ibid.*, 6 Sep. 1945, pp. 3-4.

"İhracatla ıthalatın ayarlanması," *ibid.*, 13 Sept. 1945, p. 3.

"Zincir ve kamaı," *ibid.*, 23 Sep. 1945, pp. 3-5.

"Ucuz evler hakkında bir teklif," *İller ve Belediyeler Dergisi* (Ankara), 30 (Mar. 1948), pp. 983-986.

"Un peu d'histoire inédite: M. Tekin Alp nous parle du Sionisme et du Judaïsme turc," *L'Etoile du Levant* (Istanbul), I/5 (20 Aug. 1948), pp. 1-2.

"İktisadi Demokrasiye doğru," *Türkiye İktisat Mecmuası* (İstanbul), 2 (Feb. 1948), pp. 22-26.

"Yine dördüncü kuvvet," *ibid.*, 4 (May 1948), pp. 10-11.

"Dış ticareti tanzim organı nasıl olmalıdır?" *ibid.*, 6 (July 1948), pp. 21-23.

"Marshall Plânı, hususî krediler ve hususî sermaye," *ibid.*, 17 (June 1949), pp. 14-16.

"Ticarethane kıralarının serbest bırakılmasından evvel ticarî mülkiyet haklarının tanınması lâzımdır," *ibid.*, 18 (July 1949), pp. 9-10.

"Yabancı sermaye neden Türkiyeye can atmıyor?" *ibid.*, 22 (Dec. 1949), pp. 14-16.

"Gündümlü ekonomide hatalı taraflar," *ibid.*, 25 (Mar. 1950), pp. 153-155.

"Memleket sanayiini kalkındırma şartları," *ibid.*, 29 (Dec. 1950), pp. 38-39.

"Ticarî mülkiyet meselesi," *ibid.*, 30 (Jan. 1951), pp. 9-12.

"Garp âleminde ve memleketimizde iş adamının rolü ve mevkii," *ibid.*, 31 (Feb. 1951), pp. 9-16.

"Sanayi politikamız ve devletçilik," *ibid.*, 32 (Mar. 1951), pp. 13-16.

"Bizde tüccar ve iş adamı hakkındaki telâkki," *ibid.*, 35 (June 1951), pp. 5-7.

"Mithat Paşa ve milli iktisat," *ibid.*, 36 (July 1951), pp. 1-4.

"İktisat işleri iktisat erbabına aittir," *ibid.*, 38 (Sep. 1951), pp. 17-18.

"Siyaset ve İktisat," *ibid.*, 29 (Oct. 1951), pp. 3-5.

"Ticari ve sinai mülkiyet," *ibid.*, 40 (Nov. 1951), pp. 3-5.

"Mesleki ahlâk, mesleki tesanüt ve mesleki zihniyet," *ibid.*, 41 (Dec. 1951), pp. 9-11.

"Ticaret ve sanayi sahalarında ikilik var mıdır?" *ibid.*, 42 (Jan. 1952), pp. 3-5.

"Türkiyenin iktisâdî kalkınması," *ibid.*, 50 (Sep. 1952), pp. 11-14.

"Ticaret fonu," *ibid.*, 54 (Jan. 1953), pp. 3-5.

"Mesken ve ticaret yerleri kıraları hakkında yeni mevzuat," *ibid.*, 55 (Feb. 1953), pp. 73-75.

"Kıralar meselesinde içtimaî zaruret hakkı," *ibid.*, 56 (Mar. 1953), pp. 131-133.

"Devletçilik," *ibid.*, 57 (Apr. 1953), pp. 221-223.

"İktisadi inkilâp," *ibid.*, 63 (Oct. 1953), pp. 633-636.

"Son günlerde şahit olduğumuz inkilâp hamleleri," *ibid.*, 64 (Nov. 1953), pp. 697-699.

"Yabancı sermaye meselesi," *ibid.*, 65 (Dec. 1953), pp. 763-766.

"Devlet işlemelerinin özelleştirilmesi ve Mister Randall'ın avamiri aşeresi," *ibid.*, 66 (Jan. 1954), pp. 827-835.

"Fert yok, cemiyet var," *ibid.*, 67 (Feb. 1954), pp. 889-891; and in *Vatan* (Istanbul) 15 Feb. 1954, p. 2.

"İktisadi inkilâp," *Vatan*, 19 Feb. 1954, p. 2.

"Genç Türk ruh ve zihniyeti," *Türkiye İktisat Mecmuası,* 68 (Mar. 1954), pp. 957-960.

"İş ticaret ve iktisat erbabı arasında tesanüt," *ibid.,* 69 (Apr. 1954), pp. 1023-1024.

"Yalnız yabancı sermayeyi değil, bütün yatırımları teşvik esastır," *ibid.,* 70 (May 1954), pp. 1085-1087.

"İktisadi kalkınmamız ve sosyal tepkileri," *ibid.,* 74 (Sept. 1954), pp. 1467-1471; and in *Vatan,* 22 Sep. 1954, pp. 2, 5.

"Ticaret ve sanat yerleri kiraları hakkında," *Türkiye İktisat Mecmuası,* 75 (Oct. 1954), pp. 1537-1539.

"İç ticaret ve iktisat erbabı arasında tesanüt," *Dünya ve Türkiye* **(İstanbul),** 56 (Oct. 1954), pp. 20, 22.

"Mesken ve iş yeri buhranları," *Türkiye İktisat Mecmuası,* 76 (Nov. 1954), pp. 1595-1598; and in *Vatan,* 12 Nov. 1954, pp. 2, 7.

"Kemalizm ve Devletçilik", *Türkiye İktisat Mecmuası,* 77 (Dec. 1954), pp. 1693-1696.

"Israel et la Diaspora: une conférence à Nice," *L'Etoile du Levant,* 331 (14 Jan. 1955), p. 2.

"M. Tekinalp (Moise Cohen) s'explique. Universalisme et isolationisme chez les Juifs de la Diaspora," *ibid.,* 333 (28 Jan. 1955), pp. 1, 4.

"L'orientation de notre jeunesse vers l'artisanat," *ibid.,* 335 (11 Feb. 1955), pp. 1-2.

"Milli Korunma meselesi : ahlâk ve zihniyet inkilâbına kat'ı ihtiyaç vardır," *Türkiye İktisat Mecmuası,* 79 (Feb. 1955), pp. 1821-1823.

"İktisadî kalkınmamızda plân meselesi," *ibid.,* 80 (Mar. 1955), pp. 1883-1885; and in *Dünya ve Türkiye,* 68 (30 Nov. 1955), pp. 17-18.

"İnkılâp rejimimiz ve sosyal inkılâp," *Türkiye İktisat Mecmuası,* 86 (Dec. 1955), pp. 2219-2222.

"İktisadî demokrasiye doğru," *ibid.,* 88 (Feb. 1956), pp. 2265-2269.

"Millî korunma kanunu ve tâdilleri," *ibid.,* 89 (Mar. 1956), pp. 2375-2378.

"Tesanütçülük ve gecekondu milyonerleri," *ibid.*, 90 (Apr. 1956), pp. 2407-2409.

"Yatırımları teşvik," *ibid.*, 93 (July 1956), pp. 2531-2534.

"Meslekî ahlâk," *ibid.*, 94 (Aug. 1956), pp. 2601-2604.

"Ziya Gökalp'te tesânütçülük," *Bilgi* (Monthly, official organ of the Teachers' Union of Turkey, Istanbul), 149 (Aug. 1959), pp. 7, 9.

BIBLIOGRAPHY

Virtually all of this book is based on Tekinalp's own writings – both manuscripts and printed works. Doubtful points were checked by interviews with his family and friends. Rare, brief references to him in the writings of others have been mentioned in the footnotes. No comprehensive work on Tekinalp has been published to date, although the following few items (arranged chronologically) may be of some use.

Ömer Barkan, "Tekin Alp, *Kemalizm*" (review), *Ülkü Halkevleri Dergisi* (Ankara), VIII/43 (Sep. 1936), pp. 62-64.

Abraham Galante, *Histoire des Juifs d'Istanbul.* II, Istanbul, Imprimerie Hüsnütabiat, 1942; 232 pp.

Id., *Türk harsı ve Türk Yahudisi: tarihî, siyasî, içtimaî tetkik.* Istanbul, Fakülteler Matbaası, 1953; 48 pp.

Cavit Orhan Tütengil, "M. Tekinalp'ın eserleri," *Kitap Belleten* (İstanbul), II/13-14 (Nov.-Dec. 1961 – publ. May 1962), pp. 13-14.

Id., "M. Tekinalp'ın yazı ve fikir hayatı ile ilgili bir belge," *Yenı Yayınlar* (Ankara), VII/4 (Apr. 1962), pp. 163-164.

Id., "M. Tekinalp ile ilgili ikinci bir belge," *ibid.*, VII/6-7 (June-July 1962), pp. 210, 211.

Id., "Sosyoloji tarihimizde Tekinalp," *Varlık* (Istanbul), 575 (1 June 1962), p. 7.

Zafer Toprak, "II. Meşrutiyet'te solidarist düşünce: halkçılık," *Toplum ve Bilim* (Istanbul), 1 (Spring 1977), pp. 92-123.

Hilmi Ziya Ülken, *Türkiye'de çağdaş düşünce tarihi.* 2nd edition, Istanbul, Ülken Yayınları, 1979; 496 pp.

Jacob M. Landau, "Tekinalp: Portrait of a Kemalist," in: Boğaziçi Üniversitesi, *Proceedings of International Conference on Atatürk, November 9-13, 1981* (Istanbul), III/47 (1981), pp. 1-8.

Id., *Pan-Turkism in Turkey: A Study of Irredentism.* London, C. Hurst, 1981; iv, 219 pp.

Id., "Moise Cohen-Tekinalp, Pioneer of Turkish Nationalism" (in Hebrew), in: *Proceedings of the Eighth World Congress of Jewish Studies, Jerusalem, 1981,* Jerusalem, The Magnes Press, 1982, II, pp. 223-228.

Zafer Toprak, *Türkiye'de "Milli iktisat" (1908-1918),* Ankara, Yurt Yayınları, 1982; 464 pp.

INDEX

The index does not comprise such often-repeated items as Moïse Cohen, M. Tekinalp, Istanbul, Salonica, the Ottoman Empire, Turks or Turkey. Nor has it been possible to include the titles of Tekinalp's articles (his books, though, are mentioned). Place names are generally listed according to international usage. The alphabetical sequence does not take into consideration the definite article (the, le, etc.).

www.ingramcontent.com/pod-product-compliance
Lightning Source LLC
LaVergne TN
LVHW020516100826
845148LV00010B/1248

* 9 7 8 1 5 9 7 4 0 4 4 8 8 *